Personal Data Privacy and Protection in a Surveillance Era:

Technologies and Practices

Christina Akrivopoulou
Democritus University of Thrace, Greece

Athanasios Psygkas
Yale Law School, USA

INFORMATION SCIENCE REFERENCE
Hershey · New York

Director of Editorial Content: Kristin Klinger
Director of Book Publications: Julia Mosemann
Acquisitions Editor: Lindsay Johnston
Development Editor: Michael Killian
Publishing Assistant: Casey Conapitski
Typesetter: Casey Conapitski
Production Editor: Jamie Snavely
Cover Design: Lisa Tosheff

Published in the United States of America by
Information Science Reference (an imprint of IGI Global)
701 E. Chocolate Avenue
Hershey PA 17033
Tel: 717-533-8845
Fax: 717-533-8661
E-mail: cust@igi-global.com
Web site: http://www.igi-global.com

Library of Congress Cataloging-in-Publication Data

Personal data privacy and protection in a survillance era : technologies and practices / Christina Akrivopoulou and Athanasios Psygkas, editors.
p. cm.
Includes bibliographical references and index.
Summary: "This book spans a number of interdependent and emerging topics in the area of legal protection of privacy and technology and explores the new threats that cyberspace poses to the privacy of individuals, as well as the threats that surveillance technologies generate in public spaces and in digital communication"--Provided by publisher.
ISBN 978-1-60960-083-9 (hardcover) -- ISBN 978-1-60960-085-3 (ebook) 1. Data protection--Law and legislation--United States. 2. Electronic surveillance--Law and legislation--United States. 3. Privacy, Right of--United States. 4. Records--Access control--United States. 5. Digital communications--United States. I. Akrivopoulou, Christina. II. Psygkas, Athanasios.
KF1263.C65P47 2011
342.7308'58--dc22

2010033436

British Cataloguing in Publication Data
A Cataloguing in Publication record for this book is available from the British Library.

Table of Contents

Section 5
Privacy Policies in the Network: Children's Privacy and the Protection of Copyright

Section 6
Data Protection and Privacy in Europe and in the European Union

Detailed Table of Contents

Digital information technologies have opened up fantastic new opportunities for ordinary people to both stand atop a virtual soapbox and reach millions and to participate in new forums for social interaction. However, as users conduct more and more of their personal and professional lives online, the distinction between public and private that has underlain the development of privacy law has begun to blur. While some traditional regulatory tools have proven adaptable, the ever increasing ability to collect and analyze that electronic information, suggests that the assumptions and policy considerations underlying privacy laws must be re-examined. Old dividing lines between public and private forums, which have long underlain the development of U.S. privacy law, cannot be readily transported into the digital realm. Instead, privacy regulations in the information age should respect and protect the ability for users of online services to control the dissemination of their personal information and compartmentalize different aspects of their online conduct.

Identity and privacy are often intertwined and, as a result, the significance of the distinction between the two concepts has been overlooked by Law. This article sheds some light upon the worrying indeterminacy between the concepts of privacy and identity in legal terminology, underlining the negative consequences that the lack of clarity and coherence in articulating the rights to privacy and identity will create in the forthcoming age of Ubiquitous Computing. In its proposal for a legal articulation between both rights, the article distinguishes between personal information that qualifies alethically (from αλήθεια [aletheia], the Greek word for truth) from the one that does not. It is based upon whether personal information represents or conveys a true fact or a truthful aspect concerning a given individual (depending on whether it has an alethic value or not) that the distinction between and the application of the rights to privacy and to identity shall be determined. As a way to test the usefulness of the alethic criteria, the paper looks into the main challenges posed by the vision of a Ubiquitous Computing world upon the rights to privacy and identity. In this context, the paper devotes particular attention to the implications of automated profiling technologies, arguing that the conceptual clarification of both the rights to privacy and identity will be crucial in order to protect and promote the autonomy and self-determination of the human person.

Lawyers find great joy in pointing out the destructive effects of digital technology on privacy and naturally expect the law to avert overexposure of people's personal information. This essay takes a different view by arguing that the trajectory of technological developments renders the expansive collection of personal data inevitable and, hence, the law's primary interest should lie in regulating the use –not the collection- of information. This does not foreshadow the end of privacy, but rather suggests a necessary reconceptualization of privacy in the digital era. Along those lines we first need to acknowledge that people increasingly sacrifice voluntarily some of their privacy to enjoy the benefits of technology. Second, the ready availability of a huge volume of personal information creates attention scarcity, such that the chances a person's privacy will be intruded are diminished. Most importantly, though, once the law accepts the inevitability of the collection of personal information, it will be best in the position to focus attention on ensuring that the collected information is appropriately used instead of wasting resources on trying to hinder in vain its collection. This more realistic approach calls for alternative means of regulation, like self-regulation or emphasis on informed consent, and facilitates the flow of information by reducing the transactional cost of its sharing and dissemination.

The electronic surveillance of public assemblies has been an issue highly debated in the Greek public arena. The circumstances that brought this internationally contested topic in the public focus were the parliamentary introduction of Law 3625/2007 in Greece and the legislative enactment of an exemption from the data protection legislation for all police activities involving data processing during public

commonly accepted. The paper that follows initiates from this understanding in order to support the following idea: if in fact there is a right to protect our genetic privacy, this is a right quite unique in its characteristics and is certainly not identified with our general presumptions about privacy. Its uniqueness lies in the fact, that apart form the dominant definition of privacy as a right to be let alone, as an individualistic right, genetic privacy protects not only the individual but also the members of his/her family. The present paper is examining the 'hereditary' and 'shared' character of our genetic information in an attempt to shape a right to genetic privacy that is based on the equilibrium of individual autonomy, family and public interest. In order to support such an argument, the premises of our genetic self are examined in connection with autonomy and its boundaries, mainly paternalism and genetic exceptionalism. Along this line, basic notions of the liberal privacy theory are critically examined, mainly the notions of control, confidentiality and consent, so as to maintain the existence of a right to genetic privacy that can enhance the individual's autonomy without founding it on its selfish, individual interests.

Abortion, one of the oldest discussion subjects in the history of law maintains its actuality in this century. The pro-life and pro-choice groups are the main actors of the current abortion debate. On the one hand, the woman rights defenders consider the issue as a matter of freedom and argue against bans on abortion practice. On the other hand, the fetal rights defenders are absolutely against abortion in any case and consider the abortion as a method of killing an innocent human being. All sides of the discussion rely on the scientific developments to assure the public opinion. The core of this semi-scientific debate today depends on the question "When does human life begin?". They aspire to shape the law concerning abortion and fetus, according to their answer to this question. Yet, this approach leads to deadlocks in theory and practice, because it is impossible to accept the legal personality of the fetus or to remove all the bans on abortion. However, it may be possible to find a solution within the legal system itself by using scientific knowledge but without establishing it on a human "rights" base. This paper argues that the pain as a criterion may be a promising point of compromise.

The aim of this work is to examine the European Court of Human Rights' (ECtHR) balancing exercise between genetic data protection and national security, under Art. 8 of the European Convention of Human Rights (ECHR). It analyzes, more specifically, the core principles of the Strasbourg Court that the Council of Europe's Contracting States are required to apply when they collect and store genetic data in order to reach specific purposes in terms of public security, such as the fight against crimes. It will emerge that the Court, in consideration of the risks that new technologies pose to an individual's data safeguards, pays special attention to the strict periods of storage of such data and requires that their collection be justified by the existence of a pressing social need and a "careful scrutiny" of the principle of proportionally between the intrusive measure and the aim pursued. This work is divided into three main parts. The first part provides a general overview on personal data protection under Art. 8, while the second and third part concentrate, respectively, on the collection of genetic data and on their storage for police purposes.

Section 4
The 'Targeted' Privacy: Ambient Technology and Tagging

Radio Frequency Identification technology has increasingly been applied within the hospital setting for various purposes. This paper argues that, while such applications may drastically improve hospital efficiency, they also may produce privacy risks that harm patients more than they help them. Further, the privacy risks associated with such technologies are difficult to comprehend. When patients' personal data is implicated, hospitals should adhere to privacy principles that promote the flow of full information and enable patients to make rational choices when they opt-in to hospital RFID applications. Otherwise, RFID hospital technologies may be implemented in ways that do not serve patients' long term privacy interests.

This chapter describes Bayan Muna et al. v. Mendoza et al., a 2009 Philippine Supreme Court petition involving the first and ongoing certiorari challenge to the Philippine government's implementation of passive Radio Frequency Identification (RFID) technology in the registration of all motor vehicles in the Philippines. As a matter of constitutional jurisprudence and policy, the passive use of RFID technology in this context does not infringe constitutionally-protected privacy expectations, entirely consistent with the Executive Branch's law enforcement powers. The paper shows how the proposed RFID tagging of motor vehicles in the Philippines satisfies the tests of reasonable expectations, and by dealing only with already publicly available information, avoids spectral fears of data mining and government abuse.

Unprecedented advances of Information Communication Technologies (ICT) and their involvement in most of private and public activities are revolutionizing our daily life and the way we relate to our environment. If, on the one hand, the new developments promise to make people's lives more comfortable or more secure, on the other hand, complex social and legal issues rise in terms of fundamental rights and freedoms. The objective of this paper is to envisage some of the main legal challenges posed by the new Ambient Intelligence technologies (AmI), in particular for the fundamental rights of privacy and data protection, while trying to sketch some possible solutions. One main direction followed is to consider, after having analyzed the possible applications of AmI technologies and the evolution of the concept of privacy, the adequacy of the current legal regulation models to respond to these new challenges. Attention will be paid to the possible use of these new technologies for security purposes, and therefore to the issue of balancing between opposed interests and rights according to the principles appropriate for a 'democratic society.

The achievement of an adequate level of privacy protection is still a demanding objective, and this is more than true for new technologies. One relatively new but increasing class of users of Internet related services, are children and young people. However, if Internet services can improve social skills and widen the knowledge minors have, it could open the doors to privacy abuse and misuse. As it would not be feasible to address all the legal and technical tools available within the privacy protection process, this contribution will focus on a specific element required by the regulation applicable both in Europe and in the US: the inclusion of a privacy policy in any website that collects personal data from users. The paper will provide an analysis of some of the privacy policies available online provided by companies that focus specifically on children as well as by social networking sites. The analysis will couple the descriptive part with suggestions to improve the level of compliance and, consequentially, the level of protection for minors' privacy.

Copyright and privacy are two fundamental values for a democratic society, since both enhance the development of each individual's personality. Nevertheless, in cyberspace, copyright enforcement and the right to informational self determination have become two clashing realities. In fact, with the arrival of digital technology, especially the Internet, rightholders, facing massive on-line copyright infringements, mainly by file-sharers on peer-to-peer (P2P) systems, started developing more and more intrusive new enforcement strategies in electronic communications as a means to identify the infringers and the committed infractions. The goal of the present paper is to study, in a context where massive unauthorized uses of copyrighted works is an undeniable reality, how the boundaries between what is public or private become fainter, whether the use of tracking software is consistent with personal data protection legislation and whether it is possible to reconcile these two human rights.

Section 6
Data Protection and Privacy in Europe and in the European Union

The focus of this paper is the new European legislation designed to harmonize domestic laws on the retention of telecommunications data for the purpose of assisting law enforcement efforts. The European Union introduced the EC Data Retention Directive in 2006. This Directive requires the retention of every European citizen's communications data for up to two years for the purpose of police investigation. There is, however, a major problem with the Directive in that it regularizes, and thereby entrenches, the practice of data retention across Europe. No systematic empirical evidence supports the introduction of such broad surveillance. The existence of data retention in principle raises concerns for data protection and the right to respect of privacy as protected under the European Convention of Human Rights (ECHR). This paper questions the proportionality of the Directive in line with data protection principles and Europe's obligations under Article 8 of the ECHR.

The present contribution aims to discuss the possibilities and limitations of the EU to provide for an effective and comprehensive data protection regime. In this respect, it presents an analysis of the data protection rules in EU law by examining the relevant constitutional and secondary law framework. It analyzes the jurisprudence of the European Court of Justice and the Court of First Instance on data protection issues, and argues that the European Court of Justice has interpreted an internal market measure (the Data Protection Directive) in such a way so as to foster the protection of fundamental rights. However, when it comes to the balancing between fundamental rights the Court leaves the question to be resolved by national courts. Finally, the contribution assesses the transborder data flows regime established by the Data Protection Directive and attempts to draw some conclusions on whether the 'adequate protection' test, ensures a high protection in such flows.

This chapter is mainly intended to outline the Romanian data protection regime governing the cross-border transfers of personal data, both to countries located in the European Union (EU) or in the European Economic Area (EEA), as well as to non-EU or non-EEA countries. In addressing the Romanian legal requirements related to international transfers of personal data, a high level insight into the background of Romanian data protection principles and main rules applicable in the broader context of pri-

Preface

THE PRIVACY-TECHNOLOGY DILEMMA IN THE AGE OF DIGITAL SURVEILLANCE

The proliferation of new technologies and their increasing use in many aspects of our lives pose a number of threats to privacy; digital networks, ubiquitous computing, ambient intelligence, automated profiling, genetics, radio frequency identification (RFID), wiretapping, closed circuit television (CCTV) cameras, digital rights management systems and similar technologies challenge the traditional confines of privacy, and on several occasions, call for its reconceptualization. In a dynamically changing technological framework one must answer the following dilemma: how to benefit from the friendly uses of technology without surrendering the individual's freedom and autonomy. The contributions that are included in the book that follows introduce exactly this dilemma, trying to propose possible solutions and answers, policies or practices that can balance the benefits of technology with the need to protect the right to privacy in an era of surveillance and digital technology.

The difficult balance between technology and privacy is a subject that has already drawn the international theoretical attention. Privacy, a relatively new right—at least for many of the European legal orders (e.g. Greece, France, Italy, Germany, Spain, Portugal)—has attracted the European theoretical attention over the past three decades exactly due to the rapid rise of technology. Nonetheless, the things are quite different in the other side of the Atlantic, beginning with the American theoretical dialogue on the subject initiated by the famous 'right to be left alone' of S. D. Warren and L. D. Brandeis. In their 'Right to Privacy' published in the Harvard Law Review in 1890, the two authors base the necessity for acknowledging an implicit right to privacy exactly in the rise of technology and the new threats that the press casts for the freedom of the individual. In the exact same way, nowadays the network, the data-banks and the technologies of surveillance present new endangerments that call for the protection of privacy.

This very idea connects the chapters in this book. Technology does not only present a possible threat to privacy. It also reflects the very contours of privacy, the reason that its protection becomes a legal and social necessity. This is the reason why the expansion of technology also analogically augments the legal acknowledgment of the social appreciation of privacy. This evolution has influenced the rise of the 'public safety' international technological surveillance, the relevant bibliography on the subject of privacy and technology over the past two decades, and especially after the September 11, 2001. Among others, some characteristic approaches are presented in Agre and Rotenberg (1997), Wagner- DeCew (1997), Brin (1998), Friedman (2000), and Austin (2003).

The contributions that follow engage to this open dialogue, by offering new theoretical proposals and mainly a modern taxonomy of privacy-technology problems as well as solutions, proposals and specific policy models. Thus, the book is divided in six sections, all of them encountering some of the most currently debated subject of the privacy-technology clash.

Section One revisits basic concepts associated with privacy, such as personality and identity, against the background of digital networks that entail potential dangers for privacy. All three chapters of this Section acknowledge the interconnectedness of digital information systems and the pervasiveness of electronic recordkeeping, and suggest alternative ways of viewing privacy and identity in these new environments.

More specifically, Bradley Tennis in Chapter 1 picks up on the idea of a redefinition of privacy in a networked world in view of the evolution of digital information technologies. He observes that traditional distinctions between public and private spheres are not readily applicable to the digital realm. The Internet, he writes, cannot be neatly categorized as either a public or a private space; it is a complex combination of semi-private, potentially overlapping spaces nestled in a public medium. Therefore, traditional regulatory tools prove ill-equipped to protect privacy and identity interests in today's networked world. Instead, these developments call for the recognition of an individual's right to control the dissemination of their personal information, and publicly project multiple personae by compartmentalizing different aspects of their online conduct.

The chapter begins by examining how the legal system has adapted to account for the manifestation of familiar information privacy concerns in the examples of anonymous speech and disclosure of personal information. With respect to the former, Tennis points out the danger that civil suits resulting in de-anonymization stifle online speech and cultural production. On the other hand, true victims of online harassment or defamation need to be protected. He argues that the requirements that the plaintiff make a strong showing that his claim is colorable and that the defendant receive notice generally strike an appropriate balance between these two concerns. When it comes to third party disclosure, Tennis suggests that the risk of extensive, detailed dossiers on users of online services being transferred to third parties highlights the need to adopt a uniform and broad definition of "personal information," strengthen notice and consent provisions, and provide users the opportunity to opt out of the data sharing provisions of a particular service's privacy policy not necessary to the production of the service. Chapter 1 then goes on to advocate a perception of privacy entailing an individual's right to publicly project multiple personae while still maintaining boundaries between them. This compartmentalization promotes the realization of and participation in a full democratic culture in that it allows a user to participate in the production of information and culture that might prove damaging or embarrassing if associated with them in other contexts. The chapter last examines potential safeguards for these privacy and identity interests. It concludes that Canadian and EU legislation with their expansive reading of "personal information" and the level of control that an individual should be able to exert over the collection, use, and dissemination of this information provide a step in the right direction.

Chapter 2 continues the inquiry into the concepts of privacy and identity. Norberto Nuno Gomes de Andrade emphasizes the need for a clear demarcation between the two rights. He criticizes overly broad definitions of the right to privacy that claim some of the definitional and constitutive characteristics pertaining to the right to identity. He then assesses the ambiguous and dynamic relationship between privacy and identity, providing examples of how privacy may obstruct identity, and identity may undermine privacy. While both the right to privacy and the right to identity have common roots in the so-called personality rights and relate to an individual's right to dignity and self-determination, they constitute two different and autonomous rights: the right to identity translates a person's definite and inalienable interest in the uniqueness of his being, whereas the right to privacy describes a personal condition of life characterized by seclusion from the public.

Building on this distinction the chapter introduces a "privacy-identity relevance" factor into the categorization of personal information. According to what Andrade calls the "alethic criterion" (from the Greek word for truth), the right to identity concerns all those personal facts -regardless of being truthful or not- which are capable of falsifying or transmitting a wrong image of one's identity, while the right to privacy comprises only those true personal facts that are part of one's private sphere and which, by one reason or the other, spill over to the public sphere. This distinction has significant implications, the author argues, in the foreseeable scenario of a Ubiquitous Computing world, and more specifically in the case of automated profiling technologies. In this context the application of the right to privacy and the right to identity will depend on the type of profile in question, that is, on whether the profile involves the disclosure of any necessarily true facts related to the subject or not. The right to privacy will play an important role in the first phase of the profiling process (the data phase), regulating the manner in which personal data may be captured, collected and stored The right to identity shall then play a crucial role in the second phase of the profiling process (the knowledge phase), allowing the individual to gain access and eventually contest on the grounds of misrepresentation the knowledge that has been constructed about him or her through such profiles.

Chapter 3 takes a more skeptical view towards the significance of privacy in the digital era. Konstantinos Stylianou endorses a version of technological determinism, whereby in the name of new technological vistas that maximize access to information privacy folds. He adopts a broad definition of privacy that would include all activity and all information that the subject has a reasonable expectation to keep to himself, the expectation to be free from unwarranted governmental or private intrusion, the option not to become the object of attention, the right to remain anonymous, and the ability to block physical access to himself. However, the author argues that privacy is overrated in a twofold sense: first, the ready availability of a huge volume of personal information creates attention scarcity thus diminishing the chances that a person's privacy will be intruded. But even when the dangers are real, as an empirical matter people are often willing to compromise their privacy for the benefits a given technology has to offer. For this reason, effective allocation of resources would mandate a shift in emphasis from regulation of collection of data to regulation of use of data. In this context, Stylianou suggests, self-regulation could be an alternative means of regulation worth considering.

The right to privacy faces new threats when it encounters demands for national security and public safety. This is the focus of Section Two of the book. Especially after September 11, there is a shift in emphasis toward fighting terrorist and other criminal activities. These demands for the protection of national and public security often explicitly call for or in practice result in relaxing privacy protections. Both chapters point out that in this environment the private easily becomes of public concern, but they are quick to highlight the dangers associated with such a shift.

Chapter 4 begins this inquiry by critically assessing the practice of video surveillance by means of CCTV systems. Haralambos Anthopoulos argues that a Greek statutory exemption from the data protection legislation for all police activities involving data processing during public assemblies is unconstitutional as it runs counter to the rights to political privacy and public anonymity. He explains that the right to data protection is enshrined in the Greek Constitution and includes within its scope of protection "sensitive data," such as those related to political views. This heightened protection enhances the freedom of political and social activity of the individual, securing his '"political privacy." In the case of public assemblies, Anthopoulos continues, the right to data protection directly correlates with the constitutionally protected freedom of assembly. By combining the two rights he advocates the creation of a new constitutional rule, according to which participants in lawful open public assemblies and demonstrations have the right not to be massively identified through the use of video-surveillance systems recording and storing their image, i.e., the "right to public anonymity." Furthermore, these constitutional provisions do not provide for any exemptions from their application for the sake of public security. Against this constitutional backdrop, the author maintains that the statutory exemption in question raises constitutional issues, especially in that it does not distinguish assemblies into a) lawful open public assemblies, b) open public assemblies where crimes are committed by random passengers or sole participants, and c) unlawful open public assemblies. The Chapter concludes by examining the jurisprudence of the European Court of Human Rights which seems to suggest that a breach of privacy can only be ascertained in the case of further processing of the collected material with the purpose of identification of persons recorded in it or when this information is made publicly available.

Melike Akkaraca Köse continues in this thematic in Chapter 5 by examining a "traditional" form of state surveillance: telecommunication interceptions. The author presents the applicable legal regime and domestic reforms introducing strict legal standards for communications surveillance. She notes that most of the problems regarding privacy occur due to the preventive surveillance of communications which may be applied for the abstractly defined crimes and without a serious ground for suspicion. However, Turkish laws do not show important disparities compared to the other telecommunications surveillance regulations in Europe. Akkaraca explains that, despite the positive legal reforms, the problems lie in the implementation of law by state officials. She then goes on to chronicle a series of wiretaps directed against high-ranked members of the judiciary, politicians and members of the public. The focus is on the "Ergenekon" case in which indictments relied on documents seized at the defendants' homes and wiretaps; these evidence collection methods have been described as dubious.

To evaluate these practices Chapter 5 employs a Foucauldian approach: the aim is to uncover the "conditions of possibility" for the widespread practice of wiretapping in Turkey by focusing on the actual power relations. According to the author, the surveillance of communications is a technique of discipline in a Foucauldian sense. Turkey's security conceptions may only be explained by a number of truth-claims developed by different powers in the society. The army is one of them: Akkaraca observes that the frequent use of surveillance techniques by the military is directly linked to the 2009 wiretapping scandal since it exhibits a well-established practice of limitless use of disciplinary techniques against individuals when the 'security' is at stake. Another power producing truth-claims about security in Turkey is the judiciary. The problem there lies in the limited approach it adopted in the cases concerning security and human rights. This situation, the author notes, encourages claims about the judiciary-military cooperation. On the other hand, the AKP ruling party produces most of the truth-claims critical toward the judicial and military discourses. The Chapter argues that the Ergenekon case is to be evaluated against this background. The question is whether the case is another stage of the conflicts of power or truly a struggle against the long-persisting stay-behind organizations.

The section is closing by Anna Tsiftsoglou's Chapter 6 presentation on the clash between data protection and public safety in the framework of the Greek dialogue concerning the legislative acknowledgement (Law 3783/2009) of public surveillance for reasons of preventing crime and protecting public security. The chapter analyzes both the Greek and EU legislation in comparison as well as it conceptualizes the concept of public safety and the basis of its 'inherent' clash to privacy.

Section Three moves the investigation to the area of medical and genetic privacy and the role of medical technology in the relevant debates. The examples discussed in this Section are genetics and abortion. The fact that the "object" of privacy protection in this domain is our own body also invites an ethical approach to these questions, which both chapters in this section adopt.

Christina Akrivopoulou in Chapter 7 examines the right to genetic privacy on the basis of the equilibrium of individual autonomy, family and public interest. She begins by presenting the individualistic aspect of the right noting that a deep knowledge of our genetic self promotes our autonomy. However, it also creates bonds with others since it represents a part of the subject's family heritage. Our genetic identity, she writes, is crucial for the family intimacy that we enjoy. This differentiates genetic information from any other type of medical information because the former bears a part of our personality, of our identity and autonomy, and is therefore not neutral. It consequently follows that the individual has a private interest in keeping it secure against threats posed by geneticism, genetic exceptionalism and genetic determinism that could provide grounds for unequal, discriminatory, or even outright totalitarian treatment of the individual. This leads to a discussion of the notion of "control" that has been proposed as the best remedy against such risks. Akrivopoulou argues that this notion is premised on a spatial or proprietary understanding of privacy that ignores the shared and ethical character of this right. Similarly, she cautions against the capacity of consent to offer "magic potion" solutions for all the choices connected to the individual's genetic privacy and freedom. The author then examines the ethical grounds for genetic privacy which she situates in autonomy while also taking into account the dignity and personality of the individual. The implications of grounding this right in autonomy –as opposed to the concept of control- is that it gives rise to the concept of free choice. Furthermore, basing a right to genetic privacy on autonomy and choice precludes the threat of paternalism as it entails the capacity of the subject to make harmful choices against his/her welfare. Last, the Chapter critically examines the liberal and communitarian approaches to genetic privacy in favor of what the author calls "genetic privacy as autonomy of care" that values the individual as well as the intimate relationships in which he/she chooses to participate in the same way, thus enabling his/her communication and formation of choices in a circle of trust instead of an isolated but private and dominant space.

Hasan Atilla Güngör in Chapter 8 focuses on a different aspect of the right to privacy, that related to abortion. He examines how scientific developments have been used both by pro-choice and pro-life groups in support of their cause, and argues that scientific claims concerning the fetus' ability to feel pain may more appropriately underpin the development of regulations in this area. The chapter begins by assessing the debates between the two groups revolving around scientific arguments about when human life begins. It presents five criteria that were developed over the years to try to answer this question as well as the scientific objections raised against them. The author notes that this scientific debate has not provided conclusive responses but rather seems to have exacerbated disagreements. He then suggests that formulating the question in terms of a clash between the unborn child's right to life and the woman's right to privacy is oversimplified and unfair: the reason is that in addition to a woman's right to privacy, other rights are also implicated, namely her rights to health and life. This does not mean, Güngör continues, that the fetus is left unprotected as it does enjoy private and public law protections. He stresses, however, that according legal personality to the fetus would lead to paradoxes and eliminate women's rights. What the chapter recommends instead is that each phase through which the fetus passes during the prenatal period be dealt through the invocation of distinctive legal categories. In this context, the author introduces the criterion of whether the fetus can feel pain. He clarifies that this does not suggest that abortion must be banned when the fetus begins to experience the feeling of pain. Rather, this criterion advocates establishing new legal mechanisms aiming to provide the least possible or even no pain for the fetus during its extraction from the mother's womb.

The section is closing with the contribution of Cristina Contartese in Chapter 9 which aims in presenting the clash between the protection of genetic data and national security in the jurisprudence of the European Court of Human Rights. By accounting several significant cases of the European Court of Human Rights, including the famous Marper vs the U.K., the author focuses on the importance of protecting the genetic privacy of the individual as well as the possible threats that the relevant technology poses against our control over our personal information.

Section Four addresses another issue of increasing importance nowadays, that of tagging (of humans and objects) and its threats to privacy. The first chapter in this Section discusses the implementation of RFID technology in the hospital setting and the different levels of privacy risks implicated in these applications. The second chapter examines a narrower case of RFID application in the registration of motor vehicles and finds that it raises no constitutional concerns. The chapter closing this Section presents legal challenges and possible directions for privacy protection in the example of the new Ambient Intelligence technologies.

More specifically, Christopher Suarez in Chapter 10 examines the privacy risks associated with the use of RFID in the hospital setting. He begins by presenting case studies suggesting that the application of this technology improves medical processes, decision making, and resource management. However, he points out that these efficiency gains do not come without privacy costs. In order to evaluate these costs, he draws on the literature on consumer RFID privacy to establish a set of principles guiding his overall analysis. The Chapter employs a utilitarian framework that attempts to balance the usefulness of the technology with the privacy harms posed by it. In this context, the author clarifies that endorsement of the technology in one area does not necessarily imply that it is endorsed by the public in all areas. Moreover, patients should have the ability to make choices relating to hospital RFID with the fullest information possible so that acceptance of the technology reflects true endorsement. Suarez adopts a proprietary conceptualization of privacy and builds on Schwartz's work to identify five principles against which to evaluate RFID hospital applications: limits on transferability, explicit opt-in defaults, right of exit, right of recourse, and institutions that ensure full information provision. The Chapter then provides some background on the few laws that currently govern hospital RFID in the United States. Some federal legislation only addresses RFID hospital privacy indirectly, and while thirteen states have passed RFID legislation as of 2010, most of it does not address RFID hospital privacy matters in a comprehensive fashion.

Against this backdrop the chapter then assesses a number of RFID hospital applications. The discussion begins with asset management. The author distinguishes between asset management for general hospital assets and that for patient assets. The latter is different because patient assets must be associated with patients to be used effectively in the hospital. Suarez address two such examples, hospital blood inventory and patient pharmaceuticals, and advocates a much more rigid privacy analysis of these applications. He then turns to the question of "human tagging." He distinguishes between implantable and external tags and highlights the more serious privacy implications associated with the former. Last, he examines RFID applications within neo-natal intensive care units, long-term care centers for the elderly, and emergency and operating rooms. In the concluding section, the author offers procedural and legal recommendations and suggests that additional pilots need to be undertaken within hospitals to assess how beneficial RFID really is.

Chapter 11 examines the implementation of RFID technology in the registration of all motor vehicles in the Philippines. It maintains that the passive use of this technology in this context does not threaten protected privacy zones in the Philippine constitution and relevant statutes. Diane Desierto first provides some background on the Land Transportation Office's (LTO) RFID tagging system: an RFID tag attached to a motor vehicle would enable LTO personnel with RFID readers to more swiftly retrieve registration information pertaining to the vehicle from the LTO databases, such as the motor vehicle file number; engine number; plate number; motor vehicle type; owner name; last registration date, etc. Petitioners in Bayan Muna et al. v. Mendoza et al. argued that this system constitutes an impermissible intrusion on people's protected zone of privacy. According to them, the threat to the right to privacy of citizens exists from its potential misuse for unauthorized governmental surveillance. However, as Desierto explains, these fears are unsubstantiated: passive RFID tags have narrow operational capabilities in that by themselves they do not store any other information about the driver of the vehicle. All that is signaled from the RFID tag to an RFID reader is a "unique serial number" that enables access to what has long been publicly-available and accessible registration information in the LTO's motor vehicle registration database. The author emphasizes the public availability of this information: even if a third party were to physically acquire an LTO personnel's RFID reader and use it to scan RFID tags on motor vehicles, he or she would not be accessing information privileged against public disclosure.

The Chapter then evaluates the constitutionality of the application of this technology based on the jurisprudence of the Philippine Supreme Court. That Court has adopted the "reasonable expectation of privacy" test enunciated by the US Supreme Court in Katz. According to this case-law, "[t]he reasonableness of a person's expectation of privacy depends on a two-part test: (1) whether, by his conduct, the individual has exhibited an expectation of privacy; and (2) whether this expectation is one that society recognizes as reasonable." In the Philippines, as Desierto points out, motor vehicle owners have long been put on notice by Congress that the LTO can physically inspect vehicles to determine their registration; therefore, they bear necessarily lower privacy expectations. The reading of a passive RFID tag attached to a motor vehicle is analogous to such routine inspection. The Chapter concludes that the implementation of a passive RFID tagging system serves a public purpose in advancing governmental efficiency through expediting and facilitating access to registration information already available to the public, without granting to the LTO any power that it does not already possess.

Chapter 12 discusses legal challenges that the new Ambient Intelligence technologies (AmI) are likely to raise with respect to privacy, and seeks to offer directions for potential solutions. Shara Monteleone first provides a definition of Ambient Intelligence as "a digital environment that proactively, but sensibly, supports people in their daily lives." Based on the use of sensors networks, wireless communications, smart devices, the central idea of AmI is to reduce the size of computers, so that they can be embedded in familiar objects, and employ the augmented computation capacity so as to provide a mixed, real-virtual experience that "should" improve the way we can benefit from our living surroundings. AmI entails privacy implications because, for example, tracking, locating, and identifying specific people in a certain environment has become essential in the new AmI systems in order to provide services according to the situations, needs and preferences of different users. The author then examines the concepts of privacy and data protection. She notes that "privacy" is still a muddled concept and that data protection legislation has introduced a more dynamic dimension of privacy that gives to data subjects the right to control the use of their personal information. The Chapter endorses Solove's pluralistic conception of privacy, whereby what we consider as entitled to privacy protection is variable according to time, values and technologies. It subsequently offers an overview of certain international and European legal instruments according to privacy and data protection the nature of fundamental rights.

Monteleone recommends the adoption of sector-based legislation at the EU level, especially in the context of AmI technologies. She explains that their new possible deployments and their convergence with other technologies could be better managed at a specific rather than a general level. This contextual approach advocates for a system of "micro-policies," without however sacrificing coherence. The author makes clear that this adaptation of privacy preferences to contexts and users should not suggest a proprietary understanding of privacy viewing privacy rights as a "package" similar to other services. Furthermore, she assesses the legal-technical approach which she finds convincing, but observes that it comes with challenges of its own. Last, the Chapter touches on the tension between privacy and security and suggests that the future development and use of AmI technologies in this context will probably exacerbate this tension.

Section Five returns to the discussion of privacy risks and protection in networks. The emphasis, however, this time is not on conceptual questions but more on specific policies, their effects and the need for reforms. The examples analyzed in this Section are the protection of children's privacy online and digital copyright enforcement.

In Chapter 13 Federica Casarosa begins by acknowledging that children might be techno-savvy but are also particularly vulnerable to privacy violations on the Internet. Increasing the safety of the online environment requires a multi-pronged approach, but the chapter focuses on one aspect of such protections: the informative privacy notices (or "privacy policies") on websites that collect personal data. The author first compares the EU and the US approaches to children privacy. In the EU the regulatory framework (most notably the Data Protection Directive) does not directly address the problem of children privacy as it applies uniformly regardless of the age of users. On the contrary, in the US the Children's Online Privacy Protection Act provides special protection for children under the age of 13. In order to evaluate against neutral and uniform criteria the privacy policies of websites based in Europe and the US, Casarosa uses as benchmark the pertinent OECD "fair information principles": collection limitation, data quality, purpose specification, use limitation, security safeguards, openness, individual participation, accountability. She further distinguishes between websites targeting children directly, websites of a general audience where children and young people are addressed only in a limited part of the website, and social networking websites. The Chapter reaches a number of conclusions: for instance, websites tried to clarify the main elements of the privacy policy; however, in terms of clarity and readability, only in few cases could the privacy policy be considered highly understandable and none of the analyzed privacy policies were directed to children. This prompts the author to suggest improvements, namely child-targeted design and multi-layered privacy policies. A layered structure would allow for notices drafted in a simple and clear structure easy for children to navigate. Providing minors with a more easily readable, and consequently understandable privacy policy, the author concludes, could improve their capability to engage in critical analysis and reach a really "informed consent" to provide their data.

Chapter 14 analyzes the tension between digital copyright enforcement and privacy. Pedro Pina notes that in the past such a conflict would be hardly imaginable. Digitization, however, has changed in quality and in quantity the possibilities of copyright infringement. Facing massive online copyright infringements, mainly by file-sharers on peer-to-peer (P2P) systems, rightholders started developing more and more intrusive new enforcement strategies in electronic communications. In turn, digital copyright laws adopted the legal-technological approach for protecting creative expression. However, intrusive technological measures created to identify online infringers might put in risk the privacy sphere of internet users, since their navigation and identification data can be collected and treated by a copyright holder. Pina reads the EU legislation in this field to assume that collecting IP addresses is a lawful rightholder's behavior if functionally directed to subsequent copyright enforcement, since in the context of P2P networks it will be the adequate means to present "reasonable evidence." On the other hand, he points to the European Union's concern over the protection of personal data and argues that IP addresses must be considered personal data. The Chapter also discusses a decision by the European Court of Justice holding that EU law does not require Member States to lay down an obligation to communicate personal data in order to ensure effective protection of copyright in the context of civil proceedings. This approach, according to the author, indicates that a balance between copyright enforcement and personal data protection is required by EU law. Last, the chapter addresses the graduated response mechanism, according to which, online warnings are sent to the subscriber potentially committing copyright infringement, whereby he/she is advised about the illegality of his/her behavior. If the infringement continues, six months after the first warning, a new one is sent. If, even so, the unlawful activity continues, in the last step of this procedure, a court may order the suspension of the broadband accounts of file-sharers of copyrighted material online. Pina suggests that this can be an appropriate alternative only if it respects the data collecting and treatment principles, and the general principles of proportionality, necessity and adequacy. The obligation of ISPs to filter data content should require a prior court decision, and the mere collection of IP addresses should similarly need previous authorization.

Different chapters have previously alluded to the protection of privacy and personal data in the European area. Authors have invoked EU law either as a part of the applicable legal regime or as a model providing directions for reform in foreign jurisdictions. The focus of Section Six is now specifically on different aspects of privacy protection in the European space. Although EU law is generally perceived to offer high standards of protection in this area, the chapters in this Section also touch on the occasional limitations of the EU legal framework in providing effective privacy protections.

Nóra Ní Loideain begins this inquiry in Chapter 15 by analyzing the Data Retention Directive (2006/24/EC). This Directive requires the retention of every European citizen's communications data, including traffic data of communications and location data of the communication devices used, for up to two years for the purpose of police investigation. The Chapter first presents the background and the origins of the Directive. Its legislative development, Ní Loideain observes, demonstrates the considerable unease among legislators and non-governmental organizations surrounding the Directive. The European Parliament's initial report to the Commission contained several proposals restricting the scope, amount of data, access to data and the period of retention as proposed by the Council, but the Council did not take into account a significant part of these proposals. The author then outlines the main provisions of the Data Retention Directive pertaining to access, the period of retention, security and oversight mechanisms, and the evaluation of the application of the Directive by the Commission. She subsequently sets out the substantive principles of European data protection legislation and explains that against this backdrop the Directive in question raises serious concerns: no systematic and reliable empirical research was carried out and used in its legislative development; the significant scope of the retention period increases the prospect of inappropriate searches by law enforcement officials and others; the data is not only accessible to "competent national authorities," but is also subject to access by members of the private sector as this communications data must be retained, processed and made accessible to each Member State by private ISPs. Ní Loideain suggests that the Directive raises further concerns under the European Convention on Human Rights as it would fail the proportionality test. No empirical evidence has been put forward to establish the necessity for such unprecedented invasions of privacy. Moreover, the Directive entrenches the practice of blanket surveillance of the communications of all citizens and not just those under suspicion. In conclusion, the author recommends that the National Data Protection Commissioners undertake annually an empirical study that would measure the effectiveness and necessity of using such retained communications data, particularly the number of times in which this information was essential in the successful prosecution of serious crime.

Chapter 16 discusses the EU data protection regime as well as the pertinent jurisprudence of the European Court of Justice. As Maria Tzanou clarifies, the protection of personal data at the EU level is increasingly conceived of as an autonomous fundamental right, distinct from the right to respect of private and family life. The Chapter first presents the constitutional framework for the EU data protection regime, that is, the relevant Treaty provisions. It then moves on to the legislative instruments: it begins with the most important data protection initiative, the Data Protection Directive, which brings together two seemingly conflicting principles, free trade and data protection. The author discusses the background of the Directive, the history of its legislative development, its scope, principles, and definitions. With respect to the latter, she criticizes certain uncertainties still existing regarding the definition of "personal data" and "processing." Other documents studied are the e-Privacy Directive that applies in the electronic communications sector, and Regulation 45/2001/EC that applies to the processing of personal data by EU institutions and bodies. Last, Tzanou addresses the Data Retention Directive which, she concludes, interferes disproportionately with the right to privacy.

The second part of the chapter analyzes the case law of the European Court of Justice in this area. The author notes that the ECJ has generally interpreted in a generous manner the Data Protection Directive to ensure a high level of protection of personal data within the EU legal order. As she puts it, the Court has interpreted an internal market harmonization instrument in such a manner that fosters the protection of a fundamental right within the EU. For example, it has adopted a wide interpretation of the protective scope of the Directive to cover activities regardless of their connection with the internal market as well as to apply the privacy safeguards to new technological developments, and in particular the Internet. Moreover, Tzanou refers to the jurisprudence of the Court requiring the balancing between data protection and other rights and principles, such as freedom of expression, transparency and public access to documents. The last section of the Chapter discusses the transfer of data to third countries which, pursuant to the Directive, depends on whether the third country in question effectively ensures an "adequate level of protection." Tzanou argues that the adequacy principle ensures, in principle, a high level of protection of the right to privacy in transborder data flows. She concludes by critically assessing the PNR cases concerning the obligation of airlines operating transatlantic flights to provide "Passenger Name Records" data to the US customs authorities.

The following chapter of this Section and the book continues on the topic of cross-border transfers of personal data. Although Chapter 17 focuses on the Romanian legal regime, the presentation therein can, in large part, be generalized to cover other European jurisdictions since Romania implements the EU legal framework for data protection. Grigore-Octav Stan and Georgiana Ghitu begin by presenting the main features of the Romanian Data Protection law transposing the EU Data Protection Directive. They discuss its scope of application and the general principles for personal data processing: good-faith and lawful processing, legitimacy, proportionality, accuracy, limitation, security. They make a special mention to the stronger protections applying to the processing of sensitive data as these categories of data are considered likely to trigger special risks for the data subject.

The chapter then examines the legal requirements with respect to trans-border data flows. For this transfer to be lawful, a two-step procedure is required that consists in identifying: (i) a legal basis for carrying out a data transfer under the national law of the country of export; and (ii) a legal basis for the international transfer so as to ensure that the transferred data will enjoy "adequate protection" in the country of import. As to the first step, the authors explain that data transfer represents a form of data processing and, consequently, a lawful transfer of personal data will have to comply with all legal requirements for processing. For example, the data subject must generally be informed of and consent to the processing. As to the second step, the authors describe that, similar to the EU Data Protection Directive, the Romanian Data Protection Law sets out the general rule that cross-border transfers of personal data are permitted only if the receiving country ensures an adequate level of protection. All the countries in the EU and the European Economic Area are deemed to offer an "adequate level of data protection." In the case of transfers to non-EU/EEA countries, the European Commission is entitled to consider that certain countries have data protection regimes providing a presumption of adequacy for personal data exports. In the absence of such an assessment, the national data protection authority is able to determine such adequacy. The authors discuss last the case of third countries not ensuring an adequate level of data protection. In this scenario, under EU and domestic law the transfer is lawful if the data controller adduces sufficient guarantees with respect to the protection of the fundamental rights of individuals. Such guarantees must result from contractual clauses included in agreements between the data exporter and the data importer.

This section concludes with Anna Pateraki's comparative approach on the subject of the implementation of the EU legislation concerning data protection in Chapter 18. The author provides an account of the current legislative position of data protection in several EU Member States as Germany, Great Britain and France, aiming in providing the reader with information regarding the different legal 'culture' in the European privacy protection.

The book in its totality had three respective aims. The first one was to engage with some of the most modern and pressing privacy and technology issues. The second one was to offer—as much as possible—an international approach on these issues, in order to combine, American and European literature in the common, globalized problem of the limits that technology is nowadays imposing upon the privacy of the individual. The third was to offer not a uniform but a pluralistic approach on the value and concept of privacy. As far as the first and second aim are concerned the book has tried to offer aspects of the privacy-technology problem, at least some of the main ones from several jurisdictions and legal traditions, knowing that they can only partly cover the rapidly evolving subject of privacy and technology. Without adopting a technophobic attitude towards the subject, the implications of the rise of technology on the protection of privacy were examined in the paradigms of cyberspace, genetic, medical privacy and abortion, surveillance in public spaces and telecommunications, tagging and identification problems from the use of ambient technology, the protection of privacy in the field of digital copyright and children's privacy, while the current subject of data protection in the EU and in specific European legal orders were analyzed. Nevertheless, numerous more subjects concerning the use of technology in the field of penal law as a means of crime detection, prevention or even penalization arise from the difficult conciliation between privacy and technology. New methods of surveillance as the electronic tracking of asylum seekers performed in Australia, the use of Carnivore, a web-surveillance used in the USA, the globalized use of Echelon, of the Global Positioning System (GPS) as well as the unauthorized use of thermal imaging devices, as shown in cases such as Kyllo vs U.S. (533 U.S. 27, 2001) present the pressing and yet constantly evolving, vast and open nature of the clash between privacy and technology. The contributions of this book examine many of these developments, leaving aside others, trying to find the advantages and disadvantages, the dead ends and the policies that we can introduce in order to manifest the ambiguities that the rise of technology creates for the privacy, freedom and autonomy of the individual. The book also offers a taxonomy of possible threats and harms to the privacy of the individual and a taxonomy of clashing aims and interests that should be taken into account when privacy values are protected. Though it is inherently fragmented, this attempt to taxonomize these extremely complex issues is finally leading the authors in a common conclusion: any attempt to 'exchange' privacy in order to serve aims such as public security, the public interest, crime prevention will ultimately result in the declination of both. The public sphere, the public aims can not sufficiently exist without the notion and protection of the privacy, the private sphere.

One of the most ambiguous subjects in the privacy rights theory is that concerning the concept and value of privacy. For many theorists, privacy is a chaotic notion, extremely vast, torn between the interest of philosophy, law, sociology, psychology and even medicine. Though, the basic aim of the book was not to address this still open theoretical and scientific debate, the multiplicity of the contributions concerning privacy seems to conclude with a pluralistic understanding of privacy as proposed in theory by the influential article of D. Solove's 'Conceptualizing Privacy', published in 2002 in the California Law Review. Under this pluralistic rubric, privacy can not be identified as a sole concept but as a network of concepts and understandings that take into account the relative social and legal transformations. This pluralistic account of privacy is presented in the book that follows, via the different approaches that the authors are adopting concerning privacy. Thus, many of the contributions adopt the traditional understandings of privacy, as (a) 'right to be left alone' or as loneliness and isolation, as (b) limited access to the self, as (c) data-privacy or control over ones personal information, as (d) intimacy and (e) personhood. At the same time, many other aspects of privacy are presented, including its relation with autonomy (most prominent in American theory and jurisprudence), its connection with personality, dignity and identity (which characterizes the European approach to privacy), its shared and 'caring' character in the intimate private sphere relations, such as the family, among others.

Nonetheless, the most important aim of the book was to present and apprehend the value of privacy in the new technological era, in order to evaluate the reason why its protection must be taken seriously in any legislative or public policy utilizing technology, or aiming in protecting public safety or public security. Privacy protects our identity, our inner self, and the relationships that we deem as important or crucial or as defining of how we have become and who we are now. It enables us to express ourselves freely, to autonomously form our choices, and to independently shape our own mode and rhythm of living. Privacy is the 'home' in which we create, in which we can be our true selves, in which we can relax, even hide from the obligations and duties of the public sphere. Privacy lies in the centre of our self and of the way we are presented and communicate with our intimates, the society, and the world. Each contribution of this book has aimed in examining this very value of privacy from a different aspect, a different point of view. It is after all the value of privacy that makes us remember that technology is not a value it self. Instead it becomes worthy only because of the aims and values that it serves.

Keeping this thought in mind, we hope that the following pages with their broad coverage of a diverse range of legal topics, various technologies and different legal orders will provide the reader with some directions to address the complex question of the interface between privacy and technology in today's world.

Christina M. Akrivopoulou & Athanasios-Efstratios Psygkas
Thessaloniki and New Haven, July of 2010

REFERENCES

Agre, P., & Rotenberg, M. (1997). Technology and privacy: The new landscape. Cambridge, MA: MIT Press.

Austin, L. (2003). Privacy and the question of technology. Law and Philosophy, 22(2), 119-166.

Brin, D. (1998). The transparent society: Will technology force us to choose between privacy and freedom? Reading, MA: Addison-Wesley.

Friedman, D. (2000). Privacy and technology. Social Philosophy & Policy, 17, 186-212.

Wagner- DeCew, J. (1997). In pursuit of privacy: Law, ethics, and the rise of technology. Ithaca, NY: Cornell University Press.

Acknowledgment

We wish to acknowledge Szilvia Papp (MA in English & American Studies, University of Szeged, Hungary) for her advice on the linguistic editing of several contributions in this book.

Christina Akrivopoulou, Democritus University of Thrace, Greece
Athanasios-Efstratios Psygkas, Yale Law School, USA

Section 1
Privacy, Identity and Personality in a World of Digital Technology

Chapter 1
Privacy and Identity in a Networked World

Bradley T. Tennis
Yale Law School, USA

ABSTRACT

Digital information technologies have opened up fantastic new opportunities for ordinary people to both stand atop a virtual soapbox and reach millions and to participate in new forums for social interaction. However, as users conduct more and more of their personal and professional lives online, the distinction between public and private that has underlain the development of privacy law to date has begun to blur. While some traditional regulatory tools have proven adaptable, the ever increasing ability to collect and analyze that electronic information suggests that the assumptions and policy considerations underlying privacy laws must be reexamined. Old dividing lines between public and private forums cannot be readily transported into the digital realm. Instead, privacy regulations in the information age should protect the ability for users of online services to control the dissemination of their personal information and compartmentalize different aspects of their online conduct.

INTRODUCTION

In 1946 Murray Leinster published a science fiction short story entitled *A Logic Named Joe* (Leinster, 1998). The eerily prescient story posits a society saturated by and utterly dependent on networked computers known as "logics." Each logic is wired to a central data repository called "the tank," containing the sum of human knowledge. One day a particular logic—the eponymous Joe—achieves sentience and undertakes to organize and correlate all the information in the tank. In the process, Joe reprograms the other logics

DOI: 10.4018/978-1-60960-083-9.ch001

so that they will not simply report facts or replay television programs: they will also answer any question posed to them by combining and analyzing information. For example, one user is given the recipe for a surefire remedy for inebriation; another is given precise instructions for disposing of a murder victim; still others are taught how to commit the perfect robbery. It is not long before the logic network is asked to locate a particular person and, in response, begins to collect and organize dossiers on everyone who uses it. Recognizing the peril of unlimited access to and correlation of information, the story's protagonist finds and unplugs Joe, thus saving civilization.

Leinster's story suggests a distinction between information that should be broadly accessible to the public and information that should not. Modern society has clearly drawn the line in a different place. For example, a quick Google search for "how to dispose of a body" turned up over seven million hits. These suggestions are not the product of the awesome correlative and deductive powers of Leinster's logic network, and so are presumably less likely to be unerringly correct, but it seems probable that helpful advice about corpse disposal is publicly available on the Internet. Nonetheless, the idea of a separation between public and private information has remained a key normative goal in the development of privacy policies and doctrines for over one hundred years. The idea is often traced to Samuel Warren and Louis Brandeis's *Harvard Law Review* article advocating the creation of a tort for breach of privacy. Warren and Brandeis observed:

The design of the law must be to protect those persons with whose affairs the community has no legitimate concern, from being dragged into an undesirable and undesired publicity and to protect all persons, whatsoever; their position or station, from having matters which they may properly prefer to keep private, made public against their will (Warren & Brandeis, 1890, pp. 214-215).

The concept of public and private spheres has persisted and become the theoretical foundation on which modern privacy regulation is based. As an increasing portion of personal life is mediated and, just as importantly, recorded by digital technologies, the practical distinctions between what is public and what is private have begun to blur. This tension has not gone unnoticed: many commentators have noted that traditional regulatory tools have proven difficult to apply in light of the incredible ease of generating, sharing, copying, transforming, and accessing digital information (Samuelson, 2000; Solove, 2001; Zittrain, 2008).

Regulating the creation and use of technology is an inherently difficult endeavor: society has rightly placed a high value on rapid technological advancement, but the concomitant development of the law to account for the effects of new technologies frequently occurs very slowly. Consequently it is crucial to create flexible, technologically agnostic rules, which in turn depends critically on a clear conception of the interests served by government regulation. For example, *Mullane v. Hanover Bank & Trust Co.* requires that forms of notice be "reasonably calculated, under all the circumstances, to apprise interested parties of the pendency of the action and afford them an opportunity to present their objections" (Mullane, 1950, p. 314). While this rule is not a complete solution by any stretch of the imagination (for example, what counts as reasonable notice in a harassment suit against an anonymous online poster?), the generality of the *Mullane* rule helps to ensure that specific regulations all serve the same overarching goal. Principles of the same sort are needed to animate laws restricting the collection, use, and transfer of personal information online. However, proposed solutions to the privacy problems spurred by the rapid development of information networks have continued to rely on establishing or relocating a boundary between public and private and have tended to be domain specific. Rather than extending the existing privacy regime with a series of ad hoc measures, it may prove more helpful to reexamine the basic assumptions motivating the protection of privacy.

I suggest that, at least with respect to digital information technologies, privacy interests are best founded on strengthened protections for the individual to control how and to what extent his online activity and electronic records can comingle. That is, meaningful privacy protections in a networked world require that it be possible for one to compartmentalize certain aspects of their character or activity. The ever increasing interconnectedness digital information systems and the ever increasing thoroughness of electronic recordkeeping make the potential for the unwelcome unification of one's identity, that is, thrusting every interaction into a public forum, a considerably more salient threat than in the predigital age. Without the development of legal and cultural frameworks to buttress the divisions that a person may choose to make between different aspects of his identities, he may withdraw from the forum or otherwise restrict his participation, limiting the considerable informational and cultural benefits that information technologies might otherwise provide.

This Essay proceeds in two parts. First, I will examine how the legal system has adapted to account for the manifestation of familiar information privacy concerns—in particular, anonymous speech and disclosure of personal information—in the context of digital information technologies. Though occasionally frustrated by insufficient attention to protecting the democratizing potential of information technologies or a muddled conception of which aspects of a user's identity should be protected, the legal system has proven relatively adaptable. In the Second Part, I will consider one of the more significant implications of the theoretical foundation I have just outlined: a privacy interest in information that a user has deliberately revealed to the public. I conclude that while certain legal regimes have made some progress in recognizing this interest, it is at root an interest that is best protected by inculcating a normative framework that respects identity fragmentation.

I. ADAPTING OLD TOOLS AND TECHNIQUES TO SAFEGUARD PRIVACY ONLINE

Even before the digital revolution, the ability of individuals to maintain control over the improper discovery, dissemination, or misuse of their identity was threatened by the potential for governments to wiretap telephone lines (Katz, 1967) or impose overly broad restrictions or burdens on speech (McIntyre, 1995); for businesses to misuse customer data (People's Bank, 1977); and for thieves to steal personal information (Mihm, 2003). However, the tremendous generativity of the Internet—that is, the potential for a vast and diverse set of producers to create and disseminate information—coupled with the ever growing capacity for data collection and analysis has multiplied these concerns and brought them to the foreground of national debates on privacy (Zittrain, 2006). This Essay will focus on two particularly clear examples: the deanonymization of online speakers and the disclosure of electronic information that has been transferred, whether deliberately or not, to third parties.

A. Anonymous Speakers

In a sense, anonymity and online communication are entirely at odds with each other: the essential goal of anonymity is to prevent the association of speech with the speaker's identity, and yet communicating online, which for better or worse is almost always a bidirectional process, requires that a user identify herself. Consequently, most online communication is conducted under a form of pseudonymity. Typically a user's IP address serves as a substitute for his identity, though he may also create other pseudonyms to interact with online service providers. A user's real identity is generally not broadcast unless he makes a conscious effort to do so. However, for most Internet users, pseudonymity is easily pierced. Generally speaking, a user may be connected to content that he either authored or received by a two-step process. First, an IP address is associated with particular content using the records of an online service provider such as a message board, blog service, or e-mail service. The IP address can often then be matched to a particular user through the records of that user's Internet service provider (ISP) (Zittrain, 2003).

To be sure, there are technical measures—such as data encryption, anonymizing proxy servers, chained anonymization systems such as Tor, or even entire networks, separate from the world wide web—that sophisticated users may employ to help disrupt the process of linking their online activity to their real identities. The existence and nature of these technologies, far from serving as a comforting reminder that censorship of the Internet is difficult, throws the need for stronger privacy protections into stark relief. Assuming that these technologies are not used solely for mischief or other undesirable activity, their very existence suggests that current regulations of the Internet are underserving the desire to engage in unscrutinized production of information and culture. This is not a particularly heroic assumption. For example, Johan Helsingus, the creator of one such anonymizing service, has noted:

It's clear that for things like the Usenet groups on sexual abuse, people need to be able to discuss their own experiences without everyone knowing who they are. Where you're dealing with minorities—racial, political, sexual, whatever—you always find cases in which people belonging to a minority would like to discuss things that are important to them without having to identify who they are (Quittner, 1994).

Moreover, these technologies are fundamentally incapable of serving as a panacea for protecting anonymous speech online. Even assuming that anonymizing technologies may be fairly easy to install and operate, it requires a certain level of savvy to recognize potential threats to anonymity, locate the correct tool to combat them, and ensure that the tool is functioning properly. Consequently, the legal system should strive to provide basic procedural safeguards to prevent abusive deanonymization.

Fifty years ago, the Supreme Court noted that "[p]ersecuted groups and sects from time to time throughout history have been able to criticize oppressive practices and laws either anonymously or not at all" (Talley, 1960). In *McIntyre v. Ohio Elections Commission*, the Court built on this reasoning, stating that "[a]nonymity is a shield from the tyranny of the majority. It thus exemplifies the purpose behind the Bill of Rights, and of the First Amendment in particular: to protect unpopular individuals from retaliation—and their ideas from suppression—at the hand of an intolerant society" (McIntyre, 1995, p. 357). The protections of the First Amendment clearly extend to preventing improper government inquiries into the identity of anonymous online posters. Although the dangers of improper government surveillance and deanonymization are quite real, that is not my focus here. This Section will instead consider the ever increasing potential for private actors to exploit digital information technologies to illegitimately stifle online speech or the production of cultural content.

Jerome Barron, writing about traditional mass media rather than the Internet, noted that the most significant danger to free speech came not from the government, but from the censorship powers of private media companies (Barron, 1967). While private interests remain the nominal gatekeepers for speech online, the nature of the threat posed by private interests to free speech has changed markedly. Barron's worry was that media conglomerates would use their stranglehold on access to viewers to curtail speech not in line with the company's objectives, but the owners of online services are "literally begging people to use their sites to talk to others, to add valuable content to their sites, and to draw other users to visit them" (Balkin, 2008, p. 938). Barron's prediction that the government would come to play a lessened role in the restriction of free speech has proven correct, but he did not anticipate the threat posed by third parties; the privacy interests in anonymous speech online are frequently threatened by civil actions initiated by other private parties. These suits stem from an abuse of asymmetry: speakers are pressured to self-censor to avoid the costs of defending themselves against a baseless claim and revealing their identity, potentially inviting further interference.

1. Strategic Lawsuits Against Public Participation

Regulations responding to baseless civil claims against anonymous online speakers, sometimes termed strategic lawsuits against public participation (SLAPPs), generally strike an appropriate balance between strong protections for privacy and the legitimate claims of civil plaintiffs. Section 230(c)(1) of the Telecommunications Act (47 U.S.C. § 230(c)(1) (2006)) provides a safe harbor for online service providers by absolving them of any liability for content authored by their users. This provision was explicitly intended to encourage the continued development of a wide variety of online services (47 U.S.C. § 230(b)(1) (2006)). Whether or not section 230 has been as effective as public policy, there is no doubt that the ecosystem of online services would look radically different in its absence. Without the immunities provided by section 230(c)(1), social networking sites such as Facebook and MySpace, blog services, and forums for online public commentary might have foundered under the strain of legal liability for their users' postings, curtailed users' freedom to post, or might never even have been developed in the first place.

Because the online service provider is shielded from liability under section 230, a party that wishes to force the removal of content he finds objectionable or embarrassing from a website is often only able to sue the (potentially unknown) author. Where these lawsuits are based on a cognizable legal claim, they should certainly be allowed to proceed. While the Internet is a powerful tool for enabling mass participation in knowledge and cultural production, it also provides a fertile new ground for harassment, defamation, and persecution. Anonymity provides a shield for both uses: there is no doubt that "[i]ndividuals say and do things online that they would never consider saying or doing offline because they feel anonymous" (Citron, 2009, p. 83). It is crucial to preserve the ability of true victims of online harassment or defamation to engage the justice system to discover the identities of their tormentors and bring legal action against them.

But not all lawsuits targeting individuals who post information online are based on a legitimate legal claim. In one particularly notable example, Barbara Streisand sued both photographer Kenneth Adelman and the web-based image hosting site Pictopia.com in 2003 to prevent publication of an aerial photo that included her house (ostensibly taken as part of a project to document coastal erosion). The suit was dismissed (Streisand, 2003). Unsurprisingly, Streisand's suit achieved just the opposite of the intended effect as people flocked to view the image after the lawsuit was made public. This led commentators to coin the term "Streisand Effect" to describe the increase in attention that information receives following an effort to suppress it. Even more troubling, although many SLAPP suits come from third parties without direct authority over the defendants, there have been examples of public officials using nuisance lawsuits to attempt to identify anonymous detractors (Doe, 2005).

In the context of civil suits arising from anonymously authored online content, safeguards against illegitimate claims hinge on a single procedural device: the "John Doe" subpoena. Such a subpoena is served on the online service provider and typically requests the IP address of the user who authored the offending content. Clearly some mechanism for balancing the needs of legitimate plaintiffs against the desire to protect the anonymity of online speakers against baseless claims is necessary: if these subpoenas are blindly authorized by the courts, then anonymous speech online is illusory. However, far from casually rubber-stamping John Doe subpoenas, courts have proven adaptable, modifying existing legal tools to balance the interests of plaintiffs with legitimate claims and anonymous speakers. While the specifics of the test for granting John Doe subpoenas are still in a state of flux, there appears to be a growing consensus for requiring that the plaintiff make a strong showing that his claim is colorable and that the defendant receive notice (Gleicher, 2008). These requirements seem to strike an appropriate balance between the legitimate claims of plaintiffs and the ability of defendants to protect against abusive law suits.

Of course, the potential for being unmasked is only one of the potential chilling factors on free speech implicated by nuisance lawsuits. Even if a John Doe subpoena is successfully quashed by an anonymous defendant, he may have incurred considerable legal expenses in fighting the subpoena. Section 425.16 of the California Civil Procedural Code offers a potential solution. In addition to creating a special motion to strike that may be exercised by the defendant unless "the court determines that the plaintiff has established that there is a probability that the plaintiff will prevail on the claim," the statute allows prevailing defendants to recover attorney's fees and costs (Cal. Civ. Proc. Code § 425.16 (West 2008)). The inclusion of an attorney's fee award is a crucial component to preventing the abuse of baseless legal claims to unmask anonymous speakers. Simply filing a nuisance lawsuit costs very little, but the potential costs to defend against even a John Doe subpoena are substantial when compared with the negligible *monetary* costs of self-censorship. An attorney's fee award simultaneously removes one of the most substantial burdens on defendants who choose to challenge nuisance suits and deters plaintiffs who would file them.

2. Abuse of the DMCA's Notice and Take-Down Procedures

The procedural tools that have arisen to combat the use of nuisance suits to curtail anonymous speech have been fairly successful, but the notice and take-down provisions of the Digital Millennium Copyright Act (DMCA) remain problematic. The DMCA affords online service providers a safe harbor from intellectual property infringement claims, on the condition that the service abides by a simple notice and take-down procedure (17 U.S.C. § 512 (2006)). Under the notice and take-down rules of the DMCA, a copyright owner may request that an online service remove material that the owner claims infringes on his copyright. The service provider is obligated to remove the material and notify the user who posted the data. The user is then given an opportunity to file a counter-notice indicating a good faith claim that the material is noninfringing. The service provider is then required to notify the copyright owner of the user's objection, and if a lawsuit is not filed within fourteen days the service provider must restore the material to the site. However, the counter-notice requires that the user both identify himself, and submit to the jurisdiction of a federal court.

Because the take-down procedures in the DMCA make filing a lawsuit unnecessary for copyright owners, anti-SLAPP provisions are useless to prevent abusive filing of infringement notices. When content that a user has posted to an online service provider such as YouTube is subjected to a take-down notice by a copyright owner, the poster has two options: reveal his identity and submit to the jurisdiction of a federal court by filing a counter-notice, or simply permit the content to be removed and allow himself to be censored. This is a fundamentally different choice than that faced by defendants in SLAPP cases. Whereas defendants in nuisance lawsuits may only avoid legal action by prospectively engaging in self-censorship, the notice and take-down provisions of the DMCA allow an individual to escape liability, in a practical sense, by simply assenting to the censorship demands of copyright holders. Pragmatically this might suggest that the procedural protections offered to SLAPP defendants should be stronger as they do not have the escape hatch that the recipients of take-down notices do. However, this conclusion underserves the value of encouraging a democratized participation in the creation of cultural products. The inability for recipients of DMCA take-down notices to challenge the claim without identifying themselves, and thereby inviting further, targeted scrutiny in the future, markedly increases the potential for the use of illegitimate notices to chill online speech.

Although the DMCA does contain provisions attempting to limit fraudulent claims of copyright infringement (17 U.S.C. § 512(f) (2006)), take-down notices continue to be abused (Electronic Frontier Foundation, 2003). It is not difficult to see why: a plaintiff served with a fraudulent take-down notice is in much the same position as a plaintiff served with a legitimate one. In each case, the plaintiff faces the choice of censorship or exposing himself to the possibility of lengthy and expensive legal action. The sensible choice for an individual speaker, particularly when the case for copyright infringement is ambiguous, is to avoid the fight. Without preliminary judicial oversight to rein in clearly abusive invocations, the DMCA's notice and take-down provisions are at odds with expansive protections for individual participation in democratic knowledge and cultural production. The ability to slink away without revealing one's identity is useless if that ability is conditioned on accepting censorship. As in the context of SLAPPS, it is critical that the law provide a means for an individual to defend himself against spurious claims without revealing his identity and thereby inviting further legal complications or social sanction.

B. Third Party Disclosure

Digitized data is collected during practically every interaction with commercial or governmental entities. This information may either be consciously transferred—for example, a user might provide an e-mail address to register for a newspaper's online edition—or unconsciously surrendered—for example, the service might keep track of which articles each user reads. Every click or keystroke that a person makes while using an online service can be recorded (Kane & Delange, 2009). As a result, online services can build up extensive, detailed dossiers on the usage habits of their users, perhaps correlated with any personal information such as age, gender, ethnicity, or other details that the user has either explicitly provided or that can be inferred. Were these records confined to the service that collected them, the privacy concerns of collection might be more easily mitigated, but information collected from the users of online services is often sold or transferred to third parties. For example, Acxiom maintains a database that "recognizes three billion consumers daily," (Kane & Delange, 2009, p. 329) and Experian, one of the major credit reporting bureaus, maintains records covering ninety-eight percent of American households with more than one thousand data items per household (Kane & Delange, 2009). Both databases were compiled by aggregating information collected by other organizations.

The potential for vast, interconnected systems of digital recordkeeping to implicate privacy concerns has been long recognized: records may be gathered and transferred without the user's knowledge; the user often has no ability to correct or remove false or misleading information; and individuals often cannot control subsequent disclosure of information that they have provided to an online service. Data privacy laws represent an attempt to reconstitute the boundary between public and private information by prohibiting the transfer of personal information in certain contexts, but the lack of a coherent underlying conception of the privacy interest implicated by the collection and dissemination of consumer information has resulted in an unwieldy regulatory muddle. American information privacy statutes often provide conflicting definitions of terms or wildly different scopes of consumer protection in different contexts, making it impossible for individuals to reliably predict how their data will be collected and used by a particular service provider. While traditional privacy tools have often proven adaptable to regulating the transfer of information to third parties or mitigating the harm of data breaches in specific domains, the interest in compartmentalization identified in this Essay suggests that the rules must be applied more broadly and fine tuned to permit greater individual participation.

1. Privacy Law Should Protect a Broad Reading of "Personal Information"

One of the key strategies for strengthening privacy protections in electronic information is reevaluating crabbed notions of what constitutes "personally identifiable information" in light of the sheer volume of data created by the proliferation of online services and social networks. Increasingly, it is becoming difficult to determine what information is safely anonymized and what information, if released, might lead to privacy breaches. For example, in 2006 America Online supplied researchers with the complete search data for 657,000 users collected over a three month period. Although efforts were taken to anonymize the data by referring to users only by an identification number, the content of some users' search histories was enough to identify them. While only a few users were able to be definitively identified, keep in mind that this incident involved the release of only a small slice of each user's activity with a particular service (Barbaro & Zeller, 2006). Some legal definitions of personal information are broad enough to cover information that may prove indirectly identifiable, but others continue to reflect the outdated notion that personally identifiable information is restricted to information that contains explicit reference to an identifiable aspect of the user's real world identity, such as a legal name or address.

The Video Privacy Protection Act (18 U.S.C. § 2710 (2006)), which deals specifically with disclosures of personal information by video rental businesses, is an illustrative example. The Act was passed in 1988 after Supreme Court nominee Robert Bork's video record rentals were published in an attempt to discredit him. The act defines "personally identifiable information" as "information which identifies a person as having requested or obtained specific video materials or services from a video tape service provider " (18 U.S.C. § 2710(a)(3) (2006)). While the scope of the act itself is extremely narrow, the definition of personal information within that scope is quite broad, covering any information which can associate a particular person with a rental.

Contrast this with the Drivers Privacy Protection Act (18 U.S.C. §§ 2721-2725 (2006)), passed to prevent state motor vehicle departments from selling information about drivers to marketers. This statute defines "personal information" much more narrowly as "information that identifies an individual, including an individual's photograph, social security number, driver identification number, name, address (but not the 5-digit zip code), telephone number, and medical or disability information, but does not include information on vehicular accidents, driving violations, and driver's status" (18 U.S.C. § 2725(3) (2006)). While the act does prohibit the transfer of information that conclusively and directly identifies an individual, it still permits a great deal of information to be disclosed. Without a uniform definition of personal information that underlies privacy law in all contexts, individuals are unable to form meaningful expectations about what information can be collected by or disclosed by third parties.

2. Notice and Consent Provisions Must Be Strengthened

California consumer protection laws provide an interesting example of the role notice plays in protecting the right of individuals to control the dissemination and use of their identifying information. Under section 1798.83 of the California Civil Code, if a customer requests it, a business must provide him with a list of the direct marketers to which the business has released personal information and a breakdown of the information released (CAL. CIV. CODE 1798.83(a) (West 2008)). While this law is limited in scope, it recognizes the right of an individual to at least be made aware of the spread of their identifying information beyond the first recipient. California was also the first state to adopt a statute requiring that businesses notify their customers of any breach of security of a system containing personal data (CAL. CIV. CODE 1798.82 (West 2008)). Almost every state has since followed suit, though the specific notice requirements vary across states and domains. For example, under section 1798.83, the customer must specifically request that a business furnish him with information about how his data may have been used. However, section 1798.82 places the burden on the service to inform customers of data breaches. The latter strategy is preferable, particularly where the consumer may be unaware that a third party even has access to their data.

It is also important that information privacy regulations pay careful attention to the type of transfer that requires notice or consent. The Gramm-Leach-Bliley Act (15 U.S.C. §§ 6801-6809 (2006)) provides an example of relatively well-structured notice and consent rules. Financial institutions are required to notify their customers that their data will be transferred to a nonaffiliated institution and to give the customer an opportunity to opt out of the transfer. However, the act also contains a number of exceptions permitting transfers related to legitimate business practices or other legal obligations to proceed without notice and explicit consent. Although the protection of an interest in compartmentalizing aspects of one's identity suggests that individuals should have a great deal of control over how their personal information is collected and used, I do not mean to suggest that that control need be absolute. Statutory exceptions for legitimate business practices or other legal obligations can be adopted consistently with the general principle that an individual should be able to control the transfer of information about him from one context to another.

3. Users Should Not Be Compelled to Agree to One-Sided Privacy Policies

Outside of the narrow contexts protected by the amalgam of federal and state information privacy laws, privacy protections for personal information in American law are typically mediated by organization-specific privacy policies. Acceptance of an online service's terms of use, including the privacy policy, is often required to access the service. The specific protections afforded by a privacy policy may vary considerably from service to service. For example, one online service may promise not to disclose user information; another might retain the right to share information amongst a collection of services owned by the same entity; and some services may retain broad rights to share user information with third parties (Kane & Delange, 2009; Zittrain, 2008). Users of online services face a considerable power imbalance in the negotiation of these privacy policies.

In many cases, the utility of a particular online service is critically dependent on the ability to collect and analyze potentially identifiable information. However, the disclosure of this information to third parties is rarely directly related to furnishing the service itself, except perhaps as a source of revenue necessary to operate it without charging a fee to users. Some theorists have contended that the market will protect—and has protected—privacy interests to the extent that consumers are concerned with privacy (Rubin, 2001). However, the wide variance in the protections afforded by privacy policies calls that claim into question; a number of polls have confirmed that consumers feel that privacy regulations are failing to provide adequate protection (Taylor, 2003).

I do not mean to lightly dismiss the financial implications of strengthening protections for individual control of personal information. Stronger protections will surely lead to fewer users consenting that their data be shared with marketers, even in aggregate or anonymized form (particularly considering the difficulties of suitably anonymizing information). However, there is no reason to suspect that every user is so sensitive about privacy as to categorically deny the dissemination of information collected by each of the online services they use. Data protection policies should be designed to allow users to protect particularly sensitive aspects of their identities without overburdening online service providers by requiring that they adhere to the strictest of all privacy standards for all users in all contexts. Simply providing users the opportunity to opt out of the data sharing provisions of a particular service's privacy policy not necessary to the production of the service without losing access to the service is an attractive middle ground between the status quo and draconian data protection schemes that hinder legitimate business practice.

II. PRIVACY IN PUBLIC INFORMATION

The legal system has proven relatively adaptable to the difficulties posed by the migration of familiar privacy problems into the online world. However, the increasing interconnectedness of information networks and the increased dependence of ordinary people on technology to mediate their social and professional lives has given rise to privacy problems without clear analogs in the predigital era. The privacy interests identified in this Essay should not be understood as entirely new principles. Rather they emerge from the reevaluation of the principles underpinning the First and Fourth Amendments in light of the unprecedented generativity and data-processing power of modern information technologies (Balkin, 2004; Zittrain, 2006). Whereas the word "privacy" typically connotes a sense of secrecy, the broad privacy interest advocated in this Essay also entails the ability to publicly project multiple personae while still maintaining boundaries between them. Preventing the coalescence of the various fragments of an individual's identity is less about jealously guarding information from public view than about ensuring that information is used and shared only within a particular context. Even though the Internet is, as a practical matter, a public forum, the ability to dissociate one's "real world" identity from online identities (as well as the ability to create multiple disjoint personae online) makes compartmentalization at least theoretically possible.

A. Compartmentalization and Democratic Culture

The conventional justification for protecting the freedom of speech, typified by the writings of Alexander Meiklejohn, is that free speech safeguards democracy by promoting full deliberation of important political issues (Meiklejohn, 1960). More recent scholarship has taken a more expansive view: for example, Jack Balkin conceives of freedom of speech as serving democracy in a broader sense by promoting the realization of and participation in a full democratic culture (Balkin, 2004). Balkin ties the idea of a democratic culture into the larger field of knowledge and information policy, the principle goals of which he identifies as:

(1) [promoting] the production and diffusion of valuable information and knowledge; (2) [developing] a healthy and vibrant public sphere of opinion and culture; (3) [encouraging] widespread participation in a culture of information and knowledge production that arises from a

broad, diverse, and antagonistic set of sources; (4) [promoting] innovation in, widespread availability of, and access to knowledge and information technologies; and (5) [developing] human capacities and human capabilities through the spread of knowledge and information technologies (Balkin, 2008, p. 941).

Balkin principally grounds the concept of democratic culture in the values underlying the First Amendment, but Jed Rubenfeld's recent work recasting the Fourth Amendment as protecting security rather than privacy also suggests latent values that support a democratic culture (Rubenfeld, 2008). Rubenfeld recognizes that in addition to a "flourishing 'public life,'" a robust democracy requires a "flourishing *personal life*" (Rubenfeld, 2008, p. 128). For the purposes of this Essay, I adopt Rubenfeld's definition of the term "personal life":

that sphere of activity and relations where people are supposed to be free from the strictures of public norms, free to be their own men and women, free to say what they actually think, and to act on their actual desires or principles, even if doing so defies public norms (Rubenfeld, 2008, p. 128).

Rubenfeld's observation is supported by the same assumption of a clear division between public and private that underlies the traditional interpretation of the protections implied by the Fourth Amendment. However, the desire to protect a person's private life, when so much of it is mediated by digital technologies, implies that promoting a democratic culture may have implications for privacy policy as well.

Democratic culture is contingent on individuals having access to information and social networks that allow them to fully express their personhood as well as the ability to participate meaningfully in those networks (Balkin, 2004). This interest implies a parallel interest in promoting the development of a rich variety of online services to mediate and structure that production (Balkin, 2008). The protection of a democratic culture therefore requires the balance of two interests: encouraging the creation of online services and encouraging their use. The first interest counsels against unnecessary restrictions on service operators. Ensuring that individuals may meaningfully compartmentalize aspects of their personality serves the second interest.

The ability to compartmentalize allows a user to participate in the production of information and culture that might prove damaging or embarrassing if associated with them in other contexts. For example, consider an employee fired for complaining about his job on their Facebook profile (Mastyszczyk, 2009), or a college applicant being rejected after universities discover questionable content that the student posted online (Hechinger, 2008). Finally, imagine a closeted homosexual outed to family and friends after a third party discovers his profile on a gay issues website or an alcoholic discovered after he begins to frequent an online support group. In each case, the injured party could have avoided any problem by simply not posting any information online, but this would unjustifiably stifle the production of information and culture—as well as the ability of the individual to fully engage with every aspect of their personhood—that is central to the protection of a democratic culture and the consistent with the latent values of the First and Fourth amendments.

The need to compartmentalize different aspects of one's life has long been a fundamental motivation for legal protections of privacy, resulting in regulations that purport to separate public and private spheres. However, the proliferation of digital information technologies has made plain the difficulties in cleanly separating private from public once a certain amount of one's interaction is conducted online. The separation of public and private is an insufficiently nuanced view of privacy in a networked world. The taxonomy of privacy theories articulated by Daniel J. Solove is instructive (Solove, 2008). Solove sorts theories of privacy into six classes based on the underlying interest that they serve: the right to be left alone, limited access to the self, secrecy, control over personal information, personhood, and intimacy. The first three of these categories can be dealt with together: all three clearly contemplate the separation of the world into two distinct contexts—public and private. Compartmentalization does not fit neatly into the group of theories defined by an interest in intimacy either. Such theories prove too narrow by failing to account for the protection of social relationships which may encourage cultural participation, but could not reasonably be considered intimate. The closest theoretical categorization is that supported by an interest in the control of personal information (Fried, 1968; Miller, 1971; Westin, 1967). The theory I advance is also rooted in control, but also countenances a very broad conception of what constitutes "personal information."

The definition of "personal information" is difficult to precisely establish, and theorists have offered a broad range of readings (Murphy, 1996; Parker, 1974). I advocate a reading that follows naturally from the same principles motivating Margaret Radin's proposal that different pieces of personal property may implicate concerns of personhood to differing degrees (Radin, 1982). It is easy to imagine that people may feel the same way about personae they develop in the course of using online services. Jed Rubenfeld has suggested that such a concept of privacy sweeps too broadly, noting that "[v]irtually every action a person takes could arguably be said to be an element of his self-definition" (Rubenfeld, 1989, pp. 754-755). It is important to note, however, that Professor Rubenfeld's article is primarily concerned with establishing the limits of the Fourth Amendment *right* to privacy as against Government intrusion. This Essay is concerned more with the positive aspects of privacy and aims to provide guiding principles for devising meaningful privacy protections in positive legal and normative development in light of the exigencies of digital technologies. Moreover, the connection between compartmentalization and the promotion of a democratic culture suggests a clear limit to the privacy interests it protects: that is, privacy should be protected inasmuch as the protection encourages increased engagement with cultural production. This clearly excludes some of Rubenfeld's more fanciful hypotheticals, such as "tonsorial preferences" (Rubenfeld, 1989, p. 755).

B. Privacy in Publicly Disclosed Information

For the first time, a significant portion of the average person's conduct may be represented in a digital form that is easily transferred and analyzed. Consequently, individuals have lost the ability to meaningfully control the collection, analysis, and transfer of their personal information—that is, the ability to meaningfully compartmentalize facets of their identity. This is best demonstrated by the development of semi-private spaces for social interaction embedded in the shared public forum of the Internet. In the absence of any meaningful ability to compartmentalize their online personae, users of online services are presented with an unpalatable choice: withdraw from participation in any online community that may prove harmful or embarrassing in another context or else simply accept that any aspect of their identity may be commingled with any other. Discussing the related privacy problems implied by cheap, widely available sensors, Jonathan Zittrain notes: "Today we are all becoming politicians. .. . Ubiquitous sensors threaten to push everyone toward treating each public encounter as if it were a press conference, creating fewer spaces in which citizens can express their private selves" (Zittrain, 2008, p. 84). In the same vein, Jeffrey Rosen writes: "[W] e have fewer opportunities to present ourselves publicly in all our complexity. Therefore, as more of our private lives are recorded in cyberspace, the risk that we will be unfairly defined by isolated pieces of information that have been taken out of context has increased dramatically" (Rosen, 2000, p. 158).

While traditional privacy tools may potentially be adapted to combat the electronic manifestations of familiar privacy concerns, digital information technologies have also raised concerns not readily analogized to old problems. The explosive growth in the use of online services to facilitate social interactions implicates a privacy interest in compartmentalization in myriad ways. For instance, college applicants may be rejected after admissions officers uncover embarrassing or questionable information posted online. Employees might be fired for criticizing their job online. Job applicants might be asked to reveal their usernames on social networking sites as part of a background check (Wolgemuth, 2009). Aspects of individuals' personal lives that were once ephemeral and witnessed only by a small number of people are now recorded, stored, and made available for everyone to discover.

Privacy regulations in the United States are generally motivated by a desire to locate and enforce a carefully delineated boundary between sensitive and nonsensitive information and between spaces that are public and those that are private. However, this distinction fails to appreciate the individualized nature of the privacy interest at stake. Users of online services may come to see the service as representing a distinct aspect of their personality. The privacy concerns implicated by the misuse of information that, while published on a public forum, is clearly intended to be restricted to a narrower context cannot be readily addressed by attempts to distinguish between purely public and purely private. Whether or not *United States v. Miller* (425 U.S. 435 (1976)) is normatively correct, it is descriptively accurate under the current regulatory regime: when you transmit information to third parties, you often surrender practical control of it. For instance, the users whose data were disclosed by America Online likely did not imagine that their search records would be retained. These users may therefore have been more comfortable including personally identifiable information, such as names or locations, in their search queries on the assumption that the data would never be collected or analyzed.

Even if we could vigorously protect the disclosure of personally identifiable information to third parties—in the broad sense advocated in this Essay—users may still lose the effective ability to compartmentalize their lives through collection and analysis of the vast amount of information left behind when they use an online service. Users of social networking services, a rapidly expanding class of online service providers (Lenhart, 2009), willingly disseminate information about themselves to the general public. Users of social networking sites are often sensitive to privacy concerns and can restrict access to their profile to their "friends" but disclosures of identifying information on one online service (or by the service itself) may also compromise a user's privacy on other services. For example, researchers at the University of Texas have developed a deanonymization system capable of identifying a user's Flickr account with his Twitter account for one third of users known to use both services (Narayanan & Shmatikov, 2009). The potential threat to effective compartmentalization created by the use of online services as a social medium goes beyond associating a user's various online personae: even if a particular user has scrupulously protected his identity on every service he uses, his friends may not be so careful.

C. Obstacles to Legal Regulation

The difficulty of meaningfully protecting privacy in a world where so much of our lives are conducted on the Internet has been termed "Privacy 2.0" by Professor Zittrain (Zittrain, 2008). Zittrain is primarily concerned with the ways in which increasingly inexpensive processing power, network bandwidth, and sensors can combine to render interactions in the real world recordable and indexable in the same way as purely virtual content. Understanding the effect of networked technologies on the physical world will surely be crucial to developing privacy policies in the twenty-first century, but privacy concerns pertaining solely to online personae and social networks cannot be ignored. Zittrain's account implicitly accepts the dominant view of the Internet as an entirely public arena. While this is not far off the mark in a purely descriptive sense, conceding that the Internet is a homogeneously public medium gives short shrift to the need for individuals to meaningfully compartmentalize aspects of their personal lives conducted online. Zittrain does, however, recognize that the terms "public" and "private" are not sufficiently subtle to support sophisticated discourse on information privacy concerns. However, Zittrain fails to extend this idea to its logical conclusion: the Internet cannot be neatly categorized as either a public or a private space; it is a complex combination of semi-private, potentially overlapping spaces nestled in a public medium.

The strategies Zittrain outlines for strengthening privacy protections online are primarily intended to foster privacy-enhancing norms. For instance, he has suggested the development of a license for personal information in the style of the Creative Commons license for copyrights. This license would permit users to tag their personal information with a license expressing the contexts in which they permit it to be used. Zittrain's proposal is interesting, but somewhat off the mark. The Creative Commons license is intended to liberalize a strict background regime, where the license contemplated here would do just the opposite. That is, Creative Commons is intended to encourage distribution and use of information, while the purpose of a privacy license would be to restrict it. Zittrain also suggests taking advantage of the vast generativity of the Internet to flood the space with data so as to contextualize any information that might be inappropriately used or disclosed. This solution entirely discounts the desirability of maintaining separate personas, instead suggesting the complete unification of the different facets of an individual's personality–just the outcome that this Essay seeks to avoid. Zittrain himself recognizes this difficulty, noting that this solution fails to protect against the disclosure of content that it simply embarrassing in and of itself.

By contrast, scholars who conceive of privacy rights in terms of the ability to control the publication of personal information often ground privacy protections in property and contract law and suggest market-based solutions (Bibas, 1994; Murphy, 1996; Samuelson, 2000; Volokh, 2000). However, in this context market-based solutions are rendered ineffective by the nature of the privacy interest at stake. Advocates of market-based solutions to information privacy tend to envision the relevant players as an individual user and a business. While market mechanisms may effectively intervene in that context, the privacy interest identified here often involves interactions between parties who have no privity of contract.

There are considerable difficulties in protecting privacy concerns in ostensibly public information through public law as well. Broadly speaking, regulations may protect a privacy interest by limiting the collection, use, or disclosure of personal information. There is a substantial tension between First Amendment jurisprudence and regulatory protection of the privacy interest in compartmentalization. Eugene Volokh describes the tension succinctly: "The difficulty is that the right to information privacy—my right to control your communication of personally identifiable information about me—is a right to have the government stop you from speaking about me" (Volokh, 2000, pp. 1050-1051). As Volokh suggests, regulations that seek to limit the disclosure of information that has already been made public quickly run into First Amendment difficulties. While there have been some narrow restrictions on the disclosure of information (for example, the Video Privacy Protection Act) broad public law regulation of personal information in the United States would have to focus predominantly on the collection or use of personal information.

However, the regulation of collection of public information is rendered somewhat impractical precisely because the information is public; there is no sensible way to separate benign from malicious collection without reference to how the data are used or disclosed. Moreover, the privacy interest identified in this Essay is justified by the furtherance of a democratic culture. The full expression of democratic culture requires not only that individuals be able to freely express themselves and "participate in the forms of meaning making that constitute them as individuals" (Balkin, 2004, p. 3), but also that they be able to collect and re-mix publicly available information to create new cultural content.

Attempts to enforce a privacy interest in preventing two different pieces of public information from being associated also run into temporal difficulties. The establishment of ex ante control mechanisms is difficult as there is no reasonable way to determine a priori whether a given collection or use will be malicious, and it is often impossible or impractical to even determine that publicly available information has been accessed or used. Therefore, traditional regulatory tools such as notice and an opportunity to block the transfer of personal information are inapplicable: the harm implied by a theory of privacy based on compartmentalization occurs only after a person's publicly available personal information is inappropriately used or introduced into an unwanted context. This suggests that a regulatory mechanism that serves a broad privacy interest in compartmentalization must be focused on deterring inappropriate use by imposing penalties ex post.

An examination of two foreign regulatory frameworks may help to suggest some promising approaches to legal protections for public or voluntarily surrendered information. In 2000, Canada enacted the Personal Information Protection and Electronic Documents Act (PIPEDA) (Personal Information Protection and Electronic Documents Act, 2000 S.C., ch. 5 (Can.)). The animating principle of PIPEDA is consistent with the principles of an expansive right to privacy: PIPEDA is intended to vigorously protect an individual right to privacy online while still allowing "organizations to collect, use or disclose personal information for purposes that a reasonable person would consider appropriate in the circumstances" (PIPEDA, part I, § 3). PIPEDA defines "personal information" broadly, deeming any "information about an identifiable individual" to be personal (PIPEDA, part I, § 2(1)). The European Union Data Protection Directive also takes an expansive view of personal information, defining it as "any information relating to an identified or identifiable natural person ('data subject'); an identifiable person is one who can be identified, directly or indirectly, in particular by reference to an identification number or to one or more factors specific to his physical, physiological, mental, economic, cultural or social identity" (Council Directive 95/46/EC, art. 2, § (a), 1995 O.J. (L 281) 31 (EU)).

Of course, broad definitions of personal information are toothless without restrictions on the collection, use, or dissemination of personal information without providing notice and giving an individual the opportunity to prevent use of his information. PIPEDA restricts all three activities. As an example, PIPEDA permits organizations to gather information about an individual without his knowledge or consent only if:

(a) the collection is clearly in the interests of the individual and consent cannot be obtained in a timely way;
(b) it is reasonable to expect that the collection with the knowledge or consent of the individual would compromise the availability or the accuracy of the information and the collection is reasonable for purposes related to investigating a breach of an agreement or

a contravention of the laws of Canada or a province;

(c) the collection is solely for journalistic, artistic or literary purposes; or

(d) the information is publicly available and is specified by the regulations (PIPEDA, part I, § 7(1)).

Similar provisions exist limiting the use and disclosure of personal information without the knowledge and consent of the individual except in very narrow circumstances, generally relating to criminal investigations or scholarly research. Though subsection (d) is a troubling and potentially open-ended exception, the general principle of PIPEDA is clear: knowledge and consent are required before personal data may be collected, used, or disclosed.

The EU Data Protection Directive takes a similarly aggressive stance on prohibiting the misuse of personal data. The directive states that personal data may only be processed when:

(a) the data subject has unambiguously given his consent; or

(b) processing is necessary for the performance of a contract to which the data subject is party or in order to take steps at the request of the data subject prior to entering into a contract; or

(c) processing is necessary for compliance with a legal obligation to which the controller is subject; or

(d) processing is necessary in order to protect the vital interests of the data subject; or

(e) processing is necessary for the performance of a task carried out in the public interest or in the exercise of official authority vested in the controller or in a third party to whom the data are disclosed; or

(f) processing is necessary for the purposes of the legitimate interests pursued by the controller or by the third party or parties to whom the data are disclosed, except where such interests are overridden by the interests for fundamental rights and freedoms of the data subject which require protection under Article 1 (1) (Council Directive 95/46/EC, art. 7, 1995 O.J. (L 281) 31 (EU)).

Both the Canadian and European statutes take an expansive reading of both the type of information warranting legal protection and the level of control that an individual should be able to exert over the collection, use, and dissemination of his personal information. Rather than reflecting the staid conception of privacy that has driven the development of U.S. privacy law, the protections offered by PIPEDA and the EU Data Protection Directive are grounded in a broad conception of privacy similar to that contemplated by this Essay. While by no means a panacea for the information privacy concerns identified in this Essay, the two statutes are a clear step in the right direction.

CONCLUSION

Traditional privacy doctrines, predicated on establishing a border between public and private, cannot readily be adapted to meet the privacy challenges of a networked world. While old tools can be modified to solve the online manifestations of old problems, the protection of a democratic culture requires the recognition of an individual's right to publicly project multiple personae. However, the widespread use of the Internet as a social medium coupled with advances in the ability to collect, organize, and analyze information have made salient different concerns about control over personal information and the ability to compartmentalize aspects of one's identity. Traditional methods of conceptualizing privacy—and therefore traditional regulatory tools—are ill-equipped to meet these challenges. Privacy in the twenty-first century must mean something more than simply designating information or spaces as purely public or purely private. Before the digital revolution, the ability to effectively separate aspects of one's personal life was enforced by the practical difficulty in collecting and analyzing personal information. These barriers have largely been erased by digital technologies, and there is no broad consensus on how privacy law should be developed, if at all, to meet the challenges posed by an increasingly networked world. While it may be the case that we will simply need to "get over it" (Sprenger, 1999) the protection of a democratic culture requires that we not give up so easily.

REFERENCES

Balkin, J. M. (2004). Digital speech and democratic culture. *New York University Law Review*, *79*(1), 1–58.

Balkin, J. M. (2008). Media access: A question of design. *The George Washington Law Review*, *76*(4), 933–951.

Barbaro, M., & Zeller, T., Jr. (2006, August 9). A face is exposed for AOL searcher no. 4417749. *The New York Times*, p. A1.

Barron, J. A. (1967). Access to the press—A new first amendment right. *Harvard Law Review*, *80*, 1641–1678. doi:10.2307/1339417

Bibas, S. A. (1994). A contractual approach to data privacy. *Harvard Journal of Law & Public Policy*, *17*(2), 591–611.

Citron, D. K. (2009). Cyber civil rights. *Boston University Law Review. Boston University. School of Law*, *89*(1), 61–125.

Doe v. Cahill, 884 A.2d 451 (Del. 2005).

Electronic Frontier Foundation. (2003). *Unsafe harbors: Abusive DMCA subpoenas and takedown demands*.

Fried, C. (1968). Privacy. *The Yale Law Journal*, *77*(3), 475–493. doi:10.2307/794941

Gleicher, N. (2008). John Doe subpoenas: Toward a consistent legal standard. *The Yale Law Journal*, *118*(2), 320–368. doi:10.2307/20454712

Hechinger, J. (2008, September 18). College applicants, beware: Your Facebook page is showing. *The Wall Street Journal*. Retrieved from http://online.wsj.com/article/SB122170459104151023.html

Kane, B., & Delange, B. D. (2009). A tale of two internets: Web 2.0 slices, dices, and is privacy resistant. *Idaho Law Review*, *45*(2), 317–347.

Katz v. United States, 389 U.S. 347 (1967).

Leinster, M. (1998). *First contacts: The essential Murray Leinster*. Framingham, MA: New England Science Fiction Association.

Lenhart, A. (2009). *Adults and social network websites*. Washington, DC: Pew Internet & American Life Project.

Mastyszczyk, C. (2009, February 26). Facebook entry gets office worker fired. *CNet News*. Retrieved from http://news.cnet.com/8301-17852_3-10172931-71.html

McIntyre v. Ohio Elections Comm'n, 514 U.S. 334 (1995).

Meiklejohn, A. (1960). *Political freedom: The constitutional powers of the people*. New York: Greenwood Press.

Mihm, S. (2003, December 21). Dumpster-diving for your identity. *The New York Times Magazine*. Retrieved from http://www.nytimes.com.

Miller, A. R. (1971). *The assault on privacy: Computers, data banks, and dossiers*. Ann Arbor, MI: University of Michigan Press.

Mullane v. Hanover Bank & Trust Co., 339 U.S. 306 (1950).

Murphy, R. S. (1996). Property rights in personal information: An economic defense of privacy. *The Georgetown Law Journal, 84*(7), 2381–2417.

Narayanan, A., & Shmatikov, V. (2009). De-anonymizing social networks. In *IEEE Symposium on Security and Privacy*, Oakland, CA. New York: IEEE.

Parker, R. B. (1974). A definition of privacy. *Rutgers Law Review, 27*(2), 275–296.

Peoples Bank of Virgin Islands v. Figueroa, 559 F.2d 914 (3d Cir. 1977).

Quittner, J. (1994, June). Anonymously yours—An interview with Johan Helsingius. *Wired.* Retrieved from http://www.wired.com/wired/archive/2.06/anonymous.1.html

Radin, M. J. (1982). Property and personhood. *Stanford Law Review, 34*(5), 957–1015. doi:10.2307/1228541

Rosen, J. (2000). *The unwanted gaze: The destruction of privacy in America.* New York: Random House.

Rubenfeld, J. (1989). The right of privacy. *Harvard Law Review, 102*(4), 737–807. doi:10.2307/1341305

Rubenfeld, J. (2008). The end of privacy. *Stanford Law Review, 61*(1), 101–161.

Rubin, P. H. (2001). Privacy in commercial world. Statement before the 106th Congress.

Samuelson, P. (2000). Privacy as intellectual property? *Stanford Law Review, 52*(5), 1125–1173. doi:10.2307/1229511

Solove, D. J. (2001). Privacy and power: Computer databases and metaphors for information privacy. *Stanford Law Review, 53*(6), 1393–1462. doi:10.2307/1229546

Solove, D. J. (2008). *Understanding privacy.* Cambridge, MA: Harvard University Press.

Sprenger, P. (1999, January 16). Sun on privacy: 'Get over it'. *Wired.* Retrieved from http://www.wired.com/news/politics/0,1283,17538,00.html

Streisand v. Adelman, No. SC 077 257 (Super. Ct. Cal. decided Dec. 31, 2003).

Talley v. California, 362 U.S. 60 (1960).

Taylor, H. (2003). *Most people are "privacy pragmatists" who, while concerned about privacy, will sometimes trade it off for other benefits.* New York: Harris Interactive.

Volokh, E. (2000). Freedom of speech and information privacy: The troubling implications of a right to stop people from speaking about you. *Stanford Law Review, 52*(5), 1049–1124. doi:10.2307/1229510

Warren, S. D., & Brandeis, L. D. (1890). The right to privacy. *Harvard Law Review, 4*(5), 193–220. doi:10.2307/1321160

Westin, A. F. (1967). *Privacy and freedom.* New York: Atheneum Press.

Wolgemuth, L. (2009, June 19). In Bozeman, giving up privacy for a chance at a paycheck. *U.S. News & World Report.* Retrieved from http://www.usnews.com/blogs/the-inside-job/2009/06/19/in-bozeman-giving-up-privacy-for-a-paycheck.html

Zittrain, J. (2003). Internet points of control. *Boston College Law Review. Boston College. Law School, 44*(2), 653–688.

Zittrain, J. (2006). The generative internet. *Harvard Law Review, 119*(7), 1974–2040.

Zittrain, J. (2008). Privacy 2.0. *The University of Chicago Legal Forum*, 65–119.

Chapter 2
The Right to Privacy and the Right to Identity in the Age of Ubiquitous Computing:
Friends or Foes? A Proposal towards a Legal Articulation

Norberto Nuno Gomes de Andrade
European University Institute, Italy

ABSTRACT

Identity and privacy are often intertwined and, as a result, the significance of the distinction between the two concepts has been overlooked by law. This paper sheds some light upon the worrying indeterminacy between the concepts of privacy and identity in legal terminology, underlining the negative consequences that the lack of clarity and coherence in articulating the rights to privacy and identity will create in the forthcoming age of Ubiquitous Computing. In its proposal for a legal articulation between both rights, the article distinguishes between personal information that qualifies alethically (from αλήθεια [aletheia], the Greek word for truth) from the one that does not. It is based upon whether personal information represents or conveys a true fact or a truthful aspect concerning a given individual (depending on whether it has an alethic value or not) that the distinction between and the application of the rights to privacy and to identity shall be determined. As a way to test the usefulness of the alethic criteria, the article looks into the main challenges posed by the vision of a Ubiquitous Computing world upon the rights to privacy and identity. In this context, the paper devotes particular attention to the implications of automated profiling technologies, arguing that the conceptual clarification of both the rights to privacy and identity will be crucial in order to protect and promote the autonomy and self-determination of the human person.

DOI: 10.4018/978-1-60960-083-9.ch002

INTRODUCTION

The incessant digitization of information concerning the human person, derived from technological developments – especially since the creation and diffusion of the Internet towards the so-called age of Ubiquitous Computing (Greenfield, 2006) - are challenging the legal conceptualization and protection of different (although not easy to separate) aspects of the human personality, such as identity and privacy. This technological trend affects the human person so intimately that many scholars go beyond the mere digitization of information to the outright *per se* digitization or *informationalization* of the human person. In this sense, Roger Clark talks of the "digital persona" (Clarke, 1994), while Luciano Floridi refers to the "inforg" (Floridi, 2007) and Stefano Rodotá alludes to the idea of "networked persons" (Rodotá, 2009, p. 81). In this way, different facets of one's personality are perceived, established and projected through information and communication technologies that mediate human interaction. Different aspects of one's personality are reduced to bits and bytes, being managed, transferred and represented through algorithms and other computing processes. With the consolidation of the information revolution and the move towards full data-based societies, everything has become a question of data, information and knowledge, including the protection of one's privacy and the definition of one's identity. Such a phenomenon leads to the complex blurring of these concepts, making sharp distinctions difficult to draw between the right to privacy and the right to identity.

This article sheds some light upon the worrying indeterminacy between the concepts of privacy and identity in legal terminology, underlining the potential negative consequences that the lack of clarity and coherence in articulating the rights to privacy and identity will create in this age of Ubiquitous Computing. It purposely resists the blurring of these legal concepts and rights, drawing the attention to the pressing need to provide a clear demarcation between the right to privacy and the right to identity. The first section of the paper provides a brief sketch describing the history of the legal conceptualization of the right to privacy, listing the main definitions of the privacy concept that have characterized its long and rich evolution. The article argues that the overly broad definition of privacy has undermined and overlooked the concept and right to identity. The relentless inflationary trend in the conceptualization of the right to privacy, as argued in the initial part of the paper, is presented as the main reason behind the need to articulate in a coherent manner the rights to privacy and to identity.

The second section of the article strives to clarify a number of misunderstandings usually made in the articulation between the legal concepts of identity and privacy. In this account, the paper demonstrates the ambiguous and dynamic relationship between privacy and identity, providing examples of how the former might favour or hinder the latter, according to the context in question. Contrary to the consensual view, proposed by Agre and Rothenberg (1997) and according to whom the right to privacy is the freedom from unreasonable constraints on the construction of one's own identity, the paper draws the attention to the fact that privacy may obstruct identity, while identity may also undermine privacy. Furthermore, the paper observes that the concordant privacy-identity nexus, advocated by the two previously mentioned scholars, conflate and blur the concepts of privacy and identity, overstretching the former and understating the latter.

The third section of the article focuses upon the common roots of the rights to privacy and identity, emphasizing the fact that they both relate to the individual's right to dignity and self-determination. Departing from their common legal ancestors, namely from the so-called rights of personality (*droits de la personnalité*), the article specifies the main (and often overlooked) differences between the right to privacy and identity, describing in detail how each of them relate to a different interest of the right to personality. In this light, the paper explains that a breach of the right to privacy mainly affects an individual's ability to control the use of her personal information, while a breach of the right to identity fundamentally affects an individual's interest in the uniqueness of her being (a person's uniqueness or individuality which defines or individualises her as a particular person and thus distinguishes her from others), as well as the ability to be recognised and to engage in transactions.

The fourth section of the paper shifts the analysis of the rights to privacy and to identity to the sphere of data protection, analysing the importance of their distinction in light of the broad concept of personal data currently established within the European Union legal framework. In order to distinguish the right to privacy from the right to identity within this context, I thus propose to establish a "privacy-identity relevance" criterion in order to distinguish two different kinds of personal data, one concerning privacy interests, and the other related to identity ones. Such criterion, which I shall term of 'alethic criteria', differentiates between personal information that is truthful from the one that it is not. In this way, and according to such criteria, it is argued that only personal information that qualifies alethically (in which there is a correspondence between the concept of personal data and the set of true facts related to the data subject) shall be protected under the right to privacy, whereas personal information that is not necessarily truthful shall be covered by the right to identity. In this way, the article demonstrates how the right to privacy is currently being over-stretched, covering the legal protection of personal data that, in reality, should be assigned to the right to identity. In this manner, according to the more delimited conceptualization of the right to privacy proposed in this paper, along with its articulation with the right to identity, it is argued that the latter should also be contemplated and enshrined within the EU data protection scheme.

The fifth and final section of the article looks into the main challenges posed by the vision of a Ubiquitous Computing world upon the rights to privacy and identity. More particularly, this section examines the implications of differentiated treatment between the rights to privacy and identity in the case of automated profiling technologies. With the creation of one seamless environment, the paper argues that the conceptual clarification of both the rights to privacy and identity will be crucial in order to protect and promote the autonomy and self-determination of the human being in a coherent and complete manner.

I. THE DOCTRINAL "STATE-OF-ART" IN THE CONCEPTUALIZATION OF THE RIGHT TO PRIVACY AND THE RIGHT TO IDENTITY: THE INFLATION OF THE FORMER AND THE DEFLATION OF THE LATTER

1.1.The Inflationary Conceptual Trend of the Right to Privacy

For over a century, the concept of privacy has intrigued numerous legal scholars and jurists from different backgrounds, triggering an outstanding body of theories, conceptualizations and definitions.

Looking at the long and rich evolution of the concept, privacy was initially (and famously) conceived, by Brandeis and Warren, as 'the right to be let alone' (1890). According to such initial vision, which profoundly influenced privacy in the United States, the right to be left alone was depicted "as part of the more general right to the immunity of the person, the right to one's personality" (Warren & Brandeis, 1890, p. 207). In this way, the underlying principle of privacy was "that of an inviolate personality" (Warren & Brandeis, 1890, p. 205). The right to be "let alone" constituted a legal metaphor used to protect the interest of privacy in cases concerning physical intrusion. Such conceptualization paved the way for the legal recognition of a right to privacy in the common law, while anchoring privacy to individual autonomy and to the freedom to shape one's own life. Furthermore, and due to its very broad character, the Brandeis and Warren conception of the right to be let alone framed the subsequent debate concerning privacy, giving rise to an extensive number of succeeding privacy conceptualizations. One of the latter contemplated the attachment of ideas of isolation and seclusion to the concept of privacy. Such notion of privacy intended, in particular, to safeguard the intrinsic need for isolation and seclusion, embodying a sort of right of being hidden from the outside world. Such conceptualization of privacy aimed at securing and preserving to each person their own private shelter, that is, their own remoteness place of intimacy, away from the pervasive world and the inquisitive eye of society. Other authors, such as Raymond Wacks (1980) and Julie C. Inness (1996), have pursued this vision of privacy, associating the latter with the protection of the intimate sphere.

Afterwards, and along with the development of sophisticated technologies capable of violating one's privacy – which have increasingly been able to detect, capture and expose a person's intimate and secluded spaces – such 'isolationist' vision of privacy became progressively outdated, as scholars began realizing that the underlying interest for isolation and seclusion was not sufficient to protect one's privacy. As such, the concept took on an activist dimension, entailing not the person's right to hide from the world (which was deemed insufficient and outdated), but a person's right to control the world in order to maintain her secret "hiding place." Confronted with a world of increasingly and inexorable pervasive technologies, legal scholars – realising that the best defence is the attack – aggressively pushed privacy through an individual's control of information. This changed the privacy paradigm from stances of passivity and seclusion to activity and control.

As a result, "privacy moved from static and exclusionary conception of private life to a dynamic process of boundary control, taking place between self and its environment" (Rannenberg, Royer & Deuker, 2009, p. 292). In other words, the concept of privacy was no longer, and not simply, articulated in contrast with the outside environment, as a right to be apart from it. These new privacy conceptions, on the contrary, embraced the environment, examining new ways to manage and control the latter in order to affirm and sustain itself. Rather than being conceptualized as a "gateway escape to secrecy and exclusion", privacy was now seen as a flexible management procedure of one's external environment. A good example of this conceptual shift can be found in the work of the environmental psychologist Irwin Altman (1975), who defines privacy as a boundary regulation process translating into a "selective control of access to the self or to one's group" (Altman, 1975, p. 18). For Altman, privacy is a matter of *dialectical boundary control*, about both opening and closing the self to others.

The move towards full data-based societies under the information age has seen more acceptance of this broader view of privacy, seen first in the publication of Westin's work (1967) and followed by later scholars. Gutwirth (2002), for instance, also views the concept of *privacy as freedom and informational self-determination*. In fact, the legal academic literature has exploded in conceptualizations and definitions of privacy, emphasizing and underlining continuous new aspects and dimensions which the latter should also take into account. Rodotà summarizes in the following paragraph the progressive inclusion of new aspects in a widening concept of privacy:

After the landmark definition by Warren and Brandeis – 'the right to be left alone' – other definitions have been developed to mirror different requirements. In a world where our data move about ceaselessly, 'the right to control the way others use the information concerning us' (A.

Westin) becomes equally important. Indeed the collection of sensitive data and social and individual profiling may give rise to discrimination; privacy is therefore to be also regarded as 'the protection of life choices against any form of public control and social stigma' (L.M. Friedman), as 'vindication of the boundaries protecting each person's right not to be simplified, objectified, and evaluated out of context' (J. Rosen). Since the information flows do not simply contain 'outbound data' – to be kept off others' hands – but also 'inbound data' – privacy is also to be considered as 'the right to keep control over one's own information and determine the manner of building up one's own private sphere.' (Rodotá, 2009, p. 78)

Far from its initial conception, privacy has been increasingly perceived as a broad and powerful instrument to be used and imposed against the world, that is, against other individuals. As Ruth Gavison observes, identifying the privacy 'being let alone' conception with the 'claim for non-interference by the state' fails to comprehend that "the typical privacy claim is not a claim for non-interference by the state at all. It is a claim *for* state interference in the form of legal protection against other individuals" (Gavison, 1979-1980, p. 438).

Among the many meanings and purposes that have been attached to the term, the right to privacy has been understood, for example, as providing the conditions to plan and make choices concerning one's private life, as granting control over's one's personal information and their use by others, as well as forbidding the distortion of one's image. Furthermore, the sweeping concept of privacy has also encompassed the freedom of though, the control over one's body, the misapprehension of one's identity and the protection of one's reputation (among other aspects). In this context, Lillian BeVier observes that "[p]rivacy is a chameleon-like word, used denotatively to designate a wide range of wildly disparate interests ... and connotatively to generate goodwill on behalf of whatever interest is being asserted in its name" (BeVier, 1995, p. 458).

1.2. The Over-Stretching Conceptualization of the Right to Privacy and Its Articulation with the Notion of Identity

Having acknowledged this important inflationary trend, this paper – nonetheless – does not aim at contributing to this continuous avalanche of privacy conceptions and definitions, but to instead refine their usages. In this context, I shall argue that the amount and the wide diversity of privacy definitions coined over time have gone clearly beyond what Rodotá has named "a process of unrelenting reinvention of privacy" (Rodotá, 2009, p. 78). As such, we have surpassed the phase of reinvention, having entered into the phase of distortion and confusion. In this context, it is appropriate to quote Julie Inness, who qualifies the world of privacy as a "chaotic" one (Inness, 1996, p. 3). Transposing physic terms to the concept of privacy, the explosion of privacy conceptions might exemplify the second law of thermodynamics: "a system reaches its death when it reaches its maximum disorder (i.e. it contains as much information as it can handle)" (Vedral, 2010, p. 58). Such death can be analogized to information overload. According to Vedral, "[t]he Second Law of thermodynamics tells us not only that a system dies when it reaches its maximum disorder, it tells us, startlingly, that every physical system must inevitably tend towards its maximum disorder" (Vedral, 2010, p. 59). In this light, the rumoured "death of privacy" will not derive from the fact that people tend to care less about it, but from the fact that scholars and legislators tend to care too much about it, overloading the concept with further definitions and additional characterizations. In physics terms, such phenomenon can be designated by the term "entropy", that is, "a quantity that measures the disorder of a system and can be applied to any situation in which there are multiple possibilities" (Vedral, 2010, p. 61). As a matter of fact, the legal doctrine and the law are contributing towards the increase of the *entropy* of the privacy concept, i.e., to its content overload and state of maximum disorder.

By disproportionally extending the scope of the right to privacy, such broadening conceptual trend not only renders the right to privacy vague and uncertain, but it also tends to occupy the conceptual space of other rights. It is precisely upon this last aspect, that is, the conceptual overstretching of the notion of privacy and its conciliation with other rights, namely with the right to identity, that this article will devote its attention. As it will be further developed in the following sections of the paper, the broadening of the notion of privacy has overshadowed the concept of identity, preventing a similar conceptual theorization of its corresponding legal right. In fact, the theoretical overstretching of the notion of privacy blurs itself with the concept of identity, "stealing" some of the latter's conceptual space.

An example of this overstretching can be found in some legal scholarship that specifically confronts the notions of privacy and identity. Here, the legal doctrine (in general terms) has painted a harmonious picture, depicting privacy and identity as two sides of the same coin, operating together towards the same purposes and objectives. Such view had its origins in Ager's and Rosenberg notion of the right to privacy as "the freedom from unreasonable constraints on the construction of one's identity" (1997, p. 6). Such perspective is linked to the rationale of data protection and to the idea that the "control over personal information is control over an aspect of the identity one projects in the world" (Agre & Rotenberg, 1997, p. 7). The link between privacy and the absence of restraints in developing one's identity has been pursued and reconfirmed by other scholars, such as Rouvroy (2008) and Hildebrandt (2006). The latter scholar, in her analysis of the connections between the concepts of privacy and identity, fails – nevertheless – to provide a clear demarcation between those two terms, presenting a scheme that privileges and endorses a very broad definition of privacy at the expense of the concept of identity.

In addressing the construction of self-identity from the perspective of the first person, Mireille Hildebrandt – developing Paul Ricoeur's thesis of narrative identity (Ricœur, 1992) - talks about two important aspects of identity that are never given, but constructed or developed: the *idem* and the *ipse* identity. As such, and while the identity of the self (ipse) has to be claimed *versus others*, the idem identity postulates that the self has to be claimed as being the *same* (idem) *over the course of time* (Mireille Hildebrandt, 2006, p. 51). Relying upon the already examined notions of environment and interaction, she argues that "[t]his type of identity presumes that humans are not born as individual persons, but develop into persons as they relate to their environment and interact with others" (M. Hildebrandt, 2006, p. 51). Such conceptualization characterizes the individual subject as a profoundly relational self, whose identity is constantly being re-built and re-shaped in interaction with one's environment and in confrontation with others. It is from this perspective that Hildebrandt broadens the notion of privacy, as the latter "can now be understood as the process of boundary negotiations that allows a person to hold together while changing; it presumes some measure of autonomy, some real contact like intimacy and some space to rebuild the self in accordance with one's past while anticipating one's future" (2006, p. 52). Such conceptualization of privacy borrows part of its rationale from Ervin Goffman's thesis of personal identity, according to whom identity should be seen as a dynamic and relational process, rather than a mere static collection of attributes. According to the sociologist, "[p]eople construct their identities ... through a negotiation of boundaries in which the parties reveal personal information selectively according to a tacit moral code that he called 'the right and duty of partial display' (Agre & Rotenberg, 1997, p. 8).

Such a link between privacy and the process of identity building does have its appealing factors, as "it goes well beyond the static conception of privacy as a right to seclusion or secrecy, it explains why people whish to control personal information, and it promises detailed guidance about what kinds of control they might wish to have" (Agre & Rotenberg, 1997, pp. 7-8). Nevertheless, such conceptualization – privacy as the absence of constraints in developing one's identity – presents two major flaws, which will be examined in detail in the following two sections of the paper. First, the idea of a right to privacy as "the freedom from unreasonable constraints in developing one's identity" is reductive and one-sided, capturing only one dimension among the many others that compose the spectrum of the intricate relationships between privacy and identity. As we shall see in the next section, the links and connections between identity and privacy are far more varied and complex than the simple conceptualization of privacy as a necessary condition for the construction of one's identity. Second, such proposed concept of (a right to) privacy blurs itself with the one of identity, assuming an overly broad character, claiming some of the definitional and constitutive characteristics that, in truth, pertain to the concept and to the right to identity. As we shall see in section IV, this is the case with facts related to the person that are not truthful and which, for such reason, should not be covered by the right to privacy.

II. IDENTITY AND PRIVACY: AN AMBIGUOUS AND DYNAMIC RELATIONSHIP

The fact that privacy tends to encompass information intimately connected to one's identity has led many authors to depict a positive and concordant correlation between these two concepts. One can in fact affirm that, in a way, "privacy protects the right of an individual to control information that is intrinsically linked to his or her identity" (Boussard, 2009, p. 252). In this case, the concepts of privacy and identity serve to define and contextualize what kind of information is closely connected to a given person, endowing her with the right to exert control over such information. In this context, privacy and identity are reciprocally used to define and "locate" one another. In this situation, moreover, both of these rights work together, pursuing the same objective, that is, the protection of (personal) information.

Counter-intuitively, however, this harmonious view of the privacy-identity nexus constitutes only one part of the story, as there also cases and situations that show the opposite, that is, the possible contradictions and conflicts between the right to privacy and the right to identity. In this light, privacy may in certain situations hinder identity, while the latter may in other circumstances obstruct the former. As a result, and as we shall see in the following, there is not a clear-cut homogenous connection between privacy and identity, but a profoundly ambiguous and dynamic relationship.

2.1. Privacy and Identity: A Concordant Relation

One useful point of departure to begin our analysis of the different connections between privacy and identity is the already alluded definition of the right to privacy proposed by Agre and Rotenberg. According to the authors, the right to privacy can be defined as "the freedom from unreasonable constraints on the construction of one's identity" (Agre & Rotenberg, 1997, p. 7).

This harmonious view postulates that "the core of privacy is to be found in the idea of identity" (M. Hildebrandt, 2006, p. 50) and that "the process of identity-building is what is at stake in privacy" (M. Hildebrandt, 2006, p. 50). Such positive and constructive connection between the two concepts derives from the modern conceptualizations of privacy as freedom and informational self-determination, as well as from sociological theories of personal identity (such as the one authored by Ervin Goffman), which characterize the latter as a dynamic and relational process (rather than a static collection of attributes). Benefiting from these two theoretical contributions, privacy as freedom and identity as a dynamic building process, a number of authors (starting from Agre and Rotenberg) depicted the right to privacy as the freedom from unreasonable constraints on the construction of one's identity.

Looking more closely into this proposed definition, the notion of privacy seems to acquire an instrumental nature, acting like a device through which one becomes free from environmental constrictions and, as such, fully prepared to construct his or her identity. In other words, privacy is perceived as a constructing tool indispensable to build one's identity. Such view, as already mentioned before, has been confirmed and developed by other scholars, namely by Hildebrandt – who affirms that "privacy is not merely about the exchange of or access to personal information, but about identity-building and identification" (2006, p. 44) - and by Rouvroy – who defines the right to privacy as the right not to be interfered in the construction of one's identity (2008).

This concordant and harmonious view of the "privacy–identity nexus" is not incorrect *per se*, as one's identity can in fact be built within and through one's privacy. Nevertheless, such view denotes two salient problems. Firstly, such concordant perspective is reductive and partial, capturing only a single dimension and neglecting many more that compose the intricate web of relationships between privacy and identity. Secondly, and furthermore, such partial definition confuses and conflates the terms, overstating the concept of privacy while undermining the one of identity (see below).

2.2. Privacy and Identity: A Conflictive Relation

The idea of the right to privacy as the right not to be interfered in the construction of one's identity seems to imply that, once the right to privacy is ensured, the right to identity will flow naturally, being immediately secured. Nevertheless, this assumption is erroneous, as the rights to privacy and identity may perfectly have their own conflicts and disagreements. Such concepts, in fact, may underline different purposes or even opposite objectives. In this light, the Ager view (confirmed and repeated by other authors) is only partially correct, at it encompasses only one possible way of articulating the right to privacy with the concept of identity, dismissing all the others.

Considering the possible intersections between identity and privacy, it is important to acknowledge that privacy can be both positively and negatively linked to identity (and vice versa). Within such wide spectrum of possible combinations, we shall see how privacy can undermine identity, as well as how identity can undermine privacy. These two cases demonstrate, as such, that the privacy-identity nexus is more complex and heterogeneous than the portrayed positive link between these two concepts, according to which privacy provides the conditions for the construction of one's identity.

2.2.1. Privacy Undermining Identity

An example of how privacy can operate against identity, contradicting to the idyllic view of privacy as providing the conditions for identity building, can be found in the case of identity theft. In fact, the argument that privacy fosters identity theft has been raised, in the context of US Law, by Lynn Lopucki (2002-2003). The clash between privacy and identity is illustrated by the case of an individual (perpetrator) who uses the biographical information related to the identity of another person to register under a given National Identity scheme and who, afterwards, benefits from the data protection regulation and privacy laws to uphold and sustain such false identity. Given that, at the time of registration, the perpetrator's biometrics will be permanently paired with biographical information that does not correspond to his actual identity; he will be able – from the moment of registration onwards - to correlate his biometric information to the identity of someone else, being considered – moreover and for all effects – as a data subject. Regarding this last aspect, and bearing in mind that the Data Protection directive defines data subject as an identified or identifiable natural person, a perpetrator whose biometrics are recorded in a given National Identity Scheme will be considered a natural person who can be identified under and within the definition of the Directive (even though such identification will lead to a different identity than the one of the perpetrator). In other words, even if all the other information that comprises identity relates to another person, the perpetrator will still be considered a data subject under the Directive. This means that the definitions enshrined in the Directive are "sufficiently wide to include an individual whose identity information has been hijacked as a result of fraud or which has been incorrectly recorded as a result of human or system error" (Sullivan, 2008, p. 304). In this sense, and as strange as it may seem, Privacy and Data Protection laws are – in this particular case - fostering fraud and negligence (in terms of false identity), creating the impression, and indeed, the presumption, that the registered identity is invariably authentic and accurate. Although privacy and data protection laws do not in themselves contemplate data fraudulently or illegally obtained, they do endure their existence and continuity when such data is registered in a given database or record. In other words, this example demonstrates how the right to privacy may actually conceal one's identity, enduring a situation of misrepresentation and identity theft. In conclusion, this situation illustrates how privacy (namely through its data protection legal framework) can act against the interests and purposes of identity, ensuring and promoting (at least until the perpetrator is not uncovered) the continuity and 'untouchability' of false identities.

As we can see, and going beyond Ager's view, privacy may not solely contribute to the formation of one's identity. In addition, and contrarily, "[c]alling the privacy right in might stand in the way of effective protection of identity" (De Hert, 2008, p. 11).

2.2.2. Identity Undermining Privacy

The reversed example, that is, the one where identity undermines privacy, can be found in the hypothetical case of a big-brother society, where the access to the most trivial services are made dependent upon the highest level of identity validation, that is, upon the disclosure of private information regarding one's identity. In this case, the constant requirement to prove one's identity, along with the level of detail in which such process is carried out, undermines any privacy expectations that the citizen may have. The prospect of having all of our movements and interactions with others traced and monitored (by the state, companies or any other entities), rendering our identities continuously visible and ascertainable to others, naturally disrupts and undermines one's privacy. This example, moreover, demonstrates how privacy and identity can be articulated as opposite and irreconcilable concepts, as the privacy of one person presupposes concealing her identity, while identity presupposes relinquishing one's privacy. In this way, one concept is defined as the contrary of the other: privacy as the subtraction of identity, and identity as the lack of privacy. Coming back to the scenario of the big-brother society, this case reveals how the rationale of identity (conceived as the result of an identification procedure) can hinder the aim and purposes of privacy.

Another example of a contrasting relationship between the concepts of identity and privacy can also be discerned through a market-oriented analysis. Through such lens, Deighton demonstrates how identity and privacy can be depicted as opposing economic goods, examining how consumers can choose how much of each they would like to consume (2003). The author draws an interesting economic correlation between these two goods, according to which the value of one affects the cost of the other, that is, the value of one is the loss of the other. According to this market-based analysis, our identity is an asset to the extent that others value access to us. In this light, "the cost of privacy is the loss of a valued identity" (Deighton, 2003, p. 137). In other words, "as the ability to prove identity quickly becomes more prized, privacy becomes more costly" (Deighton, 2003, p. 145). The contrast drawn between identity and privacy is evident, as the choice for one is always made to the detriment of the other. As Deighton observes, privacy and identity are both states of mind and mutually exclusive: at any moment a person is either private or identified.

2.3.Privacy and Identity: Conflating and Confusing Concepts

The second problem with the concordant view of the "privacy-identity nexus" concerns the fact that it conflates and confuses the two notions, overstretching the concept of privacy while understating the one of identity.

In this light, the view according to which the right to privacy consists upon "the freedom from unreasonable constraints on the construction of one's identity" (Agre & Rotenberg, 1997, p. 7) reduces the process of identity building to the private sphere, forgetting that identity is also (and mainly) built in the public arena, that is, while one interacts and relates to others. In this way, such view imprisons the concept of identity to a private dimension, forgetting that identity encompasses both the public and the private sphere. As Gatter notes:

Identity is constantly created by ourselves and those around us. This process happens in the privacy of our homes, in the public arena of the workplace, the schoolyard, the classroom, the athletic arena, and the public square. It is both conscious and accidental, active and passive. (Gatter, 2003, p. 462)

Likewise considering the fact that the identity building process is an intrinsically dynamic and relational process, it is important to note that our identities are not only shaped by our privately held monologues, but also (and mainly) by the dialogues we entertain with the others. In this manner, identity is both public and private. One could even affirm that it is not in the presence but, instead, in the absence of privacy that identities are actually shaped and built. As such, and contrarily to the concordant privacy-identity view, identities do not arise from an exclusively personal vacuum, but from a shared social melting pot.

There is a current conceptual confusion between the notions of privacy and identity, as the former is being defined and articulated with characteristics and features that, in actual fact, pertain to the concept of identity. Properties and aspects normally assigned to the concept of identity, such as its social, contextual and dynamic characteristics, are now being transferred to the concept of privacy. This process wipes out any conceptual autonomy between these two terms, as aspects previously and directly associated with identity are now applied in the definition of privacy which, furthermore, is then described as an instrument providing the necessary space for the construction of identity. In other words, if privacy is equated to the conditions through which one develops his or her identity, and if those conditions encompass also the properties attached to the concept of identity (dynamic, social, contextual), then any significant conceptual difference existing between privacy and identity fades away. It is exactly this definitional disarray that explains the conceptual overstretching of privacy and the consequent undermining of the identity concept.

In this light, the definition of "the right to privacy as the freedom from unreasonable constraints in developing one's identity" presents two major flaws, the one of overstretching the concept of privacy, and the other of restricting the concept of identity. As such, and while the concept of privacy is substantially enlarged, encompassing all aspects related to the process of identity building, the concept of identity is restrained to the private sphere. Such proposed articulation between privacy and identity, in this way, distorts and corrupts the true meaning and substance of both concepts. But what exactly differentiates privacy from identity, what autonomous meaning can be attributed to one and to the other? The next section is devoted to answering such question.

III.RIGHT TO IDENTITY AND RIGHT TO PRIVACY: COMMONALITIES AND DIFFERENCES (COMMON ROOTS, DIFFERENT INTERESTS)

In order to adequately distinguish the right to privacy from the right to identity one must first dig into their origins and seek to understand what they have in common. In other words, one must revisit the root of these concepts, that is, their ancestral family tree: the rights of personality. As such, we shall first indicate the commonalities between these rights, stressing afterwards their differences and divergences.

3.1.Commonalities: Privacy and Identity as Personality Rights

Both rights to privacy and identity derive from a larger set of rights named personality rights. Following Neethling's study of this particular category of rights:

[t]here is general consensus that personality rights are private law (subjective) rights which are by nature non-patrimonial and highly personal in the sense that they cannot exist independently of a person since they are inseparably bound up with his personality. From the highly personal and patrimonial nature of personality rights it is possible to deduce their juridical characteristics: they are non-transferable; unhereditable; incapable of being relinquished or attached; they cannot prescribe; and they come into existence with the birth and are terminated by death of a human being. As such, personality rights form a separate category of rights, distinguishable from real, personal and immaterial property rights which are patrimonial rights that can exist independently of the personality. (Neethling, 2005, p. 223)

In this context, identity and privacy – as members of the personality rights family – both relate to an individual's right to dignity and self-determination. As such, they both configure dignity interests that all of us possess.

3.2.Differences

Within the category of personality rights, privacy and identity constitute two different and autonomous rights. In order to effectively proceed to distinguishing the right to privacy from the right to identity, our attention should be devoted to the articulation of a general right to personality, on the one hand, and the specific personality rights, on the other. It is upon the concretisation of specific rights of personality that one will find the differences between such rights. In this account, moreover, such differences relate to distinct interests of personality guiding each of the personality rights. Neethling explains:

The precise description of those interests of personality which the law protects is very important for ... determining how a personality interest, like privacy, differs from other personality interest –

like identity, dignity, reputation, etc. (Neethling, 2005, p. 217)

In light of the particular logic rooted within the category of personality rights, identity is perceived as an interest of personality. Identity can be defined as a "person's uniqueness or individuality which defines or individualises him as a particular person and thus distinguishes him from others" (Neethling, 2005, p. 234). In this account, identity is manifested in various *indicia* by which that particular person can be recognised. Such *indicia*, in other words, amount to the facets of one's personality which are characteristic or unique to him or her, such as one's life history, character, name, creditworthiness, voice, handwriting, appearance (physical image), and etcetera (Neethling, 2005, p. 234). As a result, the right to identity translates a person's definite and inalienable "interest in the uniqueness of his being." According to such conceptualization, a person's identity is infringed if any of these *indicia* are used without authorization in ways which cannot be reconciled with the true identity one wishes to convey.

Privacy also configures an interest of personality. In fact, the large scope attributed to the right to privacy, namely in the United States, goes back to Warren and Brandeis and to the acceptance in the US of the idea of personality rights (fact which did not occur in many other common law countries). As Neethling further explains:

In this regard Warren and Brandeis laid the foundation for the recognition of the right to privacy as an aspect of the more general right to personality. However, the right to privacy in the USA does not only protect privacy but extends much wider, so much so that this right to be left alone portrays surprising similarities to the general right of personality in Germany. (Neethling, 2005, pp. 216-217)

Such initial conceptualization, one may suppose, explicates the current inflationary trend in the conceptualization of a right to privacy (which we saw in section I), explaining the excessively encompassing and general scope of the right to privacy.

Coming back to the configuration of privacy as an interest of personality, privacy (differently from the identity interest) has been defined as a "personal condition of life characterised by seclusion from, and therefore absence of acquaintance by, the public" (Neethling, 2005, p. 233). In these terms, privacy can only be breached through the unauthorised acquaintance by third persons of one's true private facts or affairs. This last aspect, as developed in further detail in section IV, underlines a very important difference between the rights to privacy and identity. As we shall see, this distinction bears important consequences in the articulation of the rights to privacy and identity within the data protection legal framework, as well as in the interpretation of the concept of personal data.

Having examined the right to identity as the right to the recognition of one's uniqueness, and recovering the conception of the right to privacy as the right to be left alone, it becomes clearer the difference and the autonomy separating these two rights. As such, while the right to identity – as the right to be recognized as a unique person - operates in conjunction, interaction and collaboration with others (as one person can only be deemed unique in comparison and contraposition with other persons), the right to privacy – as the right to be left alone – operates in solitude, renouncing the presence of others. Both rights do take into account, in their definition, the third persons' element, but while identity requires their presence, privacy demands their absence.

In addition, the right to privacy and the right to identity exhibit other important differences. In this way, and following Claire Sullivan's study on this subject (Sullivan, 2008), the right to identity has an allegedly absolute nature in comparison with the conditional one of the right to privacy. According to Sullivan, identity constitutes an essential human trait, whereas privacy amounts to a desirable condition or state. In this way, the right to have one's individuality recognised and respected (the right to identity) is a fundamental human right, which cannot simply be balanced against the public interest. As a consequence, a person's identity can never legitimately be removed or unilaterally changed – even on the ground that it is in the public interest to do so. A person's claim to privacy, on the contrary, is subject to possible exceptions, as privacy configures a conditional right requiring the balancing of personal interests against those of the broader community (national security and law enforcement, public interest considerations, etc). In addition, and as Sullivan also notes, the right to identity does not necessarily expire with the person's death. In fact, the right to identity continues after death, whereas the right to privacy is generally considered to cease on death.

Another important (and pragmatic) difference between the rights to identity and privacy lies upon the fact that the right to identity - as a right to have one's identity recognised - often represents the fulfilment of a necessary condition to access public and private services and goods. In this sense, and taking especially into account the many technological advancements in the field of electronic identity, the right to identity represents the right to have one's identity recognised before third parties, allowing that person to engage in transactions and benefit from a myriad of different services. Such particular feature of the identity concept is usually referred to as the legal or administrative identity of a person. In fact, such "civil identity is the instrument societies use to determine whether persons have legal access to certain goods and services" (De Hert, 2008, p. 1). In this way, the right to identity determines an individual's ability to transact under a given National Identity Scheme (NIS), being used to prove one's identity. This feature of the right to identity has no parallel in the right to privacy. This difference between the right to identity and the right to privacy reflects, moreover, an important distinction between the correspondent concepts, according to which "identity is claimed in order to assert particular entitlements, while privacy is sought in order to evade particular impositions" (Deighton, 2003, p. 139).

IV. RIGHT TO PRIVACY AND RIGHT TO IDENTITY WITHIN THE EU DATA PROTECTION LEGAL FRAMEWORK: PERSONAL DATA AND THE ALETHIC CRITERION

4.1. Identity and Privacy within a Data Protection Legal Framework

Everything comes down to data and information. The fact that practically all aspects of one's personality[1] can now be represented, scrutinized, processed, digitized and recorded, circulating in the information society in the form of binary digits and algorithms, turns the task of distinguishing the legal concepts of privacy and identity into an even harder one. Despite this increasing difficulty, it is of utmost importance to distinguish such concepts, not only for the sake of the coherence and operability of the legal system, but especially for the sake of attaining a complete and solid protection of all the different aspects related to an individual's personality.

As already mentioned, there is a great indeterminacy in legal terminology between the concepts of privacy and identity. Such indeterminacy, greatly fuelled by doctrinal approaches which fail to grasp the underlying differences between such concepts, is – moreover - reflected at the legislative and regulatory levels, namely within the legal framework of data protection. This section demonstrates the relevance of the distinction between identity and privacy at the level of data protection regulation.

The key concept used in this section in order to illustrate the difference between the right to privacy and identity, as well as the importance of safeguarding the autonomy of both rights, is the concept of personal information[2] and personal data, while the background to which this conceptual legal differentiation will be applied is the EU Data Protection legal framework. In this regard, and for the sake of simplicity, the right to data protection remains at a secondary level, depicted as a procedural right while the rights to privacy and identity assume a more substantial nature. This differentiation does not intend to undermine the important values and roles attached to the right to data protection, but rather to keep the focus of our analysis on the right to identity and privacy, including the data protection legal framework as a mere case-study, a field of application where the importance and the salience of the differentiation between those two rights can be adequately demonstrated. In this context, the main question that I shall entertain here is whether the concept of personal data indistinctively involves the right to privacy and the right to identity, or, whether a teleological distinction should be made within the concept of personal data. I submit that there is a difference, although overlooked, between protecting personal information through an identity rationale and through a privacy rationale (it is important to note that personal information can also be protected through different legal expedients, such as through criminal sanctions, law of contract, copyright [intellectual property law]). Such difference can be clearly assessed by looking at the already alluded distinction between a breach of the right to privacy and a breach of the right to identity.

4.2. The Distinction between the Right to Privacy and the Right to Identity

As briefly mentioned in section III, the right to identity is infringed if a given person makes use of someone's identity *indicia* in a way contrary to the latter's true identity, that is, in the case of his or her identity being falsified or an erroneous image of his personality is conveyed; while the right to privacy is only infringed if true private facts related to a person are revealed to the public. Following this reasoning, Giorgio Pino asserts that:

[t]he first feature of the right to personal identity is that its protection can be invoked only if a false representation of the personality has been offered to the public eye. This feature makes it possible to distinguish the right to personal identity from both reputation and privacy. In the first case, indeed, it can be noted that the false statements must not be necessarily defaming: personal identity can be violated also by the attribution of (false) merits. In the case of privacy, instead, legal protection does not concern the correct exposure of the personality to the public eye, but rather the interest of the subject not to be exposed. (Pino, 2003, p. 11)

In a more concrete manner, Neethling summarizes the distinction between identity and privacy in the following manner: "[i]n contrast to identity, privacy is not infringed by the untrue or false use of the indicia of identity, but through an acquaintance with (true) personal facts regarding the holder of the right contrary to his determination and will" (Neethling, 2005).

Therefore, at the heart of the distinction between the right to privacy and the right to identity we find two important elements: 1) whether the facts concerning a given person are truthful or not; and 2) whether such person wants to keep them private or not. In this regard, it is important to stress that while the right to identity concerns all of those personal facts - regardless of being truthful or not – which are capable of falsifying or transmitting a wrong image of one's identity, the right to privacy comprises only those true personal facts that are part of one's private sphere and which, by one reason or the other, spill over to the public sphere. Through such distinction it is easy to conclude that the infringement of one's identity is much more difficult to evaluate and assert in comparison with the violation of one's privacy. In this way, while the violation of the latter can be externally and objectively evaluated, as it concerns a set of true (and thus demonstrable) facts related to the person; the violation of one's identity is more complex to determine as it involves the alleged correction of a dissonance between the way a person perceives herself (in her inside, as her 'true' identity) and the identity that has been attributed to her by the outside. This particular conceptualization, furthermore, corresponds to the notion of privacy advocated by writers such as Archard, who defines privacy as "limited access to personal information", that is, "the set of true facts that uniquely defines each and every individual" (2006, p. 16). In this regard, David Archard affirms that "[t]he most plausible definition of privacy that strives to meet the conditions of coherence and distinctiveness is one, endorsed by many writers, of limited access to a specified personal domain. Furthermore, this domain is also normally understood in terms of 'personal information', the set of true facts that uniquely defines each and every individual" (Archard, 2006, p. 16).

4.3. The Concept of "Personal Information"

Transposing this essential distinction between privacy and identity to the field of data protection, the key concept one should examine is the one of "personal information." In this account, it is of utmost importance to assert if the definition of personal information for the purposes of privacy – as a collection of true facts associated to a given individual - matches the definition of personal information envisaged by the data protection regulation framework. In order to make such an assertion it is imperative to examine the concept of personal data, as applied and interpreted according to current EU law.

The definition of personal data contained in Directive 95/46/EC (henceforth "the data protection Directive" or the Directive) reads as follow: "Personal data shall mean any information relating to an identified or identifiable natural person ('data subject'). Such definition, enshrining a very broad notion of "personal data," aims to include all information concerning an identifiable individual, that is, all information which may be linked to an individual. In Opinion 4/2007, the Article 29 Data Protection Working Party (Art. 29 WP) proceeded to an exhaustive analysis of the concept of personal data (according to the data protection directive), providing a number of important clarifications concerning the wide interpretation that such broad concept demands. As such, Art. 29 WP advanced the following definition of personal data: "From the point of view of the nature of information, the concept of personal data includes any sort of statements about a person. It covers "objective" information, such as the presence of a certain substance in one's blood. It also includes "subjective" information, opinion or assessments" (2007, p. 6). Furthermore, Art. 29 WP stated explicitly that "[f]or information to be 'personal data', it is not necessary that it be true or proven" (2007, p. 6). In other words, the concept of personal data – as envisaged by the Directive - does not follow any necessary true condition, encompassing any information relating to a person, regardless of being true or false, factual or invented, accurate or imagined. In order to qualify as personal information, the latter must "only" relate to an identified or identifiable natural person, and not necessarily convey any truthful information regarding or defining the data subject.

Taking into account the already mentioned difference between the right to privacy and the right to identity, according to which the former concerns true facts while the latter deals with false data (or de-contextualized), the following conclusion can already be formulated: a large portion of personal data currently being processed concerns a person's identity, and not necessarily her privacy. Moreover, this means that the rules on the protection of personal data (defined as any information, truthful or not, relating to an identified or identifiable person) go clearly beyond the protection of privacy, covering also the protection (and promotion) of one's identity. Contrary to the uniform stand adopted by the EU data protection regulation, which "does not distinguish different sorts of personal data on the basis of such a thing as 'intrinsic privacy-relevance'" (De Hert & Gutwirth, 2009, p. 25), I thus propose to establish a "privacy-identity relevance" criterion in order to distinguish two different kinds of personal data, one concerning privacy interests, and the other related to identity ones. In this particular point it is interesting to note that, contrarily to the EU data protection regulation scheme, the European Court of Human Rights ECtHR) makes a "distinction between personal data that fall within the scope of Article 8 ECHR and personal data that do not. In the eyes of the Court there is processing of personal data that affects private life and processing of personal data that does not affect the private life of individuals" (De Hert & Gutwirth, 2009, p. 24).

4.4. The "Alethic" Criterion

Returning to the EU data protection legal framework, the first important step here proposed is to distinguish personal information that qualifies alethically (from *αλήθεια* [*aletheia*], the Greek word for truth) from personal information that does not. As such, the rights to identity and privacy should be distinguished, at the data protection level, through the analysis of the alethic nature of personal information in question. In other words, it is based upon whether personal information represents or conveys a truth or a falsehood (depending on whether it has an alethic value or not) that the processing of personal data will be deemed relevant to identity or privacy (purposes). The truthful condition or the alethic value refers to the correspondence between, on the one hand, what the content or message embedded in the information conveys or describes, and – on the other hand - the personal fact related to the subject supposedly conveyed or described. This reasoning presents the following advantages: refrains the broadening conceptual trend of the right to privacy; proposes a more restricted definition for the latter; provides an autonomous conceptual space for the right to identity to thrive; and contributes to a clearer demarcation between the different scopes of application assigned to each of those rights.

As a result, and following this logic, the right to privacy would only be summoned if the personal information to which it is concerned qualifies as truthful, while the right to identity would apply in all those cases in which personal information does not present a necessary truth-condition.

It may seem awkward, at least initially, to regulate the processing of information supposedly related to one's intimacy according to a right to identity perspective, and not privacy, even though such information ultimately conveys a falsehood. This is so, because people tend to react to the disclosure of private information (regardless of being truthful or not) as a violation of one's privacy. Nevertheless, it is important to bear in mind that privacy has nothing to do with information that, despite allegedly disclosing private facts or aspects concerning a given person, and despite being attached to a given person, does not convey any truthfulness regarding that subject. The reason for this is very simple: if the disclosure of any false information regarding our intimacy would be covered by the right to privacy, our privacy would ultimately be shaped and constructed by outsiders, encompassing any kind of information that third persons could forge and invent about ourselves. Our intimacy would be open to debate and subject to re-construction by any other person. In this light, it is the right to identity that should be used. Contrarily to the right to privacy, it is the right to identity the appropriate forum to deal with the processing of this kind of information, constituting the proper legal instrument to correct any eventual dissonance between the identity that others attribute to a given person and the identity that such person wants to effectively project (the true identity).

Identity is not necessarily about truth or objectivity; identity, instead, is about imagination, projection and representation. Furthermore, the alethic difference here portrayed, as we shall see in the following section, bears important consequences in the forthcoming scenario of Ubiquitous Computing (namely with regard to the construction and dissemination of automated profiles), ensuring a complete and flawless protection of one's personality.

V.THE CHALLENGES OF UBIQUITOUS COMPUTING

5.1.The Ubiquitous Computing Scenario

Ubiquitous Computing represents a vision of the form and means computing will take in the forthcoming years. Aspects and facets of this vision have been also called by the terms 'pervasive computing', 'physical computing', 'tangible media', 'everyware', 'ambient intelligence' and 'the internet of things' (among others). It conveys the idea of an aspiring reality – automated, intelligent, imperceptible, and omnipresent. The Ubiquitous Computing scenario represents a foreseeable future stage in which the "internet", as we know it – in the shape of a network of computers, will gradually envelope the physical environment (Andrade, 2010). In this sense, it is "a vision of processing power so distributed throughout the environment that computers per se effectively disappear" (Greenfield, 2006, p. 1). Such technological setting underlines, in this manner, the passage from the present internet structure (which currently covers only a limited number of output devices) to a world where a wide array of miniaturized computing devices (processors, tags, tiny sensors) will be integrated into a multiplicity of everyday objects, seamlessly blending in the environment. According to such anticipated vision, "we will communicate directly with our clothes, watches, pens, and furniture – and these objects will communicate with each other and with other people's objects" (Bohn, Coroama, Langheinrich, Mattern & Rohs, 2005, p. 5)

Departing from technological advances in the fields of miniaturization, computing power, embedded intelligence and wireless connectivity, the new and exciting environment of Ubiquitous Computing will be characterized, on the one hand, by its invisibility, discretion and unobtrusiveness and, on the other hand, by its sensitivity, interactivity and responsiveness. In short, the fundamental paradigm of Ubiquitous Computing is that computers disappear from the user's landscape and consciousness, receding in the background. In this way, computers and other processing and "intelligent" devices (such as sensors, tags and actuators) will merge into our surroundings, working discreetly and unobtrusively in the backstage.

5.2.The Challenges of Ubiquitous Computing: The "Ego-Mirror" Effect

As one can easily imagine, the Ubiquitous Computing scenario presents a wide array of unprecedented challenges and threats to both our privacy and identity. Among the many different transformations that such vision promises to bring, and focusing namely on the ones regarding the relationship concerning the human person and the world, I shall concentrate upon a specific one, which I would call the "Ego-Mirror" effect. Such term describes one of the most worrying consequences deriving from the full accomplishment of the Ubiquitous Computing vision, that is, the fact that the external world will resemble more and more the individual person with whom it interacts. The environment, in this way, will increasingly mirror and emulate ourselves, shaping itself to the facets of our personality and traces of our idiosyncrasy, losing much of its diversity and heterogeneity. Analysing how the vision of Ubiquitous Computing could potentially and fundamentally change the environment in which we live, Araya made the following observation:

By this weaving of extensions of ourselves into the surroundings, significant parts of the environment lose important aspects of their otherness and the environment as a whole tends to become more and more a subservient 'artifact'. This artifact, which the world immediately surrounding us becomes, is almost entirely 'us' rather than 'other.' (Araya, 1995)

In this way, and as a consequence of the implementation of the Ubiquitous Computing vision, we will live more and more in an environment adapted and similar to ourselves, rather than enriched by the presence of others. The environment will potentially lose many of its aspects related to the otherness, becoming a progressively more ego-centric and ego-biased environment. One of the main instruments through which the Ubiquitous Computing will trigger such ego-mirror effect will consist in the creation of profiles.

5.3. Profiling Technologies and Identity

The creations of profiles have an intimate connection with the topic of identity, presenting new perils and posing novel challenges to the right to identity. In order to understand how such profiles operate and what kind of impact can they exert upon one's identity, it is important to bear in mind – first of all - that each of our identities resides as much inside ourselves as well as outside, in the minds and eyes of the others. And secondly, one should also understand that our identities are mainly manifested in our social actions and behaviours. As an intrinsically dynamic and relational process, pieces of our identity emerge from the actions we perform and the habits we engage into, while being observed (and compared) by others. It is through the conversation between the "I" and the "others" in the social arena that identity is built. Ricoeur, who we met previously, illustrates this idea through the notions of idem and ipse identity, which Hildebrandt summarises in the following manner:

Idem (sameness) stands for the third person, objectified observer's perspective of identity as a set of attributes that allows comparison between different people, as well as unique identification, whereas ipse (self) stands for the first person perspective constituting a 'sense of self'. Their intersection provides for the construction of a person's identity. (Mireille Hildebrandt, 2009, p. 274)

Taking into account the above mentioned "ego-mirror" effect, one can then affirm that the *idem* element runs the risk of being seriously undermined in a Ubiquitous Computing world. It is precisely here that automated profiling practices come into action.

In terms of definition, "the term profiling is used to refer to a set of technologies that share at least one common characteristic: the use of algorithms or other mathematical (computer) techniques to create, discover or construct knowledge out of huge sets of data" (Mireille Hildebrandt, 2009, p. 275). In a more technical fashion, profiling can be defined as:

the process of 'discovering' patterns in databases that can be used to identify or represent a human or nonhuman subject (individual or group) and / or the application of profiles (sets of correlated data) to individuate and represent an individual subject or to identify a subject as a member of a group (which can be an existing community or a 'discovered' category. (M. Hildebrandt & Gutwirth, 2008, p. 18)

According to a profiling practice *modus operandi*, our actions and behaviour patterns will increasingly be captured and stored by a growing apparatus of sensors and computers (the ubiquitous computing machinery), scattered all around the environment. Many fragments of our identities will inevitably drift away from us, metamorphosing into profiles, stereotypes and categories constructed by such technological armoury. The problem with such profiles is that, rather worryingly, very few of us (if any, at all) can actually have access to them. Profiles, in reality, tend to remain locked away from the profiled persons (based upon whom they were actually constructed), lying and hiding beneath algorithms and computing processes. The other problem raised by such profiles is that, further than being inaccessible to the profiled persons, those profiles do influence to a great extent one's further behaviour and actions.

Within the forthcoming scenario of Ubiquitous computing, along with the so-called automated profiling technologies, it is important to note that these new technical developments are adding new purposes and functions to the technological apparatus surrounding us. In this account, and to better understand the technological changes that are already occurring, one should bear in mind two different perspectives on how experts approach the concept of identity: the process perspective (identity for identification) and the structural perspective (identity as representation). While according to the former perspective, identity can be linked to privacy and to data protection (as a person's own privacy is intimately linked to the fact of being identified or not), the structural perspective strays away from privacy, underlining a different feature of the concept of identity – the representative feature. As the latter perspective shows, and going back to the new purposes and functions of the technological apparatus surrounding us, what is becoming increasingly important is how data and information are being used to represent someone, and not to merely identify him or her. In other words, the issues raised by the processing of personal information cannot only be about disclosing information involving someone's privacy, but also of using such information to construct and represent someone else's identity. And this is one of the big challenges brought by the forthcoming stage of Ubiquitous Computing through the construction of profiles. It is exactly here that privacy and identity must be coherently articulated.

The application of these profiles upon a person (directing unconsciously her own behaviour and decisions) do not always constitute a question of personal data (as such profiles can amount to knowledge and not data), and they can involve either a question of privacy or identity (namely with regard to group profiling and indirect individual profiling). Following the distinction proposed in section IV, the application of the right to privacy and the right to identity depends on the type of profile in question, that is, on whether the profile involves the disclosure of any necessarily true facts related to the subject or not. In this light, individual profiling that merely serves to individuate a person and which is directly applied to the person whose data have been used to construct the profile will, in principle, only raise privacy issues, being thus covered by the right to privacy. As for more complex profiles, such as group and indirect profiling, they will be covered by the right to identity. In the sense that group and indirect profiles are used to infer preferences, habits or other characteristics that the profiled person may be found to have or not, they do not convey a necessary true-condition, presenting instead the possibility of misrepresenting the profiled individual. Thereby, they should be covered by the right to identity. Taking into account the complexity and the novelty of the latter kind of profiles, we shall now focus upon the relation between such profiling practices and the right to identity.

5.4. Profiling Technologies and the Articulation between the Rights to Privacy and Identity

In this light, the main problem with the construction of profiles resides not only on the invasion of privacy that takes place with profiling practices, but also (and mainly) on the impact they may exert on identity-building. As Hildebrandt argues, "the knowledge produced by these techniques can be used to give people reasons to rebuild their identities in ways that turn them into profitable consumers, assimilated foreign residents or – more generally – citizens who fit well into the scenarios of our policy-makers and marketing managers" (2006, p. 56). In this way, the most serious problem caused by the advance and proliferation of profiling technologies goes beyond the mere disclosure of personal information to governmental bodies, marketing companies, commercial organizations or justice authorities; the main problem comes afterwards, when the personal data is collected, aggregated and correlated, giving rise to knowledge about a person. Such knowledge, compressed in the form of profiles, will subsequently be re-directed and applied to that very same person, influencing and conditioning not only her everyday life, but also her own sense of identity. Taking into account the almost imperceptible and unobtrusive *modus operandi* of the Ubiquitous Computing machinery, such influence will be practically unconscious to that person, rebuilding and reshaping her identity without the latter even noticing it.

One other problem deriving from automated profiling techniques concerns the nature of the information obtained. As a matter of fact, and although being based on data, profiles may constitute knowledge. The transformation of data into knowledge is done through data-mining software, which scans the collected, stored and aggregated data, discovering patterns or correlations (that is, profiles). Those patterns, although based upon a person's collected data, reveal information that was not known before about that given data subject. As such, more than the revelation of information, such profiling techniques give rise to the creation of new information about the profiled person, namely about one's preferences, habits and lifestyle. The 'twist' here is that "[i]n many cases this new information is not based on a hypothesis that is tested against the data in the database, but emerges after applying algorithms that produce correlations between often insignificant data" (Mireille Hildebrandt, 2006, p. 48). And it is exactly at this point that we witness the transformation of data into knowledge, as this information does not derive from the mere capture or disclosure of personal data, but instead from a complex re-elaboration of such data, done through automated processes involving correlations and probabilities. The picture becomes even more complex when personalized profiles are combined and correlated into group profiles, a type of knowledge which "consists of sets of correlations that indicate relationships between different data in terms of probabilities" (Mireille Hildebrandt, 2006, p. 49).

As mentioned before, the legal answer to several challenges and problems posed by such profiling techniques require a solid articulation between the right to privacy and the right to identity. In this way, the right to privacy (namely within the legal framework of data protection) will play an important role in the first phase of the profiling process (the *data phase*), regulating the manner in which personal data may be captured, collected and stored (in this context, it is important to bear in mind that the data subject will be, most of the times, unaware of the whole personal data collection process). Subsequently, and taking into account that much of this personal data can be lawfully collected (namely the one assembled in public places or for legitimate purposes), the right to identity shall then play a crucial role in the second phase of the profiling process (the *knowledge phase*), allowing the individual to gain access and eventually contest (on the grounds of misrepresentation) the knowledge that has been constructed about him or her through such profiles. Whenever such knowledge does not qualify alethically, in the sense that it does not convey or represent a necessary true-condition about the profiled person, it is a task for the right to identity to regulate the construction and application of those profiles. Therefore, the right to privacy shall only apply in the case of personal information that qualifies alethically and objectively, while any other information (which conveys false or de-contextualized information, or that presents no-alethic value at all) shall be covered by the right to identity. In the context of more sophisticated profiling technologies (such as the case group and indirect profiles), the knowledge produced has no alethic value, neither conveying a truth nor a falsehood regarding the subject. Such knowledge, produced on the basis of a set of correlations articulated upon patterns discovered in a person's data (and, many times, combined and correlated with data pertaining to other persons, as in the case of group profiles), constitutes not a set of true facts, but a calculation of risks, predictions, generalisations, inferences, probabilities and likelihoods.

5.5. The Self-Fulfilling Prophecy of Profiles and the Right to Identity

As such, the problem we are faced with is the one of the self-fulfilling prophecy of profiles, that is, the fact that those set of probabilities and likelihoods about a person tend to, afterwards, verify themselves, becoming a reality. As Hildebrandt observes in the case of behavioural profiling, "it is important to note that a person might end up locked into her own past behaviours, because the profiler bases its dealings with the person on what is inferred from data collected from past interactions" (Mireille Hildebrandt, 2009, p. 285) In other words, despite the fact that such profiles do not have a necessary-true condition, they acquire it afterwards. Despite not being truthful, they inevitably become truthful. In fact, and "[i]nterestingly, the deployment of profiles implies matching them with new data, that will either confirm or falsify the patterns that have been found, thus allowing continuous fine tuning or even reconstruction of the profiles" (Mireille Hildebrandt, 2009, p. 278). We are thus in front of a right to identity problem, as profiles do not limit themselves to project an image of one's identity (a probabilistic one), they are effectively imposed upon the profiled person, providing the latter with no means to either control or even acknowledge their very own identity building process (as data processors and controllers tend to act invisibly in a Ubiquitous Computing setting). In other words, there is the peril of identity misrepresentation being carried out by the application of profiles. The interesting aspect here is that such misrepresentation is conveyed not to others (at least not only) but to oneself. It is not in the eyes of others or in public light that such identity misrepresentation takes place, but in our own eyes and private light (and without one even being aware!).

Combining the "ego-mirror" effect of Ubiquitous Computing with the "self-fulfilling prophecy" of automated profiling practices, we arrive at an endless closed loop, according to which the environment increasingly looks like us and we increasingly look like the environment. We continuously follow information that the environment has generated about us, reinforcing the view that the environment has of ourselves. In such process, we tend to resemble more and more the environment while the latter tend to resemble more and more ourselves. Such deadlock situation carries also with it a sort of "Autonomy Trap": "[i]nasfar as a person is not aware of this knowledge she may be 'trapped' or 'manipulated' into certain behaviours about which she would have thought twice if she realized the deliberate appeal to her inferred preferences" (Mireille Hildebrandt, 2009, p. 285). It is my conviction that a solid and coherent articulation between the right to privacy and identity will certainly contribute to avoid the trap and break the closed loop.

CONCLUSION

The relationship between privacy and identity is complex, intricate and cumbersome. Privacy and identity are often intertwined and, as a result, the significance of the distinction between the two concepts has been overlooked. Rather inevitably, the interests behind the right to privacy and the right to identity can overlap and enter into conflict in many aspects, fact which only adds complexity to the exercise of providing a clear distinction between both of these rights. A good example of such overlap, complexity and potential conflict can be found in the right to known one's own descent and parentage, as the right to know one's parent involves both the privacy of the parents and the identity of the child. As Neethling notes:

> *it seems that the right to know one's own descent is not a specific independent right of personality, but rather an aspect of a person's right to privacy (in the sense of his right of access to and therefore control over his .own personal information: his right to informational self-determination), or of his right to identity (which should include the power to know one's own real identity). (Neethling, 2005, p. 237)*

In this context, and aware of such difficulties, the article – acknowledging that the significance of the right to identity has been obscured by the focus on privacy - attempted to underline the most significant differences between the concepts and the rights to privacy and the right to identity.

The manner in which these terms have been legally treated seems to render them interchangeable, fact which – as this article strives to demonstrate – is erroneous and dangerous, carrying important negative consequences.

The articulation between the right to privacy and the right to identity assumes undeniable importance, especially in terms of resolving the shortcomings and insufficiencies of the right to privacy, which – as said before – has been overstretched, as well as in the context of reaffirming and consolidating the right to identity. Regarding EU Law, namely within the EU Electronic Communications legal framework, studies have precisely identified this "expansionist" problem of the right to privacy, arguing that the latter presents 'stretch marks" (Lusoli, Maghiros, & Bacigalupo, 2009)

As such, the view of a right to privacy entailed in this article goes against those macro and broad-encompassing perspectives advocates by scholars such as William Prosser, who argued that the invasion of privacy comprises four different torts: intrusion upon the plaintiff's seclusion or into his private affairs; public disclosure of embarrassing facts about the plaintiff; publicity placing the plaintiff in a false light in the public eye; and, appropriation, for the defendant's advantage, of the plaintiff's name or likeness. Such perspectives, as argued in the article, run the risk of overlapping with other pre-existing rights, namely (although among others) the right to identity. In this sense, and as noticed by Archard, "[p]rivacy needs then to be defined in ways that resist its reduction to some other interest" (Archard, 2006, p. 15)

It is important, nonetheless, to articulate and not replace. In this way, the proposed introduction of a "privacy-identity relevance" within the ambit of personal information, by discerning whether it presents and alethic value or not, aims to be a step in such articulation. As such, one should not pronounce the death of privacy and acclaim the rise of identity, but to understand their common roots and underlying connections.

In this light, there is a complementary role in the relationship between identity and privacy, but such complementarity has been incorrectly, and with detrimental consequences, stated at the micro-level of the individual rights, that is, in the conceptualization of privacy. The complementarities between privacy and identity should be seen at a more macro level, not within the definition of the right to privacy but within the broader conceptual umbrella of the idea of personality, namely through the clear distinction and articulation of its different interests and rights.

REFERENCES

Agre, P., & Rotenberg, M. (1997). *Technology and privacy: The new landscape*. Cambridge, MA: MIT Press.

Altman, I. (1975). *The environment and social behavior: Privacy, personal space, territory, crowding*. Monterey, CA: Brooks/Cole Pub. Co.

Andrade, N. N. G. (2010). Technology and metaphors: From cyberspace to ambient intelligence. *Observatorio (OBS*). Journal*, *4*(1), 121–146.

Araya, A. A. (1995). *Questioning ubiquitous computing.* Paper presented at the ACM 23rd Annual Conference on Computer Science, Nashville, TN.

Archard, D. (2006). The value of privacy. In Claes, E., Duff, A., & Gutwirth, S. (Eds.), *Privacy and the criminal law* (pp. 13–31). Antwerp, Belgium: Intersentia.

BeVier, L. R. (1995). Information about individuals in the hands of government: Some reflections on mechanisms for privacy protection. *The William and Mary Bill of Rights Journal*, *4*(2), 455–506.

Bohn, J., Coroama, V., Langheinrich, M., Mattern, F., & Rohs, M. (2005). Social, economic, and ethical implications of ambient intelligence and ubiquitous computing. In Weber, W., Rabaey, J. M., & Aarts, E. H. L. (Eds.), *Ambient intelligence* (pp. 5–29). Berlin: Springer. doi:10.1007/3-540-27139-2_2

Boussard, H. (2009). Individual human rights in genetic research: Blurring the line between collective and individual interests. In Murphy, T. (Ed.), *New technologies and human rights.* Oxford: Oxford University Press.

Clarke, R. (1994). The digital persona and its application to data surveillance. *The Information Society*, *10*(2), 77–92. doi:10.1080/01972243.1994.9960160

De Hert, P. (2008). A right to identity to face the Internet of Things. [Also on the CD of Commission Nationale française pour l'Unesco, Ethique et droits de l'homme dans la societé d'information. Actes, synthèse et recommandations, 13-14 septembre 2007, Strasbourg.] Retrieved from http://portal.unesco.org/ci/fr/files/25857/12021328273de_Hert-Paul.pdf/de%2BHert-Paul.pdf

De Hert, P., & Gutwirth, S. (2009). Data protection in the case law of Strasbourg and Luxembourg: Constitutionalisation in action. In Gutwirth, S., Poullet, Y., De Hert, P., Terwangne, C., & Nouwt, S. (Eds.), *Reinventing data protection?* Dordrecht, The Netherlands: Springer. doi:10.1007/978-1-4020-9498-9_1

Deighton, J. (2003). Market solutions to privacy problems. In Nicoll, C., Prins, C., & Dellen, M. J. M. v. (Eds.), *Digital anonymity and the law: Tensions and dimensions*. The Hague: T.M.C. Asser Press.

Floridi, L. (2007). A look into the future impact of ICT on our lives. *The Information Society*, *23*(1), 59–64. doi:10.1080/01972240601059094

Gatter, K. M. (2003). Genetic information and the importance of context: Implications for the social meaning of genetic information and individual identity. *Saint Louis University Law Journal*, *47*(2), 423–462.

Gavison, R. (1979-1980). Privacy and the limits of law. *The Yale Law Journal*, *89*(3), 421–471. doi:10.2307/795891

Greenfield, A. (2006). *Everyware: The dawning age of ubiquitous computing*. Berkeley, CA: New Riders.

Gutwirth, S. (2002). *Privacy and the information age*. Lanham, MD: Rowman & Littlefield Publishers.

Hildebrandt, M. (2006). Privacy and identity. In Claes, E., Duff, A., & Gutwirth, S. (Eds.), *Privacy and the criminal law* (pp. 43–57). Antwerp, Belgium: Intersentia.

Hildebrandt, M. (2006). Privacy and Identity. In E. Claes, A. Duff & S. Gutwirth (Eds.), *Privacy and the criminal law* (pp. x, 199). Antwerp, Belgium: Intersentia.

Hildebrandt, M. (2009). Profiling and AmI. In Rannenberg, K., Royer, D., & Deuker, A. (Eds.), *The future of identity in the information society: Challenges and opportunities* (pp. 273–313). Berlin: Springer. doi:10.1007/978-3-642-01820-6_7

Hildebrandt, M., & Gutwirth, S. (2008). *Profiling the European citizen: Cross-disciplinary perspectives*. New York: Springer.

Inness, J. C. (1996). *Privacy, intimacy and isolation*. Oxford: Oxford University Press. doi:10.1093/0195104609.001.0001

Lopucki, L. M. (2002-2003). Did privacy cause identity theft? *The Hastings Law Journal*, *54*(4), 1277–1298.

Lusoli, W., Maghiros, I., & Bacigalupo, M. (2009). eID policy in a turbulent environment: Is there a need for a new regulatory framework? *Identity in the Information Society*, *1*(1), 173–187. doi:10.1007/s12394-009-0011-9

Neethling, J. (2005). Personality rights: A comparative overview. *The Comparative and International Law Journal of Southern Africa*, *38*(2), 210–245.

Party, A. D. P. W. (2007). Opinion 4/2007 on the concept of personal data (pp. 1-26).

Pino, G. (2003). *Il diritto all'identità personale: Interpretazione costituzionale e creatività giurisprudenziale*. Bologna, Italy: Il mulino.

Rannenberg, K., Royer, D., & Deuker, A. (2009). *The future of identity in the information society: Challenges and opportunities*. Berlin: Springer. doi:10.1007/978-3-642-01820-6

Ricœur, P. (1992). *Oneself as another*. Chicago: University of Chicago Press.

Rodotá, S. (2009). Data protection as a fundamental right. In Gutwirth, S., Poullet, Y., De Hert, P., Terwangne, C., & Nouwt, S. (Eds.), *Reinventing data protection?* (pp. 77–82). Dordrecht, The Netherlands: Springer. doi:10.1007/978-1-4020-9498-9_3

Rouvroy, A. (2008). Privacy, data protection, and the unprecedented challenges of ambient intelligence. *Studies in Ethics, Law, and Technology*, *2*(1), 51. doi:10.2202/1941-6008.1001

Sullivan, C. (2008). Privacy or identity? *International Journal of Intellectual Property Management*, *2*(3), 289–324.

Vedral, V. (2010). *Decoding reality: The universe as quantum information*. Oxford: Oxford University Press.

Wacks, R. (1980). The poverty of privacy. *The Law Quarterly Review*, *96*, 73.

Warren, S. D., & Brandeis, L. D. (1890). The right to privacy. *Harvard Law Review*, *4*(5), 193–220. doi:10.2307/1321160

Westin, A. F. (1967). *Privacy and freedom* (1st ed.). New York: Atheneum.

ENDNOTES

1. Such wide array of personality aspects includes also elements about oneself that the person is not even aware of. In this particular,

see section V of this article on automated profiling technologies

2 The concept of information here analysed is restricted to and solely concerns the definition of personal information enshrined in the European Union legal framework for data protection (and not to any other taxonomical or philosophical take on the concept of information). In this sense, the definition and the application of the alethic quality of such information refers to the actual facts that correspond to a person's life story and personality.

Chapter 3
Hasta La Vista Privacy, or How Technology Terminated Privacy

Konstantinos K. Stylianou
University of Pennsylvania, USA

ABSTRACT

Lawyers find great joy in pointing out the destructive effects of digital technology on privacy and naturally expect the law to avert overexposure of people's personal information. This essay takes a different view by arguing that the trajectory of technological developments renders the expansive collection of personal data inevitable, and hence the law's primary interest should lie in regulating the use—not the collection—of information. This does not foreshadow the end of privacy, but rather suggests a necessary reconceptualization of privacy in the digital era. Along those lines we first need to acknowledge that people increasingly sacrifice voluntarily some of their privacy to enjoy the benefits of technology. Second, the ready availability of a huge volume of personal information creates attention scarcity, such that the chances a person's privacy will be intruded are diminished. Most importantly, though, once the law accepts the inevitability of the collection of personal information, it will be best in the position to focus attention on ensuring that the collected information is appropriately used, instead of wasting resources on trying to hinder in vain its collection. This more realistic approach calls for alternative means of regulation, like self-regulation or emphasis on informed consent, and facilitates the flow of information by reducing the transactional cost of its sharing and dissemination.

I. INTRODUCTION

"Congratulations on your colonoscopy" shouted Alan Shore in the courtroom making Judge Nora Lang blush with embarrassment. Too much information? "This is just information I was able to obtain from websites which employ the business standard for Internet security" he went on to explain (Boston Legal, Season 2, Episode 13).

Have we really reached a point where such sensitive information is so easily accessible to a fluffy

DOI: 10.4018/978-1-60960-083-9.ch003

non-tech savvy lawyer? And if what confuses you is the imaginary setting I use to ask the question consider the real case of Justice Antonin Scalia of the United States Supreme Court, for whom -as of last spring- we know his home number, the movies he likes, his food preferences, his wife's personal e-mail address, and what his grandchildren look like. You can thank Professor Joel Reidenberg and his students at Fordham Center on Law and Information Policy for that (Cohen, 2009).

What these two cases, and countless others both in the real and the TV world, have in common is the underlying facilitating effect of technology. And most often in egregiously intrusive cases like the above our almost instinctive reaction is to look for ways to limit the pervasiveness of technology. We fail, however, to see that in a historical perspective the trajectory of technological developments invariably attacks the notion of privacy, and –I argue- will continue to do so. There is indeed no reason to believe that, since technology has progressively enabled us to access more and more information, some of which private, we can somehow prevent this pattern from continuing into the future.

This is a theory of technological determinism in the realm of privacy. My argument is that digital technology, as best exemplified by digital networks, is bound to clash with privacy, and that the more it advances the fainter the privacy will become. Part II will explain the deterministic interaction between technology and privacy. In so doing I will show how privacy has materially shrunk due to the pressures exerted by new technologies and I will try to prove that this tendency will continue into the future. In the third part my aim is twofold: first, establish that privacy is overrated and that people in fact often give it up (deliberately or not) when this is accompanied by benefits, and second, offer general principles of how the law and people should approach the new concept of minimized privacy.

II. THE DETERMINISTIC INTERACTION OF TECHNOLOGY AND PRIVACY

1. Introducing Technological Determinism

Technological determinism is a charming, yet highly contested theory that never really found the acceptance it deserved in the humanities. This is partly attributable to the lack of a generally agreed on definition; as a result supporters of technological determinism are dispersed and uncoordinated (Bimber, 1994, p. 80). For some it states nothing more than the obvious, namely that technology has a role in fixing the form or the configuration of something (Winner, 1978, p. 75). As Heilbroner puts it "that machines make history in some sense ... is of course obvious" (1967, p. 335). So obvious indeed that he rushes into the next sentence to explain that it is equally clear "that they do not make *all* of history" (Heilbroner, 1967, emphasis added).

On the other end of the spectrum technology is given the role of society's base, the fundamental and most important condition that effects a change (White, 1949, p. 366). In that sense social interactions, market forces and regulatory choices are mainly directed by technology. Needless to say that this radical view of the fate of human existence is both hard to accept and probably easily refuted. What does for example the invention of antibiotics (voted as the most important invention of the 20th century, see Lemelson-MIT Survey, 1999) say by itself for the evolution of the human kind? The extension of longevity is a direct corollary of antibiotics, but this is merely a fact. The meaning and ramifications of an extended lifetime for the human kind do not inadvertently flow from the invention of antibiotics itself. Most importantly, though, the problem with the extreme form of technological determinism is the difficulty we face when trying to reconcile the edifice of human logic with the no-choice state extreme technological determinism leaves us with. As Lafollette and Stine explain "[a] new technology presents society with new capabilities, accompanied by new moral *dilemmas*; ...technological developments represent neither *automatically* reliable nor necessarily positive outcomes" (1991, p. 1, emphasis added). This line of thought seems reasonable and is further confirmed by everyday practice as to when, where and how we *choose* to use technology.

In-between the two extremes (technology as the defining factor of change and technology as a mere tangent of change) and in a multitude of combinations falls the so called soft determinism; that is, variations of the combined effect of technology on one hand and human choices and actions on the other (Smith & Marx, 1994, p. xiii). The scope of soft determinism is unfortunately so broad that it loses all normative value. Encapsulated in the axiom "human beings do make their world, but they are also made by it," soft determinism is reduced to the self-evident (Winner, 1978, p. 88).

By now I have brought myself in a precarious position: I pledged to preach the deterministic effects of digital technology on privacy, yet at the same time I admit that technological determinism is either too extreme to be tenable or too obvious to be of value. I believe a compromise can be reached by mixing soft and hard determinism in a blend that reserves for technology the predominant role only in limited cases, one of which is the one at hand –privacy. Naturally, it is impossible to disregard the important contribution of political will, market choices and user habits in how technology ends up affecting our lives (Volti, 2006, pp. 271-283). However, my argument is that there are indeed technologies so disruptive that by their very nature they cause a certain change *regardless* of other factors. Some points of clarification are due here.

First, neither all technologies nor technology *per se* are determinative. This is the fundamental difference with hard determinism, which suggests that technology in general has a determinative effect. On the contrary, I use technological determinism here to refer to only *specific* technologies that are tied with *specific* results. One of these technologies is digital processing and one of these results is the elimination of privacy. One of course would reasonably ask what technologies are then deterministic. There is no easy answer to this question but in any case it is outside the scope of the analysis undertaken here. Though one could imagine a pattern behind deterministic technologies and use it to predict which nascent technologies will have deterministic effects (and maybe also what these effects will be), things get even more complicated considering that a technology can be deterministic in one context (say in Europe) but not in another (say in the USA) (Flichy, 2007, p. 24).

Second, since the specific technology is deterministic it leads to a result regardless of other factors. This is not to say that other factors are absent, but merely that the said technology is a *sufficient* condition to incur the change. This is the fundamental difference with soft determinism, which sees change as a *confluence* of a variety of factors, merely *one* of which is technology.

Lastly, and in relation to the preceding point, it needs to be stated that, while the end result is predetermined by the transformative technology itself, the details of how this result will be brought about as well as its precise configuration may be spelled out by the rest of the factors through complex interactions among them. The margin left for the rest of the factors to fill in the intermediate details, however, does not change the determinative nature of a given technology.

To synthesize what I have presented so far consider the example of the microwave technology as applied in American telecommunications. There is a wide consensus that the introduction of the microwave technology, which allowed the exchange of information (video, voice etc) via the electromagnetic spectrum over the air, is the primary cause of the end of AT&T's long-distance calls natural monopoly (Nuechterlein & Weiser, 2005, pp. 14-15). The reason is that microwaves significantly dropped the cost of laying a long-distance network (which would normally be deployed on landlines) thereby allowing for the entry of competitors in the field. The primary rationale behind natural monopolies is to avoid duplication of the very costly required infrastructure, which would be wasteful due to the economies of scale and scope utilities like telecommunications exhibit (Geddes, 2000, p. 1183). Once the technological potentials for viable competition became available the quintessential reason of having a monopoly regime collapsed and the marked transitioned into competitive mode, despite the vehement opposition by established interests (most notably AT&T, see FCC, 1959, §148). The details of how the new scheme would work were laid down by the ensuing regulatory and market decisions, but the general direction of liberalization was already in place owing to the dynamics that the new technology had created. While there was no objective or extrinsic reason why the microwave technology would not be treated the same as the wireline system, the new dynamics were impossible to ignore and it is highly unlikely that the regulation of microwaves would be so uninspired as to merely replicate a network system analogous to the wireline system. The new technology innately carried a well-defined change in its shell.

Now that we are past the fundamentals of technological determinism I will use the remaining space of this part to explain why the advancement of digital technology is ineluctably bound to have a destructive impact on privacy.

2. Technological Progress and the Inescapable Loss of Privacy

As mentioned in the previous part it is hard –if not impossible- to predict which technologies are deterministic. This is mainly because knowing the future end result with which the technology is tied is a *sine qua non* to concluding on the deterministic nature of a given technology. And as we all know seeing into the future is a risky business. But for the purposes of telling whether digital technology has a predetermined destructive effect on privacy, it is enough to provide adequate evidence that, if put into a continuum, forms a consistent line toward less privacy. This argument presupposes that past dynamics will continue into the future, a theory that is safe to follow in lack of self-contradictory evidence. Unless of course one is inclined to adopt Hume's objections to causation, but I am willing to run that risk.

We also need to come up with a working definition of privacy. Technological determinism necessitates a broad view of privacy for it is a theory oblivious to the definitional differences among national legislations and, besides, privacy is inherently "a broad, abstract and ambiguous concept" (Griswold v. Connecticut (1965), Justice Black's dissent, p. 509). Under that broad understanding privacy would include all activity and all information that the subject has a reasonable expectation to keep to himself, the expectation to be free from unwarranted governmental or private intrusion, the option not to become the object of attention, the right to remain anonymous, and the ability to block physical access to himself (Gavison, 1980, pp. 428-436; Frombolz, 2000, pp. 463-464). An attack to privacy therefore should be construed as a violation, deprivation or limitation of any of the above rights and options. Additionally, since privacy is largely based upon a person's expectations and is experienced as an expression of individual autonomy (Henkin, 1974, p. 1425) any *threat* of loss of privacy or any precarious situation that endangers privacy should also count as an attack to privacy.

So the question now to ask is why digital technology results in the multiplication of threats or actual violation of privacy rights. The answer is to be found in the differences that digital technology bears in comparison to the previous real and analog world. In the analog era collecting personal information meant *physical* access. Access either to files where private information was retained or access to the premises where the person was.

Digital technology changed the playfield in that it allowed cheap, instant and accurate transfer of information without regard to the size or type of the information quantum or the distance between the place where the information was collected and the place where it was transmitted or processed. Since in the digital world a bit is a bit, meaning that all information is treated the same by the machines that collect, read, process, store and transmit it, the proliferation of digital technology in general entailed a concomitant spawning of devices that could be used or were exclusively designed for the collection of (personal) information. Examples range from voice recorders to surveillance cameras, to radio-frequency identification tags (*see*Froomkin, 2000, p. 1468-1501). But the exemplary application of technological determinism is to be found in digital networks and this will be my focus here.

As a first step consider the email. It became popular alongside the commercialization of the Internet and it wouldn't be a hyperbole to say that today almost all Internet users have an email address. What is interesting is that almost half of the total number of Internet users (also) has a web-based mail address, like@yahoo.com.In fact, the three major webmail services, Yahoo Mail, Hotmail and Gmail cumulatively count 700 million users, which translates to about 45% of the total Internet population. All the messages sent and received through a webmail service circulate freely in the Internet's wires and reside not on the local user's computer but on the remote servers of the provider company. This means that interception of and access to the emails can be obtained from anyone and anywhere in the world with standard PC equipment at a cost of less than $400. To contrast that with the real world the analogy of accessing one's mail would involve stalking and attacking the postman or breaking into the person's home. I am not trying to make an argument of legality –both actions are clearly illegal- but merely show how much easier it is to access someone's emails when they are stored online than to access his mail locked in a drawer. Understandably, one needs special expertise to hack into someone's account, but so does a burglar. On top of that, and most importantly, the potential pool of burglars is strictly localized[1] whereas the potential pool of hackers is 1,6 billion Internet users, the decisive element here being that the intruder needs to have *physical* access to the content he wishes to get hold of.

Imagine now that, instead of only your emails being stored online, you also start uploading the entire content of your hard drive. While on first thought this sounds like something that no rational user would do, in fact it is called online backup (or remote backup service) and it is currently estimated to support a $715 million market and growing (Chandler, 2008). At the same time a recent trend dating back to the early 00s allows users to upload selected personal information about themselves, usually accompanied by pictures, and share them with their friends. In only a matter of half a decade the most popular of these services, Facebook, grew to include more than 400 million active users, with more than 3 billion photos uploaded to the site each month (Facebook, 2010).

But all these technologies and services aside, the example that probably best illustrates how vulnerable privacy has become is cloud computing. Since cloud computing is more of a marketing term only a loose definition can be given here: a scalable network of servers on which users store data and use its processing power to run applications and services whose output is transmitted to the user's computer (Chappell, 2008). Arbitrary as it may sound, there is no commentator in the literature that has not emphasized the perils cloud computing poses for privacy (see for example Smith, 2010). And for a good reason indeed because cloud computing allows the user to emulate his personal computer online, including the applications he used to run locally and the data he used to store locally. So take GoogleDocs for instance. To use it the user connects to the application online, types the document online and saves it online, precisely as he would do with Microsoft Word on his own personal computer. The difference is that the software, the storage and the processing power all reside in "the cloud," somewhere, that is, in Google's data farms. To put it in a nutshell cloud computing is about completely migrating online.

Now if we follow the pattern behind the technological evolution of digital networks, it must be obvious even to the eyes of the layman that the more technology progresses the more information escapes our *immediate physical control*. The element of physicality makes a world of difference, especially when it comes to illegal acts. No better case illuminates this point than digital piracy; although the net financial harm is the same in both cases, almost everyone has probably succumbed to digital piracy at least once, while very few would break the law by stealing a real CD from a music store (Stylianou, 2009, pp. 394-395). Similarly, while it would require a true criminal mind to break into someone's house and steal information, sending out a phishing email to commit identity theft suddenly sounds more innocuous. This reduced disapprobation in conjunction with the relative easiness technological intrusion comes with, is enough to render privacy readily susceptible to destructive attacks.

I do acknowledge, however, that some information put online can be encrypted and password protected and hence well guarded from unauthorized access. Yet we often fail to see how much personal information we give away voluntarily and for free. I will come back to this point later; suffice it to say here that we should not understand the clash between technology and privacy as a war between what individuals want and what technology imposes, but rather as a conflict of interests between privacy rights and technological benefits and capabilities. In this vein privacy simply ends up limping behind other priorities, most notably technological progress and the craving for new products and services. This is precisely the quintessence of technological determinism, namely that *in the name of new technological vistas which maximize access to information privacy folds*. Whether our life becomes more transparent voluntarily (e.g. Facebook) or contrary to our will (e.g. government surveillance) is immaterial. In either case the bottom line is that we keep inventing and adopting technologies that along with all their benefits compromise our privacy.[2]

Once we fully come to terms with this inevitability we can embark on a reconceptualization of what privacy means in the digital world and how to reconcile the unstoppably galloping technological progress with the projections of ourselves in the future. This is the focus of the next section.

III. A NEW MIND FRAME FOR PRIVACY IN THE DIGITAL WORLD

1. Setting the Hierarchy: The Real Value of Privacy

Privacy is overrated, but we have yet to realize it. By that I don't mean that privacy has ceased to be important, but rather that in relative values it is ultimately not as big a concern as is commonly perceived. This misperception stems from the fact that when asked, people always appear worried about the transparency of their personal lives. For example a recent cloud computing survey by Microsoft found that "more than 90 percent of [the] people are concerned about the security, access and privacy of their own data in the cloud" (Microsoft, 2009). But at the same time the same survey showed that 90 percent of Americans are using some form of cloud computing (Microsoft, 2009). Combine the two and the conclusion to be drawn is that people's choices suggest that the potentials of a new technology outweigh the privacy costs. Similarly while many people have expressed their unease with privacy protection in social networking sites, we see an explosive growth in the information they post online and the activities –some of them very intimate- they undertake in the frames of digital social networks (Ito et al., 2009, pp. 13-34).

This trend toward more sharing of personal information is justified by the offsetting effects of technology. People acknowledge the overwhelming benefits of technology and yield to them at the expense of privacy. The benefits can be varied. A study for example showed that Facebook users are inclined to divulge increasingly more personal information based on the belief that there will be a concomitant increase in their popularity (Christofides, 2009, p. 343).

In a different setting, users of the Gmail service were enticed to sacrifice some of their privacy in exchange for more inbox space. When Gmail was first introduced in 2004 it was severely criticized for its data retention policy and its ad-supported scheme, whereby users' emails were scanned for keywords so that personalized advertisements could be fed to them (Miller, 2005, passim). These concerns notwithstanding, when it became known that Gmail's capacity would be 1GB compared to the meager 4-10MBs Yahoo! and Microsoft (Hotmail) offered, users started flocking to Gmail. Today, Gmail remains the most pervasive email platform but its users pool nevertheless counts 150 million users, ranking third behind Yahoo! and Hotmail.*

A change in moral and social standards can also result in a downgrading of privacy. The ongoing study about the future of the Internet conducted by the Pew Internet and American Life Project and Elon University is very helpful at this point. Every two years participants are asked to discuss possible scenarios for 2020 with regard to Internet issues. In the 2006 survey 46 percent of the respondents agreed that the benefits of greater transparency would outweigh the privacy costs and 49 percent disagreed (Anderson & Rainie, 2006, pp. i-ii). Interestingly, in the 2008 survey the percentage of the people that disagreed with the statement that "in 2020 people are even more open to sharing personal information … [and] are generally comfortable exchanging the benefits of anonymity for the benefits they perceive in data being shared…" dropped to 44 percent (Anderson & Rainie, 2008, p. i).

It seems that in final analysis people are not completely hostile to the overriding effects of technology despite their *prima facie* objections. Naturally, if we were given the choice to be able to enjoy all the benefits of digital social networking without compromising our privacy at all, Facebook would be the ideal digital world. However, given the present state of affairs, I want to take the previous arguments one step further and suggest that some *involuntary* leak of private information is not necessarily as evil as we seem to think.

Take behavioral advertising for example. Behavioral advertising involves the automated collection of web browsing data from advertisers who then use it to serve targeted advertisements to consumers. As expected, the large majority of users reject behavioral advertising for fear of privacy intrusion (Turow et al., 2009, p. 3). But this finding has to be read in a context. The same survey also concluded that users would still oppose behavioral advertising even if their anonymity was guaranteed (Turow et al., p. 4). This implies that users are hostile toward behavioral advertising in general, regardless of whether it is intrusive or not. This is possibly because advertisements of any kind are usually a nuisance to them, so why not avoid them altogether if given the option?

Most importantly, though, we need to ask a more fundamental question and I will state it here in general terms: why is it in the end so important for us to protect our private data from being collected and/or used? The importance of this question lies in that we can demystify privacy if we acknowledge that sharing private information is less risky than what we usually think. As Jeffrey Reiman has put it "a threat to privacy is only worrisome insofar as privacy is valuable or protects other things that are valuable. No doubt privacy is valuable to people who have mischief to hide, but that is not enough to make it generally worth protecting" (Reiman, 1996, p. 29). Reiman has nicely summarized the three pillars of the philosophical core of privacy, which can help us identify the reasons why we abominate the erosion of privacy: a) the *extrinsic loss of freedom*, also noted by other scholars as emanating from the right to *autonomy*, that is being able to choose for one's self what information becomes available (Westin, 1966, p. 1022), b) the *intrinsic loss of freedom*, that is the emotional state of knowing that one is free to make choices, c) the *symbolic function of privacy*, that is the institutional structure of privacy in society, and lastly d) in what he calls *the risk of psycho-political metamorphosis* –namely the impoverishment of inner life due to total visibility (Reiman, 1996, pp. 35-44).

I do not plan to take issue with any of the above justifications for privacy, which in any case I find at least to a certain extent valid. I do want, however, to qualify these common privacy concerns in a way that better reflects how technology threatens privacy. My position is that technology has made it indeed so easy to collect personal data that in many cases they have lost their individual value, and instead function merely as statistical or ancillary data. I am not claiming that the collected information does not amount to adequate data to synthesize a person's profile –quite the contrary (Picker, 2009, pp. 24-35), but rather that the true identity of a particular person is in principle indifferent to the aggregator of the information and hence no concern is warranted. In the case of behavioral advertising, for instance, a user's personal browsing history could potentially reveal a lot about his personality and life, but it is in fact seen as nothing more than input to the advertiser's algorithm that will calculate which advertisement is more relevant to serve (*cf.* O'Reilly, 2004 for Gmail's advertisement system). Another example is Google Street View, which provides 360° horizontal panoramic views from a row of positions along many streets in the world. This service necessarily pictures real people without their consent and in some cases they are caught in embarrassing situations like entering a sex-shop or being arrested (BBC, 2009). While I could concede that this constitutes an ad hoc invasion of privacy, it is important to note that the technology itself is not directly threatening to the individual, because, despite its technical *capability* of surveillance, the *probability* that it will be used for such purposes makes it practically innocuous. When millions of people have been randomly photographed in the street, a particular person's shot does not amount to invasion of privacy in essence, because there is nothing unique, specific or interesting about that particular person being photographed instead of someone else.

The risk about the further use and misuse of the collected information is a different issue, which I discuss in passing right below. For now and to conclude, my argument in this part could be summarized in these two strands: that privacy is likely overestimated, often because we fail to put the loss of privacy in perspective thereby exaggerating the potential –but rarely realizable- dangers, and that even when the dangers are real, people are often willing to compromise their privacy for the benefits a given technology has to offer. Seen in this light it is no wonder that the trajectory mandated by technological developments overlooks, bypasses or straightforwardly eliminates privacy policies.

2. Securing Privacy in a Technologically Pervasive Environment

In this last part my endeavor is to reconcile the increasingly intrusive technology with the privacy interests as traditionally understood. Acknowledging the deterministic effects of technology is no excuse to sit idle and surrender to the march of intrusive technologies under the pretext that this is destined to happen. I repudiate this absolutist view, and in fact, I do not think that we will ever consent to passively waive the triptych of privacy: protecting privacy of individuals against intrusive governments, protecting personal or private information, and protecting places deemed personal or private (Nissenbaum, 2004, pp. 125-131). However my major disagreement lies in the means with which we will secure this triptych. I favor a shift in emphasis from regulation of *collection* of data to regulation of *use* of data. This shift is predicated precisely upon the fact that technology is making it increasingly easy to collect data (often legally) and therefore I'm afraid that regulation in the direction of controlling the collection of information will lead to a waste of resources that could be allocated elsewhere. In this new framework we reserve an important role for the law, but it is also social and technological norms that will significantly shape the new privacy protection context. In the words of Google's chief economist, Hal Varian, "[p]rivacy is a thing of the past. Technologically it is obsolete. However, there will be social norms and legal barriers that will dampen out the worst excesses" (quoted in Anderson & Rainie, 2006, p. v).

These social norms in the real world are easy to discern. In most countries people don't keep their window curtains closed, even though they know that they can be seen through the window. However, social norms mandate that it is not polite to stare through an apartment's window. Also, people usually think that there is no reason for someone to stare through their windows, and therefore the need to take precautionary measures is mitigated. In fact, these statements hold even more truth in the urban environment where people's relationships are less intimate and the opportunities to peek through a window are so abundant that they lose value.

The analogy to the contemporary digital environment is not hard to see. As the digital population grows bigger and more and more activities are added to our digital lives, our digital footprint becomes bigger but at the same time diluted. It is decades now that Herbert Simon, the pioneering American political scientist, pointed out that "a wealth of information creates a poverty of attention" (Simon, 1971, p. 40). Indeed, from the standpoint of the aggregator of information the vast volume of available information alone makes zeroing in onto one individual highly unlikely and practically useless. To go back to the Scalia experiment, what shields us from exposure is the fact that we are not as important -and perhaps provocative- as Justice Scalia is. When it comes to the average person privacy is ensured by attention scarcity, not by impediments in the collection of information. As technology advances our lives will increasingly be transformable to collectible data, so abundant in fact that aggregators will probably find it uneconomical to collect all of them (Steeves, 2008, p. 337). A good example of what was once unimaginable but today can constitute collectible information is the thermal images of one's presence in his house using an infrared camera. Regardless of whether this information is legal to obtain without a warrant, the key point is that in a real case such data was enough to alarm the police that a person may be cultivating marijuana (Kyllo v. United States, 2001; *see contra* R. v. Tessling, 2004 (Canada's Supreme Court)). This profuseness of information coupled with the law's notorious lag (or even complicity, *see*Rubenfeld, 2008) in deciding upon what constitutes protectable personal information –reasonably so as technology and human ingenuity is always a step ahead– is good grounds to argue that focusing on controlling the collection of information may no longer be an efficient policy, for the collection *will* take place one way or another (Brin, 1998, pp. 8-9).

Attention scarcity as described above ensures that information is harder to collect, and hence it serves as a means of securing privacy at the stage *before* information comes into custody. As we can see it is not a legal measure, but rather an endogenous quality of the digital networks architecture, or in other words an embedded safety valve to ameliorate the danger of privacy intrusion. On top of technology's inherent limitations, people and the market can also adopt measures to limit exposure. For example once people accept that their private information is easy to collect they may want to consider the alternative of providing false or incomplete information (*cf.* Palfrey, 2008, Appendix C, p. 39; Burkell et al., 2007, p. 2; Ben-Ze'ev, 2003). The market can contribute its own share to this effort by helping consumers reach decisions regarding how much personal information they share or by making sure that consumers give their informed consent to the use of their personal information (Borenstein, 2008, pp. 24-25).

This approach of privacy admittedly leaves many theoretical issues unresolved. It completely marginalizes autonomy as the foundation of privacy (Cohen, 2000, pp. 1424-1428), and it is disrespectful to contextual integrity by treating all information the same regardless of the context in which it was collected and the context that it will eventually be used (Nissenbaum, 1998, pp. 581-586). This criticism is valid but it misses the point. Taking for granted that technology steadily facilitates the collection of information, the critique against a legal regime that does not maximize precautionary measures to combat the collection of information (and one that hence takes into account autonomy and contextual integrity) is misplaced. While of course the collection of information cannot be left unregulated, under the theory of technological determinism the law's primary response should focus on the stages *after* the information has been collected. The post-collection stage includes the use, processing and further transmission of the collected information. To take the case of behavioral advertising, a law influenced by technological determinism would loosen the restrictions placed on a website that collects anonymous information from the web history of the user, but would impose strict rules on what the company could do with the collected information, like for example that the company cannot use the information for purposes other than serving targeted advertisements.

There are two gains in this approach: first, it facilitates the flow of information and diminishes the transactional costs. Economic analysis of law would suggest that, when it is not imperative to keep information private –as in the case of anonymous web history data- removing free flow restrictions serves the public interest, as it allows the maximization of the information's value (Posner, 1978, pp. 394-397, 401-404). Second, for legislation to be effective it needs to stay in touch with the reality it purports to regulate. In a world where information *will* be collected, the law should consider focusing on more realistic measures without naively negating the power of technology and the determination of the market and the people to get what they want in the end. Again, this is not to suggest that regulation of the collection of information should cease to exist, but rather that the post-collection treatment of information is equally, if not more, important. In this vein, EU's new privacy rules that require the user's consent for every storing of information, or gaining of access to information in the user's terminal equipment, are in complete dissonance with the Internet's reality (*see* art. 5(3), Directive 2009/136/EC). Requiring the user to consent to the storing of every cookie on his computer is burdensome not only for the website operators but for the user himself. The pace of transactions on the Internet, the automated nature of the process of communication and the transactional customs on the Internet render EU's new measure utterly unrealistic and counter-productive. Instead, the EU should opt to facilitate the communication between web-services and users by allowing the installation of cookies, while at the same time commit to the protection of consumer privacy by prohibiting –for instance- surreptitious secondary uses of the cookies, sharing of collected information with other entities, long-term storage of cookies and any other measures that would ensure the limited and targeted utility of freely-flowing cookies.

Another flexible approach along the lines of more lenient regulation on the collection of information would be to promote self-regulation (Swire, 1997). For example in a laudable initiative led by the American Association of Advertising Agencies the advertisements industry asks that "[t]hird Parties and Service Providers ... give clear, meaningful, and prominent notice on their own Web sites that describes their Online Behavioral Advertising data collection and use practices" (AAAA et al., 2009, II.A.1). Self-regulation does not necessarily imply that the rule of law will be marginalized, but rather that the new privacy protection scheme will be a joint effort between those who possess the technological potentials and the state (Sinclair, 1997). In this scheme the final format of the regulation will fall somewhere between the two extremes of minimal protection pushed by the market and maximum protection pushed by the state.

From the preceding discussion it seems reasonable to infer that the thrust behind technological progress is so powerful that it is almost impossible for traditional legislation to catch up. While designing flexible rules may be of help, it also appears that technology has already advanced to a degree that it is able to bypass or manipulate legislation. As a result, the cat-and-mouse chase game between the law and technology will probably always tip in favor of technology. It may thus be a wise choice for the law to stop underestimating the dynamics of technology, and instead adapt to embrace it.

IV. CONCLUSION

This essay does not mean to suggest that the law is impotent. The herein presented theory of technological determinism simply highlights that technology may under certain circumstances develop its own independent path, which the law should not disregard, but rather adapt to it. In the case at hand, namely the intersection of digital technology and privacy, the first step is to reassess what privacy means in the digital world. It goes without saying that in interacting with technology people would prefer to keep most of their private information undisclosed, but this is not the right benchmark to use. Rather we need to look at how much privacy people are ready to sacrifice to enjoy the benefits of technology. What technological determinism teaches us so far is that people will always react negatively to more intrusive technology, but in the end they will probably succumb. Once we have established the true value of privacy, and given the dynamics of technology, the law should focus on producing legislation that facilitates the exchange of information on the one hand, but prevents misuse of that information on the other. This, in other words, translates into placing more emphasis on regulating what entities can do with the collected information, and into a gradual relaxation of regulation that hinders the collection of personal data. That said, this paper acknowledges that both types of regulation are necessary to provide a full framework of privacy protection.

ACKNOWLEDGMENT

I wish to thank Ms. Melina Kapeliou for her unconventional help in the completion of this essay.

REFERENCES

American Association of Advertising Agencies, Association of National Advertisers, Council of Better Business Bureaus, Direct Marketing Association, and Interactive Advertising Bureau. (2009). *Self-regulatory principles for online behavioral advertising*. Retrieved from http://www.iab.net/media/file/ven-principles-07-01-09.pdf

Anderson, J., & Rainie, L. (2006). *The future of the Internet II*. New York: Pew Internet. Retrieved from http://www.elon.edu/e-web/predictions/2006survey.pdf

Anderson, J., & Rainie, L. (2008). *The future of the Internet III*. New York: Pew Internet. Retrieved from http://www.elon.edu/docs/e-web/predictions/2008_survey.pdf

BBC. (March 20, 2009). *Google pulls some street images*. Retrieved from http://news.bbc.co.uk/2/hi/7954596.stm

Ben-Ze'ev, A. (2003). Privacy, emotional closeness, and openness in cyberspace. *Computers in Human Behavior, 19*, 451–467. doi:10.1016/S0747-5632(02)00078-X

Bimber, B. (1994). The three faces of technological determinism. In Smith, M. R., & Marx, L. (Eds.), *Does technology drive history? The dilemma of technological determinism*. Cambridge, MA: MIT Press.

Borenstein, J. (2008). Privacy: A non-existent entity. *IEEE Technology and Society Magazine, 27*(4), 20–26. doi:10.1109/MTS.2008.930565

Brin, D. (1998). *The transparent society: Will technology force us to choose between privacy and freedom*. New York: Perseus Books.

Burkell, J., Steeves, V., & Micheti, A. (2007). *Broken doors: Strategies for drafting privacy policies kids can understand*. Ottawa, Canada: On the Identity Trail. Retrieved from http://www.idtrail.org/files/broken_doors_final_report.pdf

Chandler, D. (2008). *Worldwide online backup services 2007-2011 forecast: A new market emerges*. Framingham, MA: IDC.

Chappell, D. (2008). *A short introduction to cloud platforms: An enterprise-oriented view*. Retrieved from http://www.davidchappell.com/CloudPlatforms--Chappell.pdf

Christofides, E., Muise, A., & Desmarais, S. (2009). Information disclosure and control on Facebook: Are they two sides of the same coin or two different processes? *Cyberpsychology & Behavior, 12*, 341–345. doi:10.1089/cpb.2008.0226

Cohen, J. (2000). Examined lives: Informational privacy and the subject as object. *Stanford Law Review, 52*, 1373–1437. doi:10.2307/1229517

Cohen, N. (2009, May 17). Law students teach Scalia about privacy and the web. *The New York Times*. Retrieved from http://www.nytimes.com/2009/05/18/technology/internet/18link.html

Directive 2009/136/EC of the European Parliament and of the Council. *Official Journal L337/11*.

Estelle T. Griswold & C. Lee Buxton v. Connecticut (1965), 381 U.S. 479.

Facebook. (2010). Press office statistics. Retrieved from http://www.facebook.com/press/info.php?statistics

FCC (1959), Allocation of frequencies in the bands above 890 Mcs, 27 FCC 359.

Flichy, P. (2007). *Understanding technological innovation: A socio-technical approach*. Northampton, MA: Edward Elgar Publishing.

Frombolz, J. (2000). The European Union data privacy directive. *Berkeley Technology Law Journal, 15*, 461–484.

Froomkin, M. (2000). The death of privacy? *Stanford Law Review, 52*, 1461–1543. doi:10.2307/1229519

Gavison, R. (1980). Privacy and the limits of law. *The Yale Law Journal, 89*, 421–471. doi:10.2307/795891

Geddes, R. (2000). Public utilities. In Bouckaert, B., & De Geest, G. (Eds.), *Encyclopedia of law and economics*. Northampton, MA: Edward Elgar Publishing.

Griswold v. Connecticut, 381 U.S. 479 (1965).

Heilbroner, R. (1967). Do machines make history? *Technology and Culture, 8*, 335–345. doi:10.2307/3101719

Henkin, L. (1974). Privacy and autonomy. *Columbia Law Review, 74,* 1410–1433. doi:10.2307/1121541

Ito, M., Horst, H., Bittanti, M., Boyd, D., Herr-Stephenson, B., Lange, P. G., & Pascoe, C. J. … Tripp, L. (2009). *Living and learning with new media: Summary of findings from the digital youth project (The MacArthur Foundation reports on digital media and learning).* Cambridge, MA: MIT Press.

Kyllo v. United States, 533 U.S. 27 (2001).

Lafollette, M., & Stine, J. (1991). Contemplating choice: Historical perspectives on innovation and application of technology. In Lafollette, M., & Kline, J. (Eds.), *Technology and choice: Reading from technology and culture*. Chicago: University of Chicago Press.

Lemelson-MIT Program. (1999). Lemelson-MIT survey finds high school students, their parents agree—and disagree—on the most important 20th century inventions [Press release]. Retrieved from http://web.mit.edu/invent/n-pressreleases/n-press-99index.html

Microsoft. (2009). Cloud computing flash poll – Fact sheet. Seattle, WA: Microsoft. Retrieved from www.microsoft.com/presspass/presskits/cloudpolicy/docs/PollFS.doc

Miller, J. I. (2005). Don't be evil: Gmail's relevant text advertisements violate Google's own motto and your E-Mail privacy rights. *Hofstra Law Review, 33,* 1607–1641.

Nissenbaum, H. (1998). Protecting privacy in an information age: The problem of privacy in public. *Law and Philosophy, 17,* 559–596.

Nissenbaum, H. (2004). Privacy as contextual integrity. *Washington Law Review (Seattle, Wash.), 79,* 119–158.

Nuechterlein, J., & Weiser, J. P. (2005). *Digital crossroads: American telecommunications policy in the Internet age*. Cambridge, MA: MIT Press.

O'Reilly, T. (2004). *The fuss about Gmail and privacy: Nine reasons why it's bogus*. Sebastopol, CA: O'Reilly. Retrieved from http://www.oreillynet.com/pub/wlg/4707

Palfrey, J. (2008). *Enhancing child safety and online technologies*. Cambridge, MA: The Berkman Center for Internet & Society, Harvard University. Retrieved from http://cyber.law.harvard.edu/pubrelease/isttf/

Picker, R. (2009). *Online advertising, identity and privacy (University of Chicago Law & Economics, Olin Working Paper No. 475)*. Retrieved from http://ssrn.com/abstract=1428065

Posner, R. (1978). The right of privacy. *Georgetown Law Review, 12,* 393–422.

Reiman, J. (1996). Driving to the panopticon: A philosophical exploration of the risks to privacy posed by the highway technology of the future. *Santa Clara Computer and High-Technology Law Journal, 11,* 27–44.

Rubenfeld, J. (2008). The end of privacy. *Stanford Law Review, 61,* 101–161.

Simon, H. (1971). Designing organizations for an information-rich world. In Greenberger, M. (Ed.), *Computers, communications, and the public interest*. Baltimore, MD: Johns Hopkins Press.

Sinclair, D. (1997). Self-regulation versus command and control? Beyond false dichotomies. *Law & Policy, 19,* 529–559. doi:10.1111/1467-9930.00037

Smith, B. (2010, January 20). Cloud computing for business and society. *The Huffington Post*. Retrieved from http://www.huffingtonpost.com/brad-smith/cloud-computing-for-busin_b_429466.html

Smith, M., & Marx, L. (Eds.). (1994). *Does technology drive history? The dilemma of technological determinism*. Mass: MIT Press.

Steeves, V. (2008). If the Supreme Court were on Facebook: Evaluating the reasonable expectation of privacy test from a social perspective. *Canadian Journal of Criminology and Criminal Justice*, *50*, 331–347. doi:10.3138/cjccj.50.3.331

Stylianou, K. (2009). ELSA copyright survey: What does the young generation believe about copyright? *Intellectual Property Quarterly*, *2009*(3), 391-395.

Swire, P. (1997). Markets, self-regulation, and government enforcement in the protection of personal information. In Daley, W. M., & Irving, L. (Eds.), *Privacy and self-regulation in the information age*. Washington, DC: U.S. Department of Commerce.

Tessling, R. v. (2004). 3 S. *CR (East Lansing, Mich.)*, 432.

Turow, J., King, J., Hoofnagle, C. J., Bleakley, A., & Hennessy, M. (2009). *Americans reject tailored advertising and three activities that enable it*. Retrieved from http://ssrn.com/abstract=1478214

Volti, R. (2006). *Society and technological change*. New York: Worth Publishers.

Westin, A. (1966). Science, privacy, and freedom: Issues and proposals for the 1970's: The current impact of surveillance on privacy. *Columbia Law Review*, *66*, 1003–1050. doi:10.2307/1120997

White, L. (1949). *The science of culture*. New York: Farrar, Straus & Giroux.

Winner, L. (1978). *Autonomous technology: Technics-out-of-control as a theme in political thought*. Cambridge, MA: MIT Press.

ENDNOTES

1 I assume that the cost of traveling to a foreign or far-away place and the processing cost of carrying out the crime at that place exceed the benefit that the burglar will get.

2 This is meant to be a descriptive statement. I am not claiming that loss of privacy is necessarily a negative outlook, as I am not endorsing the opposite view either.

* The reasons it only ranks third are unrelated to technology. Yahoo and Microsoft had a significant lead-time advantage during which they managed to build a robust and extensive clientele. Also, Yahoo! and Hotmail took advantage of economies of scope and networking effects by bundling their email services with Instant Messaging capabilities.

Section 2

Defining the Private and the Public:

Political Anonymity and the Technology of Security and Surveillance

Chapter 4
The Electronic Surveillance of Public Assemblies:
Political Privacy & Public Anonymity in Greece

Haralambos Anthopoulos
Hellenic Open University, Greece

ABSTRACT

The electronic surveillance of public assemblies has been an issue highly debated in the Greek public arena. The circumstances that brought this internationally contested topic in the public focus were the parliamentary introduction of Law 3625/2007 in Greece and the legislative enactment of an exemption from the data protection legislation for all police activities involving data processing during public assemblies. This paper will argue that the electronic surveillance of public assemblies affects both the privacy of political views (political privacy) and the activism (public anonymity) of a citizen. Along this line, the paper offers a combined analysis of the right to data protection [Art. 9A] and the right to free assembly [Art. 11] as acknowledged in the Greek Constitution (1975/86/01/08). As underlined, both rights constitute the basis for the protection of political privacy and public anonymity and preclude any legislatively posed limitations to their enjoyment. In the end, three key cases of the European Court of Human Rights shed light to the legitimacy of such a 'panoptic' surveillance of public assemblies.

I. INTRODUCTION: THE ELECTRONIC SURVEILLANCE OF PUBLIC ASSEMBLIES

The electronic surveillance of public assemblies has been a controversial topic in the Greek public arena, particularly during the parliamentary discussion of Law 3625/2007. This Law exempted all police activities involving data processing during public assemblies from their obligation to protect the fundamental principles deriving from the rights to privacy and data protection (Art. 8). This paper argues that such a form of surveillance of the citizens' political activism affects the values protected under the Greek Constitution, particularly the right to data protection and the freedom of assembly. In order to examine this issue in depth, we pursue a three-level analysis: a) we analyze the content

DOI: 10.4018/978-1-60960-083-9.ch004

of both the right to data protection [Art. 9A of the Greek Constitution] and freedom of assembly [Art. 11 of the Greek Constitution], separately and combined, and discuss the concepts of *political privacy* and *public anonymity,* and the way they guarantee the protection of public assemblies, b) we examine how the legislative exemption *affects* such constitutional values and guarantees and c) we use three *key cases of the European Court of Human Rights* to further examine the legitimacy of the electronic surveillance of Greek public assemblies.

II. THE ELECTRONIC SURVEILLANCE OF PUBLIC ASSEMBLIES: THE GREEK CONSTITUTIONAL GUARANTEES [ARTICLES 9A AND 11]

a. The Right to Data Protection and the Concept of 'Political Privacy'

One of the most perceptive choices of the Constitutional Revision of 2001 was the acknowledgment of the right to data protection, as an enhanced version of the right to privacy (Art. 9(1), section b of the Greek Constitution) in the new Art. 9A of the Greek Constitution. It is exactly this new right that enables us nowadays to ground a solid argumentation against the constitutionality of Art. 8 of the above mentioned Law 3625/2007. Thus, it was rightly supported in the Greek constitutional theory (Venizelos, 2001) that the scholarly underestimation of novel constitutional provisions, such as the right to data protection, that ultimately strengthened the constitutional protection of fundamental rights, gestated the 'danger of interpretational misunderstandings' (ibid, p. 476-477). The introduction of new fundamental rights in the constitutional text has received positive (Anthopoulos, 2001; Contiades, 2002) and negative reactions. As far as the latter are concerned, it is characteristically noted (Manitakis, 2007) that *'it is wrong (...) to suggest that a fundamental right does not possess constitutional power or weight, when not established explicitly in the constitutional text'* (ibid, p. 19). Indeed, fundamental rights do exist even if not specifically integrated in the constitutional text (Anthopoulos, 1992), but at any rate their specific constitutional acknowledgment renders their interpretation a much more firm and secure enterprise. Otherwise, if the legitimized by the popular sovereignty constitutional legislator does not guide their interpretation, the judiciary will on a case-by-case basis.

The right to data protection as acknowledged in Art. 9A of the Greek Constitution is identified as an individual's 'informational self-determination' (Anthopoulos, 2004, pp. 520-521). This concept, which was initially introduced by the German Federal Constitutional Court (Skouris, 1996, p. 117; Gerontas, 2002, p. 69) is clearly reflected in the text of Art. 9A of the Greek Constitution: *'Everyone has the right to protection from the collection, processing and use, especially with technical means, of his personal data, as provided by law'* (Mitrou, 2001, p. 83; Sotiropoulos, 2006, p. 118). A very substantial element of this right is the enhanced protection of 'sensitive data,' meaning data referring to *'racial or ethnic origin, political views, religious or philosophical views, association with syndical unions, health, social welfare and erotic life, as well as association with any groups related to the above'* (Article 2 section b, of the Law 2472/1997 concerning the "Protection against the process of Personal Data"). Therefore, any legislative modification that would weaken the acquired level of the protection of sensitive data would be subjected to the highest level of scrutiny according to Art. 25(1) of the Greek Constitution, since it interferes with the very core of the right to data protection (Sotiropoulos, 2006, p. 119).

The enhanced legislative and constitutional protection provided to data related to political views and association with syndical unions, which are deemed as 'sensitive,' may at first seem awkward, since in a democratic state there should be no normative barriers to the publication and transparency of any data related to the public sphere (Rodotà, 2006, p. 108). Their accession which lays not only to the scope but in the core of the novel right to data protection, finds its constitutional *ratio* in the very need to protect the individual from any harsh political discrimination based on such data (Rodotà, 2006, p. 108) – a practice that has been common in Greek history, at least until 1974 and the fall of the military dictatorship of 1967-1974 (Samatras, 2004, p. 20). Such a form of discrimination may exist even in a democratic state, especially against those considered as 'enemies' of the political and constitutional establishment, despite them acting within the fields of legitimacy (Dorsen, 2003, pp. 1276, 1293; Neumann, 1953, p. 1989).

The protection from the collection and further processing of such data thus enhances the freedom of political and social activity of the individual, securing his 'political privacy.' 'Political privacy' (Baldassare, 1974, p. 163) is an aspect of 'public anonymity,' that guarantees the protection of privacy in public spaces (Alivizatos, 2005, p. 14; Moreham, 2006, p. 606). In particular, the aspect of 'political privacy' protects the person's freedom to participate in the political process and the public sphere. In this respect, the decision of the German Federal Constitutional Court in the classic *Census* case (BVerfGe, 65, 1983) is very characteristic. According to the Court, *'if someone suspects that his participation in an assembly, a protest or in any group action is being recorded by an administrative authority and fears about the possible consequences, he is very likely to abandon the exercise of the fundamental rights protecting such activities.'*

Indeed, the ability of public authorities to use citizens' information concerning their legal, political and social activities against them, contradicts the basic assumptions of a democratic state, among which central role bears the protection of the citizens and their freedom to participate in the social and political sphere (Article 5(1) of the Greek Constitution). The fear of such an unlawful practice causes a 'psychological restriction' of fundamental rights, a 'chilling effect' (Fotiadou, 2006, p. 35) that may force citizens, as the German Federal Constitutional Court underlined, to abandon the exercise of their political freedoms and rights.

b. The Right to Data Protection and the Concept of 'Public Anonymity'

The freedom of assembly and in particular the freedom of open public assemblies (Tsiris, 1988, Bakopoulos, 1995, Sarafianos, 2004, p. 326, Kaltsonis, 2007, p. 35) and demonstrations is identified as the basic form of social protesting movements in Europe. Examples would include Greece (e.g., the movement against the revision of Article 16 of the Greek Constitution and the establishment of private higher education in Greece), Italy (the *girotondi* movement) and France (the movement against the 'first-employ contract,' see Anthopoulos, 2006). The freedom of protesting is coming back in our era as the most pressing means of expression of the public opinion and as this paper submits it finds its 'indirect guarantee' in the right to data protection (Donos, 2002, p. 11).

In the case of public assemblies, it is evident how the right to data protection (Art. 9A of the Greek Constitution) directly correlates with the freedom of assembly (Art. 11 of the Greek Constitution). By combining the two rights we could create a new constitutional rule, according to which participants in lawful -i.e., peaceful and disarmed- open public assemblies and demonstrations (Art. 11(1) of the Greek Constitution), that have not been prohibited according to the constitutional limitations (Bakopoulos, 1995, p. 160) concerning the protection of socio-economic life (Art. 11(2) of the Greek Constitution), aiming solely to express political views, ideas, syndical or civil protests, have the right not to be massively identified through the use of video-surveillance systems recording and storing their image. Thus, it could be argued that all participants in lawful open public assemblies reserve their 'right to public anonymity.'

Specifically, the 'right to public anonymity' prohibits the correlation of images and names of the assembling parties or protestors as a product of further processing of the CCTV-recorded optical data. As Christopher Slobogin further explains, the right to public anonymity ensures that someone, even when standing or moving in public spaces will remain nameless –unmarked before the state authorities, being part of the undifferentiated crowd, as long as he doesn't commit or attempt to commit illegal actions (Slobogin, 2002, p. 213). Thus conceived, the right to public anonymity represents the enhancement of the freedom of assembly (Art. 11 of the Greek Constitution) due to the guarantees established by the right to data protection. This right secures all participants in open public assemblies from any harsh discrimination against them by the state, due to their political views or their participation in syndical or other movements; as such, it serves as a constitutional barrier to the creation of a 'panopticon,' under which the freedom of assembly would be diminished (Slobogin, 2002, p. 240).

At this point, it is interesting to note that even before the Constitutional Revision of 2001 similar arguments had been expressed also by Greek constitutional law scholars. Particularly, serious concerns had been expressed about the legitimacy of image-processing in lawful open public assemblies by the police as well as the identification, the recording and storage of protestors' ID information (Pararas, 1996, pp. 46-47). Those concerns become even more relevant now, under the new Art. 9Α of the Greek Constitution, regarding the recording and storing of images through video-surveillance systems.

The right to public anonymity, as analyzed above, precludes the identification of citizens in public assemblies or protests *by the police forces*, though not by the rest of the crowd. We could argue *in extremis* that such a right exists in order to ensure the transparency of the social presence of the participants in open public assemblies or the protestors, but not the disguise of their identity (with masks, hoods, helmets or other covers). The exact wording of Art. 11(1) of the Greek Constitution does not leave any space for the legal prohibition of participation in open public assemblies of citizens disguising their identity, as long as they exercise this freedom 'peacefully and disarmed.' This practice, however, is contradictory to both the logic and the *ratio* of the right to public anonymity.

III. THE ELECTRONIC SURVEILLANCE OF PUBLIC ASSEMBLIES: THE CONSTITUTIONALITY OF THE LAW 3625/2007 (ART. 8)

a. The Contradiction of the Law 3625/2007 (Art. 8) and Article 9A of the Greek Constitution

The provision of Art. 8 of the Law 3625/2007 is problematic, first of all in terms of the novel Art. 9A of the Greek Constitution. The latter establishes, as previously described, the right to data protection as an autonomous constitutional right, with a specified substantive content, the core of which consolidates the fundamental principles of the Data Protection Law 2472/1997 (the legitimacy principle, the principle of engaging purpose, the necessity principle, the principle of data retention for definite duration, the responsibility principle, the advanced protection of sensitive data principle etc.); its exercise is guaranteed, in all its spectrum, by an Independent Authority, the Greek Data Protection Authority, established for this sole purpose (Sotiropoulos, 2006, p. 206; Mantzoufas, 2006, p. 260).

The electronic surveillance of open public assemblies is not in itself unconstitutional, but it must respect the above stated fundamental principles of the Data Protection Law 2472/1997. Specifically, electronic surveillance is permitted by the Law as far as: a) it respects the proportionality rule (Art. 4(1) section b' of the Law 2472/1997) so that recording is limited to only those data necessary for a targeted purpose, meaning only those related to the commitment of criminal actions, b) it allows the retention of data for a limited time period (Art. 4(1) section d' of the Law 2472/1997), c) it acknowledges a designated processor (Art. 4(2) of the Law 2472/1997) and d) subjects the whole procedure to the supervision of the Data Protection Authority (Art. 19 of the Law 2472/1997), even if the processor has no obligation to either notify the data subject or to obtain a permission from the Data Protection Authority. All the above guarantees for data protection are absent from Art. 8 of the Law 3625/2007.

Another important issue is whether the Data Protection Law 2472/1997 applies to processing operations concerning public security, defense, State security and the activities of the State in the areas of criminal law. The constitutional legislator during the 2001 Constitutional Revision was aware of the fact that the EU legislator had intentionally left State security and criminal matters outside the scope of Directive 95/46/EC and thus in the Member-States' discretion to include such matters within this scope. He was also aware that the Greek common legislator in the end was differentiated in this respect from the option given by the Directive, since the Law 2472/1997 did not specify any exemptions of this kind from its scope (Mittleton, 2002, p. 47). Furthermore, due process of law in Art. 9A of the Greek Constitution does not allow the common legislator to *ignore the protection assigned by the Constitution to personal data for the sake of public security*. As it has been shrewdly observed in the Greek literature (Alivizatos, 2007), 'the possibility of such a deviation afforded as an option to the national legislator by article 3(2) of the Directive 95/46/EC is not debatable for Greece due to the constitutional protection of all personal data –with no exemptions– by the Independent Authority established under article 9A of the Greek Constitution.' As a conclusion, the issue of whether public security and especially the activities of the State in areas of criminal law, fall under the scope of our national data protection legislation has already been resolved by Art. 9A of the Greek Constitution, which does not provide for any exemptions from its application.

In this respect, the Greek Constitution provides a higher level of protection than the EU Law, possibly even more than the European Convention of Human Rights (ECHR). In the case that EU law clashes with the fundamental rights established under the Greek Constitution, *Art. 28(3) of the Constitution*, which does not allow for any restrictions on the exercise of our national sovereignty if human rights and the foundations of our democratic state are jeopardized, *functions as a limit to EU law* (Venizelos, 2005, p. 16). Consequently, the danger of breaching Art. 28(3) of the Greek Constitution by EU law in the area of State security becomes more and more visible (Venizelos, 2007, p. 232).

b. The Contradiction of the Law 3625/2007 (Art.8) and Article 11 of the Greek Constitution

The most serious issue that Art. 8 of the Law 3625/2007 poses in relation to Article 11 of the Greek Constitution is, that it does not distinguish assemblies into a) *lawful* open public assemblies, b) open public assemblies where *crimes are committed by random passengers or sole participants* and c) *unlawful* open public assemblies.

According to Art. 8 of the Law 3625/2007, video-surveillance systems can operate during open public assemblies as long as the police and the Attorney General assess that the presence of a serious risk to public order and security will occur, namely that there is a strong likelihood that crimes against life, property, public safety etc. will be committed within the open public assembly. However, every open public assembly, due to its nature, involves the possibility of such a risk – and that is why Art. 11(2) of the Constitution allows the presence of police forces only in the case of open public assemblies.

In our view, the possibility of a 'present' risk (as provided by Art. 8 of the Law 3625/2007) is not sufficient in order to constitutionally justify the electronic surveillance of an open public assembly. Indeed, there has to be a 'specified' risk which is exhibited through the commitment of flagrant crimes (Simeonidou-Kastanidou, 2007). In this case, as in any other case where security clashes with our fundamental rights, the principle of proportionality (Article 25(1) section d of the Greek Constitution) and particularly the criterion of the 'least harmful measure' must be respected (Anthopoulos, 2005, p. 109; Katrougalos, 2006, p. 368). The view that public safety and state security are values ranked higher than the right to data protection cannot be grounded in the Greek Constitution, which does not impose a hierarchy on rights nor does it treat the exercise of fundamental rights as a 'civil matter' but as a major component of the protection of the public interest.

Furthermore, a measure closer to the ratio of Article 11 of the Greek Constitution would be to not operate the CCTV system if crimes are committed *by sole participants or random passengers* who could be arrested and ousted by the police forces. Sole violent incidents not supported by the majority of the participants cannot justify the dissolution of the assembly, the peaceful character of which should be judged in general (Tsiris, 1988, p. 117). This argument is also grounded in Art. 189 of the Greek Criminal Code, which punishes 'whoever participates in a public assembly of a crowd which united commits crimes' for disturbance of public peace. The same rule applies in the case of armed sole participants who can be removed and arrested by the police, without the dissolution of the assembly, since the latter does not lose its armless character due to an arm carrying minority (Bakopoulos, 1995, p.104). On the other hand, if the open public assembly has been prohibited according to Article 11(2) of the Greek Constitution and is actually taking place against this prohibition, it is considered as unlawful and thus illegal (see also Art. 171 of the Greek Criminal Code), and it can be dissolved solely on this ground (Tsiris, 1988, p. 146). In this context, video-surveillance does not raise any constitutional issues.

At any rate, the electronic surveillance of open public assemblies cannot have a 'deterrent' character. In this case it would deter not only the commitment of crimes but also the participation in constitutionally protected activities, which after all constitute the political nature of the freedom of assembly. Instead, it should only have an investigatory character, aiming to assert any crimes committed and the location of criminals.

This does not suggest that the installation and operation of CCTV systems in public spaces for purposes of crime control is in itself unconstitutional. The Greek Data Protection Authority, in its Decision No. 51/2007, supported that the installation and operation of such a system in a public square (Korolis Square in the Municipality of Drosia) in Attica, Greece was contrary to the principle of proportionality. The Data Protection Authority noted in this case that in the specific public space 'no vandalizing or damage had taken place for a long time' (Fotiadou, 2007, p. 503). Nevertheless, in designated high crime areas, the use of CCTV systems could be justified regardless of the commitment of actual crimes, as long as the freedom of assembly is not affected. We could include here the use of CCTV systems in athletic complexes for the purpose of prevention and suppression of crimes during football, basketball or volleyball games under the First League of the National Championship (Art. 41E of the Law 2725/1999) (Papadopoulou, 2006, p. 69). After all, according to the more precise opinion, fan gatherings for the purpose of watching sports games do not fall under the concept of assembly under Art. 11 of the Constitution. The freedom of assembly as guaranteed by the Greek Constitution also protects gatherings that may not have a strictly political character, as long as the purpose of influencing the public opinion is common for all the participants involved (Tsiris, 1988, pp. 99-100; Bakopoulos, 1995, pp. 85-86).

Art. 8 of the Law 3625/2007 specifies that the CCTV-collected material can only be used as evidence before the interrogator, the district attorney or the Court. Any material irrelevant to the purpose of asserting committed crimes 'is destroyed with an order of the competent District Attorney.' Speaking before the Greek Parliament, during the discussion of Art. 8, the former Minister of Justice underlined that this provision was added in order to *'assure any skeptical citizen that no massive storage of personal data will follow.'* This provision affords some guarantees; however, it would have been more effective if it had specified the maximum retention period permitted for all collected material proven irrelevant – a maximum of 24 hours, in order to comply with the principle of 'personal data retention for limited and definite duration' (Sotiropoulos, 2005, p. 135).

That remark by the former Minister of Justice gives us the opportunity to comment, in the context of constitutional law, on what Häberle calls 'the self-consciousness' of subjects whose fundamental rights were breached (Häberle, 1993, pp. 190-191). With this term he refers to the way citizens apprehend restrictions of their fundamental rights, judging whether they constitute a breach of rights, and whether such a breach is major or minor one. As a matter of fact, the above provision, even in its 'polished' version, triggered plenty of reactions and negative connotations ('Big Brother is Watching You' etc.). Greek citizens, even if justifiably alert for the violent incidents taking place within overall peaceful open public assemblies, do not seem persuaded on the necessity or the rationality of hundreds or thousands of innocent protestors being videotaped for the purposes of identifying or arresting a minority of criminals. The constitutional review of such a provision should take into account this very element, that is to say, the weak social legitimization of such a legislative choice (Tsatsos, 1994, p.286), which may be even irrelevant to human rights law elsewhere, however in Greece it is considered a serious fundamental rights violation.

IV. THE ELECTRONIC SURVEILLANCE OF PUBLIC ASSEMBLIES IN EUROPE: THE JURISPRUDENCE OF THE EUROPEAN COURT OF HUMAN RIGHTS

The subject of electronic surveillance of public assemblies has also been examined by the European Court of Human Rights (hereinafter 'the Court') from different angles. In *Peck v. The United Kingdom* (28.01.2003), video-surveillance of public spaces was not considered itself as contrary to the right to privacy (Article 8 ECHR). Nevertheless, a breach of privacy was found in the dissemination of collected personal data to the broad public, after their transmission by their processor -a municipal authority- to a TV channel that broadcasted the scenes recorded by the CCTV system. After all, *Peck* had to do with sensitive aspects of 'public anonymity' (suicide attempt in a public space), which was not at any rate related to the participation in public assemblies.

In *Friedl v. Austria* (31.01.1995), a case more relevant to our subject, the court examined whether the photographing and videotaping of people participating in a sit-in demonstration protesting against the conditions of homeless people in Vienna constituted a breach of the right to privacy. The sit-in demonstration had been dissolved with a court decision on the basis that its organizers had not obtained the necessary permission and the photographing and videotaping were done during its dissolution by the police with the purpose of avoiding the commitment of criminal offences. The court ruled that there was no breach of Article 8 ECHR in this particular case by claiming that the personal data collected *via* photographing and videotaping were not further used for the identification of the sit-in demonstration participants, but were merely retained in the administrative records of the police without any further processing.

Accordingly, in *Pierre Herbecq & Thé Association Ligue des Droits de l'Homme v. Belgium* (14.01.1998), the court ruled that the use of CCTV systems for monitoring public spaces does not constitute a breach of Article 8 ECHR *per se* in the event that no recording, storage or further processing of the collected material takes place.

What can thus be deducted from *Friedl* and *Herbecq* is, that a breach of Article 8 ECHR can only be ascertained in the case of *further processing* of the collected material with the purpose of identification of persons recorded in it or *via* its making publicly available, like it happened in *Peck*. Commentators of the Court's jurisprudence on Article 8 ECHR detect some hesitance of the Court to exercise strict scrutiny in cases of a breach of the right to privacy, if this is precisely provided by law and aims at the protection of public order and crime prevention (De Hert, 2005).

V. CONCLUSION

The electronic surveillance of public assemblies is contrary to both citizens' political privacy and public anonymity, as exercised in public spaces and guaranteed under the Greek Constitution. The provisions of the Law 3625/2007 and the exemption it introduced restrict the protection of privacy in public spaces, thus precluding the citizens, who wish to peacefully exercise their political rights. In the end, it should be noted that the relevant jurisprudence of the European Court of Human Rights recognizes a violation of privacy under Art. 8 ECHR, also *a contrario*, only in those cases where a further processing of the collected material took place.

REFERENCES

Alivizatos, N. (2005). Privacy and disclosure [in Greek]. *Mass Media & Communication Law Review*, *1*, 14–23.

Alivizatos, N. (2007, December 16). Human rights in danger: The hidden side of the amendment on cameras. *Ta Nea* [in Greek]. Retrieved November 11, 2009, from http://www.tanea.gr/default.asp?pid=2&ct=1&artid=48419

Anthopoulos, H. (1992). *The constitutional right to freedom of conscience* [in Greek]. Thessaloniki: Sakkoulas Publications.

Anthopoulos, H. (2001). *New dimensions of fundamental rights* [in Greek]. Athens, Thessaloniki: Sakkoulas Publications.

Anthopoulos, H. (2004). Data protection and freedom of information [in Greek]. *Revue Hellénique des Droits de l'Homme*, *22*, 519–554.

Anthopoulos, H. (2005). State of prevention & the right to security. In H. Anthopoulos, X. Contiades & T. Papatheodorou (Eds.), *Security & human rights in the age of risk* [in Greek] (pp. 109-135). Athens-Komotini: Ant. N. Sakkoulas.

Anthopoulos, H. (2006). Freedom & decency of work. The 'first-employ contract' before the French Constitutional Court. Comment on Case CC 2006-535DC (30.03.2006). [in Greek]. *Administrative Law Review*, *3*, 349–355.

Bakopoulos, G. (1995). *Freedom of assembly in Greek, French & British Public Law* [in Greek]. Athens-Komotini: Ant. N. Sakkoulas.

Baldassare, A. (1974). *Privacy e Constituzione*. Rome: Bulzoni.

Contiades, X. (2002). *The new constitutionalism and fundamental rights after the 2001 revision* [in Greek]. Athens-Komotini: Ant. N. Sakkoulas.

De Hert, P. (2005). Balancing security & liberty within the European human rights framework: A critical reading of the court's case law in the light of surveillance & criminal law enforcement strategies after 9/11. *Utrecht Law Review*, *1*(1), 68–96.

Donos, P. (2002). The data protection authority & its role in the advanced protection of human dignity. In Donos, P., Mitrou, L., Mittleton, P., & Papakonstantinou, E. (Eds.), *The data protection authority & the advanced protection of human rights* [in Greek]. Athens, Thessaloniki: Sakkoulas Publications.

Dorsen, N., Rosenfeld, M., Sajò, A., & Baer, S. (2003). *Comparative constitutionalism – Cases & materials*. Eagan, MN: West Group.

Fotiadou, A. (2006). *Balancing freedom of speech* [in Greek]. Athens, Thessaloniki: Sakkoulas Publications.

Fotiadou, A. (2007). Protection of municipality property v. protection of citizens' privacy: Comment on data protection authority decision 51/2007 [in Greek]. *Administrative Law Review*, *4*, 503–508.

Gerontas, A. (2002). *Citizen's protection from electronic processing of personal data* [in Greek]. Athens, Thessaloniki: Sakkoulas Publications.

Häberle, P. (1993). *Le Libertá Fondamentali Nello Stato Constituzionale*. Rome: Carocci.

Hrysogonos, K. (2003). *Civil & social rights* [in Greek]. Athens-Komotini: Ant.N.Sakkoulas.

Igglezakis, I. (2003). *Sensitive personal data* [in Greek]. Athens, Thessaloniki: Sakkoulas Publications.

Kaltsonis, D. (2007). Political & social restrictions of freedom of assembly [in Greek]. *Utopia*, *75*, 53–74.

Katrougalos, G. (2006). Freedom & security in the 'society of risk' [in Greek]. *Legal Review*, *54*, 360–374.

Manitakis, A. (2007). The necessity of constitutional revision in between majoritarian parliamentarism and revisional consensus [in Greek]. *Constitution (Foundation for the United States Constitution)*, *1*, 3–20.

Mantzoufas, P. (2006). *Constitutional protection of personal data in the age of risk* [in Greek]. Athens, Thessaloniki: Sakkoulas Publications.

Mitrou, L. (2001). Right to data protection: A new right? In D. Tsatsos, E. Venizelos & X. Contiades (Eds.), *The new constitution* [in Greek] (pp. 83–103). Athens-Komotini: Ant.N.Sakkoulas.

Mittleton, F. (2002). The right to informational self-determination and public safety. In Donos, P., Mitrou, L., Mittleton, P., & Papakonstantinou, E. (Eds.), *The data protection authority & the advanced protection of human rights* [in Greek]. Athens, Thessaloniki: Sakkoulas Publications.

Moreham, N. (2006). Privacy in public spaces. *The Cambridge Law Journal*, *65*(3), 606–635. doi:10.1017/S0008197306007240

Neumann, F. (1953). The concept of political freedom. *Columbia Law Review*, *53*(7), 901–935. doi:10.2307/1119178

Papadopoulou, N. (2006). Electronic surveillance of sports fans: The contradiction of article 41E of Law 2725/1999 to higher legal rules (article 8 of the European Convention of Human Rights, articles 9, 9A & 5 of the Greek Constitution). In Thessaloniki Bar Association, *Scientific Review* [in Greek].

Pararas, P. (1996). *The Greek Constitution & the European Convention of Human Rights* [in Greek]. Athens-Komotini: Ant. N. Sakkoulas.

Rodotà, S. (2006). *La Vita e Le Regole*. Milano, Italy: Feltrinelli.

Samatras, M. (2004). *Surveillance in Greece: From anticommunist to consumer surveillance*. New York: Pella Publishing.

Sarafianos, D. (2004). Freedom of assembly. In Tsapogas, M., & Hristopoulos, D. (Eds.), *Human rights in Greece: 1953-2003* [in Greek]. Athens: Kastaniotis.

Simeonidou-Kastanidou, E. (2007, December 11). Cameras in public assemblies. *Ta Nea* [in Greek]. Retrieved November 11, 2009, from http://digital.tanea.gr/Default.aspx?d=20071211&nid=6844132

Skouris, V. (1996). *Orientations in public law I* [in Greek]. Thessaloniki: Sakkoulas.

Slobogin, C. (2002). Public privacy: Camera surveillance of public places & the right to anonymity. *Mississippi Law Journal, 72*, 213–299.

Sotiropoulos, V. (2006). *Constitutional protection of personal data* [in Greek]. Athens, Thessaloniki: Sakkoulas Publications.

Sotiropoulos, V., & Armamentos, P. (2005). *Personal data: An interpretation of law 2472/1997* [in Greek]. Athens, Thessaloniki: Sakkoulas Publications.

Tsatsos, D. (1994). *Constitutional law* (*Vol. A*). Athens: Ant. N. Sakkoulas. [in Greek]

Tsiris, P. (1988). *The constitutional guarantee of freedom of assembly* [in Greek]. Athens: Ant. N. Sakkoulas.

Venizelos, E. (2001). Overview of the constitutional revision. In D. Tsatsos, E. Venizelos, & X. Contiades (Eds.), *The new constitution* [in Greek] (pp. 473 - 484). Athens-Komotini: Ant. N. Sakkoulas.

Venizelos, E. (2005). The relationship between the Greek Constitution & EU Law after the Signing of the Treaty Establishing a European Constitution & the Greek Constitutional Revision of 2001 [in Greek]. *Hellenic European Law Review, 1*, 1–36.

Venizelos, E. (2007). Les Formes Modernes de Crises de l'État de droit démocratique. Le binôme 'liberté/securité' comme garantie et sapement des droits fondamentaux. *Annuaire International des Droits de l'homme, II*, pp. 227-234.

Chapter 5
Telecommunications Interception in Turkey:
Rights to Privacy vs. Discourses of Security

Melike Akkaraca Köse
Marmara University, Turkey

ABSTRACT

The paper discusses telecommunication interceptions in Turkey as a state surveilling itself as well as its citizens. While surveillance of state officials including the judiciary indicates a perception of threat from inside the state, these perceptions overlap with the 'deep state' phenomenon in Turkey. Despite the 2005 legal reforms which introduce strict legal standards for communications surveillance, current political developments reveal that wiretapping remains as a commonly used micro-power application. The paper, by utilizing Foucault's theory, aims to uncover the 'conditions of possibility' for the use of this disciplinary technique in Turkey with a certain focus on the actual power relations and discourses of truth.

I. INTRODUCTION

In recent years, wiretapping has become a scandalous issue in Turkey in a period surprisingly following the 2005 legal reforms regarding surveillance over communications and despite the fact that the legal standards set by the new national regulations are similar and in some respects even higher than the European standards. Both the phenomenon of wiretapping and its dilemmatic timing may be elaborated thoroughly only if telecommunications interception as a commonly used method in Turkey is situated within the socio-cultural, political and historical background which have contributed to its *raison d'être*. The complexity of the mentioned background which is obscured further by the never-ending power-conflicts and the nature of surveillance as a micro-power application, make a Foucauldian approach to the issue even more valuable since it provides the necessary guiding light to the details which are mostly neglected in the relevant theoretical debates.

Telecommunication interceptions may be perceived as a side-product of the collaboration between technology and law for the sake of security and it may be claimed that it repeats

DOI: 10.4018/978-1-60960-083-9.ch005

its well-known global pattern in Turkey as well. Within this context, it straightforwardly poses the challenge to find a delicate balance between the rights to privacy and public interest. Yet, the direct link between surveillance and criminal law complicates, if not prevents, an effective democratic or international control over the wiretapping as an administrative tool. That becomes the point where the political and the personal coincide and where the private becomes a public concern. It may be maintained for some extreme cases that the 'intimacy' of security forces overcomes the intimacy of the individual.

While a state surveilling its own citizens is already quite challenging for the privacy debate, this paper is a modest attempt to discuss the telecommunication interceptions in Turkey as a state surveilling itself as well as its citizens. A state surveilling its political, judicial and administrative officers probably refers to a state which perceives security threats from inside and these threat perceptions overlap with the "deep state" phenomenon of Turkey as if it is a self-fulfilling prophecy. The first section of the paper purely concentrates on its legal dimension and lays down the current domestic legal reforms and the related jurisdiction in detail, and concludes with a brief comparison of the regulations in other countries with Turkey. At the end of the section, the international standards laid down by the European Union and by the case-law of the European Court of Human Rights will be discussed critically.

The second section deals with the political developments of the last two years which paved the way to the sensational outbreak of wiretapping practice directed to the judiciary among the others. This part is by and large based on the newspaper articles due to the lack of sufficient academic resources as well as to the better reflection of political sentiments in the media discourse. Unfortunately, it has not been possible to present it with a comparison of the conflicting discourses of different newspapers, which may be an interesting subject for further work in this field. In the same section, the infamous court case on the Turkish 'deep state' network is briefly introduced with a special emphasis on its criminal evidence collecting method which is largely based on the wiretapping.

The third section is more than a debate on the conclusions of the previous sections through the Foucauldian lenses. It is, rather, an endeavor to unveil the local circumstances which are rooted in the past and have led to the events summarized in the second section and to resolve the apparent inconsistency between the legal (the first section) and the political (the second section), by utilizing Foucault's theory. In other words, its modest objective is to uncover the 'conditions of possibility' for the widespread practice of legal/illegal wiretapping in Turkey by focusing on the actual power relations, whether in conflict or in collaboration, through elucidating the 'techniques of power' and the discourses of truth used and developed by these powers at the intersection of the rights to privacy and to security.

II. REGULATION OF TELECOMMUNICATION INTERCEPTIONS BY LAW: TURKEY AND THE WORLD

a) Telecommunications Surveillance in Turkish Law and Jurisdiction

The right to privacy is a constitutionally protected right in Turkey. Article 20 of the Turkish Constitution regulating Privacy of Individual Life states that "[e]veryone has the right to demand respect for his or her private and family life. Privacy of an individual or family life cannot be violated." Restriction and limitation of these rights are possible in exceptional circumstances by governmental authorities, the police, Courts and by some other legal entities. However, such particular restrictions must be legitimized with a court's decision. Article 22 preserves the secrecy of communication and states that:

Unless there exists a decision duly passed by a judge on one or several of the grounds of national security, public order, prevention of crime commitment, protection of public health and public morals, or protection of the rights and freedoms of others, or unless there exists a written order of an agency authorized by law in cases where delay is prejudicial, again on the above-mentioned grounds, communication shall not be impeded nor its secrecy be violated. The decision of the authorized agency shall be submitted for the approval of the judge having jurisdiction within 24 hours. The judge shall announce his decision within 48 hours from the time of seizure; otherwise, seizure shall automatically be lifted.

Currently, interception/surveillance of telecommunications is regulated in the section 5 of Criminal Procedure Code, No. 5271 (CMK, which came into effect on June 1, 2005 and replaced the 1995 law no.4422). According to Article 135 which bears the title "detection, monitoring and recording of communication," the communications of the suspect or the accused may be detected, monitored or recorded by means of telecommunications if during a crime investigation, there is *strong suspicion* that a crime has been committed and there are *no other means* of collecting evidence, with *the decision of the judge* or where a delay is detrimental with the decision of the public prosecutor. In such case, the public prosecutor shall immediately submit his decision to the judge for approval and the judge shall decide on this matter within twenty four hours, at the latest. Upon expiry of this period or if the judge denies approval, such measure shall be lifted by the public prosecutor immediately. The same article also envisages a list of offences (crimes listed in Art. 131 of the CMK) for which this sanction can be imposed lawfully (*'catalog offences'*). This list ranges from counterfeiting of money to trafficking of drugs and to establishing an organization with the aim of committing crimes. With a Regulation in 2005, a unit was set up called Telecommunications Directorate (TIB) with the purpose to centralize, from a single unit, the surveillance of communications and the execution of warrants to intercept communications.

In addition to communications surveillance for investigation purposes, communications may also be intercepted for intelligence purposes (preventive surveillance of communication for deterrence of crimes). Preventive telecommunications surveillance is based on Turkish Law No. 5397 (2005) and may be conducted only in the cases that there is a certain danger that a crime may be committed. In cases where delay would be disadvantageous, through the written order of the Director General of Security or Chief of the Intelligence Department, the General Commander of Gendarmerie, or the National Intelligence Organization (MIT) undersecretary or MIT deputy undersecretaries, telecommunications can be intercepted and monitored. Still a court order is needed within 24 hours after the interception order given by those authorities. The intercepted communications for prevention of crime may not be used as legal evidence in criminal proceedings but may only provide ground for starting an investigation.

However, the scope of preventive telecommunications surveillance is much more broad and loose. There is no strict condition for existence of strong criminal suspicion and the listed crimes are quite different. Most of the problems as regards to privacy occur due to the preventive surveillance of communications which may be applied for the abstractly defined crimes (e.g. crimes against state security and state secrets, spying actions, and terrorist activities, among others listed in the CMK, Art. 250) and without a serious ground for suspicion and without *ultima ratio* clause. Especially, the organizations established to commit a crime have a special position at this sanction since only the establishment of the organization without the realization of the aimed crime is itself regarded as crime (Şen, 2010; Yardımcı, 2009). Decisions for preventive surveillance can be made for a maximum of three months; these may be extended in the same way for a further three-month period a maximum of three times. For ongoing danger stemming from a terrorist organization's activities, the judge might see fit to extend the duration by three-month periods more than three times if deemed necessary.

In the last two years, some major High Court decisions have been issued in Turkey in regard to communication interceptions. The Ankara 11th High Criminal Court granted in June 2008 both the Gendarmerie and the MIT the authority to view countrywide data traffic retained by telecommunication-service providers. Subsequently, the Supreme Court of Appeals overruled the Ankara court's decision and stated that "no institution can be granted such authority across the entire country, viewing all people living in the Republic of Turkey as suspects, regardless of what the purpose of such access might be" (Freedom House, 2009). In 2009, the Constitutional Court cancelled the provision which stipulated that the director of TIB be appointed by the Prime Minister on the ground that it is contrary to the Constitution since the decision for appointment of senior executives is required to be approved by both the President and the Prime Minister in order to guarantee the protection of public officers against political authority by assurance of impartiality of the President.

Another important judicial decision came from the Council of State in December 2009. According to the 2802 Judges and Prosecutors Law, the crimes committed by the judges and prosecutors during or related to the performance of their duties may be investigated with permission by the Ministry of Justice and the Ministry inspectors. The Ministry of Justice Inspection Board Regulation (2007) gave the power to intercept communications to the Ministry inspectors during the investigations against judges. However, this provision has been found incompatible with the laws since the Criminal Procedures Acts and Law no.5397, which regulate telecommunications interceptions in detail, do not provide any legal ground justifying such an authorization of the inspectors. In short, the Council of the State annulled the provision and established that the communications by the judges cannot be intercepted by the Ministry of Justice for investigation purposes.

Overall, the 2005 regulations of communication interception may be regarded as positive legal developments in terms of the protection of private life. According to the TESEV report on Security Sector and Democratic Oversight (Almanac Turkey, 2006):

The limitation of intelligence authority to only certain types of organized crime, the requirement for the existence of certain danger that might arise in the future, and the establishment of an efficient judicial and civilian supervision mechanism along with a custody and control mechanism over said records is important for the protection of individual rights and freedoms from excessive intervention by the state, as well as the efficient elimination of threats and dangers against the state and society. Moreover, owing to this central structure, the monitoring of persons by all three intelligence units (National Security Organization (Milli İstihbarat Teşkilatı, MİT), police intelligence and gendarmerie intelligence) at the same time or at different times will be prevented, thereby eliminating the possibility of long-term interference in people's private lives (p. 152).

However, the legal regulations still need to be complemented with the proper implementation of law by state officials. As stated in the report above, there is a wide public belief that only devotion to law and ethics would prevent the police and the gendarmerie from independent illegal monitoring of individuals and institutions without permission from the central authorities. It would be difficult to instill the belief that the state does not monitor anyone illegally, while the right to privacy and private communications remains rather problematic in practice, despite the constitutional and judicial guarantees (Almanac Turkey, 2006).

b) Telecommunications Interception in the World: A Comparative Legal Approach

Before focusing on the political aspects of the issue, it may be useful to make a brief comparison with the related legal regulations in other countries. In terms of legal regulations, Turkish laws do not show important disparities from the other telecommunications surveillance regulations in Europe. According to the MPI study (as cited in Schwartz, 2004) which examines sixteen countries, mostly European but also Canada, New Zealand, Australia and the USA, the states examined restrict use of telecommunications surveillance by law enforcement agencies to situations in which other tactics will fail to gather the needed information. Telecommunications surveillance may be applied only for the investigation of a limited number of serious crimes, which are listed *ex ante* in the criminal code as being significant enough to justify surveillance. Telecommunications surveillance is generally permitted only by judicial authorization. In most of the national laws, there is an emergency exception, which allows prosecutors to authorize telecommunications surveillance for which judicial authorization has to be obtained afterwards. Additionally, the MPI Study (Schwartz, 2004) found that courts in the surveyed countries rarely refuse requests for surveillance -a finding that may be claimed to be probably valid for Turkey relying on the extensive number of legal surveillance of communications including the judges and prosecutors, despite the lack of report concerning the issue.

In terms of preventive surveillance, there are some European states which, similarly to Turkey, grant explicit legal authority to law enforcement officials to engage in preventive telecommunications surveillance (Schwartz, 2004). In those countries, preventive surveillance lacks any connection to a specific criminal act such as proof that a crime has taken place or is likely to occur; rather, its focus is on investigating organizations that are devoted to ongoing criminal behavior. For example, Italy allows "a preventively oriented collection of information." France and the Netherlands also permit these kinds of wiretaps. In France, "administrative" wiretaps do not even require judicial authorization (maximum 1,540 per year).

On the other hand, the UK, the USA and Australia have been taking very restrictive measures regarding the protection of privacy rights in telecommunications for the last ten years. For example, the UK is unusual amongst democratic states in allowing politicians to authorize interception. It is categorized as 'endemic surveillance society' by Privacy International in 2007 and is listed among the countries with the worst records regarding communication interception (Privacy International, 2007). Another country where telecommunication interceptions were made easier recently by new legislative regulations is Australia (Bronitt & Stellios, 2006). In 2006, the federal Parliament amended the Telecommunications Interception Act (TIA) 1979. According to the new law, which is the most significant expansion of the communication surveillance powers since 1960, interception may be based not upon reasonable suspicion that the person has committed or will commit serious offences, but rather on "mere involvement in those offences." "B-Party" warrants may be issued to innocent third parties who are likely to communicate with individuals involved in the serious offence under investigation.

In the USA, the real problem about the privacy of telecommunications seems to have occurred after the terrorist attack of September 11th, 2001. President Bush authorized, later admitted that he did (Rubenfeld, 2008), the NSA (National Security Administration) to conduct warrantless wiretaps on communications where one party was located outside the United States and the other party inside the United States by a secret executive order which had not been shared neither with Congress nor the public (Schwartz 2008, 2009). In August 2007, Congress enacted amendments to FISA through the Protect America Act (PAA) of 2007, which is an administration-friendly bill with an effect of authorizing the NSA surveillance program. After the PAA expired in 2008, the Congress enacted the FISA Amendments Act of 2008 (FAA), which allows government collection of information from U.S. telecommunications facilities where it is not possible to know in advance whether a communication is purely international or whether the communication involves a foreign power or its agents.

c) The Critical Assessment of the Standards Adopted by Europe

At the EU level, there are three different directives which may concern the interception of communications: namely, Directive 95/46/EC, Directive 97/66/EC, and Directive 2002/58/EC. In Directive 95/46/EC on personal data processing, it is expressly stated that activities regarding public safety, defense, national security, state security or criminal law fall outside the scope of Community law and of the Directive. Directive 97/66/EC on the protection of privacy in the telecommunications sector goes further in the clear exemption provided for the interception and states that "this Directive shall not affect the ability of Member States to carry out lawful interception of telecommunications, for the protection of public security, defense, State security…and the enforcement of criminal law." The only novelty of Directive 2002/58/EC on privacy and electronic communications, which is written in a similar way as regards to communications interception, is the inclusion of the European Convention for the Protection of Human Rights and Fundamental Freedoms (ECHR). In the 2002 Directive, it is underlined that confidentiality of communications is guaranteed in accordance with the ECHR and the constitutions of the Member States. The Member States may adopt legislative measures to restrict the scope of the privacy rights when such restriction constitutes a necessary, appropriate and proportionate measure within a democratic society to safeguard a legitimate aim. (Art. 5).

The main restriction by the EU on telecommunication interceptions in criminal issues is respect of the ECHR and its Court's rulings. Therefore, I think it is necessary to focus on the level of protection provided by the European Court of Human Rights. Art.8 of the Convention affirms that everyone has the right to respect for his private and family life, his home and his correspondence. There shall be no interference by a public authority with the exercise of this right except such as is in accordance with the law and is necessary in a democratic society in the interests of national security, public safety or the economic well-being of the country, for the prevention of disorder or crime, for the protection of health or morals, or for the protection of the rights and freedoms of others.

The legitimacy of state interference with privacy, for example through interception of communications, is dependent on three conditions: it should be in accordance with the law, pursued for a legitimate aim, and necessary in a democratic society. 'In accordance with the law' is the legality condition and it refers primarily to the existence of a legal basis for the interference. Additionally, the law in question should comply with three qualitative criteria in order to pass the legality condition. The qualitative criteria require the legal basis to be accessible (published), foreseeable (sufficiently detailed) and consistent with the rule of law (providing remedies for citizens).

When it comes to the second condition to pursue a legitimate aim, the Court has generally been reluctant to challenge the legitimate aim referred to by states. It has been frequently argued that this condition has been a clause of formality, that it is generally enough for states to refer to one of the aims and that different standards of scrutiny are applied by the Court for different categories of human rights (De Hert, 2005). It is rightly claimed that state activities such as the fight against serious forms of criminality or terrorism are usually not subjected to the strictest standards of scrutiny. States enjoy a margin of appreciation in this area. Another criticism is that the Court's approach to Article 8 is too procedural: the Court transforms Article 8 into a source of procedural rights and conditions instead of using it to prohibit unreasonable exercise of power (De Hert, 2008).

Another problem in the Court's case-law is directly related to telephone tapping. Telephone tapping does not seem to have the place it deserves in the judgments, although the Court clearly states that "tapping and other forms of interception of telephone conversations represent a serious interference with private life and correspondence" (ECHR, Huvig v. France, judgment of 24 April 1990, §32, as cited in De Hert, 2005, p.79) The requirement 'necessary in a democratic society' does include the requirement of subsidiarity (are there other less intrusive means available?) as well as the requirement of proportionality (does the aim justify the means?). In most Member States, communication interceptions may only be used as a last resort when no other technique is sufficient (principle of subsidiarity). De Hert (2005) asks whether the criteria really exist in the minds of the Strasbourg judges and concludes that 'a careful analysis of the Article 8 ECHR case law shows that the Court almost never relies on this criterion borrowed from the Article 10 ECHR case law' (p.93).

III. A BRIEF LOOK AT THE POLITICAL STAGE

a) A Big Ear Listens To Us!

In mid 2008, when the Turkish Constitutional Court (TCC) was expected to give its decisions about two politically sensitive cases (the closure case against the ruling party (Justice and Development Party, hereafter AKP) directed against their anti-secular activities, and another one on constitutional changes sponsored by the government allowing Islamic headscarves to be worn in universities), the TCC Vice President (Osman Paksüt) argued that his conversations were illegally being tapped by the police following him with a car. Although it was denied by the Security General Directorate, the chief public prosecutor in Ankara launched an investigation into the alleged tapping ("Prosecutor in Action", 2008). Opposition parties and Turkey's top jurists accused the government of exerting pressure, on the eve of crucial rulings, on the judiciary through the illegal wire-tapping of judges and other public servants ("Hands off", 2008).

Two weeks after, the secretary general of the main opposition party (Republican People Party, hereafter CHP) claimed that his office was bugged by security officials. The CHP charged the government with creating a dictatorship of fear and, in return, the AKP accused them of being paranoid and speaking nonsense. The easily raising suspicion about wiretapping had a political background in Turkey where Watergate-style surveillance is, as Bozkurt states (2008), part of political scene. Even prime ministers have not been exempt from illegal tapping, although it is not possible to understand clearly who taps whom and why.

The recent wiretapping scandal of Turkey which grew like a snowball with each step taken by the conflicting major powers against each other is the most transparent one since it developed through first judiciary *vs.* government and later judiciary *vs.* judiciary row. The dispute between the government and judges escalated more when the TCC annulled, in the beginning of June 2008, the constitutional amendments lifting the ban on the wearing of the headscarf in universities and, in return, Prime Minister Erdoğan accused the judges of taking the national will hostage while some officials proposed to scrap the court's powers.

June and July were no better than May. Just after the TCC's decision on the headscarf in June and before the Court's decision about the closure of the AKP at the end of July, the third wave of detentions came under the 'Ergenekon' case on July 1. The detentions ordered on June 29 but carried out on July 1, just hours before the Supreme Court of Appeals' chief prosecutor presented his oral evaluations regarding the AKP closure case to the 11 judges of the Constitutional Court, led the opposition parties to question the objectivity of the Ergenekon case (Kanlı, 2008a). Among the people taken into custody were some important public figures, including two retired four-star generals, two outspoken journalists and the head of Ankara's chamber of commerce. This time it was the turn of the AKP to defend that the judiciary and the police are independent and cannot be interfered with, while the opposition argued that the government had directed the case to suppress political "dissidents." The way and timing of the detentions have been criticized fiercely by many people. Kanlı (2008b) explains the situation as follows:

The probe was tainted with what appeared arbitrary and rather awkward detentions, gross violation of individual rights during detentions and the humiliation detained people were subjected to. Leaks to as well as a disinformation campaign launched in the pro-government media outlets amounting to character assassination and, unfortunately, evidence concocting created an impression that the government was acting in a revanchist understanding and trying to revenge for the closure case from anti-government elements...The absence of an indictment after 13 months and remarks of those released from detention complaining that no serious questioning was done but they were questioned mostly about their mobile telephone conversations – which were apparently all recorded – further tainted the credibility of the case.

It is needed to give some information about Ergenekon case since both the wiretapping scandal and the political controversy behind it actually became crystallized in this court case. Since it was first launched in June 2007, the Ergenekon case has become the largest and most controversial judicial investigation in recent Turkish history. The official-legal name of the case is not the "Ergenekon case" as is frequently and excessively used, but the "case against the infringement of article 313 of the Turkish Penal Code: establishment of a criminal organization" (Ünver, 2009). Little was known by the public until January 2008 because of a press embargo imposed to safeguard the investigation. On 21 January 2008, news broke of a major operation by Turkish police against an ultra-nationalist network known as Ergenekon (Turkey's Dark Side, 2008). The suspects include people from the military, intelligence community, politics, executive branches, academia, media, and civil society. The first indictment claimed that Ergenekon was the Deep State, and that it had been responsible for many "bloody operations" and that it aimed "to provoke a serious crisis, chaos, anarchy, terrorism and insecurity and that, even if it has been only partially successful, the organization has been an obstacle to the development of the country' (Jenkins, 2009, p.56).

Since the first Ergenekon indictment, which was revealed on July 15, 2008, not only the content of the indictment but also the source of the content became a subject of discussion. For proof of the existence of Ergenekon, the indictment relied heavily on documents seized at the defendants' homes and wiretaps. Silk Road report (Jenkins, 2009) criticizes it openly: "the hundreds of pages of transcripts of wiretaps – which were mostly fragments of conversations culled from what must have been thousands of hours of telephone surveillance – did not contain a single reference to the speakers' involvement with a covert organization, much less to Ergenekon; even though, in almost every case, the speakers were clearly unaware of the possibility that their conversations might be being recorded" (pp. 57-58). The European Union warned that the case's evidence collection methods — what the police refer to as "technical pursuit" — involved procedures that were considered illegal, such as wiretaps and surveillance of electronic correspondence without a warrant. Some critiques argued that almost three fourths of the indictments include phone conversation transcripts, which cannot be presented as evidence before the court as they were collected through means illegal under Turkish law (Ünver, 2009).

On the other hand, another privacy issue occurred by the publication of the indictment ("Ergenekon Indictment", 2008) as many of the disclosed wiretappings may be subject to charges of violation of privacy at the European Court of Human Rights. The 2,500-page-long Ergenekon indictment was criticized for containing irrelevant information on the accused and many wiretappings of people not on the list of accused in the lawsuit. Academics and lawyers noted that phone conversations unrelated to the lawsuit should have been excluded from the indictment all along. Additionally, the records of telephone calls particularly either by the defendants or by those criticizing the investigation have frequently appeared in pro-government newspapers and websites. Government officials have dismissed suggestions that the transcripts were based on wiretaps by AKP sympathizers in the Turkish National Police. The failure of the government to try either to investigate the sources of the leaks of wiretaps into the public domain has inevitably created a climate of fear amongst a large proportion of the Turkish population (Jenkins, 2009).

b) Wiretapping the Judges: The Judiciary vs. the Judiciary

At the second half of 2009, the wiretapping maze turned into a scandal of tapped judiciary. Due to the Ergenekon case, there was already a belief/concern in the society that the judiciary was divided politically and had lost its impartiality, especially because of so many telecommunication interception decisions taken by the judges against the suspects at Ergenekon case, most of whom are public figures known for their critical attitude towards the government. A major public controversy about the wiretappings was provoked by the statement of the Minister of Justice in April 2009 that 70,000 telephones had been monitored by the state in the last three years, many of which were related to Ergenekon case.

In July 2009, the Constitutional Court gave a landmark decision on telecommunications interception. In August 2008, the wife of TCC vice-president, Ferda Paksüt, testified as part of an ongoing investigation into Ergenekon and was listed among the suspects in the second Ergenekon indictment (March 2009). In November 2008, it was determined by the Ankara public prosecutor that her conversations had been intercepted by the court order under the Ergenekon investigations. The same month, Ergenekon prosecutor Zekeriya Öz filed a criminal complaint against TCC vice-president Paksüt on the grounds that he had assisted the alleged Ergenekon gang by leaking information regarding several cases, including the closure case against the ruling party, to his wife and sent records of phone conversations between Ferda and Osman Paksüt to the Constitutional Court as evidence. However, the TCC, in July 2009, decided not to launch an investigation of court member Osman Paksüt, stating that the evidence against him was obtained illegally as he was being monitored without court approval ("Top Court's Decision", 2009). The evidence was actually obtained from telephone conservations made on the phone owned by his wife, Ferda Paksüt, which was being monitored. The TCC stated that a separate court decision for wiretapping was required in order for the recorded statements of another person using a legally tapped phone to be used as evidence. With this latest decision, the top court set a new precedent regarding surveillance.

Osman Paksüt also filed a criminal complaint with the Justice Ministry against the Ergenekon prosecutors for the same reasons ("Top Court's Decision", 2009).

Another judicial conflict aroused at the end of July 2009 when the appointment of 87 new judges and prosecutors would be made by the Supreme Board of Judges and Prosecutors (hereafter HSYK). In the HSYK's meeting, the members claimed ("Judicial Board Criticizes", 2009) that there were various complaints against Ergenekon prosecutors and judges, and demanded their replacement. They also decided to take the controversial court decisions on the ongoing Ergenekon case to the Supreme Court of Appeals because of the allegations that these court decisions violated human rights. The issues subject to the HSYK's decision included wiretapping and searching in the absence of the proper legal conditions, among the others. The ministry had also still not answered the HSYK's requests to examine the criminal complaints leveled against Ergenekon prosecutors. In return, the ministry reacted to the HSYK with a written statement, saying that the board had exceeded its limits by asking for information on judicial issues and by making decisions about the Ergenekon case. According to the ministry, the board had authority neither to interfere in issues that fall under the authority of the ministry and courts, nor to take court decisions to the Supreme Court of Appeals ("Tensions rise", 2009).

On August 2009, Judge Osman Kaçmaz of Sincan's 1st High Criminal Court, who was under the Justice Ministry investigation, filed a criminal complaint to the Ankara Chief Public Prosecutor's Office against the inspectors for applying illegal methods to obtain evidence about him, on the grounds that the confidentiality of his private life was being violated. That he was illegally wiretapped and that his private telephone conservations derived from this wiretapping were used by the inspectors were among his complaints. Kaçmaz was known for his ruling that President Abdullah Gül should be tried in the "missing trillion" case. Right after this complaint, the Ministry of Justice announced that he was under investigation as part of the probe into Ergenekon since July and that his rulings were under inspection since September, 2008, long before his controversial decision involving the President ("Sincan Judge", 2009).

It may be claimed that the wiretapping scandal of Turkey reached its peak point in November 2009. On November 9, the Justice Ministry requested the disbarring of two top Turkish jurists -controversial Sincan 1st High Criminal Court Chief Justice Kaçmaz and YARSAV President Eminağaoğlu- upon the conclusion of its investigation into a series of questionable rulings stretching back to 2008. Just three days after, Kaçmaz sent a report prepared as a result of an examination of the records of the Telecommunications Directorate, which is responsible for conducting wiretaps, to the Supreme Court of Appeals. The complaint leading to the investigation was made by the YARSAV President Eminağaoğlu and the investigation was ordered by the Judge Kaçmaz (Kanlı, 2009). The findings of the investigation into the records of the Telecommunications Institute shook the judiciary and the whole country ("Judicial decision on wiretapping", 2009): Istanbul Chief Prosecutor Engin, under whom all prosecutors of the Ergenekon case are working, Sincan Chief Judge Kaçmaz and the Supreme Court of Appeals switchboard had been wiretapped since November 2008 as part of the Ergenekon case, along with several other judges and prosecutors upon an order from the Justice Ministry Inspection Committee. Though it was not in its jurisdiction, a high criminal court ordered the wiretapping of the Court of Appeals. HSYK's acting Chief Özbek told reporters that fearing punishment by the political authority, the top judges of some courts felt compelled to accept wiretapping requests coming from Justice Ministry investigators.

c) The Reactions to the Surveillance of the Judiciary

There were different reactions from the judiciary and the government. Immediately, the Justice Ministry made an explanation and stated ("more than 50 Judiciary Members", 2009) that 56 judiciary officials were wiretapped in the ongoing investigation into an alleged gang called Ergenekon. According to the ministry's statement, 69 judicial officers were tapped within the last five years, while 56 of them were for Ergenekon. The Justice Ministry had allowed these officials to be investigated in two decisions dated April 15, 2008 and September 5, 2008. However, the Justice Ministry refuted that the telephones belonging to members of the Supreme Court of Appeals and to the Prosecutor Engin were wiretapped. In response, the Supreme Court of Appeals announced ("Judicial decision on wiretapping", 2009) that it launched a preliminary investigation in line with the report sent by the First High Criminal Court in Sincan. According to the Court of Appeals Law, court members' phones can only be tapped with the special permission of the Court Presidency. The head of the Council of State, the top administrative court, criticized the wiretaps, as efforts to pressure the judiciary ("more than 50 Judiciary Members", 2009). HSYK's acting Chief Özbek noted that the judiciary has turned into an institution that is trying to defend itself and announced that they would pursue this issue since decisions on wiretaps should not be made by the Justice Ministry's chief inspectors.

On the other hand, Prime Minister Erdoğan criticized the reaction of judicial members against the wiretapping. He said ("Wiretapping scandal", 2009) that "it is clear whose attitude is wrong if the judicial institutions or officials don't respect the court's decisions [to grant permission for the wiretaps]. Above all, the judicial members should respect the court's decisions." The second reaction from the government was legislative ("Gov't to increase penalties", 2009). The Justice Ministry drafted a new set of regulations which would impose severe punishments (a prison sentence of up to seven years) against illegal wiretapping. Another response of the government was the announcement of statistical data of wiretapping. The Justice Ministry announced ("Ministry announces", 2009) that 113,270 people over the last three years and 32,852 people in 2009 had been wiretapped, including 12,988 people from the 2009 group who were sent a letter notifying them of this and saying no crime had been detected. No crime was detected in 11.4 percent of the wiretapping cases; Courts across the country requested the surveillance of the phones of 33,037 people in 2009. The Telecommunications Directorate objected to 185 of the requests. An interesting strategy adopted by government members concerning the wiretapping scandal was the attempt to show that the wiretapping is a fact of this country by referring to the illegal wiretappings conducted against them. First Prime Minister Erdoğan announced that he had been wiretapped illegally. Later, Turkish Justice Minister Sadullah Ergin said that he was a victim of phone tapping in 2001 during the founding of the Justice and Development Party, or AKP ("Justice minister", 2009).

On the judicial side ("Tension rises", 2009), the chief prosecutor office of the Supreme Court of Appeals demanded the tapping records from the Telecommunication Directorate to examine the connection between the ruling government and the wiretapping incidents and to determine whether there has been "illegal wiretapping by the political order." On the other hand, the Council of State gave a very significant decision in December 28 and stopped the implementation of the Justice Ministry Inspection Board's 98/ç regulation that permitted the wiretapping and technical surveillance of judicial personnel. YARSAV had filed a case with the Council of State against the implementation of the clause. The court held ("Court: tapping judges", 2009) that the regulation in question does not give the ministry the authority to conduct the wiretapping of the judges and prosecutors and that a new law would be necessary to permit any such surveillance.

Nowadays, the Chief Public Prosecutor Office in Ankara is conducting its investigations about the claims that the telephones of the Court of Appeals and the Court of State were wiretapped illegally. The central telephone and communication systems of the Supreme Court of Appeals in February 2010 and of the Council of State in Ankara in March 2010 were examined by a team of experts led by Ankara Deputy Chief Public Prosecutor. Additionally, the offices of the Telecommunications Directorate (TİB) in Ankara were searched the third time after a warrant was issued by the Ankara 9th Criminal Court under the same investigation at the end of March 2010. On the political side of the story, the public agenda is occupied with only one topic: the new draft prepared by the ruling party for constitutional amendments and for reforms of the judicial system. It seems that the dispute between the government and the judiciary will not end with this scandal but may have just started.

IV. THE SECURITY OF BIO-POWER AND A SOCIETY OF DISCIPLINE: FOUCAULDIAN ANALYSIS

a) Conflicts of Power in Turkey: Truth-Claims about Security

There are several reasons to take the theoretical approach and tools from Foucault to analyze the wiretapping scandal in Turkey. First of all, the historical, social and political background of the issue shows high complexity with a number of accidental factors which pave the way to the current situation by affirming, in a way, the claim that the surveillance is historically, spatially and culturally located (Wood, 2009) and, secondly, the deep political divisions among the parties to the controversy lead to the production and diffusion of sometimes clashing truth-claims, which may force any author to take a side in this highly political issue. Therefore, I will keep my focus on a rather modest objective to uncover the 'conditions of possibility' for the widespread practice of legal/illegal wiretapping in Turkey. In other words, my question is as follows: what circumstances in dispersed and seemingly unconnected fields of social activity combine in such a way as to give rise to this outcome? (Hunt & Wickham, 1994, p. 6)

The surveillance of citizens for security reasons is not a new phenomenon in Turkey. On the contrary, it has always been a commonly used method by the intelligence services, the police, the gendarmerie and some 'stay-behind' bodies (Almanac Turkey, 2006). However, it has rather been a topic of conspiracy theories and journalistic inquiries until its legalization, partly in 1995 and more thoroughly in 2005; while its target, and its justification at the same time, has been the threats coming from the politico-criminal organizations against the internal security, its direction has been, most of the time, the individuals. The amplification and multiplications of the internal threat-conceptions have occurred due to the rise of leftist-socialist movements in the 70s, the radical Islamic groups, and the Kurdish separatist movement since the 80s (Yücel, 2002). The discourses of security emphasized the protection of the Republic, unity of the State, democracy and secularism: the domestic enemies were always portrayed as dangerous, ready to perform violent operations which posed an imminent threat to be suppressed. In short, it is not possible to narrate the history of internal security policies as an overview of legislative history on the basis of state initiatives, since the security policies and techniques were used, or abused, both by the deep-state networks in Turkey (Ünver, 2009) and by the administrative and security forces which have not been always under the full control of the state (Almanac Turkey, 2006).

Instead, in the evaluation of the communication surveillance in Turkey, to focus on the actual power relations, whether conflicting or collaborating, and on the 'techniques of power' would lead us to more fruitful conclusions. As Foucault underlines:

I don't want to say that the state isn't important; what I want to say is that relations of power, hence the analysis that must be made of them, necessarily extend beyond the limits of the state. In two senses: first of all because the state, for all the omnipotence of its apparatuses, is far from being able to occupy the whole field of actual power relations, and further because the state can only operate on the basis of other, already existing power relations. (Foucault, 1991, p. 64)

Actually it is the National Security Council Law (1983) which includes the 'power' into definition of the national security: its duty is to monitor and to evaluate *the national elements of power* that can affect the national security policy of the state. However, 'power' as a term in this paper does not mean all the time negative and repressive. Power does not always exclude, repress, censor or conceal. Power also produces reality and rituals of truth; power circulates, functions and forms networks.

The surveillance over communications is a technique of discipline in a Foucauldian sense. In an example given by Foucault about Penal Law, he describes the collaboration of the law with the disciplinary mechanisms. The law is framed by a series of supervisions, checks, inspections, and varied controls so that, even before the crime is conducted it is possible to identify whether or not it will be. In short, the mechanisms of surveillance and correction are the disciplinary mechanisms. The disciplinary mechanism refers to a series of adjacent (detective, medical, and psychological) techniques within the domain of surveillance, diagnosis, and the possible transformation of individuals so that the culprit as a third personage, appears within the binary system of the code, and at the same time, outside the code, and outside the legislative act that establishes the law and the judicial act that punishes the culprit (Foucault, 2007). For Foucault, discipline is the distinctive form of modern power, with its special emphasis on the technique of 'surveillance' embracing the methods of observation, recording and training (Hunt & Wickham, 1994).

The state of disciplinary society is actually one step in Foucault's trilogy. When he explains the birth of bio-politics or the governmentality with a new form of power, which is called bio-power, a new understanding of security is developed using new techniques without leaving the already developed disciplinary mechanisms behind. He asserts that there is not the legal age, the disciplinary age, and then the age of security. But the governmentality makes the old armatures of law and discipline function in addition to the specific mechanisms of security. Again quoting from him:

the law prohibits and discipline prescribes, and the essential function of security, without prohibiting or prescribing, but possibly making use of some instruments of prescription and prohibition, is to respond to a reality in such a way that this response cancels out the reality to which it responds – nullifies it, or limits, checks, or regulates it. I think this regulation within the element of reality is fundamental in apparatuses of security. (Foucault, 2007, p. 69)

While bio-politics deals with the population as a political, biological, scientific and economic problem, its technology of security tries to control the series of random events that can occur in a living mass, to predict the probability of those events, to compensate for their effects and it aims to achieve an overall equilibrium that protects the security of the whole from the internal dangers (Foucault, 2003). The concept of security was about the well-being of the population in general so that it required state intervention with the essential function of ensuring the security of the natural phenomena of economic processes or processes intrinsic to population. Similarly, the concept of national security is defined very comprehensively in the Ministry of National Defense website so as to include almost all policy areas: "The protection of the state's constitutional order, national existence and integrity and all of its political, social, cultural and economic interests and its treaty rights in the international arena against all threats both internal and external" (as quoted in Almanac Turkey, 2006).

Turkey's security conceptions may only be explained by a number of truth-claims developed by different powers in the society. The truth as understood here and as explained by Foucault is a *regime* of truth. Each society has its regime of truth, its general politics of truth: that is, the types of discourse which it accepts and makes function as true. But, especially in western societies, there is a battle for truth or at least around truth about its status and the economic and political role it plays. According to Foucault, truth is not separated from power. It is linked in a circular relation with systems of power: they produce and sustain truth and truth induces and extends effects of power. Therefore, the truth is 'the issue of a whole political debate and social confrontation' (Foucault, 1991, p. 73).

The army is one of the great political apparatuses which produces and transmits truth (Foucault, 1991, p. 73). In Turkey, the army has long considered itself, and been considered by most of the people, as the guardian of the secular and unitary Republic. For those purposes, it was actively involved in politics by the *coup d'états* until 1983 and through the National Security Council between 1983 and 2003 legal reforms (Jenkins, 2007). Two security threats, separatism and fundamentalism, against which the military frequently underlined its determination to fight contributed to the dissemination of a discourse on specific interpretations of nationalism and secularism: the Silk Road Paper (Cornell & Karaveli, 2008) states that secularism, and obviously nationalism, carries existential connotations for many in the military ranks. Concerning 'securityness of secularism,' the control function (as to control both the religion and those in opposition with alternative visions about the state-religion relations) and the transformation function (as the protector of the modernization project) of secularism (Bilgin, 2008) seemed to play some role in the military's security strategy. While the military has used its hegemony over truth about who is secular and what is a threat to secularism quite frequently during the Republic's history, its own conceptions of secularism went through some transformations since the first military coup in 1960 (Cizre, 2003).

The particularly strong position of the army in Turkish politics also arises from the vital role it plays against the PKK terrorism. A state of emergency has been operated in southeast Turkey due to the armed conflict with the PKK for nearly two decades. Violation of human rights and curtailment of several democratic freedoms for the local population has accompanied the long period of emergency. The principal role of the military in the fight against terrorism also produced a certain understanding of 'true' nationalists and the internal enemies by an extensive list of the criminal acts which target to divide the unitary Republic. Questioning the reality of all these discourses of truth is not within the scope of this paper. However, the frequent use of surveillance techniques by the military through its own expanded intelligence networks, political espionage and counterintelligence activities of its own within the context of security strategy is directly linked to the 2009 wiretapping scandal of Turkey since it exhibits a well-established practice in Turkey about the limitless use of disciplinary techniques against individuals when the 'security' is at stake. Just to dare to criticize this practice has, in the past, been sufficient to label the critic as an enemy of the state, as happens still.

Another power producing truth-claims about security in Turkey is the judiciary. Especially the decisions of political party dissolutions by the Constitutional Court which are 25 in total provide a rich resource about the judicial understanding of security in Turkey. Since most of these decisions were given against the parties either with separatist/Kurdish, communist or Islamic background, the threats against the state's indivisible unity and secularism are defined by the Turkish judiciary in several incidents. While the Turkish Constitutional Court has become an important secularizing/securitizing power in the Turkish political system by continually outlawing anti–secularist/separatist/revolutionary political forces and parties, this role has been criticized as a manifestation of the politicization of the judiciary (Hirschl, 2006), which may be observed as a side effect of judicialization of politics by the legal and political system itself (Shambayati, 2004; Hirschl, 2004). Although institutions such as the judiciary might remain structurally independent, as Shambayati (2004) underlines, their active participation in the political decision-making process undermines their ability to act as impartial arbiters. The Headscarf and AKP cases recently in the Constitutional Court re-initiated the public discussions about the impartiality of the judiciary.

The problem about the judicial truth regime of secularity/security in Turkey arises from its conflict with the socio-political reality or powers. The parties which were dissolved had the support of 15–20% of the voters and were re-established by different names after the dissolution. It may be claimed that constitutional normativity should not be confused with the political reality. However, the Court is taken into the political conflict more with each decision. As stated by some authors before, relying on the judicial process to resolve divisive political issues may not reduce tensions. Instead it has the potential of creating new ones since the judicial process creates absolute "winners" and "losers" with a method based on finding "Truth" and establishing guilt (Shambayati, 2004).

The regime of truth developed by the judicial power about secularism/regime-security is perceived by some as collaboration between the secular state elites: the judiciary, they claim, comes with decisions always favorable for the guardians of regime (i.e., the military). There may be different reasons for such a collaboration of powers. According to one explanation, which sounds to be a power-centered one, even the political tension itself, growing from some dissenting social groups to the Court's decision, is generated to justify the unelected guardians' threat perception and to legitimize the continuation of its guardian role. An appearingly regime-threatening political instability becomes a mechanism for preserving the division of sovereignty between elected and unelected institutions (Shambayati, 2004). According to the "hegemonic preservation" thesis detailed by Hirschl (2006), the judicialization of mega-politics is the result of a common strategy undertaken by secular and relatively cosmopolitan elites (not limited to the military, therefore making the thesis relatively more realistic for Turkey) fearful of the growing popular support for principles of theocratic governance which poses a major threat to their cultural propensities and policy preferences. Drawing upon their disproportionate access to and influence over the legal arena, social forces in polities facing deep division along secular-religious lines aim to ensure that their constitutionally protected secular values are less effectively contested. The results have been an unprecedented judicialization of foundational collective identity, particularly in the realm of religion and state questions, and the consequent emergence of constitutional courts as important guardians of relative secularism, modernism, and universalism in countries such as Egypt, Pakistan, Israel, India, Malaysia and Turkey (Hirschl, 2004; Hirschl, 2008)

The thesis above which seems to emphasize the control function of secularism may be contrasted with a transformation function approach adopted by Shambayati (2009) later. He claims that Turkey's Constitutional Court has been set up by the 1982 Constitution as an administrative agent not to safeguard the immediate interests of the ruling elite but to transform the society in the direction of a civilizing mission and to create a new political culture according to the State's fundamental values as well as to defend this mission against potential challengers (Shambayati, 2009). However, as is analyzed by Shambayati himself, it is not the Court to blame for judicial activism. It is the judicial structure, safeguards, and competences given and non-given to courts by the political/military actors which produces particular patterns in legislative-judiciary relations. Hirschl maintains that portraying courts and judges as the source of evil is misguided since the expansion of judicial power (e.g., through constitutionalization or the establishment of judicial review) does not develop separately from the concrete social, cultural, political, and economic struggles but becomes both an integral part and an important manifestation of those struggles (Hirschl, 2004).

I agree with Hirsch partly because it is not the existence of judicial review itself which reflects the internal struggles but these struggles make it problematic. Because it may easily be claimed that the judicial review of the Turkish Constitutional Court over the principle of secularism represents a good example for constitutional democracy; that it is a necessity for the protection of secularism in countries where religious affiliation is a pillar of collective identity, for the prevention of majoritarian tyranny (Tezcur, 2007) and it is, in any way, a part of the global judicialization of politics. Therefore, the problem may be lying somewhere else for Turkey: the need for a constitution which reflects a *consensus* on the common values and principles, for a society or at least a majority which keeps and supports this *consensus* and for a judiciary which provides a balanced protection for all the values and rights with an equal weight. In other words, if the truth regime of the Constitutional Court about security would be sustainable and would find popular support, not only the Court but the judiciary in general should reflect a proper balance between the state interest, values and rights. Yet, it is not the case for Turkey. To even further this claim, the judiciary may accomplish its normative transformation role for the society only in this way.

The argument above may be summarized as follows: The regime of truth of the Turkish judiciary is problematic not mainly because of its long-debated secularism decisions but more because of the limited approach it adopted in the cases concerning security (and security forces of the state, including the military, police, and intelligence) and human rights and freedoms (Aydın, 2004). This situation encourages the claims about the judiciary-military cooperation. As Tezcur (2009) explained in detail, the Courts do not foster judicial activism in the service of civil liberties and human rights and rarely supervise the vast executive powers claimed by the military and infrequently hold members of the state security responsible for illegal behavior. Citizens have lacked basic judicial protections against arbitrary detention, torture, and state-sponsored killings, especially during the early 1990s. The European Court of Human Rights (ECHR) often finds Turkey guilty for human rights abuses. Moreover, the judiciary has frequently persecuted political dissidents who publicly challenge the ideological commitments of the regime (p. 307).

However, it is again not completely the fault of the Courts. The reasons are various: the legal system and the laws, the pressures from the political/non-political actors and the Constitution itself. As Tezcur explains (2009), it seems to be 'the result of hierarchical and informal pressures that cultivate a culture of discipline and intimidate the members of the judiciary from acting more liberally' (p. 307-308). I assert, as Tezcur does, that the solution to the conflict between the judicial and the political in such an environment is not to get rid of judicial review for secularism, but to establish a judiciary system not intimidated by the politicians and a stronger judicial review for protection of human rights, minority rights and egalitarian principles as well as secularism, which is sanctioned by a democratically written liberal constitution and not guarded by non-elected institutions (Tezcur, 2007).

Where does the AKP stand in this picture? First of all, most of the truth-claims critical to the judicial and military discourses are produced by the AKP and by the pro-government voices including academicians and media. Conception of power only in negative terms would not be quite helpful in the case of a political party with a high majoritarian support. Most of the democratic and legal reforms for the harmonization with the EU have been conducted in the period of AKP government. Most of the issues which were considered as a political taboo were opened to public debate during its rule. A number of minority policies have been initiated by the AKP. Even foreign policy began to pursue a more active and liberal road. Opponents argue that all these reforms actually serve a secret agenda which aims toward an Islamic authoritarian regime change. In other words, truth discourses of the AKP are not 'true' but conceal a hidden bad intention which may not be expressed since some discourses are forbidden. Another argument is that these reforms were needed and helpful to the AKP both for its survival in a liberalized and more tolerant political/legal environment and for gaining the support of the EU for its political power that is vulnerable to the judicial and military institutions. It is also accused of conducting some democratization reforms just to weaken the main power in opposition: the military (Jamal, 2008).

The Ergenekon case is to be evaluated against this background. As a judicial action against the 'deep state' of Turkey, the case has been welcomed by the democrats whatever their political stand. Very soon, however, doubts have risen that the case turns into a power instrument for the AKP to weaken and threaten the secular elite and the military as well as to suppress the opposition in the parliament and in the public. The question is whether the case is another stage of the conflicts of power or truly a struggle against the long-persisting stay-behind organizations. Again the same question confronted the public: what is the truth? Who tells the truth? The Ergenekon case has been transformed into a factor which divides people according to their attitude to the case and even created deeper dilemmas within one and the same person about how to interpret the process. Arrests of many academics, civil figures and journalists only aggravated this public confusion and division while contributing to the perception of a political power in a constant effort of disciplining the society.

Another argument commonly asserted is that the government which is in trouble with the judiciary (as the party closure, the presidential elections, and the headscarf cases show) started a contra-judicial struggle against the secular elites. However, the question is whether this juridical war is legal. The fact that the evidence for the case were gathered mainly through wiretapping and these records were frequently published in their full length in the pro-government media even before the preparations of the indictments led the public to paranoia of constant surveillance of their communications. The wiretapping of the judiciary revealed a deep division within the judiciary and it showed that the Ministry of Justice had overstepped its legal limits in the investigation of judges.

b. Security Justifies Discipline: Discipline Cooperates with Power

How and why did Turkey have a wiretapping scandal subsequent to the 2005 legal reforms on telecommunications interception, which had set certain standards, some of which are even higher than the European ones, for privacy rights? To refer to Foucault for the functions of law in the society would contribute to our understanding of this seemingly dilemmatic event. Modern law operates between Foucault's concepts of government and discipline. Law acts as an interface through which governmental decisions can take effect by adjusting the operations and arrangements of the disciplinary mechanisms. Law, by connecting itself to both poles of the bio-power, in justifying itself, it masks the need for each of these forms of power to legitimate themselves (Tadros, 1998). The disciplinary mechanism is the law framed by mechanisms of surveillance and correction (Foucault, 2007). I will try to put it plainly: the argument of Foucault is that modern order and power is comprised of two systems: of state law on the one hand and the disciplines on the other (Beck, 1996, p. 494). The relation between the law and disciplinary mechanisms is a kind of reciprocal support. First of all, the judicial apparatus gives the already existing disciplinary mechanism legal justification as far as it regulates the technique (Foucault, 1991, p. 237). As explained before, the wiretapping was already a very common technique used by diverse powers in Turkey, before its legalization. Secondly, the disciplinary techniques support the law to function, as can be seen in the trilogy of police-court-prison. Thus the code of law is connected to the disciplinary network through the mechanisms of the trial (Tadros, 1998). Therefore legal regulation of communication interceptions in Turkey may serve criminal law more than it will serve the protection of privacy rights. As Foucault argues:

The general juridical form that guaranteed a system of rights that were egalitarian in principle was supported by these tiny, everyday, physical mechanisms, by all those systems of micropower that are essentially nonegalitarian and asymmetrical which we call the disciplines... The real, corporal disciplines constituted the foundation of the formal, juridical liberties (Foucault, 1991, p. 211).

Thirdly, the democratic characterization of law and the rule of law masks the real importance of control of the populace through the disciplines (Beck, 1996, p. 494). In other words, the rights justify the disciplinary practice (Foucault, 2003, p. 37). A disciplinary technique -or a counterlaw, as Foucault sometimes calls it- such as wiretapping becomes 'the effective and institutionalized content of the juridical forms' (Foucault, 1991, p. 213). The theory of sovereignty and the organization of a legal code centered upon it have allowed a system of right to be superimposed upon the mechanisms of discipline in such a way to conceal its actual procedures, the element of domination inherent in its techniques (Foucault, 1980, p. 105). This may also explain the increase of the punishments for the crimes relating to the privacy of communications as a first reaction from the government to the scandal of judiciary-wiretapping. In conclusion, the legal protection of privacy rights in Turkey will not be enough, if it is not supported by the attitude/practice of the micro-powers applying the wiretapping techniques and of the great powers governing them.

The 2005 legal reforms in Turkey also attempted to centralize the wiretappings in a center called Telecommunications Directorate (TIB). A step which was hailed, for it might mean to take under control the illegal wiretapping which was believed to be a frequent practice in Turkey. From a Foucauldian viewpoint, it points to the inductive tendency of major powers, i.e., a power working to incite, reinforce, control, monitor, optimize, and organize the forces under it, rather than dedicated to impeding them, making them submit, or destroying them (Foucault, 1991, p. 259). In other words, it is very well expected that at one point when it brings a certain political utility, the techniques and procedures at the lower levels are invested, annexed or colonized by global mechanisms and, finally by the entire system of the State. Therefore, it was not surprising that the government with a strong majority slipped into the play of these technologies of power, which were at once relatively autonomous and made them part of the whole (Foucault, 2003, pp. 31,33).

Just at this point, it may be better understood how even judges were wiretapped, including the prosecutor who conducted the Ergenekon case. Many reasons may be listed: the divisions in the society and institutions along lines such as secular/conservative, pro-government/contra-government, pro-military/contra-military, and an extreme distrust to each other among the divisions; the mistrust of the government toward judges; the power struggle between the judiciary and the executive; the unimaginable depth of the Deep state… Nevertheless, it also has a connection with the nature of surveillance as a disciplinary technique. Disciplinary power is organized as a multiple, automatic, and anonymous power. It means that, although surveillance rests on individuals, it functions from the top down, but also to a certain extent from the bottom up. Foucault describes in a way an uncontrollable mechanism and power. It may hierarchically have a head, however it is the apparatus as a whole that produces power. In this sense, it leaves no zone of shade and constantly supervises the very individuals who are entrusted with the task of supervising (Foucault, 1991, p. 193). This definition about the nature of modern panoptic organizations may make more understandable the confession of the Prime Minister that his communications were intercepted, too.

However, all these explanations may still not be enough for the widespread tapping of communications of even judges and public prosecutors. For that, the concept of security should be brought back to the analysis. In Foucault's historical analysis, security as an issue is born with the increase in free circulation of people and goods. And Foucault adds that freedom is nothing else but the correlative of the deployment of apparatuses of security. An apparatus of security cannot operate well except on the condition that it is given freedom. Consequently, the governmentality as a mode of power deals with

circulations to take place, of controlling them, shifting the good and the bad, ensuring that things are always in movement, constantly moving around, continually going from one point to another, but in such a way that the inherent dangers of this circulation are cancelled out. No longer the safety (sûreté) of the prince and his territory, but the security (sécurité) of the population and, consequently, of those who govern it (Foucault, 2007, p. 93).

It would be useful to remember that the mobile phone usage rate in Turkey is 92% and that freedom of expression has been expanded as a part of harmonization efforts with the EU. As Foucault assumed for another period and geography, the regulation and securitization of the free movement of communication became much more significant in Turkey, while the speeches and discourses are circulating through the apparatus of technology and laws.

The security/governmentality works differently from the law and the discipline. It organizes circulation, eliminates its dangerous elements, makes a division between good and bad circulation, and maximizes the good circulation by diminishing the bad. This is only possible for the circulation of communications by their interception and regular monitoring. The systems of security need to use the disciplinary mechanisms. Foucault underlines that with the new mode of power called security

[t]here is a considerable activation and propagation of the disciplinary corpus. For in order actually to guarantee this security one has to appeal, to take just one example, to a whole series of techniques for the surveillance of individuals…; in short one has to appeal to a whole disciplinary series that proliferates under mechanisms of security and is necessary to make them work (Foucault, 2007, 22).

Now, in a country, where the concept of security frequently implied, and implicitly justified, the suspension of laws, rights and procedures for the people who threaten it; where the micro-powers always found the right to replace the system of justice with their subjective judgments; where the disciplinary practices such as wiretapping have been extensively used to preemptively control the threats -no matter if it is only the ideas, to coerce the 'dissidents' as well as to 'normalize' the society in the direction of the unwritten but well-known norms, what happens if a power with a popular support just re-writes the definition of concept of security, if it produces a new regime of truth about the state and regime security and if it has the sufficient control over the technologies of micro-powers, the mechanisms of discipline and the legislative mechanism? A party with enough power and with a popular political support is re-writing the concept of security without changing the rules of game.

V. CONCLUSION

The Ergenekon case deals with the 'deep state' of Turkey, which could have occurred and developed probably because of the conditions discussed above. These conditions prepared and sustained the mature soil for it to come up. If a judicial and political endeavor for demolishing this deep network makes use of the same soil, it cannot take the country out of the vicious circle, but it just creates a new one. Unfortunately, this seems to be the case. A 'normalized' society with the techniques of discipline for decades watches the familiar collaboration of a system of procedure-less justice with this process.

It is certain that the international law and environment do not give handy support, or a model, to Turkey for a proper implementation of the telecommunication interceptions in the criminal area. Neither the European Union nor the European Court of Human Rights seem eager to put restrictions on the Member States regarding the measures taken for a very sensitive issue like national security. On the contrary, some recent legal and administrative developments in countries such as the UK, the USA or Australia set legitimizing examples for the more restricted rights to privacy in the struggle against organized crime and global threats. Turkey is just in the middle with higher legal standards than these countries but with worse implementation than many European countries.

Alternatively, the domestic democratic control mechanisms over the excessive use of administrative, political or judicial powers seemed to be handicapped, not recently but for a long time due to the normalizing functions of a long-term application of the disciplinary mechanisms over the society. As Foucault foretold long ago, the techniques of discipline and discourses born of discipline colonize the procedures of law in 'normalizing' societies. (Foucault, 2003, pp. 38-39). A dilemmatic double function of the concept of security contributes to the social inertia against the violations of rights and procedures: first, the mystifying and legitimizing effect of justifications based on state security; second and contrarily, most of the measures contrary to due process are perceived as an acceptable struggle against the powers which had used the first type of justification for their criminal interests. On the other side of the coin, the critics of undue surveillance have often remained silent in the face of similar abuses of power in the past. Bill Park (2009) reminds that 'the manipulation of the judicial process, intimidation of the media, habitual corruption, and an inclination to conspiracy theory were inherited rather than invented by those currently in power in Turkey.'

Nevertheless, there is something which can be surely maintained for the current state of society. There is an atmosphere of paranoia surrounding people and arising from the ambiguity of the conflict deeply rooted into all segments of the state. This fear, as Taipale (2004) elaborates, is not the surveillance itself but 'that data relating to the individual will be mismanaged or misinterpreted with real-world consequences to that individual' (p. 148). As discussed throughout this paper, it is not only the doubts about the indiscreet surveillance over communications which may come upon any telephone conversation but also the doubts about the 'truth' of a country where the multiple relations of powers are indissociable from ever-increasing discourses of truth.

REFERENCES

Aydın, S., & Keyman, E. F. (2004, August). *European integration and the transformation of Turkish democracy*. EU-Turkey Working Papers, No. 2. Brussels: Centre for European Policy Studies. Retrieved from http://www.ceps.be

Beck, A. (1996). Foucault and law: The collapse of law's empire. *Oxford Journal of Legal Studies, 16*(3), 489–502. doi:10.1093/ojls/16.3.489

Bilgin, P. (2008). The securityness of secularism? The case of Turkey. *Security Dialogue, 39*(6), 593–614. .doi:10.1177/0967010608098211

Bozkurt, G. (2008, May 31). The corridor. *Hurriyet Daily News*. Retrieved from http://www.hurriyetdailynews.com/h.php?news=the-corridor-2008-05-31

Bronitt, S., & Stellios, J. (2006). Regulating telecommunications interception and access in the twenty-first century: Technological evolution or legal revolution? *Prometheus, 24*(4), 413–428. .doi:10.1080/08109020601030001

Cizre, U. (2003). Demythologyzing the national security concept: The case of Turkey. *The Middle East Journal, 57*(2), 213–229.

Cizre, Ü. (Ed.). (2006). *Almanac Turkey 2005: Security sector and democratic oversight.* İstanbul, Turkey: TESEV. Retrieved from http://www.tesev.org.tr/UD_OBJS/PDF/DEMP/Almanak-2005-Ingilizce-Tam%20Metin.pdf

Cornell, S. E., & Karaveli, H. M. (2008, October). *Prospects for a 'Torn' Turkey: A secular and unitary future?* Washington, DC: Central Asia-Caucasus Institute & Silk Road Studies Program. Retrieved from http://www.silkroadstudies.org/new/docs/silkroadpapers/0810Turkey.pdf

Court: Tapping judges and prosecutors' phones prohibited. (2009, December 29). *Hurriyet Daily News.* Retrieved from http://www.hurriyetdailynews.com

De Hert, P. (2005). Balancing security and liberty within the European human rights framework. A critical reading of the Court's case law in the light of surveillance and criminal law enforcement strategies after 9/11. *Utrecht Law Review, 1*(1), 68–96.

Ergenekon indictment may trouble Turkey. (2008, September 3). *Hurriyet Daily News.* Retrieved from http://www.hurriyetdailynews.com

Foucault, M. (1980). *Power/knowledge selected interviews and other writings of Michael Foucault (1927-77)* (Gordon, C., Ed.). Brighton, UK: Harvester Press.

Foucault, M. (1991). *The Foucault reader* (Rabinow, P., Ed.). London: Penguin Books.

Foucault, M. (2003). *Society must be defended. Lectures at the Collège de France, 1975-1976* (Macey, D., Trans.). New York: Picador.

Foucault, M. (2007). *Security, Territory, Population. Lectures at the Collège de France, 1977-78* (Burchell, G., Trans.). Basingstoke, UK: Palgrave Macmillan.

Freedom House. (2009). *Freedom on the Net 2009 – Turkey*. Geneva, Switzerland: The Office of the United Nations High Commissioner for Refugees. Retrieved from http://www.unhcr.org/refworld/docid/49d47595c.html

Gov't to increase penalties against illegal wiretapping. (2009, November 17). *Hurriyet Daily News.* Retrieved from http://www.hurriyetdailynews.com

'Hands off,' judiciary tells government. (2008, May 22). *Hurriyet Daily News.* Retrieved from http://www.hurriyetdailynews.com

Hirschl, R. (2004). Constitutional courts vs. religious fundamentalism: Three Middle Eastern tales. *Texas Law Review, 82*, 1819–1860.

Hirschl, R. (2006). The new constitutionalism and the judicialization of pure politics worldwide. *Fordham Law Review, 75*(2), 721–754. Retrieved from http://law2.fordham.edu/publications/articles/500flspub9554.pdf.

Hirschl, R. (2008). The judicialization of mega-politics and the rise of political courts. *Annual Review of Political Science, 11*(1), 93–118. doi:10.1146/annurev.polisci.11.053006.183906

Hunt, A., & Wickham, G. (1994). *Foucault and law*. London: Pluto.

Ian, B. (2009). Regulation of converged communications surveillance. In Neyland, D., & Goold, B. (Eds.), *New directions in surveillance societies and privacy* (pp. 39–73). Exeter, UK: Willan.

Jamal, A. (2009). Democratizing state-religion relations: A comparative study of Turkey, Egypt and Israel. *Democratization, 16*(6), 1143–1171. .doi:10.1080/13510340903271779

James, N. J. (2004). Handing over the keys: Contingency, power and resistance in the context of s 3LA of the Australian Crimes Act 1914. *The University of Queensland Law Journal, 23*(1), 7–21.

Jenkins, G. (2007). Continuity and change: Prospects for civil–military relations in Turkey.

International Affairs, 83(2), 339–355. doi:10.1111/j.1468-2346.2007.00622.x

Jenkins, G. H. (2009, August). *Between fact and fantasy: Turkey's Ergenekon investigation*. Washington, DC: Central Asia-Caucasus Institute & Silk Road Studies Program. Retrieved from http://www.silkroadstudies.org/new/docs/silkroadpapers/0908Ergenekon.pdf

Judicial board criticizes Justice Ministry over investigations. (2009, July 29) *Hurriyet Daily News*. Retrieved from http://www.hurriyetdailynews.com

Judicial decision on wiretapping shakes judiciary. (2009, November 12). *Hurriyet Daily News*. Retrieved from http://www.hurriyetdailynews.com

Kanlı, Y. (2008a, July 2). The empire of fear. *Hurriyet Daily News*. Retrieved from

http://www.hurriyetdailynews.com/h.php?news=the-empire-of-fear-2008-07-02

Kanlı, Y. (2008b, July 8). Cost of Uncertainty. *Hurriyet Daily News*. Retrieved from

http://www.hurriyetdailynews.com/h.php?news=cost-of-uncertainty-2008-07-08

Kanlı, Y. (2009, November 12). Empire of fear or the AKP's Turkey. *Hurriyet Daily News*. Retrieved from http://www.hurriyetdailynews.com/n.php?n=empire-of-fear-or-akp8217s-turkey-2009-11-12

Karakas, C. (2007). *Turkey: Islam and laicism between the interests of state, politics, and society*. PRIF Reports, No. 78. Frankfurt, Germany: Peace Research Institute Frankfurt (PRIF). Retrieved from www.hsfk.de/downloads/prif78.pdf

Lagerwall, A. (2008). *Privacy and secret surveillance from a European Convention perspective*. Unpublished master's thesis, Stockholm University, Sweden. Retrieved from http://www.adbj.se/2009/ht_2009_Anders_Lagerwall.pdf

Minister of justice: 'my phone has been tapped, too'. (2009, December 1). *Hurriyet Daily News*. Retrieved from http://www.hurriyetdailynews.com

Ministry announces number of people tapped. (2009, November 19). *Hurriyet Daily News*. Retrieved from http://www.hurriyetdailynews.com

More than 50 judiciary members tabbed. (2009, November 13). *Hurriyet Daily News.* Retrieved from http://www.hurriyetdailynews.com

Park, B. (2009, September). Ergenekon: Power and democracy in Turkey. *Open Democracy.* Retrieved from http://www.opendemocracy.net/article/ergenekon-power-and-democracy-in-turkey-0

Privacy International. (2007a). *PHR 2006- Republic of Turkey*. London: Privacy International. Retrieved from http://www.privacyinternational.org/article.shtml?cmd[347]=x-347-559483

Privacy International. (2007b). *Leading surveillance societies in the EU and the world 2007.* London: Privacy International. Retrieved from http://www.privacyinternational.org/article.shtml?cmd[347]=x-347-559597

Prosecutor in action to relieve court members' 'plight'. (2008, May 17). *Hurriyet Daily News.* Retrieved from http://www.hurriyetdailynews.com

Rubenfeld, J. (2008). The end of privacy. *Stanford Law Review, 61*(1), 101–161.

Schwartz, P. M. (2003). German and U.S. telecommunications privacy law: Legal regulation of domestic law enforcement surveillance. *The Hastings Law Journal, 54*(4), 751–804.

Schwartz, P. M. (2004). Evaluating telecommunications surveillance in Germany: The lessons of the Max Planck Institute's study. *The George Washington Law Review, 72*(6), 1244–1263.

Schwartz, P. M. (2008). Reviving telecommunications surveillance law. *The University of Chicago Law Review. University of Chicago. Law School, 75*(1), 287–315.

Schwartz, P. M. (2009). Warrantless wiretapping, FISA reform, and the lessons of public liberty: A comment on Holmes's Jorde lecture. *California Law Review, 97*(2), 407–432.

Şen, E. (2010). *Türk Hukunda Telefon Dinleme, Gizli Soruşturmacı, X Muhabir*. Ankara, Turkey: Seçkin.

Shambayati, H., & Kirdis, E. (2009). In pursuit of "contemporary civilization": Judicial empowerment in Turkey. *Political Research Quarterly, 62*(4), 767–780. .doi:10.1177/1065912909346741

Shambayati, H. (2004). A tale of two mayors: Courts and politics in Iran and Turkey. *International Journal of Middle East Studies, 36*(2), 253–275. doi: 10.1017.S0020743804362057

Sincan judge investigated as part of Ergenekon probe. (2009, August 6). *Today's Zaman.* Retrieved from http://www.todayszaman.com

Tadros, V. (1998). Between governance and discipline: The law and Michel Foucault. *Oxford Journal of Legal Studies, 18*(1), 75–103. doi:10.1093/ojls/18.1.75

Taipale, K. A. (2004). Technology, security and privacy: The fear of Frankenstein, the mythology of privacy and the lessons of King Ludd. *Yale Journal of Law and Technology, 7*(123), 125–201.

Tension rises in the judiciary. (2009, December 1). *Hurriyet Daily News.* Retrieved from http://www.hurriyetdailynews.com

Tensions rise between Turkish judicial board, Justice Ministry. (2009, July 30). *Hurriyet Daily News.* Retrieved from http://www.hurriyetdailynews.com

Tezcur, G. M. (2007). Constitutionalism, judiciary, and democracy in Islamic societies.

Polity, 39(4), 479–501. .doi:10.1057/palgrave.polity.2300086

Tezcur, G. M. (2009). Judicial activism in perilous times: The Turkish case. *Law & Society Review, 43*(2), 305–336. doi:10.1111/j.1540-5893.2009.00374.x

Top court's decision on Paksüt to challenge Ergenekon prosecutors. (2009, July 19). *Hurriyet Daily News.* Retrieved from http://www.hurriyetdailynews.com

Turkey's dark side: Party closures, conspiracies and the future of democracy. (2008, April 2). *European Stability Initiative (ESI).* ESI Briefing Berlin – Istanbul. Retrieved from http://www.esiweb.org/pdf/esi_document_id_104.pdf

Ünver, H. A. (2009). *Turkey's "deep-state" and the Ergenekon conundrum.* The Middle East Institute, Policy Brief, No. 23. Retrieved from http://www.mei.edu/Portals/0/Publications/turkey-deep-state-ergenekonconundrum.pdf

Wiretapping scandal still echoes in Turkish capital. (2009, November 16). *Hurriyet Daily News.* Retrieved from http://www.hurriyetdailynews.com

Wood, D. M. (2009). The 'surveillance society': Questions of history, place and culture. *European Journal of Criminology, 6*(2), 179–194. .doi:10.1177/1477370808100545

Yardımcı, M. M. (2009). *İletişimin Denetlenmesi.* Ankara, Turkey: Seçkin.

Yücel, G. (2002, February). *New dilemmas of Turkish national security politics: Old and new security concerns and national development in the post-1980 era.* Paper presented at the Fourth Kokkalis Graduate Student Workshop at JFK School of Government, Harvard University. Retrieved from http://www.hks.harvard.edu/kokkalis/GSW4/YucelPAPER.PDF

Chapter 6
Surveillance in Public Spaces as a Means of Protecting Security:
Questions of Legitimacy and Policy

Anna Tsiftsoglou[1]
University of Athens, Greece

ABSTRACT

The Greek Data Protection Authority (DPA) was asked in July 2009 to review a proposed legislation that was exempting personal data processing via camera installations in public spaces from the scope of the Greek Data Protection Law 2472/1997. Such an exemption was justified, among other reasons, for the protection of public safety and crime prevention. This paper examines the legitimacy of this security measure from two angles: European and Greek Law. Furthermore, our analysis focuses on questions of privacy, the concept of public safety and its application, as well as the DPA's role in safeguarding citizens' privacy even in city streets.

I. INTRODUCTION: QUESTIONS OF LEGITIMACY AND POLICY

In July 2009, the Greek Data Protection Authority ('DPA') was asked to draft an opinion regarding a proposed legislation concerning the electronic surveillance of public spaces. According to the proposed legislative provision (art.12(1) of Law 3783/2009), all competent public authorities processing personal data via a closed-circuit television ('CCTV') system installed in public spaces in Greece for the purposes of state security, defense and public safety were exempted from the scope of the national Data Protection Law 2472/1997, thus also from DPA supervision. To examine the legitimacy of this new security policy, the DPA pursued a three-level analysis: Greek national law (constitutional and legislative), European law (European Convention on Human Rights, EU Charter of Fundamental Rights, Convention 108 of the Council of Europe and Directive 95/46/EC) and comparative law (France, Germany and Austria). In the present study, we will focus on the European and Greek national law analysis of the proposed legislative provision.

DOI: 10.4018/978-1-60960-083-9.ch006

II. SURVEILLANCE IN PUBLIC SPACES AND THE EUROPEAN PUBLIC ORDER

a. The Scope & Exemptions of Directive 95/46/EC

Directive 95/46/EC of the European Parliament and the Council on the protection of individuals with regard to the processing and free movement of personal data ('the Directive') explicitly exempts (Art. 3(2)) from its scope all activities falling outside the range of EU Law. Such activities were traditionally classified under the former 2nd and 3rd EU Pillars (Craig & De Burca, 2003, pp. 44-52). At any case, they included data processing for the purposes of public order, defense, state security and criminal action. After Lisbon Treaty entering into force in Dec. 2009, such actions are still left virtually to their entirety to State regulation (Van Raepenbusch, 2008, pp. 461-463).

In the cases C-317/04 & C-318/04 ('the PNR cases'), the European Court of Justice ('ECJ') ruled that the transfer of airline Passenger Name Records (PNRs) by airline carriers to the US Customs and Borders Control for the purposes of state security and crime prevention cannot be considered as an internal-market affair (thus not classified under the former First Pillar) but may fall under the exemption of Art. 3(2) of the Directive (pp. 54-59). The PNR cases encompass a strong political flair (De Leon, 2006, pp. 327-328) due to the important role assigned to the European Parliament in the decision-making yet provocatively set aside, in the end. The exemption of PNR data transfer from the level of data protection provided by the Directive creates precedent in favor of protecting state security (Sotiropoulos, 2006, p. 949).

Thus, member-states retain the power to regulate if and how the level of data protection provided by the Directive will be enforced in these sensitive areas of state action. Such discretion is in accordance with the notion and the economically-oriented purposes of the European legislator. Nevertheless, it leaves space for possible arbitrariness by the national legislator as well as it leads to the creation of heterogeneous data protection levels in the European area of security (Sicilianos, 2001, pp. 123-141). This may be pointed as one of the Directive's main weaknesses (Robinson et al., 2009, pp. 36-38) since it leaves the member-states the freedom to regulate this field *ad hoc* boundlessly, while it extends its protective shield exclusively to internal market affairs. Greece did not adopt the above solution, but rather subjected the complete spectrum of personal data processing to the protective level provided by the Directive (Alivizatos, 2007), even in areas not originally covered by it.

b. The Right to Data Protection within the EU Public Order

On a European public order level, the right to data protection is *autonomously* established also in other legally binding statutes (Sicilianos, 2001, pp. 123-141; Papadimitriou, 2007). Firstly, it is established in the Convention 108 of the Council of Europe for the Protection of Individuals with regard to Automatic Processing of Personal Data ('Convention 108') (Art. 1). Convention 108, applicable also to the public sector thus to police activity too (Art. 3(1)) offers the member-states the discretion to derogate from the principles of legitimate data processing provided by the Convention, if a state measure is considered to be 'necessary in a democratic society' for the purposes of state security and the regulation of criminal law issues (Art. 9(2)). Regarding Convention 108 we should note that:

a) The term 'necessary measure in a democratic society' refers in its wording to the European Convention on Human Rights ('ECHR'). In the ECHR jurisprudence the term 'necessary measure' is a relative concept, and should be judged *in concreto* for each country and within a specific political context (Explanatory Memorandum, section 56).

b) The Council of Europe adopts a 'traditional' definition of state security as *'protection of national sovereignty against internal or external threats'* (Explanatory Memorandum, section 56).
c) The 'major interests of the State' justifying exemptions from the protective level of the Convention are *listed exhaustively* and do not allow the states to regulate differently.

Additionally, Recommendation R (87)15 of the Committee of Ministers of the Council of Europe, an important *soft law* legal resource, also provides principles regarding data processing, applicable in the public sector.

Finally, the right to data protection is independently established in the legally binding EU Charter of Fundamental Rights ('The Charter'), in Art. 8, which provides personal data processing principles (Art. 8(2)) as well as the subjection of data processing to the supervision of an independent authority (Art.8(3)). The incorporation of this right within the Charter, an *'international legal text that has received the most diverse influences and has received inspiration from a wide number of sources more than any other legal document'* (Gerapetritis, 2002, p. 920), which also *'signifies a clear turning point of the EU by placing the individual'*, instead of policies, *'at the heart of the European evolution'* (Gerapetritis, 2002, p. 912), is of particular importance. It signifies that the right to data protection, along with the rest of the rights incorporated in the Charter, provides a privacy rights-based constraint on the exercise of the EU power – *'a matter of principle, for a political entity with the power of the EU'* (Craig, 2002, p. 217).

c. Data Protection as an Aspect of Privacy within the ECHR

The right to data protection is protected also under Art. 8(1) ECHR, as an aspect of the right to privacy. Regarding public spaces in particular, the European Court of Human Rights ('ECtHR') recognizes a right to privacy. In *Peck v. the United Kingdom* (28.01.2003), ECtHR ruled that the mere monitoring of people in public spaces via CCTV, without any further processing of data, does not constitute breach of privacy (p.60). However, any further processing of this material, such as storing or unauthorized dissemination, may raise such issues (Alivizatos, 2005, pp. 15 and 22).

Art. 8(2) ECHR has as follows:

'There shall be no interference by a public authority with the exercise of this right, except such as in accordance with the law and is necessary in a democratic society in the interests of national security, public safety or the economic well-being of the country, for the prevention of disorder or crime, for the protection of health or morals, or for the protection of the rights & freedoms of others'.

The above provision, as interpreted recently by the ECtHR places *conditions* for the legitimacy of the interference to the exercise of the right to privacy by a public authority:

a) be in accordance with the law, meaning:
   1. to have a legal foundation in the national law of the member-state
   2. the legal provision should have specific quality elements: accessibility (*Khan v. the United Kingdom*, 12.05.2000, pp. 26-28; *P.G. & J.H. v. the United Kingdom*, pp. 37-38), foreseeability (*Amann v. Switzerland*, 16.02.2000, pp. 55-62; *Peck v. the United Kingdom*, p. 66; *S & Marper v. the United Kingdom*, 04.12.2008, pp. 95-99) and provide safeguards against arbitrariness (*P.G.*

& J.H. v. the United Kingdom, p. 62; *Rotaru v. Romania*, 04.05.2000, pp. 59-60; *Association for European Integration & Human Rights and Ekimdzhiev v. Bulgaria*, 28.06.2007, pp. 85-93).

b) be necessary in a democratic society, meaning:
   1. there is a pressing social need for the establishment of a restriction, and the measure is considered to be *sufficient* and *relevant.*
   2. it complies with the principle of proportionality stricto sensu, meaning the measure should be *proportional* to the achievable aim (*Peck v. the United Kingdom*, pp. 79-85; *Weber & Saravia v. Germany*, decision on the admissibility, 29.06.2006, pp. 107-118).

c) be justified by one or more of the following legitimate aims: national security, public safety, the economic well-being of the country, prevention of disorder or crime, protection of health or morals, or the protection of the rights and freedoms of others.

III. SURVEILLANCE IN PUBLIC SPACES AND THE GREEK PUBLIC ORDER

a. The Concept of Public Safety: Legitimate Aim and Legislative Tool

The concept of 'public safety' is crucial for specifying the aim of the relevant legal provision [Art.12(1) of Law 3783/2009]. Its clarification is also important, since it is perceived differently by people especially in the context of the city environment. Ball (2002), for example, when discussing about the use of CCTV systems in public spaces, comments on the differing public attitudes towards the concept of safety in the city: *'Cities, by their nature, are uncertain places [...]. People want to be safe in the cities, but they do not necessarily want the city itself to be safe, and any attempt to manage and homogenize the space detracts from its social richness'* (Ball, 2002, pp. 575-578).

The DPA gives the following definition of public safety: *'the obligation of the State to take the appropriate measures for the protection and the efficient exercise of civil rights'*. The concept of public safety as an obligation to protect rights is founded, according to the Authority, on the generic clause of Art. 25 (1), Sec. 1 of the Greek Constitution ('The rights of man as an individual and as a member of the society as well as the principle of the social state are guaranteed by the State. All agents of the State shall be obliged to ensure the unhindered and efficient exercise thereof') (Papaioannou, 2007, p. 729; Anthopoulos, 2005, pp. 113-114). DPA thus comprehends public safety *not as a self-existent good*, but rather as the 'concentration of fundamental legitimate goods individually protected within their own constitutional limits'. It rejects, thus, two contradictory theoretical but also practical schemes, security viewed either as an *individual* good (Hrysogonos, 2006; Kamtsidou, 2006; Anthopoulos, 2005, pp. 113-126; Katrougalos, 2006) or as a *public* good (Mantzoufas, 2006; Kourakis, 2006). It further confuses *human security* with the *security of the state*. We could argue that security hereby used as a restriction to the exercise of the fundamental right to privacy, is more closely related to the second concept.

Public safety constitutes an indispensable aspect of security of the state. If we followed a traditional definition (Manesis, 1980, p. 390) state security consists of maintaining order within the state (*internal* security or public safety) and protecting the independence and sovereignty of the state among other states (*external or national* security). Moreover, the security of the state viewed as the protection from internal or external threats sustains the very core of the State's existence (Manesis, 1980, p.391). Furthermore, the relationship of security and freedom – in our case, privacy –resembles an issue of 'drawing limits'

(Manesis, 1980, pp. 392 and 417) while achieving the balance in this relationship constitutes 'one of the major issues of our era'.

The contemporary version of security also contains the element of 'risk'. In the post-modern times, state security has been promoted to the protection of the state from 'whichever source the threat may originate' (Papaioannou, 2007, p. 731). The priority in the modern 'state of prevention' (Anthopoulos, 2005, pp.109-113) is now given to the protection of goods from possible risks threatening them (Mantzoufas, 2004). In the risk society, risk -objectively observable though not easily predictable- helps us grasp the magnitude of state security. The size of security, a function of risk, is constantly being edified and transformed within specific socio-political factors (Manoledakis, 2004, p. 26) and hazard conditions. As a consequence, the continuous transformation of the concept of state security may lead legislators to constant transformations of legitimate aims. Thus, extensive data processing today may be justified for the purposes of state security but may become outdated once risk will not be evidently present to manage.

b. The Right to Data Protection [Art. 9A Con.]

The right to data protection is established in the Greek Constitution, after the Constitutional Revision of 2001, under the new Art. 9A, which provides the following: *'All persons have the right to be protected from the collection, processing and use, especially by electronic means, of their personal data, as specified by law. The protection of personal data is ensured by an independent authority, which is constituted and operates as specified by law'*. The right to data protection is not a novel right, however (Venizelos, 2002; pp. 148-150, Mitrou, 2001). On the contrary, it standardizes values already developed by the jurisprudence or pre-existed within the Greek or the European public order. Firstly, it encompasses the jurisprudence of the German Federal Constitutional Court (Pararas, 2001, pp. 64-65; Vlahopoulos, 2007, pp. 60-61), specifically the judgment in its notable decision on the Census case (BVerfGe, 65, 1983). There, the Court introduced the concept of 'informational self-determination', the essence of which rests in *the ability of the person to determine him/herself if, when and under what circumstances his or her personal data shall be made public*. This concept could be applied in various contexts, even in the case of electronic surveillance of public assemblies (Anthopoulos, 2007, pp. 721-723).

In addition, Art. 9A of the Greek Constitution incorporates certain values already established under the Greek Constitution of 1975, like the value of human dignity, [Art. 2(1)], free development of personality [Art. 5(1)] and privacy [Art. 9] with which it is closely related in its concept and application (Akrivopoulou, 2009, pp. 430-439). Additionally, Art. 9A formalizes principles found in legally binding international texts (Sotiropoulos, 2006, pp. 109-118; Mitrou, 2001, pp. 92-94; Venizelos, 2002, pp. 148-150) like those provided by Directive 95/46/EC for data protection and Convention 108 (1981) of the Council of Europe. Such principles governing the processing of personal data are also included in Law 2472/1997, the most notable of which being the principles of fair and lawful processing, proportionality, purpose specification (Art. 4) and the supervision of personal data processing by an independent authority (Art 15). Finally, similar principles can be found in the now legally binding Charter (Papadimitriou, 2007, pp. 218-219) in Arts. 7 (right to privacy and family life) and especially 8 (right to data protection). The latter establishes, among others, the principle of fair and lawful processing (Sect. 2) and assigns the supervision of data protection rules appliance to an independent authority (Sect 3).

At any case, every restriction of a fundamental right must respect the general conditions set by Art 25(1) of the Greek Constitution and the related jurisprudence of the Hellenic Council of State regarding permissibility of restrictions, and particularly:

a) to be founded in law; the term 'law' may refer either to the procedures of the parliament (Vegleris, 1982, pp. 22-25; Manitakis, 1994, pp. 348-357) or to the procedures of the executive body exercising its regulatory authority (Manitakis, 1994, pp. 348-357; Hrysogonos, 2003, pp. 74 - 82).
b) to be justified by compelling public interest aims.
c) to be linked with the proposed legitimate aim and to be sufficient and relevant with the aim.
d) to not affect the very core (essence) of the right

c. The Role of the DPA within the Modern Greek Democracy

The allocation of powers to an independent administrative authority like the DPA is a relatively novel issue in the Greek public order. Such practice is closely related to the broader role of independent authorities in our modern democracy and to the concept of agencification as a means of *new public management* (Flogaitis, 2006, p. 112). The establishment of independent administrative authorities received wide applause as an important step in the modernization of the Greek Public Administration by instituting decentralized bodies with extensive powers and appointing experts with personal and functional independence to handle cases of their expertise (Art. 101A(1) of the Greek Constitution). Such modernization was initiated, firstly in the common legislation (the Greek Competition Authority being the first Greek Independent Public Authority established by Law 702/1977), and then Constitutionally for an exclusive group of five Independent Agencies (including the Data Protection Authority [Art.9A of the Greek Const.] and the Authority for Communication Security and Privacy [art.19(2)]). It is worth noting here, on a comparative note, that in the US, which is the origin of this administrative model, independent regulatory authorities are created by the Congress, thus by the common legislator, and are not established by the US Constitution (Strauss, 2003, pp.159-160). Strauss (2003) furthermore claims that '*the American Constitution and the general national statutes concerning the responsibilities given to governmental agencies or the procedures required of them neither define nor distinguish among the various forms the Congress creates*' (p. 160). The 'innovation' of the Greek legislator to include independent authorities within the constitutional text, makes it harder to control their influence or to even abolish them. Certainly not a solution followed by the American legislator.

Venizelos, the parliamentary majority rapporteur during the 2001 Constitutional Revision, claims that the Parliament was led to vote for the *constitutional* establishment of Anglo-Saxon-type independent authorities in Greece for various reasons. The most important was to shield some fundamental rights with additional guarantees but also to transfer several political responsibilities to 'neutral/apolitical' bodies so as to lift the heightened political burdens on sensitive issues from the Government (Venizelos, 2008). Alivizatos insists that both the sensitive nature and the rapidly shifting parameters of certain issues called for technocratic management and could not be left over to political manipulation (Alivizatos, 2001, p. 121). However, the wide institutionalization of independent authorities in Greece received skeptical reviews, mostly due to the democratic deficit characterizing such bodies (Venizelos, 2001, pp. 479-480; Kozyris, 2003, pp. 39-40).

The DPA has a prominent supervisory role in Greece. Particularly, its mission as an independent supervisory body / watchdog but also as an 'institutional guarantee' (Manesis, 1961, pp.15-17; Venizelos, 2008) of the right to data protection is established under Art. 9A Sect. b' of the Greek Constitution ('*The protection of personal data is ensured by an independent authority*'). On the other hand, its competence is *strictly defined by Law* ('*...which is constituted and operates as specified by law*'), hereby meaning Law 2472/1997. The proper specification of DPA's mission is especially important for future judicial decisions, since erroneous constitutional interpretations of the DPA's mission may lead to perilous expansion of its allocated powers (Stratilatis, 2004, pp. 558-559). It lays in the discretion of the common legislator to regulate (Art. 15-22) everything concerning the formation, operation and allocation of powers to the DPA. The competence of an administrative body, such as the DPA, involves powers towards specified aims, which the DPA has the right and the obligation to exercise only according to law. The DPA's powers are confined by law, according to the principle of legality (Spiliotopoulos, 2007, pp. 151-152; Dagtoglou, 2004, pp. 529-531). Consequently, the Greek Constitution establishes the mission, though not the action framework of the DPA.

The DPA's supervisory role could be lawfully limited, though strictly within the boundaries prescribed by the Constitution (Mitrou, 2008, pp. 123-124). Since the DPA is considered an institutional guarantee of the right to data protection, the common legislator could not limit the DPA's powers to the point that it practically extinguishes it. The amended provision of article 3(2) of the section c' of the Law 2472/1997, which removes from the supervision of the DPA all the personal data processing by the competent public authorities (Taylor, 2003, p.86) via CCTV for the purposes of state security, defense and public safety, may raise serious issues of unconstitutionality. Those issues are relative to the amount of public authorities competent to process personal data, the range of data processing for the specific legislative aims and the scope of such an exemption from the supervision of the DPA. At any case, the existence of a fully independent supervisory body like the DPA is provided as a guarantee both by the Greek Constitution and by international legislation against state arbitrariness. As such, the limitation of DPA's allocated powers must take place with additional legislative caution.

D. CONCLUSION

Surveillance in public spaces as a security measure must observe all relative national and European legislative principles. Furthermore, it must respect the constitutional role of the DPA as a guarantor of the right to data protection. In this sense, the proposed legislative provision has three central issues, according to the DPA's Opinion. *Firstly, it does not cite a specific legitimate aim.* According to the DPA the vague referral to the aim of 'public safety' and 'especially the protection of people or goods' is very generic and leaves space for multiple interpretations. Particularly, the absence of a specified aim renders the application of proportionality test more difficult for the courts. However, the DPA wrongfully concludes that the provision should have included risk criteria for the specification of time and space to install and operate CCTV systems, since their enactment rests on the discretion of the competent authorities. The legislator should enrich the provision with safeguards against arbitrariness, as ordained by the ECtHR. *Secondly, the provision does not comply with the quality standards of law shaped by the ECtHR jurisprudence regarding the restrictions of the Art 8(2) ECHR.* The proposed provision is not foreseeable; it is not precise on the terms and conditions of processing personal data, with the exception of collected data and their destruction procedure, or on security measures of processed data. The data processor is also not specified. *Lastly, the provision does not cite sufficient safeguards against arbitrariness.* The DPA suggests that the proposed legislation does not provide sufficient safeguards, but instead removes the existing ones, by exempting a specific field of state action from the supervision of the DPA. However, in this point rests the only counter-argument against the evaluation of the provision as fully inadequate: it offers some safeguards. Specifically, it assigns the supervision to a body with functional independence, the District Attorney, and further provides criminal sanctions in case that this regulation is breached. And this is something that the DPA fails to underline.

E. REFERENCES

Akrivopoulou, C. (2009). *Between privacy & autonomy: Reconstructing the right to privacy* [in Greek]. Unpublished PhD thesis. Retrieved December 17, 2009, from http://invenio.lib.auth.gr/record/113367?ln=el

Alivizatos, N. (2001). Privacy and transparency: A difficult conciliation. In Sicilianos, L., & Gavouneli, M. (Eds.), *Scientific and technological development & human rights*. Athens: Ant.N.Sakkoulas.

Alivizatos, N. (2005). Privacy and disclosure [in Greek]. *Mass Media & Communication Law Review, 1*, 14–23.

Alivizatos, N. (2007, December 16). Human rights in danger: The hidden side of the CCTV Regulation. *Ta Nea* [in Greek]. Retrieved November 11, 2009, from http://www.tanea.gr/default.asp?pid=2&ct=1&artid=48419

Anthopoulos, H. (2005). State of prevention & the right to security. In H. Anthopoulos, X. Contiades & T. Papatheodorou (Eds.), *Security & human rights in the age of risk* [in Greek] (pp. 109-135). Athens-Komotini: Ant.N.Sakkoulas.

Anthopoulos, H. (2007). The right to public anonymity – Data protection, freedom of assembly and electronic surveillance of open public assemblies [in Greek]. *Administrative Law Review, 6*, 719–728.

Ball, K. (2002). Elements of surveillance: A new framework & future directions. *Information Communication and Society, 5*(4), 573–590. doi:10.1080/13691180208538807

Craig, P. (2002). The community rights and the charter. *European Review of Public Law, 14*(1), 195–225.

Craig, P., & De Burca, G. (2003). *EU law: Text, cases & materials*. Oxford: Oxford University Press.

Dagtoglou, P. (2004). *General administrative law* [in Greek]. Athens-Komotini: Ant.N.Sakkoulas.

De Leon, P. (2006). The fight against terrorism through aviation: Data protection versus data production. *Air and Space Law, 31*(4-5), 320–330.

Flogaitis, S. (2006). Multilevel governance and administrative reform in the 21st century [in Greek]. *Administrative Law Review, 1*, 110–115.

Gerapetritis, G. (2002). EU charter of fundamental rights: A case study. *European Review of Public Law, 14*(1), 881–924.

Hrysogonos, K. (2003). *Civil and social rights* [in Greek]. Athens-Komotini: Ant.N.Sakkoulas.

Hrysogonos, K. (2006). The fundamental right to security [in Greek]. *Revue Hellénique des Droits de l'Homme, 32*, 1209–1223.

Kamtsidou, I. (2006). The fundamental right to security of the person [in Greek]. *Revue Hellénique des Droits de l'Homme, 32*, 1225–1239.

Katrougalos, G. (2006). Liberty and security in the 'Age of Risk': The case of electronic surveillance [in Greek]. *Legal Review, 54*, 360–374.

Kourakis, N. (2006). Liberty and security: Their static and dynamic limits [in Greek]. *Legal Review, 54*, 1217–1226.

Kozyris, P. (2003). The ‘independence’ of the independent authorities in Greece – Issues and perspectives. In P. Kozyris & S. Megglidou (Eds.), *The ‘independence’ of the independent authorities: Thoughts and hopes on a new institution – Symposium proceedings* [in Greek] (pp. 25-40). Athens - Komotini: Ant.N.Sakkoulas.

Manesis, A. (1961). *The constitutional guarantees* (*Vol. II*). Athens, Thessaloniki: Sakkoulas Publications. [in Greek]

Manesis, A. (1980). The issue of state security and liberty. In *Constitutional Theory & Practice* [in Greek] (Vol. I), 390-417. Athens-Thessaloniki: Sakkoulas Publications.

Manitakis, A. (1994). *Rule of law and judicial review of constitutionality* [in Greek]. Athens, Thessaloniki: Sakkoulas Publications.

Manoledakis, I. (2004). State security or freedom? In Manitakis, A., & Takis, A. (Eds.), *Terrorism & human rights: From state security to the insecurity of law* [in Greek]. (pp. 23–41). Athens: Savalas Publications.

Mantzoufas, P. (2004). Security and prevention in the age of risk: Introductory questions and questionings on the constitutional state. In *Honorary Volume for the 75th Anniversary of the Council of State* [in Greek] (pp. 55-72). Athens-Thessaloniki: Sakkoulas Publications.

Mantzoufas, P. (2006). *Constitutional protection of rights in the society of risk* [in Greek]. Athens, Thessaloniki: Sakkoulas Publications.

Mitrou, L. (2001). The right to data protection: A new right? In D. Tsatsos, E. Venizelos & X. Contiades (Eds.), *The new constitution: Proceedings of the conference on the revised Greek constitution of 1975/1986/2001* [in Greek] (pp. 83-103). Athens-Komotini: Ant.N.Sakkoulas.

Mitrou, L. (2008). The regulation of law 3625/2007 – Is surveillance in public spaces excluded from the data protection authority’s control? In I. Kamtsidou (Ed.), *The electronic surveillance of public spaces – Symposium proceedings* [in Greek] (pp. 101-150). Athens-Thessaloniki: Sakkoulas Publications.

Papadimitriou, G. (2007). The articulation of national, international and EU protection of fundamental rights in Europe. In *Constitutional Studies* [in Greek]. *Vol. I*). Athens, Thessaloniki: Sakkoulas Publications.

Papadimitriou, G. (2007). *Constitutional studies* [in Greek]. *Vol. II*). Athens, Thessaloniki: Sakkoulas Publications.

Papaioannou, Z. (2007). The electronic surveillance of public assemblies by the police authorities [in Greek]. *Administrative Law Review, 6*, 729–751.

Pararas, P. (2001). The Greek Constitution & the European Convention of Human Rights [in Greek]. Athens-Komotini: Ant.N.Sakkoulas.

Robinson, N., Graux, H., Botterman, M., & Valeri, L. (2009). *Review of the European Data Protection Directive*. Retrieved January 6, 2010, from http://www.ico.gov.uk/upload/documents/library/data_protection/detailed_specialist_guides/review_of_eu_dp_directive.pdf

Sicilianos, L. (2001). International protection of personal data: Privacy, freedom of information or both? In L. Sicilianos & M. Gavouneli (Eds.), *Scientific and technological development & human rights* (pp. 123-141). Athens-Komotini: Ant.N.Sakkoulas.

Sotiropoulos, V. (2006). *The constitutional protection of personal data* [in Greek]. Athens, Thessaloniki: Sakkoulas Publications.

Sotiropoulos, V. (2006). Comment on ECJ Decisions C-317/04 & C-318/04. *The Constitution, 3* [in Greek], 938-952.

Spiliotopoulos, E. (2007). *Administrative law textbook* (Vol. I) [in Greek]. Athens-Komotini: Ant.N.Sakkoulas.

Stratilatis, K. (2004). The mission of the data protection authority under the Greek Constitution [in Greek]. *Revue Hellénique des Droits de l'Homme*, *22*, 555–588.

Strauss, P. (2003). The United States experience with independent regulatory commissions. In P. Kozyris & S. Megglidou (Eds.), *The 'independence' of the independent authorities: Thoughts and hopes on a new institution – Symposium proceedings* [in Greek] (pp. 159-184). Athens - Komotini: Ant.N.Sakkoulas.

Taylor, N. (2003). Policing, privacy & proportionality. *European Human Rights Law Review*, (Special issue), 86–100.

Van Raepenbusch, S. (2008). The institutional revision by the Lisbon Treaty: The legal emersion of the European Union [in Greek]. *Hellenic Review of European Law*, *3*, 459–488.

Vegleris, P. (1982). Limitations on human rights [in Greek]. Athens-Komotini: Ant.N.Sakkoulas.

Venizelos, E. (2001). Overview of the Constitutional Revision. In D. Tsatsos, E. Venizelos & X. Contiades (Eds.), *The new constitution* [in Greek] (pp. 473 - 484). Athens-Komotini: Ant.N.Sakkoulas.

Venizelos, E. (2002). *The Revisional Acquis* [in Greek]. Athens-Komotini: Ant.N.Sakkoulas.

Venizelos, E. (2008). The independent regulatory authorities. In *Constitutional law textbook* [in Greek]. Athens-Komotini: Ant.N.Sakkoulas.

Vlahopoulos, S. (2007). *Transparency of state action and data protection* [in Greek]. Athens-Komotini: Ant.N.Sakkoulas.

ENDNOTE

1 E-mail address: tsiftsoglou[at]gmail[dot]com.

Section 3

Genetics, Medical Technology and Its Threats to Privacy, Individual Autonomy and Freedom

Chapter 7
Genetic Privacy:
A Right between the Individual, the Family and the Public Interest

Christina M. Akrivopoulou
Democritus University of Thrace, Greece

ABSTRACT

Privacy is a right with many aspects. Although, a uniform approach on privacy is quite often sought, a consensus is growing that there are not only one but many privacy rights. This chapter explores whether there is in fact a right to protect our genetic privacy, since this is a right quite unique in its characteristics and is certainly not identified with our general presumptions about privacy. Its uniqueness lies in the fact, that apart form the dominant definition of privacy as a right to be let alone, as an individualistic right, genetic privacy protects not only the individual but also the members of his/her family. The present paper is examining the 'hereditary' and 'shared' character of our genetic information in an attempt to shape a right to genetic privacy that is based on the equilibrium of individual autonomy, family and public interest. In order to support such an argument, the premises of our genetic self are examined in connection with autonomy and its boundaries, mainly paternalism and genetic exceptionalism. Along this line, basic notions of the liberal privacy theory are critically examined, mainly the notions of control, confidentiality and consent, so as to maintain the existence of a right to genetic privacy that can enhance the individual's autonomy without founding it on its selfish, individual interests.

I. INTRODUCTION: IS GENETIC PRIVACY AN INDIVIDUALIST RIGHT AFTER ALL?

At the core of the constitutional and philosophical debate, privacy is sometimes considered to be an individualistic right. Thus, a right exclusively orientated in protecting the private goals and aspirations of the individual. In that context privacy bears an unsocial, narcissistic meaning, which is setting apart the subject from society or even from its intimates. As Richard Posner (1981) supports, privacy in this perspective is not a right worth of constitutional acknowledgment or value,

DOI: 10.4018/978-1-60960-083-9.ch007

but a protective veil, an asylum for the subject to adopt illegal activities or cover unsocial endeavors.

Nevertheless, as far as genetic privacy is concerned the term 'individualistic' can be highly contested. The right to genetic privacy is considered to be quite new, since it is connected to the relatively recent technological evolution of decoding the human DNA. The right to genetic privacy brought forward a new aspect of the human self, a rather comprehensive and peculiarly, not individualistic one. The human genome contains not only the information based on which we are distinguished from the others but also the information that define our roots, our family heritage, our parental co-belonging. From this point of view the right to genetic privacy sets a question mark: to whom our genetic decisions lie with, to what extent can we consider them a 'private matter' when our human genome contains information that we share with our parents, siblings, ancestors and predecessors. In two words, having a right to genetic privacy does or does not give the subject the autonomy to drive its genetic identification by his/her own will?

Let us get acquainted with the 'shared' privacy that the human genome entails using two uneven paradigms. In the case Paulík *versus Slovakia* (European Court of Human Rights (ECHR), Decision of 10.1.2007) the ECHR handled the following circumstances: the applicant had a sexual encounter with a woman in 1966, who gave birth to a daughter on December 17th of the same year. The applicant denied his paternity and the mother of the girl pursued him in the national courts, which asserted his paternity based on a medical test known as 'blood hereditary test', a sexology report and several witnesses. Consequently, the applicant was legally acknowledged as the biological father of the girl in 1970 and supported her financially ever since. To a certain point and when she was a teenager, the applicant started to develop a personal bond with her, which evolved in a familial relationship. At 2004 the applicant and his daughter quarreled over a financial subject. The quarrel led them to take a DNA test which proved without any doubt that he was not her biological father. The applicant turned to the national courts which insisted on the 1970 decision on the grounds that the legal acknowledgment of his paternity was in fact irreversible (*res juridicata*). Thus, they denied the applicant's wish to cut any legal, biological or material relationship with his legal but not biological daughter. The applicant then applied to the ECHR in order to protect his right to privacy under Article 8 of the European Convention of Human Rights.

This legal-real life scenario underlines several observations connected to genetic privacy. The applicant's right to his identity, thus his privacy, has been severely inflicted because he has falsely adopted the qualities of a father. The Paulík *versus Slovakia* case not only points out the importance of the genetic evolution regarding the individual's self-determination but also the close connection between our biological and our ethical identity. The applicant, Paulík, was imposed with an identity that he did not select: the powerful and symbolic identity of a father. Regardless the actual ties that he developed with his legally acknowledged daughter, what mattered the most was the biologically truth of the physical bond connecting them as parent and child. Thus, genetic privacy is a matter of individual privacy, of personal identity and of choices for the subject. But it is also a matter of intimacy, of connecting and co-belonging in a biological and material sense. Not only Paulík but also his daughter was inflicted in this sense. She also had to bear the symbolic identity of the daughter and to suffer of a broken familial bond. What was violated was their shared right to their genetic heritage and their biological family ties.

The second paradigm is much more fetched. It concerns the case of Roche and De Code Genetics Inc. which in 1998 unveiled a scheme for entering all medical records of Iceland into a database, in order to conduct population genomics research by effectively simulating a population. Under the 'Health Sector Database' Act, the Icelandic parliament issued the license to create of a genetic database called 'Icelandic Healthcare Database' (IHD) to Roche and De Code Genetics Inc., which aimed at decoding genomically hereditary diseases. The public genetic scheme of Iceland was in fact an extensive genetic experiment on the whole population. Why was Iceland selected by this American Incorporation in order to perform this vast genetic research? Iceland is a small country of approximately 300.000 inhabitants. It is originated from the 8th a.c. century, from a small colony of Vikings and their Irish slaves. Since then a total of approximately 850.000 habitants have lived in the island-country. There are complete genealogical files for about 600.000 of them, enabling each Icelandic citizen to trace his/her ancestors back to even a thousand years in many cases. This highly ambitious experiment was based on the public health-care structure of Iceland organized very well by a file-system, as well as on the fact that the population bore 'familial' characteristics. Iceland was in fact a closed society with the minimum amount of immigrants and mixed families.

What was in fact the key to the success of the 'Icelandic experiment' is that this whole nation could indeed be considered as a 'family tree'. Thus, it presented an excellent field for researching hereditary diseases and analyzing the DNA of the population. The 'Icelandic Experiment' projects a macro paradigm of the relation between the genetic identity of the individual and its family, its intimates. In the case of Iceland, the common culture and common genealogy could unveil genetic information for a whole nation, consequently. In the Icelandic case, the question posed form the beginning is magnified. Is genetic privacy an individualistic right or a 'shared' right? Indeed, how complex can the role of the autonomy of the individual become, since in view of the Icelandic macro-paradigm, even if the subjects do not consent to their genetic scrutiny, the same result could be achieved by decoding the DNA of their family? Moreover, the *post mortem* problems that the 'Icelandic paradigm' is setting out are critical in this sense. Where there, if any, rights of the diseased, and if our answer to this question is a positive one, who could claim them and under which circumstances?

The main focus of this paper is to examine the 'shared' circumstances of genetic privacy in order to pursue a right that guarantees the integrity of personal autonomy, without jeopardizing the advantages of technological evolution, as well as the protection of public interest. Thus, the paper will support the thesis that at the core of genetic privacy always lies the right of the individual 'to know' any genetic information that may cause one harm, as well as the right to be protected from any discrimination based on one's genetic identity. The paper contains five parts-arguments: a) the specific traits that distinguish genetic information from any other personal or medical information, b) the boundaries of the genetic autonomy of minors and c) of adults, concerning the protection of the family, the public interest and of private autonomy, d) the problems of confidentiality and disclosure of genetic information related to the subject of control and autonomy over genetic privacy, e) the value of founding a right to genetic privacy on personal autonomy and its main assets, informed decision, right 'to know' and non-discrimination.

II. THE UNIQUE CHARACTER OF GENETIC INFORMATION AND ITS CONNECTION TO IDENTITY AND AUTONOMY

Information in general bears a unique trend. It can be created by many and thus be co-shared; it can be transferred easily and in the era of globalization almost rapidly and if controlled, can be used by indefinite subjects for a number of positive or even negative ends. The meaning of information is closely connected with the democratic theory, because of its enormous significance for the realization of political freedom and participation as well as for pubic criticism. In this view information is identified with transparency, public accountability and democratic control (Sunstein 2007; Solove, 2004; Cole, 2005). The hugest problem that the acknowledgment of a modern right to control, access, use or process of information is facing, is the fact that it is difficult to define its subject, and thus to determine a relationship of 'ownership' as far as information is concerned. Literally, the current augmentation of data-banks, the vast expansion of cyberspace, the dynamic role that the mass media plays in the information era, render the understanding of a right to information as a traditional individual one more and more difficult. If information is to be controlled by its subject, its owner, if it is considered to be 'property' of an individual is a highly ambiguous matter nowadays. What are the reasons of such an ambiguity? A large part of what we can today describe as our personal information, including our genetic information-is shared with others. Certainly, in the course of our lives not all the information that we create is a part of our individual biography, many of it is constructed by our familial or intimate ties. To write for example in our autobiography that our husband was an alcoholic, in many ways lies in our freedom to reveal information concerning our privacy, our intimate relationships (Solove, 2002). After all such facts in many ways have the ability to construct our identity, our personality.

More importantly the technological evolution defies the 'proprietal' character, this classic liberal bond, between the subject and its personal, intimate information, the ones we usually acknowledge legally as 'sensitive'. Truly, if cyberspace can be deemed as gigantic information data-base, who can question that it contains mainly personal information of e.g. consumers (Akrivopoulou & Stylianou, 2009). Moreover, who can doubt that from the moment that a little bit of information is out in the cyberspace, its subject has entirely lost its right to possess and control it use. The combination of information and technology has diminished the core characteristic that each right bears, the ability of power and control that entails for its subject. Moreover, it is extremely threatening for the privacy and especially the autonomy of the individual. If anyone can ultimately access or posses our personal information in what way can we still be defined as independent, self-drived and autonomous human beings?

Those are the reasons why the use of the term personal or sensitive 'data' instead of information in the legal literature on privacy is a two edged knife. It is not as simple to apply in legal science the fact that the current form of information is technologically constructed as to connect a legal norm with a factual reality. It also implies the acceptance of several implications such us, the free flow of information, their digital procession and their ability to disconnect form their subject or to be disclosed etc. It entails an understanding of information as computer data, as neutral facts, with no origin, no subject, no control, data that can flow freely by the drive of their own or in the end by anyone's will. The understanding of information as data, is detaching the right to control one's personal information from its autonomy.

In order to define a right to genetic privacy, we must first define what kind of information can be considered to be genetic. The answer to that is a simple one. Our genetic information is what we call chromosomes. Each of us possesses a number of twenty three chromosomes, which we inherit by half from our mother and father. The information that our chromosome contain are extremely comprehensive. Each chromosome carries a set of particular genes, which are responsible for the operation of every human cell. This genetic 'diary' is a set of combined coded information which we call DNA or genome. Why an individual has an interest in decoding his/her genome? In many cases our DNA carries several 'defective' genes. In cases that those genes are inherited in two copies or even as a 'dominant' one, the individual might suffer by a number of diseases such as anemia or cystic fibrosis (Laurie, 2002). In this blueprint an individual has a significant interest to be informed on his/her genetic material in order to exercise his/her right to marriage, family and especially reproduction as well as in order to plan his/her future life. Knowledge of genetic disorders enables the individual to better deal with or even avoid future illnesses. At the same thread the evolution of medical research can enlighten even more this process, since in the future it would be possible to detect a genetic component in a number of disorders that today we consider to be of psychological or social origins, such as alcoholism (Fendrick, 2008-2009).

On the one hand the capacity of genetic information to predict ones' medical future is what mainly differentiates it from any other medical information. Surely medical information in general can only identify but not predict a future illness or disorder, but mainly can provide with their causes and thus could affect their prevention or cure. Though in many cases our genetic decoding can only give us probabilities and not certainties it can nevertheless provide the individual with the immense capacity to plan his/her own future and guide his/her health and body choices, by understanding the inner depth of his/her physical identity. Given that the human body is considered to be the central mediator of autonomy and individual privacy (Thomas, 1992), any decision and choice concerning its future health can be considered as private. In that sense the deeper our knowledge of our genetic self becomes the further our autonomy is emancipated.

What distinguishes genetic information from any other medical information is that it represents a part of an individual's identity, meaning it represents a part of the subject's family heritage. We become who we are by connecting and communicating with the others, those we call intimates. Our familial genetic information can be represented as a form of such a bond, as a medium of communication. Thus, genetic information can foster a very intimate notion of identity, between an individual and his/her family. Each of us is characterized by his/her genetic links, his/her 'family resemblances'. Genetic ties and common genetic characteristics have the capacity to form a special kind of intimacy for a person which is a great part of our cultural heritage in modern western societies. It separates the individual from those with whom such a connection does not exist, while it is keeping together those with whom a genetic interconnection does in fact exist. The Paulík case clearly underlines this argument. Though the applicant, Paulík have believed for half a lifetime that he was the true father of his judicially acknowledged as such daughter, it was in the end the genetic truth that he was seeking. This truth had the ability to destroy any factual or legal tie that he had created in the meantime. Thus, our genetic identity is crucial for the family intimacy that we enjoy. As Laurie (2002) puts it, 'the "Gene" has the status of a cultural image' since it is not only identified with the notion of family tree but is also identifying the role of the specific individual in it, e.g. the father, the grandfather etc.

At this point we can underline the following: what differentiates genetic from medical information is that is so much more than information. Genetic information bears a part of our personality, of our identity and autonomy. It cannot be deemed us neutral. On the contrary, one could say that it is extremely comprehensive. This was the central argument in Marper *versus U.K.* of the ECHR. The ECHR faced a case of retention of genetic information by the British police forces according to the Police and Criminal Evidence Act of 1984 (known as the PACE). The applicants, a minor S and an acquitted adult, Marper applied in the ECHR requesting protection under article 8 of the Convention. The reason was that the two applicants' DNA material was retended although they were both found to be innocent or acquitted. The U.K. government claimed the retention of their genetic data justified, for reasons of public interest and pubic safety, namely prevention of crime and terrorism.

In its decision the ECHR emphasized the chief characteristic of genetic data, distinguishing them from any other personal or even medical information. The ECHR noted the extremely comprehensive nature of DNA data, thus their capacity to unveil the subject's ethnic identity, family relations and hereditary diseases, central traits of a person's right to privacy and identity. Those characteristics forced the ECHR to underline that the retention of this information could severely affect the autonomy of the individual, since it entailed an indefinite loss of his/her genetic self-definition. What the ECHR should have added is that genetic information is not exactly neutral because they are so comprehensive and thus the entity (state or private) that gains control over it can literally control the individual itself e.g. by discriminating against him/her.

At the end, the very characteristic that distinguishes genetic from medical or any other information is its ability to be identified with one specific individual. An individual's complete genome can link to his/her family but it is ultimately unique. It can not be copied or cloned. Thus, from an ethical point of view our genetic self is part of what we can call authentic, or different in ourselves, it is part of what we can call identity, which means to differentiate us even from our family members. At the same time this unique trend augments extremely the utility of genetic information for reasons of preserving the public safety. This trait is what clearly and without a doubt renders genetic information the character of sensitive, personal or private 'data'.

III. PROTECTING GENETIC INFORMATION BETWEEN THE INDIVIDUAL, THE FAMILY AND THE PUBLIC INTEREST

Delineating genetic autonomy as a means to construct a right to individual privacy is difficult exactly because decisions concerning genetic information implicate moral reasons, the balancing of opposing rights, and the values of community, as well as the complex control that family members co-share over it. A characteristic example is the case of the 'Frozen Embryos' tried by the Tennessee Circuit Court. A couple the Davises had performed 'Cryopreservation' an evolution of the IVF process of producing a test-tube baby. In the IVF process, eggs are removed from a woman's ovaries and are fertilized by sperm insemination. Afterwards, they are returned to the woman's uterus. In 'normal' circumstances at least one of the fertilized eggs will attach to the uterine wall and a pregnancy will follow (Horsey & Biggs, 2006). Nevertheless that was not the case of the Davises and that was the reason why they proceeded with the 'cryopreservation' procedure during which pre-embryos are frozen in order to be preserved for future use. 'Cryopreservation' ultimately enhances the probabilities of a successful pregnancy far more tan the simple IVF process. The couple went through with the 'Cryopreservation' but before a pregnancy could occur they decided to get a divorce. The problem remained: what would be the future of their frozen pre-embryos? Mrs Davis wanted the pre-embryos to be donated claiming her right to privacy, thus her right to make autonomous choices concerning her reproductive freedom. From the opposite side Mr Davis also claimed his right to privacy and autonomy emphasizing that imposing the role of the father on him was an undue burden.

The case shows emphatically a number of the dead ends that genetic privacy is facing when familial choices concerning genetic material or information are examined. Apart from the questions concerning the autonomy of the couple, ethical questions could be raised as far as the pre-embryos were concerned. What exactly is a pre-embryo, is it a person, is it an object of ownership, thus property? As Alderman and Kennedy (1997) observe and according to the Guidelines of the American Fertility Society, they were in fact 'an interim category, they were human tissue deserving of special respect because of their potential for human life.' But wouldn't that mean that one could also add in this case the role of public interest in the preservation of the pre-embryos?

The Court acknowledged that though the federal Tennessee Constitution did not enlist a right to privacy, this was indeed deducted by a number of provisions concerning personal autonomy and individual liberty (e.g. freedom to worship, freedom of speech etc.) as well from the First, Third and Ninth Amendment of the U.S. Constitution (Alderman & Kennedy, 1997). The Court applied the Supreme Courts Webster reasoning to the case concluding that a right to procreation is indeed a core part of an individual's right to privacy and that accordingly it protects a) the right to procreate and b) the right not to procreate. Those twin rights representing the Davis opposing interests in the case. Moreover, the Court underlined, that since the pre-embryos were in storage and the decision did not involve choices connected with Mrs Davis bodily integrity, the former spouses were deemed as equals as far as their reproductive autonomy was concerned. The Court repeated an argument developed in former abortion cases such as Roe and Casey, claiming that parenthood was indeed an undue burden in the identity of the individual (Alderman & Kennedy, 1997). Weighing the states interest in preserving the pre-embryos the Court noted that the protection of compelling life is not compelling until viability (about six months of pregnancy). The reason why the Court leaned towards the right of Mr Davis not to procreate was mainly because Mrs Davis right of privacy was not bodily mediated. The pre-embryos were detached from their mother and they were meant to be donated to third parties.

This complex, yet interesting case unveils the problematic of genetic autonomy. The first question concerns bodily integrity. We can in fact agree that core parts of it are the privacy and autonomy manifested and mediated by our body. Thus, genetic decisions are private and autonomous decisions because they are intimately connected with our bodily integrity and health. The problem though arises, when an individual's body is considered as a part of its subject. In such cases as the 'Frozen Embryos' one, such a conception can restrain the autonomy of the individual. This is a matter closely connected with the very idea of creating DNA data-banks. If we consider our genetic information or material as items, then the creation of such entities could be justified. But how genetic information that –as we have noted above- has the capacity to enclose the kind of information that differentiate an individual even by his family members, thus can authentically identifying him, can be considered being an 'item', thus only the external physical part of one's self?

Clearly Davis *vs Davis* set a point for the genetic autonomy of the individual. Nevertheless, it overlaps with a more unifying concept of what genetic integrity and genetic identity means: not to shutter the genetic self in bits and pieces, in genetic data or information or material but to preserve its unity even beyond the human body. Our genetic self -as our human self- should not only be preserved physically but mainly ethically (Downie and Macnaughton, 2007). The second problem that Davis *vs Davis* set forward is the common control of the spouses over genetic information. As McLean (2010) underlines, in such cases 'control of the information may be more problematic because of the interests that others may have in sharing it.' This shared control over genetic information in many cases is reflected when according to the special circumstances, the cooperation between family members is necessary in order to predict accurately the genetic constitution of the subject. In fact two kind of genetic tests exist: a) the genetic ones where a 'defective' gene can be examined without the cooperation of anyone but the interested subject, b) the linkage tests, where the test results are based in the comparison of genetic samples taken from at least two members of a family (Laurie, 2002). The second kind, the linkage tests is clearly affecting both the individual's autonomy as well as the genetic results that can be seriously undermined by the lack of cooperation between the members of a family.

In those cases, nevertheless, the autonomy of the individual is inherently restricted and a balancing of opposing interests should be performed in order to maintain a right to genetic privacy.

Another problem that Davis *vs Davis* highlights is the following: if the protection of an embryo's rights is at stake, what is the case with the limited genetic autonomy of minors? Relatively, what boundaries can society set on the freedom of the adult family members to make choices concerning the genetic autonomy of a child? It is well known for example that Jehovah's Witnesses decline blood transfusion and the use of red and white blood cells or platelets of plasma for their children. In several cases such practices have been considered to violate aspects of the child's freedom, respect for liberty, security and life as they are acknowledged by national constitutions and international law, mainly the Convention of the Rights of the Children as well as the States' positive obligation to protect those rights (e.g. case 2009 of the Canadian Supreme Court, A.C. *vs Manitoba, Director of Child and Family Services*). Though it could be sustained, that the adult's autonomy entails from many aspects their right to make choices, even harmful ones concerning their health, body or life (such as abortion or euthanasia) the same argument cannot be articulated as far as minors are concerned. For example, to what extent are the parents responsible while performing *in vitro* fertilization (IVF) coupled with pre-implantation genetic diagnosis (PGD) not to make the most beneficiary for their child's future genetic decisions, even by excluding certain embryos that appear to bear genetic deficiencies? The positive answer to such a dilemma does not nevertheless give the parents the right to determine their children's characteristics, e.g. for purely aesthetic or genetistic reasons. This is the barriers that society, ethics and deontology sets to the control that the parents retain over the limited autonomy of their offsprings. It is also the difference between what we can call genetic research and *genetism*.

As far as the genetic privacy of children is concerned, McLean (2010) is true to observe that 'parents have both the right and the responsibility to act in the best interests of their children, and this may include gathering the most accurate information available about their current and future health.' It must be observed, nevertheless, that preserving the best interest of the child should involve the protection of his/her health and bodily integrity as well as his/her moral and psychological integrity. Thus, testing a child for Phenylketonuria (PKU), a treatable condition is much different than testing him/her for cancer. In the second case an unbearable pschycological burden can be imposed on the child's psyche. In such cases the child can also suffer form stigmatization or discrimation and it may be for his/her best interest to perform such genetic testing in older ages. Serious problems can also be caused by the fact that many genetic predictions involve probabilities and not certainties about a child's future health. This could be preferable in the cases where genetic testing can offer mainly probabilities, not certainties, or when a probable disease may also be triggered by other socio-psycho causes. Furthermore, at this point we must differentiate between the consequences of predictive genetic testing in general and during childhood in particular (Elliston, 2007). The latter is connected with health decisions prior to adulthood and thus prior to the full gain of autonomy of the child.

Moreover, a right to genetic privacy is differentiated since matters concerning the genetic constitution in the children-parents relationship matters are deemed to be part of the family domain at first. The most problematic one is the case of adulthood, where the individual cannot have a right or claim to the privacy and confidentiality of his/her genetic information that has already been lost. The above remarks clearly show that in the case of children's genetic privacy it is harder to use the notion of right and more that of responsibility or limited autonomy. Parents on their behalf cannot claim or control the child's autonomy without taking account his/her prior consent or at least his/her informed opinion. Thus, in order to respect the integrity and liberty of a child, he/she should participate and communicate in any genetic decision involving his/her welfare. The parents can claim a right to act in the best interest of the child. A right limited by the objective values by which both law and the society define what is in a child's best interest.

To what extent does the state have the power to limit parental authority over the genetic privacy of a child? According to the ECHR, parental authority over children is considered to be a private issue regulated by Article 8 of the European Convention of Human Rights. Thus, the State's authority must be deteriorated by their negative obligation to protect children from harm. In any case the child can partly enjoy a right to genetic privacy. That way the protection of the dignity and freedom of a child imposes on the parents the limitation of using his/her genetic information among family members and for health reasons only, in order to avoid their future discrimination and stigmatization.

IV. THE 'CONSTITUTION' OF GENETIC PRIVACY: CONTROL, CONSENT AND DETERMINISM IN GENETIC INFORMATION

In theory there is criticism against the main argument supported above, that genetic is not differentiated from any other medical information and that insisting on its unique character is in fact a form of 'genetic exceptionalism' (Gostin & Hodge, 1999). 'Genetic exceptionalism' exists indeed in the cases where the human genome is considered to be the basis of unlawful discrimination especially on ethnic grounds. A characteristic case of 'genetic exceptionalism' is the recently uncovered case of Roma sterilization in the former Czechoslovakia. Indeed, information has been uncovered that between 1970 and until the early 90's Roma women were systematically sterilized under a Czechoslovak government program aiming at reducing the high birth rate of Roma women, a population considered to be 'unhealthy' and 'second class' citizens. According to the facts gathered by the European Roma Rights Centre (EPRC) based in Budapest, the authorities of the former Czechoslovakia coerced the Roma women into sterilization either unknowingly, by offering large financial incentives or, in some cases by threatening to remove their existing children from their custody. This unlawful and totalitarian suppressing practice was revealed in 2003 when Roma women begun coming forward and lodged complaints to the Ombudsman, claiming that they have been victims of forced sterilization, which were found to be justified (also see the case A.S. *vs Hungary*, CEDAW/C/36/4/2004, of 14 August 2006).

In K.H. and Others *vs Slovakia* ECHR (of 28 April 2009, no 32881/04) eight women, all members of the Roma community of Slovakia complained about the infringement of their right to informational privacy, thus of their right to full access to their medical records that can prove that they have been victims of this unlawful practice. The ECHR underlined the 'efficacy' that lies at the core of the protection of human rights under the European Convention. Thus, determining that the scope of state obligations under Article 8 is to offer practical and effective protection to any interest regarding the private (personal and medical information) or family life (information concerning the reproductive autonomy of the individual).

The case of the Romas underlines a notion made in philosophy by Michel Foucault known as 'biopolitics'. In his well known three volume work 'History of Sexuality' (1979) the famous writer refers to the term 'biopolitics' in order to describe a form of governance based on the regulation of the population via *biopower,* thus the application of political power in all aspects of human life, especially those concerning life, death, disease and reproduction. If closely interpreted, biopower can be conceptualized as the practice of sovereignty in biopolitical conditions. This notion has been contested in theory by Antonio Negri and Michael Hardt (2000) who, in their influential work 'Empire' have used the term 'biopolitical' in order to describe an anticapitalist revolutionary practice in which the individuals use their life and body as weapons in order to resist 'biopower' (e.g. suicide terrorism is the most tragic form of this practice). What both accounts clearly show is that bio-control can considerably empower its subject, whether that is the autonomous individual, the society or the sovereign. As Mclean (2010) points out, '...genetic information has real significance for individuals and societies, and indeed other organizations, such as industry.' Testing, researching and controlling genetic information which can predict the future medical state of and individual and control his/her life and death decisions can become an extremely powerful social, political and economical tool.

A huge threat to genetic privacy is posed by the recent development in data bio-banks, mainly utilized for reasons of public safety (Khadija, 2009). Those banks contain bio-metric information, namely fingerprints and DNA material (cellular samples). The uniqueness of these kinds of information is that they can not only identify an individual but that they can also confirm and verify with complete accuracy this identification (Nelkin & Andrews, 1999). Such banks exist in many European countries, such as the United Kingdom, Austria, Belgium, Finland, France, Germany, Hungary, Ireland, Italy, Luxemburg, the Netherlands, Norway, Poland, Spain and Sweden (also EDNAP, European DNA Profiling Group and ENFSI, Network for Forensic Science Institutes). In the European Union, the use of biometric data was proposed as a means to safeguard border controls between the countries participating in the Schengen Agreement (1985-). Specifically due to their common agreement, the European countries participating in the Schengen Area agreed in harvesting the biometric data of the visa applicants, storing them in the VIS information data banks for non- Schengen citizens (e.g. Norway who has activated the measure since January 1st 2009).

Another form of genetic Data-Banks is described above in the 'Icelandic experiment'. Those are formed as Health Database Organizations (HDOs) public and private, regulated by the state or by profit or non profit non-governmental organizations. Those Data-Banks contain primary genetic information harvested by individual medical files, or secondary genetic information available from insurance companies, state programmes and public health surveillance. Those Data-Banks beyond their possible threats for the privacy of the individual serve valuable scopes of public interest, such as public health, patient care and mainly scientific and academic research (Taylor, 2007). In theory, Wagner DeCew (2004) has proposed three alternative policy strategies in an effort to balance between genetic privacy and the public interest concerning the storing and processing of genetic data: a) a welfare state policy based on governmental guidelines and centralized data-bases, such as e.g. the EU policy, b) a liberal policy based in the corporate self-regulation and c) a hybrid policy based on private and public deliberation.

The use of genetic information mainly for public safety reasons underlines the above mentioned argument: genetic information is not only a means of medicine and namely it's not neutral in character. Thus it can be used to serve public-political or financial purposes, purposes of power. Genetic material is an ideal tool for identification and thus an irresistible tool for public safety, crime preventive and anti-terrorist policies. The question is at what cost for the privacy of the individual? As Gostin (1995) suggests the problems with genetic privacy rise not by the storing but by the processing of such data since, '...although the ability to identify a named individual in a large population simply from genetic material is unlikely, the capacity of computers to search multiple data bases provides a potential for linking genomic information to that person. It follows that non-linked genomic data do not assure anonymity and that privacy and security safeguards must attach to any form of genetic material.'

On the basis that genetic information is not neutral follows that the individual has a private interest in keeping it secure. A serious threat on the individual is posed by *geneticism* and by genetic *determinism.* Genetism identifies the individuals with their genes, subdividing them according to their genetic characterists by promoting the conviction that biological differences can be construed as the basis of unequal treatment. Such a theory could have an endangering implementation in the health insurance section affecting the social character of public policies as well as the significance of the individual's social dignity. In its turn, genetic *determinism* points out that genetic information can serve not only scientific or medical purposes, but also purposes possibly serving social prejudices and discrimination. Thus, there is some research according to which the basis of homosexuality is biological (as Laurie (2002) puts it, is there in fact a 'gay-gene'?). Such research can enshrine the argument that our sexuality is not a choice but a biological factor; can also support the prejudiced and discriminative opinion that homosexuals are not biologically 'completed' or 'normal' (Laurie, 2002). Determinism can be used also to enhance criminal policy arguments, concerning e.g. the genetic nature of certain crimes e.g. pedophilia.

The notions of control and autonomy are extremely attached to the privacy rights debates and thus could not be a part of any discussion concerning the protection of genetic privacy. Retaining the 'control' over our genetic privacy is considered to be the best remedy against the risks posed by 'geneticism' and 'genetic determinism' as described above. The notion of 'control' is used as an 'external' tool that can protect or delineate the core privacy concept. Thus, privacy cannot be described as control but it can be protected if the subject's control remains intact. On the other hand, the loss of this control entails the partial or total loss of privacy protection for the individual. The notion of control refers to a territorial or spatial understanding of privacy in which the subject's right is considered to be of proprietal worth. Conceptualizing privacy as space, as territory or as property entails the risk to understand its loss as economical and not ethical. That way, for example, the subject has the contractual freedom to disclose genetic information (since they are in metaphor a commodity) in exchange for financial benefits, without taking into account that this information is also linked to other members of one's family and that this disclosure can be offending or even infringing for their dignity, personality etc.

Using the notion of the 'control' that the subject bears over his/her genetic privacy we diminish the shared and mainly ethical character of this right. Our self becomes an owned subject and parts of its integrity can be given up like commodities, such as our valuable genomic information. Such an understanding poses limits on the genetic privacy of the individual only as far as he/she chooses to. This notion is adopted by Article 7 and 9 of the 'Universal Declaration of the Human Genome and Human Rights' adopted by UNESCO in 1997, where it is stated that, '(Art. 7) Genetic data associated with an identifiable person and stored or processed for the purposes of research or any other purpose must be held confidential in the conditions set by law' as well as that '(Art. 9) In order to protect human rights and fundamental freedoms, limitations to the principles of *consent* and confidentiality may only be prescribed by law, for compelling reasons within the bounds of public international law of human rights'. On this account, via the notion of *consent,* the genetic privacy of the individual acquires an individualist, atomistic character. Consent as far as genetic privacy is concerned is thus identified with the absolute control of the individual over his/her genetic personality.

Consent as far as the right to privacy is concerned it is considered to be a 'magic potion' for all the choices connected to the individual's genetic privacy and freedom. According to many theorists consent is identified with freedom. Nevertheless, this is not true. Freedom is a condition prior to consent. Is an employee free when he/she offers his/her consent to disclose medical and genetic information to his/her employer in order to be insured? Is a minor free when his/her parents offer their consent to genetic testing? Is there consent to give when an individual chooses to be cloned, or the clone does not have the right to be free? What happens in life-death decisions such as the case of 'Terri Schiavo' where the interested party cannot declare his/her consent in choosing death instead of a troubled life (Caplan & McCartney & Sisti, 2006)? In the end what is the analogy between the doctor-god and the well informed patient in health, or life decisions?

Consent bares the same contractual characteristics of the notion of control and it reduces the human self to *dominium.* Consent can be used as a tool to legitimize or delegitimize ethical decisions concerning the individual but not in a substantial way. That is why the consent of Jehovah Witnesses does not seem to make their medical decisions concerning their minors appearing to be either rational or justified. Moreover, genetic choices always involve others, the family or the society. The society and its values are part of who a certain individual is; it affects and is affected by his/her decisions. Thus, genetic decisions are deteriorated also by social values that protect the abstract individual and the society itself. The decision to become a society of both men and clones can not be deemed as a solely individual or atomistic choice. This is why genetic cases are as unique as the human genome. Each one of them is different and entails balancing between the individual's interest, the society values and the family members' rights.

V. THE ETHICAL GROUNDS FOR GENETIC PRIVACY: BETWEEN AUTONOMY AND PATERNALISM

In order to found the right to genetic privacy as an individualistic right its intrinsic moral value for the individual must be established. This ground is nonetheless the autonomy of the individual. Autonomy (*αυτονομία*) is a word of Greek origin, meaning self-governance. Autonomous is he/she who lives by his/her own (*αυτός*) rules, by his/her self-made norms (*νόμος*) (Friedman 2003; Laurie, 2002). The relation between privacy and autonomy is considered to be different on the two sides of the Atlantic. In the U.S. legal culture autonomy and privacy are in many cases identified. This is the reason why it is more accurate to talk of *privacy rights* than of a right to *privacy* as far as the American jurisprudence and theory is concerned. Thus *privacy* is presented like a matrix in which privacy rights are fostered. That is why it is easy to talk and differentiate among more than one privacy concepts. Privacy in the American understanding can be seen as informational privacy, as intimacy, as limited access to the self, as anonymity, as right to be let alone (Brandeis & Warren, 1890), as genetic privacy etc. What is extremely interesting in this conceptualization is that privacy is not presented as a uniform right, but as a network of rights or conditions of privacy.

On the contrary in the European legal culture autonomy is the common moral ground of rights. There, the specific numeration of rights, in the form of constitutional 'catalogues'-unusual in the American tradition where rights are specified by the jurisprudence- differentiates the relation between autonomy and privacy. Privacy is described as an instance, amongst many of the individual's autonomy (Eberle, 2002). Moreover, other linked concepts such as personality and dignity unify the protection of the individual. In this understanding dignity represents the core, the very essence of the individual's rights and the ultimate boundary of their protection. Personality protects the individual's outer self, the freedom to make choices concerning his/her social and public life, whereas the right to privacy protects our inner self, our private contours, our freedom to make choices concerning our body, our style of life and our sexual and intimate relations. Privacy is focused on our identity and our diversity. It is the right which protects a person as a unique entity.

Addressing the 'European rights' talk' one could say, that grounding a right of genetic privacy on autonomy is completed only if the dignity and personality of the individual are taken into account. Privacy is connected with the genetic information of the individual for namely three reasons: a) our human genome is the core of our biological identity and diversity, the main interests that privacy protects, b) the value of our genetic information can only be measured subjectively, according to our personal private understanding, c) genetic information defines our intimate choices, concerning our body and our most intimate-familial relation, the main domain that privacy protects. Nevertheless, dignity has a role to play also in the integration of the protection of our genetic selves. Dignity deteriorates privacy both from the inside and the outside. Dignity obliges us from the outside to protect the human self as an entity in itself, as a subject and not as an object. This, for example, means that the individual cannot be submitted to any harvesting of his/her genetic material that objectively infringes its dignity, e.g. by violence, or against his/her will, or in order to be used for unlawful, stigmatizing, racist and degrading causes. Analogically, dignity obliges the individual from the inside to value and use his/her genetic identity and information for scopes that do not infringe the relative societal values, e.g. the icon of human self as unique, and thus as not an object of genetic experimenting or cloning. Along the same line of thought, the personality of the individual enhances the protection of our genetic self in the social and public sphere, in our work relationships or in our political participation. In that line the use of biometric controls as a means of identification in the working place is infringing for the individual's personality (see the Directive no 115/2001 and the Decision 59/2005 of the Greek Data Protection Authority).

Grounding a right to genetic privacy on autonomy make one wonder how is that different from deeming to the individual the ability to control his/her genetic information? The difference lies in the concept of *free choice*. Whereas the notion of control is closely connected with the conception of the individual as an owner of its self, with the ability to control the use or loss of his/her genetic information as commodities, or objects, autonomy links genetic privacy to the ethical integrity of the individual and to the ability to make free choices (Akrivopoulou, 2009). Naturally, this ability is controlled by the law as far as minors or e.g. patients in a coma are concerned. Nevertheless, the genetic autonomy of the individual, due to its shared character can ground lawful interests and judicial claims even in *post mortem* cases. Thus in the case Ragnhildur Guðmundsdóttir *vs The State of Iceland* (151/2003) the Icelandic Supreme Court underlined, that a daughter bore a legitimate interest in the transfer of her dead father's medical files into the 'Health Sector Database', due to the hereditary and thus 'shared' character of such information.

As a specific instance of one's autonomy genetic privacy should be valued for two sets of reasons. According to the first, genetic privacy should be valued because of the general grounds that privacy is deemed to be important in any legal order. According to the second, genetic privacy should be valued because of the sensitive, personal and intimate for the individual character of such information. Privacy rights as Jean Cohen (2002; Glendon, 1991) puts it, are in fact an 'invisible shield' for the individual protecting freedom, self-governance, independence and his/her self expression. Privacy nourishes intimacy, the ability of the individual to form its life whether alone or in relationships according to his/her own choices and personal rhythm. Privacy positively enhances those qualities by negatively defending them against public and private scrutiny, pressure and exploitation (Berlin, 1958). It enables the individual to keep intact its identity without being obliged to conform to public values or social interests. Privacy should be enjoyed by the individual because it enables him/her to live by his/her own set of values, apart form the prejudice and judgment of the others (DeCew, 1997).

The loss of genetic privacy entails a series of potential dangers for the individual. The loss of information concerning our genetic privacy makes us vulnerable and thus inclined to conform, or leads us to private decisions based on sentiments of threat and fear. The very loss of private information causes anxiety and concern to its subject, especially over their future and potential uses (see e.g. the judgment Reklos & Davourlis *vs Greece*, ECHR, 15 Janouary of 2009, no 1234/05). In the case of genetic information where the future evolution of bio-technology leaves the ways in which they could be used obscure, these concerns become even more pressuring for the individual. Generally, medical information and especially genetic information allows possibilities of aggregation, economical exploitation and misuse. As Wagner DeCew (2004) underlines, 'in such cases, the potential harms from disclosure range from embarrassment, loss of self-esteem, social stigma, isolation, and psychological distress to economic loss and discrimination in such areas as employment, child custody, insurance housing, and immigration status'.

What nevertheless differentiates the foundation of privacy on autonomy and not on the notions of e.g. control or consent of the individual is the fact that this connection can furthermore shield him/her from the threats that *paternalism* poses. Paternalism represents an inherent conflict between the privacy and autonomy of the individual, medical ethics, the objective welfare of a patient as well as the values that a society construes as significant. Basing a right to genetic privacy on autonomy and choice entails the capacity of the subject to make damaging or even harmful choices even against his/her welfare. A characteristic paradigm of *paternalism* was shown above in the Witnesses of Jehovah's of denying blood transfusion. Nevertheless, such a conception of the autonomy of the individual presupposes that the patient has the capacity and maturity of choice and that he/she had the right to make a medically informed decision. That is why, in the majority of 'paternalism' cases as Laurie (2002) points out, 'the patient is deemed to be incapax and therefore unable to exercise her autonomy.'

Nevertheless, the risk of 'paternalism' does not exist only in specific cases where genetic autonomy clashes with the well-being of the individual but is also present in the social understanding of what is deemed as genetically 'normal', 'majoritarian' or even 'politically correct'. The conception of genetic privacy as a basis for the autonomy of the individual obliges even in cases where the patient can not literally offer his/her consent or state his/her objection to testing or treatment, e.g. he/she is unconscious or in a coma, to take account of his 'supposed' will. Therefore his/her general attitude for or against genetic research can be evaluated, or even his/her convictions or religious choices must be examined prior any medical choices are taken. In this understanding, *paternalism* and the right to genetic privacy can ultimately clash only in those cases that the doctor's do not facilitate the patients right to choose under his/her perceptive of best interest.

VI. AN INDIVIDUAL'S RIGHT TO GENETIC PRIVACY ON THE BASIS OF CARE

In many cases privacy as a concept is defined as *secrecy*. A quite similar related concept concerning especially medical privacy is *confidentiality*. Both bear the same basis since they are commonly concerned with the matter of information security but neither of them can be identified with privacy, or even more as genetic privacy. First of all what is considered to be secret or confidential does not necessarily have to be private. For example military secrets are considered to be secret or confidential but they can only be regarded as matters of a public and not private character (Solove, 2002). The same observation holds for medical or genetic information. To consider it as confidential or as secret does not mean that its content is not of public nature or that its does not have public consequences. For example the information that an epidemic disease has suffered a genetic mutation and therefore can even result in the death of those inflicted by it, can hardly be considered as secret or confidential. Secrecy and confidentiality basically differ in their following attribute: while secrecy represents privacy as a veil that sets apart public and private, confidentiality, based on this dichotomy, it mainly focuses on the relationship of trust and loyalty developed by professional ethics in preserving the secrecy and security of information (Prudil, 2006; Laurie 2002). As far as genetic privacy is concerned this relationships is deteriorated by the trust developed between the doctor and his/her patient.

From a theory of rights point of view, the basic reason for which confidentiality can not be identified with genetic privacy is the fact that its protective scope is reduced to the two parties involved, the doctor and the patient. The main consequence of such a counterfeit is that if the doctor breaches his/her obligation of confidentiality, theoretically apart from him/her every other party does not have the legal or ethical obligation to disclose any information concerning the genetic self of the individual. This notion leaves the concept of privacy 'empty' and depending completely on the secrecy or disclosure of the genetic information of the individual. This is the theory of the 'wall' as narrated by the classic liberal theory of privacy: privacy is considered us a 'neutral' concept that is delineated according to an absolute private/public division (Cohen, 2002). Thus any information, private or personal in nature that passes the 'wall' setting apart private from public, is considered to be as public, none regarding its substantial character or the unlawful means used for their disclosure. Consequentially if a piece of information concerning our human genome is disclosed according to the 'wall' theory it 'loses' its personal, sensitive, private etc. quality.

Nevertheless, rights, the right to genetic privacy amongst them have their own substantial content, a moral and not a neutral or procedural one as this approach implies. Moreover, at the core of the protection guaranteed by fundamental rights is their capacity to protect the individual from any possible infringement, or threat posed by the others or the state, no matter where it originates from. Thus, their enforcement can not be limited exclusively in the doctor's-patient relationship. In many cases, the relational, familial character of genetic privacy may even enforce the disclosure of such information to family members. Additionally, rights relate to both the concepts of freedom: positive and negative. Thus, not only they shield their subjects against possible threats, but they also enable them to enjoy a number of competences, such as the free development of the personality, the nourishment of one's identity, even so the appreciation of interpersonal and intimate relationships.

Under the theory of 'wall' rubric the right to genetic privacy can only be considered being a defense mechanism, a negative freedom of the individual. Nonetheless, confidentiality may be not identified as the right to genetic privacy of the individual but it represents one of its very important instances. Confidentiality is guaranteeing the respect for the secrecy of the individual's genetic choices (Poste, 1999). That way it is extremely important for the autonomy of the subject since not only secures the privacy of information concerning their identity, intimacy and personality but mainly because of the promise of trust, that confidentiality entails, enables the individual to take genetic and medical choices without the fear of disclosure. As Gillon (1994) characteristically underlines, '[t]hus maintaining confidentiality not only respect's patient's autonomy but also increases the likelihood of our being able to help them.' A characteristic example is the confidentiality which covers medical information concerning HIV/AIDS or other 'stigmatizing' diseases. There, the promise of confidentiality has always the ability to enable the choices of the patient to enter therapy etc.

The familial and relational character of genetic privacy sets boundaries to the obligations deriving from the duty of confidentiality. Confidentiality can not be considered as absolute as far as family member rights are concerned. Article 9 of the 'Universal Declaration of the Human Genome and Human Rights' of the Unesco clearly states that, 'In order to protect human rights and fundamental freedoms, limitations to the principles of consent and confidentiality may be prescribed by law, for compelling reasons...'. Therefore, according to the 'American Society of Human Genetics Social Issues Subcommittee on Familial Disclosures' the preconditions for breaching confidentiality are connected with the notion of possible harm for the family members. In such cases, a) a doctor has the right to warn the interested relatives when they are identifiable, b) when the harm is extremely likely to occur, c) and when this harm could, according to accepted medical standards, be reduced if early monitored, d) if any attempts to encourage the patient him/her self to disclose in the above cases the genetic facts have failed. In such cases, an avoidable but serious risk or harm for the family members is the decisive factor for the lawful breach of confidentiality. According to the American jurisprudence (e.g. cases as Pate *vs Threkel*, Fla 1995, Safer *vs Pack*, NJ 1996) in such cases a 'duty to warn' or even a 'duty to rescue' is obligatory for the doctor.

One should, nevertheless, point out that genetic defections can not be categorized as any other transferable diseases or conditions. Genetic abnormalities can transcend generations, in many cases they are linked with possibilities and not probabilities, or can even be co-defined by other unforeseen factors such as environmental and living conditions. Moreover as far as genetic information is concerned the difference between adults and minors is critical, since the first category always has the ability and maturity to decide for themselves and moreover has full access in familial genetic information by self-testing. In the end, in many cases genetic information concerning possible but not certain harm can put an undue burden on family members. In those cases the interested party may exercise his/her right 'not to know' his/her genetic heritage. This right is guaranteed by Article 5 of the Unesco 'Universal Declaration on the Human Genome and Human Rights' which states that '[t]he right of every individual to decide whether or not to be informed of the results of genetic examination and the resulting consequences should be respected.' In theory there is controversy concerning this rights. Some theorists contain that the right 'not to know' our genetic constitution is in fact part of the right to 'know' it. Along this line, the individual is genetically autonomous to make his/her genetic choices. Nonetheless there are voices who underline that in those cases that genetic information can pose a threat for the others, this right should be limited.

The controversy concerning the right to 'not to know' is in reality the core of the right to genetic privacy controversy. This right can be seen via two quite different approaches. The first is the liberal one which points out that a right to genetic privacy is in fact a right of genetic autonomy. Following this perception the individual's right to genetic privacy entails its ability to control his/her genetic information by means of confidentiality and informed consent. The core of this autonomy is guaranteed not only for adults but also for minors as well as for those unable to express their will (e.g. patients in a coma) as long as they're deemed to be mature enough to make such choices or every possibility to receive their possible consent has been made. Even in the cases that this conception of a right to genetic privacy is not considered to be absolute, one can accept that it can be limited only as far as a willing or unwilling 'loss' of genetic information has occurred. According to this understanding the greatest threat concerning genetic privacy is *paternalism*, the 'fear' that the genetic choices of the individual could be made against or prior to his/her own will. Under this rubric, the understanding of the control of the individual over his/her genetic truth, secrets or choices as a priority against any other existing familial or social or even public interest and value lies at the core of a right to genetic privacy.

On the contrary, the communitarian approach to a right to genetic privacy is emphasizing its interpersonal character, especially the dependencies which evolve within families with inherited genetic disorders. The main threats that one can pose on such a conception of a right to genetic privacy is the 'selfish' individual self and the empowerment of *geneticism*. This theoretical understanding is critical as opposed to the liberal approach which considers the individual as the sole, sovereign of his/her genetic self. Indeed, it points out that genetic decisions are not individual decisions as long as they have impacts on the family members of the subject involved. By choosing his/her right not to know the individual can cause serious harm to his/her intimates e.g. children. That way he/she is excluding them from choices that can possibly be connected with their health or quality of life, in many cases by making them vulnerable as far as future endangerment and harm are concerned. Often, this insufficient attention to the consequences that a genetic disorder may cause, can often impose an undue burden on others, e.g. for example to possibly prevent giving birth to children with potential mutations in the mitochondrial DNA, which in the most serious cases can even cause muscular weakness, or even be fatal.

The main counterfeit to this approach is that it is deeming the right to privacy not only as a right but also as a 'duty' for the individual, in a *paternalistic* way. Thus, the individual in order to form the 'right' and 'just' choices for him/herself must always take into account the agency and autonomy of the others, namely the family members. This disadvantage is balanced as Gilbar (2007) puts it because, 'the individual has an interest in maintaining familial relationships and living in a community with which he or she can identify.' Nonetheless, a third approach is here proposed over a relational right to genetic privacy, based on both autonomy and the notion of *care* on which the familial relationships are construed on. This approach points out that autonomy is not necessarily the basis of our atomistic and selfish perceptions of 'good' and 'bad' as far as our health, our genetic self and our future life is concerned. It is also the foundation for forming relationships that are characterized by intimacy and care as those constructed amongst the family members. Such a conception of a right to genetic privacy can provide a principled, ethical guidance for the complex problems of genetic privacy. Under this veil, the individual can form his/her decisions unconditionally but always aiming apart from his/her private interest to his/her family and social welfare, with care to their freedom and ethical values.

One could say that a serious medical, health problem triggered by one's defected genome is becoming unburdened when it leads the subject to family or social 'isolation'. The genetic privacy as the *autonomy of care* can leave the individual hurt but not alone, even if that means that he or she chooses to give up parts of it in order to enable the agency and space of others. *Care* does not lead to paternalism neither is considered to be a duty of the individual e.g. to inform in any case the members of his/her family of their genetic truth. Instead it liberates the individual to choose to develop intimate relationships of trust with the members of his/her family and to share the burden and obligations, the stigma, the possible discriminations and the fear of his/her genetic truth. Genetic privacy as *autonomy of care* values the individual as well as the intimate relationships in which he/she chooses to participate in the same way, thus enabling his/her communication and formation of choices in a circle of trust instead of an isolated but private and dominant space. Genetic privacy as autonomy of care is thus, based on the communication and dialogue between the family members and in the sense that genetic decisions are decisions which challenge our socially set ethical values to their very core. Each micro-genetic decision can become a macro-genetic decision affecting the society itself.

VII. CONCLUSION

A characteristic example of the relation between micro and macro genetics is pictured in the recent genetic research preformed by a genetics research team at the Newcastle University. The Newcastle scientists have developed a technique which enables them to replace defective mitochondria during an IVF (in vitro fertilization) procedure. The research team used newly fertilized eggs, removed the nuclei from the father's sperm and the mother's egg, which contain the parents DNA, excluding the defected mitochondria. Then the nuclei were put into another egg from which the nucleus has been removed, in order to retain the healthy mitochondria. Thus, the embryo was literally construed by three parents, its natural ones and a third, the donor of the healthy mitochondria egg. The solution that this technique offers to those born with defected mitochondria DNA can be considered monumental. Researches show that one in 6,500 children is born with mitochondrial disease and might suffer, as mentioned above, from serious or even fatal diseases (e.g. heart failure). The problem lies with the uncertainty of such a prediction since, one the other hand, a large presentage of children born each year with mutations in the mitochondrial DNA is asymptomatic or mildly diseased.

Nevertheless, this case shows vividly the relation between micro and macro genetic choices. The choice to use such a technique may be for the welfare of the children involved only if serious diseases are predicted to result from genome defections; otherwise an undue burden concerning the unborn child may be posed concerning his/her origin, and its right to know his ancestors. Such cases, involve always apart from the specific individual, the family, society and its values as well (Gavaghan, 2007). As far as genetic research is concerned the ice between technophobia, ethics, religion and the autonomy and privacy of the individual is extremely thick and the choices to be made often challenge our perceptions of existence, dignity and humanity. Genetic research has the ability to alter the very meaning of the beginning, the birth, and the end, the death of life as strictly matters of 'private' significance, both in a negative and positive way. It also poses serious threats of genetism, paternalism, bio-politics and bio-control on the individual's fundamental freedoms.

It is only on the 20th of May 2010 that the famous biochemistry entrepreneur James Craig Venter has announced in the AAS Science periodical, the creation of the first 'artificial' genome as follows: '[w]e report the design, synthesis, and assembly of the 1.08-Mbp *Mycoplasma mycoides* JCVI-syn1.0 genome starting from digitized genome sequence information and its transplantation into a *Mycoplasma capricolum* recipient cell to create new *Mycoplasma mycoides* cells that are controlled only by the synthetic chromosome. The only DNA in the cells is the designed synthetic DNA sequence, including "watermark" sequences and other designed gene deletions and polymorphisms, and mutations acquired during the building process. The new cells have expected phenotypic properties and are capable of continuous self-replication' (Gibson, 2010). What could probably be considered as a historic moment for the treatment of many disease can also makes us wonder, if this undoubtedly major breakthrough leaves intact our human, autonomous and free self or whether it surrender its absolute control to 'biopolitics' in Foucault's sense.

Under these conditions, preserving the genetic privacy, the genetic autonomy of the individual seems to be the only prominent path, the only possible answer in order to protect the human self at its core, in its very freedom. Nonetheless, this genetic privacy does not necessarily has to lead to the 'hard' conception of an atomistic, selfish, narcissist individual in constant conflict for maintaining his/her genetic sovereignty, but to a much more 'mild' concept that puts him in the centre of care: for his/her physical and ethical integrity, for his intimates, the family, and for his/her sense of social co-existing and belonging as a concrete and yet as an abstract human being.

REFERENCES

Akrivopoulou, C. M. (2009). *Between autonomy and intimacy: Redefining the right to private life (Art. 9(1) of the Greek Constitution 1975/86/01/08)*. Thessaloniki: Aristotle University of Thessaloniki. Retrieved from http://invenio.lib.auth.gr/record/113367?In=el

Akrivopoulou, C. M., & Stylianou, A. (2009). Navigating in internet: Privacy and the transparent individual. In Politis, D., Kozyris, P., & Igglezakis, I. (Eds.), *Socioeconomic and legal implications of electronic intrusion* (pp. 122–135). Hershey, PA: Information Science Reference. doi:10.4018/978-1-60566-204-6.ch007

Alderman, E., & Kennedy, C. (1997). *The right to privacy*. New York: Vintage Books.

Berlin, I. (1958). Two concepts of liberty. In *Four Essays on Liberty* (1969 ed.). Oxford: Oxford University Press.

Brandeis, L., & Warren, S. (1890). The right to privacy. *Harvard Law Review*, *4*, 193–220. doi:10.2307/1321160

Caplan, A., McCartney, J. J., & Sisti, D. (Eds.). (2006). *The case of Terri Schiavo: Ethics and the end of life*. New York: Prometheus Books.

Cohen, J. (2002). *Regulating intimacy: A new legal paradigm*. Princeton, NJ: Princeton University Press.

Cole, R. (2005). Authentic democracy: Endowing citizens with a human right in their genetic information. *Hofstra Law Review*, *33*, 1241–1303.

Downie, R., & Macnaughton, J. (2007). *Bioethics and humanities: Attitudes and perceptions*. London: Routledge-Cavendish.

Eberle, E. J. (2002). *Dignity and liberty: Constitutional visions in Germany and the United States*. Westport, CT: Praeger Press.

Elliston, S. (2007). *Best interests of the child in healthcare*. London: Routledge-Cavendish.

Fendrick, S. (2008-2009). The role of privacy law in genetic research. *A Journal of Law & Policy for the Information*, *4*, 803-820.

Foucault, M. (1979). The history of sexuality: *Vol. I. An introduction*. London: Penguin Books.

Friedman, M. (2003). *Autonomy, gender, politics*. New York: Oxford University Press. doi:10.1093/0195138503.001.0001

Gavaghan, C. (2007). *Defending the genetic supermarket: The law and the ethics of selecting the next generation*. London: Routledge-Cavendish.

Gibson, D. G., Glass, J. I., Lartigue, C., Noskov, V. N., & Chuang, R. Y. Algire1, M. A., ... Venter, J. C. (2010, July 2). Creation of a bacterial cell controlled by a chemically synthesized genome. *AAS Science.* Retrieved from http://www.sciencemag.org/cgi/content/abstract/science.1190719

Gilbar, R. (2007). Communicating genetic information in the family: The familial relationship as the forgotten factor. *Journal of Medical Ethics*, *33*, 390–393. doi:10.1136/jme.2006.017467

Gillon, R. (1994). Medical ethics: Four principles plus attention to scope. *British Medical Journal*, *309*, 184–188.

Glendon, M. A. (1991). *Rights talk: The impoverishment of political discourse*. New York: Free Press.

Gostin, L. O. (1995). Genetic privacy. *The Journal of Law, Medicine & Ethics*, *23*, 320–330. doi:10.1111/j.1748-720X.1995.tb01374.x

Gostin, L. O., & Hodge, J. G. Jr. (1999). Genetic privacy and the law: An end to genetics exceptionalism. *Jurimetrics*, *40*, 21–58.

Hardt, M., & Negri, A. (2000). *Empire*. Cambridge, MA: Harvard University Press.

Horsey, K., & Biggs, H. (2006). *Human fertilization and embryology: Reproducing regulation*. London: Routledge-Cavendish.

Khadija, R. P. (2009). Comparative architecture of genetic privacy. *Indiana International Journal & Comparative Law Review*, *19*, 89–170.

Laurie, G. (2002). *Genetic privacy: A challenge to medico-legal norms*. Cambridge: Cambridge University Press. doi:10.1017/CBO9780511495342

McLean, S. A. M. (2010). *Autonomy, consent and the law*. London: Routledge-Cavendish.

Nelkin, D., & Andrews, L. (1999). DNA identification and surveillance creep. *Sociology of Health & Illness*, *21*, 687–706. doi:10.1111/1467-9566.00179

Posner, R. A. (1981). *The economics of justice and the criterion of wealth*. Cambridge, MA: Harvard University Press.

Poste, G. (1999). Privacy and confidentiality in the age of genetic engineering. *The Review of Law & Politics*, *4*, 25–32.

Prudil, L. (2006). Privacy and confidentiality: Old concept, new challenges. *Medicine and Law*, *25*, 573–580.

Solove, D. J. (2002). Conceptualizing privacy. *California Law Review*, *90*, 1087–1155. doi:10.2307/3481326

Solove, D. J. (2004). *The digital person*. New York: New York University Press.

Sunstein, G. R. (2007). *Republic.com 2.0*. Princeton, NJ: Princeton University Press.

Taylor, M. J. (2007). Regulating personal data in a shared world: Limitations of the EU's approach to data protection. *Personalized Medicine*, *4*, 471–477. doi:10.2217/17410541.4.4.471

Thomas, K. (1992). Beyond the privacy principle. *Columbia Law Review*, *92*, 1431–1516. doi:10.2307/1122999

Wagner DeCew, J. (1997). *In pursuit of privacy, law, ethics and the rise of technology*. Ithaca, NY: Cornell University Press.

Wagner DeCew, J. (2004). Privacy and policy for genetic research. *Ethics and Information Technology*, *6*, 5–14. doi:10.1023/B:ETIN.0000036155.29288.f9

Chapter 8
Autonomy, Abortion and Pain Criteria:
An Ethical Approach

Hasan Atilla Güngör
Istanbul Kultur University, Turkey[1]

ABSTRACT

Pro-life and pro-choice groups are the main actors in the current abortion debate. On the one hand, the defenders of women's rights consider the issue as a matter of freedom and argue against bans on abortion practice. On the other hand, the fetal rights defenders are absolutely against abortion in any case and consider abortion a method of killing an innocent human being. Both sides use the scientific developments to influence public opinion. The core of this semi-scientific debate today depends on the question "When does human life begin?" Participants aspire to shape the law concerning abortion according to their answer to this question. Yet, this approach leads to deadlocks in theory and practice, because it is impossible to accept the legal personality of the fetus or to remove all the bans on abortion. However, it may be possible to find a solution within the legal system itself by using scientific knowledge, but without establishing it on a human "rights" base. This paper argues that using pain as a criterion may be a promising point of compromise.

I. INTRODUCTION

Abortion, as a subject in the common interest of medicine, law, religion and moral philosophy, has been one of the most important ethical issues in the last century and apparently it continues to steam a challenging debate in this century as well, along with the others at the crossroad of ethics and science such as "stem cell researches". The efforts of the interested parties to influence the abortion-related legislation in the direction of their moral or religious judgments have carried the subject into the public sphere by making it even more popular and more controversial. Due to the increasing popularity of the subject, some uncompromising legal expectations of the parties which do not accord with the reality of law and human rights are sometimes ignored. Conse-

DOI: 10.4018/978-1-60960-083-9.ch008

quently, the need to guarantee several significant values does not reflect on the legal praxis; thus for example some maintain that the fetus' legal personality must be acknowledged during the prenatal period and that as a result women's right to abortion must be banned.

Although the demand for acknowledging a legal personality to the fetus may not be satisfied within the current system of law and of human rights, that does not mean that any effort in realizing its protection is hopeless for as long as a common basis can be found on objective, scientific facts. I argue at this paper that the scientific claim concerning the fetus' ability to feel pain may offer the shared ground desired for any legal regulations related to abortion. In this study, I will briefly present the discussion on abortion and the influence of technological and scientific developments on this debate. Subsequently, it will be explicated that the availability of abortion for a woman as an option is not only required in order to realize her right to privacy but also her right to life. The following section will focus on various examples from the legal mechanisms developed in different legal systems concerning the protection of the fetus during the prenatal period. Accordingly, it will be elaborated why it is not viable to legalize the claim that the fetus must be recognized as a person and must have the right to life. Lastly, this study will face the questions of "how the fetus can be protected within the system of positive law" and "whether the fetus' ability to feel pain" may be used as a criterion for the legal regulation of abortion.

II.EVERLASTING DISCUSSION: ABORTION AND THE "BEGINNING OF LIFE" CRITERION

The ever-fevered debate on abortion is largely based on the conflict between the moral judgments which the parties attempt to rationalize by drawing upon the scientific developments. On the one hand, there are the defenders of woman rights who contend the wrongfulness of the restrictions over abortion and consider the abortion as an indispensible part of women's autonomy; on the other hand, there are pro-life groups which generally uphold the religious arguments and consider the abortion as an act of killing an innocent human being. Since the stands taken by each party seek to protect two opposite moral values, abortion may be understood, according to the value one chooses to protect, as a means of freedom or it may be regarded as a murder, no matter why and when it is committed.

At this point, it is needless to say that the moral approach and the values adopted by the legislators are of vital importance for the interested parties of the debate. That is because, these moral judgments are legitimized and put into effect in the society only via legislative regulation. Thus, the interested and opposed factions work in order to increase the public support for their arguments and thereby to influence the legislative process according to their preferences. That's why the subjects of abortion and the legal status of the fetus have been brought to the public attention through a number of different, real cases. This is especially true for the USA as it may be observed in legendary court cases such as Roe *v. Wade* or in acts such as "The Unborn Victims of Violence Act".

Nevertheless, it should be noted that even a strong public support favored by moral judgments as well as a positive legislation in compliance with these value choices, are not sufficient to legitimize them; for example in order to ground the right to abortion in the non-justifiability of an interest in protecting the fetus or to value the latter at the expense of the woman's right to autonomy. Especially pro-life groups which argue that the fetus during the prenatal period must enjoy the same rights as a postnatal individual have tried to prove scientifically that there is no difference between a fetus and a born individual. In response, women rights defenders have worked hard to refute these arguments by using scientific facts also. Consequently, though the relative debate initiated as a conflict between inherently opposing moral arguments and judgments it consequently eveloped as a clash between scientific arguments.

In the core of this theoretical conflict lays the question of when the human life starts, i.e. who may be identified as a person. The seemingly easy answers to these questions conceal some of their important legal consequences, because a "person" is identified as a being that bears legal rights. In this case, the question is actually at which period of the human formation, this being may be entitled to some interests that ought to be legally protected. Thus, for instance, if the pre-natal period is accepted as the beginning of legal personality, any interventions against the fetus during this period would be defined as an assault and battery as it is the case for the ones born. More directly, abortion would be regarded as an act of murder and would be considered as illegal no matter what its causes; no matter for example, whether a woman's life or health is in danger or whether she has gotten pregnant by having been raped. On the other hand, if it is accepted that the legal personality of the fetus starts in the postnatal period, any intervention made against the fetus, even 10 minutes prior to the birth, would not be considered as an assault against a person.

The 'rationality' of law itself as far as the concepts of person and personality are concerned, as briefly discussed above, requires the evaluation of the relative scientific facts, as a necessary but insufficient element of any legislative process related to the subject. Accordingly, the U.S., Federal Supreme Court evidently employed scientific facts for the justification of the aforementioned Roe *v. Wade* decision in 1970. However, it should be noted that the tendency of the law to utilize scientific facts regarding abortion and the fetus is actually even older. For instance, a scientific criterion known as "Quicken" has been introduced in the 12th century in Great Britain for the punishment of any acts damaging the fetus and it is still in use in some of the U. S. (e.g. Arkansas, Washington, Michigan, Florida, Nevada and Rhoe Island.) (Lugosi, 2007).

The basis of the "Quicken" criterion derives from the common law idea that when an unborn child moves for the first time, it attains "animation" or a soul. Therefore, when the pregnant woman perceived the first movement of the fetus, this was considered as an evidence that the child was alive (McQueeney, 2005). In the early Common Law systems, this criterion was functioning as the threshold in order to determine whether an act against a fetus constituted a crime. After this 'moving' phase, any damage experienced by the fetus could be also the subject of a separate crime besides those committed exclusively against women. Additionally, it was not possible prior to this phase to bring any penal suit against acts that could cause damage to a fetus. To sum up, the Early Common Law did not consider the killing of the fetus as a murder since it accepted in principle that its legal personality starts with birth, but nevertheless acknowledged it as a serious crime requiring prison sentence on the basis of the 'Quicken' principle (Brobst, 2006).

The "Quicken" criterion is exposed to serious criticisms due to the usage of information based on semi-scientific legal observations (Holzapfel, 2002). In addition to the criticism that according to this approach even one movement may be regarded as a sign for being a living creation, it is also impossible for a mother to be expected to feel or realize the first movement of the fetus. Scientific facts based on ultrasound images show that the earliest movements occure at the 5.5 weeks of gestional age. It is realistically impossible for the mother to feel this movement. The fetus' first movement can be perceived by the mother from approximately 16 to 18 weeks of gestitation. (Burgess & Tawai, 1996).

The argument, which defends that "the conception" should be accepted as the beginning of legal personality is more familiar particularly because it is supported by the Catholic world, although scientific facts are also used to support it. According to this argument, life, from the conception-penetration of a sperm into an ovum- should be protected by the law as a moral value. The argument is constructed as follows: the individual must have some distinctive features that differentiate her from all others (even her relatives), in order to be acknowledged as a person. Considering the human development, it is observed that the aforesaid individuating features occur during the conception. At this phase two cells coming from the mother and the father, carrying different genetic information, combine and create a new structure. This structure at the same time builds up a different, unique genetic code independent from the sources from which it was created. After the formation of the genetic code and because the development and distinctive qualifications of that structure have been biologically specified, the main element determining the personhood has emerged. Therefore, since it is with the conception that a single, unique and distinctive structure comes into existence ontologically, it is the conception that must be recognized as the beginning of the human life (Lugosi, 2007; Noonan, 1970).

Nevertheless, the scientific world has ascertained about 30-35 years ago not only how and during which periods the fertilization is occurring but has also established that a specific moment of conception does not actually exist. As opposed to what it was believed before, the fertilization occurs over a period of 12-24 hours. If the stages are described from the very beginning, for example, the sperm needs to stay in the female reproductive organ for about 7 hours in order to realize the fertilization. Sperm which gets ready to go to the ovary after the 7-hour waiting time reaches the ovum after a 10-hour progression; whereas the entrance into the ovum is a quite complex and biochemical process. After nearly a period of 24-hour, the fertilized ovum called the zygote comes into being. However, another period of 24-hours required to complete the formation of a diploid individual. (Shanon & Wolter, 1990; Beller & Zlatnik, 1995).

As explained above, there is not a moment which may be defined as the specific moment of conception. The sperm is entering into the ovum and the occurrence of impregnation is a process lasting for days. It is even more remarkable that the zygote does not bear the genetic efficiency to become an embryo itself, even though the ovum has been impregnated in this phase, i.e. it has become a zygote. At this stage it is neither self-contained nor self-sufficient to develop by itself (Shanon & Wolter, 1990).

In this period, which is called pre-embryo phase, just as it is not possible to note any genetic individuality of the zygote, it is also impossible to mention its ontological oneness. That is because it is possible that the zygote could be divided in two within the period of 14-15-days before reaching the uterus. In this phase, during which the formation of twins takes place, the possible self-division of the organism into two independent single structures prevents us from concluding on the zygote's ontological oneness. Thus, and because it is impossible to deter a distinctive structure genetically or ontologically, it is depicted that this phase cannot be recognized as the beginning of life (Shanon & Wolter, 1990).

Consequently to the secular allegation that the conception is the beginning of life on the grounds of scientific facts, another argument (which is called the "Gastrulation phase" argument) has claimed, that the settlement of the fetus into the uterus is in fact the decisive time criterion as far as the beginning of life is concerned. The "Gastrulation phase" argument introduces a new understanding in the discussion and poses serious criticisms to the previous approach by arguing against the precise definition of the moment of conception. The core of these criticisms is the idea that the impregnation phase cannot provide the zygote's genetic and ontological oneness and that a distinctive structure may come into being only with the transition of the fetus into the uterus. This is because the risk for division, which exists before the settlement, disappears as soon as the zygote is placed in the uterus while it continues to develop under the control of its own genetic structure. Therefore, the fetus becomes a genetically and ontologically distinctive structure in this phase. Another important characteristic of this period is that the cells of the organism differentiate in order to build up certain parts of the body (Gilbert, Tyler & Zackin, 2005; Shanon & Wolter, 1990).

The first objection put forward against the "Gastrulation phase" argument is that the scientific facts which assert that "the zygote cannot divide itself in two, making therefore impossible to bear twins after the "Gastrulation phase" is not correct. According to the authors who object to this view, the organism may still divide itself in this phase. Extraordinary twin formations known as the *Siamese twin* can occur after the zygote is emplaced in the uterus. This means that the organism, though hardly probably, has nonetheless the potential to create two different beings in this phase (Irving, 1999).

The authors that propose the conception or "Gastrulation phase" are basing the formation of the individual only on biological factors and thus they do not define the 'real' formation of the individual. For it is not possible to maintain that the character of the individual is formed only upon her genetic code. In addition to her characteristics which are shaped according to her unique genetic code, the main characteristics that make the individual distinctive are formed and specified by the relationships she develops socially in the public sphere. Therefore, it is unwise for some scholars to base their arguments on individuality exclusively on biological data, thus putting aside the characteristics formed via the interaction with the social environment.

Another criterion proposed in order to determine the beginning of human life via the use of scientific data is the beginning of brain's functioning. According to this view, the personality of an unborn child should be recognized legally and its right to life has to be acknowledged, when the human brain actually starts functioning. However, the supporters of this view do not always agree at certain points. Their most important disagreement concerns the very core of their argument, thus what should be understood as "brain's functioning".

One of the first scholars who have favored this criterion is Baruch Brody. In his theoretical approach, Brody initiates a connection between the criteria which are used to determine the existence of death and the existence of life. For Brody, if the conditions of death are absent, we may be assured that a certain human is actually alive. Accordingly, the first emergence of these characteristics points to the beginning of human life with a simple reasoning. If we employ brain death in order to define the death of a human, we may accept brain's functioning as the beginning of human life. Claiming that electrical activities in the fetus' brain can actually be detected about 6 weeks after conception (Brody, 1975). Brody's approach has been exposed to serious criticisms because it is uncertain whether this activity indicates only that the brain cells are alive or that serves as a clear evidence that the brain is able to fulfill its own functions. Thus it remains ambiguous in which respect and framework his contribution can be utilized

As far as the question of which electrical activities produced by the brain qualify as "brain functions", another cleavage occurs among the authors who acknowledge the beginning of brain's functioning as a criterion of life. Some of them maintain that an ordinary electrical activity can be considered as sufficient in order to consider it as the beginning of life, whereas others insist on the existence of regular cerebral activities that can specifically indicate the existence of consciousness. Certain authors, who argue that recordable unorganized electrical activities only indicate that brain cells are alive, claim that it is more important for the beginning of life to detect regular signals denoting human brain functions. Unorganized electrical activities may also be produced by other living cells not belonging to a brain in a way as not to reveal that the brain actually functions. Yet, the brain is regarded as criterion because of the meaning assigned to its function (Bonin, 2002).

On the other hand, the functional activity of the brain is possible only through the development of some structural features. Therefore, measuring the only the electrical activities of the brain in itself cannot be considered as sufficient criterion for establishing the beginning of life. Additionally, this is a condition that our brain and nervous system can reach only when they have acquired a certain level of maturity. In order to discover when this level of maturity has been reached, we need to understand how our brain and nervous system develop during the period of pregnancy. Both the embryonic brain and the spinal cord are formed in the 3rd week of pregnancy. But this primitive structure does not have the efficiency to perform any neurologic function in this phase. In the 5th week, the first nerve cells come into existence. Even though it is extremely rare, synapses, nerve cells bound to each other, are formed for the first time in the 6th week and from the 7th week reflex movements are possible to be ascertained, depending on each fetus' speed of development. When the 12th week is reached, reflex movements can be observed in all the embryos. However, the most important period for the development of the nervous system is the 20th week of the fetus' development because in this phase the connection of neural pathways through the thalamus to neocortex is occurring. This allows stimuli to be received and the creation of thalamus, a region of the brain which enables the integration of the nervous system is completed (Gilbert, Tyler & Zackin, 2005; Shanon & Wolter, 1990). That means that the necessary groundwork is ready for the brain to fulfill its functions. However, even among the authors who agree up to this point, the views concerning the precise time of actual brain function as well as the actual period that regular electrical activities may be observed, differ: these periods may vary from the 22th week to the 35th week of gestation from one author to the other (Bonin, 2002).

The last focal point in the discussion concerning abortion and the fetus's beginning of life, within this scientific framework, is the criterion called "viability", i.e. the capability of living. This criterion is the most current of the above-mentioned arguments and is formed in such a way as to reinforce the very concept of the individual. "Viability" exists when the fetus acquires the ability by itself to survive outside or without its mother's womb. In other words, a fetus is deemed as viable when it is not depending upon its mother's body in order to maintain its life. Probably one of the most important reasons for propounding this criterion is the fact that premature babies, coming into the world through the preemies between the 20th and 23rd weeks of pregnancy, can be kept alive by medical support. Therefore, it may be supported that the fetus has the necessary features that enable it to survive even if it leaves its mother's body, 3,5 months earlier than expected. The basic claim of the viability criterion is that this moment, namely the moment that the fetus acquires all the necessary features to survive by itself, should be accepted as the beginning of life. This is because the fetus in this phase is -at least theoretically- no longer a part of its mother and has the capacity of living by itself and bears its own structural features (Crum & McCormack, 1992; Beller & Zlatnik, 1995; Bonin, 2002).

Nonetheless, the viability criterion is also subject to various criticisms. Thus, it is suggested that a standard moment for the fetus to acquire its structural features is impossible to determine, due to the fact that each fetus has a different speed of development (Noonan, 1970). Actually, the growth of each baby in its mother's womb varies depending on various factors such as nutrition. Hence, it is not possible to determine a uniform standard moment, valid for each and every pregnancy. On the other hand, even the notion of the fetus's "viability" seems quite unclear. "Viability" enables the fetus to be kept alive by benefitting from all the up to date technological developments or is the condition in which the fetus can actually survive in an environment without the possible use of medical technology? The answer is generally that the use of technology is required. However, some other problems arise in this case. If as "viability" of the fetus we understand its ability to be alive due to the assistance of medical technology, then the fertilized ovum *in vitro*, outside of the mother's body, should also be accepted as an individual that can live independently from its mother. Independency from the mother and surviving by means of medical support are also available in this kind of fertilization (Crum & McCormack, 1992). Nevertheless, in the case that the fertilized ovum is replaced in the mother's womb, this creature which seemed as independent from its mother will depend on her again and consequently the personality that the fetus had *in vitro* will no longer exist. Under these conditions the fetus' personality or its right to life will become blur and relative.

As discussed earlier, the reflection on the scientifically based arguments propounded by the pro-life and pro-abortion groups shares the same consequence of the moral discussion concerning these issues; namely disagreement. I strongly believe that carrying the subject from the moral platform to the scientific area does provides us with firm and secure answers and solutions. On the contrary it seems to deepen even more the existing conflict. However, in my opinion the main obstacle stems from shaping this problem in the form of a clash between the right to life, namely of one's own child, against the woman's right to privacy, in terms of abortion. This contrasting point of view doesn't pay justice for either of the two sides of the respective argumentation, as I will further sustain.

III. A WOMAN'S RIGHT TO PRIVACY VS. THE UNBORN CHILD'S RIGHT TO LIFE; AN UNFAIR PROPOSITION

As opposed to the common view, I claim that a woman's right to abortion and access to abortion facilities (i.e. hospitals, clinics) does not only refer to her right of control over her body, neither it is exclusively connected with the enjoyment of her right to privacy. A wide range of rights, related to a woman's right to abortion, including her right to life, may be realized and protected only if she can fully enjoy her free access to abortion facilities. Hence, to simplify the matter into a choice between an "unborn child's" right to life and a woman's right to privacy as identified with her right to control her own body, can lead us to hasty and unfair conclusions. In this context, abortion is not only a right but a vital necessity for women all over the world.

Nonetheless, women, ultimately, may not benefit from the established secure abortion facilities due to two basic reasons. First, abortion is forbidden in some legal systems or it is permitted only under exceptional circumstances. Secondly, women may abstain from having an abortion because of material or spiritual reasons, even though abortion is legally permitted. In certain regions of India, it has been observed that abortions cannot be virtually performed due to the high social pressure, although the legal system itself, allows their performance. However, the inability to enjoy the right to abortion, regardless of the reasons, gives rise to a series of quite important human rights problems. One of the primary reasons for a woman's claim to abortion is most probably that her existing pregnancy endangers her health or life. Sometimes the mere continuation of a pregnancy may really put a woman's life at risk due to a number of reasons. In such cases, the woman's will to carry on with her pregnancy should definitely be respected on the basis of her right to privacy. Yet, a woman's decision to terminate her pregnancy should be respected, as well. This respect to the woman's choice, to her autonomy and decisional privacy, in such cases can prove to be essential in order to protect her rights to life and health.

The connection between the right to privacy on the one hand and the right to life and health is also established in the international human rights law. For instance, it is unacceptable that an abortion may not be performed, because it is considered to be illegal if the pregnancy may seriously endanger a woman's health according to the European Commission of Human Rights and the European Court of Human Rights (i.e. case of Paton *vs. United Kingdom*, 1980). The United Nations Commission on Human Rights (UNCHR) expressed a similar opinion in the United Nations 28th General Comment. The Commission during its annual evaluation concerning the international practices regarding the violation of the right to life, has called the respective U. N. member states to take the necessary steps in order to protect women from illegal abortion practices (UN Human Right Commission, 2000). Furthermore, the UNCHR in several decisions, after observing the relative abortion practices of U.N. member states has established a clear connection between abortion ban and the right to life. In its decision, Llantoy *vs Peru* (2005) the UNCHR, held that abortion bans, result in human rights abuse. Therefore, it may be concluded that nowadays it is recognized by the international human rights law that abortion bans pose a serious threat on a woman's right to life and to health.

The statistical data of the World Health Organization on this issue may be summarized as follows: about 210 million pregnancies occur in a year and 80 million of them are unplanned. Nearly 46 million of 80 million pregnancies are terminated due to women's choice. Only 27 million of these operations are performed within a legal framework that permits them, while 19 million of them are considered to be illegal and are performed in unsecure abortion facilities due to abortion bans or the inability to freely access legal and appropriate abortion facilities for other reasons, namely social or religious. Every year, 68.000 of 19 million unsecure abortions result in the death of pregnant woman. Regionally, most of these deaths occur in Asia, which counts 34.000 'abortion' deaths per year. Africa follows with 29.800 deaths every year, while Latin America and the Caribbeans come third to this sad statistics with annually 3.700 'abortion' deaths. The number of deaths in the continent of Europe is estimated in 300 per year (World Health Organization, 2004).

It is clearly not possible to realistically claim, that a practice that caused the death of 68.000 women yearly does not negatively influence the rights to life and health. This view can be strongly supported by the characteristic Romanian example. With the adoption of a more restrictive abortion legislation by the Romanian government in 1966, a considerable increase was observed in the rate of deaths, resulting from abortion in Romania. While 20 deaths were the result of abortions in 1966, compared to 100.000 healthy births, this rate increased in 1970 to 60/100.000, nearly to 100/100.000 in 1974 and to 150/100.000 in 1983. In 1989, the rate of 'abortion' deaths decreased due to the re-legalization of abortion. This rate decreased to 60/100.000 in 1990, to 40/100.00 in 1992 and to 20/100.000 in 1997 (World Health Organization, 2004). A similar research was conducted in the Republic of South Africa. After the legalization of abortion in 1966, there was a decrease from 16,5% to 9,7% in the rate of health problems arising from unsecure and unhealthy abortion applications (Lancet, 2006).

Another human rights problem related to the inability of free access to secure abortion facilities is honor killings and suicides, which are not widely known but are substantially important to be ignored. In the cases of pregnancies which are disapproved by society, for example pregnancies due to extramarital affairs or rapes, a woman may be killed even by her family members because she has dishonored the tribe or clan in which she belongs. In other cases, a woman who is afraid of being killed may commit suicide or be forced to commit suicide. Therefore, providing safe, available and secure conditions for women to freely access abortion facilities and informing them about their rights is of vital importance. As a matter of fact, the UNCHR, observing the abortion practices of Ecuador had the opportunity to explain that the suicides of many young women living in the country were directly related to the fact that abortion was legally forbidden (UN Human Rights Committee, 1998). In the evaluations made for several other countries by both the UNCHR and other UN bodies concerned with the human rights protection, one can find many similar texts depicting a direct connection between human rights abuse and abortion bans, difficulties in accessing secure abortion or lack of information concerning this subject (Güngör, 2007).

The Inter-American Convention on Human Rights seems to uphold that abortion bans are considered to be violating for human rights, namely the right to life and health. On the contrary, it contains that those bans should continue to exist for the sake of protecting the human rights of the fetus, especially its right to life, as acknowledged by Article 4 of the Convention. The Latin American countries which act in a conservative manner as far as the subject of abortion is concerned, due to their conservative catholic social structure, constitute a considerable number of contracting countries to this convention. According to the Article 4 establishing the right to life in this Convention, "from the moment of conception right to life shall be protected in general by law". Only through this sentence, it may be concluded that a fetus has the right to life in its mother's womb and has interests protected by law, since it acquired a legal personality by the moment of conception. Thus, according to the Convention, it may be supported that abortion is forbidden from the moment of conception.

In 1981, an applicant, a private individual appealed to the Inter-American Commission on Human Rights arguing that by legislatively allowing abortions the legal system of the USA, abused the Inter-American Convention, namely Article 4. In this complaint, better known as the "Baby Boy" case, the Commission, after analyzing the concerned regulations of the American Declaration of the Rights and Duties of Man and the Inter-American Convention on Human Rights concluded that the right to life cannot be so widely interpreted as protecting the fetus. Although abortion is not recognized as a human right in international law, the legal identification of the right to life as protected by law from the moment of conception cannot in any way be interpreted as an argument in favor of judicial or legislative abortion bans. In this context, the most significant argument that the pro-life supporters can draw from the international human rights law inevitably has become disfunctional.

Dissimilarly to the examples given above, the Inter-African Convention of Human Right recognizes abortion as a right in the Protocol attached to this Convention. In the "Protocol of the African Charter on Human and People Rights' on the rights of women in Africa (date of adoption 11.07.2003)", the governments of the member states are asked to take the necessary measures in respect of guaranteeing the right to abortion, if the pregnancy is a result of a sex crime or an incest relationship, or in those cases it negatively influences a woman's physical and spiritual state, or sets a woman's life at risk. Considering the main international conventions on human rights we mentioned above, we should conclude that the national legislative efforts not only should not ban abortions, but instead they should guarantee the secure, free and easy access of the interested women to abortion facilities. The Inter-African Convention on Human Rights has acknowledged abortion as an autonomous right. Thus, it is clear that at least in terms of human rights, a legislative ban on abortion should not even constitute an option.

Furthermore, this approach poses some challenging questions; "Should abortion not be restricted in any way?" or "To protect a woman's right to privacy, should abortion be allowed in any period of pregnancy?" A positive answer to these questions would mean that any legislative regulation aiming to protect the fetus before its birth should not be accepted. In other words, within the context of protecting a woman's autonomy and freedom, it would be possible to unlimitedly dispose even a baby who can actually survive without a mother. Certainly this kind of reasoning as well as the conclusions that it leads to can be seriously conflicted in exactly the same way as abortion cannot be understood as a problem solely concerning a woman's right to privacy.

IV.IS THE FETUS LEFT UNPROTECTED FOR THE SAKE OF THE WOMAN'S LIBERATION?

Nonetheless, it is impossible to argue that the fetus is left totally unprotected in the current, modern legal systems for the sake of guaranteeing the woman's liberation. On the contrary, the respective national legislative regulations seem to adopt the same standards, thus maintain a balance between the woman's rights and public interest in protecting the fetus. This legal trend for protection may be clearly traced not only in the public but in the private law, also.

In terms of private law, the most rooted and widespread protection in the history of law is the protection of the rights that the fetus's is entitled in the prenatal period but can actually enjoy only after birth, a protection existing even in Roman Law. These legislative regulations, acknowledged in the vast majority of the legal systems, exist in the law of inheritance and protect the fetus' right only in the condition of it being born alive. The peculiarity in this circumstance is that this protection is not associated with the fetus as it exists in its mother's womb, but with the fetus that lives to be born. Thus, if a fetus dies before birth, the inheritance is not succeeded to the fetus' heirs, i.e, unlike the death of a living born baby. Subsequently, that means that the protected rights belong to the fetus that is born alive and not to the unborn one hosted in its mother's womb. Accordingly, the child, for example, whose father was killed prior to birth or who was handicapped due to an intervention which occurred in the prenatal period, can lawfully claim a fair compensation (Oğuzman, Seliçi & Oktay, 1993) -naturally these demands have no legal basis if the fetus is not born alive.

Another case recently recognized in the U.S.A. private law, is known as the claim to "Wrongful Birth". In this case, a child who is born handicapped claims compensation due to his dissatisfactory life from the mother or the doctor who allowed her "wrongful birth". The case of "Wrongful birth" has started being acknowledged also in the European legal orders (Morris & Saintier, 2003; Hensen, 2005). In short, it should be noted that the national legislative regulations concerning the fetus have improved its protection over time, on the basis of it being born alive. In the field of public law, the measures concerning the fetus's protection can be grouped in two categories. The first one concerns the restrictions placed on abortion and the other, the criminalization of intentional or negligence interventions directed to the fetus by third parties. Such interventions are regarded as crimes penalized by criminal law. Just like in the field of private law field, these measures are common for almost all modern legal systems. Therefore, one could say that various legislative regulations aiming to protect the fetus do exist in both the fields of public and private law. Additionally, these regulations inevitably place certain restrictions for the woman's right to privacy as far as abortion is concerned.

At this point, it seems necessary to underline an important detail different from the discussion made above. The restrictions posed to abortion do not aim at directly protecting the fetus' interests. The fetus is not considered to be a rightholder in any legal system and neither is it possible for it to become one. This impossibility may be better understood if the probable unreasonable results of the fetus becoming a rightholder could be demonstrated. At first, if the fetus is regarded as a rightholder, it will share the common legal status with any born individual. Thus, any kind of external intervention to its well-being will constitute an illegality. In that case, necessarily abortion should be completely banned and consequently many of women's rights, especially their right to life, would be -one could modestly say- endangered if not completely annihilated.

One proposed and possible solution for the protection of women's right to life, is to provide some exceptions to abortion bans, i.e. that it may be allowed, in order to protect a woman's life or health. Although it seems reasonable at first, this approach may trigger a series of discriminating implications. If newborn individuals and fetuses share the same legal status and if it is conceivable or possible to sacrifice one's life for the sake of the other's–accepting the exceptional application of abortion- it literally means that it is possible and reasonable to legally regulate the following norm: any individual can lose her life for another on the basis that her life is hiererchized as more valuable regardless of a legitimate and justifiable reason. The same could be argued about the harvesting of organs belonging to an ordinary citizen in order to maintain the life of a very important scientist. Therefore, it is impossible for a fetus and a born individual to share the common legal status of a rightholder and thus for both to bear a legal personality. Some problems may also rise in other fields of law. Because certain interests protected depend upon the fetus being born alive, if we assert its legal personality they should be recognized even before its birth. Thus, for example the fetus which dies in its mother's womb should leave its inheritance rights to its own heirs. Such an understanding could create an inheritance share undesired by the first deceased. Or it will be possible for a mother to receive a compensation for her loss of support due to the death of the fetus' father before its birth, even though the living birth could not occur in the end. In other words, she will be compensated on the fetus's account, though it will not be born alive.

Recognizing the fetus' legal personality creates impasses as far as legal certainty is concerned. In the very early periods of pregnancy, even when the woman herself is not aware of her pregnancy, criminal and legal sanctions may be imposed on a woman due to some of her own behaviors that can be proven to be damaging for the physical integrity of the fetus or even cause its death. This danger could apply not only regarding the expectant mother but also for third parties. Since the mother's legal responsibility concerning her obligations of care towards the fetus could be considered to be the same as her duties towards her born children, her actions should be then defined in public law and criminal law in a similar way.

It is possible to further examine analogous examples. But the idea I would actually like to underpin is that recognizing the fetus as an individual is not possible within the law's own reality. On the other hand, the law is influenced by the meaning and the value that a certain society attributes to the fetus although its own reality precludes the acknowledgement of a fetal personhood. This influence may be observed in the wording of the relative legislation as well as in the legal terms and expressions used. For example, in some of the USA, acts against the fetus are defined as murder and their punishments are close or equivalent to those concerning the ones born alive. These legislative regulations merely reflect the States evolutions on the subject. Thus, those States that recognize any act that causes the fetus's death as murder, have amended their respective legislation in order to punish them only exceptionally –mainly because the abortion ban became unconstitutional in the USA after the *Roe v. Wade* decision. Thus, some of the USA may reflect their opinions about the fetus' status in the related legislation, as indicated in Roe *v. Wade* as long as this opinion does not hinder the woman's right to abortion. In other words, even though the fetus can be legally and formally defined as having a legal personality, the related legislation in some of the USA is functionally protecting in fact, the States' interest invested in the fetus's existence.

A legislative regulation, in parallel with those enacted in some of the USA and yet in contrast with the general tendency of the rest European legal systems, can be found in the Dutch Criminal Code. In the Article 82a of the Dutch Criminal Law, where the concept of murder is defined, it is clearly stated that a fetus which is considered as viable without depending on its mother's body should be included in this definition. Additionally, the crime of illegal abortion is acknowledged separately by the Dutch Criminal Code under the Article 296. Hence, the acts directed to end a fetus' existence basically constitute two different types of crime according to the Dutch Criminal Code If those acts take place at the moment that the fetus can be considered as viable, they can be regarded as murder. However, if these acts occur at a the time prior to the fetus's being considered as viable, they constitute the crime of illegal abortion under the Article 296 of the Dutch Criminal Code (Gevers, 2006). Nonetheless, if the mother's life is at risk, the viability of the fetus, whose existence has ended due to an abortion is not taken into account according to the Article 82a of the Dutch Criminal Code (Dorscheidt, 1999).

As explained above, the Dutch law shares the approach adopted by certain of the USA. Consequently, the legislative regulations in favor of the fetus's protection are considered to be reflections of the society's invested interest in the fetus' existence. Parallely with the increasing of public campaigns and awareness concerning this issue, the national legislators assume even more protective and appropriate attitudes towards the protection of the fetus; moreover, these attitudes would be reflected in legislation even if not reflected in legal reality, as in the case of the USA and the Netherlands. It should be once more underlined, that a woman's right to privacy, to abortion in those cases, is restricted for the sake of the interests that society has invested in the fetus that are not the interests of the fetus itself. If this debate focuses on the benefit which the fetus has or should acquire from the social interests in its existence – I personally believe that this is the direction that the relevant debate currently took– it will be impossible and even undesirable to take claims claims inconsistent to the current legal reality seriously and even more- to expect certain rational and efficient results from their legal regulation. When the claim to acknowledge the fetus' personality and its right to life becomes the main element of this debate, it is only natural that the reaction of the women's rights supporters would be to reject this argument completely, since it does not accord with the reality of law. To put it bluntly, the shift of the focus in the current debate about rights –either the fetus's or women's- drags this issue into theoretical declinations which may be impossible to put into practice in any legal system while at the same time it marginalizes the benefit possible gained by their practical enforcement. Therefore, the legislative regulations concerning the protection of both the fetus and the women have to be applicable in legal practice and based on the objective information drawn from scientific facts as much as possible. Only in this way, it may be feasible to create a common ground on which the benefits propounded by both of the parties could be balanced and protected.

V. WHAT KIND OF PROTECTION DO WE NEED FOR THE WOMAN AND THE FETUS?

It is obvious that the use of concepts such as 'right' and 'personality' in order to support the moral demand for the fetus's protection within the framework of human rights and positive law, is not an appropriate approach to follow. But an individual as a biological being and mainly as human must be treated and protected within the framework of human rights during the prenatal period as well as afterwards; the same arguments stands for a woman's right to privacy at the same period. Its protection represents both a moral and legal requirement in the sense that it comes as a natural consequence of the principle that considers human rights as the basis of all positive law regulations in positive law. Accordingly, a solution to this challenge can inevitably be provided within the framework of human rights and positive law.

The most commonly accepted method by many legal orders concerning the fetus's protection nowadays, is to impose legal sanctions on any of the interventions realized by third persons and by the expectant mother against the fetus under certain conditions. The underlying justification for such a protection might vary from the recognition of the fetus as a rightholder or the protection of the public interest showed regarding the fetus's existence. Regardless of the justification, the selection of the sanctions to be imposed as well as the specific content of the conditions necessary in order to assess the legality of any interventions against the fetus are the factors which determine their practical consequences. In other words, not the legal wording itself but the protection provided underneath it, is what matters more. The claim that the fetus should be considered as a rightsholder results probably from the fact that the effectiveness of its current protection as provided in many national legal orders is debatable in some cases. Unfortunately, it is evident that the relevant national legal regulations are in some cases undeniably in contrast with the sense of justice.

Let us take a common legal approach adopted by many countries, including Turkey, towards the deliberate murder of a fetus. According to the Turkish law, the deliberate murder of the fetus, for example, a day before its birth is regarded as an aggravated case of the crime of illegal abortion or of intentional physical harm depending on the characteristics of the incident. In the case of the crime of illegal abortion, the sanction is imprisonment for 5-10 years and for the latter, the imprisonment is extending from 2-6 years. However, if the same act takes places only a while after the birth, for example about 30 seconds later, the perpetrator shall be sentenced to life imprisonment because the crime is then defined as murder. One could observe that essentially and substantively, no change has occurred within a day in the quality of the creature that has been killed. The difference exists only in the law's own reality and logic. The creature is recognized as a human being and an individual only after it leaves its mother's womb, whereas the same creature is not legally regarded as a human being or an individual while it still remains inside its mother. In reality, only a spatial difference stands for this significant change from the legal point of view. The reason is that any act realized before the fetus leaves its mother's womb, is actually regarded as an act directed to its mother's bodily integrity – i.e. the direct addressee of the intervention is not the fetus. On the contrary, after leaving its mother's body, the consequences of the act resulting in the murder of the fetus is considered as a more severe one, because the victim is acknowledged as a creature that owns a concrete legal personality. As indicated above, this is the case not only for Turkey but for many of the Continental legal systems. However, severe punishments are not necessarily prescribed only for the crimes that have been committed against a discrete and 'actual' rightholder in a specific legal order. It is possible to find some legal examples that are incompatible with the logic discussed above; thus, there are crimes that can be committed neither against an 'actual' individual, nor are their punishments lighter than the ones prescribed for the crimes committed against 'actual' individuals.

The legal debate concerning the fetus's protection cannot be limited only to the questions concerning the severity of sanctions. The thought that the fetus is not dealt with due regard in positive law surpasses the mere subject of the severity of sanctions and brings about the following idea:

the matter of the protection of the fetus calls for legislative regulative efforts in certain societies. The formation process of "The Unborn Victims Violence Act" known as "Laci and Conor's Law" in the USA is probably the best example of such a situation. During the lawsuit of a person, who had killed his 8 months pregnant wife and thus also the fetus in its mother's womb, a public discussion begun concerning the question of whether the perpetrator of the crime had committed two murders or one. In fact, this discussion could not really affect the case in its legal consequences, because the perpetrator would anyhow be imposed to the severest punishment, namely life imprisonment, due to the fact that he had killed his wife. As a result, the court adjudged that only one murder had occurred. Yet, with the influence of the intense discussion and the pressure of the public opinion, this incident initiated the formation of the federal legislation known as "The Unborn Victims Violence Act", which, similarly to the legislative efforts mentioned above, attempts to protect the fetus as a rightholder.

In the USA, during the past three decades, the legal sanctions prescribed for crimes against the fetus aggravated up to capital punishment, stem from the strong social support to the claim for the protection of the fetus' right to life and the political effectiveness of the American public opinion. In this frame, it is indeed remarkable that the legal wording used for the normative specification of the crimes against the fetus is the same as the one used for the crimes against 'actual' persons. Moreover, in certain legal orders, only by including the fetus into the concept of a "victim", can the crimes committed against any individual be applied to the acts against the fetus. In terms of normative law technique, these modes of crime, as mentioned before, look out for the society's and not the fetus's legal interests.

Overall, the motive hidden behind the public frustration concerning this issue, is the idea that the positive law does not show the necessary respect that the fetus deserves as a stage in the process of human life, from a formal or contextual point of view. The basic argument of this paper certainly does not include the dogmatic approaches of the pro-life groups which are mainly based on religious arguments. Nevertheless, in order to strengthen this perspective, it is futile to voice the basic argumentation of the religious dogmas that participate in this debate, emphasizing nonetheless that it does not accord with the law's own reality. The main counterfeit of this 'religious' argumentation is that it aims at enclosing a whole maturing process, through which a creature turns from a cell into a viable, human organism in one and only legal category. On the contrary, it should be understood that each phase in this 'maturing' process demands a different legal category and a separate and specific legislative regulation. In order to realize this, it is necessary to deal with the legislative regulations with regard to their quality and substance, setting aside the formal demands and use the information provided by technology and thereby science in order to specify and specifically handle the several phases the fetus passes through and consequently to take into account the unique qualifications that the fetus bears in each one of them. Only such an approach has the ability to direct the national legislators to adopt efficient legislative regulations in order to offer the fetus real protection and the respect it deserves from the positive law as a creature representing a certain stage of human life.

VI. THE FETUS'S PAIN AS A RESTRICTIVE CRITERION FOR ABORTION

It can be supported that the process the fetus passes through during the prenatal period as well as the qualifications that it acquires at each phase must be dealt via the invocation of separate and distinctive legal categories. However, it is vital to carefully specify both the qualifications of these phases and the normative conclusions that can be drawn by them, mainly because this categorization can possibly restrict –to a certain extent at least- the woman's liberation. Besides, it is obvious that more objective approaches based on scientific facts are necessary if we take into account that it is already quite difficult to legislatively find a balance commonly accepted by all interested parties on the subjects of "abortion" and the acknowledgment of the "fetus' legal personality", mainly because the opposite views supporting them are not only differently but also dogmatically expressed.

In this sense, I think that two are the most important qualifications that the fetus acquires during the pregnancy process, that can be significant as far as the relevant legislative regulations are concerned These are "viability" and the "ability of feeling pain", which have already been adopted to some extent by positive law. These two qualifications, which may easily be used for the regulation of both the methodical (i.e. the use of anesthesia in order to prevent the fetus from suffering) and the temporal (i.e. the definition of the phase after which abortion should be banned) aspects of the abortion process, may also provide us with the necessary and commonly accepted by all the interested parties, criteria. The 'viability' criteria have already been used as the basic elements in determining the time limits for a legally justified abortion in the well known decision *Roe v Wade* of United States of America Supreme Court, and as a threshold for the protection of the fetus against interventions during the prenatal period in an analogous way to the born babies according to the Dutch legal order.

The main questions on which I would like to dwell in this part are the following two: first, whether the fetus's "feeling pain" may, or should, be used as a criterion as far as abortion and the woman's liberation are concerned; second, in what way is it feasible to balance this criterion with the actual interests of both the fetus and the woman. In this frame, the "viability" qualification briefly mentioned above will not be discussed in detail at this point, namely because it goes beyond the scope and focus of this paper. The important question nevertheless is whether it is possible for the fetus to feel pain at any phase of the pregnancy? And if it is really possible, how can this phase be detected? These questions and others alike are in fact not easy to answer. In what way can we determine by certainty whether another person, human or pre-human being feels pain or not? It does not seem possible within today's scientific capacities to ascertain whether a fetus has the ability of feeling pain or not. Therefore, with the help of certain indications barely, we can only make some assumptions on whether a fetus feels the pain or not. Certainly, these estimations will be based on the facts presented by science and technology.

The primary scientific facts necessary in order to estimate the existence of pain in the fetus, concern the phase in which the anatomical characterists that enable us to feel the sense of pain are developed, namely the development of the nervous system. Nevertheless, one could observe that the respective literature is differentiated. Thus, there are authors claiming that a fetus can experience the feeling of pain even from the 8th week of gestation Others argue that the necessary anatomical characteristics that enable us to sense the feeling of pain are actually developed in far later periods and the ones claiming that the existence of a nervous system is not sufficient but it is needed to function at the same time, in order for the fetus to feel pain. Consequently, in the respective literature various time periods, starting from the 18th week of gestation are proposed in order to estimate the beginning of the feeling of pain (Benatar & Benetar, 2001). On the contrary to this approach, there are authors claiming that the fetus does not have the capacity of feeling pain in any way and, thereby, they support the view that the use of methods such as anesthesia, in order to prevent the fetus from suffering is needless (Derbyshire, 1999).

Yet, in its publication, the International Association for The Study of Pain (IASP) which may be regarded as one of the most competent associations in this area, argues the contrary:

The available scientific evidence makes it possible, even probable, that fetal pain perception occurs well before late gestation. Those attempting to deny or delay its occurrence must offer conclusive evidence for the absence of fetal pain at given levels of maturity. When developmental time is translated across animal species to humans, it is clear that functionally effective patterns of sensory processing develop during the second trimester. Thalamocortical interactions located in the subplate zone persist into maturity, thus providing a functional template for subsequent cortical processing. Several lines of evidence indicate that consciousness depends on a subcortical system and that certain contents of consciousness are located in cortical areas. These subcortical structures, which develop much earlier than the cortex, may play a pivotal role in sensory perception. Our current understanding of development provides the anatomical structures, the physiological mechanisms, and the functional evidence for pain perception developing in the second trimester, certainly not in the first trimester, but well before the third trimester of human gestation. (Anand, p.3).

Evidently, the Association does not intend to put an end to the current discussion on the issue in its publication. Neither does it underestimate or consider other equally significant scientific findings meaningless. However, while this claim is propounded on satisfactory grounds by several scientists, it is impossible to ignore it or to think that it won't influence also the relevant legal framework also. In fact, as recently as in April 2010, the State of Nebraska accepted a law banning abortion after the 20th week of gestation due to the fact that the fetus can actually feel the pain, although it is highly probable that the respected legislations would face problems concerning its constitutionality. Putting aside the questions concerning the extent to which this legislative effort will be applicable in the end or its compatibility with the woman's human rights, it should nonetheless be noted that it is one of the first legislative bill on the basis of the "pain" criterion.

Scientific conclusions stating that the fetus most probably can feel pain before its birth have apparently added a new dimension to the legal conflict between the fetus and the woman. Even though, it is not yet and beyond any doubt proven that the fetus feels pain before its birth, a high probability does exist and that makes pain a factor that has to be taken into account in the abortion debate. In positive law, to cause pain to any other living creature is sanctioned. To give another example from the Turkish legal order, the Animal Protection Act in its first article, expresses as the main aim of the Act as; "... *to provide animals with comfortable life conditions and good and convenient treatments, enable the best protection for animals against pain, suffering and torture and prevent any grievances of them...*" Can any of us consider this legally defined scope which intents to prevent and thus protect animals especially from pain, odd? Really, isn't it quite natural for any rational and sentient person to react against any pain experienced by any being or living creature, human or not? Thus, the human sensibility against any actions causing fetal pain during the prenatal period renders the legislative regulation in this field necessary; a regulation that can meet the standards of both sides in the abortion controversy and can also acknowledge the need for a 'pain sensitive' approach on the subject. In this framework, the need for the fetus to be protected from pain represents a strong interest for the society which can be balanced and even leveled towards the woman's right to privacy.

Nevertheless, the main point expressed in this contribution is not that abortion must be banned in the period where the feeling of pain begins to be perceived by the fetus and that consequently the woman's right to privacy must be limited by a legislative prohibition on abortion at this certain stage of the pregnancy. Moreover, I agree with the view that recognition of the fetus' personality and its right to life before its birth is inconsistent to the 'born alive principle' and could eventually lead to the abuse of a woman's rights or could even result in various other problems for the respected legal orders. Therefore, I do not maintain that the fetal pain perception phase should be considered the threshold for the definition of the beginning of the fetus's right to life and thus of its legal personality. However, I claim that the possible existence of a phase during pregnancy where the fetus can actually experience the 'feeling of pain' should lead us to new regulations as far as abortion is concerned. What I really mean is that it is necessary to establish new legal mechanisms, aiming at providing the least possible or even no pain for the fetus during its extraction from the mother's womb, beginning from the phase in which pain perception starts, rather than to subject abortion to a much more strict regulation. Even if it is does not seem highly possible that the differences concerning the legislative regulation of abortion amongst diverse societies could disappear in a short period of time, at least certain standards that could prevent the feeling of pain by the fetus, during its extraction from the woman's body, could be developed. I absolutely maintain that the pain criteria could not construe the basis for regarding the protection of the fetus as a value superior to the pregnant woman's right to privacy.

The pain criteria offer a new approach to the protection of the fetus, not as important in method as in substance. In order to protect the fetus by using the pain criteria, it does not seem to bes necessary to either invoke that it has the right to lifeor to prove that it owns a legal personality. If our societies attribute a certain value to any being, human or pre-human they must make sure that this does not result in a human rights violation (i. e. the protection of the fetus must not result in the limitation of the woman's liberation). Nonetheless, the effort for the legal recognition of values which go beyond the law's current logic and reality does not merely call for legal amendments but also for a radical transformation of the very grounds of the current legal system.

REFERENCES

Anand, K. J. S. (2006, June). Fetal pain? *Pain: Clinical Updates*, *14*(2), 1–4.

Beller, F. K., & Zlatnik, G. P. (1995). The beginning of human life. *Journal of Assisted Reproduction and Genetics*, *12*(8), 477–483. doi:10.1007/BF02212909

Benetar, D., & Benetar, M. (2001). A pain in the fetus: Toward ending confusion about fetal pain. *Bioethics*, *15*(1), 57–76. doi:10.1111/1467-8519.00212

Bonin, D. (2002). *Defense of abortion*. Cambridge, UK: Cambridge University Press. doi:10.1017/CBO9780511610172

Brobst, J. A. (2006, Spring). The prospect of enacting an unborn victims of violence act in North Carolina. *North Carolina Central Law Journal*, 127–171.

Brody, B. (1975). *Abortion and the sanctity of human life*. Cambridge, MA: MIT Press.

Brody, B. (1988). *On the humanity of the fetus. What is a person?* (pp. 229–250). Clifton, NJ: Humana Press.

Burgess, J. A., & Tawai, S. A. (1996). When did you first begin to feel it? Locating the beginning of human consciousness. *Bioethics*, *10*, 1–26. doi:10.1111/j.1467-8519.1996.tb00100.x

Crum, G., & McCormack, T. (1992). *Abortion: Pro-choice or pro-life?* Washington, DC: American University Press.

Dorsheidt, J. (1999). The unborn child and the UN Convention on Children's Rights: The Dutch perspective as a guideline. *The International Journal of Children's Rights*, *7*, 303–347. doi:10.1163/157181899920494426

Gever, S. (2006). Abortion legislation and the future of the 'counseling model'. *European Journal of Health Law*, *13*, 27–40. doi:10.1163/157180906777036355

Gilbert, S., Tyler, A., & Zackin, E. (2005). *Bioethics and the new embryology: Springboards for debate*. Sunderland, MA: Sinauer Associates.

Güngör, H. A. (2007). Yaşam Hakkı. Unpublished doctoral thesis. Istanbul Kultur University, Turkey.

Hensen, W. F. (2005, Winter). The disabling impact of wrongful birth and wrongful life action. *Harvard Civil Rights-Liberties Law Review*, pp. 141-196.

Holtzapfel, M. (2002, Summer). The right to live, the right to choose, and the Unborn Victims of Violence Act. *The Journal of Contemporary Health Law and Policy*, 443–445.

Human Right Commision. (2000). General Comment 28: Equality of Rights Between, Men and Women, 68th Session.

Inter-American Commission on Human Rights. (1981, October 6). Annual Report 1980-1981. OEA/Ser.L/V/II.54, Doc. 9 rev. 1.

Irwing, D. (1999). When do human beings begin? Scientific myths and scientific facts. *International Sociology and Social Policy*, *19*(3/4), 22–46. doi:10.1108/01443339910788730

Lancet. (2006, November 4). Executive summary of sexual and reproductive health series.

Lugosi, C. I. (2007). Conforming to the rule of law: When person and human being finally mean the same thing in fourteenth amendment jurisprudence. *Issues in Law & Medicine*, *22*, 119–303.

Morowitz, H. J., & Trefil, J. (1992). *The facts of life: Science and the abortion controversy*. Oxford, UK: Oxford University Press.

Morris, A., & Saintier, S. (2003, Summer). To be or not to be: Is that the question? Wrongful life and misconception. *Medical Law Review*,167–191. doi:10.1093/medlaw/11.2.167

Noonan, J. T. (1970). *An almost absolute value in history. The morality of abortion: Legal and historical perspectives*. Cambridge, MA: Harvard University Press.

Oğuzman, M. K., Seliçi, Ö., & Oktay, S. (2005). *Kişiler Hukuku*. Istanbul, Turkey: Filiz.

Shah, M. K. (2001). Inconsistencies in the legal status of unborn child: Recognition of a fetus as a potential life. *Hofstra Law Review*, *29*(3), 931–969.

Shanon, T. A., & Wolter, A. B. (1990). Reflection on the moral status of the pre-embryo. *Theological Studies*, *5*, 603–626.

UN Human Right Commission. (2000). General Comment 28: Equality of Rights Between, Men and Women, CCPR/C/21/Rev.1/Add.10, 68th Session.

UN Human Rights Committee. (1998, August 18). CCPR/C/79/Add.92, Ecuador.

ENDNOTE

1 I am utterly grateful to the editor Christina M. Akrivopoulou for the linguistic editing of this paper.

Chapter 9
Balancing the Protection of Genetic Data and National Security in the Era of New Technology:
The Role of the European Court of Human Rights

Cristina Contartese
University of Bologna, Italy

ABSTRACT

The aim of this work is to examine the European Court of Human Rights' (ECtHR) balancing exercise between genetic data protection and national security, under Article 8 of the European Convention of Human Rights (ECHR). It analyzes, more specifically, the core principles of the Strasbourg Court that the Council of Europe's Contracting States are required to apply when they collect and store genetic data in order to reach specific purposes in terms of public security, such as the fight against crimes. It will emerge that the Court, in consideration of the risks new technologies pose to an individual's data safeguards, pays special attention to the strict periods of storage of such data and requires that their collection be justified by the existing of a pressing social need and a "careful scrutiny" of the principle of proportionally between the intrusive measure and the aim pursued. This work is divided into three main parts. The first part provides a general overview on personal data protection under Article 8, while the second and third part concentrate, respectively, on the collection of genetic data and on their storage for police purposes.

I. INTRODUCTION

In the era of new technologies, where collecting, storing and disclosing data is easier and faster and where sensitive data, such as genetic information, can be extracted, personal data deserve a special attention in the context of the more general right to privacy, where the protection of personal data falls. Privacy, in order to preserve human dignity, serves mainly three purposes: individuality, inti-

DOI: 10.4018/978-1-60960-083-9.ch009

macy, and liberty (Chadwick, 2006). However, in society, privacy is not an absolute right. Other values, such as national security, compete with it. States, in their domestic legislation, therefore, have to establish the compromise, that technology is creating complexities between the different interests at stake. The aim of this paper is to investigate to what extent the European Court of Human Rights (ECtHR) protects a particular category of personal data, that is, genetic data, under Art. 8 of the European Convention of Human Rights (ECHR). As it is known, DNA, which is unique in each person, stands for deoxyribonucleic acid and contains full genetic information of an individual. Over recent years, in the Council of Europe's Member States, there has been considerable practice towards compiling a comprehensive national DNA database. This latter can serve two possible objectives, that is, investigative purposes and/or the mere inclusion in a database. In the first case, DNA information has a forensic value, being a powerful tool for the investigation of offences, as it can determine the innocence of a person suspected of having committed an offence as well as providing probative evidence of guilt. In the second case, the aim is to enlarge the inclusiveness of the database itself. This work examines, more specifically, when the collection and retention of genetic data, by a State, is perceived necessary in order to reach specific purposes in terms of public security, such as the fight against crimes. In other words, it seeks to provide how the ECtHR balances the right to protection of genetic data and a State's necessity to guarantee national security against crimes, in consideration of the risks new technologies pose to an individual's information safeguards. This work is divided into three main parts. The first part provides a general overview on personal data protection under Art. 8, while the second and third part concentrate, respectively, on the collection of genetic data and their storage for police purposes.

II. THE RIGHT TO PERSONAL DATA PROTECTION UNDER THE ECHR

Under Art. 8, par. 1 of the ECHR, providing that 'everyone has the right to respect for his private and family life, his home and his correspondence', the right to respect for 'private life' is 'a broad term not susceptible to exhaustive definition' (*Peck v. United Kingdom*, para. 57). As indicated by the Court, elements such as gender identification, name, sexual orientation and sexual life are important elements of the personal sphere protected by Article 8, as well as the right to personal development, to establish and develop relationships with other human beings and the outside world. Art. 8 imposes two categories of obligations, that is a "negative" and a "positive" obligation. The "negative" obligation refers to avoiding interference with Art. 8, par. 1 unless the conditions in Art. 8, par. 2 are satisfied. The "positive" obligation indicates taking actions to protect individuals' private life, particularly against interference by third persons. According to the doctrine, five sub-categories of private life interest can be identified from within the Art. 8 jurisprudence:

First, there are the three "freedoms from" rights (the first two of which correspond loosely with traditional private law conceptions of "privacy") – the right to be free *from* interference with physical and psychological integrity, *from* unwanted access to and collection of information, and *from* serious environmental pollution. Then there are the "freedoms to" – the right to be free *to* develop one's identity and *to* live one's life in the manner of one's choosing" (Moreham, 2008).

It is, in fact, accepted that protection of personal information is part of the "privacy" interest. "Personal data", under the Council of Europe Convention of 1981 for the protection of individuals with regard to automatic processing of personal data ("the Data Protection Convention"), is defined as "any information relating to an identified or identifiable individual" (Art. 2).

The notion of personal data is, therefore, broad and comprise any kind of information that can relate to identified or identifiable persons. The Council of Europe has displayed special attention not only to automatic processed data, but also to data used in criminal proceedings, insurance purposes, privacy on the Internet, medical data, etc. In this regard, it has adopted several Recommendations that are important, despite their not binding value, since they illustrate the principles that the Contracting States should apply on these issues, such as Recommendation No.R (87) 15 of the Committee of Ministers to Member States regulating the use of personal data in the police sector (17 September 1987) and Recommendation No. R (92)1 on the use of analysis of deoxyribonucleic acid (DNA) within the framework of the criminal justice system (10 February 1992). It has also promoted some international conventions, such as the Convention for the protection of human rights and dignity of the human being with regard to the application of biology and medicine, known as the Oviedo Convention (4 April 1997).

The Court has clearly recognized the relevance of protecting personal data, stating that "the protection of personal data is of fundamental importance to a person's enjoyment of his or her right to respect for private and family life, as guaranteed by Article 8 of the Convention" (*M.S. v. Sweden,* 1997), and that the domestic law must afford appropriate safeguards to prevent any such use of personal data as may be inconsistent with the guarantees of this Article. With respect to the fight against crimes in our technological era, where the notion of personal data extends to different electronic means, such as ATMs, credit cards, GPS-equipped vehicles, emails, mobile phones, the Court has specifically observed that "the protection afforded by Article 8 of the Convention would be unacceptably weakened if the use of modern scientific techniques in the criminal-justice system were allowed at any cost and without carefully balancing the potential benefits of the extensive use of such techniques against important private-life interests" (*S. and Marper*, para. 112).

As it is known, the right to privacy and to respect for private life is not an absolute right, unlike other provisions of the Convention, as established by Art. 15. In some cases, the Court is required to balance the respect for private life with the other rights protected by the Convention, such as the balancing exercise between the freedom of expression, established by Art. 10, and the right to privacy under Art. 8. In other cases, the right to privacy is subject to certain conditions expressly specified by the same Art. 8, par. 2. The Court, when it establishes that there has been an interference with one of the rights in Art. 8, par. 1, has to ascertain if the interference is justified. In order to satisfy Art. 8, par. 2, three requirements have to be met. Firstly, the interference must be "in accordance with the law", which means that the national law must be compatible with the rule of law; secondly, a measure has to pursue one of the "legitimate aims" specified in Art. 8, par. 2, that is "the interests of national security, public safety or the economic well-being of the country, for the prevention of disorder or crime, for the protection of health or morals, or for the protection of the rights and freedoms of others"; thirdly, a measure must be "necessary in a democratic society", that means that the interference must correspond to 'a pressing social need' and be proportionate to the legitimate aim pursued.

In the next sections, the purpose is to specifically analyze to what extent a State can legitimately collect genetic information of its citizens in order to pursue policies of national security, and whether it can store the information obtained. Although these two different aspects of privacy, that is collection and retention of personal data, are, from a practical point of view, "inextricably intertwined", they can also be conceptualized. Part of the doctrine, referring to DNA information, specifies that "the aspect of privacy violated by the former is bodily integrity or personal privacy; it overrides the autonomy of the individual to make decisions as to the uses to which their body should be put. The issue raised by retention and future use of DNA samples so obtained concerns some aspect of informational privacy" (Roberts & Taylor, 2005). The latter, in particular, "appears to involve an interference with privacy by virtue of the loss of control over personal information that is involved" (Roberts & Taylor, 2005). With this distinction in mind, we approach, in the next section, the legal issues that genetic data collection raises.

III. THE COLLECTION OF GENETIC DATA UNDER THE ECHR

The collection of genetic data in criminal proceedings poses several legal issues as their use is constantly expanding. The taking of such data, which began, mainly, for the most serious offences, has progressively expanded to include new applications for forensic analysis, such as familial searches. In order to establish to what extent a State can legitimately collect the genetic data of its citizens for national security concern, the Court has, firstly, to ascertain if there was an interference with private life. Secondly, if this is justified under Art. 8.

a. The Collection of Personal Data as an Interference with Private Life

The first core issue that the Court clarified in its jurisprudence was whether the collection of personal information amounts to an interference with private life under Art. 8. It is uncontroversial, for the Court, that the coercive taking of personal information, containing unique and sensitive information, such as a sample of DNA and cellular material, amounted to 'an intrusion upon the applicant's privacy' (*Van der Velden v. Netherlands*, para. 2) even though the applicant was aware of the collection of their data. In more general terms, the Commission, in *Peters v. Netherlands*, where the applicant was submitted to a compulsory urine test in order to ascertain the presence of drugs in his body, established that 'compulsory medical intervention even if it is of minor importance, must be considered an interference with the right of respect for private life'. The Commission reached the same conclusion in *X v. Netherlands* (App. No. 8239/78), related to the taking of a blood sample from a driver for an alcohol test. From the ECtHR's case-law, it emerged that the notion of interference, applied to the collection of personal data, is a broad one. In fact, although the collection of data with the consent of an individual can be distinguished from one which takes place without his/her knowledge, according to the Court, 'private-life considerations may arise once *any systematic or permanent record* comes into existence of such material from the public domain' (*Copland v. UK*, para. 57).

For this reason, the collection of personal information relating to a person's telephone, as well as to their email and internet usage at work, *without their knowledge,* amounts to an interference with an individual's private life, even though aiming at ensuring that the facilities provided by a publicly funded employer were not abused (*Copland v. UK*, para. 44). Files gathered by the security services on a particular individual fall within the scope of Art. 8, even when the information has not been collected by any intrusive or covert method (*Rotaru v. Romania*, para. 43-44). A permanent record of a person's voice by taping of telephone conversations, relevant to identifying that person in the context of other personal data, must be regarded as concerning the processing of personal data about the applicants (*P.G. and J. H.*, para. 59), while the taking of photographs at a public demonstration in a public place and retained by the police in a file does not amount to an interference with private life as no action had been taken to identify the persons photographed on that occasion by means of data processing (*Friedl*, para. 49-52) as well as the monitoring of a person's actions in a public place by the use of photographic equipment which did not record the data would not in itself give rise to an interference (*Peck*, para. 50). The decision in *Lüdi v. Switzerland* is more controversial as the Court held that the use of an undercover police officer did not interfere in the private life of the applicant who was involved in a large-scale drug-smuggling network as he must have been aware that he was committing a serious offence and ran the risk of encountering an undercover police officer (*Lüdi v. Switzerland,* para. 40).

In brief, with the sole exception of *Lüdi*, that part of the doctrine has interpreted as a decision which applied only to situations where the police use an undercover officer to conduct a test-purchase effectively merely confirming the guilt (Gillespie, 2009), the ECtHR recognized that collection of personal data, with or without the knowledge of the person involved, constitutes an interference under Art. 8 when it is pursued with the aim of identifying, specifically, a person. The automatic processing of personal data, therefore, amounts constantly to an interference.

b. The Expression "in Accordance with the Law"

Although a State's measure is considered as an interference by the Court, the Convention recognizes that such a measure could be in the interest of national security and the prevention of disorder and crime. This is why the Court's examination has to ascertain that domestic law provides protection against arbitrary interference with an individual's right under Article 8. The first standard that the Court sets up in relation to the collection of personal information is the requirement that this practice is 'in accordance with the law'.

The expression "in accordance with the law" not only requires that the impugned measure should have some basis in domestic law, but it also refers to the *quality of the law* in question, requiring that it should be *accessible* to the person concerned and *foreseeable* as to its effects (*Kopp v. Switzerland*, para. 55). In order to fulfill the requirement of foreseeability, 'the law must be sufficiently clear in its terms to give individuals an adequate indication as to the circumstances in which and the conditions on which the authorities are empowered to resort to any such measures' (*Copland*, par. 46). In particular, referring to interceptions, the Court holds that the law has to display special precision, and outlining the issue of technology development, it establishes that "it is essential to have clear, detailed rules on the subject, especially as the technology available for use is continually becoming more sophisticated" (*Kopp v. Switzerland*, para. 72).

The notion of "in accordance with the law", therefore, displays three requirements, that is, the legal basis in domestic law; accessibility of the law; and the foreseeability of the law. In the *Amann* case, where the applicant's telephone call was intercepted fortuitously by the police, the Court reaches the conclusion that interference with the private life of the applicant cannot be considered to have been "in accordance with the law" since Swiss law did not establish sufficiently the scope and conditions of exercise of the authorities' discretionary power in case of persons monitored "fortuitously" as "necessary participants" in a telephone conversation (*Amann*, para. 61-62). In *P.G. and J.H.*, the Court reaches the same conclusion about both the use of covert listening devices in private place and in the police station. Concerning the first, at the time of the events, there existed no statutory system to regulate the police's use of covert listening devices at private place as these measures were governed by the Home Office Guidelines, which were neither legally binding nor directly accessible to the public, while in relation to police station, there were domestic provisions concerning covert surveillance on police premises, but no statutory system existed to regulate the use of covert listening devices by the police on their own premises (*P.G. and J.H. v. UK*, para. 37, 63). In *Taylor-Sabori*, where part of the prosecution case against the applicant consisted of the contemporaneous written notes of the pager messages which had been transcribed by the police, the Court established that, at the time of the events, there was no statutory system in existence to specifically regulate the interception of pager messages transmitted via a private telecommunication system (*Taylor-Sabori v. UK*, para. 19). In *Klass v. Germany*, the Court guarantees substantial safeguards to the applicant, stating that "factual indications" have to be present before surveillance can be undertaken (*Klass v. Germany*, para. 40).

Finally, Art. 8 requires that the collection of personal data is "necessary in a democratic society". Among the ECtHR's case-law, *Z. v. Finland* offers a significant example of this notion. Here, the Court finds that the seizure of the applicant's medical records, concerning HIV status, in order to include them in the investigation file as evidence in domestic proceedings, was supported by relevant and sufficient reasons. Such information was among the variety of data that could be relevant in the proceedings, and therefore, their taking override the applicant's interest for respect to private life (*Z. v. Finland*, para. 109-110).

Another legal issue that the collection of genetic data raises is whether such a measure, after a sentence has been imposed, has to be regarded as a further penalty. In *Van der Velden*, the applicant, besides the alleged violation of Art. 8, complained under Art. 7 of the Convention that the taking of a sample of cellular material and the storage of DNA profile amounted to an extra penalty in respect of the sentence he received for his conviction. The Court, therefore, examined whether this measure was a "penalty". It concluded that given the fact the measure operates completely separately from the ordinary sentencing procedures, and was not severe, such a measure did not amount to a "penalty".

From the analysis of the ECtHR's case-law, it emerges that the Court paid special attention to the future development of technology in relation to States' practice of collecting personal data for investigative and criminal purposes. Advances in technology, in fact, have transformed the way this practice can be conducted. States are, therefore, required to provide detailed and specific legislation each time a new technique is applied. While the taking of genetic data has not specifically been addressed by the ECtHR, from its jurisprudence, it could be inferred that DNA samples could be coactively taken from a person if such a measure emerges as relevant for national security. However, new techniques have emerged, such as the "DNA dragnet", that is the collection of DNA from a large group of individuals, who fit the general description of the offender, to search for the perpetrator of a crime. The legitimacy of this practice could be challenged under Art. 8 as it implies an indiscriminate collection of personal information from people who are not neither charged nor convicted of an offense. Probably, the Court would not exclude the use of genetic data from these categories of individuals as far as the circumstances of the case warrant such action. That is, this technique would be justified only for the most serious offenses and, therefore, it could not be applied to any kind of crime.

IV. GENETIC DATA RETENTION UNDER THE ECHR: THE PRINCIPLE OF PROPORTIONALITY BETWEEN PRIVATE AND PUBLIC INTERESTS

As stated above, a DNA database contains genetic profiles that the police, when necessary, use to verify if they match with a crime scene. The main legal issues that the existence of such a database poses are related to the length of time a person's genetic information can be retained, and to a State's legitimacy to expand it, for public interests concerns, with profiles of non convicted persons. In the ECtHR's case-law, the leading case is *S. and Marper*, in which the Court investigates if the UK's automatic retention of DNA samples, profiles and fingerprints from those persons who had been suspected, but not convicted, of any offences is a breach of the right to a private life under Art. 8 of the Convention. The issue to be analyzed by the Court is whether the retention of fingerprint and DNA data of persons who are not convicted of any criminal offences, was necessary in a democratic society. The Court, in fact, does not question that "the fight against crime, and in particular against organized crime and terrorism, which is one of the challenges faced by today's European societies, depends to a great extent on the use of modern scientific techniques of investigation and identification. The techniques of DNA analysis were acknowledged by the Council of Europe more than fifteen years ago as offering advantages to the criminal-justice system (see Recommandation R (92) 1 of the Committee of Ministers)" (*S. and Marper v. UK*, para. 105).

As noted by the Court, the UK legislation on data retention for investigative and criminal matters, specifically England, Wales and Northern Ireland, but not Scotland, represented, among the Council of Europe's Member States, an isolated case. In fact, while a majority of its Member States allows the compulsory taking of fingerprints and cellular samples in the context of criminal proceedings only for limited periods of time, the UK Police and Criminal Evidence Act (PACE) allowed, at the time of the decision, the indefinite retention of fingerprint and DNA material of any person of any age *suspected* of any recordable offence.

a. The Retention of Genetic Data as an Interference

In *S. and Marper*, the first question that the Court had to analyze is whether the mere retention of cellular samples, DNA profiles and fingerprints amounts to an interference with the applicants' right to respect for their private lives, within the meaning of Article 8 § 1 of the Convention. Taking into consideration the nature and scope of the information contained in each of these three categories of the data, the Court believed it was appropriate to examine the issue of retention of cellular samples and DNA profiles separately, on one hand, and fingerprints, on the other. In relation to cellular samples and DNA profiles, the Strasbourg Court displayed a deep concern for the developments in the field of genetics and information technology. The Court, maintaining the view expressed in *Van der Velden*, articulates its concern on the fact that, 'given the use to which cellular material could conceivably be put in the future, the systematic retention of that material was sufficiently intrusive to disclose interference with the right to respect for private life'.

Concern about the conceivable use of cellular material in the future is not the only element that influences the Court in concluding that there is an interference with Art. 8. The Court recalls that both cellular samples and DNA profiles contain highly personal and sensitive information about an individual. They provide the unique genetic code of each individual and also, for example, information about health. Other elements, such as the possible infrequency of familial searches, the safeguards attached, the fact that profiles are intelligible only with the use of computer technology and capable of being interpreted by a limited number of persons, do not affect the conclusion of the Court. This latter stated, in fact, that the retention of both cellular samples and DNA profiles discloses an interference with the applicants' right to respect for their private lives, within the meaning of Art. 8, para. 1 of the Convention.

The UK Courts, in *S. and Marper*, on the issue of the interference of the three categories of data with the right to respect for private life, found that retention of fingerprints and DNA profiles reveal only limited personal information, and that the benefits in achieving the aim of prosecuting and preventing crime are greater than the risks. Therefore, they concluded that there was no interference with Art. 8 or there was, at most, a very modest interference (see *S. and Marper*, para.

13-25). As pointed out by the doctrine, this finding is a disappointing aspect of the UK decisions (Roberts A., Taylor N., 2005). Nevertheless, it is interesting to note that, in reaching this finding, the UK Courts relied on two decisions of the former European Commission of Human Rights on the retention of fingertips and photographs, that is *McVeigh, O'Neill and Evans v United Kingdom* and *Kinnunen v Finland*. In *McVeigh*, the Commission did not reach a clear position on the issue of interference of fingerprints retention with Art. 8, stating that 'it is open to question whether the retention of fingerprints, photographs and records of such information amounts to an interference with the applicants' right to respect for private life under art. 8(1) of the Convention', while in *Kinnunen*, the Commission found that the retention of fingerprints and photographs in connection with a charge of fraud was not an interference with Art. 8 as they did not contain any subjective appreciations which called for refutation.

The *S. and Marper* case also revealed to be useful on the issue of fingerprints because it clarified the approach of the Court in this respect. The key element is whether the data at issue, despite their content and future potential use, enter in a data-processing system. The Court stresses that the applicants' fingerprint records are personal data which contain certain external identification features as personal photographs or voices samples. The fact that personal data enter in a data-processing system could give rise to private life considerations. While in *Friedl*, the Commission, addressing special attention to the fact that the photographs did not enter in a data-processing system and that the authorities did not intend to identify the persons photographed by means of data-processing, considered that the retention of anonymous photographs that have been taken at a public demonstration did not interfere with the right to respect for private life, in *P.G. and J.H.*, the Court considered that the recording of data and the systematic or permanent nature of the record could give rise to private-life considerations even though the data in question may have been available in the public domain or otherwise.

In *S. and Marper*, the Court reached the conclusion that the general approach taken in respect of photographs and voice samples should also apply to fingerprints. The Court accordingly concluded that 'the retention of fingerprints on the authorities' records in connection with an identified or identifiable individual may in itself give rise, notwithstanding their objective and irrefutable character, to important private-life concerns' (*S. and Marper*, para. 85-86). Therefore, the Court reiterated that the storing, by a public authority, of information relating to an individual's private life amounts to an interference within the meaning of Article 8. Neither the subsequent use of the stored information nor the difference between sensitive and not sensitive data has bearing on that finding (*Amann*, para. 69-70).

b. The Interference as "Necessary in a Democratic Society"

The most relevant issue that the Court had to analyze on the retention of genetic data is the existence of justification for the interference with an individual's private life, that is, whether the retention of fingerprints and DNA information is necessary in a democratic society. In *S. and Marper*, while it is not questioned that the retention policy is 'in accordance with the law' and pursues a legitimate aim, that is detection and prevention of crime, the Court had to establish, under Art. 8, par. 2, whether the UK had properly balanced national security concerns and the competing interests of preserving respect for private life. The principle of proportionality requires a "careful scrutiny" of the measures adopted by the State, that is a consideration on whether the degree of interference is higher than necessary to achieve that aim. With regard to national security, the core principles in the protection of personal data, which are particularly sensitive, such as genetic information, require "the retention of data to be proportionate in relation to the purpose of collection and insist on limited periods of storage" (*S. and Marper*, para. 107). These principles, consistently applied by the Contracting States, are indicated in relevant instruments of the Council of Europe, such as the Data Protection Convention, Recommendation R (87) 15 of the Committee of Ministers regulating the use of personal data in the police sector, and Recommendation No. R (92) 1 of the Committee of Ministers on the use of analysis of DNA within the framework of the criminal justice system. The Court outlined that the strong consensus existing among the Contracting States on this issue is of considerable importance and narrows the margin of appreciation left to the respondent State in the assessment of the limits of the interference with private life. Moreover, it stressed the responsibility of the UK in this field, stating that 'any State claiming a pioneer role in the development of new technologies bears special responsibility for striking the right balance in this regard' (*S. and Marper*, para. 112).

Therefore, the Court's conclusion was that the respondent State overstepped its margin of appreciation as the blanket and indiscriminate nature of retention of the fingerprints, cellular samples and DNA profiles of persons suspected but not convicted of offences, failed to strike a fair balance between public and private interests. Accordingly, the UK approach to genetic data retention is a disproportionate interference with the applicants' right to respect for private life and could not be regarded as necessary in a democratic society. The Court has also expressed special concern, from a social point of view, on the inclusion of unconvicted persons in the DNA databases. In particular, the Court recognized the risk of stigmatization since persons who have not been convicted of any offence and are entitled to the presumption of innocence, are treated in the same way as convicted persons. In case of minors, the retention of unconvicted persons' data could result harmful, given the special situation and the importance of their development and integration in society.

It is worth noting that the UK has recently modified its legislation on data retention, in the Crime and Security Act 2010 (April 2010), as a response to the Strasbourg's decision. In establishing the periods of genetic data storage, the UK displays special regard to the age of data subjects, distinguishes between 'qualify offences' and 'other recording offences', and between persons convicted or charged and those who give voluntarily data. However, the UK legislation may still be in violation of the Convention as the 6-year limit for retention of an innocent person's DNA does not take into consideration the specific circumstances of the unconvicted persons under the age of 18.

c. The Consistency of ECHR's Jurisprudence on Genetic Data

In *Van der Velden*, the applicant complained that a mouth swab was taken after being sentenced to six years' imprisonment for robbery as, under the Dutch law, a sample of cellular material can be taken from a person who has been convicted of an offence carrying a statutory maximum prison sentence of at least four years, and can be retained for twenty or thirty years, in relation to the severity of the offence. Here, the Court, following the same reasoning as it did in *S. and Marper,* reached the conclusion that the retention of genetic data was 'necessary in a democratic society'. In relation to the alleged violation of Art. 8 ECHR, the Court displayed a special sensitivity for the retention of cellular material and DNA profiles. In fact, recalling that, in *Kunnunen v. Finland* case, the former Commission found that fingerprints 'did not contain any subjective appreciations which might need refuting', and therefore, that the retention of that material did not constitute an interference with private life, the Court specified that:

while a similar reasoning may currently also apply to the retention of cellular material and DNA profiles, the Court nevertheless considers that, given *the use to which cellular material in particular could conceivably be put in the future*, the systematic retention of that material goes beyond the scope of neutral identifying features such as fingerprints, and is sufficiently intrusive to constitute an interference with the right to respect for private life set out in Article 8 § 1 of the Convention.

However, although the Court reached the conclusion that the taking of cellular samples constitutes an interference with the private life of the applicant, it held that the measure at issue is "necessary in a democratic society". The Court, in *Van der Velden*, underlined that:

in the first place [...] there can be no doubt about the substantial contribution which DNA records have made to law enforcement in recent years. Secondly, it is to be noted that while the interference at issue was relatively slight, the applicant may also reap a certain benefit from the inclusion of his DNA profile in the national database in that he may thereby be rapidly eliminated from the list of persons suspected of crimes in the investigation of which material containing DNA has been found.

Consistently with its previous case law, the Court concluded that taking of a mouth swab, in order to obtain cellular material, amounts to interference in the right to respect for private life. Because of the use to which this material could conceivably be put in the future, its systematic retention goes beyond the scope of neutral identifying features such as fingerprints, and is sufficiently intrusive to constitute interference in the right to respect for private life. However, it is not unreasonable for the obligation to undergo DNA testing to be imposed on all persons who have been convicted of offences of a certain seriousness. In particular, the Court focused on positive aspects of DNA data retention on detection and prevention of crime.

Comparing *S. and Marper* with *Van der Velden*, which are not in contrast to the ECtHR recent case law, remarkable differences emerge. At first glance, the key difference relies, obviously, on the fact that in *S. and Marper* the applicants have not been convicted of any crime, while in *Van der Velden*, the applicant had been sentenced to six years' imprisonment. Moreover, the Dutch law, unlike the UK legislation, was proportionate in relation to the nature and gravity of offences and any special circumstances under which the offence was committed. The Court reiterated this position on three recent judgments of 17 December 2009, concerning the automatic processing of personal data for police purposes, and having France as respondent State, that is, *Bouchacourt v. France*, *M.B. v. France*, *Gardel v. France*. Here, the Court concluded that, although the automatic processing of personal data for police purposes constitutes an interference with Art. 8, there was a fair balance between the private and public interests in consideration of the severity of the offences committed and the limited time of storage foreseen by the French law.

The ECtHR's case law on genetic data retention is interesting for several reasons. First of all, this is an affirmation of the importance of personal privacy rights in individuals' relationship with their State, even in the context of crime prevention (Beattie, 2009). In fact, the UK's mere reasoning on national security concern was not sufficient to justify an intrusion in a person's private life. Secondly, it underlines the need for the State to provide compelling justifications for genetic data retention. Finally, the Court stressed, once again, how problematic the use of genetic information could be with the constant progress of technology. If it could still be questionable whether fingerprints retention amounts to an interference with a person's private life under Art. 8, as stated in *Kinnunen* and recalled in *Van der Velden*, the same cannot be said about cellular material for the use to which they could conceivably be put in the future. It is also significant the Court's call to the 'special responsibility' of a country in developing DNA technology and how this affects the principle of proportionality.

V. CONCLUSION

With the progress of new technology, one of the most delicate issues, in the context of national security and more specifically of criminal proceedings, is States' opportunity to seize and store genetic information of individuals who have been convicted or charged with an offense. As pointed out, national DNA database is, at first glance, an attractive proposition in facilitating detection and prevention of serious crimes, however, this practice can potentially undermine an individual's freedom and raise legal, ethical and social problems. Therefore, protection of personal data creates a dilemma for the domestic authorities. States are required to establish, in their legislation, the right balance exercise between privacy and national security.

This paper has aimed to stress the important role of the ECtHR's jurisprudence in establishing the principles to fairly balance genetic data protection and public security. In fact, while the Court has clearly expressed the importance of collecting and storing genetic data in the fight against crimes, at the same time, it has clarified that such a purpose does not constitute a blanket justification for their unlimited use and expansion. The contribution of the ECtHR, in its consistent jurisprudence, set up how the benefits have to be assessed with privacy interests. According to the Court, the mere retention of personal data by public authorities, however obtained, are to be regarded as having direct impact on the private-life interest of an individual concerned, irrespective of whether subsequent use is made of the data. In the era of new technology, the Strasbourg Court has paid a special regard to the relationship between sensitive information and technology as the Convention is "a living instrument that must be interpreted in light of present day conditions". Only the existence of a "pressing social need for the interference", which requires the application of the principle of proportionality between a particular objective to be achieved and the means used to pursue that objective, can justify collection and retention of genetic data. Moreover, it has recognized that any State, which takes a leading role in developing scientific technologies to fight crime, has a special responsibility for striking the right balance between competing public and private interests.

REFERENCES

Akrivopoulou, C. M. (2009, May 11-13). The jurisprudence of the ECHR as a common European constitution. Working paper presented at *The Many Constitutions of Europe* conference, Centre of Excellence in Foundations of European Law and Polity Research, Helsinki, Finland.

Beattie, K. (2009). S and Marper v. United Kingdom: Privacy, DNA and crime rrevention. *EHRLR, 2009*(2), 229.

Chadwick, P. (2006). The value of privacy. *EHRLR, 2006*(5), 495-508.

Colussi, I. A. (2011). Dati genetici e forze di polizia: intersezioni europee. In L. S. Rossi (Ed). *La protezione dei diritti fondamentali: Carta dei diritti UE e standards internazionali: xv Convegno, Bologna 10-11 June 2010 / SIDI,* Società italiana di diritto internazionale, Napoli: Editoriale scientifica (forthcoming).

Colvin, M. (Ed.). (2002). *Developing key privacy rights*. Oxford, UK: Hart.

Delany, H., & Murphy, C. (2007). Towards common principles relating to the protection of privacy rights? *EHRLR, 2007*(5), 568-582.

Fanuele, C. (2007). Un archivio centrale per i profili del DNA nella prospettiva di un "diritto comune" europeo. *Diritto penale e processo, 13*(3), 385.

Gillespie, A. A. (2009). Regulation of internet surveillance. *EHRLR, 2009*(4), 552.

Janis, M. W., Kay, R. S., & Bradley, A. W. (Eds.). (2007). *European human rights law: Text and materials* (3rd ed.). New York: Oxford University Press.

Moreham, N. A. (2008). The right to respect for private life in the European Convention on Human Rights: A re-examination. *EHRLR, 2008*(1), 44.

Roberts, A., & Taylor, N. (2005). Privacy and the DNA database. *EHRLR, 2005*(4), 373.

Rothstein, M. A., & Talbott, M. K. (2006). The expanding use of DNA in law enforcement: What role for privacy. *The Journal of Law, Medicine & Ethics, 34*, 153. doi:10.1111/j.1748-720X.2006.00024.x

Scaffardi, L. (2009). Le banche dati genetiche per fini giudiziari e i diritti della persona. In Casonato, C., Piciocchi, C., & Veronesi, P. (Eds.), *Forum biodiritto 2008 La circolazione dei modelli nel biodiritto*. CEDAM.

Tracy, P. E., & Morgan, V. (2000). Big Brothers and his science kit: DNA databases for 21st century crime control? *The Journal of Criminal Law & Criminology, 90*(2), 635. doi:10.2307/1144232

Warbrick, C. J. (1998). The structure of Article 8. *EHRLR, 1998*(1), 32.

Williams, R., & Johnson, P. (Eds.). (2008). *Genetic policing: The use of DNA in criminal investigations*. Cullompton, UK: Willan.

APPENDIX: TABLE OF CASES

Amann v. Switzerland (App. No. 27798/95), judgment of 16 February 2000

Bouchacourt v. France (Application n. 5335/06), judgment of 17 December 2009

Copland v. United Kingdom (App. No. 62617/00), judgment of 3 April 2007

Friedl v. Austria (28/1994/475/556), judgment of 26 January 1995

Gardel v. France (App. No. 16428/05), judgment of 17 December 2009

Kinnunen v. Finland (App. No. 24950/94), decision of May 15, 1996

Kopp v. Switzerland (13/1997/797/1000), judgment 25 March 1998

Kruslin v. France (App. No. 11801/85), judgment of 24 April 1990

Leander v. Sweden (App. No. 9248/81), judgment of 26 March 1987

Malone v. United Kindgom (App. No. 8691/79), 2 August 1984

M.B. v. France (App. No. 22115/06), judgment of 17 December 2009

McVeign, O'Neill and Evans v. United Kingdom (App. Nos 8022/77, 8025/77, 8027/77), decision of December 12, 1979

Peck v. United Kingdom (App. No. 44647/98), judgment of 28 January 2003

Rotaru v. Romania (App. No. 28341/95), judgment of May 4, 2000

S. and Marper (Apps. Nos. 30562/04 and 30566/04), Grand Chamber judgment of 4 December 2008

Taylor-Sabori v. United Kingdom (47114/99), judgment of 22 October 2002

Van der Velden v. Netherlands (App. No. 29514/05), decision of 7 December 2006

Z. v. Finland (9/1996/627/811), judgment of 25 January 1997

Section 4

The 'Targeted' Privacy:

Ambient Technology and Tagging

Chapter 10
Radio Frequency Identification in Hospitals:
Balancing Hospital Efficiency and Patient Privacy

Christopher A. Suarez
Yale Law School, USA

ABSTRACT

Radio Frequency Identification (RFID) technology has been applied increasingly within the hospital setting. This chapter argues that, while such applications may drastically improve hospital efficiency, they also may produce privacy risks that harm patients more than they help them. Further, the privacy risks associated with RFID technologies are difficult to comprehend. When patients' personal data is implicated, hospitals should adhere to privacy principles that promote the flow of full information and enable patients to make rational choices when they opt-in to hospital RFID applications. Otherwise, RFID hospital technologies may be implemented in ways that do not serve patients' long term privacy interests.

INTRODUCTION

Although Radio Frequency Identification (RFID) technology has been in existence for over 50 years, it was not recommended for use in many applications until recently because it is still relatively expensive and underdeveloped. As consultants and investors saw the potential moneymaking opportunities that could arise from RFID, however, there has been a substantial push for its continued development. Starting with Wal-Mart's 2004 mandate to its top 100 suppliers requiring them to use RFID in their supply chains, a huge buzz was created that envisioned all sorts of RFID applications (Fanberg 2004). Meanwhile, consumer privacy advocates rolled up their sleeves, pointing out a myriad of privacy concerns posed by particular

DOI: 10.4018/978-1-60960-083-9.ch010

applications of RFID. They asserted that, while RFID is a technology that can produce tangible benefits, the negative privacy implications of RFID implementations may not be worth those benefits.

In this chapter, I evaluate the privacy implications of RFID applications in the hospital setting. Many hospital RFID applications have not been thoroughly discussed in the literature, and the proposed applications within hospitals are highly nuanced and varied. Some of them, for example, involve sensitive ethical issues relating to human tagging—meanwhile, others raise issues on how we should deal with extremely sensitive personal information. Indeed, RFID tags can be designed to store personal information or contain unique identifiers that can be linked to large amounts of data stored on servers. Any discussion of hospital RFID privacy, therefore, requires an examination of various RFID hospital applications.

In addressing the privacy concerns that arise from the applications of RFID within hospitals, I employ a utilitarian framework that attempts to balance the usefulness of the technology with the privacy harms that are posed by it. The ultimate goal is not to justify deployments of RFID for RFID's sake—rather, it is to determine the privacy drawbacks to each RFID application while suggesting ways that RFID implementations may maximally alleviate privacy concerns. Such concerns may be alleviated via both legal and procedural means. In some cases, implementing RFID technology may be worth it if the technology provides benefits to individuals that outweigh a largely mitigated set of privacy concerns. In other cases, however, the privacy concerns may be impossible to overcome—or be unknown—and those concerns may outweigh the benefits of the technology.

Once the decision is made to implement RFID in the hospital setting, there are several technological choices that need to be considered. Some issues that have privacy implications include whether active or passive RFID tags are used, the type of information that is stored on the tags, the read/write capability of the tags, the encryption capability of the tags, and the frequency at which the tags transmit data. While these technical choices are beyond the scope of this analysis, all of them have a direct bearing on the privacy implications of the technology.

Because many hospital RFID applications are in pilot phases and have not yet been fully implemented on a large scale, it is impossible to legitimately analyze the full extent of benefits that each RFID application confers to society. Further, the ultimate form of many RFID implementations in hospitals remains unseen. While many hospital RFID applications have been proposed and implemented, future applications may alter the balance of considerations made in this analysis. By addressing a wide variety of hospital RFID applications, I hope to address the full range of privacy issues that may be presented by both present and future applications. These issues need to be brought out up front in order to ensure that RFID hospital implementations adequately tradeoff efficiency and privacy in both the near and far term.

This paper proceeds as follows. In Part I, I discuss the general arguments that justify RFID use in the hospital setting. Next, in Part II, I assess the literature on consumer RFID privacy and use a proposed deontological framework to establish the principles that are used to evaluate various RFID applications. I also use the literature to confirm that the principles are consistent with those established by well-known privacy advocacy groups and discuss the principles in the context of the legal considerations that affect RFID policy. Part III provides the reader with some background on the few laws that currently govern hospital RFID in the United States. In Part IV, I discuss several hospital RFID applications, providing recommendations on how we may best benefit from each application while ensuring the privacy of patients. Finally, I provide general conclusions and recommendations in Part V.

I. THE BENEFITS AND COSTS OF RFID IN HOSPITALS

There are several reasons that RFID technologies are valuable within the hospital setting. Most importantly, RFID is well-suited to the operational needs of the hospital environment. Standard hospital operating procedures, in particular, are improved by RFID because it can be integrated seamlessly into existing infrastructures. For example, medical instruments are subjected to extreme temperatures during sterilization. Although many technologies malfunction in the presence of such temperatures, RFID tags can tolerate them. Items within the hospital are also exposed to unique materials such as water, blood, and other materials. Since RFID signals can be designed to travel through such impediments, RFID can overcome those obstacles (Fishkin and Lundell 2006).

Given the fast-paced, cluttered environment that is the hospital, moreover, it is also essential that any new technology infrastructure does not present a significant burden to nursing staff, doctors, and other health care professionals. RFID facilitates this goal because it is non-obtrusive and easy to use. Its signals can travel through walls or floors, allowing readers to be stored in locations that are hidden from sight. RFID scanners, unlike barcode scanners, do not require direct lines of sight to receive information. This allows items to be identified with little or no action from hospital personnel. Further, RFID tags, even when expensive, are reusable for long periods of time (Banks et al., 2007, pp. 314-315).

Pilots within hospitals have verified that RFID and other wireless technologies can increase hospital efficiency. This is unsurprising because the non-obtrusive nature of the technology prevents it from getting in the way of the day-to-day operations of the hospital. Data from RFID-tagged patients shows that the technology improves medical processes, decision making, and resource management (Janz et al., 2005, pp. 132-148). A case study of a Taiwan hospital that used RFID to track SARS patients found that RFID has the potential to contribute to general operating efficiency, good medical service, and patient safety (Wang et al. 2006). A study from Cisco, finally, revealed that the implementation of wireless LANs within hospitals made hospital workers almost 27% more productive (2003).

A seamlessly-integrated RFID solution within a hospital may also promote better patient care. If operating efficiency in the hospital is improved, doctors may have more time to interact with their patients, which would allow them to have more meaningful doctor-patient relationships. The University of Chicago Comer Children's hospital purchased an RFID implementation to "enable [its] staff to spend more quality time with [its] patients and less time manually performing administrative tasks such as billing and reordering" (Mobile Aspects, 2005, p. 1).

Much of the value from hospital RFID results from improved asset management. If assets are more effectively utilized in the hospital, costs are reduced significantly. Workflow management may also be improved. And, if an RFID system can quickly identify and locate pieces of medical equipment needed for a critical test or procedure, it prevents needless delays that may, in some cases, be the difference between life and death.

However, these benefits do not come without privacy costs. The tags may increase efficiency by not requiring a direct line of sight to be read, but this also means a malicious third party could have an easier time reading the information on a tag with his own reader. Sensitive patient information is either stored on the RFID tags themselves or on a third party database that is associated with the data on the tags. Should hospitals endorse a system that could expose the information on tags to such third parties? An additional problem is that, in some cases, hospital customers may not know that RFID technology is in their presence. Does a patient waive his or her right to privacy when entering the hospital, or should zones of

RFID use be clearly demarcated by the obvious presence of readers?

I ask whether these privacy drawbacks outweigh the increase in hospital efficiency asserted by proponents of hospital RFID. After establishing privacy principles, I provide the current legal landscape and discuss the tradeoffs between privacy and efficiency associated with several proposed hospital RFID solutions.

II. PRIVACY PRINCIPLES, CONSTRAINTS, AND CONSIDERATIONS

The focus of this work, ultimately, is on finding ways to address the privacy concerns that are raised by RFID opponents while still promoting the benefits that RFID could confer unto society. Because most implementers of RFID focus on generating new and interesting applications of the technology, they often fail to consider fully privacy principles that should guide RFID hospital implementations in the US. This section establishes these principles. In the next section, I apply these principles to the various applications that are discussed. I then consider them in the context of legal constraints that govern RFID in the US and provide support for them by comparing them to privacy principles that have been established by the Electronic Privacy Information Center (EPIC) and the RFID privacy literature.

A. Establishing a Set of Overarching Legal Principles

To establish a set of principles that guides this analysis, I employ a utilitarian framework that considers both the short and long term implications of implementing RFID technology. Since most hospital patients would appreciate benefits that come from improved hospital efficiency and patient care, they could be willing to immerse themselves in an RFID-enabled hospital. If patients demonstrate support of the technology, its use in the hospital arena should be allowed. This support, however, is subject to significant constraints.

First, endorsement of the technology in one area does not necessarily imply that it is endorsed by the public in all areas. Most Americans, for example, are not likely to be comfortable in a world that allowed them to be ubiquitously tracked on the streets or in their homes—and, as RFID applications continue to become more widespread, Katherine Albrecht and others argue that an imperceptible "RFID Revolution" could potentially permeate all of society (Albrecht and McIntyre, 2005, p. 219). My principles, therefore, should not be susceptible to slippery slopes that facilitate additional RFID applications without the public's consent.

Second, acceptance of RFID technology in the hospital setting may not even represent true acceptance—especially if patients are unaware of its potential privacy drawbacks. Because of the uncertainty inherent in RFID's implementation, neither patients nor implementers of the technology can completely understand the overall benefits and risks of the technology's use at this time.

A major issue that one should consider in establishing analytical principles in this context is the information asymmetry problem. A limitation of the utilitarian framework is that it assumes that individuals make fully informed, rational choices. However, when information asymmetries or uncertainties exist, these fully informed choices are not possible, and individuals are only able to base their decisions on what they know, perceive, and understand in the world. In the behavioral economics literature, one problem that inhibits rational decision-making is referred to as the availability bias. People generally construct their perceptions of likelihood based on the mental availability of instances of specific harms (Meyer, 2006, pp. 160-61). Absent explicit knowledge of privacy harms from RFID in the hospital setting, therefore, people will tend to underestimate its risks. Nevertheless, implementers of RFID will inevitably know a lot more about the privacy implications of the technology than will patients, and they have an opportunity to communicate their understanding of those privacy risks to patients. Patients should be told about those risks, since this would provide them with a better ability to make rational choices relating to hospital RFID. As privacy scholars have noted, for example, "[n]ot knowing key pieces of information, such as which firms are interested in purchasing personal information and to what ends, disadvantages an individual so that rational evaluation of personal information-revealing strategies is impossible" (Magid et al., 2009, pp. 36-37).

The public knows little about RFID—it is a complex technology that is not widely discussed amongst laypersons. Poignant examples that indicate society's lack of RFID knowledge appear in a study by Strickland and Hunt (2005). In this study, a general acceptance of RFID use for toll collection was revealed despite the fact that its associated data management practices were unknown. This is a problem, since states can easily use basic mathematical calculations based on RFID tracking to give speeding tickets and implicate criminals. If people know that their data could be used in this way, it is far less likely that they would accept the technology without opposition. Most merely see the advantages of speeding through the toll lane without stopping to pay a tollbooth attendant—and this makes sense considering that they are completely unaware of any broader implications of the technology. Similarly, in the hospital RFID context, patients may only hear about the benefits of RFID in hospitals and accept it in a similar manner that does not allow them to consider full information about the technology. And, unlike toll collection data, the information that could be collected using hospital RFID is far more sensitive on a personal level.

This chapter previously alluded to some instances where RFID has already been piloted within hospitals. It is doubtful that there have been significant efforts within these hospitals to inform customers of the privacy risks associated with the technology. If patients continue to accept RFID hospital implementations without full information, we risk perpetuating a dangerous situation in which patients who obtain more information later on could retaliate. Indeed, patients may not have accepted RFID technology in a hospital setting had they fully understood the privacy risks. As RFID continues to be implemented within hospitals, patients could eventually be forced to accept implementations of the technology on-face and without consent. Indeed, "[g]iven the growing prevalence of privacy-invading devices, individuals have succumbed to a sort of inevitability about disclosures" (Magid et al., 2009, p. 50).

This development is concerning because "inevitable disclosure" not only skirts around patient rights, but could also lead to public frustration and retaliation that could have been prevented if the right steps had been taken in the first place. Further, a sense of inevitable disclosure could cripple patients' sense of control over their personal privacy. To be legitimate, a fully-informed public should make a rational choice to be "on-board" the technology.

Implementers of RFID technology have the responsibility to make the technical design choices that are in the best interest of patients before implementing the technology. By making it a point to optimize patient privacy within RFID systems themselves, implementers will do their part to reduce impacts that could arise as a result of information asymmetries. Design choices in various facets of an RFID system should not be made blindly and without the consideration of privacy rights. In theory, systems that are perfectly designed would reduce the information asymmetry problem to a triviality since the system would then be "privacy perfect." Such an assumption, however, is overly optimistic—it is better to assume that our systems will not protect privacy perfectly and that we must complement privacy-friendly system designs with additional privacy safeguards. Moreover, regardless of the robustness of RFID privacy protections within a system, we must reinforce our notion of a fully-informed patient cohort: that is required if we are to achieve a utilitarian ideal.

This means that regulation—and the law—has a role in ensuring that citizens are proactively educated about the privacy risks of various technological applications, including RFID in the hospital. This also means that consumers should be notified—both individually and collectively—when privacy breaches occur. Frequent notification may artificially inflate perceptions of privacy risks or trigger availability biases, but it would be normatively better for the public to overestimate privacy harms than to underestimate them.

There are several reasons a regime that overestimates privacy is desirable. Like Paul Schwartz (2009), I advocate a principle of first, do no harm. Unlike him, however, I would not frame the primary harm as privacy regulation, thereby warranting a parsimony principle of minimal regulation (Schwartz, 2009, p. 928). Rather, the harm from the vantage point of one who wants the legal regime to accurately track society's privacy preferences would be a world in which the public's opportunity to express its privacy norms or values could be derailed—a world that allows for coerced acceptance of or naïve reliance on privacy-harming technological advances. Daniel Solove (2009) explains that "the government could gradually condition people to accept wiretapping or other privacy incursions," which could artificially alter society's privacy expectation (Solove, 2009, p. 73). Further, governments—both federal and state—could under-regulate and fail to inform the public of privacy risks of emerging technologies. If this occurs, another form of coercion could occur as people gain reliance interests in technological innovations and become too invested in a particular application to recover the privacy rights they would have preferred to assert in the first instance. They also may succumb to the aforementioned sense of inevitability and fail to push back on any harms arising from the technology for that reason.

Why overestimate privacy risks when doing so could undercut economic benefits or efficiency gains? The simple answer is that the private sector will always be motivated to maximize profits. Absent regulation, the private sector will not always be motivated to maximize privacy in a world filled with incomplete information. By erring towards a regime that overestimates privacy risks, we place a burden on industry to self-regulate the technologies and methods that are used to transfer and store information. If privacy harms are somewhat overestimated as a result of reduced information asymmetries between consumers and private actors, these actors will more proactively work to reduce the likelihood of privacy breaches in order to minimize the impact of perceived information privacy risks on their profits. Although consumers may still gain reliance interests in technological innovations and applications, increases in a technology's popularity over time will be a more accurate reflection of that technology's fully-assessed privacy risks. The market itself could solve for adequate privacy protection without the need for inefficient, *reactive* government regulation that would otherwise be necessary.

Assuming the provision of full information could ensure better measurement of society's privacy preferences, however, how should federal and state privacy law be balanced? First, hospital regulation at the federal level should always promote notification of information privacy risks and breaches in all sectors, especially for technologies or applications where privacy implications are uncertain. Privacy risk education could flow from a federal office or agency that studies the privacy risks and benefits of emerging technologies. It would be efficient for a single federal agency to perform such broad privacy risk and educational assessments instead of a patchwork of state notification and privacy research hubs.

The foregoing discussion reveals several principles that drive the remaining analysis of this paper. These principles should viewed with an eye towards conceptualizing privacy as a form of personal property—as Schwartz argues, "[p]ersonal information is an important currency in the new millennium" (2004, p. 2056). It is therefore crucial that our privacy principles prioritize patient ownership over hospital (or private) ownership with respect to any RFID technologies that may incorporate the use of personal data—health or otherwise. The five property elements Schwartz describes—inalienabilities, defaults, right of exit, damages, and institutions—provide an excellent frame to articulate these privacy principles for hospital RFID applications.

Principle 1: Limits on Transferability

Called *inalienabilities* by Schwartz, this privacy principle emphasizes that data obtained from RFID tags should be protected from arbitrary transfers to third parties. This principle emphasizes that the hospital patient always has ownership and dominion over the data on an RFID tag. This means that implementers must first receive *opt-in* permission from someone who is tagged before their data can be used by that party. Moreover, this third party, upon being granted permission, cannot transfer or sell information about that person to others for any purpose unless authorized to do so. A single opt-in should not be viewed as an all-or-nothing proposition where a hospital or similar medical providers "assume[s] full control of information after consent is demonstrated..." (Magid et al., 2009, p. 49). Treating information this way prevents individuals from making rational economic calculations about whether to reveal personal information in particular contexts or situations. This principle arises out of a general concern that a market of transferable information is very likely to be made possible with the proliferation of RFID.

Principle 2: Explicit Opt-In Defaults

There should be a default option that requires hospital patients to opt-in to any forms of RFID data use that may be associated with their personal information. Requiring patients to opt-in places the burden on implementers who will need to convince their customers to use the technology. Presumably, it will lead to a more informed citizenry that is told why the technology is beneficial as well as why the technology has some potential drawbacks.

Three considerations should be emphasized when discussing opt-in defaults. First, opt-in defaults are only valuable to the extent that opt-in choices accurately reflect preferences and are not subject to the information asymmetry problem. Second, and as will be addressed in Part V, there are certain situations (infants, the elderly, and in the ER) where RFID hospital implementations may not be able to obtain legitimate "opt-in" from patients. Finally, to the extent that bifurcated systems can be maintained in the hospital setting—those that allow patients to use the RFID system while still allowing others to opt-out—such systems should be maintained.

Principle 3: Right of Exit

Once someone opts-in to using RFID technology in the hospital, there should also be a right of exit. Although someone may have felt that the technology was initially worthwhile, it should not be assumed that this initial consent gives the technology provider an unlimited right to use RFID to associate information with a person. Indeed, people may opt-in, discover drawbacks of RFID, and then wish to opt-out of the technology. This is yet another reason why opt-in cannot be an all-or-nothing proposition. If customers do not have this exit right, we may reach a point at which a critical mass of consumers has little to no recourse against companies who fail to protect privacy.

Principle 4: Right of Recourse

Invasions of privacy rights should be associated with some level of compensatory damages and an ability to seek retribution for privacy harms inflicted on a particular person or group of persons. Although it may be difficult to pinpoint an individual who steals personal information or data using RFID technology in a particular case, a liability rule can be placed on hospitals that fail to create the technological infrastructures that adequately protect privacy. Thus, even if a party outside of the hospital were to use technological know-how to steal patient data using an RFID reader, the affected person would always be able to secure recovery from a solvent—and available—party. Current privacy law sets liquidated damages that are quite steep to discourage violations—for example, the Video Privacy Protection Act allows a court to "award ... actual damages but not less than liquidated damages in an amount of $2,500." People should know about their right to seek recourse—whether it is from the hospital itself or from the individuals who steal personal data.

Principle 5: Institutions that Ensure Full Information Provision

Institutions should be created that regulate and enforce RFID privacy provisions. Schwartz advocates the creation of a Data Protection Commission that would fill a more general oversight function. The United States is the only large Western nation that has failed to create such an independent privacy commission (Flaherty, 1989, pp. 394-97). Consistent with the discussion above, one major role of such a commission would be to ensure that consumers were armed with full information. Thus, it would ensure that consumers had notice of the presence of RFID technologies in hospitals, that accurate information about the technology was communicated, and that consumers have an authentic choice to opt in and out of the technology as they please.

B. Supporting the Principles

Assuming the above principles are adopted, they must withstand the scrutiny of both the general public and consumer interest groups. This section compares and contrasts these principles with those that have been articulated by various privacy groups.

First, the Electronic Privacy Information Center (EPIC) has established privacy principles regarding health information privacy. Marc Rotenberg, EPIC's President, gave a talk in 1994 entitled *Privacy and Security for Medical Information Systems*. In this talk, he emphasized several principles that can be applied to RFID in the health care industry. These principles emphasized a code of fair information practices, controlling secondary use, controlling the use of an identifier, patients' right of access, and oversight and enforcement.

Each of EPIC's principles can be associated with the general principles introduced above. First, a code of fair information practices emphasizes the responsibility of data holders to their subjects, and, in addition, the duty to keep data subjects fully informed about the use of their personal information. This principle is somewhat connected to the principle of opt-in defaults because these defaults have the primary goal of forcing data holders to share information with their subjects, but neither such codes nor such defaults are enough. These measures do not ensure that consumers are fully informed about privacy and the use of their data. As such, it is important that any opt-in policy is coupled with other safeguards to ensure that fair information practices exist and are met.

Second, EPIC recommended in 2005 to the Department of Health and Human Services that RFID implementations in the healthcare setting should contain the minimum data possible to function effectively. This is a technical consideration, as the amount of data stored on tags and servers is a system design choice. Minimization measures would promote the principle of inalienability.

Another important consideration noted by Rotenberg, finally, is controlling the use of identifiers. All RFID tags have identifiers that—using either a random number or some other combination of data—serve to identify individuals or items that are associated with the tag. Although the context in 1994 was different—the goal was solely to address identifiers within medical record databases—the controlled use of identifiers is *even more critical* in the RFID world because so many RFID implementations in hospitals emphasize the use of a unique ID to be associated with tags on each item or patient. Such a unique ID needs to be chosen carefully and implemented in a proper way. For example, were a social security number chosen as a unique ID in an RFID implementation, a malicious third party could intercept that information and use it to exploit that person's banking and credit records. Strict control of identifiers also promotes the inalienability of patients' private data.

Beyond EPIC, Lisa Sotto, former vice chair of the Data Privacy and Integrity Advisory Committee of the US Department of Homeland Security, advocates the adoption of an RFID Code of Conduct in the medical industry. Although HIPAA, federal and state laws, and the Fair Information Practices established by the Federal Trade Commission (FTC) provide some privacy protections that cover RFID implementation in the healthcare field, she believes that such a code of conduct would offer an additional layer of protection that would be more specifically and clearly tailored to address specific concerns about RFID (Sotto 2005). Indeed, such a code of conduct has recently been created by the American Medical Association in the context of implantable RFID chips created for medical use (Bacheldor 2007). Such a code, however, does not extend more broadly to other hospital RFID applications.

Upon a simple examination of each portion of Sotto's proposed code of conduct, it too is almost directly in line with the five proposed principles. The code would require notice, opt-in, and the ability to review and amend data stored on an RFID tag. Further, Sotto's proposed code would call for instruction on chip deactivation, which would be another way that patients could exercise a right of exit. Finally, she emphasizes privacy accountability and enforcement. These ideas are all consistent with the notion that RFID data is the personal property of hospital patients and not the hospital.

III. LEGAL CONSIDERATIONS

Currently, there is little law that affords consumers privacy protections with respect to RFID implementations in hospitals. Although the Fourth Amendment of the United States Constitution prohibits "unreasonable searches and seizures," the Supreme Court has long established that the Fourth Amendment only applies to government actors (Sommer, 2009). Thus, the Constitution places no limits on private hospitals or medical providers. Further, there are not any Federal statutes that directly address RFID privacy issues. As Paula Bruening of the Center for Democracy and Technology has noted:

It is more effective and efficient to begin at the outset of the development process to create a culture of privacy and that establishes the key business and public policy decisions for respecting privacy in RFID use before RFID is deployed rather than building in privacy after a scandal or controversy erupts publically (Bruening 2004).

Nevertheless, some federal legislation addresses RFID hospital privacy indirectly. In addition, bills addressing RFID-related issues have been proposed at the state level.

A. Federal Legislation and Regulations

The main bill that is referenced when discussing RFID privacy concerns is the Health Insurance Portability and Accountability Act of 1996 (HIPAA). After HIPAA was passed, it was amended to include *Standards for Privacy of Individually Identifiable Health Information,* also known as the "privacy rule." The privacy rule sets forth several guidelines that control how medical patients' personally identifiable information may be distributed. This personally identifiable information is known as "protected health information" (PHI).

The limitations the rule places on PHI have several implications on RFID implementations. And because HIPAA applies to "any health care provider who transmits health information in electronic form…," it applies to hospitals.

The privacy rule implicitly requires that PHI be stored in centralized databases and not on RFID tags themselves. This is because the privacy rule protects PHI held in any form of media, and the information stored on RFID tags is susceptible to third party adversaries who may attempt to read it. Even in the presence of encryption, a third party with the proper decryption tools could, in theory, collect patient information with a specially designed reader. By storing the PHI in central databases within a given health care facility, the information is not accessible within public areas, and this provides an extra layer of protection of third party intrusion. The ubiquity of RFID in the hospital setting facilitates many points of entry for the random hacker who could attempt to collect information from individuals who may be tagged (whether the tagging is under the skin or via a bracelet).

The information protected under HIPAA extends beyond medical information about a given patient. This is because the protected information can also include information that identifies the individual or for which there is a reasonable basis to believe can be used to identify the individual (45 C.F.R. § 160.103 (2009)). Thus, even if an RFID tag does not contain any medical information about a patient, the identifier on an RFID tag must also be protected. Identifiers such as social security numbers, phone numbers, or publicly available hospital identification numbers may not be used to identify a patient on RFID tags. Only "de-identified" information may be included on tags, and the de-identification of such information must usually be verified via a formal determination by a qualified statistician (45 C.F.R. § 164.514(b) (2009)). Once information is conveyed in a de-identified form, it is virtually impossible to determine the person from whom the information originated. As studies have shown, however, de-identification is virtually impossible since seemingly de-identified data may be re-identified in some instances (Sweeney, 1998).

Although the use of the protected health information is regulated, the privacy rule does not extend to all uses of PHI. In general, the PHI cannot be disclosed unless the individual who is the subject of the information (or the individual's personal representative) authorizes such disclosure in writing. The information can also be disclosed by the entity that holds the information for the purposes of its *internal* treatment, payment, and health care operations as long as it is not disclosed to third parties. However, hospitals must also disclose the "protected" information to the US Department of Health and Human services when it is undertaking a compliance investigation, as well as to certain entities for "national priority purposes"—these may include law enforcement and public health activities (45 C.F.R. § 164.502(a) (2009); 45 C.F.R. § 164.512 (2009)).

Finally, the privacy rule requires that medical providers provide a notice of their privacy practices. Given the principle of full information adopted in this chapter, any provision that promoted disclosure is beneficial. There are specific provisions in the rule that, for example, require the privacy notice to be descriptive in the ways the provider may use and disclose personal information. The notice must inform patients of their rights, including the right to complain to HHS (45 C.F.R. § 164.502(a)-(b) (2009)).

Moreover, one additional federal law may be construed to apply to RFID technologies in some circumstances (Sommer, 2009). The Electronic Communications Privacy Act (ECPA) regulates electronic communications. ECPA makes it a crime for any person who, "intentionally intercepts, endeavors to intercept, or procures any other person to intercept or endeavor to intercept, any wire, oral, or electronic communication" (18 U.S.C. § 2701 et seq. (2009)). To the extent that intercepted communications between an RFID tag and reader are construed as "electronic communications" under the act, one could argue that ECPA applies. Courts have not resolved this matter, however.

Finally, federal regulatory agencies—including the Federal Communications Commission (FCC) and Federal Trade Commission (FTC)—have directly addressed some RFID issues through other regulations. The FCC, for example, can regulate RFID through its regulatory authority over the frequency spectrum. Thus, it may allocate particular frequency ranges to RFID uses. For example, operation in the 433.5-434.5 MHz band is restricted to RFID uses "limited to commercial and industrial areas such as ports, rail terminals, and warehouses" (47 C.F.R. § 15.240 (2009)). Further regulations can explicitly expand particular portions of the spectrum to hospital RFID applications.

The FTC, meanwhile, issued a report in 2005 discussing the implications of RFID applications on consumers. Although the FTC does not currently have the authority to issue formal RFID privacy regulations, it argued that "the goal of such programs should be transparency," and that notice should be "clear, conspicuous, and transparent" (FTC, 2005, p. 22). It concluded that "consumer education is a vital part of protecting consumer privacy" (p. 23). The report also highlighted the fact that industry regulations and policing can play a role in RFID regulation, but the FTC would serve the public well by educating the public on these matters.

B. State-Level Laws

Although several state RFID laws either have been proposed or are on the books, most of these do not address RFID hospital privacy matters in a comprehensive fashion. According to the National Conference of State Legislatures (NCSL), thirteen states have passed RFID legislation as of 2010.

Of these current laws, four of them directly address RFID chip implantation. As I discuss later, chip implantation may be an effective tool to improve medical efficiency. Nevertheless, some are quite fearful of the ethical and moral implications of chip implantation. Thus, under these laws, employers or other institutions are not allowed to require chip implantation of their employees or patients (National Conference of State Legislatures, 2010).

Most of the other laws, however, are less directly connected to RFID hospital privacy issues. Many are concerned with RFID use in drivers' licenses or passports. Nevertheless, some of these laws bear some relevance to the privacy principles advanced in this chapter. For example, Michigan's RFID privacy law governing its RFID-enabled drivers' licenses adopts the principle of minimization by only allowing a single unique ID to be stored on the license—this unique identifier is also encrypted. Moreover, there is a notice provision. An applicant must sign a declaration acknowledging an understanding of RFID technology before an "enhanced" drivers license is issued (Mich. Comp. Laws § 28.304 (2009)). Nevada, in addition, has a law prohibiting the malicious capturing, reading, or storing of RFID information on a form of identification without the person's knowledge or consent (Nev. Rev. Stat § 205.461-205.4675 (2009). To the extent that these ideas can be transferred to legal requirements governing hospital RFID, state legislatures have provided some useful starting points for future RFID hospital privacy laws.

Although RFID-related legislation has not yet been proposed without controversy or mild shortcoming, these early pieces of legislation are fostering public discourse that will allow privacy and other concerns to be vetted out more fully. In New Hampshire, for example, such dialogue has already occurred. There, an RFID bill was amended to create a privacy commission to investigate RFID privacy issues further. This privacy commission released a report in 2008 that contained many useful recommendations. Although the report did not discuss hospital RFID, it proposed regulations that directly addressed chip implantation and illegal uses of RFID readers (2008). These sorts of conversations and reports could help move additional reform forward.

C. Opposition to Legal Remedies

Despite the seeming power of legal measures to enforce RFID privacy, sheer passage of laws will not necessarily guarantee the privacy of hospital patients in the United States. If the public and consumer privacy advocates do not support such laws, they may not be taken seriously. And if doctors and medical practitioners do not support laws that protect RFID rights, it is unlikely that the laws will be enforced. The FTC report on RFID technologies, further, emphasized the importance of industry regulation (2005).

Any incremental legal protections that are analogous to the HIPPA rule will also need to be justified to physicians to be effective. In a 2005 *Health Affairs* article, Slutsman et al. released the findings of a study that revealed significant discontent among doctors when it came to the privacy rule. Despite being very familiar with the privacy rule, for example, only one of four physicians felt that medical record privacy is a serious problem. Meanwhile, a minority of doctors believed that the privacy rule helped maintain the privacy of medical records. Some (roughly one-third) believed that the rule would *impede medical research* (Slutsman et al., 2005). This has negative implications because, besides indicating that the rule may be ineffective, studies have suggested that physicians will ignore or not fully implement legal requirements that they do not agree with (Siegal et al., 2001, pp. 63-78). Such resistance to future RFID privacy regulation could frustrate privacy protections and promote physician discontent that may inhibit those doctors' ability to perform their jobs effectively.

Nevertheless, the study did also find that organizations with more procedural privacy practices in place were about seven times more likely than those with fewer provisions to do a very good job at protecting privacy, and also that such organizations were about five times more likely to *not interfere* with physicians' abilities to care for patients and consult their colleagues (Slutsman et al., 2005). Thus, while there may be a general frustration with additional legal privacy protections on the part of doctors, effective compliance with the provisions probably is in the best interest of patients. Nevertheless, the effectiveness of the law should be continually examined, and something should be done to counteract the negativity doctors have expressed towards efforts such as the privacy rule.

Because of the general discontent doctors have expressed toward legal privacy protections, it will be especially important to educate doctors and other medical personnel—not just patients—on RFID technology before undertaking any RFID deployment. The median age of doctors today is quite high, and it is likely that most of these doctors will not understand or have much of an interest in this technology. Thus, doctors are likely to become frustrated or confused if the implementation of RFID technologies requires them to cut through any additional red tape. While this red tape may be burdensome to physicians, however, they are more likely to be accepting of it once they fully understand the rationale behind adoption of the technology.

Beyond doctors' discontent, Katherine Albrecht and Liz McIntyre (2005) argued in *Spychips* that government and legal intervention in the RFID privacy realm is not a viable solution. They contend that there is a lack of political willpower to oppose RFID, citing a Republican Taskforce that stated that "RFID holds tremendous promise…and should not be saddled prematurely with regulation." Meanwhile, Congressmen have funneled American tax dollars to support RFID research (pp. 204-205). From examples such as these, Albrecht and McIntyre assume that lawmakers will succumb to corporate pressures, refusing to support any legislation that limits RFID usage. To date, their prediction has been realized. As this section has illustrated, RFID privacy legislation is minimal at both the federal and state level. Nevertheless, much of the problem remains due to a general lack of awareness of the technology's wide-ranging implications.

At this time, most patients who have received implantable RFID chips are sufferers of Alzheimer's disease, diabetes, and other chronic illnesses (Banks et al., 2007, p. 316). However, use of such chips could proliferate. For this reason, government intervention should complement any efforts the public may take to assert RFID privacy rights. In particular, the government should maintain a role in information provision. It is unrealistic to assume that a substantial proportion of the public will appreciate the nuances of their privacy rights, just as it is unrealistic to assume that a substantial proportion of the public will be able to name their Congressional representative. While most consumers of RFID would probably be concerned if they truly understood the privacy issues that are intertwined with RFID, most are completely oblivious to the concept of RFID—let alone its privacy risks.

Despite the substantial privacy concerns associated with the implantable VeriChip, for example, the public has only become more supportive of the chip. Although only 9% said they would put it in their bodies after the initial announcement, 19% said they would after FDA approval. And, once Tommy Thompson joined the VeriChip board, the rate went up to 33% (DeNoon 2005). Corporations who are creating value-added solutions with high profit-margins are not necessarily going to listen to the relatively small number of consumers who actively voice their concerns against RFID. Absent a catastrophic event involving an individual's—or a group's—compromised privacy, consumers are unlikely to exercise broad, concerted action independently.

Although Gillette, Proctor and Gamble, and others have succumbed to consumer pressure to back away from consumer deployments of RFID, such scenarios are less realistic in the hospital setting. Medical care is unlikely to be resisted by consumers in moments of urgent medical need. While people can easily switch between products in the supermarket that may or may not be privacy friendly, it is not so simple to switch hospitals or medical providers on a whim.

Most importantly, the reality is that RFID is being implemented in hospitals *right now*, and whether or not that reality is desired by privacy advocates, it needs to be acknowledged. The time frame needed to coalesce enough citizens to have an effect on corporations is far too great, and the only way to make corporations begin conforming to privacy guidelines will be to increase awareness of RFID and strengthen our laws.

IV. INTRODUCTION OF HOSPITAL RFID APPLICATIONS

I now turn to a discussion of proposed RFID hospital applications. With the exception of the first application (asset management), most of these applications have not been formally implemented within any major hospital. I therefore hope to create an awareness of the potential uses of RFID based on what we know right now—however, the uncertainties associated with the technology may mean that the technology is *never implemented* in some of the ways described. Meanwhile, there may be future hospital RFID applications that are not considered here. These examples mainly serve to contextualize many of the privacy issues that may arise from implementing RFID in the hospital in different ways.

A. Asset Management

The first major use of RFID in the hospital setting is for asset management. Hospitals are often lent assets such as hospital beds or monitoring equipment that are owned by third-party vendors. Such third party vendors would like to have the ability to track their property. In addition, some hospitals own their own machines, beds, surgical tools, and other equipment, and the internal tracking of such items can be quite useful in any efforts to bolster the overall efficiency of hospital operations.

Asset management has been the most pioneered application of RFID in hospitals because the primary incentive motivating RFID implementations is a positive return on investment (ROI). In an interview with Dr. In Ki Mun, a hospital researcher at MIT, I was told that the primary implementations of RFID at the hospital level are in asset management because the ROI for this application is estimated to be particularly high—in a mere 2-3 years, investors can expect positive returns. Meanwhile, Mike Dempsey, the founder and CTO of Radianse, claims that a deployment using their systems typically has a breakeven ROI somewhere between 11 and 18 months (Goth, 2006). These time frames are short enough to convince members of hospital boards to invest now.

A survey of the literature on RFID in hospitals verifies this. As early as 2004, Agility Healthcare Solutions made a five year pact with three Virginia hospitals to track mobile hospital equipment. In one of these hospitals (Bon Secours), it was estimated that a positive return on investment would be obtained within one year of deploying the system. This is unsurprising because, according to the CEO of Agility Healthcare, equipment management is a "universal problem in hospitals" (Collins 2004). One of the highlighted advantages to the Agility implementation is that its readers are linked wirelessly to the hospitals central networks, allowing reader positions to be reconfigured without reinstalling cabling. This is beneficial since hospitals reconfigure layouts frequently. Several other hospitals, including Beth Israel in Boston, Washington Hospital Center in Washington DC, continue to use RFID to track assets (Brown, 2007, pp. 157-58).

Many in the hospital field doubt the economic viability of hospital RFID implementations, even in areas of asset management. According to Provizio Research in 2004, most hospitals expressed a desire to rely on bar code technology for at least six more years. The main reason for this was that it was difficult to justify the cost outlay for "the more expensive, but clearly promising, RFID technology" (Jaques, 2004). And although RFID can be more easily integrated into existing infrastructures than before, the current IT infrastructure of most hospitals still makes it easier to use bar codes.

In September 2005, moreover, a similar study by Spyglass Consulting group revealed that RFID—particularly passive RFID—is not ready for use in the healthcare sector. In interviewing more than 100 healthcare organization professionals, that study revealed that less than 23 percent of RFID healthcare solutions are passive,[1] and that many of these professionals did not see a strong business case for the passive RFID due to the cheaper bar code alternative, a lack of industry standards, and a lack of government or industry mandates. Many also expressed concerns about expanding existing network infrastructures and about the scalability of the technology—there is a desire to use existing wireless networks over using an independent, dedicated RFID network (Monegain, 2005). But these concerns have been addressed in current implementations—both Alexandra Hospital in Singapore and Jacobi Hospital in New York utilize viable active tag implementations, and Beth Israel has successfully deployed its system over its standard 802.11 wireless network (Brown, 2007, pp. 157-58).

Ultimately, there is general agreement that RFID will eventually replace barcodes. This is because the potential advantages to it are so substantial. Besides the utility asset-tracking gives a hospital in terms of item recovery and efficient operation, asset-tracking may also allow for applications that may benefit the hospital in other ways. For example, some hospitals have attempted pilots where they tag medical practitioners and associate those practitioners with objects for educational purposes. In a pilot with the University of Washington Medical School, students wore small RFID readers in a glove—two antennae in the gloves allowed for easy tracking of the sequences of objects used by students in simulations. The records of such sequences can be used to assess student performance, and this is one of many ways that RFID may be used to not only monitor behavior in the hospital, but provide an educational function as well. If, for example, a student picked up the wrong tool for a given operation, an alarm could sound that guarantees that another, more experienced doctor may properly intervene. In this sense, RFID adds another layer of protection against medical error (Fishkin and Lundell 2006).

The application of RFID in hospital asset management is relevant to our privacy discussion for multiple reasons. First, the continued use of RFID for asset management will certainly pave the way for the use of RFID technologies in other ways that may more directly impact patient privacy. By creating RFID-enabled infrastructures within hospitals, for example, asset management applications will make it easier to move towards a system that integrates human tagging. Second, there are some direct patient privacy implications to consider at the asset level. While the tracking of general assets such as monitoring devices and hospital beds may not appear to impact patient privacy, there are ways that directly tracking patients will have such an effect. For example, a tracked hospital bed may be associated with a patient who sleeps in a bed during a given night. Meanwhile, the device that monitors that patient's heart rate can also be associated with the patient as it is wheeled around the hospital with the patient attached. As such, measures must be taken by hospitals to ensure that such associations are not made without the knowledge or consent of a patient. In these instances, patients should know that RFID is being used and tracked items should not be directly associated with patients without full information and consent.

Despite the potential invasions of patient privacy that may result from asset management applications, these invasions are minimized if RFID-tagged assets are never associated with particular patients. However, such a sweeping policy is only possible when discussing asset management for *general hospital assets.* The unique nature of the hospital environment also promotes another form of asset, which I call *patient assets*. *Patient assets* are different from general assets because they *must* be associated with patients to be used effectively in the hospital. Because such associations are inherently necessary with patient assets, I address the additional privacy concerns that arise from them.

Two hospital RFID applications involving *patient assets*—hospital blood inventory and patient pharmaceuticals—already have been considered and implemented in pilot forms. I therefore address these applications in the following sections. A third patient asset, breast milk, is addressed in a later section on neo-natal intensive care units.

B. Hospital Blood Inventory

Current processes for hospital blood transfusions involve both paperwork and the use of bar codes. These processes have generally worked to this point, but proponents of using RFID in hospital blood inventory procedures argue that RFID could greatly improve the efficiency of such processes. The line of sight requirement of bar codes, for example, slows down hospital blood inventory processes because it requires that, in some cases, many bags be individually scanned to find a correct match to a particular patient. RFID tagging would allow many blood bags to be queried at once, making it easier to track down and locate a blood bag that may be needed for a transfusion. Moreover, RFID tags are less susceptible to wear than are bar codes, and their use can increase general staff mobility and efficiency, improve data collection, and increase general hospital staff access to blood data.

Because blood-handling processes currently require a number of manual steps which may be eliminated with RFID, proponents also argue that RFID would reduce errors that result from the blood transfusion process. Errors in the blood identification process, meanwhile, can have very harmful effects. This is because incorrect blood transfusions sometimes lead to death or the transmission of harmful diseases such as hepatitis or HIV. While erroneous blood transfusions are known to occur at a rate of about one in every 12,000 units, experts argue that the error rate is actually much higher since many "near miss" incidents go unreported. In a 6-month RFID blood tagging pilot at San Raffaele Hospital in Italy, meanwhile, *no errors* were observed in the blood transfusion processes that were part of the pilot (Dalton et al., 2005).

In the pilot at San Raffaele hospital, the following procedures were used during blood donations and transfusions. For a transfusion, patient information, including a photograph, was stored on wristbands that were given to each patient that entered a blood donation area. The relevant data on these tags would then be copied to the blood bag tag that corresponded to the donation. After the donation is made, finally, the staff member compares the full blood bag and wristband via a personal digital assistant. Assuming patient data is initially written to the RFID tag correctly, this procedure ensures that the correct blood bags are associated with the correct patients. For a transfusion, patient data on a wristband is matched with the data on the blood bag for verification, and the transfusion takes place. If the match fails, an alarm sounds and the transfusion does not take place (Dalton et al., 2005).

Because blood transfusion involves patient assets, we must be much more rigid in our privacy analysis of this application. In the San Raffaele pilot, there was no discussion of an opt-in default whatsoever. Any patient who was either donating or retrieving blood from the blood bank there was automatically subjected to the use of RFID-tagged blood. Implicitly, there was no right of exit in this implementation either, since all patients who used the hospital for blood transfusion needed to go through the RFID pilot. However, especially in the context of pilots such as these, it is not difficult to give patients the option to store their blood either with or without RFID tags—blood bags had been identified without RFID for years, and hospital personnel understand the procedures involved. Patients, meanwhile, should at minimum know that the blood they are donating is tagged—it didn't appear that those involved in this pilot were told about what was going on behind the scenes. These steps need to be taken sooner rather than later to ensure that a fully informed citizenry accepts the technology.

Meanwhile, certain aspects of the San Raffaele RFID blood pilot are concerning because the system's design did not minimize avoidable privacy risks. In particular, the tags that associated with the patients' blood did not contain the minimum information possible. The tags in the system contained information about each patient's blood type, a picture, and other personally identifiable information. While this may have made it easier for system designers—for example, this design could make it easier to cross-checking blood samples with patient records—this particular aspect of the design is worrisome. The tags associated with blood bags could be designed to protect privacy much more if they only contained unique identifiers associated with given samples of blood.

Moreover, the tags that were used in this implementation were writable—information about a patient and their blood type was written to the tags during the process of tagging and identifying blood samples. By using tags of this nature, there is room for third party adversaries to write invalid or mischievous information to tags. While this would appear to be an unlikely possibility, it is something that could legitimately happen and this is a flaw in this RFID implementation.

C. Patient Pharmaceuticals

Another application on the horizon involves the tagging of patient pharmaceuticals. In hospitals where thousands of medications are administered on a daily basis, it is important that the correct patients receive the correct medications. Because RFID aids in verification procedures, it could serve as an extra layer of protection in ensuring that the wrong drugs are never administered to patients. It is also important that patients receive the proper dosages of their medications, and RFID systems can help gauge how much medication patients are taking. In a society that is increasingly concerned about the presence of counterfeit drugs, positive identification of all drugs is a pressing issue.

CVS Pharmacy has been a leader in the tagging of pharmaceutical products through its participation in an RFID trial called project Jump Start. CVS was interested in the project because over 70% of its revenue stems from prescription drug sales. In addition, CVS wanted to get on board early to ensure that any RFID standards made with respect to pharmaceuticals considered the *specific needs* of pharmacy retailing—these needs include a consideration of the specific privacy and security requirements of pharmacy retailing (Garfinkel et al., 2005).

Project Jump Start uses electronic product codes (EPCs) to track shipments of drugs, and it is possible that these individual EPC codes could be associated individual customers. However, the initial roll-out of Project Jump Start has only tagged bottles that contain 90-100 or more tablets—these are the bottles of pills that are broken and placed into smaller bottles by pharmacists. The tags used in this project, moreover, have an adhesive backing and perforations that make them easily removable by either the pharmacist or consumers. By taking these steps, CVS has implemented its pilot in a way that can still increase efficiency in the supply chain while avoiding infringements of privacy at the individual consumer level. One cannot assume, however, that all implementers of pharmacy RFID will design their systems in this manner. CVS was cognizant of privacy, going so far to say "if people [developing this technology] don't understand privacy, this thing is going to be stopped dead in its tracks" (Garfinkel et al., 2005).

In general, there are several privacy considerations in using RFID with pharmaceuticals. First, a system that contains RFID tagged prescriptions must not allow adversaries to associate customers' prescriptions with specific customers—this is because pharmaceuticals, like blood bags, are patient assets. The ability to know who is prescribed what medicine has immense privacy implications because, beyond knowing the medication itself, the adversary would also be able to infer diseases or medical conditions that are afflicting a customer or members of a customer's family. Moreover, all forms of *personally identifiable* medical information are protected under HIPAA. Thus, CVS could face legal trouble if it installed a faulty RFID system. Finally, consumers should have the right to *opt-out* of an RFID tagged prescription upon purchase.

Although CVS could improve privacy by taking some of the steps above, it only deals with consumers who purchase drugs at its stores, and its primary goal is to improve supply chain efficiency. While the same motivations may exist for some who are in charge of hospital pharmacies, hospitals may have a broader interest in tagging pharmaceuticals. Tagged prescriptions, for example, could be associated and verified with patients at bedside by nurses who may be administering drugs. This, in fact, could eventually become standard practice within hospitals as it becomes the most efficient and cost-effective thing to do. Because of this possibility, patients should understand that these future implications of tagging pharmaceuticals, and they should be given an option to not use them. Because drug information is already printed on bottles, and patients frequently administer drugs to themselves, there is not a strong argument for tracking prescription bottles throughout the hospital. Even if there is some marginal health gain to be realized by individual patients by tracking their drugs using RFID, an educated patient should be able to make an informed decision as to whether or not he wants his drug bottle to be tagged.

Despite these concerns about broader tracking of prescriptions within the hospital, there may be legitimate reasons for tagging pharmaceuticals. For example, if drugs are to be taken by patients at certain times of the day, or there is a limit on how many times a drug should be administered to a patient, RFID may be a valuable tool to identify that a prescription bottle was taken from the patient's bedside at the wrong time of the day. This could sound an alarm that informs nurses that a patient may have improperly taken a drug. It also may be useful for patients who take several prescriptions and must keep track of all of them. Measures beyond RFID, however, can be taken to solve those types of problems. This is because most patients are capable of reading labels and administering drugs to themselves, and the efficiency gains from this use of RFID tagged pharmaceuticals do not appear to be great. The tracking of such drugs within the hospital may be a more feasible option for those who are incapacitated or face unique challenges, but this still does not provide a reason to track pharmaceuticals absent consent and adequate privacy protections.

Overall, while a well-implemented RFID blood inventory system could improve hospital efficiency and provide a good service to patients and the hospital, the tagging of pharmaceuticals should be primarily used for inventory management in the ways employed by companies such as CVS. Once a hospital pharmacy is assured that it has the correct drugs, it does not make sense to make associations between pharmaceuticals and patients within the hospital who are prescribed to receive those drugs, especially given the privacy risks that could result from tagging patient assets.

D. Tagging of Humans

There are several types of "human tagging" that could be implemented within hospitals. First, the tagging can occur at two distinct levels, since tags can either be external in the form of a wearable device or internal implants under the skin of the patient. This external tagging is occurring in hospitals right now: Alexandra Hospital in Singapore tracks all "patients, visitors, and staff entering the hospital" using an ID card (Brown, 2006, p. 157). Jacobi Hospital in New York, moreover, issues wristbands encoded with a patient ID number to all patients upon check-in. These wristbands are accessed by tablet computers that have their own RFID readers.

The circumstance of a patient who is tagged is relevant in discussing privacy. For example, the circumstances surrounding a patient who is casually admitted to the hospital are distinct from those surrounding someone who is urgently rushed to the emergency room. Circumstances surrounding the tagging of children and the elderly differ as well. I therefore examine several different forms of human tagging in this analysis. First, I discuss the privacy measures we believe should be considered for implantable versus external tags, and then go into the issues of tagging different people facing different circumstances.

1. Implantable RFID: The VeriChip

While the tagging of babies, the elderly, and other humans has presented some concerns, the most controversial of all applications has been *implantable* RFID. As mentioned before, this is the one form of RFID in the medical field that has been explicitly banned by state statutes. The *Verichip* is an implantable RFID device that is about the size of a grain of rice and contains a unique ID number. Proponents argue that this device has invaluable applications to the medical field because it can be used as a fail-safe identifier in the case of an emergency. If, for example, a person is unconscious upon arrival to the hospital emergency room, that person can still be easily identified in the event that the hospital has a *VeriChip* compatible reader. The chip's unique identifier can be associated with a database that contains a person's medical records, ensuring that the hospital properly obtains a person's blood type, medication history, and other important information. And, according to Arthur Caplan, director of the Bioethics center at the University of Pennsylvania, "you are more likely to die or be harmed by lack of medical information about you than by people knowing too much about your medical information—in an emergency, it's important for doctors to know what your allergies and medical problems are…." (DeNoon, "Chip Implants", 2005).

Moreover, this chip may be used to identify elderly patients - those suffering from dementia or Alzheimer's disease. An example of this is described in a March 2006 Washington Post article, in which Roxanne Fischer explained that she had the *VeriChip* implanted in her 83 year old mother. Roxanne did this in case she could not be reached in the event of an emergency, and implanting the device in her mother gave her "tremendous peace of mind." Although few people have implanted the chips as of now, *VeriChip* has offered extensive incentives to hospitals to deploy the infrastructure for the technology—for example, it provides free readers to hospitals that sell the chip (Stein 2006). A new company, PositiveID, now holds the rights to the *VeriChip*.

Overall, this particular application has not been received well, and the reasons for this are clear. First, such chips could make it easier for unauthorized third parties to access medical records. Mainly, however, some fear that the chips will lead to an Orwellian society in which individuals are constantly monitored—unlike other solutions, the chips are permanently readable and cannot be turned "off." Moreover, people like Richard Smith (Internet and privacy consultant in Boston) say that "it's not a secure chip—there's nothing to stop someone from accessing the code and cloning the chip to access records." In fact, Westhues cracked the *VeriChip* in less than two hours in 2006 (Ulatowski, 2008, p. 647). Finally, who can access the databases that store medical information? Given a unique ID and access to PositiveID's VeriMed database, it is not difficult for a third party to obtain someone's medical records. This, actually, is a problem with all centralized databases. While PositiveID claims that privacy is its utmost priority, its interest is also to make profit. Therefore, concerns about the *VeriChip* must be assessed sooner rather than later. This is especially true as the technology becomes increasingly popular—at a medical convention in 2006, 172 new physicians elected to offer the VeriMed ID system (and therefore the *VeriChip*) to patients, representing a 300% increase over its previous adoption (*VeriChip* Press Release, 2006).

Despite concerns with the VeriMed system, however, *VeriChip* and its successor corporation have been mindful of privacy. The *VeriChip* tag only contains a random identifier that does not contain any personal information, and one must explicitly opt-in to receive the chip. Although the chip is implanted, there is technically an opt-out possibility since the chip may be removed through a "simple procedure." Depending on a patient's privacy preferences, moreover, the patient may choose the extent of data stored on the VeriMed servers. Finally, because the VeriMed system employs passive tags, tracking is difficult because a reader must be within 2.5 inches of a person to read the tag.

Under a utilitarian framework, however, one desires that hospitals provide full information to patients regarding the *VeriChip*'s overall implications. For those RFID applications that will stay within a given hospital's confines (wristbands, tagged blood etc.), these implications do not usually extend beyond the hospital, and the information provided may not need to be very extensive. However, the privacy implications of *VeriChip* extend beyond the hospital domain and to areas well outside the hospital—this is especially due to the difficulty of "turning off" the chip absent a medical procedure.

With more robust institutions that enforce standards of system design to ensure privacy, approval of RFID hospital systems will eventually become more stringent and we will be able to prevent more privacy harms before they happen. It is dubious that the FDA, in approving the *VeriChip*, undertook a broad consideration of its privacy implications during the approval process. And, because *VeriChip* has not seen widespread implementation yet, we are uncertain as to how broad the privacy effects from its current design will be. Because of these uncertainties, and the *potential* for particularly strong privacy effects in this case, we need strong institutions along with laws that maintain patients' rights to seek compensatory damages if they are misinformed.

2. Neo-Natal Intensive Care Units

One of the more tailored RFID applications considered within hospitals is that within neo-natal intensive care units (NICUs). This is because NICUs present several unique challenges to patient identification. Unlike a typical hospital stay for an adult, during which a person is likely to stay in the same hospital bed for a period of several days, hospital stays for babies in the NICU are rotated throughout a facility based on sensitive aspects of each patient's condition. For example, a patient may be on a warming table one day, in an incubator the next day, or in a bassinet on another day depending on his or her condition. This transitory nature of patient stays in the NICU requires robust identification. Moreover, it is very difficult to tell children apart during the nascent stages of their development. Gender is not apparent, and the babies do not have distinct facial characteristics. Finally, children often come to the NICU with identical or similar sounding surnames—according to one study, this factor alone is a distinct risk possibility approximately 51% of the time a NICU is in operation (Gray 2006).

Misidentification raises serious ethical and practical concerns. For example, Simpson et al. (2004) found that approximately 25% of the medication errors in a British NICU were associated with identification errors. In addition, Suresh et al (2004) found that 11% of errors reported to a voluntary error reporting system in Vermont were associated with patient errors. Once we know that a significant number of errors in the NICU are attributable to misidentification and we acknowledge that these errors pose harmful health consequences, this is a serious issue.

Despite the need for robust identification, the identification of babies in the NICU also must not be intrusive so as to infringe on the health of the infant. The skins of babies in the NICU, for example, are very sensitive to touch and to light. Therefore, any identification measure that makes physical contact with the skin needs to be used with caution—along those lines, identification methods should not force the doctor or nurse to need to physically move the patient, since this movement may do physical harm to the child. It may also interrupt the patient's *stasis*—studies have shown that the conditions in the NICU should simulate conditions in the mother's womb as much as possible, and any exogenous forces that force movement may inhibit the child's normal development.

When visiting a NICU at Beth Israel, I was told that patient identification numbers were assigned sequentially. While this is an easy method of assignment, studies of medical error indicate that many common identification errors in medical records stem from flipped digits or the fact that a single digit may be off by one or two numbers. As such, numbering children sequentially in the

NICU may be a risky proposition, especially when a set of triplets in the NICU—already practically indistinguishable—receives such sequential numbers. Moreover, there is no checkdigit at the end of patient identification numbers that are given out at Beth Israel Deaconness and other hospitals. Thus, there is no way to independently verify that the number corresponding to a given patient is legit (Gray et al. 2006).

Besides identifying the neonates themselves, identifying key NICU items such as breast milk is critical. This is because, when babies stay in the NICU, they are commonly separated from their mothers. The emphasis on identifying breast milk results from past problems that were caused by giving breast milk from an incorrect mother to an infant. Things that contribute to these errors, Gray notes, are incorrectly labeled specimens, difficult-to-read handwritten specimen labels, errors in verification of patient/aliquot identification, and systematic problems with the storage of the aliquots. These facts, combined with the reality that over 40,000 breast milk feeds are given in the average NICU each year, make it unsurprising that breast milk errors are frequent and of concern.

Another issue of misidentification in the NICU relates to the aforementioned used of wristbands. A study by Howanitz et al. (2002) that surveyed over 200 hospitals found that roughly 7% of patients face identification problems resulting from wristbands—of these errors, 71% of them were a result of missing wristbands and the other 29% resulted from incorrect, missing, or incomplete information associated with those bands. Note that this 7% number reflects the rate of misidentification from wristbands of *general patient cohorts.* In the cohort of NICU patients, this rate may be much higher due to the aforementioned concerns of lacerating the sensitive skins of infants and the general difficulty of finding a suitable attachment point for the wristband on the infant. This means that many bands are affixed to patients' charts or incubators and that could lead to even more misidentification.

There are several potential benefits to applying RFID to this area. However, there is once again a substantial amount of uncertainty since babies within NICUs have never actually been tagged—this makes our utilitarian framework difficult to apply, since individuals who are subjected to the technology will not be able to make rational choices about its use. What we do know is that, if the benefits conferred unto infants are worthwhile, systems must be designed with particular care in this area. Some bodies of research speculate that RFID may present adverse health risks to individuals. The general nature of neonates may make them particularly susceptible to these risks. Thus, if an implementation of RFID were to exist in the NICU, its existence and implications should be fully explained to parents who should then be given the option (on behalf of the patient) to use a wristband that does or does not include RFID. While the tagging of breast milk can be addressed by taking measures similar to those we suggest for blood bags, NICU RFID implementations raise far more complex issues that will need to be addressed as they arise.

3. Care for the Elderly: Long Term Care Centers

Another interesting application of RFID that has been considered is within the realm of long-term care centers for the elderly. In long-term care centers, elderly patients may experience symptoms of dementia or Alzheimer's disease, and this may result in their wandering away from the point of care. Although there are generally safeguards in long-term care centers to prevent such "escapes," these safeguards only extend to the care wards themselves—it may useful to employ a technology that can be applied when, for example, dementia patients are taken away from the facility by family or friends—however, measures are already in place in most long-term care centers to address that problem, so the real benefit of RFID is unlikely to come there.

Nevertheless, if RFID could adequately monitor the elderly population more generally, this may reduce the need for some long-term care centers in the first place. Given the impending baby boom and the demand that the rapidly growing elderly community will place on limited health care resources, hospitals could shift resources away from long-term care and towards broader applications in the home or elsewhere. Because long-term care is currently very resource intensive and often mandates that patients be separated from their families, this may be a good reason to apply RFID to patients who are experiencing such symptoms.

Most of the RFID solutions that have been proposed to facilitate long term care in the home focus on the ability to do "OKness" checking. A tagged elderly person lives in a home in which almost all items are tagged—prescription drugs, the telephone, and maybe even the TV remote control would be tagged in such scenarios. A close relative can then verify that the elderly patient takes his or her medicine at the prescribed time, and that other portions of the patient's "daily routine" are executed normally. If the patient diverts from his or her usual routine, the RFID system could be configured to set off an alarm that would notify a relative, nurse, or doctor. In addition, assuming that the patient was tagged, long periods of patient activity could be flagged by the system. For patients who are largely capable of living on their own, but are experiencing the initial signs of dementia or Alzheimer's, an RFID system may provide the elderly patient with an alternative to living in a nursing home that would probably be much more desirable (Fishkin and Lundell, 2006).

Despite these benefits, such a system could raise several privacy issues. If RFID systems, for example, contained readers that are able to read tags throughout the entirety of homes, the systems would have to be designed so that the tags placed throughout the home were unreadable. We would not want an adversary sitting in the bushes outside a tagged patient's house to be able to track the rich elderly patient's every move. Maybe the tagged patient in this case has a substantial store of money in the house or other valuables, and this adversary could use the RFID system to gauge the likelihood of a successful burglary. Moreover, the system needs to be designed so that the readers cannot successfully read the tags from outside the home where the system is implemented. If we were in a world where adjacent houses employed these systems, we would not want two separate systems to be able to identify patients and items outside of their domain.

Additionally, the opt-in default for a system like this would, in many cases, not be exercised by the patients themselves. Because of this, relatives who make decisions for elderly patients need to be fully informed about the technology, just as mothers do when they are presented with the possibility that their babies are tagged with RFID. Serious ethical debates are raised when relatives try to make decisions "on behalf of" elderly or incapacitated patients, however, so it may be necessary to gauge public response to this form of RFID before implementing it. Finally, while such systems may be useful and indeed necessary, it is important to reaffirm the importance of personal interaction in taking care of the elderly. If implemented, RFID should not be used solely to give relatives "peace of mind" and an excuse to not check up on or take care of their relatives.

4. Emergency Room and Operating Room RFID

Obviously, the opt-in provisions have their limitations, as I have stressed how these provisions break down when there is a lack of full information. *Spychips,* moreover, makes a valid point when it questions how legitimate consent actually is in the context of a hospital emergency room. In that context, people want to obtain care immediately and they will sign just about anything. It may have been somewhat unethical, therefore, for the Memphis Regional Medical Center to have conducted RFID trials in their operating room in which they claimed to obtain "consent" (Albrecht and McIntyre, 2005, p. 111). That is not to say that there is no room for legitimate ways to obtain an individual's consent in this area. Knowing that initial consent may not be legitimate, the hospital can later follow up with a patient to ensure that there is a willingness to be tagged. If efficiency gains within the ER and OR are significant—especially given the need for rapid service in this area—it may be worth relaxing opt-out provisions for these patients.

Empirically, however, RFID can promote tangible benefits in emergency department. Because every second counts in the emergency room, the efficiency gains from RFID in this area may have an even greater impact on patient health. At the emergency department at Christina Care in Wilmington, Delaware, for example, an RFID tracking system "was able to reduce the average length of stay for admitted patients by 36 minutes in the [emergency] department and to reduce the average length of stay for patient[s] released from the [emergency department] by 14 minutes" (Banks et al., 2007, p. 315). But it is not clear if this implementation has sought to protect privacy.

There are some final concerns that are raised by RFID applications in the ER and OR. For many patients, the ER is the only option for medical care. The poor oftentimes do not have insurance and are unable to make everyday appointments with doctors at hospitals, meaning that these patients disproportionately seek the ER. In addition, any patient facing an emergency must always go to the ER. Because of this, many patients who are subjected to the ER do not have any choice in the first place. Thus, if an RFID enabled ER exists in a hospital, and all patients are required to be tagged in that ER, there are many patients who could effectively have no choice. And, while patients may obtain increased health benefits from an RFID enabled ER or OR, they should be given the option to opt-out wherever possible. Most importantly, every effort should be made to ensure that care provided to those who opt-out is of comparable quality to the care given to those who do not opt-out. This is possible in the context of an RFID-enabled OR or ER. If an OR is enabled to use RFID tools and instruments, and much of the efficiency gains are realized from the tagging of these items, failing to tag the patient alone should not substantially impact patient care. If it would impact patient care, and substantially more utility is gained from the necessary tagging of the patient, it may be a worthwhile consideration to relax opt-out provisions.

V. CONCLUSION AND RECOMMENDATIONS

Privacy is a legitimate concern raised by RFID, and this chapter has highlighted several areas where hospital RFID implementations may negatively impact patient privacy. Nevertheless, RFID also has the potential to increase operating efficiency, improve quality of care, and reduce medical error.

If we knew how significant the benefits of implementing RFID really were, we would be in a better position to assess the tradeoffs between privacy and the public good to determine an "ideal" policy. Unfortunately, we do not. Although asset management RFID pilots have indicated that significant ROI benefits can be realized by some hospitals, the realization of positive ROIs in other hospitals is uncertain. And, although RFID has increased operating efficiency in some hospital pilots, the extent of RFID's positive impact remains blurry. Thus, additional pilots need to be undertaken within hospitals to assess how beneficial RFID really is. Ideally, such pilots will be designed in ways that will allow us to grasp the maximum benefits RFID confers.

Meanwhile, as we continue to assess the viability of RFID in the hospital setting, implementers of RFID should not do so hastily. Hospitals should be held accountable for infringements of patient privacy, and this accountability should extend to the technical design choices that are made by implementers.

After gaining a better understanding of the costs and benefits RFID provides in various hospital applications, we will be better able to assess privacy tradeoffs and make clear-cut recommendations. For example, in situations where time is of the essence, such as when patients are rushed to the ER, it may be worth relaxing opt-out provisions if that makes the difference between life and death. In other situations where RFID does not make as direct an impact on an individual patient's health, hospital efficiency may be inhibited somewhat by additional bureaucratic red tape that serves the interest of privacy.

Meanwhile, there needs to be an acknowledgment that RFID is here to stay. In a survey of over 300 healthcare providers released in November 2005, roughly 74% of them anticipated investment in RFID by 2007. The FDA also continues to affirm its recommendation made in February 2004 that the entire pharmaceutical supply chain use RFID. Most recently, the 2010 RFID Journal Live conference featured an entire track of panel discussions devoted to applications of RFID in the health care and pharmaceutical industries. At this conference, speakers were slated to discuss issues related to both pharmaceutical tracking and asset management.

The goal of this chapter is simply to begin an interesting discourse on hospital RFID privacy. It has provided several recommendations that should be taken into account by all parties who are concerned about this technology. In searching for the appropriate balance between hospital efficiency and patient privacy, the literature reveals evidence both for and against RFID hospital implementations, and this ultimately raises more questions than answers. The law, meanwhile, has little to say on the topic. Future research will seek to empirically assess the adequacy of privacy protections in both current and future RFID hospital implementations. Further, such research will attempt to accurately gauge hospital patients' true preferences in this area. Once we have a better sense of these preferences and patients are able make fully-informed, rational choices to use RFID in the hospital, we can be confident that we are striking the right balance between hospital efficiency and patient privacy.

REFERENCES

Albrecht, K., & McIntyre, L. (2005). *Spychips: How major corporations and government plan to track your every move with RFID*. Nashville, TN: Nelson Current Publishers.

Banks, J., Pachano, M., Thompson, L., & Hanny, D. (2007). *RFID applied*. Hoboken, NJ: John Wiley & Sons. doi:10.1002/9780470168226

Brewin, B. (2004, November 15). RFID gets FDA push. *Federal Computer Week*. Retrieved April 24, 2010, from http://fcw.com/articles/2004/11/14/rfid-gets-fda-push.aspx

Brown, D. E. (2007). *RFID implementation*. New York: McGraw-Hill.

Bruening, P. J. (2004, July). *RFID technology: What the future holds for commerce, security, and the consumer*. Testimony before the Subcommittee on Commerce, Trade, and Consumer Protection of the House Committee on Energy and Commerce, Washington DC. Retrieved April 24, 2010, from http://cdt.info/testimony/20040714bruening.pdf

Cisco, Inc. (2003). Wireless LAN benefits study. Retrieved April 24, 2010, from http://newsroom.cisco.com/dlls/2003_NOP_WLAN_Benefits_Study.pdf

Collins, J. (2004). Hospitals get healthy dose of RFID. *RFID Journal*. Retrieved April 24, 2010, from http://www.rfidjournal.com/article/view/920http://www.rfidjournal.com/article/view/920http://www.rfidjournal.com/article/view/920http://www.rfidjournal.com/article/view/920http://www.rfid-journal.com/article/view/920

Dalton, J., Ippolito, C., Poncet, I., & Rossini, S. (2005). *Using RFID technologies to reduce blood transfusion errors*. White Paper by Intel Corporation, Autentica, Cisco Systems, and San Raffaele Hospital. Retrieved April 24, 2010, from http://www.cisco.com/web/IT/local_offices/case_history/rfid_in_blood_transfusions_final.pdfhttp://www.cisco.com/web/IT/local_offices/case_history/rfid_in_blood_transfusions_final.pdfhttp://www.cisco.com/web/IT/local_offices/case_history/rfid_in_blood_transfusions_final.pdfhttp://www.cisco.com/web/IT/local_offices/case_history/rfid_in_blood_transfusions_final.pdfhttp://www.cisco.com/web/IT/local_offices/case_history/rfid_in_blood_transfusions_final.pdf

DeNoon, D. (2005, July 27). Chip implants: Better care or privacy scare? *WebMD Medical News*, Retrieved April 24, 2010, from http://www.webmd.com/healthy-aging/news/20050727/chip-implants-better-care-privacy-scarehttp://www.webmd.com/healthy-aging/news/20050727/chip-implants-better-care-privacy-scarehttp://www.webmd.com/healthy-aging/news/20050727/chip-implants-better-care-privacy-scarehttp://www.webmd.com/healthy-aging/news/20050727/chip-implants-better-care-privacy-scarehttp://www.webmd.com/healthy-aging/news/20050727/chip-implants-better-care-privacy-scare

Fanberg, H. (2004). The RFID revolution. *Marketing Health Services, 24*(3), 43–44.

Federal Radio Frequency Device Regulations, 47 C.F.R. § 15.240.Federal Trade Commission. (2005, March). *Radio frequency identification: Applications and implications for consumers*. Workshop report from the Staff of the Federal Trade Commission. Retrieved April 24, 2010, from http://www.ftc.gov/os/2005/03/050308rfidrpt.pdfhttp://www.ftc.gov/os/2005/03/050308rfidrpt.pdfhttp://www.ftc.gov/os/2005/03/050308rfidrpt.pdfhttp://www.ftc.gov/os/2005/03/050308rfidrpt.pdfhttp://www.ftc.gov/os/2005/03/050308rfidrpt.pdf

Fishkin, K., & Lundell, J. (2006). RFID in healthcare. In Garfinkel, S., & Rosenberg, B. (Eds.), *RFID: Applications, security, and privacy*. Reading, MA: Addison-Wesley.

Flaherty, D. H. (1989). *Protecting privacy in surveillance societies: The Federal Republic of Germany, France, Canada, and the United States*. Chapel Hill, NC: University of North Carolina Press.

Garfinkel, S., DeAlmo, J., Leng, S., McAfee, P., & Puddington, J. P. (2006). RFID in the pharmacy: Q&A with CVS. In Garfinkel, S., & Rosenberg, B. (Eds.), *RFID: Applications, security, and privacy*. Reading, MA: Addison-Wesley.

Goth, G. (2006). Tuning in to RFID. *Healthcare Informatics*. Retrieved April 24, 2010, from http://www.healthcare-informatics.com/ME2/dirmod.asp?sid=&nm=&type=Publishing&mod=Publications:Article&mid=8F3A7027421841978F18BE895F87F791&tier=4&id=B02C8A8740984CD7A7FDA241D324FAC1http://www.healthcare-informatics.com/ME2/dirmod.asp?sid=&nm=&type=Publishing&mod=Publications:Article&mid=8F3A7027421841978F18BE895F87F791&tier=4&id=B02C8A8740984CD7A7FDA241D324FAC1http://www.healthcare-informatics.com/ME2/dirmod.asp?sid=&nm=&type=Publishing&mod=Publications:Article&mid=8F3A7027421841978F18BE895F87F791&tier=4&id=B02C8A8740984CD7A7FDA241D324FAC1http://www.healthcare-informatics.com/ME2/dirmod.asp?sid=&nm=&type=Publishing&mod=Publications:Article&mid=8F3A7027421841978F18BE895F87F791&tier=4&id=B02C8A8740984CD7A7FDA241D324FAC1http://www.healthcare-informatics.com/ME2/dirmod.asp?sid=&nm=&type=Publishing&mod=Publications:Article&mid=8F3A7027421841978F18BE895F87F791&tier=4&id=B02C8A8740984CD7A7FDA241D324FAC1

Gray, J. E., Suresh, G., Ursprung, R., Edwards, W. H., Nickerson, J., & Shiono, P. H. (2006). Patient misidentification in the neonatal intensive care unit: Quantification of risk. *Pediatrics*, *117*(1), 43–47. doi:10.1542/peds.2005-0291

HIPAA Privacy Rule. 45 C.F.R § 160.103 (2009).

HIPAA Privacy Rule. 45 C.F.R. § 164.502(a) (2009).

HIPAA Privacy Rule. 45 C.F.R. § 164.502(a)-(b) (2009).

HIPAA Privacy Rule, 45 C.F.R. § 164.512 (2009).

HIPAA Privacy Rule. 45 C.F.R. § 164.514(b) (2009).

Howanitz, P. J., Renner, S. W., & Walsh, M. K. (2002). Continuous wristband monitoring over 2 years decreases identification errors: A College of American Pathologists Q-tracks study. *Archives of Pathology & Laboratory Medicine*, *126*(7), 809–815.

Janz, B. D., Pitts, M. G., & Otondo, R. F. (2005). Information systems and health care II: Back to the future with RFID: Lessons learned — Some old, some new. *Communications of the Association for Information Systems*, *15*(1), 132–148.

Jaques, R. (2004). Hospitals reluctant to deploy RFID. *Computing*. Retrieved April 24, 2010, from http://www.computing.co.uk/vnunet/news/2124641/hospitals-reluctant-deploy-rfidhttp://www.computing.co.uk/vnunet/news/2124641/hospitals-reluctant-deploy-rfidhttp://www.computing.co.uk/vnunet/news/2124641/hospitals-reluctant-deploy-rfidhttp://www.computing.co.uk/vnunet/news/2124641/hospitals-reluctant-deploy-rfidhttp://www.computing.co.uk/vnunet/news/2124641/hospitals-reluctant-deploy-rfid

Journal, R. F. I. D. (2010). *RFID Journal Live! Conference Brochure*, Retrieved April 24, 2010, from http://www.rfidjournalevents.com/live/live2010_brochure.pdfhttp://www.rfidjournalevents.com/live/live2010_brochure.pdfhttp://www.rfidjournalevents.com/live/live2010_brochure.pdfhttp://www.rfidjournalevents.com/live/live2010_brochure.pdfhttp://www.rfidjournalevents.com/live/live2010_brochure.pdf

Meyer, R. J. (2006). Why we under-prepare for hazards. R. J. Daniels, D. F. Kettl, & H. Kunreuther (Eds.), *On risk and disaster: Lessons from Hurricane Katrina* (pp. 153-174). Philadelphia: University of Pennsylvania Press.

Mich. Comp. Laws § 28.304 (2009).

Mobile Aspects. (2005, February 9). *University of Chicago Comer Children's Hospital selects Mobile Aspects: RFID solutions deliver a higher quality of patient care, safety, and operational efficiency* [Press release]. Retrieved from http://www.mobileaspects.com/news_media/pressrelease/press_release_02.09.2005_University_of_Chicago.pdfhttp://www.mobileaspects.com/news_media/pressrelease/press_release_02.09.2005_University_of_Chicago.pdfhttp://www.mobileaspects.com/news_media/pressrelease/press_release_02.09.2005_University_of_Chicago.pdfhttp://www.mobileaspects.com/news_media/pressrelease/press_release_02.09.2005_University_of_Chicago.pdfhttp://www.mobileaspects.com/news_media/pressrelease/press_release_02.09.2005_University_of_Chicago.pdf

Monegain, B. (2005, September 12). Study: Passive RFID not ready for prime time in healthcare. *Healthcare IT News*. Retrieved April 24, 2010, from http://www.healthcareitnews.com/news/study-passive-rfid-not-ready-prime-time-healthcarehttp://www.healthcareitnews.com/news/study-passive-rfid-not-ready-prime-time-healthcarehttp://www.healthcareitnews.com/news/study-passive-rfid-not-ready-prime-time-healthcarehttp://www.healthcareitnews.com/news/study-passive-rfid-not-ready-prime-time-healthcarehttp://www.healthcareitnews.com/news/study-passive-rfid-not-ready-prime-time-healthcare

National Conference of State Legislatures. (2010, January). State statutes relating to radio frequency identification (RFID) and privacy. Retrieved April 24, 2010, from http://www.ncsl.org/default.aspx?tabid=13442http://www.ncsl.org/default.aspx?tabid=13442http://www.ncsl.org/default.aspx?tabid=13442http://www.ncsl.org/default.aspx?tabid=13442http://www.ncsl.org/default.aspx?tabid=13442

Nev. Rev. Stat. §§ 205.461-205.4675 (2009).

New Hampshire Commission on the Use of Radio Frequency Technology. (2008, November). *Final report*. Retrieved April 24, 2010, from http://www.gencourt.state.nh.us/statstudcomm/reports/1812.pdfhttp://www.gencourt.state.nh.us/statstudcomm/reports/1812.pdfhttp://www.gencourt.state.nh.us/statstudcomm/reports/1812.pdfhttp://www.gencourt.state.nh.us/statstudcomm/reports/1812.pdfhttp://www.gencourt.state.nh.us/statstudcomm/reports/1812.pdf

Rotenberg, M. (1994, October). *Privacy and security for medical information systems*. Paper presented at American Health Information Management Association National Convention.

Schwartz, P. M. (2004). Property, privacy, and personal data. *Harvard Law Review*, *117*, 2055. doi:10.2307/4093335

Schwartz, P. M. (2006). Privacy inalienability and personal data chips. In Strandburg, K., & Raicu, D. S. (Eds.), *Privacy and technologies of identity: A cross-disciplinary conversation* (pp. 93–114). New York: Springer. doi:10.1007/0-387-28222-X_6

Schwartz, P. M. (2009). Preemption and privacy. *The Yale Law Journal*, *118*, 902.

Siegal, G., Siegal, N., & Weisman, Y. (2001). Physicians' attitudes toward patients' rights legislation. *Medicine and Law*, *20*(1), 63–78.

Simpson, H. S., Lynch, R., Grant, J., & Alroomi, L. (2004). Reducing medication errors within the neonatal intensive care unit. [Special fetal neonatal issue]. *Archives of Disease in Childhood*, *89*(6), F480–F482.

Slutsman, J., Kass, N., McGready, J., & Wynia, M. (2005). Health information, the HIPAA privacy rule, and health care: What do physicians think? *Health Affairs*, *24*(3), 832–841. doi:10.1377/hlthaff.24.3.832

Solove, D. (2008). *Understanding privacy*. Cambridge, MA: Harvard University Press.

Sommer, K. (2009). Riding the wave: The uncertain future of RFID legislation. *Journal of Legislation*, *35*, 48.

Sotto, L. J. (2005). An RFID code of conduct. *RFID Journal*. Retrieved April 24, 2010, from http://www.rfidjournal.com/article/view/1624/http://www.rfidjournal.com/article/view/1624/http://www.rfidjournal.com/article/view/1624/http://www.rfidjournal.com/article/view/1624/http://www.rfidjournal.com/article/view/1624/

Stein, R. (2006, March 15). Use of implanted patient-data chips stirs debate on medicine vs. privacy. *Washington Post*. Retrieved April 24, 2010, from http://www.washingtonpost.com/wp-dyn/content/article/2006/03/14/AR2006031402039.htmlhttp://www.washingtonpost.com/wp-dyn/content/article/2006/03/14/AR2006031402039.htmlhttp://www.washingtonpost.com/wp-dyn/content/article/2006/03/14/AR2006031402039.htmlhttp://www.washingtonpost.com/wp-dyn/content/article/2006/03/14/AR2006031402039.htmlhttp://www.washingtonpost.com/wp-dyn/content/article/2006/03/14/AR2006031402039.html

Strickland, L. S., & Hunt, L. E. (2005). Technology, security, and individual privacy: New tools, new threats, and new public perceptions. *Journal of the American Society for Information Science and Technology*, *56*(3), 221–234. doi:10.1002/asi.20122

Suresh, G., Horbar, J. D., Plsek, P., Gray, J., Edwards, W. H., & Shiono, P. H. (2004). Voluntary anonymous reporting of medical errors for neonatal intensive care. *Pediatrics*, *113*(6), 1609–1618. doi:10.1542/peds.113.6.1609

Sweeney, L. (1998). *Re-identification of de-identified medical data. Testimony before the National Center for Vital Health Statistics on the subject of medical data and privacy*. Baltimore, MD: HIPAA.

Ulatowski, L. M. (2008). Recent development in RFID technology: Weighing technology against potential privacy concerns. *Journal of Law and Policy For The Information Society*, *3*, 623.

U.S. Department of Health and Human Services. (2003, May). *OCR privacy brief: Summary of the HIPAA privacy rule*. Retrieved April 24, 2010, from http://www.hhs.gov/ocr/privacy/hipaa/understanding/summary/privacysummary.pdfhttp://www.hhs.gov/ocr/privacy/hipaa/understanding/summary/privacysummary.pdfhttp://www.hhs.gov/ocr/privacy/hipaa/understanding/summary/privacysummary.pdfhttp://www.hhs.gov/ocr/privacy/hipaa/understanding/summary/privacysummary.pdfhttp://www.hhs.gov/ocr/privacy/hipaa/understanding/summary/privacysummary.pdf

VeriChip. (2006). *VeriMed patient identification*. Retreived April 24, 2010, from http://www.verimedinfo.com/files/Patient_VM-003R2(web).pdfhttp://www.verimedinfo.com/files/Patient_VM-003R2(web).pdfhttp://www.verimedinfo.com/files/Patient_VM-003R2(web).pdfhttp://www.verimedinfo.com/files/Patient_VM-003R2(web).pdfhttp://www.verimedinfo.com/files/Patient_VM-003R2(web).pdf

VeriChip. (2006, March 20). *VeriChip Corporation expands infrastructure rollout of VeriMed patient identification system — 172 new physicians elect to offer VeriMed ID system to patients* [Press release]. Retrieved from http://www.redorbit.com/news/health/435457/verichip_corporation_expands_infrastructure_rollout_of_verimed_patient_identification_system/http://www.redorbit.com/news/health/435457/verichip_corporation_expands_infrastructure_rollout_of_verimed_patient_identification_system/http://www.redorbit.com/news/health/435457/verichip_corporation_expands_infrastructure_rollout_of_verimed_patient_identification_system/http://www.redorbit.com/news/health/435457/verichip_corporation_expands_infrastructure_rollout_of_verimed_patient_identification_system/http://www.redorbit.com/news/health/435457/verichip_corporation_expands_infrastructure_rollout_of_verimed_patient_identification_system/

Wang, S., Chen, W., Ong, C., Liu, L., & Chuang, Y. (2006). RFID applications in hospitals: A case study on a demonstration RFID project in a Taiwan hospital. In *Proceedings of the 39th Hawaii International Conference on System Sciences*.

ENDNOTE

1 Passive RFID tags do not have their own internal power sources. They are powered by the signals that are read by the tags and have short read ranges. Active RFID tags, on the other hand, are powered by their own battery sources and can propagate signals much farther than passive RFID tags.

APPENDIX: SUMMARY OF RECOMMENDATIONS

Figure 1.

Procedural Recommendations
1. Patients need to have the ability to make fully informed, rational choices as to whether or not they wish to participate in RFID pilots and implementations within hospitals
2. Implementers should not be allowed to assume that acceptance of RFID technology by patients in some areas implies acceptance in other areas.
3. Implementers need to ensure that systems conform to design principles that minimize privacy risks. Procedural privacy safeguards should complement these system designs.
4. Strong limits of information transfer should be observed, and patients should both know and have control over data that is associated with RFID tags. Even if tags themselves do not store information and personal information is stored on isolated databases, implementers need to consider insider abuse and all potential opportunities that personally identifiable information can be seen by unauthorized persons.
5. The opt-in default should be strongly observed because it promotes the dissemination of information to patients and allows them to make rational choices. The principle of full information underlies much of our analysis, and we believe that providing patients and the community full information leads to levels of public scrutiny that are necessary to ensure that RFID systems are protecting privacy in the public's interest. When patients do not opt-in, hospitals should offer bifurcated solutions.
6. The right of exit should also be strongly observed.
7. A framework should be created that allows patients to seek compensatory damages in the event their protected information is leaked or disseminated unjustifiably. Our utilitarian discourse requires this, and it is in the best interest of patients to have recourse against delinquent implementations.
Legal Recommendations
1. Institutions should be created that protect data privacy. Such institutions should have staff members that specialize in RFID privacy issues. This could take the form of a "Data Protection Commission" or some other form. These institutions could enforce RFID system design standards that minimize privacy risks and outline protocol that should be followed by hospitals and other health organizations that implement RFID solutions.
2. Laws should bolster HIPAA and existing laws to protect RFID privacy rights, but not in ways that are overly restrictive on the development of RFID applications. For example, laws should focus on scrutinizing the ways RFID systems are implemented, not on the fact that RFID is used in general.
3. The law has a role in ensuring that full information is provided. Patients, doctors, and the community will need to understand the motivation for passing laws. It is possible that patients, doctors, and the community at large will not take laws seriously if they do not understand the rationale for them. Laws need to have legitimacy to be effective, and legislatures need to give any laws that are passed legitimacy by communicating these rationales to their constituents and to doctors.
4. Lobbying should be regulated. Patients need to understand the nuances of the debate because corporations have substantial lobbying power. Corporate and lobbyist considerations should not outweigh *actual* constituent concerns. Legitimate proxies for public opinion need to be assessed before inaccurately assuming what the public believes based on the overrepresentation of some concentrated interest

Chapter 11
Privacy Expectations in Passive RFID Tagging of Motor Vehicles: *Bayan Muna et al. v. Mendoza et al.* in the Philippine Supreme Court

Diane A. Desierto
Yale Law School, USA & University of the Philippines College of Law, Philippines

ABSTRACT

This paper describes Bayan Muna et al. v. Mendoza et al., a 2009 Philippine Supreme Court petition involving the first and ongoing certiorari challenge to the Philippine government's implementation of passive Radio Frequency Identification (RFID) technology in the registration of all motor vehicles in the Philippines. As a matter of constitutional jurisprudence and policy, the passive use of RFID technology in this context does not infringe constitutionally-protected privacy expectations, entirely consistent with the Executive Branch's law enforcement powers. The paper shows how the proposed RFID tagging of motor vehicles in the Philippines satisfies the tests of reasonable expectations, and by dealing only with already publicly available information, avoids spectral fears of data mining and government abuse.

I. INTRODUCTION

For a postcolonial and post-dictatorship democracy such as the Philippines (Desierto, 2009), governmental acquisition and use of information almost always conjures fears of reversion to a police state. In 1998, the Philippine Supreme Court struck down an initial governmental attempt to implement a national ID system *(Ople v. Torres et al.,* 1998) due to the lack of previous legislative enactment, but the Court also declared in *obiter dicta* that the proposed national ID system violated an already jurisprudentially-recognized *(Morfe v. Mutuc,* 1968) constitutional right to privacy. The same *obiter dicta* stressed provisions in the 1987 Philippine Constitution (CONST. (Phil) art. III, secs. 1, 2, 3(1), 6, 8, 17) and Philippine statutes (Civil Code Arts. 26, 32, 723; Revised Penal Code Arts. 229, 290-292, 280; Republic Act Nos. 4200, 1405, and 8293; Rule 130(C), Sec. 24, Revised Rules of Evidence) that explicitly recognized the right to privacy as well as its various facets. In 2006, however, the Court upheld an Executive Branch measure that created a multi-purpose

DOI: 10.4018/978-1-60960-083-9.ch011

uniform ID system applicable to governmental agencies and entities that had, up to then, issued separate ID cards to private citizens availing of basic governmental services such as health insurance (through Philhealth), pensions (through the Government Service Insurance System or Social Security System, or GSIS and SSS, respectively), and licensing of motor vehicles (through the Land Transportation Office or LTO) *(Kilusang Mayo Uno et al. v. The Director General et al.,* 2006). The unanimous Court in *Kilusang Mayo Uno et al. v. The Director General et al.* (2006) ruled that this multi-purpose uniform ID system did not violate the right to privacy, since the system would only consolidate information already publicly available in government agencies; there were adequate safeguards that already protected such information and controlled its use; and the system served an important public policy in promoting the efficient delivery of basic governmental services.

In the last quarter of 2009, the Land Transportation Office (LTO) commenced implementation of a passive Radio Frequency Identification (RFID) tagging system for all motor vehicles in the Philippines, as part of the LTO's ongoing comprehensive Information Technology (IT) Project involving centralized driver licensing, motor vehicle registration, law enforcement and traffic adjudication, among others (*The Philippine Star,* 2009). The passive RFID tagging system forms an intrinsic part of the automated processes for identifying motor vehicles, stopping colorum vehicles, and identifying motorists that do not comply with LTO's traffic and motor vehicle emissions regulations (Ruiz, 2010). It is a limited or "passive" implementation of RFID technology (Weinberg, 2007-2008, p. 782; Werbach, 2007, p. 2330; Quirk, 2006; Magid et al., 2009, p. 10), since the tags used do not have any internal battery or global positioning system (GPS) capability (Noda, 2010; Paredes, 2010; Pascual, 2009).

Likewise, these tags do not emit any signal. In the LTO's implementation of the passive RFID tagging system, non-battery powered identification tags or strips would be attached to a motor vehicle and a device called an RFID reader. The RFID reader would be used by LTO officers to identify vehicles by sending a radio frequency signal to the RFID tag. The tag then sends back via radio waves an identifying code to the RFID reader. The RFID reader then downloads pertinent information from the existing database of the LTO which identifies the motor vehicle. This process occurs almost instantaneously, with only the following information appearing on the LTO officer's RFID reader screen: the RFID unique code, Motor Vehicle File Number, Engine Number, Chassis Number, Plate Number, Motor Vehicle Type, Color, Make, Series, Year Model, Body Type, Motor Vehicle Classification, Franchise, Route, Owner/Organization Name, Last Registration Date, and Alarms (settled & unsettled) (Pascual, 2009). These data have long been publicly available at the LTO offices for physical inspection.

By end of 2009, however, several groups filed a petition before the Philippine Supreme Court (subsequently docketed as *Bayan Muna et al. v. Leandro R. Mendoza, Secretary of the Department of Transportation and Communications et al.,* under G.R. No. 190431) challenging the LTO's implementation of the passive RFID tagging system, alleging, among other grounds, the violation of motorists' rights to privacy (Ruiz & Panesa, 2010). An overwhelming majority of transport groups and organizations filed a motion for intervention with the Supreme Court, supporting the implementation of the RFID system (Punay & Ronda, 2010; Ronda, 2009; *Business Mirror Online,* 2009). Pending the dispute, the Philippine Supreme Court issued a temporary restraining order on LTO's nationwide implementation of the RFID tagging system (Dalangin-Fernandez, 2010), but did not order the LTO to reimburse fees already collected upon implementation of the project (*ABS-CBN News,* 2010). The LTO has publicly declared that it would respect the Supreme Court's temporary restraining order (Ronda, April 2010). As of this writing, *Bayan*

Muna et al. v. Mendoza et al. remains pending at the Philippine Supreme Court.

This paper examines the alleged privacy infringement of passive RFID tagging of motor vehicles within the context of the Philippine constitutional right to privacy. It shows that passive RFID tagging of motor vehicles, as limited by the LTO to publicly-available data points, does not threaten protected privacy zones in the Philippine constitution and relevant statutes.

II. BACKGROUND ON THE LTO IT PROJECT AND THE PASSIVE RFID TAGGING OF MOTOR VEHICLES

A. Background on the LTO IT Project and the Passive RFID Tagging System

The LTO initiated computerization of its motor vehicle, licensing, and other functions as early as 1997, when it entered into a Build-Operate-Own (BOO) contract with Stradcom Corporation for the design, construction, and maintenance of an Information Technology system (the LTO IT Project) pursuant to Republic Act No. 6967 (as amended by Republic Act No. 7718), otherwise known as the Philippine Build-Operate-and-Transfer (BOT) Law, and its counterpart administrative rules and regulations. Under the BOO contract, Stradcom would own, operate, and maintain all facilities of the LTO IT Project at no cost to the government, while LTO would continue to manage the processing of its transactions (Noda, 2010). As required in Sec. 2(d) of the Philippine BOT Law, the LTO IT Project was officially recommended for approval by the National Economic Development Authority (NEDA), and thereafter approved by the President of the Philippines.

The LTO IT Project is a system-wide concession consisting of various components, such as the Driver's Licensing System (DLS); the Motor Vehicle Registration System (MVRS); Law Enforcement and Traffic Adjudication System (LETAS); Manufacturers, Assemblers, Importers and Dealers Reporting System (MAIDRS); Automated Driver's License Examination System (ADLES); and Revenue Collection System *(The Philippine Star,* 2009). Since its inception, the LTO IT Project has been able to provide interconnectivity between the LTO Central Office, and numerous district offices nationwide, regional offices, driver's license renewal centers, mobile e-patrol service vans, and the law enforcement units of the LTO (Ong, 2009). After over a decade of computerization and improvement in its service efficiency, the LTO received distinction as the only agency of the Philippine government with an ISO:2001 (one of the International Organization for Standardization's key International Standards) certification (*Sun Star,* 2010).

The LTO launched the passive RFID tagging of motor vehicles in 2009 as part of the ongoing implementation of the LTO IT Project, specifically for the Motor Vehicle Registration System (MVRS) and the Law Enforcement and Traffic Adjudication System (LETAS). An RFID tag attached to a motor vehicle would enable LTO personnel with RFID readers to more swiftly retrieve registration information pertaining to the vehicle from the LTO databases, specifically, the: 1) motor vehicle file number; 2) engine number; 3) chassis number; 4) plate number; 5) motor vehicle type; 6) color; 7) series; 8) year model; 9) body type; 10) motor vehicle classification; 11) franchise; 12) route; 13) owner name; 14) last registration date; 15) alarms (settled and unsettled); and 16) other data deemed necessary. Enabling the automated retrieval of this information would greatly support the LTO's law enforcement capabilities, since LTO personnel could more easily detect and apprehend colorum vehicles (or public utility vehicles that operate without a franchise), as well as motorists that do not comply with regulations on emissions testing (*See* DOTC Circular No. 2009-06; LTO Memorandum Circular No. ACL-2009-1199; June 16, 2009 Memorandum of Agreement (MOA) between DOTC and STRADCOM; Weinberg, 2008, pp. 246, 257-258).

Instead of having to physically check and match a vehicle's observable registration information with the information contained in the LTO databases, LTO personnel can determine on the spot if there are discrepancies between the vehicle's apparent information and the LTO databases' registered information. Should such discrepancies be detected, LTO personnel can immediately report the violation and pursue authorized law and/or traffic enforcement measures (Republic Act No. 4136, as amended). In essence, the passive RFID tag fulfils the functions of the LTO's previous validating tags, which also enabled previous LTO personnel to countercheck a vehicle's registration information by going directly to the LTO Offices. The Philippine Congress had long delegated legislative authority to the LTO to issue such validating tags and stickers (and exact corresponding reasonable fees) for purposes of renewing the registration of motor vehicles (Republic Act No. 4136, Section 17, last paragraph), as well as to "at any time examine and inspect any motor vehicle *to determine whether such motor vehicle is registered*, or is unsightly, unsafe, overloaded, improperly marked or equipped, or otherwise unfit to be operated because of possible excessive damage to highways, bridges and/or culverts" [Republic Act No. 4136, Section 4(6)].

B. Legal Authority for the Administrative Issuances Underlying the Passive RFID Tagging System

DOTC Circular No. 2009-06; LTO Memorandum Circular No. ACL-2009-1199; June 16, 2009 Memorandum of Agreement (MOA) between DOTC and STRADCOM collectively comprise the administrative issuances for the LTO's implementation of the passive RFID tagging system for motor vehicles in the Philippines. These administrative issuances were based on the statutory and administrative authority of the Department of Transportation and Communications (DOTC) and the Land Transportation Office (LTO).

On April 13, 1987, President Corazon C. Aquino issued Executive Order No. 125-A amending Executive Order No. 125 entitled "Reorganizing the Ministry of Transportation and Communications, Defining its Powers and Functions and for Other Purposes." Section 5 of E.O. 125, as amended by E.O. 125-A enumerated the powers and functions of the Department of Transportation and Communications as follows:

Sec. 5. Powers and Functions. To accomplish its mandate, the Department shall have the following powers and functions:

(a) Formulate and recommend national policies and guidelines for the preparation and implementation of integrated and comprehensive transportation and communications systems at the national, regional and local levels;
(b) Establish and administer comprehensive and integrated programs for transportation and communications, and for this purpose, may call on any agency, corporation, or organization, whether public or private, whose development programs include transportation and communications as an integral part thereof, to participate and assist in the preparation and implementation of such program;
(c) Assess, review and provide direction to transportation and communication research and development programs of the government in coordination with other institutions concerned;
(d) Administer and enforce all laws, rules and regulations in the field of transportation and communications;
(e) Coordinate with the Department of Public Works and Highways in the design, location, development, rehabilitation, improvement, construction, maintenance and repair of all infrastructure projects and facilities of the Department. However, government corporate entities attached to the Department

shall be authorized to undertake specialized telecommunications, ports, airports and railways projects and facilities as directed by the President of the Philippines or as provided by law;

(f) Establish, operate and maintain a nationwide postal system that shall include mail processing, delivery services, and money order services and promote the art of philately;

(g) Issue certificates of public convenience for the operation of public land and rail transportation utilities and services;

(h) Accredit foreign aircraft manufacturers and/or international organizations for aircraft certification in accordance with established procedures and standards;

(i) Establish and prescribe rules and regulations for identification of routes, zones and/or areas of operations of particular operators of public land services;

(j) Establish and prescribe rules and regulations for the establishment, operation and maintenance of such telecommunications facilities in areas not adequately served by the private sector in order to render such domestic and overseas services that are necessary with due consideration for advances in technology;

(k) Establish and prescribe rules and regulations for the operation and maintenance of a nationwide postal system that shall include mail processing, delivery services, money order services and promotion of philately;

(l) Establish and prescribe rules and regulations for issuance of certificates of public convenience for public land transportation utilities, such as motor vehicles, trimobiles and railways;

(m) Establish and prescribe rules and regulations for the inspection and registration of air and land transportation facilities, such as motor vehicles, trimobiles, railways and aircrafts;

(n) Establish and prescribe rules and regulations for the issuance of licenses to qualified motor vehicle drivers, conductors, and airmen;

(o) Establish and prescribe the corresponding rules and regulations for the enforcement of laws governing land transportation, air transportation and postal services, including the penalties for violations thereof, and for the deputation of appropriate law enforcement agencies in pursuance thereof;

(p) Determine, fix and/or prescribe charges and/or rates pertinent to the operation of public air and land transportation utility facilities and services, except such rates and/or charges as may be prescribed by the Civil Aeronautics Board under its charter, and, in cases where charges or rates are established by international bodies or associations of which the Philippines is a participating member or by bodies or associations recognized by the Philippine government as the proper arbiter of such charges or rates;

(q) Establish and prescribe the rules, regulations, procedures and standards for the accreditation of driving schools;

(r) Administer and operate the Civil Aviation Training Center (CATC) and the National Telecommunications Training Institute (NTTI); and

(s) Perform such other powers and functions as may be prescribed by law, or as may be necessary, incidental, or proper to its mandate or as may be assigned from time to time by the President of the Republic of the Philippines. (Italics supplied).

Under paragraph 'm' and 'o', respectively, the DOTC may prescribe rules for land registration and the enforcement of laws governing land transportation. E.O. 125, as amended by E.O. 125-A was issued by the late President Corazon C. Aquino in the exercise of her legislative power (*MMDA, et al. vs. Viron Transportation Co.*, 2007). The LTO is also empowered to issue LTO Memorandum Circular No. ACL-2009-1199. The LTO Chief occupies the position of Assistant Secretary and under Sec. 11, Chapter 2, of Book IV of E.O. 292

otherwise known as the Administrative Code of 1987, the Assistant Secretary shall perform such duties as may be provided by law or assigned to him by the Secretary. The issuance and promulgation of the implementing rules and regulations of the passive RFID tagging system was assigned by the DOTC to the LTO under the Memorandum of Agreement dated June 16, 2009 between the DOTC/LTO and STRADCOM Corporation. Section 3.1(c), Article III of the MOA provides that the LTO shall "[i]ssue guidelines, rules and regulations governing the implementation of this Agreement in so far as it would (sic) the process of the LTO IT Project's systems."

III. THE PRIVACY CHALLENGE IN *BAYAN MUNA ET AL. V. MENDOZA ET AL.* TO PASSIVE RFID TAGGING OF MOTOR VEHICLES

Among other challenges brought against the legality of the passive RFID system, the Petitioners in *Bayan Muna et al. v. Mendoza et al.* argued that the RFID system constitutes an "impermissible intrusion on people's protected zone of privacy" (*Bayan Muna et al.* Petition, 2009, paras. 26-27). According to them, the threat to the right to privacy of citizens exists from its potential misuse: "[g]iven the correct and exact configuration, the technology could be used by government operatives or malicious elements for information gathering, tracking and surveillance. Neither is it reassuring that as per the LTO's implementing rules, the tags will store 'other data deemed necessary' --- a most ambiguous category" (Salamat, 2009). On the other hand, the Commission on Human Rights subsequently expressed its opinion that the LTO's passive RFID system contained sufficient safeguards and would not violate motorists' right to privacy (Ronda, January 2010). The Commission on Human Rights (CHR) is an independent constitutional office created under the 1987 Philippine Constitution with powers, among others, to "investigate, on its own or on complaint by any party, all forms of human rights violations involving civil and political rights" [1987 Philippine Constitution, art. XIII, sec. 18(1)]. The CHR confirmed that the RFID tags to be used in the LTO IT Project would not be able to track the location or movement of vehicles or their occupants, and that the tags could not have any global positioning capability (Ronda, January 2010).

Clearly, the *Bayan Muna et al.* petitioners' challenge to the passive RFID system involves informational privacy, or "an individual's ability to avoid disclosure of personal matters" (Magid et al., 2009, p. 13). In this case, they assail the possibility of disclosing personal information from the passive RFID tagging of motor vehicles, such as an individual's movements, location, and other activities. The threat to the right to privacy, according to the petitioners, stems from the potential expansion of the RFID system into an unauthorized governmental surveillance. These factual surmises, however, are nowhere supported by the actual narrow operational capabilities of passive RFID tags (Weinberg, 2007-2008, pp. 781-783; Hilliard & Kuzin, 2005; Eschet, 2005, p. 306). The LTO's passive RFID tags can only amount to surveillance if third parties possess readers that can read the tags *and* access the LTO's encrypted databases, *and* if the third party also simultaneously employs extensive visual tracking systems (Eschet, 2005, p. 312). As the following subsections show, however, it is factually improbable for this scenario to materialize. In any event, the features of the LTO's passive RFID system fully satisfy reasonable expectations of privacy as defined under Philippine law and jurisprudence.

A. Features and Safeguards of the Passive RFID System

DOTC Circular No. 2009-06, LTO Memorandum Circular No. ACL-2009-1199, and the June 16, 2009 Memorandum of Agreement (MOA) between DOTC and STRADCOM, rule out the threat of unauthorized access to information read from the passive RFID tags and the corresponding LTO databases. The June 16, 2009 MOA defines RFID as "a method of identifying unique items using radiowaves, through the use of a reader which communicates with an RFID tag, which holds unique digital information in a miniature microchip" (Memorandum of Agreement, 2009, clause 1.13). The RFID tag is only a "sticker to be attached on a motor vehicle's windshield [with] a miniature micro-chip and antenna...hav[ing] the following characteristics: (i) 64-bits unique tag ID; (ii) 128-bits customer-specific tag; (iii) frequency range of 902 to 928 MHZ; (iv) over 100,000 reads and writes; and (v) tamper-proof" (June 16, 2009 Memorandum of Agreement, clause 1.14). Obviously, the passive RFID tag by itself does not store any other information about the driver, occupant, or the owner of the vehicle. It is a passive device that does *not* have its own radio transmitter or location sensing circuit (such as global positioning system/GPS triangulation) and is only fixed to motor vehicles, and *not* individuals. The RFID tag's extremely limited memory cannot store personal information. All that is signaled from the RFID tag to an RFID reader is a code or "unique serial number" that enables access to what has long been publicly-available and accessible registration information in the LTO's motor vehicle registration database (DOTC Circular No. 2009-06; LTO Memorandum Circular No. ACL-2009-1199, clauses 2.12-2.15).

The RFID reader is defined as a "fixed or mobile device that emits radio waves, and receives signals back from an RFID Tag. The RFID reader passes the signal received or information in digital form to a computer system" (June 16, 2009 Memorandum of Agreement, clause 2.13). The RFID reader has a limited reading range of not more than ten (10) meters, much less than the reading range of CCTV cameras that are already used for reading license plate numbers of vehicles traversing several public roads and thoroughfares in the Philippines. Only LTO personnel will have use of RFID readers as part of the Motor Vehicle Registration System (MVRS) and the Law Enforcement and Traffic Adjudication System (LETAS) of the LTO IT Project.

Finally, the passive RFID system, as a continuation of the March 26, 1998 BOO Agreement between the DOTC/LTO and Stradcom, likewise binds the parties to the same confidentiality obligations under Philippine law. The data retrieved by an RFID reader "shall specifically be used only for the intended purpose" (June 16, 2009 Memorandum of Agreement, clause 5.1 at p. 9; DOTC Circular No. 2009-06, LTO Memorandum Circular No. ACL-2009-1199). The scope of the passive RFID system is clearly described as a mere "[e]nhancement of the LTO IT Project's systems, particularly in Motor Vehicle Registration System and Law Enforcement and Traffic Adjudication System...[and] integration of RFID technology... in the PETC [private emission testing center] system" (DOTC Circular No. 2009-06, clauses 1.0-1.2, at p. 1). The passive RFID system's project purposes expressly and narrowly refer only to the motor vehicle registration process, such that information accessed by the authorized user of the RFID reader will necessarily be limited to the LTO's IT Project database on motor vehicle registration. It bears stressing that long before the implementation of the passive RFID system, the LTO has already made such motor vehicle registration information available to the public since 1987 (LTO Memorandum Circular No. 87-038, otherwise known as Guidelines in the Verification of Motor Vehicles, 6 November 1987).

Given these circumstances, the threat of any unwarranted disclosure is remote. Even if a third party were to physically acquire an LTO personnel's RFID reader and use the same to scan RFID tags on motor vehicles, he or she will not be accessing information privileged against public disclosure. The only data points the third party could obtain using an RFID reader are those already publicly and physically available at the LTO offices, namely the: 1) motor vehicle file number; 2) engine number; 3) chassis number; 4) plate number; 5) motor vehicle type; 6) color; 7) series; 8) year model; 9) body type; 10) motor vehicle classification; 11) franchise; 12) route; 13) owner name; 14) last registration date; 15) alarms (settled and unsettled); and 16) other data deemed necessary. While the petitioners in *Bayan Muna et al.* seek to capitalize on the inclusion of the phrase "*other data deemed necessary*" as the potential source of data misuse and unwarranted disclosure (Petition, 2009, paras. 112-113), they overlook that the RFID readers can only access information contained in the LTO IT Project databases, which only contain matters pertaining to the registration of motor vehicles. The phrase "*other data deemed necessary*" must be read in conjunction with the RFID reader's limited ability to access general motor vehicle registration information, and nothing more.

B. Philippine Legal Framework on Privacy and Reasonable Expectations Test

Privacy is both a constitutional and statutory right in the Philippines (*Morfe v. Mutuc,* 1968; Cortes, 1970; Tan, 2008). Core rights on informational privacy are frequently predicated on express provisions of the 1987 Philippine Constitution, such as the due process clause ("*[n]o one shall be deprived of life, liberty, or property without due process of law*", CONST., art. III, sec. 1); the search and seizures clause ("*[t]he right of the people to be secure in their persons, houses, papers, and effects against unreasonable searches and seizures of whatever nature and for any purpose shall be inviolable*", CONST., art. III, sec. 2); and the privacy of communications clause ("*[t]he privacy of communication and correspondence shall be inviolable except upon lawful order of the court, or when public safety or order requires otherwise, as prescribed by law*", CONST., art. III, sec. 3, para. 1). The Philippine Civil Code recognizes causes of action for damages arising from breaches of the right to privacy (Civil Code, Arts. 26, 32, 723), while the Revised Penal Code criminalizes revelation of secrets by public officers, private individuals' discovery of secrets through seizure of correspondence, revelation of secrets with abuse of office, and revealing industrial secrets (Revised Penal Code, Arts. 229, 290-292). The Philippines also has laws on anti-wiretapping (Republic Act No. 4200); bank secrecy (Republic Act No. 1405); protective anonymity measures for rape victims (Republic Act No. 8505, sec. 5); privacy and confidentiality of child and family cases (Republic Act No. 8369, sec. 12); information security against hacking and piracy of copyrighted works under the Electronic Commerce Act (Republic Act No. 8792). This latter statutory category crucially applies in the proposed implementation of the passive RFID tagging system. Section 27(4) of the Electronic Commerce Act explicitly requires government agencies that transact governmental business using electronic data messages or electronic messages to specify, among others, the "control processes and procedures appropriate to ensure adequate integrity, security and confidentiality of electronic data messages or electronic documents or records of payments." In the Philippines, it is the Commission on Information Communications and Technology (CICT) that serves as "the primary policy, planning, coordinating, implementing, regulating, and administrative entity of the executive branch of Government that will promote, develop, and regulate integrated and strategic ICT systems and reliable and cost-efficient communication facilities and services", with a mandate, among others, to "preserve the rights of individuals to privacy and confidentiality of their personal information" (Executive Order No. 269, Sec. 2).

In interpreting the right to privacy, the Philippine Supreme Court has adopted the *Katz* "reasonable expectation of privacy" test (*Katz v. United States,* pp. 351-355) for determining the lawfulness of challenged government regulations resulting in information disclosure (*Ople v. Tor-*

res, 1998). To recall, the *Katz v. United States* test repudiated *Olmstead v. United States'* restrictive requirement of actual physical trespass of property for a 'search' to exist in the constitutional sense (*Olmstead v. United States,* pp. 466-469), in favor of a privacy-based analysis that calibrated individuals' expectations of privacy with governmental safeguards against third-party interception of private information (Winn, 2009, pp. 1-3).

The *Ople* majority, speaking through then Associate (later Chief Justice) Reynato Puno, held that "[t]he reasonableness of a person's expectation of privacy depends on a two-part test: (1) whether, by his conduct, the individual has exhibited an expectation of privacy; and (2) whether this expectation is one that society recognizes as reasonable." The Court qualified this test with the recognition that "[t]he factual circumstances of the case determine the reasonableness of the expectation. However, other factors, such as customs, physical surroundings and practices of a particular activity, may serve to create or diminish this expectation...As technology advances, the level of reasonably expected privacy decreases. The measure of protection granted by the reasonable expectation diminishes as the relevant technology becomes more widely accepted" (*Ople v. Torres,* 1998). The *Ople* test of "reasonable expectation of privacy" has been applied in subsequent cases that assailed governmental measures on the basis of the right to privacy, such as random drug testing (*Social Justice Societ et al. v. Dangerous Drugs Board et al.,* 2008); the uniform ID system (*Kilusang Mayo Uno et al. v. The Director-General et al.,* 2006); search of moving vehicles (*Epie Jr. et al. v. The Hon. Nelsonida T. Ulat-Marredo et al.,* 2007); and routine inspections (*Caballes v. Court of Appeals,* 2002).

C. Testing Reasonable Expectations in the LTO's Passive RFID System

In the Philippines, motor vehicle owners have long been put on notice by Congress, through the Land Transportation and Traffic Code, that the LTO can inspect vehicles to determine their registration (Republic Act No. 4136, Section 4(6), as amended). Motor vehicle owners thus bear necessarily lower privacy expectations when it comes to determining the due registration of motor vehicles, and the LTO's enforcement of other laws and issuances on safety regulation. As the text of LTO Memorandum Circular No. ACL-2009-1199 makes clear, inspections can be reasonably anticipated during the process of registration, renewal of registration, and emission tests thereafter. The reading of a passive RFID tag attached to a motor vehicle is analogous to LTO personnel's routine inspection of motor vehicles to determine registration and compliance with LTO regulations, traffic laws, and other motor safety regulations.

At best, the physical inspection of the exterior of the vehicle (where the RFID tag is attached) comprises a bare and minimal intrusion (if indeed it is an intrusion) that does not violate the right to privacy. The Philippine Supreme Court has declared that visual searches inherent in routine inspections do not violate privacy interests within the constitutional right against unreasonable searches and seizures:

Routine inspections are not regarded as violative of an individual's right against unreasonable search. The search which is normally permissible in this instance is limited to the following instances: (1) where the officer merely draws aside the curtain of a vacant vehicle which is parked on the public fair grounds; (2) simply looks into a vehicle; (3) flashes a light therein without opening the car's doors; (4) where the occupants are not subjected to a physical or body search; (5) where the inspection of the vehicles is limited to a visual search or visual inspection; and (6) where the routine check is conducted in a fixed area (Caballes v. Court of Appeals, 2002).

The passive reading of the signal or digital code from the RFID tag by the authorized user of the RFID readers can, and should, be seen as one such permissible visual inspection.

Finally, in surveying the context of privacy expectations in the Philippines with respect to RFID use, contemporaneous practices might also be taken into account. RFID technology has already been in use and publicly accepted in the Philippines even before the LTO's implementation of the passive RFID system, such as for toll payments in the South Luzon Expressway (the E-Pass), the EC Tag in the North Luzon Expressway, as well as for access cards, authentication cards, ePassports, and private companies' inventory and supply chain management systems (Noda, 2010). No public objections have been raised against these similar uses of RFID technology.

D. Public Purpose and Data Protection

The Philippine Supreme Court recently articulated several badges or indicia of a possible infringement on individuals' reasonable expectations of privacy. In the 2006 case of *Kilusang Mayo Uno et al. v. The Director General et al.*, the Court denied a privacy challenge to a Presidential measure (Executive Order No. 420, "Requiring All Government Agencies and Government-Owned and Controlled Corporations to Streamline and Harmonize their Identification (ID) Systems, and Authorizing for such Purpose the Director-General, National Economic Development Authority to Implement the Same, and for Other Purposes"), that sought to impose a unified multi-purpose ID system applicable to all government agencies and government-owned and controlled corporations that issued ID cards to their members. E.O. 420 specified fourteen data points to be collected from private individuals under the unified multi-purpose ID system: the individual's name, home address, sex, picture, signature, date of birth, place of birth, marital status, names of parents, height, weight, two index fingermarks and two thumbmarks, any prominent distinguishing features like moles and others, and the tax identification number. E.O. 420 listed the following general safeguards:

Section 6. *Safeguards.*– The Director-General, National Economic and Development Authority, and the pertinent agencies shall adopt such safeguards as may be necessary and adequate to ensure that the right to privacy of an individual takes precedence over efficient public service delivery. Such safeguards shall, as a minimum, include the following:

a. The data to be recorded and stored, which shall be used only for purposes of establishing the identity of a person, shall be limited to those specified in Section 3 of this executive order;
b. In no case shall the collection or compilation of other data in violation of a person's right to privacy shall be allowed or tolerated under this order;
c. Stringent systems of access control to data in the identification system shall be instituted;
d. Data collected and stored for this purpose shall be kept and treated as strictly confidential and a personal or written authorization of the Owner shall be required for access and disclosure of data;
e. The identification card to be issued shall be protected by advanced security features and cryptographic technology; and
f. A written request by the Owner of the identification card shall be required for any correction or revision of relevant data, or under such conditions as the participating agency issuing the identification card shall prescribe."

E.O. 420 stated that the adoption of a unified multi-purpose ID system was necessary to ensure the attainment of the following objectives:

a. To reduce costs and thereby lessen the financial burden on both the government and the public brought about by the use of multiple ID cards and the maintenance of redundant database containing the same or related information;
b. To ensure greater convenience for those transacting business with the government and those availing of government services;
c. To facilitate private businesses and promote the wider use of the unified ID card as provided under this executive order;
d. To enhance the integrity and reliability of government-issued ID cards; and
e. To facilitate access to and delivery of quality and effective government service.

Writing for the unanimous Court, Associate Justice Antonio Carpio applied the "reasonable expectations of privacy" test and held that E.O. 420 did not violate such expectations. Using a textual and contextual scrutiny of E.O. 420, Justice Carpio characterized the disclosure requirements under E.O. 420 as "benign and cannot therefore constitute violation of the right to privacy." The information to be disclosed under E.O. 420 appeared mere "routine for ID purposes, data that cannot possibly embarrass or humiliate anyone." Justice Carpio stressed that E.O. 420 "applies only to government entities that already maintain ID systems and issue ID cards pursuant to their regular functions under existing laws…[it] *does not grant such government entities any power that they do not already possess under existing laws*" (Italics supplied). Most importantly, E.O. 420 "makes the existing sectoral card systems of government entities like GSIS, SSS, Philhealth and LTO less costly, more efficient, reliable, and user-friendly to the public" (*Kilusang Mayo Uno et al. v. The Director-General et al.*, 2006). Clearly, the Court's privacy analysis of data protection and public purposes in *Kilusang Mayo Uno* accepts the objective of promoting governmental efficiency as a licit and sufficiently compelling state interest for information access or disclosure. In the same case, the Court recognized the fundamental importance of LTO's licensing functions: "[t]he integrity of the LTO's licensing system will suffer in the absence of a reliable ID system."

Applying the Court's methodological lens in *Kilusang Mayo Uno* to the LTO's proposed implementation of passive RFID tagging, it is evident that the LTO has provided for similarly-worded data protection safeguards. As previously discussed, information accessed by the RFID reader from the passive RFID tag on a motor vehicle is limited only to publicly-available registration information at the LTO IT databases, and are to be used (following the language of Executive Order No. 420 in *Kilusang Mayo Uno*) only for the "intended purpose" of verifying motor vehicle registration and compliance with LTO regulations on registration, safety, and emissions testing. Likewise, the LTO does not gain any power that it does not already posses in implementing the passive RFID tagging system, since the Land Transportation and Traffic Code expressly authorizes the LTO to physically inspect motor vehicles for compliance with LTO registration and other regulations, as well as issue validating tags for purposes of renewal of motor vehicle registration.

Finally, the implementation of a passive RFID tagging system does not create new information, but advances governmental efficiency through expediting and facilitating access to registration information already available to the public. In this case, precisely because the information accessed through the RFID reader is **already publicly-available**, there is an implicit concession of the existence of a compelling interest in ensuring the availability of such information for law enforcement and monitoring compliance with traffic rules and regulations. In the 1964 case of *Morfe v. Mutuc*, the Philippine Supreme Court did not hesitate to reject a privacy challenge against a statutorily-required disclosure of financial information in a statement of assets and liabilities, there being a rational relationship between the disclosure and the objectives of the statute (the Anti-Graft and Corrupt Practices Act of 1960). A similar rational relationship demonstrably subsists in the implementation of the passive RFID system under DOTC Circular Number 2009-06; LTO Memorandum Circular Number ACL-2009-1199; and the June 16, 2009 Memorandum of Agreement between DOTC and STRADCOM. Using passive RFID tagging affords LTO personnel immediate access to publicly-available registration information of motor vehicles while patrolling Philippine roads and thoroughfares, and in so doing, supports the efficient discharge of the LTO's monitoring and regulatory functions under the Land Transportation and Traffic Code (Republic Act No. 4136, sec. 4).

IV. CONCLUSION

Bayan Muna et al. v. The Director-General et al. presents a significant example of technology-influenced privacy analysis. Much of the spectral fears about data misuse concerning the LTO's proposed implementation of passive RFID tagging in motor vehicles throughout the Philippines arise from unfamiliarity with the technology's capabilities and limitations. As this paper has shown, allegations of governmental surveillance can be belied with a systemic view of the actual contours of passive RFID technology in the LTO's verification of registration information as part of the LTO's ongoing IT Project. During the LTO's previous consultations with the transport industry sector, the overwhelming majority of transport groups in the Philippines confirmed understanding of the passive RFID system and expressed support for its use to more expeditiously detect and curtail colorum practices (vehicle owners operating as public utilities without a franchise or license). No less than the Philippine Constitutional Commission on Human Rights has already issued an opinion that this particular limited use and scope of RFID technology does not violate the constitutional and statutory rights to privacy of individuals. The Philippine Commission on Information Communications and Technology has not issued any privacy objections to this particular use of RFID technology. The opinions of these vital stakeholders, agencies, and constituencies should bear persuasive significance in the eventual resolution of *Bayan Muna et al. v. The Director General et al.*

Moreover, the proposed passive RFID tagging of motor vehicles in the Philippines should also be viewed alongside the actual climate of motorists' reasonable expectations of privacy and the extensive data protections already provided under the 1987 Philippine Constitution and the relevant statutes. Motorists and/or vehicle owners, unlike the general mass of individuals, have lower expectations of privacy in operating their vehicles in public roads and thoroughfares because the LTO has the continuing duty, under the Land Transportation and Traffic Code and related laws, to physically inspect vehicles for compliance with motor vehicle registration, safety regulations, and emission level regulations. CCTV (closed circuit television) cameras (which have a greater (and potentially more intrusive) viewing and reading range than an RFID reader's range for reading a passive RFID tag on a motor vehicle) have already been deployed in many key areas of Metropolitan Manila as part of crime prevention and traffic enforcement measures, with no privacy objections raised (Kwok, 2010; *Philippine News Agency,* 2008). Most importantly, the nature of the information to be elicited through passive RFID tagging nowhere appears to be personal information contemplated in the right to privacy. The passive RFID tagging of motor vehicles in the Philippines will simply enable LTO personnel to access motor vehicle registration information that has been made publicly-available at the LTO's physical offices since 1987. Considering this factual context alongside the Philippine legal framework on data protection, the *Bayan Muna et al.* petitioners' privacy challenge remains doubtful.

REFERENCES

ABS-CBN News. (2010, January 13). LTO not ordered to reimburse RFID collection. Retrieved May 19, 2010, from http://www.abs-cbnnews.com/nation/01/13/10/lto-not-ordered-reimburse-rfid-collection

Bayan Muna et al. Petition in *Bayan Muna et al. v. Leandro R. Mendoza et al.*, G.R. No. 190431, (pending before the Supreme Court of the Republic of the Philippines)

Blas, F. *Ople v. Ruben D. Torres, et al.*, G.R. No. 127685, July 23, 1998 (en banc), *citing* Burrows v. Superior Court of San Bernardino County, 13 Cal. 3d 238, 529 P 2d 590 (1974). See Katz v. United states (1967), 389 U.S. 347, 350-352, 88 S. Ct. 507, 19 L. Ed. 2d 576; People v. Krivda (1971) 5 Cal. 3d 357, 364, 96 Cal. Rptr. 62, 486 P. 2d 1262; 8 Cal. 3d 623-624,105 Cal. Rptr. 521, 504 P. 2d 457. Retrieved May 19, 2010, from http://www.lawphil.net/judjuris/juri1998/jul1998/gr_127685_1998.html

Business Mirror Online. (2009, September 27). Transport leaders back RFID project. Retrieved May 19, 2010, from http://businessmirror.com.ph/index.php?option=com_content&view=article&id=16552:transport-leaders-back-rfid-project&catid=26:nation&Itemid=63

Caballes v. Court of Appeals, G.R. No. 136292, January 15, 2002.

DOTC Circular No. 2009-06

Cortes, I. (1970). *The constitutional foundations of privacy*. Quezon City, Philippines: University of the Philippines Law Center.

Dalangin-Fernandez, L. (2010, January 12). Supreme Court stops RFID. *Philippine Daily Inquirer.* Retrieved May 19, 2010 from http://newsinfo.inquirer.net/breakingnews/nation/view/20100112-246939/Supreme-Court-stops-RFID

Desierto, D. (2009). A universalist history of the 1987 Philippine constitution (I). *Historia Constitucional/Electronic Journal of Constitutional History, 10*, 383-444. Retrieved on May 19, 2010 from http://www.historiaconstitucional.com/index.php/historiaconstitucional/article/viewFile/236/209

Eschet, G. (2005). FIPs and PETs for RFID: Protecting privacy in the web of radio frequency identification. *Jurimetrics*, *45*, 301–331.

Executive Order No. 269 (Creating the Commission on Information Communications and Technology), 12 January 2004. Retrieved on May 19, 2010 from http://www.ops.gov.ph/records/eo_no269.htm

Hildner, L. (2006). Defusing the threat of RFID: Protecting consumer privacy through technology-specific legislation at the state level. *Harvard Civil Rights-Civil Liberties Law Review*, *41*, 133–176.

Hillard, D., & Kuzin, J. (2005, January). RFID experiences important growth and regulatory attention. *National Edition.*

Jesus, P. *Morfe v. Amelito Mutuc as Executive Secretary et al.,* G.R. No. L-20387, January 31, 1968 (en banc). Retrieved on May 19, 2010 from http://www.lawphil.net/judjuris/juri1968/jan1968/gr_l-20387_1968.html

Katz v. United States, 389 U.S. 347 (1967).

Kwok, A. (2010, March 2). Installation of more CCTV cameras on expressways pushed. *Philippine Daily Inquirer.* Retrieved on May 19, 2010, from http://newsinfo.inquirer.net/breakingnews/metro/view/20100302-256270/Installation-of-more-CCTV-cameras-on-expressways-pushed

Lorenc, M. (2007). Comment: The mark of the beast: U.S. Government use of RFID in government-issued documents. *Albany Law Journal of Science & Technology*, *17*, 583–614.

Magid, J. M., Tatikonda, M. V., & Cochran, P. L. (2009). Radio frequency identification and privacy law: An integrative approach. *American Business Law Journal*, *46*, 1–54. doi:10.1111/j.1744-1714.2009.01071.x

Maragay, F. (2010, January 13). Birth pains of a high-tech project. *Manila Standard Today.* Retrieved May 19, 2010, from http://www.manilastandardtoday.com/insideOpinion.htm?f=2010/january/13/felmaragay.isx&d=2010/january/13

LTO Memorandum Circular No. 87-038, otherwise known as Guidelines in the Verification of Motor Vehicles, 6 November 1987). June 16, 2009 Memorandum of Agreement (MOA) between DOTC and STRADCOM *EpieJr. et al. v. The Hon. Nelsonida T. Ulat-Marredo*, et al., G.R. No. 148117, March 22, 2007.

LTO Memorandum Circular No. ACL-2009-1199

MMDA., *et al. vs. Viron Transportation Co.,* G.R. No. 170656, 15 May 2007. Retrieved May 19, 2010, from http://www.lawphil.net/judjuris/juri2007/aug2007/gr_170656_2007.html

Act No. 3815, (otherwise known as the Revised Penal Code of the Philippines), December 8, 1930, as amended.

Noda, T. (2010, February). Service breakthroughs: Anytime, anywhere. *Computerworld Philippines.* Retrieved May 19, 2010, from http://computerworld.com.ph/service-breakthroughs-anytime-anywhere/

Olmsteadv. United States, 277 U.S. 438 (1928).

Ong, E. (2009, November 1). Stradcom and LTO get close to people. *Manila Bulletin.* Retrieved May 19, 2010, from http://www.mb.com.ph/node/227466/

Paredes, D. (2010, January 25). On STRADCOM and the LTO. *Business Insight Malaya.* Retrieved May 19, 2010 from http://www.malaya.com.ph/01252010/edducky.html

Pascual, F., Jr. (2009, October 20). Facts and figures on RFID car tags. *The Philippine Star.* Retrieved May 19, 2010, from http://www.philstar.com/Article.aspx?articleid=515822

Philippine News Agency. (2008, February 22). Metro Manila crimes and traffic to be monitored by 56 CCTV cameras. Retrieved May 19, 2010 from http://www.encyclopedia.com/doc/1G1-180007363.html

Privacy International. (2009). Privacy in Asia: Final report of scoping project. Retrieved May 19, 2010, from http://www.privacyinternational.org/issues/asia/privacy_in_asia_phase_1_report.pdf

Punay, E., & Ronda, R. (2010, January 12). Transport groups file support for RFID project before Supreme Court. *The Philippine Star.* Retrieved May 19, 2010 from http://www.philstar.com/Article.aspx?articleId=540015

Quirk, R. (2006, August 30). Commentary: Techlink: Barcodes on steroids. *The Daily Record* [Baltimore, MD].

Remo, M. (2010, January 29). MMDA, WB sign 'bus reduction' for carbon credits project. *Philippine Daily Inquirer.* Retrieved May 19, 2010, from http://newsinfo.inquirer.net/breakingnews/metro/view/20100129-250154/MMDA-WB-sign-bus-reduction-for-carbon-credits-project

Republic Act No. 386, (otherwise known as the Civil Code of the Philippines), June 18, 1949, as amended.

Republic Act No. 1405 (otherwise known as an Act Prohibiting Disclosure of or Inquiry into Deposits with any Banking Institution and providing penalties therefor), September 9, 1955, as amended.

Republic Act No. 4136 (otherwise known as the Land Transportation and Traffic Code), June 20, 1964, as amended.

Republic Act No. 4200 (otherwise known as An Act to Prohibit and Penalize Wire Tapping and other Related Violations of Privacy of Communications, and for other purposes), June 19, 1965, as amended

Republic Act No. 6957, July 9, 1990, as amended by Republic Act No. 7718, (otherwise known as the Philippine BOT Law), May 8, 1994. Retrieved May 19, 2010, from http://www.neda.gov.ph/references/RAs/RAs%207718%20or%20the%20BOT%20Law.pdf

Republic Act No. 8293 (otherwise known as the Intellectual Property Code of the Philippines), June 6, 1997, as amended

Republic Act No. 8369, (otherwise known as the Family Courts Act of 1997), October 28, 1997

Republic Act No. 8505 (otherwise known as the Rape Victim Assistance and Protection Act of 1998), February 13, 1998

Republic Act No. 8792 (otherwise known as the Electronic Commerce Act), June 14, 2000

Revised Rules of Evidence, Rules 128-134, Philippine Rules of Court [1997]

Ronda, R. (2009, December 31). Transport groups back LTO's RFID project. *The Philippine Star.* Retrieved May 19, 2010, from http://www.philstar.com/Article.aspx?articleId=536960&publicationSubCategoryId=65

Ronda, R. (2010, January 4). CHR says RFID tags wn't violate motorists' privacy. *The Philippine Star.* Retrieved May 19, 2010, from http://www.philstar.com/Article.aspx?articleId=537889

Ronda, R. (2010, April 12). LTO chief to respect Supreme Court ruling on RFID. *The Philippine Star.* Retrieved May 19, 2010, from http://www.philstar.com/Article.aspx?articleid=565639

Ruiz, J. C. (2010, January 6). Motorists assured on RFID plan. *Manila Bulletin.* Retrieved May 19, 2010, from http://www.mb.com.ph/articles/237228/motorists-assured-rfid-plan

Ruiz, J. C., & Panesa, E. F. (2010, January 11). RFID stirs protests. *Manila Bulletin.* Retrieved May 19, 2010, from http://www.mb.com.ph/node/238026/rfid-stirs-protests

Salamat, M. (2009, December 20). Solons, Drivers Ask SC to Void Anomalous RFID Project. *Bulatlat.* Retrieved May 19, 2010, from http://www.bulatlat.com/main/2009/12/20/solons-drivers-ask-sc-to-void-anomalous-rfid-project/ and http://www.satur4senator.com/news/2009/12/15/solons-drivers-ask-high-court-void-rfid-project

Social Justice Society et al. v. Dangerous Drugs Board et al., G.R. No. 157870, November 3, 2008 (en banc).

Stanton, J. M. (2008). ICAO and the biometric RFID passport. In Bennett, C. J., & Lyon, D. (Eds.), *Playing the identity card: Surveillance, security and identification in global perspective* (pp. 253–267). New York: Routledge.

Sun Star. (2010, May 19). LTO unveils modernized services. Retrieved May 19, 2010, from http://www.sunstar.com.ph/manila/lto-unveils-modernized-services

Tan, O. (2008, June). Articulating the complete Philippine right to privacy in constitutional and civil law: A tribute to Chief Justice Fernando and Justice Carpio. *Philippine Law Journal, 82*(4), 78–238.

The Constitution of the Republic of the Philippines [1987], Constitutional Commission, Quezon City, Philippines

The Philippine Star. (2009, November 2). Technology brings LTO into the 21st century. Retrieved May 19, 2010, from http://www.philstar.com/ArticlePrinterFriendly.aspx?articleId=519585

Torres, T. (2010, January 11). Transport groups to SC: Car ID system OK. *Philippine Daily Inquirer*". Retrieved May 19, 2010, from http://newsinfo.inquirer.net/breakingnews/nation/view/20100111-246744/Transport-groups-to-SC-Car-ID-system-OK

Uno, K. M., et al. *v. The Director General et al.*, G.R. No. 167798, April 19, 2006 (en banc). Retrieved May 19, 2010, from http://www.lawphil.net/judjuris/juri2006/apr2006/gr_167798_2006.html

Weinberg, J. (2008). RFID and Privacy. In Chander, A., Gelman, L., & Radin, M. J. (Eds.), *Securing privacy in the internet age* (pp. 245–269). Stanford, CA: Stanford Law Books.

Weinberg, J. (2007-2008). Tracking RFID. *I/S: A Journal of Law & Policy for the Information Society, 3*, 777-836.

Werbach, K. (2007). Sensors and sensibilities. *Cardozo Law Review*, *28*, 2321–2371.

Winn, P. (2009). Katz and the origins of the 'Reasonable Expectations of Privacy' test. *McGeorge Law Review*, *40*, 1–13.

Chapter 12
Ambient Intelligence:
Legal Challenges and Possible Directions for Privacy Protection

Shara Monteleone
European University Institute, Italy

ABSTRACT

Unprecedented advances of Information Communication Technologies (ICT) and their involvement in most of private and public activities are revolutionizing daily life and our relationship to our environments. If, on the one hand, the new developments promise to make people's lives more comfortable or more secure, on the other hand, they raise complex social and legal issues in terms of fundamental rights and freedoms. The objective of this paper is to envisage some of the main legal challenges posed by the new Ambient Intelligence technologies (AmI), in particular for the fundamental rights of privacy and data protection, while trying to sketch some possible solutions. After analyzing the possible applications of AmI technologies and the evolution of the concept of privacy, the chapter considers the adequacy of the current legal regulation models to respond to these new challenges. Attention will be paid to the possible use of these new technologies for security purposes, and therefore to the issue of balancing opposed interests and rights according to the principles appropriate for a democratic society.

INTRODUCTION

The central question(s) of this study could be formulated as follows: which (new?) privacy issues have been raised by the recent developments of intelligent computing, especially by those used for security purposes? And, therefore, which safeguards can be drawn?

DOI: 10.4018/978-1-60960-083-9.ch012

It is possible to specify the main questions into the following sub-questions: a) are there any conceptual and juridical changes with regard to the right(s) of privacy related to the ICT developments of the last decades? b) Is the current legislation appropriate for covering the new challenges of AmI and which are, possibly, the main enforceability issues? c) What kind of solutions can be suggested (legal – new/old – technical measures, both)? d) What is the European policy on this issue (and, in particular, is the adoption of the Lisbon Treaty going to introduce relevant changes)?

Finally, a general question could be posed on the role of the law in a 'democratic society,' as it is facing the new technologies threatening for fundamental rights (for instance, should the law protect the individual against such threats or ignore them)?

If, on the one hand, the new developments promise to make people's lives more comfortable or more secure (Cook et al., 2009), on the other hand, complex issues arise in terms of fundamental rights and freedoms - among which, the right to privacy- traditionally protected, although in different ways, by the Constitutions of the EU Member States (Leenes et al., 2008). In this sense, privacy could also be seen as an example of those fundamental rights that are challenged by new technologies, "the process of which is faster and more difficult to regulate compared to traditional technologies" (Boisson de Chazournes et al., 2009). In particular, serious concerns for privacy (and related rights) of the individuals seem to arise from the increasing diffusion of devices allowing the 'mobility' and also the remote identification and control of items, persons and interests, due to their stronger capability to invade into the private sphere and their general 'reluctance' to be subjected to legal restraints (Dix, 2005).

It might be helpful to start this paper with a brief overview of the recent developments in AmI technologies in order to identify, besides the opportunities they promise, the threats they pose to privacy and data protection right(s), after having briefly considered the doctrinal evolution of the legal concept of privacy and having analyzed the related legal sources.

It will be useful, for this purpose, to consider, on the one hand, i) the 'adequacy' of the legal principles and requirements, acknowledged by the European Data Protection Regulation, to ensure legal safeguards for individuals (enforceable in Courts) and, on the other hand, ii) their practical applicability: a basic requirement of the Data Protection, such as the consent, is difficult or even impossible to be put in practice in AmI environments, where sophisticated technologies operate often without the subject's intervention.

Since the main legal concerns about privacy and data protection arise from the use of new technologies for purposes that may conflict with those of privacy (for example, in order to protect free speech, marketing or security aims), it is worth considering the legitimacy and the necessity of this kind of measures, as well as their proportionality according to the current legal framework (particularly, human rights law and EU data protection law) and their jurisprudential interpretation.

In exploring the main current European regulation, a short account of the legal grounds granted to privacy protection by the Lisbon Treaty will be given (e.g., the binding value of the Charter of Fundamental Rights of Nice). Finally, the paper wishes to contribute to the debate on the opportunity to achieve a legislative reform in the field and, possibly, on the criteria to be adopted for balancing privacy and other 'opposed' rights (e.g., security).

1. THE AMBIENT INTELLIGENT (AMI) ENVIRONMENT. OPPORTUNITIES AND LEGAL ISSUES

1.1. The AmI Applications

When the computer revolution started some decades ago, probably nobody could expect that the capabilities and intelligence, only imagined in science fiction films, would become a reality. Technologies, which were used until now in a passive way, are becoming active and personalized in order to respond to individual needs or desires: we are going towards a world where people are surrounded by easy-to-use interfaces embedded in everyday objects, capable of responding to individuals in a seamless, unobtrusive and invisible way (Wright et al., 2008).

The expressions Ambient Intelligence, or ubiquitous or pervasive computing, created by computer-science researchers around the world, indicate a quite recent discipline that, taking the advantage of important changes in the Information Communication Technologies, aims at bringing 'intelligence' to our everyday life environments, making them responsive and sensitive to us (Aart et al., 2003). More commonly, these terms essentially mean the same thing: "a digital environment that proactively, but sensibly, supports people in their daily lives" (Cook et al. 2009). Based on the use of sensors networks, wireless communications, smart devices (with the miniaturization of microprocessors), the central idea of AmI is, on the one hand, to reduce the size of computers, so that they can be embedded in familiar objects (mobile phones, GPS navigator, home equipments); on the other hand, to employ the augmented computation capacity and the spreading availability of the devices – technology distributed around us –in order to provide a mixed, real-virtual experience that 'should' improve the way we can benefit from our living surroundings.

While we are becoming accustomed to sensors that control temperature or lighting in modern houses, the possibilities of Ambient Intelligence go much further than that, allowing to combine more than one electronic device in order to interact in an 'intelligent' way with the users, that is, to be adaptive and responsive to features, behavior and acts of users, thus providing personalized services and anticipating their needs. The relevance of these technologies, their invasive nature and the fact that they rely on the collection and processing of personal data make privacy right safeguards and data protection regulations applicable. What is more difficult to say is to what extent and in which manner they should be applied.

Though it is impossible to refer to all the studies devoted to the development of Ambient Intelligence in this paper, it could be useful to underline some of their main features, especially those related to the privacy issues discussed in this paper. Those are *sensing, reasoning and acting,* as identified by Cook et al. (2009). The *sensing* capability of AmI allows the interaction between technology and the real world and relies on a variety of sensors employed. Environment and user's characteristics are *perceived* by a software algorithm, that uses these data to *reason* and *act* consequently in order to change the environment. Thus, the development of profiling and personalization algorithms is crucial for the success of an AmI system (De Vries, 2010). It is possible to immediately argue that, as long as the perception of movements, temperature, position, pressure remain anonymous (in the sense that the system doesn't need to identify a specific person in order to operate), relevant legal issues of privacy and data protection are not raised, at least, not directly.

The problem is that tracking, locating and identifying specific people in a certain environment (i.e., on the basis of their features, devices or other distinctive means) has become essential in the new AmI systems, in order to provide services according to the situations, needs and preferences of the different users. Tracking people and items is performed, for example, by using technological means (such as Radio Frequency Identification -Rfid- tags) that require individuals and items to be 'tagged' (De Vries, 2010), that is, to be continuously followed, monitored, guided, with consequences in terms of invasion of private life and profiling, especially if they are combined with other technological measures (motion sensors, cameras, microphones, unique identification number). Profiling in itself is not forbidden by current EU legislation. The legitimacy of the profiling activity is, nevertheless, defined by specific legal requirements (in particular, lawfulness and limited finality). The increasing use of Rfid for different applications (logistics, access control, etc.), due to the cost reduction of computing and communications, which will facilitate exchanges of information among smart and small devices, shows that we are already living in an AmI world.

As it has been argued, AmI will directly affect our lives in many ways, as individuals, as professionals and as citizens. Accordingly, safeguards for privacy-related rights (i.e., anonymity, identity, non-discrimination and non-manipulation etc.) should be ensured in various situations of the individual, whether they are private or public. Broader considerations of the current society should be taken into account in order properly to address all the issues raised by these technologies and before they become ubiquitous. Besides the invisibility, accessibility and other technical innovations, attention should be paid to the increasing concerns for security after 11 September 2001 and to the weakening of public control on this evolution (Wright et al., 2008).

Further developments in computer science, which are going to surpass the limits of the existing technologies (i.e., to ensure a proper and exact identification of people, to avoid imprecision and failure of sensors perception, Cook at al. 2009), together with the convergence of different media and different systems, are making the situation more complex and worrying for several reasons. First, the existence of blurred concepts in the current EU data protection regulation (such as that of 'personal information') renders its application difficult in practice. Moreover, identifying people with their precise names or addresses is becoming needless, since, in order to create a profile and to provide customized services, it may be sufficient to know, in some cases, only the identification number of their computer device, while in others, merely the categories to which a person is likely to belong (Wright, Gurtwirth, et al., 2009). Furthermore and foremost, the increasing use of biometric data (fingerprints, but also eye retina or smell), for both security and non-security purposes (that sharpens the issue of conflict between rights) guarantee an exact identification of the individual involved.

In order to be adaptive and act unobtrusively but in an appropriate way (e.g. completing a task when it is supposed to be needed by the subject that interacts with the system, as explained by Simpson et al., 2006), an AmI system needs to work well in terms of reasoning capability, the features of which are extremely relevant in privacy-related debates. For example, the ability to model users' behavior, to predict and recognize activities in the environment, the ability of decision-making on behalf of the individuals based on their profile settings are aspects that clash with some of the main principles of privacy and Data Protection (as discussed later, necessity, finality, minimization, proportionality), leaving aside the relative ethical and social considerations (Marx, 2001).

The scientific literature regarding the advances of the technologies in this context is quite rich even if only few applications of AmI projects have already been fully implemented. A broad overview of the different projects developed in Europe (as well as in the rest of the world, particularly in the U.S.A. and in Japan) is illustrated in the SWAMI report (Wright et al., 2008). Within it, also a first example of Ambient Intelligence "vision" promoted by the European Union and commissioned in 2000 to the Information Society Technologies Advisory Group (ISTAG). This vision has constituted the basis for the following research agenda within and without Europe alike.

The scenarios for possible applications and activities that these technologies are expected to provide are manifold and involve private as well as public spaces. Some examples are the smart homes (e.g., for the intake of proper food), hospitals (for the intake of medicines/health monitoring and assistance), transportation (for increased safety, e.g. controlling the driver's behavior), smart office or campus (for information services or use of remote facilities). First of all, it is essential for the AmI system, in order to function appropriately, to be aware of the subject's preferences, intentions, and needs in order to 'act' automatically (that is to anticipate, interrupt or suggest to the subject). The AmI system will rely on a human-computer interaction (using intuitive interfaces) that nowadays includes voice, facial and emotion recognition. In this framework, the computers will actually be everywhere, invisibly integrated in everyday items and more autonomous from a direct input of the subject.

It is easy to imagine how this bears upon the effectiveness of legal preconditions of data protection such as the previous consent and the information obligation. With this aim, some projects tried to verify the enforceability of these requirements through the design of *ad hoc* technical tools (such as the "privacy agent" software (Le Metayer & Monteleone, 2009), which is able to provide automated consent for the processing of personal data). Recently, the European Data Protection Supervisor adopted an Opinion on the usefulness of "privacy by design", which is considered a key tool to ensure citizens' trust in ICT (Opinion EDPS, 2010).

It is possible to identify some main threats to privacy and related rights on the basis of the different components of an AmI system: hardware, pervasive wireless communications between computers, intuitive interfaces, embedded intelligence controlling interfaces and communications. The main problem deriving from hardware components is their miniaturization (becoming difficult to be noticed and easy to lose or steal, with the relevant risks for the data stored in it). The centralized storage of data is therefore considered risky and unlawful regarding the protection of privacy, due to the possibility of combining data gathered from other parts of the system (Wright et al., 2008) or due to unauthorized access thereto. Ubiquitous communications imply the wireless transmission of a large amount of data. In this case the reduction and the encryption of data transmitted could be used as safeguards - a task that could be performed automatically, according to the principle of necessity and depending on the purpose of the communication. Doubts about the possibility to achieve anonymity derive from the increasing use of unique identifiers (IP addresses, Bluetooth device ID, RFID tags), enabling the tracking of communications between devices (embedded into personal items) and users.

Future developments require, therefore, better protection mechanisms. Advanced interfaces would be able to interpret the users movements, face features and emotions so that the 'embedded intelligence' could reason about how to use the personal data gathered (providing suggestions or acting autonomously on behalf of the user). The main concerns for the user's privacy seem to derive from the lack of control on the logging of the interactions, the possibility they are accessed by an unauthorized person, as well as the undue use of sensors (fake biometrics or identity theft).

Some solutions to these counterfeits would be to charge the embedded intelligence with the task of automatically selecting the privacy policy appropriate for the particular context in which it is used and minimizing the relative use of data. Also, to adopt security systems that allow continuous recognition of the owner of a specific device (unobtrusive but reliable biometrics, more user-friendly than a password or PIN codes) or to permit the user easily to switch off functions when he/she wants (Gutwirth, 2007).

Another interesting aspect (that is not possible to account in this paper) concerns the reliability and security of the system that should be normally addressed by encryption techniques. These techniques are difficult to use in an AmI context because they run counter to the principle of minimal resources, which is typical of such technologies. The risks of technical errors and the misleading capacity of the system could also affect the protection of individual privacy and some of the existing projects are focused on that disadvantage, for example designing specific devices in order to secure the information transmission or to be able to preserve location data private, or to employ biometrics in order to ensure privacy (Vildjiounaite, 2006).

1.2. Social and Legal Expectations of Privacy

The amount of data collected by cameras and biometric systems through the use of automated devices and their 'intelligent' use in order to provide personalized services, clearly, gives rise, as mentioned above, to privacy and data protection problems. In particular, collection, storage, processing of communication and diffusion are activities legally acknowledged according to the European data protection regulation, which establishes their minimum limits and requirements, regardless of the technologies employed in practice. Furthermore, the invasive nature of some technological solutions give rise to compliance issues with regard to traditional privacy principles, such as proportionality or the 'purpose limitation' that are set in international conventions, particularly the European Convention of Human Rights (see *infra*).

Although the afore-mentioned features of AmI are presented by scientists as a way to make surroundings more adaptive and helpful for the users (e.g., reducing the individual's efforts in performing certain tasks), or even to address important challenges such as environmental protection, health care or transportation (as stressed at the OECD Experts Conference, 2010), the same AmI advocates could not avoid taking into account the privacy concerns and indeed, they became more responsive towards them (Cook, 2009).

This paper necessarily focuses on the legal aspects of these technological advances, even though we cannot disregard completely some of the socio-political issues at stake, which also have legal implications (Marx, 2001; Lyon, 2007). Marx, in particular, warns about the increasing use of science and technology for acquiring social control. "The control has become softer and less visible, partly because it is built-in... partly because of the more sophisticated use of deception" and it became, according to him, more extensive (by, e.g., blurring traditional institutional and organizational borders) and more intensive (by, e.g., passing the boundaries of distance and darkness or by breaking physical barriers – factors that traditionally protected liberty and privacy).

According to Marx, the increase of social control via engineering is related, on one side, "to concerns over issues such as crimes, terrorism, border control, economic competitiveness," and, on the other, "to the technical developments in electronics, computerization, artificial intelligence[...]; paradoxically increased expectation and protection of privacy have furthered reliance on external, distance-mediated, secondary technical means, that identify, register, classify, validate or generate grounds for suspicion." The idea of Marx is that we should assure the control of technology rather than the reverse. This assumption appears relevant also for the success of the legal-technical approach, which is currently quite popular among European jurists and scientists in the general debate on data protection (Poullet, 2005a).

Especially after 09/11, security and predictability trends seem to have increased dramatically in our society, in parallel with the (less diffused) fear of witnessing the realization of a total-surveillance society, a sort of Bentham's/ Foucault's 'Panopticon', several times denounced by legal-sociologists (Lyon & Zureik, 1996). The use of GPS in mobile phones and other location-aware services, for business or governmental security purposes, although presenting many benefits, have raised concerns amongst privacy advocates as far as the risks of unwanted and unwarranted surveillance are concerned. These risks are doomed to increase in a world of AmI, where intelligent devices will be able easily to detect people, places, movements. This is probably a challenge for the legislative authorities, which have to ensure that proper safeguards are adopted in order to avoid the unauthorized and abusive access to the data collected, especially in the frame of a blurring private and public distinction (Wright et al., 2008). Among others, Rouvroy (2009) critically evaluates this strong emphasis that modern societies place on security and prevention issues that seems drastically to erode the protection of the right to privacy, especially when it is combined with the use of invasive technologies.

2. PRIVACY AND DATA PROTECTION: CONCEPTS AND LEGAL CATEGORIES

Before discussing the particular emphasis that now paid to security interests, as reflected in the recent adoption of legal security measures by several international and European institutions, it is appropriate to consider briefly the concept and the right of privacy itself. It will be sufficient to evoke here the main values founding the privacy right(s) as they can be deduced from the main legal rules aiming at protecting it/them.

The legal literature focusing on privacy issues is very broad, but not yet necessary elucidative as far as the exact definition or the expansion of this right, as defined by the legal texts (national and supranational), is concerned. Some juridical interpretations have been given by the national Constitutional or European Courts (Sudre, 2005), and by opinions and assessments made by the administrative entities set for the regulation and protection of this right (National and European Data Protection Authorities), but they have not been of much assistance in clarifying the normative content of the right.

The beginning of a legal debate on privacy as autonomous right of the individual is traditionally ascribed to the North American doctrine developed at the end of the nineteenth century (following the publication of Warren and Brandeis' well known article, 'The right to privacy' (Warren, Brandeis, 1890)). At that time it corresponded to what later became its essential but not exclusive component, the "right to be let alone," that is, the right to protect the confidentiality of one's private sphere against public or private interferences. From that moment on, the concept and the right of privacy have undergone a significant evolution, due to the socio-economic developments and, much more, due to the introduction of the Information Communications Technologies into daily life.

With the development of the Information Society, and the indispensable flow of information across the national boundaries, the main focus, especially of the EU regulative approach (*infra*), has become the protection of personal data, considered even more important than the protection of a *strictu sensu* privacy right. Data protection legislation has introduced a more dynamic dimension of privacy that gives to the citizen/users of communications the right to control the use of their personal information in the modern Information Society. Often used as synonymous terms, privacy and data protection are, therefore, different concepts (as confirmed by the different legal grounds in the Charter of Fundamental Rights of the EU, *infra*), but, since their relative domains are blurring, it is not possible to recognize two distinct, autonomous rights. In my view, they could be illustrated as circles, sometimes concentric, sometimes intersecting.

The lack of a wider regulation of privacy right(s) and the almost exclusive attention to the issues concerning data protection has been regarded as one of the limits posed by the community approach (Lugaresi, 2004), on the grounds that it would put too much importance on the economic aspect of privacy (personal data seen as a valuable and negotiable or merchandized matter), thus overshadowing other components of privacy, for example solitude, the intimacy of personal relationships, not being under constant surveillance, self-determination and autonomous choice. According to the proponents of this view, data protection alone would not satisfy all the expectations of a subject's privacy, the latter being also functional for the protection of other individual and social rights (Rouvroy, 2008). In particular, as highlighted by some American scholars, informational privacy would grant collective benefits through the promotion of decisional autonomy and deliberative democracy (Cohen, 2000).

For this reason, although Europe could boast of a general legal framework on data protection (missing in the United States of America) and stronger juridical safeguards, it does not yet seem to have found yet a meaningful answer to the fact that privacy is still a "conceptual muddle." As underlined by Keats Citron and Henry (2010), without a deep understanding of privacy "decision-makers will have great difficulty identifying, defining and protecting against socially detrimental incursions on privacy". It may be enough to think about law enforcement agencies supplying our digital data to marketing companies or about governments accessing our social-network profiles, in order to comprehend the dangers involved for the individual's autonomy.

2.1. A (New) Pluralistic Conception of Privacy

Among other *understandings* of privacy, one particularly interesting is that provided by Daniel Solove (2008), who criticizes all scholarly attempts to choose a common denominator of privacy, as too narrow or too broad, with the risk of creating a privacy conception either over-inclusive or too vague and thus unable to respond to important privacy problems. He suggests, therefore, to "understand privacy as a set of family resemblances, not reducible to a singular essence." The author offers a pragmatic approach and a pluralistic conception of privacy (not only in relation to the activities of collection, but more in respect of the processing, storage and dissemination of data), especially useful because it is focused on the specific and concrete problems of privacy, instead of producing a holistic approach to it. Briefly, in Solove's *method*, privacy is a family of interrelated yet distinct things, and this is why similar activities could have different privacy implications.

In that frame, what we consider as entitled to privacy protection is *variable,* according to time, values and technologies. This pluralistic and contingent theory of privacy requires, not only a level of *generality* that ensures extensive applicability, but also enough of stability in order to be legally useful; this could be achieved, in Solove's view, by *focusing* on privacy problems, thus on a taxonomy of activities (that he divides in four non-definitive groups) that the law should guarantee.

From the lesson taught by Solove, we learn also that our concerns for the right to privacy should not overshadow society's interest for privacy protection. The judges and the legislators should balance privacy against other interests in concrete contexts (1) and protect it when it ensures the best outcomes for the society (2). The pragmatist view of Solove allows us to recognize a more complete and useful value of privacy, as a bringer of social benefits, like in the case of an invasive police search: in this case there is a societal interest (not only an individual's one) in avoiding unjust searches, the interest in ensuring that police forces will follow a legally justified procedure before conducting invasive searches (Keats Citron & Henry, 2010).

As Keats Citron and Henry argue, Solove's societal view of privacy (his "visionary pragmatism") can help legislators and jurists to face technologies of our time in a thorough manner and guide them better in balancing privacy and other legally protected interests. According to Keats Citron and Henry, one way to apply this pragmatic approach is to oblige decision makers, judges and legislators, to explain their assessment of the interests they are balancing and the reason why society would benefit from a particular outcome. The adoption of this approach could, for instance, have brought the Italian Tribunal of Milan to a more accurate (and maybe different) argument in the recent and debated sentence in the Google case (Tribunal of Milan, Criminal Section, sentence n. 1972 of the 24/02/2010), in which three Google executives were convicted for data protection crimes, as the consequence of the users' uploading of a video containing sensitive data (Sartor & Viola de Azevedo Cunha, 2010).

Keats Citron and Henry go beyond the Solove's taxonomy and suggest considering not only the privacy values but also the possible harms that its protection may cost, measurable on a case by case basis (e.g., harms from disclosure and harms from seclusion): not an uncritical acceptance of privacy protection but also the consideration of its negative social costs (e.g., a drug user's privacy and her son's safety). That way, according to the authors, some control on decision-makers discretion would be better ensured.

Thus, a consideration follows: looking at the violations of those values that the law aims to protect should make privacy both a concept more connected to reality and a less abstract notion that can guarantee the development of the appropriate legal and practical protection. The use of technical solutions, acting *ex ante*, could be more effective than *ex post* balancing in some cases (Keats Citron & Henry, 2010). Additionally, the technological solutions could better address some of the privacy problems described in Solove's taxonomy.

2.2. Identity and 'Contextual Integrity' in Information Age

Even though they cannot be considered the same, the right to privacy is often also associated, conceptually and legally, with the right to (personal) identity. The latter is understood, on the one hand, as the right to be able to identity oneself in every circumstance and not be forced into doing so (in the Information Society this right is acknowledged via the notions of anonymity and 'pseudonymity'), and, on the other side, as the right not to be misrepresented (Hoikkaanen et al., 2010), as the "truth of person," weighable only against a prevalent public or private interest (M. Hildebrandt, 2005). It can be noted that the meaning of this interest, for the scope of this paper, is connected to the concepts of decisional privacy and 'contextual integrity' (Hoikkaanen et al., 2010) that should assume more relevance in the AmI debate.

Some kinds of technology affect the capacity of the individuals to control their personal data and their identification. The risk of erroneous processing of personal data is particularly high on the Internet as well as in sophisticated Ambient Intelligence scenarios, because of the possibility that these kinds of technologies have to use personal data and act unobtrusively. In these contexts, one of the main interests of the related subject could be to reinstate the situation correctly, i.e., the *status quo* regarding his/her personal data. However, the risks that the misuses of data can provoke are more serious, as far as identity theft, discrimination, social exclusions or even stigmatization are concerned. The right to privacy becomes therefore, also an instrument in order to ensure the ability to exercise other fundamental rights and values of a democratic society. Some of the main components of a privacy right are, in fact, the self-determination and the decisional autonomy of the subject in the context of his/her social and political life (Rouvroy, 2008).

It has been argued (Buttarelli, 1997) that it should be taken into account, especially in ICT contexts where we deal with electronic identity(ies), that the individual's identity has a changeable nature. Therefore, the subject or entity that collects the individual's personal data (even if legitimately) could acquire a significant power over him/her that should be compensated by the acknowledgment of proper safeguards in order to ensure that the disclosure or use of such data reflects the true identity of people. Recently, the proliferation of Identity Management Systems (IdM) has been promoted in the marketplace, providing users with different available digital identification techniques, different identifiers, and different levels of assurance. Nonetheless, this evolution guarantees neither the awareness of how they actually work, nor the ability appropriately to manage them. More and enhanced information about their functioning and about the effects of the related choices seems, therefore, necessary (Hoikkaanen, et al., 2010).

Conceptually, the concept of identity could be considered wider than the concept of privacy, even if, paradoxically, it is being protected by the right to privacy. Indeed, the two main aspects of identity correspond to the two traditional prerogatives of privacy: its defensive and its offensive aspect, freedom and confidentiality (Dreyer, 2005). The ensemble of these two aspects justifies the nature of fundamental right of privacy as well as its acknowledgement by international and European legal instruments.

3. CURRENT REGULATION AND LIMITS

Considering briefly the legal framework in this field, it is opportune to mention those provisions of the relative international and European texts that give to privacy and data protection the nature of fundamental right(s), but are also characterized by some enforceability issues, especially in the context of the new ICT. Among the many International Treaties that protect the right to privacy, we should mention Art. 17 of the International Covenant on Civil and Political Rights (ICCPR), Art. 8 of the European Convention of Human Rights (ECHR), both protecting the right to private life, and the Convention of the Council of Europe for the protection of individuals with regard to the Automatic Processing of Personal data (no. 108, Strasbourg Convention of 1981). The latter, though being of European origin, can also be ratified by States that do not belong to the Council of Europe (Bygrave, 2008).

Although not directly contemplated by the ECHR, data protection has been recognized by the European Court of Human Rights as included in the right of privacy *ex* Art. 8, as well as restricted on the same grounds (Art. 8,2): law requirements, necessity, specific purposes (such as public security) and proportionality (the latter is derived from the interpretation of the Court of Strasbourg). This set of safeguards should be taken into account especially in the development of new technologies, which aim to detect objects and people for purposes that cannot always be deemed 'legitimate.' Within the European Union, we should mention the Charter of Fundamental Rights of Nice, which contains two distinct articles on privacy and data protection: the importance of this Charter has increased especially because of its binding value after the recent adoption of the Lisbon Treaty (see *infra*).

Since the emerging of ICT technologies and in order to integrate the existing and limited privacy regulation (that does not include the private sector, nor the right to access or correct personal data), the European framework has been enriched by several legal acts dedicated to data protection (such as the Directive 2002/58/EC on privacy and electronic communications and the Directive 2006/24/EC on Data Retention). The Directive 95/46/EC (Data Protection Directive) is the first EU instrument that contains general binding rules concerning privacy and data protection and that has been implemented (although with discrepancies) by all Member States, even if, at a national level, some of them had adopted earlier domestic legislation aiming at offering data protection to their citizens.

One of the main innovations of this Directive has been the founding of National Data Protection (DP) Authorities, with regulatory and control powers, as well as of an advisory group (DP Working Party, so called "Art 29"), with the task of helping in applying data protection rules also to new technologies (for example, Article 29 DP WP on RFID technology, or the Working Document on biometrics).

Multidisciplinary studies have pointed out that some aspects of data protection are not protected by the legal guarantees provided for the privacy right(s), and this would have been the reason for the adoption of a specific European DP regulation (Wright, Gutwirth et al., 2008).

Nevertheless, though we cannot forget that the Single Market is the first objective of the Community regulation in general, including the DP regulation, and that this would justify the Community's major attention for data protection (economically valuable for marketing and transaction purposes), the right to privacy nowadays does not seem to be limited to the sole ability to control one's data. On the contrary, it aims at including a wider sphere of the individual's personal behavior as well as at protecting the "dominion" over the context in which the individual exercises all of his/her fundamental freedoms (Rodotà, 1997). This particular aspect of the right to privacy is characteristically evident in its clash with the use of the new information technologies.

While privacy protection instruments could be seen as protecting the 'opacity' of the individuals against the interference of private and public powers, the Data Protection regulation system has introduced 'transparency tools' (Gutwirth, 2009; Wright et al., 2008), which allow a controlled interference with the individual's private autonomy (through the legal acknowledgment of a balancing system and of procedural safeguards). In spite of the DP Directive's 'young age,' the general principles included therein have been deemed, also in the recent official reviews, as suitable to be applied even to new technologies (European Commission, COM (2007) 87). Most of these principles are stated in Arts. 6 and 7 of the Directive or are derived from the jurisprudential interpretation of the same Directive. They recall and enrich the principles of the ECHR (specific purposes principle; data minimization principle; fair treatment principle; unambiguous consent). Furthermore, the Directive provides for legal requirements and establishes rights and obligations.

Nevertheless, several issues of implementation and efficacy still remain, especially in relation with the development of a hyper-technological world. Two classes of problems could be immediately pointed out with regard to these principles. First of all, at the level of their abstract formulation, their interpretation has not been univocal in the last years, since consequent conflict issues regarding other legal principles (e.g., security purposes) have occurred. Secondly, a thorny issue relates to their concrete implementation, especially in the virtual society of the Internet as well as in the new scenarios proposed by AmI technologies, where data protection rules risk being just misled; new threats arise if we consider the growing up of the "Internet of the things" (*infra*). This is why Liu (2009) underlines the need to set clearer criteria in the evaluation of DP principles, such as the proportionality of processing biometric data (e.g., the distinction between identification and verification in biometrics).

In this context a deeper reflection on the current regulatory framework appears to be necessary (Wright, Gutwirth et al., 2009). The legal analysis developed in the last decade concerning the Data Protection regulation system has, in particular, underlined the need, on the one hand, of improving and extending the context of certain legal notions (such as that of the 'personal data'), and, on the other hand, of achieving adequate specificity in the Data Protection regulation system. Sector-based legislation at the EU level would be valuable "in order to apply those principles to the specific requirements of the technology in question" (European Commission COM (2007) 87). This could prove to be extremely useful as far as the development of AmI technologies is concerned. Indeed, their new, possible deployments and their convergence with other technologies and systems could be better managed at a specific rather than a general level mainly related to their functional and not technological aspects.

3.1. An "Internet of the Things" and Profiling Issues: A Need of DP Differentiated Regulatory Regimes?

It has been shrewdly observed that with 'intelligence' embedded everywhere, an "Internet of the things" increases the possibilities for collecting and aggregating data. Similarly, the continuing advances in computing power will increase data-mining and analysis (Wright, Gutwirth et al. 2009). The collection and processing of profiling-data has been recognized in recent years as a threat for privacy especially when the access to such data is likely for unauthorized persons (in this sense data protection coincides with security protection, according to Keats Citron and Henry, 2010) or when they are communicated to third parties, due to the risks for these data to be used for purposes other than the original ones (breach of the 'limited purpose' principle).

Other concerns could emerge from discriminatory practices, similar to the online dynamic pricing and price discrimination that remain lawful marketing practices unless they are conducted without the will of the subject or in violation of individuals' fundamental rights. In this last case they are considered to constitute negative discrimination. The same issues and concerns could be raised in the AmI environment, where the possibility to track the users across different contexts, such as workplace, home and entertainment venues is of crucial importance. Therefore, in the AmI environment the risk of possible erosion in the autonomy of the individual is higher as well as his/her right to diversity according to different situations and circumstances (Leenes, 2008). That is probably one of the principal meanings that we should ascribe to the right of privacy today.

Though privacy issues related to the Internet are beyond the scope of this paper, relevant connections are nevertheless possible and necessary, not only due to the similarity of some problems online and offline, but because the Information Society is becoming more and more digitalized and a larger amount of data is actually disclosed in the virtual world (Daskala & Maghiros, 2007). Individuals, families and homes are increasingly connected to the Internet and this raises policy concerns in relation to the protection of their identity, privacy and security (Punie, 2005). The situation is becoming even more complex to define and regulate if we take into account the augmented possibilities of data diffusion offered by the convergence of technologies and media, that consequently blur the boundaries of our offline (e.g., that of AmI) and online worlds (the Internet).

Ronald Leenes, considering profiling and 'dataveillance' (surveillance of and through personal data) as pressing issues of Internet today, argues that it is possible (and more useful) to differentiate between several types of 'identifiabilities,' depending on the domain in which they occur or on other factors such as their goals, relations, issues and effects (Leenes, 2008). The different kinds of 'identifiability' could raise different concerns that ought to be addressed in a different way by the regulatory regime (i.e., different Data Protection-related obligations and rights, such as consent, information, etc.). These differences are not taken into consideration by the current legal framework but they could benefit from different regulatory regimes and, eventually, create a common ground between the privacy and the industrial advocates. Leenes's assumption is also interesting as far as the matter of AmI is concerned, in particular for his reflections regarding what he calls *Recognition-Identifiers* (e.g., a password) and *Classification*-identifiers (referring to the cases individuals are classified on the basis of preexisting profiles or categories) and for the practical issues surrounding them, such as the possible uses of the derived profiles (Hildebrand and Gurtwirth, 2007).

The opaqueness of data processing in AmI due to the ability of the system to capture and process data in an automated and hidden fashion is one of the reasons for its success. What happens if this unawareness extends also to the same kind of unrevealed and unfair practices that are today used on the Internet (such as behavioral targeting, stereotyping)? Can a legal requirement such as the consent be deemed appropriate and useful in such kind of situations? Therefore, it seems that recognizing the concerns deriving from the use of AmI mechanisms in different contexts could enable us to find different and differentiated data protection rules. Another relevant issue is which form these rules should have, e.g., hard law or soft law.

I wonder if this assumption could bring us to consider the updating of notions such as 'personal data' and 'identifiable person' -that are comprised in current legal provisions and are, as mentioned above, quite broad and unclear- necessary in order to 'deconstruct' them. I also wonder if this could be in line with the view that underlines the importance of making technologies, such as those used in AmI, 'relative' depending on the context and people involved (see below).

3.2. Legal Requirements and Implementation Issues

One of the main general principles of privacy and data protection is the 'fair processing' of data (Art. 6 DP Directive), that underpins all the other specific requirements. A "decent treatment of people in society" represents a core value of data protection (Leenes, 2008), and implies that people know when and for what purposes their data are collected. The 'purpose specification' and 'purpose limitation' principles are essential in the context of privacy and data protection, and their implementation relies on enacted and applied requirements of transparency. In other words, whatever the context (online or offline, the Internet or AmI), the controller (i.e., the subject who, according to the European Directives, decides the scopes and modalities of data processing) should clearly specify the reasons of the data collection and the modalities of their use. This requirement derives directly from the information obligation provided by the DP Directive, the implementation of which is not always achievable in the ICT environment and in particular in AmI scenarios. Despite a quite extensive legislation on data protection and -in a minor way- on privacy, there are still practical difficulties in its implementation (as testified, for example, by the Art 29 DP Working Party, Opinion 1/2010 on the concept of "controller").

Regarding the compliance of the new technologies, including those used in AmI environments, to the legal parameters it appears necessary not only to ensure that the existing legislation is applicable to new mobile services and that it is implemented in a uniform way in all Member States, but also that an appropriate new regulation should be adopted, where necessary (Poullet, 2005b). As argued by Hoikkaanen et al. (2010), it is important to distinguish the contexts and the typology of the data collected in each of them. Consequently, the legislation should be able to take into account this contextualization and identify the different requirements. AmI technologies require policy-making to be more contextual "without jettisoning coherence" (Wright & Gutwirth, 2009). The fact that new technologies are blurring the boundaries between private and public sectors (e.g., working from one's home) makes the protection of privacy more difficult. Whilst the European Court of Human Rights has stated, in this regard, that the protection of private life should also be extended to the professional life based on the criterion of a 'reasonable expectation of privacy' (Halford v. United Kingdom, 27/05/1997), this issue is still ambiguous in Europe, as proved by the differentiated jurisprudence decisions of the national Courts and DP Authorities.

In AmI environments where people and items are connected to each other and are always online it will be more difficult to apply the principle of reasonable expectation of privacy. Thus, it becomes more and more urgent to adopt a clearer interpretation of the notion of private life and its additional legal protection (Wright et al.,

2008). An appropriate direction to follow in the DP regulatory system appears to be that of relative and *ad hoc* rules, yet responding to general common grounds. In order to answer to the need of safeguards arising from the emergence of AmI, one approach could be to adopt a system of "micro-policies," instead of domain policies (Wright et al., 2008) that could better fit with the specific circumstances, the specific technologies and individuals. Therefore, it will be a challenge in the future to instantiate a coherent use of these micro-policies (Wright).

3.3. Contextualizing Privacy and Other Possible Responses

Many privacy problems and issues seem to derive from the type of the AmI technology used in practice, from its more or less pervasive character (e.g., video-cameras and biometrics), from its context (airport or home), or from the purposes it serves (e.g., security or entertainment scopes). In general, the most critical aspects seem to be connected, as mentioned above, to the reduced control that the individuals have over their private sphere and personal data, especially if the AmI system allows them to share information with third parties and gives them the capacity to monitor or access the collected data even when such practices are considered to be unlawful. Indeed, such practices clash with the two cornerstones of DP regulation, the principle of consent and the 'purpose limitation.'

Many authors underline that AmI technologies are particularly risky in terms of privacy and data protection, due to their nature and their tendency to collect detailed personal data that are stored and shared (Rodotà, 2009; Wright, 2005). What is to happen then? Do we have to renounce the future technological progress or do we have to totally abandon our privacy concerns (Le Metayer, 2009)?

In the debate among scientists and lawyers, it is interesting to recall here the thesis (Joinson et al., 2006) that affirms the need to customize privacy as any other preference service on the basis of the context of AmI environments or the features of people. That is to say that privacy should be influenced by the context in which it is adopted.

The advantage of such an approach relies on the reduced detailed personal information that is necessary in order to satisfy the user's needs, inferring the needed data from previously processed and profiled data (Cook et al. 2009). Nevertheless, 'constitutional' doubts stay on the ground with regard to this view, if proper safeguards are not established. One thing is, in my view, the adaptation of privacy preferences to contexts and users. Another is to consider privacy rights as a 'package' that could be acquired as other services (and maybe with the option to 'take or leave' it). As stressed elsewhere (Le Metayer & Monteleone, 2009), the latter approach would be more in line with a proprietary view of privacy, which recognizes a contractual nature of the consent to data processing and considers data as objects of transactions (Bibas, 1994). This view has been criticized by many scholars in Europe (Poullet, 1991; Bianca & Busnelli, 2007), because it seems to fail to ensure those privacy-related rights, such as the right to take free and autonomous choices, the individual's decisional autonomy, which are considered as essential to a vivid democracy (Rouvroy, 2008).

3.4. A Legal-Technical Approach

As mentioned above, one of the main privacy and data protection issues is the safeguarding of the implementation of the related rules, especially in the context of ICT applications. In order to find possible solutions and based on the presumption that the best data protection could only be achieved by a legal-technical approach (Poullet, 2008), some research projects, founded by the EU, have been trying for years, to develop technologies with the ability to enhance the privacy of user (the so-called *Privacy Enhancing Technologies*, P.E.T.), few of which have so far achieved significant results (Kosta et al. 2008; Wright et al. 2008). Acting directly at the level of the technical designs and standards, the aim of these projects is to anticipate the level of privacy protection, in order to produce 'conformed' technologies and to have a regulation from the *inside* rather than from the *outside* of the technologies. The idea is to put in practice what many scholars have been predicting for some years, namely that the solution to technology is technology itself (Poullet, 2001).

Though such an approach seems extremely convincing, I am inclined to believe that there are problems to be solved and privacy threats that should be avoided that especially derive from its possible deviations. First comes the issue of transforming legal provisions into technical standards, thus into 'codes', since legal rules are not easily translatable into computer-logical rules. Secondly, the technical ruling (programming) could be considered to be an autonomous rule-making process (Leenes, Koops et al., 2008), rendering, therefore, difficult to decide which role should be assigned to it, integrating or replacing the traditional law (Lessing, 1999). A third issue derives from automated data-mining and data-analysis, especially when supporting computerized decision-making (that brings us back to the discriminatory profiling as discussed above). Finally, it could be not so trivial to consider the implications of an all-preventive (*ex ante*) approach (which would replace a repressive one) on the values of self-determination and the decisional autonomy of the individual, as an underlying right to privacy.

It can be affirmed that these implications should be taken into account in the development of new AmI scenarios if it is true that the success of AmI will depend on how secure it can be made, how privacy and other rights of individuals can be protected and how individuals can come to trust the intelligent world that surrounds them (Friedewald et al., 2007; Sartor, 2006). Finally, two main goals should be achieved: to allow the development of new technologies and to ensure the protection of the individuals' rights threatened by them. Research has highlighted the importance of designing technologies for people instead of making people adapt to technology (Wright, 2009). In this respect, the afore-mentioned technologies inspired by the idea of 'privacy by design' could play a crucial role in its protection (Le Metayer, 2010).

The debate on which legal and/or technical instruments should be adopted for a better implementation of data protection requirements is still open (Poullet, 2005c; Le Metayer - Monteleone, 2009). The law is, however, expected to play a crucial role in these new technologies, possibly "looking into the future scenarios in order to identify adequate legal responses" (Fernandez-Barrera et al. 2009).

4. PRIVACY VS. SECURITY ISSUES

One of the possible conflicts between the right to privacy and other rights is the clash between privacy and security. It is possible to find many traces of the increasing attention for public security interests in the current international and European policies. The Convention of Budapest on Cybercrime and the Data Retention Directive 24/2006/EC are some examples. Regarding EU policy, these trends are becoming very 'strategies,' as we can observe in several hard and soft law legal documents (e.g., most recently, the Council of the European Union Stockholm Program).

Although the issue of possible conflict between fundamental rights and security is not new (Zucca, 2008), the post-09/11 effects have tremendously sharpened it, especially as far as privacy and data protection are concerned (De Hert, 2005). Some of the counter-terrorism measures already adopted by the U.S. as well as by the EU raised several doubts about their 'constitutional' legitimacy (Sheinin et al., 2009) and about the balancing principle as a proper approach for such a dilemma. Amongst them, particularly interesting, for their possible and predictable connection with AmI scenarios are the new types of detection technologies, the aim of which is to empower the practices of the fight against terrorism. Privacy issues seem to arise not only from the increasing resort during the last decade to these mechanisms but mainly from the invasive character of the new technologies that enables them to penetrate more deeply into the private sphere of the individuals than ever before (e.g., body scanners). Constitutional challenges raised by these detecting technologies are pointed out by Leenes et al. (2008), in particular with respect to the rights to intimacy, inviolability of the body and of the home.

It is not difficult to imagine that the situation could become thornier with the future development and use of AmI technologies for these purposes (Maghiros, 2003). Some authors (Friedewald et al., 2007) argue not only that AmI technologies tend to go beyond the currently existing privacy guarantees, but also that they are changing our expectations of privacy, in terms of its diminution, given that these technologies become a common part of our life. In other words, we are becoming more and more used to see our privacy limited (like, possibly, with the increasing use of social networks as 'normal' and as an essential part of many social relationships), and, worst, to be commonly considered as potentially 'suspicious,' as demonstrated by the increasing use of detection technologies.

As has been argued, there are no simple solutions to reach the right balance between privacy and security, just as there are no simple solutions to ensure that AmI is beneficial for citizens, industry and governments as well. The only alternative seems to be to address those (emerging) threats one by one and to make everyone involved in safeguarding his/her privacy, identity and security (Wright et al., 2008). Legal and philosophical debates in the context of balancing privacy and security have been lit up both by advocates of the so called "I've got nothing to hide" argument and its opponents: to agree with the latter means recognizing that the issue at stake is not to fully accept or to totally renounce the relative security and surveillance policies, but to verify the related oversight procedures that governments are expected to put in place (Solove, 2007).

It might be useful to evoke here that the European DP Directive does not apply to data processing carried out for the purposes of public security, defense and activities in the area of criminal law (the so called 'third pillar' of the pre-Lisbon Treaty). After several debates on the opportunity to extend data protection also to these areas of action, the European Council has adopted a Framework Decision in 2008 (2008/977/JHA), defining the data subject's rights in the context of criminal investigation and other police practices (including profiling): the right to be informed, the right to access, rectify or erase data, activities that should also be made known to third parties to whom the data have been disclosed and a specific obligation to ensure a high quality of data is also provided for, in order to guarantee the correctness of the consequent profiles (Wright et al., 2008). Nevertheless, as stressed by the EDPS (EDPS PressNews, 2008; Opinion 2009/C 128/02), this decision only covers police and judicial data exchanged among Member States or EU authorities and not to domestic data, leaving the level of protection unsatisfactory.

This situation is likely to change thanks to the recent entry into force of the Lisbon Treaty.

Even in the absence of a specific EU regulation addressing the processing of personal data for security reasons, some protection may be obtained through the recognition of the binding nature of the EU Charter of Fundamental Rights (as stated by the Lisbon Treaty), and consequently its applicability in contexts traditionally excluded by the Data Protection regulation system. I believe, in fact, that it is possible to assign to this Charter a 'horizontal effect' in the European area, in the same way other human rights instruments have in International Law (Kamminga & Sheinin, 2009).

It is interesting to notice how the ECHR, although recognizing the violation of the fundamental right of privacy, has recently arrived to quite different conclusions in terms of the 'legitimacy' of security and investigative measures (that is, *ex* Art. 8 of the ECHR, necessity and proportionality of the public interference in private life for a democratic society). Characteristic are the examples of the decisions Bykov v. Russia (n. 4378/02) and S. and Marper v. UK (nos. 30562/04 and 30566/04), the latter addressing also the adequacy of the safeguards aimed to avoid abuses in the processing of and access to biometric data. These discrepancies are also due to the lack of uniformity on the further employment of evidence gathered through procedures that have infringed the right to privacy (Wright et al., 2008). The need for more clarity is even more urgent if we think about the increasing recourse to electronic evidence as judicial proof, the lawfulness of its collection being often contested.

CONCLUSION

To conclude, after having analyzed some possible applications of AmI technologies, it is possible to affirm that, while the main concern of computer scientists is to render the AmI systems as widely accepted and useful for the society as possible (Cook et al., 2009), the main concern of the legal theory is instead to verify, on the one hand, the legitimacy of these technologies according to the existing values deriving from the fundamental rights protection and, on the other, to find out possible legal responses, in order to 'balance' the apparently opposite values (security and predictability, on one side, privacy and identity, on the other). Some steps have been taken in this direction in order to enhance privacy while developing new automated technologies, but several legal issues remain to be addressed. One direction could be, as discussed above, the adoption of relevant sector-based rules, more adaptive to AmI contexts and privacy needs.

It could be premature to define the effects of the enforcement of the Lisbon Treaty at a European level as far as privacy and data protection are concerned, but at least one relevant benefit can already be mentioned: the binding value of the Charter of Fundamental Rights of Nice and its horizontal effect and consequently its applicability in contexts traditionally excluded by the Data Protection Regulation system or in which the right to privacy is limited, (art 8 (2)ECHR).

The norms contained in the Charter must be taken into account from now on, when implementing (or defining) general or specific rules regarding privacy and data protection.

Further research should be conducted in order to find suitable safeguards for privacy and related rights in parallel with the developments of AmI technologies and their diffused use. The law should still play the role of ensuring the respect of fundamental values and rights, without which a 'democratic society' would be nothing more than empty words.

REFERENCES

Aarts, E., & Encarnacao, J. (2006). *True visions: The emergence of ambient intelligence*. London: Springer Verlag.

Aarts, E., & Marzano, S. (2003). *The new everyday: Views on ambient intelligence*. Rotterdam, The Netherlands: 010 Publishers.

Augusto, J. (2007). Ambient intelligence: The confluence of pervasive computing and artificial intelligence. In Schuster, A. (Ed.), *Intelligent computing everywhere*. London: Springer Verlag. doi:10.1007/978-1-84628-943-9_11

Bianca, C. M., & Busnelli, F. (2007). *La protezione dei dati personali*. Padova, Italy: Cedam.

Bibas, S. (1994). A contractual approach to data privacy. *Harvard Journal of Law & Public Policy*, *17*, 591–611.

Boisson de Chazournes, L. (2009). New technologies, the precautionary principle and public participation. In Murphy, T. (Ed.), *New technologies and human rights*. Oxford: Oxford University Press. doi:10.1093/acprof:oso/9780199562572.003.0005

Buttarelli, G. (1997). *Banche dati e tutela della riservatezza*. Milano, Italy: Giuffrè.

Bygrave, L. (2008). International agreements to protect personal data. In Rule, J. B., & Greenleaf, G. (Eds.), *Global privacy protection*. Cheltenham, UK: Edward Elgar Publishing.

Clemens, B., Maghiros, I., Beslay, L., Centeno, C., Punie, Y., Rodriguez, C., & Maser, M. (2003). Security and privacy for the citizen in the post-September 11 digital age: A prospective overview. Report to the European Parliament Committee on Citizens' Freedom and Rights, Justice and Home Affairs (LIBE), Institute for Prospective Technological Studies, Seville, Spain. Retrieved from http://cybersecurity.jrc.es/docs/libe%20study/libestudy%20eur20823%20.pdf

Cohen, J. E. (2000). Examined lives: Informational privacy and the subject as object. *Stanford Law Review*, *52*, 1373–1438. doi:10.2307/1229517

Cook, D., Augusto, J. C., & Jakkula, V. R. (2009). Ambient intelligence: Technologies, applications and opportunities. *Pervasive and Mobile Computing*, *5*(4), 277–298. doi:10.1016/j.pmcj.2009.04.001

Cremona, M., & De Witte, B. (2008). *EU foreign relations law: Constitutional fundamentals*. Oxford: Hart.

Daskala, B., & Maghiros, I. (2007). *Digital territories: Towards the protection of public and private spaces in a digital and ambient intelligence environment* [IPTS report]. Luxemburg: OPOCE.

De Hert, P. (2005). Balancing security and liberty within the European human rights framework: A critical reading of the court's case law in the light of surveillance and criminal law Enforcement Strategies after 9/11. *Utrecht Law Review*, *1*(1), 68–96.

De Vries, K. (2010). Identity, profiling algorithms and a world of ambient intelligence. *Ethics and Information Technology*, *12*(1), 71–85. doi:10.1007/s10676-009-9215-9

Dix, A. (2005). Le tecniche Rfid. In G. Rasi (Ed.), *Innovazioni tecnologiche e privacy*. Rome: Ufficio grafico dell'Istituto Poligrafico e Zecca dello Stato.

Dreyer, E. (2005). Le respect de la vie privée objet d'un droit fondamental, *Lexis-Nexis Juris-Classeur, 5*(18).

Ducatel, K., Bogdanowicz, M., Scapolo, F., Leijten, J., & Burgelman, J. C. (2001). Scenarios for ambient intelligence in 2010. Final report EUR 19763, EC-JRC, IPTS, Seville, Spain. Retrieved from http://cordis.europa.eu/fp7/ict/istag/home_en.html

European Commission. (2007). Communication on the follow-up of the work program for better implementation of the Data Protection Directive [COM (2007) 87 final]. Retrieved from http://ec.europa.eu/justice_home/fsj/privacy/docs/lawreport/com_2007_87_f_en.pdf

European Council. (2008, November 27). Framework Decision 2008/977/JHA on the protection of personal data processed in the framework of police and judicial cooperation in criminal matters. Retrieved from http://eur-lex.europa.eu/LexUriServ/LexUriServ.do?uri=OJ:L:2008:350:0060:0071:EN:PDF

European Data Protection Supervisor. (2009). Opinion on the Communication from the Commission to the European Parliament, the Council and the European Economic and Social Committee towards a European e-Justice Strategy. *Official Journal of the European Union* (2009/C 128/02).

European Data Protection Supervisor. (2010). Opinion of the European Data Protection Supervisor on promoting trust in the information society by fostering data protection and privacy. Retrieved from http://www.edps.europa.eu/EDPSWEB/webdav/site/mySite/shared/Documents/Consultation/Opinions/2010/10-03-19_Trust_Information_Society_EN.pdf

Fernandez-Barrera, M., Gomes De Andrade, N. N., De Filippi, P., Viola De Azevedo Cunha, M., Sartor, G., & Casanovas, P. (2009). *Law and technology: Looking into the future*. Florence: European Press Academic Publishing.

Friedewald, M., Vildjiounaite, E., Puniec, Y., & Wright, D. (2007). Privacy, identity and security in ambient intelligence: A scenario analysis. *Telematics and Informatics*, *24*(1), 15–29. doi:10.1016/j.tele.2005.12.005

Gutwirth, S. (2007). Biometrics between opacity and transparency. *Annali dell'Istituto Superiore di Sanita*, *43*(1), 61–65.

Hildebrand, M., & Gurtwirth, S. (2007). *Profiling the European citizen*. London: Springer.

Hildebrandt, M. (2005). Privacy and identity. In Claes, E., Duff, A., & Gutwirth, S. (Eds.), *Privacy and the criminal Law*. Antwerp, Belgium: Intersentia.

Hoikkaanen, A., Bacigalupo, M., Compano, R., Lusoli, W., & Maghiros, I. (2010). New challenges and possible policy options for the regulation of electronic identity. *Journal of International Commercial Law and Technology*, *5*(1).

Joinson, A. N., Paine, C., Reips, U. D., & Buchanan, T. (2006). The role of situational and dispositional variables in online disclosures. Paper presented at the Workshop on Privacy, Trust and Identity Issues for Ambient Intelligence. Retrieved from http://www.cs.st-andrews.ac.uk/~pst/pti-ai-workshop/programme/joinson-privacy.pdf

Kamminga, M. T., & Sheinin, M. (2009). *The impact of human rights law on general international law*. Oxford: Oxford University Press. doi:10.1093/acprof:oso/9780199565221.001.0001

Keats Citron, D., & Henry, L. M. (2010). Visionary pragmatism and the value of privacy in the twenty-first century. *Michigan Law Review*, *108*, 1107–1126.

Kosta, E., Zibushka, J., Scherner, T., & Dumortier, J. (2008). Legal considerations on privacy-enhancing location based services using PRIME technology. *Computer Law & Security Report*, *24*(2), 139–146. doi:10.1016/j.clsr.2008.01.006

Le Métayer, D. (2010). Privacy by design: A matter of choice. In Gutwirth, S., Poullet, Y., & De Hert, P. (Eds.), *Data protection in a profiled world*. London: Springer. doi:10.1007/978-90-481-8865-9_20

Le Metayer, D., & Monteleone, S. (2009). Automated consent through privacy agents: Legal requirements and technical architecture. *Computer Law & Security Report*, *25*(2), 136–144. doi:10.1016/j.clsr.2009.02.010

Leenes, R. (2008). Do you know me? Decomposing identifiability. *Tilburg University Legal Studies Working Paper* no. 01/2008.

Leenes, R., Koops, B. J., & de Hert, P. (2008). *Constitutional rights and new technologies: A comparative study*. The Hague: T. M. C. Asser Press.

Lessing, L. (1999). *The code and other laws of cyberspace*. New York: Basic Books.

Lugaresi, N. (2004). Protezione della privacy e protezione dei dati personali: i limiti dell'approccio comunitario. *Giustizia amministrativa* no. 03/2004. Rome: Istituto poligrafico e Zecca dello Stato.

Lyon, D. (2007). *Surveillance studies, an overview*. Cambridge: Polity.

Lyon, D., & Zureik, E. (1996). *Computer, surveillance and privacy*. Minneapolis, MN: University of Minnesota Press.

Marx, G. T. (2001). Technology and social control. In Smalser, N., & Baltes, P. (Eds.), *International encyclopedia of the social and behavioral sciences*. Oxford: Elsevier.

OECD. (2009, June 8-9). Using Sensor-based Networks to address Global Issues: Policy opportunities and Challenges. OECD Experts conference, Lisbon, Spain. Retrieved from http://www.oecd.org/document/41/0,3343,en_2649_34223_42616233_1_1_1_1,00.html

Pilia, R. (2002). *Tutela della privacy informatica e protezione dei dati personali: un'analisi comparata. Studi economico-giuridici della Facoltà di Giurisprudenza dell'Università degli Studi di Cagliari*. Torino, Italy: Giappichelli.

Poullet, Y. (1991). *Le fondement du droit à la protection des données nominatives: propriétés ou libertés. Nouvelles technologies et propriété*. Paris: Thémis.

Poullet, Y. (2001). *Conclude a contract through electronic agents? Electronic Commerce – DER Abschlub von Vertragen im Internet*. Baden Baden, Germany: Verlagsgesellschaft.

Poullet, Y. (2004). The fight against crime and/or the protection of privacy: A thorny debate? *International Review of Law Computers & Technology, 18*(2), 251–273. doi:10.1080/1360086042000223535

Poullet, Y. (2005a). The internet and private life. In Kenyon, A. T., & Richardson, M. (Eds.), *New dimensions in privacy law*. Cambridge: Cambridge University Press.

Poullet, Y. (2005b). Pour une troisième génération de réglementations de protection de données. *Jusletter, 3*(22).

Poullet, Y. (2005c). Comment réguler la protection des données? Réflexions sur l'internormativité. In *P. Delnoy, Liber amicorum*. Bruxelles: Larcier.

Punie, Y. (2005). The future of ambient intelligent in Europe: The need for more everyday life. In Silverstone, R. (Ed.), *Media, technology and everyday life in Europe: From information to communication*. London: Ashgate Publishers Ltd.

Rodotà, S. (1997). *Repertorio di fine secolo*. Rome: Laterza.

Rodotà, S. (2009). *La vita e le regole, tra diritto e non diritto*. Milano, Italy: Feltrinelli.

Rouvroy, A. (2009). Privacy, data protection, and the unprecedented challenges of ambient intelligence. *Studies in Ethics, Law, and Technology, 108*(2), 116–122.

Sartor, G. (2006). Privacy, reputation and trust: Some implications for data protection. *EUI Working Papers*, Law no. 2006/04. Florence, Italy: European University Institute.

Sartor, G., & Viola de Azevedo Cunha, M. (2010). The Italian Google-case: Privacy, freedom of speech and responsibility for user-generated contents [Working paper]. *Social Science Research Network*. Retrieved from http://papers.ssrn.com/sol3/papers.cfm?abstract_id=1604411

Scheinin, M. (2010). Report of the special rapporteur to the Human Rights Council of United Nations on human rights and counter-terrorism [A/HRC/13/37]. Retrieved from http://www2.ohchr.org/english/issues/terrorism/rapporteur/srchr.htm

Sheinin, M. (2009). *Law and security: Facing the dilemmas. EUI working papers, Law 2009/11*. Florence, Italy: European University Institute.

Simpson, R., Schreckenghost, D., LoPresti, E. F., & Kirsch, N. (2006). Plans and planning in smart homes. In Augusto, J. C., & Nugent, C. D. (Eds.), *Designing smart homes: The role of artificial intelligence*. London: Springer- Verlag. doi:10.1007/11788485_5

Solove, D. (2007). "I've got nothing to hide" and other misunderstandings of privacy. *The San Diego Law Review, 44*, 745.

Solove, D. (2008). *Understanding privacy. Harvard*. Harvard University Press.

Sudre, F. (2005). La "construction" par le Juge européen du droit au respect de la vie privée. In Sudre, F. (Ed.), *Le droit au respect de la vie privée au sens de la Convention européenne des droits de l'homme*. Brussels: Bruylant.

Vildjiounaite, E., Mäkelä, S. M., Lindholm, M., Riihimäki, R., Kyllönen, V., Mäntyjärvi, J., & Ailisto, H. (2006). Unobtrusive multimodal biometrics for ensuring privacy and information security with personal devices. In *Pervasive Computing* [Proceedings of the 4th International Conference, PERVASIVE 2006, Dublin, Ireland, May 7-10, 2006]. Berlin-Heidelberg: Springer.

Warren, S., & Brandeis, L. (1890). The right to privacy. *Harvard Law Review, 4*(5), 193–220. doi:10.2307/1321160

Wright, D. (2005). The dark side of AmI. *The Journal of policy, regulation and strategies for Telecommunications, 7*(6), 33-51.

Wright, D., Gutwirth, S., Friedewald, M., De Hert, P., Langheinrich, M., & Moscibroda, A. (2009). Privacy, trust and policy-making: Challenges and responses. *Computer Law & Security Report, 25*(1), 69–83. doi:10.1016/j.clsr.2008.11.004

Wright, D., Gutwirth, S., Friedewald, M., Vildjiounaite, E., & Punie, Y. (2008). *Safeguards in a world in ambient intelligence*. London: Springer.

Zucca, L. (2008). *Constitutional dilemmas*. Oxford: Oxford University Press. doi:10.1093/acprof:oso/9780199552184.001.0001

Section 5

Privacy Policies in the Network:

Children's Privacy and the Protection of Copyright

Chapter 13
Privacy Policy Improvements to Protect Children Privacy

Federica Casarosa
Robert Schuman Centre for Advanced Studies, Italy

ABSTRACT

The achievement of an adequate level of privacy protection is a demanding objective, especially for new technologies. One relatively new but increasing class of users of Internet related services consists of children and young people. However, if Internet services can improve social skills and widen the knowledge minors have, it could open the doors to privacy abuse and misuse. As it would not be feasible to address all the legal and technical tools available within the privacy protection process, this chapter will focus on a specific element required by regulation and applicable both in Europe and in the US: the inclusion of a privacy policy in any website that collects personal data from users. The paper will provide an analysis of some of the privacy policies available online provided by companies that focus specifically on children and by social networking sites. The analysis will couple the descriptive part with suggestions to improve the level of compliance and, consequentially, the level of protection for minors' privacy.

1. CHILDREN ON THE INTERNET: NAIVE AND TECHNO-SAVVY

The achievement of an adequate level of privacy protection is still a demanding objective, and this is more than true for new technologies. The pervasive presence of information and communication technologies (ICTs) in our life and the increasing importance they have in our working and leisure time pushes for a more comprehensive understanding of problems and risks and, at the same time, for a more focused analysis of the needs and specificities of each class of data subjects.

One relatively new but increasing class of users of ICTs, and in particular of Internet related services, is children and young people. Statistics show that currently the percentage of children using Internet significantly overcomes the corresponding percentage of young adults (age 18-24), in a similar time period (Eurobarometer,

DOI: 10.4018/978-1-60960-083-9.ch013

2007). Moreover, social studies also acknowledge that minors are more and more interested in new technologies, and Internet in particular offers them new forms of socialization not available before. Through e-mail exchanges, online surfing, virtual games, chats and other services, minors are now increasingly able to relate to others living in faraway places, to meet different people and learn about their lives, their history, games and many other topics which can enhance their own knowledge of reality in unprecedented and unparalleled ways (Simpson, 2003).

If Internet services can improve social skills and widen the knowledge minors have, it could open the doors to privacy abuse and misuse. However, we should not interpret the Internet as evil, and we should not overestimate the risks online, as, though complex and multifaceted, in most cases these are not significantly different than those children face offline. Moreover, some of these risks do not necessarily arise from the technology itself but result from offline behaviors that are extended into the online space (Staksrud and Livingstone, 2009; Home Office task force on child protection on the internet, 2008). Youngsters are always attracted to new experiences and the Internet is an ideal playground where they can search for the service that mostly fits their needs and interests, and eventually switch to a new one as soon as they get bored. This approach pushed Internet Service and Content providers to differentiate their products and services so as to gather as many users for the longer time possible. As a matter of fact, minors leave traces of their passage and provide information about themselves. This, given the expanded possibilities to collect, organize and store thousands of data (Art 29 WP, 2009), can provide the materials for databases that include detailed profiles which can be used (directly or indirectly) for marketing purposes. Thus, websites can build in systems to help them monitor and understand children preferences, so as to have the possibility to tailor the content and the services upon minors identified interests, and push those interests into specific buying trends through the way in which the content and the services are provided (Stevees, 2006; Edwards, 2008; Kerr and Stevees, 2005).

From the policymaker perspective, this framework raises two level of difficulties: on the one hand, it is not possible to define a 'one size fits all' rule applicable to all possible services and devices through which the data are collected, not only due to differentiation of services provided to users, but also to convergence of media, which allow users to interact through different devices, such as mobile phones, personal digital assistants, game consoles and PCs. On the other hand, the policy approach should not only focus on a single tool to achieve the level of privacy protection required. Increasing the safety of the online environment is an objective that should include all the previous and subsequent phases which are linked to online connection. Namely such an effort should entail the education and awareness raising actions in schools and at home, the provision of technical and legal tools that can help children and young people to manage their online experience and, in the worst case scenario, to react to potential harm.

Obviously, it would not be feasible to address all the legal or technical tools available at the different stages; instead, this paper will focus on a specific element required by the regulation applicable both in Europe and in the US: the inclusion of an informative privacy notice, the so-called privacy policies, on any website that collects personal data from users (par. 2). The paper will provide an analysis of some of the privacy policies available online provided by companies that focus specifically on children and by social networking sites to which generally young people are more and more attracted (par. 3). This part will also try to show the differentiation among privacy statements addressed to children, those addressed to young people, and finally those addressed to adults, including parents and guardians. The analysis will couple the descriptive part with suggestions to improve the level of compliance and, consequentially, the level of protection for minors' privacy (par. 4).

The objective of this contribution is to identify ways that could potentially help websites reduce the privacy concerns of their users – mainly parents and caregivers – by emphasizing matters that the different class of users could more easily understand; this might help websites build strong trusting relationships with their users being them minors or adults.

Concerning terminology, though different terminology is used in order to define minors under 18 years old, such as tynies, tweenies, children, kids, with reference to different age span, in this paper we will stick to a simpler distinction between children and young people, whereby the former category includes all people up to 13 years old, while the latter includes people between 13 and 18 years old. There is no specific reason to differentiate in legal terms, at least in Europe, however, this distinction will help us in particular when dealing with US legislation, namely the Children's Online Privacy Protection Act, 1998, that provides for different legal consequences in case websites collect data from people under or over 13 years old.

2. CHILDREN PRIVACY AS A POLICY OBJECTIVE

The proliferation of the Internet allows websites to reach potential users all around the world, thus the flow of data and personal information could go beyond country borders. Therefore, a company located in one country with one privacy regulation can share or transfer personal information about the users of its website located in another country with a different privacy regulation.

Given this framework, the present paper will focus on two jurisdictions, namely Europe and the United States, in order to provide a comparison between the current regimes of children privacy protection in these two cases.

2. 1. The European Approach to Children Privacy

Although the European Union has been a forerunner in tackling children protection issues, as the first steps date back to the Green Paper on the protection of minors and human dignity in informational and audiovisual services (EU Commission, 1996a), the current framework does not directly address the problem of children privacy. In particular, the Green Paper provided an analysis of the legislation and policies in force at national, European and international level, pushing forward some guidelines to provide a more flexible regulatory framework capable to face the characteristics of the new services. At the same time, the European Commission published a *Communication on Illegal and Harmful content on the Internet* (EU Commission, 1996), in which such concepts were defined.

The basic framework concerning privacy at European level is the Data protection Directive 95/46/EC (EU Commission, 2003; Bennett, 1992; Carey, 2009; Cammilleri-Subrenat & Levallois-Barth, 2007; Gutwirth, 2009). The Directive requires that data be processed fairly and lawfully. This implies a high level of transparency in the process: companies collecting and processing personal data must publish their data protection policy where the data treatment characteristics should be described in a detailed way. Data must only be collected 'for specific, explicit and legitimate purposes.' However, this obligation is not further specified in case of children data, where the ability of minors to understand privacy policies presented by the websites can be more limited, or at least different given their age (Bartoli, 2009). Moreover, the directive adds other principles for the fair treatment of data: the possibility to access and correct the data, the need to keep the data updated, and the possibility to object to the data treatment. Again, no distinction in case of children data treatment is included in the directive; thus, children have the same rights as adults concerning their data, though usually less knowledge about it.

The Directive should be read in conjunction with Directive 2002/58/EC, the so-called Privacy and Electronic communication directive. In particular, the latter comes into play when third parties store information or gain access to information stored in the terminal equipment of a subscriber or a user (art. 5, par. 3). In terms of children privacy protection, however, this Directive does not help either, as it applies regardless of the age of the user and imposes uniform rules on data controllers concerning, for instance, the storing of cookies on the computer of the child. Nonetheless, such obligations would only provide an indirect positive effect on children privacy, as usually children will use parents' or schools' computers where such data processing would have been already refused by the administrator of the computer.

In order to comply with this wide set of rules, websites should shape not only their privacy policies but eventually their website architecture, e.g. including an age verification filter, and the like.

2. 2. The U.S. Approach to Children Privacy

After the Federal Trade Commission (FTC) 1998 report concerning the risks entailed in current online marketing practices, in particular towards children, the U.S. Congress enacted the Children's Online Privacy Protection Act (hereinafter COPPA) (Garber, 2001; Killingsworth, 2000; Slaughter-Defoe and Wang, 2009). COPPA applies to commercial websites and online services targeting children aged under 13 and to general websites that have actual knowledge that they may collect data from children aged under 13. Under this regulation, websites are not only obliged to comply with the five essential Fair Information Principles (FIPs), defined by the FTC, but they also have to comply with an opt-in system that requires a verifiable parent consent to the data treatment.

Practically, the website must take reasonable steps to ensure that the parent receives notice of the willingness of their child to access a website, which asks for personal data, such as name, address, city code, etc., and at that point the parent should give their consent to access and consequently to the data treatment. For instance, the website can ask for the email address of a parent in order to send them a request that provides as follows:

"*Your child has created a free account on AAA, and now needs your permission to start playing. During the registration process, we have asked the email of the guardian of the child for the purpose of sending the password to that email and have parental consent prior to accessing the environment.*

To complete the registration on AAA and get access to the virtual world, we provide you with the following password, which you can change once inside AAA if you click on the option MY ACCOUNT".

However, the obligation of parental consent should be appreciated and verification tools should be proportional to the type of data treatment as exceptions are included in the regulation. For instance, up to 2002, the FTC interprets the verifiability of parental consent as "*if the operator uses the information for internal purposes, a less rigorous method of consent is required. If the operator discloses the information to others, the situation presents greater dangers to children, and a more reliable method of consent is required*" (FTC, 2006). Accordingly, the FTC assumed that placing children under surveillance as they play and collecting their personal information in order to market products to them was inherently benign and posed only a slight risk of harm (Kerr and Steeves, 2005).

Moreover, websites are required also to state that collection of children's personal data may be pursued. Parents should be informed of what the website owners intend to do with the information and whether or not they intend to disclose the children's personal information to third parties. For this purpose, website owners must display online a 'clear and prominent' notice of the site's information practices.

Recent developments of this regulation focus still on this point, and in particular current public consultation ask for opinions on additional technological methods to obtain verifiable parental consent that should be added to the COPPA Rule, on whether any of the methods currently included should be removed, and on what challenges operators face in authenticating parents (FTC, 2010).

3. PRIVACY POLICIES: USEFUL TOOLS TO ENHANCE TRUST

In general terms, a privacy notice is the oral or written statement that individuals are given when information is collected about them. Although different terminologies have been used to defined such statements, such as 'privacy policies', 'privacy statements', 'privacy notices', and 'information practice statements', at the end of the day their meaning is the same. Thus, in this contribution we will use uniformly the term privacy policies.

From a practical standpoint, the inclusion of a privacy policy within a website can increase transparency, and thus increase the level of trust of consumers towards the enterprise; it can also motivate the enterprise "*to reflect on their declared corporate privacy undertakings in their business process.*" (Clarke, 2010). From this perspective, the privacy policy should help individuals understand how information will be used and what the consequences of this are for them. From a legal standpoint, the provision of a privacy policy can also help articulate and eventually limit legal responsibilities when it complies with the data protection laws applicable.

As a minimum, a privacy policy should provide information about the data treatment and the data controller, but it can also include further information such as data subjects' access rights or security arrangements. The content of the privacy policy, however, is mainly based on the data protection legislation applicable to the data controller and/or data subject.

As stated above, the approaches by European and U.S. regulations concerning the list of items to be included in a privacy policy differ; however, they are both based on a common concern about the way in which any data subject could get knowledge about how to control the quality, use and further disclosure of his/her own data to other individuals and/or organizations. From a more general perspective, the possibility that inconsistencies across the different regulatory regimes, mainly across European countries but also at the global level, might become a restraint on trade was the trigger for a codification of common principles; this could serve as a framework for countries to use when drafting and implementing their laws, including rules at to the information to be included in the privacy policies. In particular, this task was pursued by the Organization for Economic Co-operation and Development (OECD) and resulted in the OECD Guidelines on Protection of Privacy and Transborder Flows of Personal Data, a document which expressed and described eight 'fair information principles': Collection Limitation, Data Quality, Purpose Specification, Use Limitation, Security Safeguards, Openness, Individual Participation, Accountability.

In order to compare on a more neutral background the privacy policies used by websites based in Europe and in U.S., we will use as benchmark the OECD principles. These principles constitute the set of substantial criteria against which we evaluate their application in practice through the privacy policy.

Concerning the European regulatory framework, the point of reference will be the Data protection directive, which has also been supported by the art. 8 of the Charter of European Fundamental Rights where the main principles were endorsed, namely, after the general statement "*everyone has the right to the protection of personal data,*" the related basic principles included are fair process; specified purposes; consent or other legitimate basis; access and rectification; control by an independent authority.

Concerning the U.S. regulatory framework, the point of reference will be the Fair Information Principles (FIPs) and their specific interpretation endorsed within the COPPA (FTC, 2000). It is worth mentioning the different source of the two, given that the former are private regulation while the latter falls into public regulation. In the U.S., since the early 1970s, governments committed to monitoring the "information practices" of organizations or, more specifically, the methods in which these organizations collect and use personal information and the safeguards they employ to ensure those practices are fair and provide adequate privacy protection. The result of this government intervention has been a series of guidelines and model codes that now represent commonly accepted principles, more formally known as FIPs.

4. ANALYSIS OF THE PRIVACY POLICIES

The selection of privacy policies to be analyzed in this study has been based on two main criteria: the type of website and the legal system they referred to.

On the one hand, the type of websites selected can fall into three categories:

- websites targeting directly children (hereinafter children website - CW), where usually the main content of the website is dedicated to a toy or a children product, and the children are interested in having the possibility to play games, socialize and communicate with other users equally interested in the same toy or product. This follows the COPPA definition which uses as factors to classify the website as targeting to kids the subject matter, language, whether the site uses animated characters, and whether advertising on the site is directed to children;
- websites of a general audience such as online broadcasting channels where children and young people are addressed only in a limited part of the website, for instance websites including children TV show and related games and gadgets (hereinafter general audience websites - GAW);
- social networking websites (hereinafter SNS) that, as the previous ones, are directed at a general audience, but they can be accessed by children and young people as well, providing them with the possibility to create online personal profiles and to communicate and share videos, images, etc. with any other user of the website.

Although these categories are not so different in terms of services provided, which always include games and competitions, chat rooms, video or photo sharing, and the like, the objectives are not exactly the same. In the first two categories brand building is the underlying objective. In this case, participation of minors, through personal data and on-site behavior, provides information about (young) consumers' taste and preferences, which can help, for instance, in defining customized marketing techniques, or different broadcasting strategies. In the third category instead, the objective is the creation of an online identity which could be shared and enriched by the communication and the participation of other users. This would improve minors' self-esteem and consciousness, as Haubenreicht (2006) notes, given that "*the multifarious steps to creating a profile can take hours, and that time spent thinking about who she is as a person can be extraordinarily valuable to her personal development.*" In this latter case, the dissemination of personal data by users, be they adult or minors, is at the very basis of the website model, including not only personal data, but also those data that are defined 'sensitive' by the European Data Protection Directive, such as "*personal data revealing racial or ethnic origin, political opinions, religious or philosophical*

Table 1. Comparison between data protection principles and policies

OECD Principles	EU Data Protection Directive	U.S. Fair Information Principles (FIPs)	U.S. COPPA FIPs
Collection Limitation	Processing is to be fair and lawful, with consent of the data subject	Choice/Consent	*Control (1).* Web sites must obtain parents' verifiable consent prior to collecting personal information from children 12 and under.
Purpose Specification	Processing is only to be undertaken for known and specified purposes	Notice/Awareness	*Notice.* A child-directed Web site must display a link to a description of its information collection practices on the home page of its site and at each area where it collects personal information from children.
Data Quality	Data is to be kept accurately and if necessary updated	Integrity/Security	*Appropriateness.* Children cannot be asked to provide personal information beyond that for which the requested information is reasonably necessary.
Use Limitation	No more personal data is to be gathered than necessary and relevant to specified purposes; data is not to be held longer than necessary to fulfill these purposes	Not included in the FIPs	See Appropriateness above.
Security Safeguards	Data is to be held securely	Integrity/Security	*Security.* Child-directed Web sites must establish and maintain reasonable procedures to protect the confidentiality, security, and integrity of all personal information provided by children.
Openness	Data controller is to be clearly identified, as the existence and purpose of the data processing	Not included in the FIPs	*Completeness.* The statement of information collection practices must completely describe: types of information collected; their use and storage; disclosure to third parties; purpose of collection; and parental rights with regard to information content and usage.
Individual Participation	Rights of data subjects, e.g. to access and correct their data, and prevent its use for direct marketing, are to be respected	Access/Participation Enforcement/Redress	*Control (2).* Parents have the right and must be given the means to review and, if desired, delete their child's personal information. Parents can allow or disallow the dissemination of their child's information to third parties.
Accountability	National supervision authorities that monitor the data protection level and start legal proceedings when data protection regulation has been violated	Not included in the FiPs	No reference in the COPPA

beliefs, trade-union membership, and the processing of data concerning health or sex life" (art. 8, par. 1). On SNS, the participation of children is usually excluded as websites provide expressly their service only to young people over 13 years old; this allows the SNS not to be subject to the aforementioned COPPA stricter obligations concerning data protection. In some cases, this age limitation is coupled with technological tools, such as placing a 'cookie' onto a user's computer to prevent the user from attempting to re-register with false age details; or using technical tools such as search algorithms to look for slang words typically used by children and young people and to identify children under 13 years old who may have lied about their age at registration; and, also offering free downloadable parental controls which allow parents to manage their children's use of the service (Staksrud & Lobe, 2010).

On the other hand, in order to emphasize differences and similarities among privacy policies, the selection of the website was also based on

Table 2. Websites selected and their main characteristics

	Enterprise Nationality	Specific for minors	Age limit
Walt Disney (CW1)	U.S.	Children and young people	None
Barbie (CW2)	U.S.	Children and young people	None
Pocoyo (CW3)	Spain	Children and young people	None
Gormiti (CW4)	Italy	Children and young people	None
Thomas the train (GAW1)	U.S.	Children and young people	None
Vai Diego Vai (GAW2)	Italy	Children and young people	None
Petite princesse (GAW3)	France	Children and young people	None
Facebook (SNS1)	U.S.	Young people	Not under 13
Netlog (SNS2)	Belgium	Young people	Not under 13
Hyves (SNS3)	Netherlands	Young people	Not under 16

nationality of the enterprises that create them, taking as a point of reference their main seat. Thus, I include both U.S. websites and European ones, the latter scattered among different countries.

The analysis will underline two types of elements: descriptive elements which will take into account the formal characteristics of the privacy policies available on the selected website (Table 3); and substantial elements which are requirements put into effect on the basis of the mentioned OECD principles (Table 4).

4.1. Results and Best Practices

From the analysis of the previous two tables, we can affirm that in general the inclusion of a privacy policy on the website, whether or not the latter is focused on children and young people, is the rule. However, the differences among the results push for a more detailed evaluation; in particular, the following arguments can be proposed:

- Except for one case (GAW3), all the other websites try to clarify in a more open way

Table 3. Formal characteristics

	Type of media	Last update	Length	Style	Reference to other doc.
CW1	Written	May 2007	1500 words	Questions & Answers	Yes
CW2	Written	June 2008	2800 words	Questions & Answers	Yes*
CW3	Written	Not specified	900 words	Solid text	No
CW4	Written	Not specified	700 words	Solid text	No
GAW1	Written	July 2008	2100 words	Paragraphed text	No
GAW2	Written	Not specified	1300 words	Paragraphed text	No
GAW3	Written	Not specified	150 words	Solid text	No
SNS1	Written	April 2010	5400 words	Paragraphed text	Yes **
SNS2	Written	February 2009	1200 words	Bullet points	Yes*
SNS3	Written	April 2009	1700 words	Questions & Answers	No

* Reference to Terms of use and Code of conduct.

** Reference to Terms of use.

the main elements of the privacy policy on the website. In terms of readability, only part of the policies analyzed tries to attract the attention of the reader through a more user-friendly visual presentation of the text, such as question and answers style or paragraphed text.

Table 4. Substantive characteristics

Website/OECD principles		CW1	CW2	CW3	CW4	GAW1	GAW2	GAW3	SNS1	SNS2	SNS3
Collection Limitation	Consent system	Opt in	Opt In	Opt in	Opt in	Opt in	Opt in	Opt in	Opt in	Opt in	Opt in
	Parent consent	Only under 13	Only under 13	Only under 14	Any under 18	No	No	No	No (no one under 13 accepted)	No (no one under 13 accepted)	Only under 16
	Possibility of denial	Yes	Yes	Yes	Yes	Yes	Yes	Yes	Yes	Yes	Yes
	Consequences of denial	Limited service	Limited service	Limited service	Limited service	Not specified	Limited service	Not specified	Refusal of service	Refusal of service	Refusal of service
Data Quality	Minimization of data	Acknowledged	Acknowledged	Acknowledged	Not mentioned	Not mentioned	Not mentioned	Not mentioned	No	Not mentioned	No
Purpose Specification	Description of data collected	Specified but open to undefined additions	Specified but open to undefined additions	Not clearly specified	Not clearly specified	Listed and defined	Listed and defined	Not specified	Listed and clearly defined	Listed and clearly defined	Generally defined
	Description of sources	From user and automatically generated	From user	From user	From user	From user, automatically generated and advertisers	From user, automatically generated and advertisers	Not specified	From user, automatically generated and advertisers	From user and automatically generated	From user and automatically generated
	Description of purposes	Shortly described	Listed and shortly described	Not connected with specific data	Listed and shortly described	Listed and shortly described	Shortly described	Not specified	Listed and described	Listed and shortly described	Listed and described
	Reference to sensitive data	No	No	No	Yes	No	No	No	No	No	No

continued on following page

Table 4. continued

Use Limitation	Length of data retention	Not specified	Not specified	Not specified	Not specified	Not specified	Mentioned but not specified	Not specified	Yes (in some cases 3 months	Yes (6 months)	Not specified
	Type of disposal	n.a.	n.a.	n.a.	n.a.	n.a.	Deletion	n.a.	Anonymization	Deletion	Not specified
	Sharing with 3rd parties	Yes	Yes (upon consent)	No	No	Yes	Yes	Not specified	Yes	Yes	Yes (upon consent)
	Request to 3rd parties to apply similar PP or principles	n..a.	No	N.a.	N.a.	n.a.	n.a.	n.a.	Yes	No	No
	Type of information shared	Mentioned but not specified	Marketing information (only for over 13)	n.a	n.a.	Marketing information	Marketing information	n.a.	All	Marketing information	Marketing information
	Liability in case of misuse	Not specified	Not specified	Not specified	Not specified	Not specified	Not specified	Not specified	No	Not specified	No
Security Safeguards	Adequate security system	Not specified	Only for credit card data	Yes, but vague	Not specified	Yes, but vague	Not specified	Not specified	Yes	Not specified	Yes, but vague
Openness	Accessibility	Link within the general privacy policy	Link at the end of webpage	Link at the end of webpage	In the registration form for purchase	Link at the end of webpage	Link at the end of webpage	Link at the end of webpage	Link at the end of webpage	Link at the end of webpage	Link at the end of webpage
	Target reader	Adult	Scattered	Scattered	Adult	Adult	Adult	Adult	Adult	Adult	Adult
	Clarity and conspicuousness	Average	Good	Good	Good	Good	Average	Poor	High	High	Good
	Entities covered	Enterprise group	Enterprise Group	Enterprise only	Enterprise group	Enterprise group	Enterprise group	Enterprise Group	Enterprise only	Enterprise only	Enterprise only

continued on following page

Table 4. continued

Individual Participation	Possibility to access and update data	Yes	Yes	Yes	Yes	Yes	Yes	Yes	Yes	Yes	Yes
	3rd party certification	Yes	No	No	No	No	No	No	Yes	No	No
	Dispute resolution system	Yes (3rd party certification)	No	No	No	No	No	No	Yes	No	No
Accountability	Legal reference	COPPA	COPPA	Spanish DP legislation	Italian DP legislation	US DP legislation	Italian DP legislation	French DP legislation	US DP legislation	Belgian DP legislation	Not specified
	Contact point	Yes	Yes	Yes	Yes	Yes	Yes	Yes	Yes	Yes	Yes

- Low level of 'legalese' terminology is generally applied on all CW and SNS; however, European websites tend usually to reference Data protection legislation acts and provisions, which does not encourage comprehension or readership.
- In the majority of cases, the privacy policy is a stand-alone text complete and comprehensive, also in the cases where minors' protection clauses are included in the more general privacy policy. However, in one case (CW1), the cross-reference between general and children focused privacy policy limited the understanding of the text, given also the extraordinary length of the general privacy policy.
- Prominence of the privacy policy tab is usually interpreted by enterprises as the mere inclusion of the tab within those corporate ones at the end of the page, without any further emphasis on such document. On the one hand, this positioning in the webpage is a common practice that users are well aware of and generally used to; on the other hand, this implicitly communicates to users/parents that the privacy policy is a fundamental part of the site. However, in all these cases the privacy policy tab is not differentiated from the other features of the page, except for CW3 where the website distinguishes the link with a different shape in which 'privacy' is written, attracting the users' attention. Another exception is CW4 where the privacy policy is included in the registration form, directly followed by the parent/adult consent request.
- Contact points are always provided for questions and information on redress mechanisms. Usually contact points are postal addresses, but in few cases, more options were provided, such email addresses and free-toll telephone numbers. On the one hand, this can increase the difficulties for the websites to handle the requests by users in a shorter time, but, on the other hand, it can increase the possibility to accommodate different users' preferences.
- Opt-in is the main consent system, in particular for CW given the obligations arising from the COPPA regulation for under 13-year old users. In case of denial of data treatment, however, only few websites

permit access to games, videos, etc. without registration. In case of SNS, denial to provide consent leads to refusal of service, given that the website is obviously based on the free flow of users' data. However, lack of registration does not mean that websites do not collect the so called non-PII, i.e. information which does not allow to personally identify users (see GAW1).

- In terms of clarity and conspicuousness, only in few cases can the privacy policy be considered highly understandable; in particular, our evaluation was based on the purpose specification items. Except for SNS, the set of data collected and corresponding purposes are not always clearly defined nor described; yet in two cases the types of data collected are included in an open list, with only few of them being explicitly justified through examples. Moreover, the same websites that acknowledge in their privacy policy a data minimization approach do not put it into practice when expressing the types of data collected and their purposes.
- Length of data retention is almost never defined (except for SNS1 and SNS2), however, this can become an issue if Art 29 Working Party does follow the same path concerning the log and cookies duration that it had with Google in 2008 (Casarosa, 2008).
- Security systems are also not very detailed in the privacy policies nor are they differentiated in terms of the type of data collected. This can be barely justified on the assumption that the explicit description of security systems can facilitate unauthorized access to data by hackers; instead, a general description of security safeguards could increase users' trust and confidence (No, Boritz, and Sundarraj, 2008).

4.2. Space for Improvements

What is evident from the previously listed points is the fact that privacy policies can be widely differentiated documents, yet complying with accepted guidelines and legal requirements at least at a basic level. Such an evaluation, however, is based on the perceptions and level of understanding of an adult – educated and used also to legal terminology – on adult-targeted privacy policies. As a matter of fact, none of the analyzed privacy policies were directed to children, neither as to their style and structure nor as to their explicit receiver. Only in the case of SNS, where youngsters' participation is more than an exception, the terminology and design is more clear and concise and, at the same time, more understandable for a younger and less educated reader.

Improvements in this direction could take into account two possible suggestions: child-targeted design and multi-layered privacy policies.

The multi-layered privacy policy has been also presented by Art 29 Working Party (2004) distinguishing between essential and further information. Essential information is to be provided in all circumstances, whereas further information should be provided "*if it is necessary to guarantee fair processing having regard to the specific circumstances in which the data are collected.*" (Art 29 WP, 2004, p. 5) The Art 29 WP supported the possibility to provide a three-layered privacy policy, to be interpreted as legally compliant with European data protection legislation if the total sum meets the legal requirements. As a matter of fact, the Opinion clearly states that "*The sum total of the layers must meet specific national requirements, while each individual layer will be considered acceptable as long as the total remains compliant*", (Art 29 WP, 2004, p. 7).

This layered structure can be useful also to improve minors' understanding of privacy policies, as the three layers could be framed not only in terms of number of information included, but also in terms of different level of understanding of users. For instance, the first layer or short notice, where at least the identity of the controller as well as the purpose of the data processing are included, can be drafted in a simple and clear structure so that also children and young people can comprehend (Burkell, Steeves, Micheti, 2007). Moreover, the additional information "*which in view of the particular circumstances of the case must be provided beforehand to ensure a fair processing*" (Art 29 WP, 2004, p. 8) can also include in the case of minors a short explanation of the three main items that they could be interested in: data collected, their use and possible share of such information with third parties. In this sense, a child-targeted privacy policy should be relatively short, written at an appropriate reading level, easy to navigate and self-contained.

Then, the second layer or condensed notice, could provide more detailed information concerning the collection, use and sharing, including all the items listed by the Art 29 WP, namely the name of the company, the purpose of the data processing, the recipients or categories of recipients of the data, whether replies to the user questions are obligatory or voluntary, as well as the possible consequences of failure to reply, the right to access, to rectify and oppose, choices available to the individual, the contact point for questions and information on redress mechanisms, either within the company itself or details of the nearest data protection agency. In this case, the style and structure of the text can be more refined, given that the target reader can be identified in an adult, and can also provide longer and more specific details; however, it should be also underlined that social studies have determined that privacy policies are written at a reading level that is also beyond the capacity of most adults (Graber, D'Alessandro, and Johnson-West, 2003).

Statistics show that children and young people are, in the majority of cases, alone in front of the computer and decide autonomously concerning the provision of their data. In particular, ICO study (2007) emphasizes that only 14% of the users between 14 and 21 years old users of SNS said they always read and understand the privacy policies. Over half of all young people said they skim read privacy policies and a further 32% said they never read them at all. However, what is encouraging is the evidence that 91% of respondents felt that privacy statements are important, with 39% saying they felt that privacy statements were 'very important, I layer my profile so that full access is only granted to a very close group of friends'. Nonetheless, 52% of all respondents felt that privacy statements 'are important, but I like to meet new people so I tend to leave some of my profile public.'

Given this framework, the possibility to provide minors with a more easily readable, and consequently understandable privacy policy could improve their capability to engage in critical analysis and reach a really 'informed consent' to provide their data. Probably the outcome would still be a flow of their data, but in this case their decisions about privacy would be directly linked to disclosure.

5. CONCLUSION

Minors are not a homogeneous class of people; this renders necessary a distinction taking into account age: children younger than 13 years or over 16 years old obviously manifest different levels of understanding of risks and harms. This distinction should also balance the polarized view of adults towards minors. In particular, children can be seen as "*vulnerable, undergoing a crucial but fragile process of cognitive and social development to which technology poses a risk by introducing potential harms into the social conditions for development and necessitating, in turn, a protectionist regulatory environment*" (Home Office task force on child protection on the internet, 2008, p. 15). At the same time, children can be competent and creative, more techno-savvy than adults acknowledge, and this could have as a consequence that society may fail to provide a sufficiently rich environment for them. Finding a position that recognizes both these characteristics is important.

In this direction, facilitating children to read and understand the privacy policies of websites could be a way to improve minors' awareness of data protection rights, and at the same time to provide them with the tools to appreciate when and how to offer their personal information for access to games and social networking sites.

Clearly, changing the format of privacy policies will not solve all the problems related to the collection and use of personal information. However, the privacy policy plays a significant role in protecting minors' online privacy, because it is one of the primary methods to ensure that minors and their parents have enough information to make informed choices about whether or not to reveal personal information. Thus, creating comprehensible privacy policies is one important step in the right direction.

REFERENCES

Article 29 Working Party. (2004). Opinion 10/2004 on more harmonised information provisions. Retrieved May 1, 2010, from http://ec.europa.eu/justice_home/fsj/privacy/docs/wpdocs/2004/wp100_en.pdf

Article 29 Working Party. (2009). Opinion 2/2009 on the protection of children's personal data (General guidelines and the special case of schools). Retrieved May 1, 2010, from http://ec.europa.eu/justice_home/fsj/privacy/docs/wpdocs/2009/wp160_en.pdf

Bartoli, E. (2009). Children's data protection vs. marketing companies. *International Review of Law Computers & Technology, 23*(1-2), 35–45. doi:10.1080/13600860902742612

Bennett, C. (1992). *Regulating privacy: Data protection and public policy in Europe and the United States*. Ithaca, NY: Cornell University Press.

Burkell, J., Steeves, V., & Micheti, A. (2007). Broken doors: Strategies for drafting privacy policies kids can understand. Retrieved May 1, 2010, from http://www.idtrail.org/files/broken_doors_final_report.pdf

Cammilleri-Subrenat, A., & Levallois-Barth, C. (2007). *Sensitive data protection in the European Union*. Brussels: Bruylant.

Carey, P. (2009). *Data protection: A practical guide to UK and EU law* (3rd ed.). New York: Oxford University Press.

Casarosa, F. (2009). Privacy in search engines: Negotiating Control. Retrieved May 1, 2010, from http://ssrn.com/abstract=1561571

Clarke, R. (2010). The effectiveness of privacy policy statements: A pilot study against a normative template. In I. Kerr, J. Gammack & K. Bryant (Eds.), *Digital business security development: Management technologies*. Retrieved May 1, 2010, from http://www.rogerclarke.com/EC/PPSE0812.html

EU Commission. (1996a). Green paper on the protection of minors and human dignity in audiovisual and information services [COM (96) 483 fin].

EU Commission. (1996b). Communication on illegal and harmful content on the internet [COM (96) 487 fin].

EU Commission. (2003). First report on the implementation of the Data Protection Directive (95/46/EC) [COM(2003) 265 fin].

Commission, E. U. (2010). Recommendation of the council concerning guidelines governing the protection of privacy and transborder flow of personal data (23.09.1980). Retrieved May 1, 2010, from http://www.oecd.org/document/18/0,2340,en_2649_34255_1815186_1_1_1_1,00.html

Edwards, L. (2008). Data protection 2.0: This time is personal. Paper presented at the Gikii2 conference, Oxford, UK. Retrieved May 1, 2010, from http://www.law.ed.ac.uk/ahrc/gikii/docs3/edwards.pdf

Edwards, L., & Brown, I. (2009). Data control and social networking: Irreconcilable ideas? In Matwyshyn, A. M. (Ed.), *Harboring data: Information security, law and the corporation* (pp. 202–226). Stanford, CA: Stanford University Press.

Eurobarometer. (2007). Safer internet for children: Qualitative study in 29 European countries. Retrieved May 1, 2010, from http://ec.europa.eu/public_opinion/quali/ql_safer_internet_summary.pdf

Federal Trade Commission. (1998). Privacy online: A report to congress. Retrieved May 1, 2010, from http://www.ftc.gov/reports/privacy3/priv-23a.pdf

Federal Trade Commission. (2000). Privacy online: Fair information practices in the electronic marketplace: A report to Congress. Retrieved May 1, 2010, from http://www.ftc.gov/reports/privacy2000/privacy2000.pdf

Federal Trade Commission. (2006). How to comply with the Children's Online Privacy Protection Rule. Retrieved May 1, 2010, from http://www.ftc.gov/bcp/edu/pubs/business/idtheft/bus45.shtm

Federal Trade Commission. (2010). Questions whether changes to technology warrant changes to agency rule. Retrieved May 1, 2010, from http://www.ftc.gov/opa/2010/03/coppa.shtm

Garber, D. (2001). COPPA: Protecting children's personal information on the Internet. *Journal of Law and Policy*, *12*, 129–187.

Graber, M., D'Alessandro, D., & Johnson-West, J. (2007). Reading level of privacy policies on Internet health web sites. *The Journal of Family Practice*, *51*(7), 642–646.

Gutwirth, S. (Ed.). (2009). *Reinventing data protection?*London: Springer. doi:10.1007/978-1-4020-9498-9

Haubenreicht, S. N. S. (2008). Parental rights in MySpace: Reconceptualising the state's parens patriae role in the digital age. Retrieved May 1, 2010, from http://ssrn.com/abstract=1217872

Home Office task force on child protection on the internet. (2008). Good practice guidance for the providers of social networking and other user interactive services. Retrieved May 1, 2010, from http://police.homeoffice.gov.uk/publications/operational-policing/social-networking-guidance/

Information Commissioner Office. (2007). Data protection: Topline report. Retrieved May 1, 2010 from http://www.ico.gov.uk/upload/documents/library/data_protection/detailed_specialist_guides/research_results_topline_report.pdf

Kerr, I., & Stevees, V. (2005, April). Virtual playgrounds and buddybots: A data-minefield for tinys & tweeneys. Paper presented at the meeting Panopticon, The 15th Annual Conference on Computers, Freedom & Privacy, Seattle, WA. Retrieved May 1, 2010, from http://idtrail.org/files/Kerr_Steeves_Virtual_Playgrounds.pdf

Killingsworth, S. (2000). Website privacy policies in principle and in practice. *PLI/Pat* 663-736.

Kuner, C. (2003). *European data protection law and online business*. Oxford: Oxford University Press.

No, W. G., Boritz, E., & Sundarraj, R. (2008). Do companies' online privacy policy disclosures match customer needs? Retrieved May 1, 2010, from http://ssrn.com/abstract_id=1082961

Simpson, B. (2005). Identity manipulation in cyberspace as a leisure option: Play and the exploration of self. *Information & Communications Technology Law*, *14*(2), 115–131. doi:10.1080/13600830500042632

Slaughter-Defoe, T. D., & Wang, Z. (2009). From "ego" to "social comparison": Cultural transmission and child protection policies and laws in a digital age. In Matwyshyn, A. M. (Ed.), *Harboring data: Information security, law and the corporation* (pp. 145–157). Stanford, CA: Stanford University Press.

Staksrud, E., & Livingstone, S. (2009). Children and online risk: Powerless victims or resourceful participants? *Information Communication and Society*, *12*(3), 364–387. doi:10.1080/13691180802635455

Staksrud, E., & Lobe, B. (2010). *Evaluation of the implementation of the Safer Social Networking Principles for the EU*. European Commission Safer Internet Programme, Luxembourg. Retrieved May 1, 2010, from http://ec.europa.eu/information_society/activities/social_networking/eu_action/implementation_princip/index_en.htm#final_report

Stevees, V. (2006). It's not child's play: The online invasion of children's privacy. *University of Ottawa Law & Technology Journal*, *3*(1), 169–188.

Turow, J. (2003). *Americans and privacy: The system is broken*. Philadelphia, PA: Annenberg Public Policy Center of the University of Pennsylvania. Retrieved May 1, 2010 from http://www.annenbergpublicpolicycenter.org/Downloads/Information_And_Society/20030701_America_and_Online_Privacy/20030701_online_privacy_report.pdf

APPENDIX: PRIVACY POLICIES (ALL RETRIEVED MAY 1ST, 2010)

Barbie

Website http://www.barbie.com/

Privacy policy http://www.everythinggirl.com/common/policy.aspx?site=barbie

Pocoyo

Website http://www.pocoyo.com/

Privacy policy http://www.pocoyo.com/v2/privacys/es/privacy.html

Gormiti

Website http://new.gormiticlub.it/

Privacy policy http://www.gormiticlub.it/club/registrati.php?controllo_eta=1

Walt Disney

Website http://disney.go.com/index

Privacy policy http://tv.disney.go.com/playhouse/mickeymouseclubhouse/index.html

Thomas the train

Website http://www.thomasandfriends.com

Privacy policy http://www.hitentertainment.com/corporate/privacy.html

Vai Diego Vai

Website http://www.nickjr.it/tv/programma.asp?id=74

Privacy policy http://www.nicktv.it/legale4.asp

Petite princesse

Website http://www.mon-ludo.fr/petite-princesse/

Privacy policy http://www.francetelevisions.fr/mentionslegales/

Facebook

Website http://www.facebook.com/

Privacy policy http://www.facebook.com/policy.php

Netlog

Website http://en.netlog.com/

Privacy policy http://en.netlog.com/go/about/legal/view=privacy

Hyves

Website http://www.hyves.nl/

Privacy policy http://www.hyves.nl/privacy/

Chapter 14
Digital Copyright Enforcement:
Between Piracy and Privacy

Pedro Pina
Polytechnic Institute of Coimbra, Portugal

ABSTRACT

Copyright and privacy are two fundamental values for a democratic society, since both enhance the development of each individual's personality. Nevertheless, in cyberspace, copyright enforcement and the right to informational self determination have become two clashing realities. In fact, with the arrival of digital technology, especially the Internet, rightholders, facing massive on-line copyright infringements, mainly by file-sharers on peer-to-peer (P2P) systems, started developing more and more intrusive new enforcement strategies in electronic communications as a means to identify the infringers and the committed infractions. The goal of the present paper is to study, in a context where massive unauthorized uses of copyrighted works is an undeniable reality, how the boundaries between what is public or private become fainter, whether the use of tracking software is consistent with personal data protection legislation, and whether it is possible to reconcile these two human rights.

I. INTRODUCTION

Until recently, the mere idea of a conflict between copyright and privacy rights would be quite surprising. The tension between these rights was indeed almost imperceptible, since the referred branches of law – both recognized as human rights and related to the development of an individual's personality as an ethical entity in articles 12 and 27 § 2 of the Universal Declaration of Human Rights – have developed autonomously, in tangentially unrelated fields, and have hence co-existed peacefully.

In fact, traditionally, the boundaries between copyright and privacy were perfectly drawn in the context of the enforcement of the patrimonial rights granted to a copyright holder. Indeed, both in the common law copyright system and in the *droit d'auteur* system, despite their different bases and principles, copyright has been drawn

DOI: 10.4018/978-1-60960-083-9.ch014

as an instrument to grant the holder, amongst other rights, the exclusive economic right to use and exploit his/her original work. This does not mean that copyright can be reduced to a mere patrimonial right. Actually, in the *droit d'auteur* approach that prevails in European legislations, the copyrightable intellectual work is considered an extent of its creator's personality and, therefore, the legal copyright regime directly regards the development of his/her personality and subsequently promotes cultural diversity. For that reason, beyond the recognition of patrimonial rights, law grants the creator moral rights over the work, such as the right to claim authorship of the work and to object to any distortion, mutilation or other modification of or other derogatory action in relation to the said work which would be prejudicial to his honor or reputation. Recently, moral rights have been introduced in common law countries in general – where they were not traditionally recognized – and, although in very limited terms, in the United States of America (USA) legislation, in particular.

Not disregarding the mixed nature of copyright, the possible conflict between that right and privacy rights could only find relevant space in the field of patrimonial rights' enforcement. If, on the one side, rightholders had the exclusive right to exploit publicly their copyrighted work, on the other side, private and non-commercial uses of the copyrighted work were free and escaped their control, since they belonged to the private sphere of its consumer.

However, with the advent of digital technology, especially the internet, this state of things has altered dramatically since rightholders, facing massive on-line copyright infringements, mainly by file-sharers on peer-to-peer (P2P) systems, started developing more and more intrusive new enforcement strategies in electronic communications as a means to identify the infringers and the committed infractions, reaching personal electronic information of consumers of online copyrighted works.

Recognizing the importance of creative contents to the digital economy, legislators have been accompanying the rightholders' efforts to strengthen copyright protection in the digital environment, by creating sectorial legislation in the field of copyright enforcement. However, cyberworld's idiosyncrasies, its specific structure and architecture, have been revealing copyright's highly porous new external boundaries that have been forcing it to leave the ivory tower where it used to stand in the old analogical world. In the digital relationship established with privacy rights, copyright's boundaries are becoming faintly outlined. In fact, considering that all data flowing through the internet is basically computer code, it is not possible for rightholders' tracking software to distinguish which collected data is public or private, lawful or unlawful, without a subsequent human-made normative evaluation. This simple example demonstrates clearly how thin the line between the exercise of a private surveillance power granted by law to the intellectual property's owner and the violation of the users' right to privacy can be.

The purpose of the present paper is precisely to present and briefly study the tension that has been arising in the digital world between new intrusive copyright enforcement mechanisms, on the one side, and internet users' privacy, on the other, and how these rights can be reconciled.

II. BACKGROUND

Technology has always been an essential element for copyright regulation. In fact, since copyright regards the protection of intellectual aesthetic creations or, in other words, immaterial goods, the exteriorization of such kind of object needs the mediation of a physical support which may transform and evolve according to the known technology. The *corpus mysticum*, *i.e.*, the copyrighted creative expression, is to be revealed by the *corpus mechanicum* that technology permits.

For that reason, copyright, *per se*, is not a tangible right, but an intangible *sui generis* property right over intellectual creations that can be embodied in tangible objects such as books or records.

When the *corpus mechanicum* was truly corporeal, it was relatively easy for rightholders to control the usages of their works. However, digitization brought the possibility of experiencing works without a corporeal fixation and has favored an enormous, global and almost uncontrolled flow of intangible information, including copyrighted content, which could easily escape rightholders' control. Nevertheless, in my opinion, the core of copyright patrimonial protection remains the same today as in the pre-digital era: rightholders have the power to exclusively exploit all the non-private usages of their creations, excluding others from using it without proper authorization and, normally, remuneration. Unlike the holders of tangible property, copyright holders do not have rights on things, namely the things where the intellectual works are embodied; for a limited period of time, they have the right to impose abstention behaviors to others, *i. e*., the right to exclude others from the use or consumption of the work without proper authorization, except in the case of mere private uses of copyrighted works or public interest concerned exceptions or limitations, such as for academic or scientific research, amongst others. Intellectual property rights, including copyright, and tangible property were, therefore, never totally equivalent.

Digitization, however, has changed in quality and in quantity the possibilities of infringement: it is possible to make huge amounts of perfect copies of (the code) of digitized works and to easily spread them globally throughout the internet, since no corporeal body is needed, unlike the analogical era.

In legal terms, digital technology, not disregarding its possible lawful uses, has thus facilitated several possible violations of patrimonial rights that copyright laws usually grant exclusively to copyright holders: the right to display the copyrighted work publicly, the right to perform works publicly, the right to publicly distribute copies of the copyrighted works or the right to reproduce the works in copies. As a consequence, technological progress has permitted the establishment of genuine parallel economies based on counterfeiting and some non-commercial uses, such as the exchange of digital files through P2P networks have grown to such an extent that they are competing with the normal exploitation of works and challenging established commercial models (Geiger, 2010, p. 4).

The impact of the internet in the copyright field was, in fact, huge and lead to an unbalanced clash between massive and globalized digital unauthorized uses of copyrighted content and the obsolete copyright enforcement legal instruments that were designed in an analogical and tangible context. Creative contents and information flowing on the internet not only wanted to be free but also seemed to be liberated from rightholders' control and from judicial reaction. As Boyle (1997) pointed out, for a long time, digital libertarians, based on the technology of the medium, the geographical distribution of its users and the intangible nature of its content, thought that the cyber world provided an unavoidable shift from a legal regime to a technological regime where speech was liberated from public or private heteronomous constrictions.

In fact, the plurilocalized distribution of the infringers and the colossal quantity of online infractions revealed how unprepared the international copyright legal system was to enforce rights in the digital context. Public enforcement mechanisms based on national courts were inefficient since they were localized (*i.e*., limited by territorial sovereignty) and merely reactive. Therefore, such circumstances left most of the infractions unpunished and did not prevent the patrimonial damages that rightholders had suffered.

Facing an insufficient state protection, rightholders started developing self-help systems based upon technological protection measures such as, *inter alia*, steganography, encryption or electronic agents like web crawlers or spy-bots, that could be able to hinder online infringements and economic losses. Clark (1996) elegantly synthesized in his famous slogan "the answer to the machine is in the machine" (p. 139) the tendency to diminish the importance of copyright in a digital environment in favor of a control-by-code based solution. According to this point of view, technology would be the most relevant instrument to lock-up access to creative expression and information in a digital environment and architectural design would become the preferred or, at least, a popular method of regulating the emerging global communication networks (Lessig, 2006).

The referred approach was, however, insufficient: technological protection measures could be circumvented by other technological devices or software. For that reason, the information and communication technologies (ICT) industry started lobbying for the enactment of new laws whereby both copyright and technology protection measures were recognized and the technological transformation of the copyright legal regime became a flagrant reality.

From the Agreement on Trade Related Aspects of Intellectual Property Rights (TRIPS) or the World Intellectual Property Organization (WIPO) Copyright Treaty and the WIPO Performances and Phonograms Treaty, at the international level, to the Digital Millennium Copyright Act (DMCA), in the USA, or the Information Society Directive (InfoSoc Directive), in the European Union – followed by subsequent transpositions into member state laws, digital copyright laws adopted the legal-technological approach for protecting creative expression by recognizing that the use of technological protection measures is a lawful means to a digital rights management system. Furthermore, the referred new generation of copyright laws provides that circumvention acts and the creation or dissemination of circumvention devices are forbidden and punished as criminal offenses. Since this kind of provisions has substantially less to do with creative expression than with copyright enforcement, some authors distinguish it from primary copyright and call it *paracopyright* (Jaszi, 1988) or *übercopyright* (Helberger & Hugenholtz, 2007). In this context, it is proper to conclude that rightholders are entitled to

three levels of cumulative protection: the first is the legal protection by copyright. The second level is the technical protection of works through measures protection techniques. The third level is the new legal protection against circumvention of technological protection measures introduced by the WIPO Treaties. (Werra, 2001, p. 77)

According to the current legal background, technology can be combined with the contractual provisions included in end user license agreements to create what can apparently be the perfect digital rights management system in view of the fact that licensors can contractually predict which users' behaviors are lawful or not and have the means to digitally control it. That is to say that in these specific cases, copyright may be overridden and substituted by the combination of technology and contract law.

However, despite their obvious advantages to rightholders – who are granted the right to create private systems of copyright monitoring – the online surveillance measures contained in digital rights management systems have the potential to undermine some fundamental rights of internet users, such as freedom of expression, including in its scope the right of access to knowledge and information, or the right to privacy or, in its multifaceted dimension, the right to informational and communicational self determination. Regarding the latter and considering that the basic functions of technological protection measures

are envisaged as follows: (i) controlling access to copyright works (and possibly other information products); (ii) restricting unauthorised reproduction (and possibly other usage) of such works; (iii) identifying the works, the relevant right–holders (and possibly the conditions for authorised usage of the works); and (iv) protecting the authenticity of the latter identification data (Bygrave, 2003, pp. 420-421),

the intrusive nature of such measures on users' privacy becomes evident. The capabilities of an ideal digital rights management system are detecting and preventing a wide range of operations, including open, print, export, copying, modifying, excerpting; maintaining records of lawful or unlawful users' behaviors and sending this information to rightholders. The collectors may then manipulate the acquired data to generate predictive profiles of infringers or lawful consumers for use in future marketing activities, or for sale to other vendors (Cohen, 1997, pp. 186-187).

As indicated above, digital rights management systems apply, in the first place, to legitimate users or purchasers of copyrighted digital works whose habits of reading, listening to or accessing copyrighted works can be monitored by rightholders: in these cases, the latter players go beyond the limits of the users' private sphere since they are capable in some cases to monitor their private tastes and behaviours (Cohen, 1996).

Given that "intellectual privacy resides partly in the ability to exert (a reasonable degree of) control over the physical and temporal circumstances of intellectual consumption within private spaces" (Cohen, 2003, p. 582) the described use of digital rights management systems may trump users' privacy rights.

However, although the scope of privacy rights cannot be reduced to the protection against intrusion, the present chapter focuses on one of the most controversial issues in this field, which is related to the use of intrusive software regarding copyright enforcement within P2P networks, where file-sharers frequently swap copyrighted content without rightholders' authorization.

P2P architecture promotes a distributed and decentralized network that enables a computer to find files directly on the hard drive of another network connected device without the need for central servers. As a result, each user can be a consumer and a supplier of files simultaneously. In such a decentralized network, the boundaries between what is public and what is private within a computer's memory grow fainter since the user consents to peers accessing the hard disk of his/her computer. Therefore, the number of potential invasions to the computer's memory and the number of unknown accesses to personal data stored in the device may increase rapidly.

If this architecture revealed itself to be an outstanding mechanism of content distribution, its connatural openness also enhances an attractive panoptic structure of private surveillance and control by rightholders seeking for copyright infringers using unauthorized content. In such a context, it becomes relatively easy to collect file-sharers' data like their IP addresses, the files stored in their computer or the record of uploads and downloads. Since the judgment over the legality of the files' content is made afterwards, it is possible that data has been collected and analyzed for nothing, with excessive harm of P2P networks users' privacy.

III. PRIVACY AND THE RIGHT TO INFORMATIONAL SELF-DETERMINATION

The advent of digital ICT has promoted a profusion of digital transmission and communication of data that, given the electronic trail that it leaves, can easily be surveyed, collected and controlled. Since a substantial part of digital data regards personal matters, safeguards against the treatment and misuse of computerized personal data are becoming increasingly important (Canotilho/Moreira, 2007, pp. 550-551).

Recent European responses to the exposed problem are inspired by a Germany Federal Constitutional Court (BVerfGE, 1983) ruling according to which, *in the context of modern data processing, the protection of the individual against unlimited collection, storage, use and disclosure of his/her personal data is encompassed by the general personal rights constitutional provisions. This basic right warrants in this respect the capacity of the individual to determine in principle the disclosure and use of his/her personal data [and consists in] the authority of the individual to decide himself, on the basis of the idea of self-determination, when and within what limits information about his private life should be communicated to others.*

This perspective recognizes the right to privacy with a broader scope than the traditional United States law understanding of this right as "the right to be left alone" (Warren & Brandeis, 1890), imposing an obligation of no trespassing.

Following Ferrajoli's teachings on the distinction between rights and their guarantees (2001), we could note that, although a negative dimension is included in the scope of the right to communicational and informational self-determination, this right is conceptualized not only as a mere guarantee of the right to privacy, but as a true fundamental right with an independent meaning; this meaning consists in the recognition of the freedom to control the use of information (if it is personal), and in the protection against attacks arising from the use of such information" (Castro, 2005, pp. 65*ff.*).

Therefore, the right to communicational and informational self-determination reveals two autonomous but intrinsically linked facets. The first one has a defensive nature, similar to the guarantee for the secrecy of correspondence and of other means of private communication, and is built as a negative right that protects the holder against interference by the State or by individuals who are responsible for processing digital or analogical data or others. The second facet constitutes a positive right to dispose of your own personal information, a power of controlling it and determining what others can, at every moment, know about you (Castro, 2006, p. 16). That is to say, the holder does not only have the right to remain opaque to others but also the right to control the use of his/her personal data and establish the terms of its use by third parties.

The right to communicational and informational self-determination is a true fundamental right, related to the development of the personality of each individual, established in article 8 of the European Union Charter of Fundamental Rights:

1. Everyone has the right to the protection of personal data concerning him or her.
2. Such data must be processed fairly for specified purposes and on the basis of the consent of the person concerned or some other legitimate basis laid down by law. Everyone has the right of access to data which has been collected concerning him or her, and the right to have it rectified.
3. Compliance with these rules shall be subject to control by an independent authority.

The Charter's legislator followed the tracks of the European Convention on Human Rights and the jurisprudence of the European Court of Human Rights, according to which "the State is not merely under the obligation to abstain from interfering with individuals' privacy, but also to provide individuals with the material conditions needed to allow them to effectively implement their right to private and family life" (Rouvroy/Poullet, 2007, p. 20).

At the European Union derivative law level, three directives directly regulate privacy matters: a) Directive 95/46/EC of the European Parliament and of the Council of 24 October 1995 on the protection of individuals with regard to the processing of personal data and on the free movement of such data; b) Directive 2002/58/EC of the European Parliament and of the Council of 12 July 2002 concerning the processing of personal data and the protection of privacy in the electronic communications sector (Directive on privacy and electronic communications); and c) Directive 2000/31/EC of the European Parliament and of the Council of 8 June 2000 on certain legal aspects of information society services, in particular electronic commerce, in the Internal Market (Directive on electronic commerce).

Through the mentioned directives, the European legislator created a legal framework to regulate the activity of electronic data collecting and subsequent treatment guided by the following principles: (a) the principle of lawful collecting, meaning that collecting and processing of data constitute a restriction on the holder's informational self-determination and are only permitted within the parameters of the law and, particularly, with the holder's knowledge and consent; (b) the finality principle, according to which data collecting and the data processing can only be made with a clearly determined, specific and socially acceptable finality that has to be identifiable in the moment when the activity is being executed; (c) the principle of objective limitation, meaning that the use of the collected data must be restricted to the purposes that were communicated to the holder, and must respect the general principles of proportionality, necessity and adequacy; (d) the principle of temporal limitation, which implies that data shall not be kept by more than the time needed to achieve the finality that justified the activity; (e) the principle of data quality, meaning that the collected data must be correct and up-to-date; (f) the principle of free access to data, according to which the holder must be able to know the existence of the collection and the storage of his/her personal data and, if he/she wants, to rectify, erase or block the information when incomplete or inaccurate; and (g) the security principle, under which the controller must implement appropriate technical and organizational measures to protect personal data against accidental or arbitrary unlawful destruction or accidental loss, alteration, unauthorized disclosure or access, in particular where the processing involves the transmission of data over a network. As it is regulated in the European Union, the right to communicational and informational self-determination gives an individual the power to control all the possible usages of his/her personal data.

In the United States of America, market regulation of privacy is prevalent. Therefore, despite the provisions of the Privacy Act of 1974, 5 U.S.C. § 552a, "with limited exceptions, the processing and transferring of data per se is not among those activities that either the state or federal governments monitor" (Garcia, 2005, p. 1238, n. 206). In fact, except for the government regulation of specific sectors like the protection of children online, all the procedures related to collecting, keeping or transferring consumer data are left to industry self-regulation. The Federal Trade Commission (FTC) has an important role in promoting fair privacy policies, but has only prosecution powers against firms that act inconsistently with their disclosed policy if existent.

Consequently, without public regulation imposing duties to data collectors, and in the absence of the collectors' disclosure of privacy policy, personal data holders may not have the information or the powers to control what personal information is collected, when or how it is collected, how it will be used, or if it will be disclosed or transferred to third parties, amongst other possible usages.

IV. DIGITAL COPYRIGHT ENFORCEMENT SURVEILLANCE MECHANISMS

One of the major pieces of European legislation in the field of copyright enforcement is Directive 2004/48/EC of the European Parliament and the Council of 29 April 2004 on the enforcement of intellectual property rights ("Enforcement" Directive). This directive does not only apply to infringements committed on a commercial scale, although some provisions – Articles 6(2), 8(1) and 9(2) – are only applicable in such cases. But even the concept of "commercial scale" proposed by the Directive is vague: in Recital (14) it is stated that acts carried out on a commercial scale "are those carried out for direct or indirect economic or commercial advantage; this would normally exclude acts carried out by end-consumers acting in good faith." There is no definition of the concepts of economic advantage or good faith, which may bring several interpretation problems, especially because in recital (15) it is recognized that the Directive should not affect substantive law on intellectual property and, consequently, the exclusive rights to distribute the work or to make it available to the public, which leaves space to a maximalist interpretation of the concept of commercial scale.

In Article 6, paragraph 1, of the "Enforcement" Directive it is stated that:

Member States shall ensure that, on application by a party which has presented reasonably available evidence sufficient to support its claims, and has, in substantiating those claims, specified evidence which lies in the control of the opposing party, the competent judicial authorities may order that such evidence be presented by the opposing party, subject to the protection of confidential information. For the purposes of this paragraph, Member States may provide that a reasonable sample of a substantial number of copies of a work or any other protected object be considered by the competent judicial authorities to constitute reasonable evidence.

In face of this provision, it seems correct to conclude that the European legislator assumed that collecting IP is a lawful rightholder's behavior if functionally directed to subsequent copyright enforcement, since in the context of P2P networks it will be the adequate means to present "reasonable evidence." Such assumption could also be supported by Article 8, paragraph 3, of the Infosoc Directive, which provides that "[m]ember States shall ensure that rightholders are in a position to apply for an injunction against intermediaries whose services are used by a third party to infringe a copyright or related right." In fact, the European Union solution was influenced by the US notice and take down solution provided for in the DMCA, § 512,(c)(3), and (h)(1), which grants the rightholders the right to "request the clerk of any United States district court to issue a subpoena to a service provider for identification of an alleged infringer." Such request may be made by filing with the clerk one notification of claimed infringement that must be a written communication provided to the designated agent of a service provider that includes substantially, amongst other elements, the identification of the copyrighted work claimed to have been infringed, the identification of the material that is claimed to be infringing or to be the subject of infringing activity and that is to be removed or access to which is to be disabled, and information reasonably sufficient to permit the service provider to contact the complaining party, such as an address, telephone number, and, if available, an electronic mail address at which the complaining party may be contacted.

One of the most controversial provisions of the "Enforcement" Directive is article 8, paragraph 1, which creates, under the epigraph "Right to information," a broad *sub pœna* that permits intellectual property holders to easily obtain the names and addresses of alleged infringers. In fact, according to the identified provision,

Member States shall ensure that, in the context of proceedings concerning an infringement of an intellectual property right and in response to a justified and proportionate request of the claimant, the competent judicial authorities may order that information on the origin and distribution networks of the goods or services which infringe an intellectual property right be provided by the infringer and/or any other person who:

(a) was found in possession of the infringing goods on a commercial scale;
(b) was found to be using the infringing services on a commercial scale;
(c) was found to be providing on a commercial scale services used in infringing activities; or
(d) was indicated by the person referred to in point (a), (b) or (c) as being involved in the production, manufacture or distribution of the goods or the provision of the services.

This right to information is considered absolutely essential to ensure a high level of protection of intellectual property as it may be the only means to identify the infringer. Nevertheless, it is not absolute: paragraph 3 (e) of article 8, expressly stipulates that paragraph's 1 provision "shall apply without prejudice to other statutory provisions which [...] govern the protection of confidentiality of information sources or the processing of personal data." In reality, European Union's concern over the protection of personal data is clearly manifested in recital 2 of the "Enforcement" Directive, where it is stated that, although the protection of intellectual property should allow the inventor or creator to derive a legitimate profit from his invention or creation and to allow the widest possible dissemination of works, ideas and new know-how, "[a]t the same time, it should not hamper freedom of expression, the free movement of information, or the protection of personal data."

One of the greatest obstacles that rightholders have been facing in this field is precisely the protection of personal data argument that is used by Internet Service Providers (ISPs) for not disclosing their clients' identity. Given the contractual relationships established with the users, ISPs are the best positioned to give an identity to the IP address collected by the rightholder. Indeed,

ISPs have developed into a relatively new form of governance in cyberspace because they maintain a substantial amount of private, consumer information regarding users' online activities, and because they often control the transmission and distribution of requested information. For these reasons, many consider the ISP the principal repository for all identifying information regarding individual users and their Web activities. (Katyal, 2004, p. 311)

In order to escape personal data collecting and treatment laws, some groups of rightholders have been defending the idea that IP addresses are not personal data and, therefore, that ISPs may disclose their clients' identity even without a previous jurisdictional decision. The main argument relied on the fact that an IP address is *per se* insufficient to identify the individual behind it.

Although several cases related to this subject have been discussed throughout Europe, one in particular has become well known. In France, on May, 23, 2007, the *Conseil d'État* revoked a decision from the *Commission Nationale de l'Informatique et des Libertés* (CNIL), according to which this independent agency had refused to give an authorization to four collective management entities regarding the use of digital devices that could automatically detect copyright infringements and forward messages to the alleged online infringers. The CNIL understood that those devices constituted disproportional measures because they were not designed just to implement occasional actions strictly limited to the specific needs of the fight against counterfeiting, but may lead to a massive collection of personal data and provide an exhaustive and continuous surveillance over the P2P networks (2005).

The *Conseil d'État* revoked that decision, announcing that the CNIL had erred in applying the law, namely on the proportionality issue, considering on the one hand, the quantitative dimension of copyright infringements on the Internet, and, on the other hand, that the survey related only to users who shared or provided copyrighted works up from a certain number. Later on, the *Cour d'appel* de Paris held that IP addresses should not be qualified as personal data and that they were not protected under the right to privacy or to informational self-determination. This understanding clearly diverges from the general understanding that IP addresses must be considered personal data. Such conclusion is, in my view, the right one and is consistent with the Opinion 4/2007 on the concept of personal data, from the Working Party set up under Article 29 of Directive 95/46/EC, whereby it considered IP addresses as data relating to an identifiable person. The Working Party stated:

Internet access providers and managers of local area networks can, using reasonable means, identify Internet users to whom they have attributed IP addresses as they normally systematically "log" in a file the date, time, duration and dynamic IP address given to the Internet user. The same can be said about Internet Service Providers that keep a logbook on the HTTP server. In these cases there is no doubt about the fact that one can talk about personal data in the sense of Article 2 a) of the Directive. Especially in those cases where the processing of IP addresses is carried out with the purpose of identifying the users of the computer (for instance, by Copyright holders in order to prosecute computer users for violation of intellectual property rights), the controller anticipates that the "means likely reasonably to be used" to identify the persons will be available e.g. through the courts appealed to (otherwise the collection of the information makes no sense), and therefore the information should be considered as personal data. (Article 29 data protection working party, 2007, p. 16)

In fact, considering that personal data is defined in Article 2 (a) of the Directive 95/46/EC as "any information relating to an identified or identifiable natural person [and that] an identifiable person is one who can be identified, directly or indirectly, in particular by reference to an identification number or to one or more factors specific to his physical, physiological, mental, economic, cultural or social identity," it will be very difficult to sustain that a person cannot be identified through an IP address. More recently, other courts' decisions have declared that IPs are indeed personal data, based on the Article 29 data protection working party opinion; but there is still an undesirable lack of unanimity over this issue.

In the case C-275/06, the Court of Justice of the European Communities decided one of the most important cases related to the discussion on the balance between intellectual property enforcement and privacy. *Promusicae*, a Spanish collective management society, asked the ISP *Telefonica de España* to reveal personal data on their users in order to enable the latter to subsequently bring civil law charges against the detected copyright infringers. Since, under Spanish law, ISPs only have to reveal personal data to judiciary authorities in cases of criminal investigations and prosecutions, the Spanish court (*Juzgado de lo Mercantil n.º 5 de Madrid*) wanted to know from the Court of Justice if that material restriction was in conformity with European Union law. Advocate-General Juliane Kokott concluded that it is compatible with Community law for Member States to exclude the communication of personal traffic data for the purpose of bringing civil proceedings against copyright infringements. Kokott noted that up to now the legislature has not considered that a more far-reaching protection of the holders of copyrights is necessary.

On the contrary, in adopting Directives 2000/31, 2001/29 and 2004/48, it provided for the unaltered continued applicability of data protection and saw no reason, when adopting the sector-specific Directives 2002/58 and 2006/24, to introduce restrictions of data protection in favour of the protection of intellectual property. Directive 2006/24 could, on the contrary, lead to a strengthening of data protection under Community law with regard to disputes concerning infringements of copyright. The question then arises, even in criminal investigations, as to the extent to which it is compatible with the fundamental right to data protection under Community law to grant aggrieved rightholders access to the results of the investigation if the latter are based on the evaluation of retained traffic data within the meaning of Directive 2006/24. Up to now that question is not affected by Community law since the Data Protection Directives do not apply to the prosecution of criminal offences. (CJEC, 2007)

In its final decision, the Court decided that EU law does not require Member States to lay down an obligation to communicate personal data in order to ensure effective protection of copyright in the context of civil proceedings. This approach is extremely relevant, since it clearly indicates that a balance between copyright enforcement and personal data protection is needed and required by European Union Law, even though isolated readings of the legislation may suggest the pre-eminence of one over the other.

V. THE GRADUATED RESPONSE: AN ALTERNATIVE ENFORCEMENT MECHANISM

Large controversy was raised in France recently over the implications of the *Creation and Internet* law for internet users' freedom of expression – a matter that shall not be treated in the present paper – and privacy. This law, also known as HADOPI law, the acronym of *Haute Autorité pour la Diffusion des Œuvres et la Protection des Droits sur Internet* (High Authority for the Diffusion of Art Works and for the Protection of Rights on Internet), embraces new normative strategies regarding the enforcement of copyright in a digital environment, such as the graduated response mechanism.

More than a sanctionatory procedure based on the direct applicability of substantial copyright rules, the graduated response is a compelling mechanism that "intends primarily to reduce the scale of infringements through an (automated) educational notification mechanism for alleged online infringers" (Strowel, 2009, p. 78). It is based on a three-strike procedure that implies ISPs cooperation with rightholders and with the High Authority.

Once the individuals behind the IPs of alleged online infringers collected by rightholders or by the High Authority have been identified, with the cooperation of ISPs, the first step of the procedure is to send online warnings to the subscriber potentially committing copyright infringement, whereby he/she is advised about the illegality of his/her behavior and also about the possibility of legal online offer of creative content. If the infringement continues, six months after the first warning, a new one is sent. If, even so, the unlawful activity continues, in the last step of this procedure, a court may order the suspension of the broadband accounts of file-sharers of copyrighted material online.

This kind of solution has been spreading throughout the world and is being discussed with similar controversy in the United Kingdom, Australia, New Zealand, Germany or Spain. Furthermore, at the European Union legislative level, after the approval in November 2009 of the telecommunications package and the insertion of the new article 3a in the text of the Directive 2002/21/EC, it seems that the graduated response mechanism has found space in future member state legislation provided that a prior fair and impartial procedure is to be guaranteed. According to the referred provision,

Measures taken by Member States regarding end-users access' to, or use of, services and applications through electronic communications networks shall respect the fundamental rights and freedoms of natural persons, as guaranteed

by the European Convention for the Protection of Human Rights and Fundamental Freedoms and general principles of Community law.

Accordingly, in the European Union, copyright infringements committed through electronic networks may lead to the application of enforcement measures against ISPs' clients. Nevertheless, measures, such as the ones provided in the graduated response mechanism, may only be taken with due respect for the principle of presumption of innocence and the right to privacy. In fact, pursuant to the new article 3a, "a prior, fair and impartial procedure shall be guaranteed, including the right to be heard of the person or persons concerned, subject to the need for appropriate conditions and procedural arrangements in duly substantiated cases of urgency in conformity with the European Convention for the Protection of Human Rights and Fundamental Freedoms," and "the right to effective and timely judicial review shall be guaranteed."

From a personal data protection point of view, solutions like the graduated response may be considered acceptable only if they respect the collecting and treatment principles discussed above and the general principles of proportionality, necessity and adequacy. For instance, a solution that imposes on ISPs the obligation of filtering data content without a court previous decision where, on an ad-hoc basis, all the factual and normative elements are available, should not be acceptable. Otherwise, all private communications, lawful or not, would be monitored by ISPs and government agencies: this would clearly violate the most basic foundations of a democratic society. Furthermore, the mere collection of IP addresses needs, at least in the European Union context, to be previously authorized, for instance, by the CNIL in France, or corresponding member state agencies. This would be an adequate way to ensure that a specific rightholder will objectively and proportionally collect IP addresses respecting the rights of the data owners providing them with a means to control the collector's actions.

VI. AN OPEN CONCLUSION

Both copyright and privacy, especially the right to informational self-determination, have been dramatically affected by new digital technologies and by the enormous quantity of massive, plurilocalized, transnational and apparently anonymous infringements that these technologies facilitate in addition to their possible lawful uses.

If the first answers to the digital challenge resembled legal capitulation ("the answer to the machine is in the machine") and assumed the death of copyright and privacy laws in cyber world, defined as a space free from external regulation by national laws, soon such a technological determinism approach had to be abandoned. In fact, considering the potential harmfulness of online infringements, the equivalence between real and digital worlds had to be proclaimed, which led to the technological transformation of the legal regimes that had to rapidly adapt to the new contexts. Modern legislations recognize that both technology and law may concur to protect copyright and privacy: beyond substantive legal provisions regarding the scope of protection and the substantial powers granted to rightholders, it is also possible to use privacy enhancement technologies and copyright digital management systems.

However, in the field of digital copyright enforcement, intrusive technological measures created to identify online infringers were developed, putting in risk the privacy sphere of internet users, since their navigation and identification data can be collected and treated by a copyright holder. In this context, it is neither possible nor correct to offer an *a priori* hierarchy of copyright and the right to privacy. Both rights are recognized as human rights that are fundamental to the development of an individual's personality. For this reason, it is not up to the ordinary legislator to decide which right should prevail in abstract terms. Seeking for a harmonization or a practical concordance between two fundamental rights when in collision is a delicate task that cannot be strictly foreseen. A fundamental right may be restricted only when this restriction is proportionate, adequate and necessary to protect another right with similar value. Consequently, one cannot *a priori* emphasize copyright's protection and importance in disfavor of privacy concerns and vice-versa.

Digital copyright is facing an enormous challenge, since the number of online infractions is growing every day, causing significant economic losses to rightholders. The seeming opacity of the right to privacy should not allow unlawful behaviors to go unpunished. However, not every infringement may permit the disclosure of personal data. This can only be authorized if it is necessary to protect a value or a right with similar or greater value. This means that, first, the collection of IP addresses needs to be previously acknowledged by law or authorized by an independent agency; subsequently, only when copyright infringement constitutes simultaneously a criminal offense, privacy rights of the alleged infringer can be proportionately sacrificed.

It is, therefore, desirable that a harmonized legal framework regarding the criminalization of copyright infringements is settled; this is a difficult task to perform, considering how connected to national sovereignty such a matter is, even at the European Union level and despite the proposed Directive on this subject. Until then litigation in courts will surely increase regarding the conflict between copyright enforcement and privacy rights and the casuistic definition of each one's scope; and legal uncertainty and insecurity will foment privacy self-regulation mechanisms, mainly through the use of privacy enhancing technology to protect users' personally identifiable information.

REFERENCES

Article 29 data protection working party. (2007). Opinion 4/2007 on the concept of personal data. Retrieved March 15, 2010, from http://www.droit-technologie.org/upload/actuality/doc/1063-1.pdf

Boyle, J. (1997). *Foucault in cyberspace: Surveillance, sovereignty, and hard-wired censors*. Retrieved March 15, 2010, from http://www.law.duke.edu/boylesite/foucault.htm

Bygrave, L. A. (2003). Digital rights management and privacy. In Becker, E., Buhse, W., Günnewig, D., & Rump, N. (Eds.), *Digital rights management: Technological, economic, legal and political aspects* (pp. 418–446). New York: Springer.

Canotilho, J. G., & Moreira, V. (2007). *Constituição da República Portuguesa Anotada* (4th ed.). Coimbra, Portugal: Coimbra Editora.

Castro, C. S. (2005). O direito à autodeterminação informativa e os novos desafios gerados pelo direito à liberdade e à segurança no pós 11 de Setembro. In *Estudos em homenagem ao Conselheiro José Manuel Cardoso da Costa* (*Vol. II*). Coimbra, Portugal: Coimbra Editora.

Castro, C. S. (2006). *Protecção de dados pessoais na Internet. Sub Judice, 35*. Coimbra, Portugal: Almedina.

CJEC. (2007). Opinion of Advocate General Kokott [Court of Justice of the European Communities Case C-275/06].

Clark, C. (1996). The answer to the machine is in the machine. In Bernt Hugenholtz, P. (Ed.), *The future of copyright in a digital environment*. The Hague: Kluwer Law International.

CNIL. (2005, October 18). Délibération no. 2005-235. Retrieved March 27, 2010, from http://www.legifrance.gouv.fr/affichCnil.do?oldAction=rechExpCnil&id=CNILTEXT000017652059&fastReqId=137369379&fastPos=1

Cohen, J. (1996). A right to read anonymously: A closer look at 'copyright management' in cyberspace. *Connecticut Law Review, 28*, 981–1039.

Cohen, J. (1997). Some reflections on copyright management systems and laws designed to protect them. *Berkeley Technology Law Journal, 12*, 161–190.

Cohen, J. (2003). DRM and privacy [Georgetown Public Law Research Paper No. 372741]. *Berkeley Technological Law Journal, 18*, 575-617. Retrieved March 27, 2010, from http://ssrn.com/abstract=372741

Ferrajoli, L. (2001). Fundamental rights. *International Journal for the Semiotics of Law, 14*, 1–33. doi:10.1023/A:1011290509568

Garcia, F. J. (2005). Bodil Lindqvist: A Swedish churchgoer's violation of the European Union's Data Protection Directive should be a warning to U.S. Legislators. *Fordham Intellectual Property. Media & Entertainment Law Journal, 15*, 1204–1243.

Geiger, C. (2010). The future of copyright in Europe: Striking a fair balance between protection and access to information. *Intellectual Property Quarterly, 1*, 1–14.

Helberger, N., & Hugenholtz, P. B. (2007). No place like home for making a copy: Private copying in European copyright law and consumer law. *Berkeley Technology Law Journal, 22*, 1061–1098.

Jaszi, P. (1998). Intellectual property legislative update: Copyright, paracopyright, and pseudo-copyright. Paper presented at the Association of Research Libraries conference: The Future Network: Transforming Learning and Scholarship, Eugene, OR. Retrieved March 27, 2010, from http://www.arl.org/resources/pubs/mmproceedings/132mmjaszi~print.shtml

Katyal, S. (2004). The new surveillance. *Case Western Reserve Law Review, 54*, 297–386.

Lessig, L. (2006). *Code 2.0*. New York: Basic Books.

Rouvroy, A., & Poullet, Y. (2008). The right to informational self-determination and the value of self-development: Reassessing the importance of privacy for democracy. In *Reinventing Data Protection: Proceedings of the International Conference*, Brussels, 12-13 October 2007. Berlin: Springer.

Strowel, A. (2009). Internet piracy as a wake-up call for copyright law makers – Is the "graduated response" a good reply? *World Intellectual Property Organization Journal, 1*, 75–86.

Warren, S., & Brandeis, L. (1890). The right to privacy. *Harvard Law Review, 4*(5), 193–220. doi:10.2307/1321160

Werra, J. (2001). Le regime juridique des mesures techniques de protection des oeuvres selon les Traités de l'OMPI, le Digital Millennium Copyright Act, les Directives Européennes et d'autres legislations (Japon, Australie). *Revue Internationale du Droit d'Auteur, 189*, 66–213.

Section 6
Data Protection and Privacy in Europe and in the European Union

Chapter 15
The EC Data Retention Directive:
Legal Implications for Privacy and Data Protection

Nóra Ní Loideain
*Office of the Director of Public Prosecutions, Ireland**

ABSTRACT

The focus of this paper is the new European legislation designed to harmonize domestic laws on the retention of telecommunications data for the purpose of assisting law enforcement efforts. The European Union introduced the EC Data Retention Directive in 2006. This Directive requires the retention of every European citizen's communications data for up to two years for the purpose of police investigation. There is, however, a major problem with the Directive in that it regularizes, and thereby entrenches, the practice of data retention across Europe. No systematic empirical evidence supports the introduction of such broad surveillance. The existence of data retention in principle raises concerns for data protection and the right to respect of privacy as protected under the European Convention of Human Rights (ECHR). This paper questions the proportionality of the Directive in line with data protection principles and Europe's obligations under Article 8 of the ECHR.

I. INTRODUCTION

States have always been faced with the difficult task of striking a balance between the constitutional rights of the citizen to privacy and security. Debate continues as to whether the surveillance of innocent citizens can be justified as 'a necessary evil' (Sewell & Barker, 2001; Marx, 1988) in the pursuit of public safety and security. Continuing developments in modern technology in the area of telecommunications have had an impact upon how serious criminals now approach their operations. An example of terrorists incorporating modern communications technology in the undertaking and planning of their attacks was demonstrated in the terrorist attacks on Madrid in 2006 where mobile phone cards were used to detonate bombs on the trains in the Madrid terrorist attacks (BBC News, 2006). The need, therefore, for balance between the competing interests of security

DOI: 10.4018/978-1-60960-083-9.ch015

and privacy has become all the more urgent. It is understandable that the State, *via* the police, would seek to utilize the power of technological advances in telecommunications and cyberspace for the purpose of safeguarding its citizens. To what extent, however, should the police be allowed to invade the privacy of citizens' communications in the interests of State security?

The EC Data Retention Directive came into force from 3 May 2006 (Directive 2006/24/EC, Article 16). This Directive requires the retention of every European citizen's communications data, including traffic data of communications and location data of the communication devices used, for up to two years for the purpose of police investigation. The Directive effectively gives investigative authorities across the European Union unprecedented access to the private lives of its citizens. This paper will set out the origins (Parts II and III) and main provisions of the Directive (Part IV). Its legislative development demonstrates the considerable unease among legislators and non-governmental organizations surrounding the Directive. The implications of the Directive for data protection and the right to respect of privacy as guaranteed under the European Convention of Human Rights (ECHR) will be then be addressed (Part V).

It is submitted that there is a major problem with the Directive in that it regularizes, and thereby entrenches, the practice of data retention in Europe. No empirical evidence has been put forward demonstrating that data retention will be effective in the fight against serious crime that would establish the necessity for such unprecedented invasions of privacy. Further, even if the retention of data can sometimes be justified, the measures under the Directive have blanket application to the communications of all citizens and not just those suspected of the commission of, or involvement with, serious crime. Hence, the proportionality of the Directive must be considered suspect. It will be recommended that the evaluation of the Directive's impact and the future development of law reform and policy governing State surveillance of telecommunications and cyberspace should be evidence-based in order to ensure the development of proportionate and effective legislation (Part VI).

II. BACKGROUND OF THE DATA RETENTION DIRECTIVE

The blanket retention of communications data for the purpose of law enforcement was a measure first proposed by the EU Telecommunications Council shortly before the 9/11 terrorist attacks upon New York and Washington D.C. in 2001. Under this early proposal, Internet Service Providers (ISPs) would be required to retain all citizens' communications data from telephones, mobile phones, faxes, emails and other internet use for up to 7 years (Lillington, 2001a). After the 9/11 attacks, the President of the United States of America sent a communiqué urging the EU to adopt provisions for the blanket retention of communications data "in the international effort against terrorism" (United States Mission to the European Union, 2001). More than thirty international civil rights organizations expressed concern to the EU Council of Ministers and U.S. President George Bush regarding the threat to civil liberties and the right to privacy posed by this unprecedented measure (Global Liberty Internet Campaign, 2001). These civil liberties organizations also highlighted the absence of such a data retention obligation for ISPs in the U.S. and pointed out that "there is a significant risk, if this proposal goes forward, that US law enforcement agencies will seek data held in Europe that it could not obtain at home, either because it was not retained or because US law would not permit law enforcement access." The opposition of the Article 29 Working Party, Data Protection Commissioners across the European Union, was more direct:

It is not acceptable that the scope of initial data processing is widened in order to increase the amount of data available for law enforcement objectives. Any such changes in these essential provisions that are directly related to fundamental human rights would turn the exception into a new rule. Systematic and preventive storage of EU citizens' communications and related traffic data would undermine the fundamental rights to privacy, data protection, freedom of expression, liberty and presumption of innocence (Letter from the Article 29-Data Protection Working Party the Council, 2001).

In 2002, the Council proposed the inclusion of a provision requiring the retention of data for law enforcement purposes in a Directive initially intended to solely update the 1995 (Directive 95/46/EC) and 1997 (Directive 97/66/EC) Data Protection Directives (Cappato, p. 3). Civil liberties organizations urged Parliament to reject the proposal on the basis that this measure should only be employed in exceptional cases and in accordance with the ECHR and the case law of the European Court of Human Rights (Coalition of Civil Liberties Organisations, 2002). A controversial amendment was still made, however, to the 2002 EC Directive on privacy and electronic communications (Directive 2002/58/EC) allowing Member States to impose an obligation upon ISPs to retain the communications data of citizens for the purpose of law enforcement. Article 15(1) of the 2002 EC Directive provides that Member States can restrict the scope of traditional privacy safeguards and adopt legislative measures for the retention of citizens' communications data. Such a restriction can be adopted if it constitutes "a necessary, appropriate and proportionate measure within a democratic society to safeguard national security (i.e. State security), defence, public security, and the prevention, investigation, detection and prosecution of criminal offences or of unauthorised use of the electronic communication system."

Data Protection Commissioners across Europe criticized the 2002 EC Directive on privacy and electronic communications for its lack of adequate and specific safeguards concerning the treatment of communications data. In particular, the Article 29 Data Protection Working Party noted that the vague conditions allowing for this unprecedented retention of data "leaves room for diverging interpretation and implementation by the Member States" (Opinion 3/2006 on the Directive 2006/24/EC, p. 2). The Working Party also stated that the transposition of a Directive on data retention must be done uniformly in order to "uphold the high standard of protection" provided by the 1995 Data Protection Directive and to comply with the requirements of Article 8 of the ECHR.

In 2004, France, Sweden, the United Kingdom and Ireland put forward a draft solely concerned with the retention of data for law enforcement purposes in the form of a Framework Decision under the EU three-pillar institutional framework's third pillar of justice and home affairs (European Council Document 8958/04, 2004). The European Commission and several other Member States on the EU Council expressed many reservations, however, regarding the legality of this Draft Framework Decision as well as the proposed legislation's scope, aim and application (Response of the Commission *et al.*, 2005, pp. 3-10).

III. LEGISLATIVE BASIS OF THE DIRECTIVE

At the time of the legislative development of the Directive, the European Union was said to rest upon the 'three pillars' established by the Maastricht Treaty. The first pillar referred to the traditional EEC Treaty matters, the second pillar dealt with common foreign and security policy, and the third pillar dealt with justice and home affairs. Actions taken under the second or third pillars were binding only to the extent that Member States had accepted them; in other words, Members States were free to opt out of any such actions. Such freedom was more limited when actions were taken under the first pillar (DeBurca, 1992; Morgan, 1994; Walker, 1998; Dashwood, 2001). Articles 2 to 6 of the Lisbon Treaty, that came into effect on the 1st December, 2009, amend the areas of Union and Member State competences and abolish the 'three pillar' legislative structure of the EU.

A major implication arising from the adoption of a Directive, a legislative measure under the first pillar, is that it would ensure that Parliament had a greater involvement in the development of the legislation. Under the legal basis of a Directive, as established pursuant to Article 251 (ex. Article 189b) of the Maastricht Treaty, Parliament is allowed the right of co-decision. The only democratically elected body in the EU is thus provided with an enhanced role in the legal instrument's scope, objectives and application. As Weatherill puts it, the key feature of the co-decision procedure is that the Council "is for the first time prevented from passing legislation against the will of the Parliament" (Weatherill *et al.*, 1999, p. 138). In contrast, under Article 39 of the Treaty Establishing the European Community, Title VI, a Framework Decision on data retention under the third pillar, as initially proposed by the Council, would have limited the role of Parliament to a right of consultation leaving the development of a pan-European measure on data retention without "the more democratic co-operation procedure" (Barnard, 2004, p. 501).

The European Parliament expressed several reservations regarding the Council's initial proposal in a report published shortly before its rejection of the Draft Framework Decision. The Parliament's main reservations consisted of the "sizeable doubts concerning the choice of legal basis," doubts regarding the proposal's proportionality as its provisions were "neither appropriate nor necessary and unreasonably harsh towards those concerned" and the "incompatibility" of the Council's proposal with Article 8 of the ECHR, the right to respect of privacy (European Parliament Session Document, 2005, pp. 6-9). The Parliament also rejected a second Framework Decision proposal on data retention put forward a few months later in September (Council of the European Union, 2005, p. 2) again on the basis that it had "sizeable doubts" about the legal nature of the Council's third-pillar measure on data retention (BBC News, 2005).

In September 2005, the Commission put forward a first-pillar proposal for a Directive on data retention for approval by both the Council and the European Parliament (Commission of the EC, Proposal, 2005). The Council only began to reconsider withdrawing their third-pillar initiative in October despite the numerous rejections of their proposal by both the Commission and Parliament (Presidency to Council on the Subject of Data retention, 2005). Furthermore, the Council clearly conveyed to Parliament that, even with the current development of a Directive on data retention, "the Framework Decision will remain on the table" (Letter to the European Parliament, 2005). Additionally, the Council's support for a Directive on data retention was conditional upon agreement being reached between the Commission, Parliament and the Council on the provisions of a Directive in two months.

The first pillar co-decision procedure provided Parliament with an enhanced role in the development of this legislation but, perhaps inevitably, only a minority of the amendments proposed by Parliament influenced the final rushed draft of the Directive.

The Parliament's initial report to the Commission contained several proposals restricting the scope, amount of data, access to data and the period of retention as proposed by the Council (European Parliament Draft Report on Data Retention, 2005). For example, Parliament proposed in its draft report that the retention of citizen's communications data *via* phone, email or other internet telephony, excluding content, should be available only for the "investigation, detection and prosecution" of *serious* crimes and not the broader purpose of the "prevention, investigation, detection and prosecution" of crime (p. 7). In a following report, Parliament successfully excluded the objective of 'prevention' from the Directive based on the rationale that "it is a vague concept and makes the retained data more vulnerable from abuses." (European Parliament Report on Data Retention, p. 9).

In relation to the amount of data, Parliament proposed the exclusion of location data from the Directive; however, the Council, while noting the proportionality concerns, insisted that location data be included on the basis that it "has repeatedly proven its value in criminal investigations and prosecutions" (Response of Council to proposals by European Parliament, 2005, p. 4). The Council did not provide systematic research from each Member State demonstrating the necessity for the retention of the location data of *every EU citizen's* communications by phone, email or other internet telephony for the purpose of law enforcement. Its justification for this unprecedented scope of surveillance was based instead on six examples where location data and records of unsuccessful calls were said to have been of assistance to law enforcement agencies. One of these examples concerned Northern Ireland, where mobile phone location data was said to have been "vitally important in pinpointing the positions of those involved in the Omagh bombing."

The Parliament's proposal concerning access to data was that access should be limited to "competent law enforcement authorities." The Parliament defined this as the "judicial authorities responsible for the detection, investigation and prosecution of serious criminal offences" (EU Parliament Draft Report on Data Retention, 2005, p. 12). The Council, however, made no note of this proposal and proposed instead that access to data be made available to an undefined but inherently larger group of "competent national authorities" (Response of Council to proposals by European Parliament, 2005, p. 7).

The different periods of data retention proposed illustrates another significant disparity between the proposals of the Council and Parliament. For example, while the Parliament proposed a retention period of 3 months of communications data, the Council recommended what is now the required retention period under Article 6 of the Directive, that is to say, up to 2 years (Response of Council to proposals by European Parliament, 2005, p. 11).

Nevertheless, after rejecting two previous proposals by the Council to introduce mandatory data retention for the purpose of law enforcement across Europe, the European Parliament approved, by a majority vote of 378 to 197, this jointly amended version of the Commission's Directive proposal in December 2005 (BBC News, 2005).

The legal basis of the Directive resulted in a challenge to the Directive by Ireland, supported by the Slovak Republic (Case-301/06 *Ireland* v *Parliament and Council* Judgment of the Court (Grand Chamber) of 10 February 2009). Ireland argued that the legislation should have been adopted as a measure under the third pillar as the objective of the Directive is "clearly directed towards the fight against crime" (para. 29). The European Court of Justice rejected this challenge. The Court found that the adoption of the legislation under the first pillar as a Directive was satisfactory, *inter alia*, for the harmonization of legislation between Member States following the disparity of previous laws on data retention introduced under Article 15 of the Electronic Communications Directive 2002/58/EC (paras. 70-72).

IV. THE MAIN PROVISIONS OF THE DIRECTIVE

The aim of the Directive is to make the data, under Article 5(2) and Article 6, concerning the communications of every citizen and legal entity, excluding content, available for the purpose of "the investigation, detection and prosecution of serious crime, as defined by each Member State in its national law." Under the Directive, ISPs are required to retain traffic and location data related to telephone calls and emails for a period of six months to two years, depending on the wishes of the Member State in question. This data contains the identification information of both parties to the communication, *via* telephone or internet, along with the time, date, and duration of these communications. The data will also identify the geographic location of the caller by identifying the position of their landline or mobile communications device. As a former chairperson of the Irish Council for Civil Liberties commentator puts it, location data is "effectively like having a tagging device on a person" (Lillington, 2001b).

a. Access

Under Article 4 of the Directive, this data will be made available to any individuals who fall under the liberal remit of "competent national authorities." This data is also likely to be exchanged between law enforcement agencies across different Member States as a result of the growth in international cooperation and mutual assistance in criminal matters (Anderson *et al.*, 1994; Benyon et al., 1996; Hebenton & Thomas, 1995; Ferola, 2002).

b. Period of Retention

A Member State may, as provided under Article 12(1), extend the current maximum period of retention beyond 2 years "if facing particular circumstances that warrant an extension." The Member State must then notify the Commission and other Member States of this action and is also required to state the grounds for taking this extra measure. The Commission may reject, under Article 12(2), the extension proposed by the Member State on the grounds that the proposal is "a means of arbitrary discrimination or a disguised restriction of trade between Member States and whether they constitute an obstacle to the functioning of the internal market."

c. Security & Oversight

The Directive also introduces several measures concerning data security and oversight mechanisms. Member States are required by Articles 7 and 9 of the Directive to designate a supervisory authority to monitor ISPs to ensure that data protection principles are adhered to in the security of retained data. Member States are required under Article 13 to ensure that the conditions providing for judicial remedies, liability and sanctions, as set out under the 1995 Data Protection Directive, are fully implemented. Article 10 of the Data Retention Directive also requires Member States to provide the Commission with statistical analysis of the Directive's impact annually. These statistics include the cases in which information was provided to the competent authorities, the time elapsed between the date on which the data was retained and the date on which the competent authorities requested the data and cases where requests for data could not be met.

d. Evaluation

Member States were required, under Article 15, to transpose this Directive by the 15th September, 2007. The Commission is required to submit to the Parliament and the Council an evaluation of the application of the Directive no later than 15th September, 2010, as provided under Article 14(1). This evaluation will take into account the statistical information provided by Member States with a view to determining whether there is a need to amend the provisions of the Directive. When undertaking this evaluation the Commission will have particular regard to the necessity to alter the period of retention or the nature of the data to be retained. Article 14 states that the results of this evaluation will be made available to public scrutiny.

V. DATA PROTECTION & PRIVACY CONCERNS

The Data Retention Directive has been the subject of criticism. Concerns have been raised regarding the Directive's proportionality, particularly its compliance with data protection principles (Hawkes, 2006; Vilasu, 2007) and the protection of privacy guaranteed by Article 8 under the ECHR (Breyer, 2005; McIntyre, 2007). It is submitted, as will be addressed below, that these concerns are legitimate.

a. Data Protection

The need for data protection legislation in Europe was largely driven by the dangers posed by data processing as experienced during the Second World War. The Nazi government initially found it difficult to identify Jewish individuals, and other "undesirables," for imprisonment and extermination as they were well integrated into Western Europe. The use of modern statistical techniques supplied by computer data processing in the form of punch-card machines, however, enabled the Nazis to deal with this "obstacle." Thus, the computer-processing numbers tattooed upon prisoners located in certain concentration camps enabled the camp's authorities to identify who was suitable for work or death. The first data protection legislation was adopted in Germany in 1970 (Wood *et al*, 2006; Kelleher, 2006; Black, 2001; Bainbridge, 1996).

The substantive principles of European data protection legislation are set out in Article 6 of the 1995 Data Protection Directive to assist governments and private bodies in their collection and management of personal information: (a) processed fairly and lawfully; (b) collected for specified, explicit and legitimate purposes and not further processed in a way incompatible with those purposes. Further processing shall not be considered as incompatible provided that Member States provide appropriate safeguards; (c) adequate, relevant and not excessive in relation to the purposes for which they are collected and/or further processed; (d) accurate and, where necessary, kept up to date; every reasonable step must be taken to ensure that data which are inaccurate or incomplete, having regard to the purposes for which they were collected or for which they are further processed, are erased or rectified; (e) kept in a form which permits identification of data subjects for no longer than is necessary for the purposes for which the data were collected or for which they are further processed. Member States shall lay down appropriate safeguards for personal data stored for longer periods for historical, statistical or scientific use. European data protection legislation also provides protection to the citizen's right to respect for private life as one of its objectives under its principal legislation is to "protect the ... right to privacy with respect to the processing of personal data" (Directive 95/46/EC, Article 1(1)). The data protection legislative framework (Directive 95/46/EC; Directive 2002/58/EC) provides that each Member State must have a Data Protection Commissioner who is entrusted with certain investigatory and supervisory functions over both the State and private data controllers.

Data Protection Commissioners also play an advisory role on matters of data protection in the European Union. Article 29 of the 1995 Data Protection Directive established the 'Article 29 – Data Protection Working Party.' The Working Party is independent, acts in an advisory capacity and consists of the Member States' Data Protection Commissioners with a representative from the EU Commission. The tasks of the Working Party are outlined in Article 30 and include the providing of expert opinion from the member state level to the Commission on questions of data protection and the promotion of the uniform application of the general data protection principles of the Directive in all Member States through co-operation between data protection supervisory authorities. Significantly, the Working Party must also advise the Commission on any Community measures affecting the rights and freedoms of natural persons with regard to the processing of personal data and make recommendations to the public, and particularly to Community institutions, on matters relating to the protection of persons with regard to the processing of personal data in the European Community.

b. Data Protection Concerns

As previously noted, the Article 29 Working Party raised serious objections to the unprecedented scope of the EC Data Retention Directive in its legislative development. The Data Protection Commissioner for Ireland, Mr. Billy Hawkes (2006), has expressed his concerns with the disproportionate nature of the Directive in that it allows "personal data of innocent citizens to be stored *in case* it is needed by the police." Hawkes (2006) also notes the absence of a proportionality test in the development of the Directive in the "lack of hard evidence" of the number of occasions where access to data was essential (p. 9). The only European empirical research carried out to assess the need and, hence, justification for such broad communications data surveillance concluded, after examining 65 police investigations in the Netherlands, that a retention period of twelve months may be desirable for law enforcement purposes (Verloop, 2005). This recommendation and the methodology of this research were strongly criticized by the Dutch Data Protection Authority (2007). The Dutch DPA pointed out that the study provided insufficient evidence of the need for a longer retention term than is used in current practice, whereby providers retain traffic data for their own commercial purposes (i.e. for transmission and billing purposes). The report's recommendations regarding internet traffic data were not based on the investigation into actual use of traffic data as the selection of investigation files did not include the use of internet traffic data. Instead, the researchers based their findings on discussions with the police and the Ministry of Justice on the desirability of a longer retention period. It was on this basis that the conclusion was reached that a retention period of one year would be desirable for the retention of all citizens' traffic data. Thus, the DPA noted that the "necessity" of a retention obligation of one year was not established as required by Article 8 of the ECHR leaving "the substantiation for the proportionality demanded by the ECHR ... accordingly absent" (p. 3).

The time retention period for surveillance of citizens' communications data may even be extended by a Member State (Article 12(1) of the Directive) beyond the period of two years. This measure is permitted provided that a Member State is faced with "particular circumstances" and notifies the Commission and other Member States immediately of this extension. The Commission will approve or reject the measures taken. This provision significantly undermines the commitment made by the time period set out in Article 6 to harmonize the scope of data protection retention across the European Union (Vilasu, 2007).

The significant scope of the Directive's retention period, in addition to the possibility of extending this period further under Article 12, increases the prospect that citizens' personal data will be the subject of inappropriate searches by law enforcement officials and others. Individuals involved in law enforcement have in the past been prone to abusing police databases of citizens' personal information for matters unrelated to criminal investigations. For example, in the United States, it has been reported that more than ninety Michigan police officers, dispatchers, federal agents and security guards have abused the Law Enforcement Information Network (LEIN), a database created for the purpose of criminal investigations. The network contains "a computerized index of documented criminal justice information concerning crimes and criminals of Statewide, as well as national interest. LEIN provides access to the National Law Enforcement Telecommunications System, the National Crime Information Centre, and various State data bases." Law enforcement officers misused information from this database to intimidate and harass innocent citizens, to produce details for police officers' child custody battles and to get personal information about women whom male police officers found attractive (Detroit Free Press, 2001). Research undertaken by the Home Office in the UK on police corruption (Miller, 2003) found evidence of misuse of police databases ranging from "low level" leaking of data by police to friends, leaks to the media particularly regarding high profile cases and serious misuse of data in the deliberate leaking of information to criminals (p.13).

It is worth noting that this data is not only accessible to "competent national authorities" of the State, under Article 4, but is also subject to access by members of the private sector as this communications data must be retained, processed and made accessible to each Member State by private ISPs. The security risks involved in the retention of large amounts of personal data in the private sector were demonstrated when staff of mobile phone company T-Mobile sold data of thousands of customers to a third party for market purposes (BBC News, 2009).

Inadequate data protection safeguards have already been the focus of a successful constitutional challenge against the transposed domestic legislation of the Directive in Germany. It was reported that a constitutional complaint was brought to the Federal Constitutional Court by 35,000 citizens. The Court held in March 2010 that the legislation contained insufficient safeguards but did not find against the principle of data retention. As part of its judgment, the Court ruled that data already collected should be deleted and that future reform of the legislation in the area should include stricter conditions for the use and storage of data (BBC, 2010).

c. Privacy Concerns under the ECHR

Article 8 under the European Convention of Human Rights (ECHR) provides for a qualified right to respect of privacy. Article 8(1) guarantees that "everyone has the right to respect for his private and family life, his home and his correspondence." The notions of "private life" and correspondence" cover telephone and e-mail communications (*Weber & Saravia v. Germany* (2008) 46 E.H.R.R. SE 47, para. 77; *Copland v UK* (2007) E.H.R.R. 253, para. 44). Article 8(2) does, however, permit interference with these private communications by a public authority with this right on a number of grounds; "such as is in accordance with the law and is necessary in a democratic society in the interests of national security, public safety or the economic well-being of the country, for the prevention of disorder or crime, for the protection of health or morals, or for the protection of the rights and freedoms of others." The principles of legality, legitimacy and proportionality under Article 8(2) must be considered by the court in order to establish whether the interference in question is justified. Any interference under Article 8(2) in relation to covert surveillance must be "in accordance with the law" (*Liberty v. United Kingdom* (2008) 48 E.H.R.R. 1; *Kruslin v. France* (1990) 12 E.H.R.R. 547; *Huvig v. France* (1990) 12 E.H.R.R. 528), it must pursue one of the legitimate aims as provided, such as the prevention of crime and must meet the proportionality test by being "necessary in a democratic society" (*Klass v. Federal Republic of Germany* (1978) 2 E.H.R.R. 214).

The legality principle under Article 8(2) requires that the legislative measure in question have some basis in domestic law; it also refers to the quality of the legislation in question, requiring the measure to be compatible with the rule of law and accessible to the person concerned who must be able to foresee its consequence for him (*Liberty v. UK* (2008), para.59). The Court has noted the requirement of "foreseeability," in the context of secret surveillance, cannot mean that an individual, or criminal, should be able to foresee when the authorities are likely to intercept their communications so that they an adapt their actions accordingly (*Weber v. Germany* (2008)).

There is, of course, a balance to be struck between the security and effectiveness of law enforcement intelligence gathering and the citizen's right to privacy. The Court has pointed out, however, that it is possible for a State to make certain details available regarding the operation and safeguards of a surveillance scheme without compromising national security (*Liberty v. UK* (2008), para. 68; *Weber v. Germany* (2008), para. 100, *Klass v. Germany* (1978)).

The Court has found that the use of information relating to the date, length and numbers dialed in telephone conversations can "give rise to an issue under Article 8" as such information constitutes "an integral element of the communications made by telephone" (*Copland v. UK* (2007), para. 43; *Malone v. UK* (1984) 7 E.H.R.R. 214). The storing of personal data relating to the private life of an individual also falls under the protection of Article 8(1) (*Amann v. Switzerland* (2000) 30 E.H.R.R. 843). Therefore, as Vincents (2007) notes, the extensive precedent of the Court involving surveillance of traditional methods of communication is "analogous to … internet communications … and contemplate some analogous European Court cases" (pp. 641-642). Thus, the retention of personal communications data, *via* phone and internet usage, under the Data Retention Directive constitutes an interference under Article 8(1). As the Court has noted (*Liberty v. UK* (2008)):

"[M]ere existence of legislation which allows a system for the secret monitoring of communications entails a threat of surveillance for all those to whom the legislation may be applied. This threat necessarily strikes at freedom of communication between users of the telecommunications services and thereby amounts in itself to an interference with the exercise of the applicants' rights under Article 8" (para. 56).

It remains to be seen whether the discretion afforded under the Data Retention Directive to allow for the transposition of its provisions in each Member State will lead to clear and detailed rules regarding the examination, storing, sharing and destruction of accessed data for law enforcement purposes, as required under Article 8(2) (*Kopp v. Switzerland* (1999) 27 E.H.R.R. 91; *Contreras v. Spain* (1999) 28 E.H.R.R. 483).

The subject matter and objective of the Data Retention Directive to retain the communications data, bar content, of every citizen who communicates by means of an electronic device across the EU for "the investigation, detection and prosecution of serious crime, as defined by each Member State in its national law" falls within the legitimate aim of the prevention of disorder or crime, as provided under Article 8(2). It is not contested that the Directive provides a legal basis for the above objective but that the scope of the Directive goes beyond what is necessary to achieve its legitimate aim in a democratic society.

It is submitted that the interference by the Directive is not, as required under Article 8(2), necessary in a democratic society. The European Court of Human Rights has held that in order for an interference to be "necessary in a democratic society," and thus compatible with the Convention, it must correspond to a "pressing social need" and be "proportionate to the legitimate aim pursued" (*Handyside v. UK*, paras. 48-49). The unprecedented scope of the Directive has not been justified through any evidence demonstrating its effectiveness in tackling serious crime or the need for its broad scope, as noted and heavily criticized by data protection authorities across the EU and privacy advocates worldwide. Undoubtedly, the EU and its Member States may consider these surveillance powers to be useful and desirable but these considerations are not "synonymous" with the meaning of 'necessary' as required under Article 8(2) (*Silver v. UK* (1983), para. 97). The measures introduced under the Directive, though unquestionably in pursuit of a legitimate ground, are excessive. There has been no attempt, political rhetoric aside, to demonstrate otherwise. The

Directive is, therefore, in violation of Article 8 of the Convention.

The requirements of Article 8 for respect of privacy hold an increased significance for the EU and its Member States since the incorporation of the ECHR in the Lisbon Treaty. The EU acceded to the ECHR with the coming into effect of the Lisbon Treaty on the 1st December, 2009 (Protocol relating to Article 6(2) of the Treaty on European Union).

d. Entrenchment of Data Retention

The Directive arguably makes some welcome changes by providing some compliance with data protection safeguards for data retention following the absence of a legislative framework for the area under Article 15 of the 2002 Directive but it does so by conceding the principle of blanket data retention. This principle is inherently inimical to the concept of privacy as protected under Article 8 of the European Convention of Human Rights.

Undoubtedly, there are times when surveillance is justified and can assist in the maintenance of public safety and security. Therefore, the law should permit derogation from the protection of privacy but only when proportionately based upon evidence that such derogation is necessary. The Council (Directive 2006/24/EC, Recital 11) has stressed the benefits of retaining communications and location data for the purpose of law enforcement. There is, however, a striking absence of systematic evidence supporting the political discourse that the introduction and scope of this data retention legislation is necessary for successful law enforcement. For example, no information has been made available regarding how the European Council arrived at the determination that two years would be an appropriate standard maximum period for retaining communications data as opposed to the six month retention period as recommended by data protection authorities. Almost a third of the Council responded negatively when asked if the absence of blanket data retention had ever obstructed the work of their law enforcement authorities (Council of the EU, Answers to questionnaire, 2002). There have also been concerns expressed by the ISP community concerning the drafting of the Directive, particularly regarding the realistic implementation of requirements made by the legislation of the industry (Durrant, 2006).

Allied to this, the Directive directs the *blanket* retention of data. Not only has the necessity for this measure not been shown, there will never be the necessity to show reasonable cause to justify the infringement of an individual's rights in any specific case because it is a blanket provision. Every individual's communications data is retained without exception. Disproportionate surveillance undermines the fundamental rights of the individual, particularly the right to privacy.

The proportionality of the Directive is the subject of a High Court challenge in Ireland. In May 2010 the Court ruled that a privacy advocacy group, Digital Rights Ireland, had *locus standi* to seek a ruling from the ECJ on the compatibility of the Directive under Article 6(1) and 2 of the EU Treaty, which provides that the EU will respect fundamental rights as guaranteed under the European Convention on Human Rights (Carolan, 2010).

e. Importance of Privacy

Several values are served by privacy including the provision of "vital space for personal growth and development and for the exercise of freedom," the right to establish and develop relationships with other human beings through the freedom of association and guarantees a necessary secluded space free from public scrutiny for those who have a contribution to make in public life (Irish Law Reform Commission, 1998, paras. 1.11-1.14). A free society requires that its individuals be free to act, speak and move as they choose without State interference providing they do not injure the legitimate interests of others, as required under Mill's 'harm principle' (Mill, 1869; Stephen, 1991).

It may be argued that the type of surveillance involved in data retention imposes no physical restraint upon this control but surveillance tends to have a 'chilling effect' (Greenfield, 1991). Metaphorically, in eroding the privacy of the individual, "the State is more like a sponge than a stone. If it wants to harm or neutralize an individual, it is more likely to achieve this goal by absorbing him rather than breaking him" (Brodeur, 1984, p. 204). One tends to limit one's actions to those that are socially approved. One is more circumspect in one's language and in one's movements. As Lustgarten & Leigh (1994) put it,

Clandestine interception or eavesdropping infringes upon a fundamental choice: with whom one chooses to speak. The only defences against it are silence and withdrawal ... Turning inward is not merely bad for the individual personality, it is destructive of a great collective value: sociability. An atmosphere in which people practice self-censorship, avoid sharing thoughts and feelings, and prefer secretiveness for reasons of safety is stultifying and fearful (pp. 39-40).

There is no burden of proof on those who assert the fundamental rights of the individual, for in a free society such rights are assumed by the very existence of that society. Rather, the burden must rest upon those who assert the need to infringe fundamental freedoms to prove the necessity for such infringements. It is on this basis that the Directive ultimately must be viewed as being flawed both in concept and in design.

VI. SOLUTIONS & RECOMMENDATIONS

The evaluation process provided under Article 14 of the Directive is a welcome measure but its value is arguably limited. The Directive has entrenched the principle and practice of blanket surveillance across the EU without demonstrating the need for such an unprecedented measure. The hasty development of such EU legislation would support Baker's observation (2009) that in relation to the area of freedom, security and justice, "far more energy has been invested in crime control and law enforcement than in safeguarding the rights of those who are on the receiving end of these processes" (p. 839).

There is an opportunity, however, provided under the evaluation framework set out by Article 14 to broaden its assessment of the Directive's operation to include not only the economic impact of the legislation but also to study its compliance with data protection principles and Article 8 of the ECHR. This expansion of the evaluation, in addition to the statistical assessment required under Article 10, would result in a review grounded in real evidence of how the powers under the Directive are operating. This empirical research would reflect the real impact and usefulness to the criminal justice system, and, therefore, the need of these surveillance measures in a democratic society. An analogous point was raised in the case of *S. & Marper v. U.K.* (2009) 48 E.H.R.R. 50.

In *Marper*, the Court upheld a complaint against a law in the U.K. which allowed for the indefinite retention of fingerprints, samples and DNA profiles from every individual arrested for a recordable offence, irrespective of whether they were subsequently charged or convicted. The U.K. Government submitted statistical evidence to support their claim that this practice constituted a proportionate measure under Article 8 of the Convention. The Court agreed, however, with the assertion of the applicants, supported by an independent Report by the Nuffield Council on Bioethics (2007), that the statistics provided by the Government were "misleading" (para.116). The report referred in particular to the lack of satisfactory empirical evidence to justify the data retention in question (para.38). The Court upheld the complaint and held that the law at issue was a disproportionate interference with the applicants' right to a private life, and was thus a violation under Article 8 of the Convention (para.125). This ruling suggests that the Court gave serious consideration to the factor of reliable empirical evidence, or lack thereof in this case, in its application of the proportionality requirement as guaranteed under Article 8(2).

It is submitted that the "National Data Protection Commissioner" of each Member State should undertake an empirical study on the application of the Data Retention Directive on an annual basis. This research would involve direct access to a randomly selected number of police and prosecution files which required requests for data provided under the provisions of the Directive. The qualitative aspect of this statistical research would focus on the links between the use of this data and investigation and prosecution outcomes and compliance by public and private bodies involved in the operation of the Directive with data protection principles and the obligations under Article 8 of the Convention. This review would be systematic and would measure the effectiveness and necessity of using such retained communications data, particularly the number of times in which this information was essential in the successful prosecution of serious crime.

This proposed review procedure is similar in principle to that of the "Security Intelligence Review Committee" (SIRC), one of two oversight mechanisms of national security surveillance in Canada. The Committee is an independent review body that reports to Parliament in annual reports on the general operation of the Canadian Security Intelligence Service (CSIS). The Committee investigates and reports on the use of warrant powers provided under the Canadian Security Intelligence Service Act 1984 (ss. 29-55). Under Section 38(a) of the CSIS Act, the Committee is required to compile and analyze statistics on the operational activities of the CSIS. In contrast to the in depth reviews of CSIS operations by the SIRC that are not subject to parliamentary oversight, it is submitted that these proposed research reports on the operations of the Directive should be subject to parliamentary scrutiny at both the domestic and European level.

Data Protection legislation already provides "Supervisory Authorities" with investigative powers to carry out inspections to ensure compliance with data protection legislation and to identify possible breaches (Directive 1995/46/EC, Article 28). The main focus of a data protection audit is to identify improvements that may be needed to ensure that the requirements of the Data Protection legislation are fully observed at all times and also identify whether there are any discernible breaches of data protection legislation evident. The empirically based review of the Data Retention Directive's impact would, therefore, be an extension of this audit capacity but would instead be compulsory to specific bodies involved with the operation of the Directive. These 'supervisory authorities' would also be ideally placed in applying the appropriate safeguards and practices when undertaking such research in order to take account of the sensitivity and confidentiality of such information. Undoubtedly, the undertaking of such a project would most likely require an increase in the capacity of these organizations, e.g. additional staff, training in statistical collation and analysis.

VII. CONCLUSION

The legislative development of the Data Retention Directive demonstrates the considerable unease among legislators, Data Protection authorities and the ISP industry surrounding the Directive. As emphasized in recent judicial challenges in Germany and Ireland, the data protection and privacy concerns first highlighted during the development of this EU law still persist. These concerns highlight the absence of a commitment to a systematic evidence-based approach essential to the development of proportionate and effective legislation in a free society. As Grayling (2007) observes, "where it is easy to pass a hasty law limiting or abolishing a liberty, it is far harder to get that liberty back" (p. 271). There is an opportunity, however, to undertake empirical research that will measure the real impact of the Directive if its scope of evaluation is expanded. This proposed expansion should include an assessment of the Directive's effectiveness, its compliance with data protection principles and the right to privacy as protected under Article 8 of the ECHR. Hopefully, the evaluation process of the Directive will not result in a missed opportunity for the civil liberties of citizens across the EU.

REFERENCES

Anderson, M., & den Boer, M. (Eds.). (1994). *Policing across national boundaries*. New York: Pinter Publishers.

Article 29 Data Protection Working Party. (2001). Letter to Mr. Goran Persson, Acting President of the Council of the EU. Retrieved from http://www.statewatch.org/news/2001/jun/07Rodota.pdf

Article 29 Data Protection Working Party. (2006, March 25). Opinion 3/2006 on the Directive 2006/24/EC. Retrieved from http://europa.eu.int/comm/justice_home/fsj/privacy/docs/wpdocs/2006/wp119_en.pdf

Bainbridge, D. (1996). *EC Data Protection Directive*. London: Butterworths.

Baker, E. (2009). The European Union's "area of freedom, security and (criminal) justice" ten years on. *Criminal Law Review (London, England)*, *12*, 833–850.

Barnard, C. (2004). *The substantive law of the EU*. Oxford: Oxford University Press.

Benyon, J. (1996). The politics of police cooperation in the European Union. *International Journal of the Sociology of Law*, *24*, 353–379. doi:10.1006/ijsl.1996.0022

Black, E. (2001). *IBM and the Holocaust: The strategic alliance between Nazi Germany and America's most powerful corporation*. New York: Crown Publishers.

Brodeur, J. P. (1984). Policing: Beyond 1984. *Canadian Journal of Sociology*, *9*(2), 195–207. doi:10.2307/3340216

Cappato, M. (2002, May). Session document on the Council common position for adopting a European Parliament and Council Directive (p. 3). Brussels: European Parliament. Retrieved from http://www.statewatch.org/news/2002/may/epamend.pdf

Carolan, Mary. (2010, May 6). European court to rule on data storage law. *The Irish Times*.

Coalition of Civil Liberties Organisations. (2002, May). Letter to the President of the European Parliament. Retrieved from http://www.gilc.org/cox_en.html

Commission of the EC. (2005, September). Proposal for a directive of the European Parliament and of the Council on the retention of data. Retrieved from http://www.statewatch.org/news/2005/sep/com-438-data-retention.pdf

Committee on Civil Liberties. Justice and Home Affairs. (2005, May). Report on the initiative for a Draft Framework Decision on the retention of data [European Parliament session document]. Retrieved from http://www.statewatch.org/news/2005/oct/ep-data-ret-june-05.pdf

Committee on Civil Liberties. Justice and Home Affairs. (2005, October). European Parliament Draft Report on Data Retention Directive. Retrieved from http://www.statewatch.org/news/2005/oct/alvaro-amendments.pdf

Committee on Civil Liberties. Justice and Home Affairs. (2005, November). *European Parliament report on data retention*. Retrieved from http://www.statewatch.org/news/2005/nov/EP_provd-preport.pdf

Council of the EU. (2002, November). Answers to questionnaire on traffic data retention. Retrieved from http://www.effi.org/sananvapaus/eu-2002-11-20.html

Council of the EU. (2005, October). Outcome of proceedings on the subject of the Draft Framework Decision on the retention of data. Retrieved from http://www.statewatch.org/news/2005/oct/council-data-ret-draft-10-oct-05.pdf

Council of the European Union. (2004, April 28). Draft framework decision [Council Doc. 8958/04]. Brussels: EC. Retrieved from http://www.statewatch.orgg/soseurope.htm

Dashwood, A. (2001). The Constitution of the European Union after Nice: Law-making procedures. *European Law Review*, *26*, 215–238.

De Burca, G. (1992). Giving effect to European Community directives. *The Modern Law Review*, *55*, 215–240.

Durrant, P. (2006, July). *Data retention directive: Some ISP observations*. Paper presented at the Irish Centre for European Law, Privacy and Data Retention Directive Conference, Dublin, Ireland.

Dutch Data Protection Authority. (2007, January). Legislative proposal (Bill) for implementation of the European Directive on Data Retention. Retrieved from www.dutchdpa.nl/downloads_adv/z2006-01542.pdf

Elrick, M. L. (2001, July). Cops tap database to harass, intimidate. *Detroit Free Press*. Retrieved from http://www.sweetliberty.org/issues/privacy/lein1.htm

Ferola, L. (2002). The fight against organised crime in Europe: Building an area of freedom, security and justice in the European Union. *International Journal of Legal Information*, *30*(1), 53–91.

Global Liberty Internet Campaign. (2001). Available from http://www.gilc.org/verhofstadt_letter.html

Grayling, A. C. (2007). *Towards the light: The story of the struggles for liberty & rights that made the modern West*. London: Bloomsbury.

Greenfield, K. (1991). Cameras in teddy bears: Electronic visual surveillance and the Fourth Amendment. *The University of Chicago Law Review. University of Chicago. Law School*, *58*(3), 1045–1077. doi:10.2307/1599996

Guild, E. (2004). Editorial. *European Law Journal*, *10*, 147–149. doi:10.1111/j.1468-0386.2004.00208.x

Hawkes, B. (2006, July). *The Data Retention Directive and data protection*. Paper presented at the Irish Centre for European Law, Privacy and Data Retention Directive Conference, Dublin, Ireland.

Hebenton, B., & Thomas, T. (1995). *Policing Europe: Co-operation, conflict and control*. Basingstoke, UK: Macmillan.

Kelleher, D. (2006). *Privacy and data protection law in Ireland*. London: Tottel.

Law Reform Commission of Ireland. (1998). *Report on privacy: Surveillance and the interception of communications*. Dublin: Law Reform Commission of Ireland.

Lillington, K. (2001, August 3). Government support for data plan at odds with own policies. *The Irish Times*.

Lillington, K. (2001, November 7). Retention of mobile call records queried [Article quotes M. Murphy, former co-chairperson of the Irish Council for Civil Liberties]. *The Irish Times*.

Lustgarten, L., & Leigh, I. (1994). *In from the cold: National security and parliamentary democracy*. Oxford: Clarendon Press.

Marx, G. T. (1988). *Undercover: Police surveillance in America*. Berkeley, CA: University of California Press.

McIntyre, T. J. (2007, November). *Data retention: Privacy, policy and proportionality*. Paper presented at the ICEL/ERA Conference on The Impact of the Fight Against Terrorism on EU Law, Dublin, Ireland.

Mill, J. S. (1869). *On liberty*. Oxford: Oxford University Press.

Miller, J. (2003). *Police corruption in England and Wales: An assessment of current evidence*. London: Home Office.

Monar, J., & Morgan, R. (Eds.). (1994). *The third pillar of the European Union*. Brussels: European University Press.

BBC News. (2005, September 27) EU phone record proposal rejected.

BBC News. (2005, December 14). EU approves data retention rules.

BBC News. (2006, March 11). Madrid awaits end to bomb probe.

BBC News. (November 17, 2009). T-Mobile staff sold personal data.

BBC News. (2010, March 2). German court orders stored telecoms data deletion.

Presidency of the EU to the Council. (2005, May). On the subject of Draft Framework Decision on the retention of data. Retrieved from http://www.statewatch.org/news/2005/jul/8864-rev1-05.pdf

Presidency of the EU to the Council. (2005, October). Note on the subject of data retention (p. 2). Retrieved from http://www.statewatch.org/news/2005/oct/council-data-retention-oct-05.pdf

Reich, N. (2005). The constitutional relevance of citizenship and free movement in an enlarged Union. *European Law Journal*, *11*(6), 675–698. doi:10.1111/j.1468-0386.2005.00282.x

Response of Commission and other Member States. (2005, February). Report on the Draft Framework Decision on the retention of data (pp. 3-10). Retrieved from http://www.statewatch.org/news/2005/apr/draft-data-retention-proposal.pdf

Response of Council of the EU to proposals by EU Parliament, Council. (2005, October). Subject on data retention (p. 4). Retrieved from http://www.statewatch.org/news/2005/oct/coun-dat-ret-28-10.-5.pdf

Sewell, G., & Barker, J. R. (2001). Neither good, nor bad, but dangerous: Surveillance as an ethical paradox. *Ethics and Information Technology*, *3*, 181–194. doi:10.1023/A:1012231730405

Stephen, J. F. (1991). *Liberty, equality and fraternity*. Chicago, IL: University of Chicago Press.

Stubb, A. (1996). A categorisation of differentiated integration. *Journal of Common Market Studies*, *34*(2), 283–295. doi:10.1111/j.1468-5965.1996.tb00573.x

UK Home Office. (2005, October). Letter to the European Parliament. Retrieved from http://www.statewatch.org/news/2005/oct/data-ret-clarke-to-cavada-17-10-05.pdf

United States Mission to the European Union. (2001, October). Retrieved from http://www.statewatch.org/news/2001/nov/06Ausalet.htm

Verloop, P. (2005, June). *Wie wat bewaart die heeft wat.* Eramus University Rotterdam Report: Investigation into the use of and need for a retention duty for historical traffic data from telecommunication traffic. Government of the Netherlands.

Vilasu, M. (2007). Traffic data retention v data protection: The new European framework. *Computer and Telecommunications Law Review, 13*(2), 52–59.

Vincents, O. B. (2007). Interception of internet communications and the right to privacy. *European Human Rights Law Review, 6*, 637–648.

Walker, N. (1998). Sovereignty and differential integration in the European Union. *European Law Journal, 4*(4), 355–388. doi:10.1111/1468-0386.00058

Weatherill, S., & Beaumont, P. (1999). *EU Law*. London: Penguin Books.

Wood, D. M. (Ed.). (2006). *A report on the surveillance society for the Information Commissioner*. London: Surveillance Studies Network.

ADDITIONAL READING

Annual Reports of the Art. 29 Data Protection Working Party. Retrieved from http://ec.europa.eu/justice_home/fsj/privacy/workinggroup/annual_reports_en.htm

Balkin, J. (2008). The Constitution in the national surveillance state. *Minnesota Law Review, 93*(1), 1–25.

Bellia, P. L. (2008). The memory gap in surveillance law. *The University of Chicago Law Review. University of Chicago. Law School, 75*(1), 137–179.

Orwell, G. (1949). *Nineteen eighty four*. London: Penguin Books.

Penny, S. (2008). Updating Canada' communications surveillance laws: Privacy and security in the digital age. *Canadian Criminal Law Review, 12*, 115.

Schwartz, P. M. (2000). Internet privacy and the state. *Connecticut Law Review, 32*, 815–859.

Westin, A. F. (1967). *Privacy and freedom.* New York: Atheneum Press.

ENDNOTE

* Legal Research Officer, Office of the Director of Public Prosecutions. This article is written in my personal capacity and should not be taken to represent the views of the Director or his Office.

Chapter 16
Data Protection in EU Law:
An Analysis of the EU Legal Framework and the ECJ Jurisprudence

Maria Tzanou
European University Institute, Italy

ABSTRACT

This chapter aims to discuss the possibilities and limitations of the EU to provide for an effective and comprehensive data protection regime. In this respect, it presents an analysis of the data protection rules in EU law by examining the relevant constitutional and secondary law framework. It analyzes the jurisprudence of the European Court of Justice and the Court of First Instance on data protection issues, and argues that the European Court of Justice has interpreted an internal market measure (the Data Protection Directive) in such a way so as to foster the protection of fundamental rights. However, when it comes to the balancing between fundamental rights the Court leaves the question to be resolved by national courts. Finally, the contribution assesses the transborder data flows regime established by the Data Protection Directive and attempts to draw some conclusions on whether the 'adequate protection' test ensures a high protection in such flows.

1. INTRODUCTION

The recent rapid developments of information and communication technologies have raised serious concerns regarding our control over personal information. Not only do we have to face what has been described as the emergence of 'the National Surveillance State' (Balkin & Levinson, 2006, p. 131), but we also have to deal with the numerous private 'Big Brothers' that are watching us (Andenas & Zleptnig, 2003, p. 765). Police, public bodies and national security forces process, collate, analyze and store vast amounts of conversations, e-mails, and Internet traffic between individuals in order to detect possible terrorist or criminal activities. This information can be further manipulated through computer matching and profiling (Bennett, 1992, p. 19). At the same time, private companies and individuals record, store and process huge amounts of data

DOI: 10.4018/978-1-60960-083-9.ch016

for various reasons, such as the surveillance of the business premises or of the employees in the context of the employment relationship, or the storing of consumer data for commercial purposes (Bolman, 2002, p. 3).

The challenge of protecting personal data is universal, and countries as well as international organizations have attempted to address it by developing different legal responses according to their economic, political and ideological priorities. One cannot speak of a universal standard of data protection, but rather of a fragmented picture of different personal data protection legal regimes. In this picture, the EU data protection regime figures prominently. Europeans tend to see privacy as a fundamental right closely tied to the protection of dignity that deserves rigorous and comprehensive legislative safeguards (Bygrave, 2008, p. 16).

Of all the human rights, privacy is perhaps the most difficult to define (Banishar, 2000, p. 1; Michael, 1994, p. 1), because its meaning varies widely according to context and environment (Webb, 2003, p. 2). Privacy protection is normally seen as a way of drawing the line at how far society can intrude into a person's affairs (Davies, 1996, p. 23). The right to privacy is enshrined in the most important international human rights instruments such as the Universal Declaration of Human Rights (Article 12), the International Covenant on Civil and Political Rights (Article 17), the American Declaration of the Rights and Duties of Man (Article V), the American Convention on Human Rights (Article 11) and the European Convention for the Protection of Human Rights and Fundamental Freedoms (ECHR). In particular, Article 8 (1) ECHR reads as follows: 'Everyone has the right to respect for his private and family life, his home and his correspondence'.

The present study will focus its attention on data protection, which refers to the management of personal information or 'the information privacy.' Privacy and data protection are not identical rights. While data protection is generally considered as an aspect of the right to privacy, it is however to be distinguished from it, since it applies to all personal data and is not limited to data related to the private or the family life of a person. This scope is illustrated by the European Court of Justice judgment in *Österreichischer Rundfunk*, where the Court held that data relating to remuneration received by an employee constitute personal data (para 64).

In this context, the present contribution presents an analysis of the data protection rules in EU law. It examines the jurisprudence of the European Court of Justice on data protection issues, and discusses the possibilities and limitations of the EU to provide for effective and comprehensive data protection.

2. THE EU DATA PROTECTION REGIME

2.1 The Constitutional Framework for the EU Data Protection Regime

The protection of personal data is recognized in primary EU constitutional law as a dimension of the right to respect for private life (Skandamis, Sigalas & Stratakis, 2007, p. 6) under Article 8 of the ECHR, as reflected in Article 6 (3) of the Treaty on European Union (TEU) which provides as follows: 'Fundamental rights, as guaranteed by the ECHR and as they result from the constitutional traditions common to the Member States, shall constitute general principles of the Union's law.' Recital 10 of the preamble to Directive 95/46 also states that 'the object of the national laws on the processing of personal data is to protect fundamental rights and freedoms, notably the right to privacy, which is recognized both in Article 8 of the ECHR and the general principles of Community law.'

Furthermore, the protection of personal data is also a 'treaty-given' right to the extent that Article 16 of the Treaty on the Functioning of the European Union (TFEU) sets out the rules on the protection of individuals with regard to the processing of personal data and on the free movement of such data applicable to the Union institutions themselves. Article 16 TFEU, which replaces Article 286 EC, stipulates that the Union institutions, bodies, offices and agencies, and the Member States when they are carrying out activities which fall within the scope of Union law, shall protect personal data and their processing activities shall be subject to the control of an independent supervisory authority.

Whereas in general the European Court of Human Rights (ECtHR) in its case law has tended to widen the scope of the right to privacy to make it cover the protection of personal data, the protection of personal data at the EU level is increasingly conceived of as an autonomous fundamental right, distinct from the right to respect of private and family life (Skandamis, Sigalas & Stratakis, 2007, p. 5). There are two recent developments in the field of European law that confirm this conclusion.

The first is the inclusion of the right to the protection of personal data in Article 8 of the EU Charter of Fundamental Rights (EUCFR). According to the Explanations of the Presidium, Article 8 is based on Article 286 EC and Directive 95/46/EC, as well as on Article 8 ECHR and on the Council of Europe Convention 108, which has been ratified by all the Member States. However, by recognizing personal data as a distinct fundamental right from the right to respect for private and family life, home and communications set out in Article 7, the Charter goes beyond these instruments (Rodota, 2007, p. 2). Not only the right to personal data protection is elevated to the level of a fundamental right in the EU legal order, but it is also included as a new generation right in the European bill of rights. This development is not immune from criticism. As Bergkamp (2002) argues, '[a]n unfortunate consequence of including this right among truly fundamental rights, such as the prohibition of torture and slavery and the freedom of expression, is that the notion of fundamental right seriously devaluates, with adverse consequences for the respect for the core human rights' (p. 33).

Moreover, it is worthwhile noting that the Charter does not limit itself to proclaim the right to data protection, but it goes further and lays down a number of data protection principles, such as the fair processing of data for specified purposes, the need of the consent of the data subject, the right of access to the data and the right of rectification. Since the Lisbon Treaty entered into force as from 1 December 2009, the EUCFR enjoys the status of EU primary law according to Article 6 (1) TEU.

The importance of this choice is reflected in the second development concerning data protection that took place in the European space. This comes from the active role that the European Court of Justice (ECJ) has undertaken to play with respect to fundamental rights in general and to the right to data protection in particular. More specifically, in its judgment in the *Promusicae* case, delivered in January 2008, the Court recognized for the first time expressly that the right to data protection enjoys the status of a fundamental right within the Community legal order (paras 61-64). It did so by looking at Article 8 of the EUCFR, which, however, at the time of the delivery of the judgment was not legally binding. It seems, that the Court in this case went one step forward from its case-law concerning the Charter: until *Promusicae*, if a right was contained in the Charter, this created a presumption that it was protected under the general principles of Community law (Dougan, 2008, p. 662). In *Promusicae* however, the fact that the protection of personal data was enshrined in the Charter was enough for the ECJ to identify it as an autonomous fundamental right.

As a fundamental right, the protection of personal data does not merely require that the EU institutions or the Member States bodies abstain from illegal interferences in the personal data. There also exists a positive obligation to secure the protection of personal data. In essence, the positive obligation presupposes the adoption of legislative measures laying down more precise rules and principles concerning the protection of personal data. This positive obligation is spelled out by Article 8 ECHR which requires that any restriction to the right to respect for private life be 'in accordance with the law.' According to the ECtHR, this 'not only requires that the impugned measure should have some basis in domestic law, but also refers to the quality of the law in question, requiring that it should be accessible to the person concerned and foreseeable as to its effects.' Similarly, the requirement that the grounds on which the processing of personal data is allowed shall be clearly and precisely laid down by the law is also another fundamental principle (see also Article 8 EUCFR). Below it will be examined whether the Union legislation concerning data protection meets these requirements.

2.2 Legislative Instruments

2.2.1 The Data Protection Directive

i. Introduction

Directive 95/46/EC (also known as the 'Data Protection Directive') constitutes the central legislative measure of the EU data protection regime. It is the first piece of legislation adopted at the EU level concerning the protection of individuals with regard to the processing of personal data, and it is still considered as the most important data protection initiative within the EU ((Bygrave, 2008, p. 31) - and the leading force of globalizing data protection in the rest of the world (Birnhack, 2008, p. 512).

ii. Background to the Adoption of the Data Protection Directive

The negotiations for the adoption of the Data Protection Directive, which took almost five years to complete, provide a good example of the different interests and approaches of the three main actors involved in the Community's legislative process (Newman, 2008, p. 119). While the European Parliament had adopted as early as the 1970s a clear 'fundamental human rights approach' (Heisenberg, 2005, p. 53), the Council and the Commission seemed more concerned with 'the promotion of a European data processing industry' (Nugter, 1990, p. 32) and the facilitation of transborder data flows.

The European Parliament had asked thrice the Commission (in 1976, 1979, and 1982) to propose a directive in order to harmonize the data protection regulations across the EC. The Commission provided a first draft of a directive harmonizing data protection legislation only in 1990. This draft was largely inspired by the German and French data protection laws, and thus had fundamental rights as its central focus. What has been characterized by Heisenberg as 'Germany's disproportionate influence' to this first Commission draft was mainly a consequence of the significant contribution of Hesse's data protection commissioner, Spiros Simitis, who acted as the Chairman of the Commission's drafting group. Simitis, who held also the Chair of the Council of Europe's Data Protection Experts Committee, was keen to emphasize the fundamental human rights aspect of the Directive that could not be traded off against other interests (Simitis, 1995, p. 447). It is hardly surprising that this position was not welcomed by certain Member States, and in particular the UK, that did not see any need for harmonization of data protection rules at the EC level. Furthermore, the Commission's proposal was severely criticized by trade and industry, on the ground that it was too bureaucratic and gave a clear priority to the protection of personal data at the expense of other public policy objectives such as the need for commercial exchange of the data.

In view of those criticisms, the Commission submitted in October 1992 a second amended draft. The tensions within the Council between the different Member States were obvious even after this second proposal. The UK continued to object to a directive that would harmonize data protection laws in Europe to a higher than the UK standard degree. However, in the end it chose to abstain, rather than to vote against the Directive. The Directive was finally signed by the presidents of the Council and the European Parliament on 24th October 1995, giving Member States a period of three years for transposition into domestic law. All Member States have implemented Directive 95/46 in their national legislation (see Status of Implementation of Directive 95/46 on the Protection of Individuals with regard to the Processing of Personal Data)

iii. Scope, Objectives and Definitions

The Data Protection Directive aims to harmonize the different national rules on the protection of personal data, by ensuring at the same time the free movement of such data. In this respect, it can be seen, on the one hand, as a 'negative harmonization' instrument to the extent that it intends to remove obstacles to the establishment of the internal market, by ensuring and facilitating free trade of data between different Member States. Nevertheless, on the other hand, it can be considered as a measure of 'positive harmonization' in that it replaces the divergent data protection regimes across the Community with a harmonized EC regulatory framework. This 'tying together' by the Directive of two seemingly conflicting principles, free trade and data protection, was not immune from criticism both from the point of view of fundamental rights protection, as well as from the standpoint of business interests (Bergkamp, 2002, p. 37). As Gutwirth (2002) characteristically observes, '[t]he European Midas is at work again: everything the Commission touches becomes a market... The concern about privacy is totally subordinate to the market prerogatives' (pp. 91-92).

These criticisms, though, seem to be rather unsubstantiated, at least if one takes into account the almost fifteen years of life of the Directive, in which it has achieved to strike a fair balance between the competing values. Insofar as its legal basis is concerned, due to the fact that Directive 95/46/EC was intended as a harmonization instrument, it was adopted under Article 95 (ex Article 100a) of the EC Treaty, which concerns the approximation of legislation relating to the internal market (see Recital 7).

Regarding its scope, the Directive applies to 'any operation or set of operations which is performed upon personal data', called 'processing' of data. According to Article 3 (1) it applies 'to the processing of personal data wholly or partly by automatic means, and to the processing otherwise than by automatic means of personal data which form part of a filing system or are intended to form part of a filing system.'

Article 3 (2) lays down the two areas where the Directive does not apply. First, processing of personal data 'in the course of an activity which falls outside the scope of Community law, such as those provided for by Titles V and VI TEU and in any case to processing operations concerning public security, defence, State security (including the economic well-being of the State when the processing operation relates to State security matters) and the activities of the State in areas of criminal law.' Second, processing of data 'by a natural person in the course of a purely personal or household activity' also falls outside the scope of application of this Directive.

[1]. Of paramount importance is the definition of the notions of 'personal data' and 'processing.' In the context of the Data Protection Directive, 'personal data' means 'any information relating to an identified or identifiable natural person ('data subject'); 'an identifiable person' is one that can be identified, directly or indirectly, in particular by reference to an identification number or to one or more factors specific to his physical, physiological, mental, economic, cultural or social identity.' (Article 2 (a)). 'The processing of personal data' ('processing') involves 'any operation or set of operations which is performed upon personal data, whether or not by automatic means, such as collection, recording, organization, storage, adaptation or alteration, retrieval, consultation, use, disclosure by transmission, dissemination or otherwise making available, alignment or

combination, blocking, erasure or destruction' (Article 2 (b)).

[2]. Those definitions, which are central to the EU Data Protection regime, are not without uncertainties. Insofar as the definition of 'personal data' is concerned, this weakness was recognized by the Article 29 Working Party which sought to provide an interpretation of this concept. It concluded that the European lawmaker intended to adopt a broad notion of personal data, nevertheless this is not unlimited. The definition of 'processing' is also problematic. More particularly, it is so broadly defined that it raises concerns as to whether the requirement that the grounds on which the processing of personal data is allowed shall be clearly and precisely laid down by the law can be satisfied.

iv. Content

Directive 95/46/EC contains a number of principles concerning the legitimate processing of personal data (Articles 6 and 7). In most cases, those go beyond the data protection principles enshrined in Convention 108 of the Council of Europe. In particular, the Directive sets out that personal data must be processed fairly and lawfully; they should be collected for specified, explicit and legitimate purposes, and not further processed in a way incompatible to those purposes; they should be adequate, relevant, and not excessive; accurate, up to date, and kept for no longer than is necessary for the purposes for which they were collected or processed. Personal data may be processed only if the data subject has given his consent; or if processing is necessary for the performance of a contract to which the data subject is party.

Furthermore, the Directive lays down when processing will be permitted, in respect to 'sensitive data' such as those revealing 'racial or ethnic origin, political opinions, religious or philosophical beliefs, trade-union membership, and data concerning sex or health life' (Article 8). It requires that information should be provided to the data subject (Article 10), and establishes a right to access to data (Article 12) and a right to object (Article 14). An innovative provision is Article 15 which grants a person the right 'not to be subject to a decision which produces legal effects concerning him or significantly affects him and which is based solely on automated processing of data intended to evaluate certain personal aspects relating to him, such as his performance at work, creditworthiness, reliability, conduct, etc'.

In Chapter III the Data Protection Directive provides for the judicial remedies to be made available to every person whose rights have been breached (Article 22) and envisages the possibility of compensation for the damage suffered (Article 23). The Directive regulates the transfer of data to third countries, which is permitted if the third country in question ensures an adequate level of protection (Articles 25-26).

Finally, it stipulates that each Member State will set up a supervisory authority responsible for monitoring the compliance within its territory with the provisions of the Directive (Article 28), and establishes a Working Party on the Protection of Individuals with regard to the Processing of Personal Data (Article 29). Those provisions clearly go beyond the stipulations of the Convention 108.

v. The Article 29 Data Protection Working Party

One of the most innovative aspects of the Data Protection Directive is without doubt the establishment of an independent EU Advisory Body on Data Protection and Privacy, the Article 29 Working Party on the Protection of Individuals with regard to the Processing of Personal Data (hereafter 'Article 29 Working Party'). The Working Party is composed of representatives of national data protection authorities, the European Data Protection Supervisor, and the Commission. Its main tasks, which are laid down in Article 30 of the Directive, consist in providing expert opinions from the member state level to the Commission on questions of data protection; in promoting the uniform application of the general principles of data protection in all Member States through co-operation between data protection supervisory authorities; in advising the Commission on Community measures affecting the rights and freedoms of natural persons with regard to the processing of personal data and privacy; and in making recommendations to the public and to the Community institutions on matters relating to the protection of persons with regard to the processing of personal data and privacy in the Community.

Even though this unique body of the EC's institutional system has only advisory competences, it has played an important role in promoting data protection issues within the Community, and has produced a significant number of reports, recommendations and opinions on privacy matters. In addition to that, it must be pointed that the Working Party enhances the co-operation and the informal exchanges of 'best practices' concerning data protection between national Data Protection authorities. In this respect, it certainly contributes to a harmonization of the interpretation of the provisions of the Data Protection Directive (Poullet, 2006, p. 208).

2.2.2 Towards a Third Generation of Data Protection Legislation: The e-Privacy Directive

On July 12, 2002, the Community lawmaker adopted a further legislative instrument that deals with the challenges posed by the new advanced digital technologies. Directive 2002/58/EC concerning the processing of personal data and the protection of privacy in the electronic communications sector (the 'e-Privacy Directive'), replaces and modifies Directive 97/66/EC concerning the processing of personal data and the protection of privacy in the telecommunications sector in order to adapt the Community legislation to the developments of the Internet, and thus to 'provide an equal level of protection of personal data and privacy for users of publicly available electronic communications services, regardless of the technologies used' (Recital 4).

The e-Privacy Directive aims at harmonizing the different national provisions on the protection of the right to privacy, with respect to the processing of personal data in the electronic communications sector while ensuring the free movement of such data and of electronic communications equipment and services in the Community (Article 1 (1)). In essence, it particularizes and complements the provisions of the Data Protection Directive with respect to the processing of personal data of natural persons in the electronic communications sector. However, it goes beyond Directive 95/46/EC in many respects, and offers a new approach to the protection of privacy in the information society. First of all, unlike Directive 95/46/EC, which applies only to the processing of data of individuals, the e-Privacy Directive also includes in its scope the protection of legal persons (Article 1 (2)). Furthermore, it contains provisions regarding unsolicited communications. According to Article 13 of the Directive, the use of automatic calling machines, fax or electronic mail for the purposes of direct marketing may only be allowed in respect of subscribers who have given their prior consent. In addition, the Directive takes into account a number of particularities of the Internet environment such as cookies, spyware, web bugs, hidden identifiers and other similar devices that may seriously intrude upon the privacy of users by entering their terminal without their knowledge in order to gain access to information, to store hidden information or to trace their activities (Recitals 6, 7, 8, 24 and 25). It allows the use of such devises only for legitimate purposes, with the knowledge of the users concerned.

Naturally, as a first pillar measure, this Directive, like the Data Protection Directive, does not apply to activities that fall outside the scope of the EC Treaty (Article 1 (3)). According to Article 5 (1) of the e-Privacy Directive, Member States shall ensure the confidentiality of communications and the related traffic data through national legislation. In particular, they shall prohibit listening, tapping, storage or other kinds of interception or surveillance of communications and the related traffic data by persons other than users, without the consent of the users concerned, except when legally authorized to do so. Furthermore, traffic data relating to subscribers and users processed and stored by the provider of a public communications network must be erased or made anonymous when it is no longer needed for the purpose of the transmission of a communication (Article 6). However, Article 15 enables Member States to adopt legislative measures to restrict the scope of the rights provided for in the Directive 'when such restriction constitutes a necessary, appropriate and proportionate measure within a democratic society to safeguard national security (i.e. State security), defence, public security, and the prevention, investigation, detection and prosecution of criminal offences or of unauthorised use of the electronic communication system.'

The e-Privacy Directive was amended on 19 December 2009 by Directive 2009/136/EC. Under the new regime, communications service providers are required to notify national data protection authorities and consumers of security breaches (Article 4 (3)); legal remedies are provided to natural and legal persons adversely affected by infringements concerning unsolicited communications (Article 13 (6)); enhanced penalties (with the possibility of adoption of criminal sanctions) are laid down for infringements of the Directive (Article 15a (1)); and national data protection authorities receive new enforcement and investigative powers (Article 15a (2, 3, 4)) .

2.2.3 Regulation 45/2001/EC

Directive 95/46/EC and Directive 2002/58/EC are addressed to the Member States and, accordingly, they do not apply as such to the EU institutions and bodies. However, Regulation 45/2001/EC on the protection of individuals with regard to the processing of personal data by the institutions and bodies of the Community and on the free movement of such data lays down the data protection rules for the EU institutions. The Regulation which is based on Article 286 EC, aims at protecting the fundamental rights and freedoms of natural persons, and in particular their right to privacy with respect to the processing of personal data (Article 2). It applies to the processing of such data by all Community institutions and bodies insofar as such processing is carried out in the exercise of activities all or part of which fall within the scope of Community law (Article 3). Regulation 45/2001 specifies the data processing obligations of the controllers within the Community institutions and bodies (Articles 5-12), sets out the rights of the data subject (Articles 13-19), provides the individuals with judicial remedies (Article 32) and establishes an independent supervisory authority, the European Data Protection Supervisor (Articles 41-48).

The European Data Protection Supervisor (EDPS) aims to promote a "data protection culture" in Community (now Union) institutions and bodies. He is the independent authority that ensures at the EU level that the fundamental rights and freedoms of natural persons, and in particular their right to privacy, are respected by the EU institutions and bodies. His tasks consist in supervising personal data processing by the institutions or bodies of the Union, in examining the data protection and privacy impact of proposed new legislation, and in cooperating with other data protection authorities, mainly within the platform of the Article 29 Working Party, in order to ensure consistency in the protection of personal data.

Insofar as his supervisory role is concerned, the EDPS undertakes prior checks on the processing of data by Union institutions and bodies and carries out inquiries on complaints received from EU staff members or from other people that allege that their data has been mishandled. Furthermore, the EDPS advises the EU institutions and bodies on data protection issues in a range of policy areas. His consultative role relates to proposals for new legislation as well as soft law instruments like communications that affect personal data protection in the EU. He also monitors new technologies that may have an impact on data protection. Overall, the contribution of the European Data Protection Supervisor in the establishment of a high level of protection of personal data can be characterized as significant (Hijmans, 2006, p. 1341).

2.2.4 Undermining Data Protection within the EU? The Data Retention Directive

i. Directive 2006/24/EC: Aim, Scope, Content

Directive 2006/24/EC (the 'Data Retention Directive') aims to harmonize Member States' provisions concerning the obligations of the providers of publicly available electronic communications services with respect to the retention of certain data which are generated or processed by them, in order to ensure that the data are available for the purpose of the investigation, detection and prosecution of serious crime, as defined by each Member State in its national law (Article 1 (1)). It applies to traffic and location data on both legal entities and natural persons and to the related data necessary to identify the subscriber or registered user, but does not apply to the content of electronic communications (Article 1 (2)).

The Directive does not include within its regulatory framework the prevention of crimes, but it requires the retention of data only for the purpose of the 'investigation, detection and prosecution of serious crime.' The text of the Directive is, however, problematic due to the lack of a definition of what constitutes 'serious crime', something which is left to be regulated by each Member State at the national level. This choice not to define the notion of 'serious crime' is to be criticized because it can result to an excessive broadening of the scope of the Directive, and therefore of the retention of data, for any crime that is to be characterized as 'serious' by each Member State (House of Lords European Union Committee, 2005, p. 18).

The categories of data to be retained are laid down in Article 5 of the Directive. They consist of data necessary: to trace and identify the source, the destination, the date, time duration and type of communication; to identify users' communication equipment; and, to identify the location of mobile communication equipment.

The Directive stipulates that the retention period will be between six months and two years starting from the date of the communication (Article 6). The fact that the Directive does not set a specific period for data retention but allows for variations raises questions as to the level of harmonization that it aims to achieve. It is possible that a data retention period of six months in one Member State and of two years in another, might affect the competition between the service providers in the common market.

ii. Assessing the Data Retention Directive with Regard to the Right to Privacy

The right to privacy is enshrined in Article 7 EUCFR, which provides that: 'Everyone has the right to respect for his or her private and family life, home and communications'. Furthermore, Article 52 (3) EUCFR stipulates that: 'In so far as this Charter contains rights which correspond to rights guaranteed by the ECHR, the meaning and scope of those rights shall be the same as those laid down by the said Convention'. Indeed, the right to private life is guaranteed in Article 8 of the ECHR and therefore the present analysis will be guided by the interpretation of this right by the European Court of Human Rights (ECtHR) in order to assess the meaning and scope of Article 7 EUCFR.

Article 8 (1) ECHR provides that everyone has the right to respect for his private and family life, his home and his correspondence. This right, however, is not an absolute right, but subject to the limitations provided for in paragraph 2 of the same Article. It should be mentioned in the first place that the (ECtHR) has adopted a broad interpretation of the protective scope of Article

8 (1) ECHR and a narrow one of the restrictions provided for in the second paragraph, thus being consistent with its case law of reading the Convention as a 'living instrument which ... must be interpreted in the light of present day conditions' (*Tyrer v UK*, para 31). The Court has also underlined that 'the protection of personal data, ... is of fundamental importance to a person's enjoyment of his or her right to respect for private and family life as guaranteed by Article 8 of the ECHR' (*Z. v. Finland,* para 95).

According to the case-law of the Strasbourg Court, an interference with the right to privacy is justified only when it is in accordance with the law, it serves a legitimate purpose, and it is necessary in a democratic society. The analysis below will examine whether the Data Retention Directive satisfies those requirements.

a. Interference with the right to respect for private life

The Court has interpreted the notion of 'interference with the right to privacy' broadly. In *Leander v. Sweden* it held that the storing by a public authority of information relating to an individual's private life amounts to an interference with the right to respect for private life (para 48). In *Amann v Switzerland* it reiterated this conclusion and added that the subsequent use of the stored information has no bearing on that finding. Furthermore, in *Klass v. Germany*, the Court reasoned that because a law permitting interception of mail created a "menace of surveillance" for all users of the postal service, and because that menace struck at freedom of communication, the law constituted an interference with the right to privacy (para 40).

In the light of the above mentioned decisions of the ECtHR, it can be concluded that the blanket retention of traffic data can be considered as an interference with the right to respect for private life, irrespective of whether these data will be used subsequently.

b. 'In accordance with the law'

According to the case-law of the Court, the requirement that an interference with the right to privacy must be 'in accordance with the law' covers two aspects. First, there must be a legal basis for the interference; secondly, the measure should be compatible with the 'rule of law'. This means that the measure should meet the standards of accessibility and foreseeability: it must be accessible to the persons concerned, and sufficiently precise to allow them reasonably to foresee its consequences. In this respect, the ECtHR held in *Kruslin v France* that 'tapping and other forms of interception of telephone conversations represent a serious interference with private life and must accordingly be based on a 'law' that is particularly precise. It is essential to have clear, detailed rules on the subject, especially as the technology available for use is continually becoming more sophisticated' (para 33).

The data retention regime seems to satisfy the requirement of being 'in accordance with the law' as it is envisaged in an accessible, detailed, and democratically enacted law- Directive 2006/24/EC. In this respect, Bignami (2007) notes that the democratic character of the law is further enhanced by the fact that it was adopted under the first pillar where 'the involvement of a directly elected legislature improves the transparency of rights-burdening rules.' However, it should be noted here that the outcome of the 'in accordance with the law' test depends also on the quality of the laws of transposition of the Directive in domestic legislations.

c. Legitimate aim

In order to be justified the interference with the right to privacy should also pursue one of the aims listed in paragraph 2 of Article 8. With regard to this requirement, the Strasbourg organs have rarely found that the processing of data is not in compliance with at least one of those aims (Bygrave,

1998, p. 273), and the purpose of 'investigation, detection, and prosecution of serious crime' can be considered as a legitimate aim.

d. 'Necessary in a democratic society'

The most disputable requirement is without doubt the test of the 'necessary in a democratic society'. According to the ECtHR, this is satisfied when the interference 'corresponds to a pressing social need' and is 'proportionate to the legitimate aim pursued' (*Leander,* para 58). Nevertheless, national authorities enjoy a certain margin of appreciation, depending on a variety of factors, such as the importance of the legitimate aim or the seriousness of the interference involved. In examining the necessity of a measure, the first test is that of effectiveness. Furthermore, it has to be taken into account whether there are less intrusive alternatives available. Finally, insofar as the proportionality requirement is concerned, the measure should not be disproportionate to the aim that it seeks to achieve.

In the light of these considerations, it seems difficult how the Data Retention Directive can satisfy the proportionality test when it stipulates the compulsory retention of traffic data of every individual, irrespective of whether he is considered to be under suspicion or not. Blanket data retention, constitutes a permanent, general recording of citizens' behavior (Breyer, 2005, p. 370). The fact that this does not cover the content of the communication does not affect this conclusion, because also traffic data can reveal a detailed picture of the communications, and the movements of individuals. Furthermore, a blanket data retention is not proportionate because it fails to take into account specific types of communication (such as the attorney-client communication), which the States already recognize as sufficiently special to warrant a higher degree of protection. Concerning the effectiveness of the measure, there is no empirical knowledge at the moment, but it seems doubtful that a generalized data retention regime will in fact reduce the crime levels in the society. Besides, it is not absolutely certain that alternative, less privacy-intrusive measures do not exist. For instance, under the so-called 'quick-freeze procedure', information can be stored on a suspected individual, and accessed at a later point by the police if they have the necessary evidence to obtain a court warrant. Finally, the maximum retention period of two years does not seem reasonable in the absence of any justification concerning its usefulness for the combating of crime. Thus, the Data Retention Directive seems to fail the proportionality test, and it is highly probable that the European Court of Justice will declare it void.

A challenge of the Directive based on the ground of violation of the right to privacy seems now possible on the basis of a preliminary reference submitted by a national court (Article 267 TFEU, ex-Article 234 EC) on the validity of this measure with respect to fundamental rights as protected in the Community legal order and the principle of proportionality.

In this respect its worth mentioning that the German Constitutional Court, in its decision of 2 March 2010 (*1 BvR 256/08, 1 BvR 263/08, 1 BvR 586/08*), found unconstitutional the law transposing the Data Retention Directive in Germany on the ground that the obligations it imposes are disproportionate. In particular, the Court held that Section 113 of the Telecommunications Act does not guarantee the security of the stored data; lacks in transparency because it imposes a direct use of the data for the investigation, detection and prosecution of a number of criminal offences that are not specified clearly; and the legal protection that it affords to the data subject is not compatible with the requirements of the German Constitution.

iii. Which Pillar for Data Retention? Challenging the Legal Basis of the Data Retention Directive

At the time of the adoption of the Directive, there were vigorous debates between the EU institutions and the Member States regarding its legal basis, and in particular whether it fell under the Community competence or it was a measure to be adopted under the framework of police and judicial cooperation.

The case was not resolved even after the adoption of the Directive as a first pillar measure. Ireland challenged it before the ECJ, on the ground that Article 95 EC was not the appropriate legal basis, because its main objective is to facilitate the investigation, detection and prosecution of serious crime, including terrorism, and thus it should have been adopted under the third pillar. The Court in its judgment disagreed and held that the Directive was adopted on the appropriate legal basis, since both its aim and its content fell under Article 95 EC. This is because the Data Retention Directive covers the activities of service providers in the internal market and does not contain any rules governing the activities of public authorities for law-enforcement purposes.

I contend that the ruling of the Court is satisfactory from a fundamental rights perspective. This is because the ECJ expressly stated in its decision that the action brought by Ireland (and therefore its judgment) related 'solely to the choice of legal basis and not to any possible infringement of fundamental rights arising from interference with the exercise of the right to privacy contained in Directive 2006/24' (*Ireland v. EP and Council*, para 57). This, in my opinion, can be read as opening up the possibility of challenging the Directive, this time, however, on the ground of violation of the rights to privacy and data protection.

2.3 An Overview of the Case Law of the European Court of Justice Concerning Data Protection

2.3.1 Interpretation of the Data Protection Directive

Since the adoption of Directive 95/46/EC the European Court of Justice has been called upon a number of times to rule on questions of interpretation of this Directive. In general terms, the ECJ has interpreted in a generous manner the Data Protection Directive, to ensure a high level of protection of personal data within the EC legal order. In essence, it has interpreted an internal market harmonization instrument in such a manner that fosters the protection of a fundamental right within the Community. In this respect, it has adopted an expansive reading of the protective scope of the Directive, which goes beyond the exercise of economic activities, and a restrictive one concerning the exemptions not covered by it. Its flexible interpretation has also permitted to apply the guarantees offered by the Directive to new technological developments, and in particular the Internet. Furthermore, when the rights of the Union citizens have been at issue, the ECJ has proved to be even more cautious in its analysis based on the fundamental EU principle of non-discrimination on the ground of nationality (Article 12 EC, now Article 18 TFEU), and has found suspicious every national measure discriminating against Union citizens from other Member States. In this case, its scrutiny of the national legislation has been stricter, and it has not hesitated to strike down such legislation as incompatible with primary Community law, even though the Member State at issue invoked the argument of the fight against crime which falls outside the scope of the Data Protection Directive.

Finally, the ECJ held recently in the case *Commission v Germany* that Germany failed to fulfil its obligations under Article 28(1) of the Data Protection Directive by making the authorities responsible for monitoring the processing of personal data by non-public bodies and undertakings governed by public law which compete on the market (öffentlich-rechtliche Wettbewerbsunternehmen) in the different *Länder* subject to State scrutiny, and by thus incorrectly transposing the requirement that those authorities perform their functions 'with complete independence.'

i. Scope of Application

A first set of questions that the Court was called upon to address concerned the scope of the application of Directive 95/46/EC. In *Österreichischer Rundfunk,* a preliminary ruling case which concerned the compatibility with Community law of an Austrian provision requiring entities which were subject to control by the Austrian Court of Audit, the Rechnungshof, to inform the latter about the salaries of their employees when they exceeded a certain level; and subsequently the Rechnungshof would publish this information in a report which contained the names of the persons and the level of their respective salaries; the Court was asked to rule whether the Data Protection Directive was applicable at all to this control activity exercised by the Rechnungshof. Unlike Advocate General Tizziano who pleaded against the applicability of the Directive, the ECJ found that it was applicable. According to the Court, 'since any personal data can move between Member States, Directive 95/46 requires in principle compliance with the rules for protection of such data with respect to any processing of data as defined by Article 3' (*Österreichischer Rundfunk*, para 40). The ECJ rejected the argument that the Data Protection Directive applies only to activities which have a sufficient connection with the exercise of the fundamental freedoms of the common market, by holding that recourse to Article 95 EC as a legal basis 'does not presuppose the existence of an actual link with free movement between Member States in every situation referred to by the measure founded on that basis' (para 41). If a contrary interpretation were to be adopted, it would make the limits of the field of application of the Data Protection Directive particularly unsure and uncertain, which would be contrary to its essential objective.

The same wide interpretation of the scope of the Data Protection Directive was reiterated in *Lindqvist,* where the ECJ stressed once more that a distinction should be made between the general objective of an act adopted on the basis of Article 95 EC and the specific situations where this act can be applied even if those are not directly linked to the internal market. The ECJ clarified that the exception of Article 3 (2) applies only to the activities which are expressly listed there or which can be classified in the same category. As a result, the Directive applies to all the other activities regardless of their connection with the internal market. Thus, it applied to the charitable and religious activities carried out by Mrs Lindqvist, who worked as a volunteer catechist in a parish of the Swedish Protestant Church. Mrs Lindqvist had published on her internet site personal data on a number of people working with her and the ECJ found this activity to fall within the scope of the Data Protection Directive.

Similarly, in *Satakunnan Markkinapörssi and Satamedia* the Court held that the processing of personal data files which contain solely, and in unaltered form, material that has already been published in the media, falls within the scope of application of Directive 95/46/EC. In this respect, the ECJ stressed that a general derogation from the application of the directive in respect of published information would largely deprive it of its effect. It would be sufficient for the Member States to publish data in order for those data to cease to enjoy the protection afforded by the Directive.

ii. The Interpretation of Specific Provisions

A second set of legal issues brought before the Court concerned the interpretation of specific provisions of the Data Protection Directive. In *Lindqvist* the ECJ ruled for the first time on a number of questions concerning the issue of the processing of personal data carried out on the Internet. It noted that information such as that published by Mrs Lindqvist on her personal website containing the name, telephone number and the working conditions or hobbies of specified people, was covered by the definition of 'personal data' of Article 2(a) of the Directive. Furthermore, the placing of this information on the Internet constituted 'processing of personal data wholly or partly by automatic means.' As far as the interpretation of sensitive personal data was concerned, the Court found that the reference by Mrs Lindqvist to the fact that one of her colleagues had 'injured her foot and was on half-time on medical grounds' constituted personal data concerning health within the meaning of Article 8 (1) of the Directive.

The ECJ was also asked to rule on the direct applicability of specific Articles of the Data Protection Directive, namely whether they could be relied on by individuals before the national courts to oust the application of rules of national law which are contrary to those provisions. It held that Articles 6(1)(c) and 7(c) or (e) were sufficiently precise and thus directly applicable. Moreover, the ECJ pronounced on the issue of whether it 'is permissible for the Member States to provide for greater protection for personal data or a wider scope than this required under Directive 95/46.' In this respect, it stressed that the Data Protection Directive envisages complete harmonization. Nevertheless, Member States enjoy a margin for maneuver in certain areas, which authorizes them to maintain or introduce particular rules for specific situations, and in any case they remain free to regulate the areas excluded from the scope of application of the Directive, provided that no other provision of Community law precludes it.

Furthermore, the Court had to deal in *Huber* with the principle of non-discrimination in the protection of personal data within the context of the Union citizenship. The case concerned a German law requiring the storage in a central register operated by the Federal Office for Migration and Refugees ('the Bundesamt'), of certain personal data of foreign nationals residing in Germany for a period of more than three months, while at the same time personal data of German citizens were stored only in local, municipal registers. The German government argued that through this storage the 'Bundesamt' assisted the public authorities responsible for the application of the legislation relating to the law on foreign nationals and the law on asylum, and that the information stored in the central register was used for statistical purposes, and for the exercise by the security and police services and by the judicial authorities of their powers in relation to the prosecution and investigation of criminal activities. In its examination of the compatibility of this national provision with Community law, the Court distinguished the justifications put forward by Germany in two categories: First, the function of providing support to the authorities responsible for the application of the legislation relating to the right of residence and the use for statistical purposes, was to be assessed with regard to the Data Protection Directive and more particularly to the condition of necessity laid down by Article 7(e). Second, the function of fighting crime was to be examined with regard to primary Community law, as it fell outside the scope of the Directive. The ECJ held that a system for processing personal data relating to Union citizens who are not nationals of the Member State concerned, having as its object the provision of support to the national authorities responsible for the application of the legislation relating to the right of residence does not satisfy the requirement of necessity laid down by Article 7(e) of Directive 95/46, unless two conditions are fulfilled: First, the data it contains should be necessary for the application by those authorities of that legislation, and second, its centralized nature should enable that legislation to be more effectively applied as regards the right of residence of Union citizens who are not nationals of that Member State. On the other hand, the storage of data for statistical purposes cannot, on any basis, be considered to be necessary within the meaning of Article 7(e). Furthermore, the Court found that the difference in treatment between Member State nationals and other Union citizens which arises by virtue of the systematic processing of personal data relating only to the latter for the purposes of fighting crime constitutes discrimination which is prohibited by Article 12 (1) EC.

Finally, in *Rijkeboer* the ECJ had to interpret the scope of Article 12(a) of the Data Protection Directive which provides for the right of access to data. Having stated that the right of access is necessary, on the one hand, to enable the data subject to exercise a number of other rights, such as the rights of rectification, erasure or blockage of data; and on the other hand, to enable the data subject to exercise his right to object to his personal data being processed or his right of action where he suffers damage, it went on to hold that Article 12(a) requires Member States to ensure a right of access to information not only in respect of the present but also in respect of the past. However, it is for Member States to fix a time-limit for storage of that information and to provide for access to that information which constitutes a fair balance between, on the one hand, the interest of the data subject in protecting his privacy, in particular by way of his rights to object and to bring legal proceedings and, on the other, the burden which the obligation to store that information represents for the controller.

2.3.2 Balancing Data Protection with Other Rights

The Court has been asked many times to balance the right to privacy and data protection with other fundamental rights and freedoms protected within the EC legal order. While it has noted the importance of all the fundamental rights at issue, it has avoided pronouncing on the final outcome of this reconciliation. Instead, it left the final decision on the matter to the (referring) national court. This is because, according to the Court, a balance must be found between the rights and interests involved at the stage of the application at the national level of the legislation implementing the Data Protection Directive in individual cases. However, it has sought to provide guidance to the national court by stressing the importance of the principle of proportionality. The ECJ has shown itself to be very sensitive in cases that concern the balancing between the freedom of expression, and more particularly, journalism, on the one hand, and data protection on the other. In these cases, it seemed ready to accept an exception from data protection rules.

In *Österreichischer Rundfunk* the ECJ had to assess whether national regulation, such as the Austrian that was at issue in the main proceedings, requiring a State control body to collect and communicate, for purposes of publication, data on the income of persons employed by the bodies subject to that control, where that income exceeded a certain threshold, was compatible with the Data Protection Directive. The competing rights at issue were, on the one hand, the right to data protection of the persons concerned, and on the other, the principles of transparency, of public access to official documents and of the proper management of public funds. The ECJ commenced its analysis by stating that the provisions of Directive 95/46/EC, 'must ... be interpreted in the light of fundamental rights, which, according to settled case-law, form an integral part of the general principles of law whose observance the Court ensures' (para 68). It then found that an interference with the right to privacy existed in the present case, and explained when it would be justified. However, the ECJ left the final decision on the matter to the national court.

In this respect, it is worth mentioning the judgment of the Court of First Instance (CFI) in the *Bavarian Lager* case. The applicant in this case challenged a Commission's decision, rejecting his application for access to the full minutes of a meeting held in the context of Article 226 EC proceedings, and the CFI was asked, essentially, to strike a fair balance between, on the one hand, the right to data protection, and on the other, the fundamental right of the European citizens to have access to the documents of the EU institutions. The Court concluded that disclosure of the names of the representatives in the Commission meeting 'is not capable of actually and specifically affecting the protection of the privacy and integrity of the persons concerned' (para 110). The CFI drew a distinction between *Bavarian Lager* and the judgment of the ECJ in *Österreichischer Rundfunk*, in that the former case fell within the application of Regulation 1049/2001, and the exception laid down by Article 4(1) (b) of that Regulation concerns only the disclosure of personal data which would undermine the protection of the privacy and integrity of the individual. The Court noted at this point that 'not all personal data are capable by their nature of undermining the private life of the person concerned' (para 119) Thus, it annulled the Commission's decision rejecting access to the full minutes of the meeting.

In *Lindqvist* the ECJ had to strike a balance between the right to data protection and the freedom of expression enshrined in Article 10 ECHR and protected as a general principle of Community law within the EC legal order. The Court noted that 'fundamental rights have a particular importance, as demonstrated by the case in the main proceedings, in which, in essence, Mrs Lindqvist's freedom of expression in her work preparing people for Communion and her freedom to carry out activities contributing to religious life have to be weighed against the protection of the private life of the individuals about whom Mrs Lindqvist has placed data on her internet site' (para 90). However, the Court again left it to the national court to ensure, in accordance with the principle of proportionality, that a fair balance was struck between the rights in question.

In *Satakunnan Markkinapörssi and Satamedia*, the Court was asked to interpret Article 9 of the Data Protection Directive, which allows the Member States to provide for exemptions and derogations for the processing of personal data 'carried out solely for journalistic purposes or the purpose of artistic or literary expression only if they are necessary to reconcile the right to privacy with the rules governing freedom of expression.' The case was a preliminary reference made in proceedings between the Finnish Data Protection Ombudsman, and the Finnish Data Protection Board, relating to activities involving the processing of personal data undertaken by Markkinapörssi and Satamedia. More particularly, Markkinapörssi collected public data from the Finnish tax authorities for the purposes of publishing extracts from them in the regional editions of the Veropörssi newspaper, and transferred the same data to Satamedia with a view to those being disseminated by a text-messaging system. The ECJ noted the importance of the right to freedom of expression in a democratic society and held that notions relating to that freedom, such as journalism, should be interpreted broadly. It then clarified that activities which involve the processing of data from documents which are in the public domain under national legislation, may be classified as 'journalistic activities' if their object is 'the disclosure to the public of information, opinions or ideas, irrespective of the medium which is used to transmit them' (para 61). Furthermore, the Court ruled that those activities are not limited to media undertakings but cover every person engaged in journalism, and may be undertaken for profit-making purposes. However, the Court left it to the national court to determine whether that was the case in the main proceedings.

The ECJ was also asked to engage in a balancing exercise in *Promusicae*. The case concerned the refusal of a commercial company, which provided internet access services, Telefónica, to disclose to Promusicae, a non-profit-making organization of producers and publishers of musical and audiovisual recordings, acting on behalf of its members who were holders of intellectual property rights, personal data of certain people whom it provided with internet access services. Promusicae sought disclosure of the above information in order to be able to bring civil proceedings against those persons, who, according to it, used the KaZaA file exchange program (peer-to-peer) and provided access in shared files of personal computers to phonograms in which the members of Promusicae held the exploitation rights. The ECJ concluded that there was a 'need to reconcile the requirements of the protection of different fundamental rights, namely the right to respect for private life on the one hand and the rights to protection of property and to an effective remedy on the other.' However, it left the task of balancing to the national court.

3. THE EXTERNAL DIMENSION OF DATA PROTECTION: TRANSFER OF DATA TO THIRD COUNTRIES

3.1 The Data Protection Directive Regime

Transborder data flows are an everyday reality in today's globalized world. They facilitate international commerce and the provision of services across borders and take place in a number of different contexts and for various reasons. For instance, a company, the administration or even an individual, may export data e.g. to perform a contract, to obtain from a third country certain technical applications (such as the backing up or storage of data), or to build up a common database concerning individuals located in different countries. The Data Protection Directive did not leave this field unregulated. The Community legislator opted for a centralized model for transfer of data to third states, which means that the Community institutions have a saying on the transborder data flows in order to ensure that personal data are protected.

More particularly, Article 25 (1) of the Data Protection Directive stipulates that the transfer to a third country of personal data which are undergoing processing or are intended for processing after transfer may take place only if the third country in question ensures an 'adequate level of protection.' Member States and Commission shall inform each other of cases where they consider that a third country does not ensure an adequate level of protection. However, it is the Commission that has the last word on the assessment of the adequacy of the protection provided by a third country. Such a decision is taken under a complex comitology procedure, which involves: a proposal from the Commission; an opinion of the Article 29 Working Party; an opinion of the Article 31 Management committee delivered by a qualified majority of Member States; a thirty-day right of scrutiny by the European Parliament to check if the Commission has used its executing powers correctly; the decision is adopted finally by the College of Commissioners.

The central question here is what constitutes an 'adequate level of protection'. According to the Methodology Paper adopted by the Article 29 Working Party (1998), the concept of adequate protection has to be distinguished from other concepts like the concepts of 'equivalent protection' or 'sufficient protection.' An assessment of the adequacy of protection entails a consideration of the specific privacy risks linked with a transborder data flow by taking into account the number and quality of the data transferred, the types of usages pursued by the transfer, the eventual onward transfers, etc. In this context, it must be pointed out that any regulatory regime including contractual provisions, self-regulatory systems or even the technology itself might be taken into consideration with regard to the assessment of the adequacy of the protection. The Directive's approach to the standard of adequate protection is characterized as open, pragmatic, relying on self-regulation, functional and risk-oriented (Poullet, 2007, p. 8). Poullet argues in particular that this attitude is the contrary to any EU imperialism as regards the way in which the protection would have to be ensured (Poullet, 2003, p. 242).

The present contribution submits that the adequacy principle ensures, in principle, a high level of protection of the right to privacy in transborder data flows. This is because the adequacy judgment is taken by a case by case approach which analyzes the protection of personal data that is 'effectively' offered by the recipient. The Commission has so far recognized Switzerland, Canada, Argentina, Guernsey, Isle of Man, the US Department of Commerce's Safe Harbor Privacy

Principles, and the transfer of PNR to the US as providing adequate protection.

However, even when there is no adequate protection, transfers may still take place under the specific circumstances provided for in Article 26. This is the case, among others, if the data subject has given his unambiguous consent to the transfer; and the transfer is necessary: for the performance of a contract; for important public interest grounds; and in order to protect the vital interests of the data subject.

The existence of these exceptions is not always enough. This is because in most cases that a third country is found not to provide an adequate level of protection, individuals may be reluctant to give their consent to the transfer of their personal data (de Hert & B. de Schutter, 2008, p. 317). The Data Protection Directive takes into account this reality by providing that a Member State may authorize a transfer of personal data to a third country which does not ensure an adequate level of protection, where the controller adduces adequate safeguards with respect to the protection of the privacy and fundamental rights and freedoms of individuals; such safeguards may in particular result from appropriate contractual clauses. In this regard, companies operating worldwide may indeed wish to establish such safeguards in order to be able to continue their commercial transactions without being dependent on the good will of the legislators in their country (de Hert & B. de Schutter, 2008, p. 317).

3.2 The *PNR* Cases

Following the terrorist attacks of 9/11, the United States passed legislation in November 2001 providing that air carriers operating flights to or from the US or across US territory had to provide the United States customs authorities with electronic access to the data contained in their automated reservation and departure control systems, referred to as 'Passenger Name Records' ('PNR data'). The PNR data comprised up to 34 fields of data, including not only names and addresses, but also contact details such as telephone numbers, e-mail addresses, information about bank numbers and credit cards, even information about meals ordered for the flights. As seen above, the Data Protection Directive stipulates that personal data can only be transferred to third countries which provide an adequate level of protection. Airlines operating transatlantic flights thus found themselves in the position of having to choose between offending either US aviation security requirements or EU data protection standards. Recognizing this situation, the Commission entered into negotiations with the US Department of Homeland Security (DHS), and upon a Decision on adequacy adopted by the Commission on 14 May 2004, on the basis of Article 25 (6) of the Data Protection Directive, the Council adopted on 17 May 2004 a Decision allowing for the conclusion of an Agreement between the Community and the US on the transfer of PNR.

The European Parliament brought an action before the Court seeking the annulment of both the Commission's Decision on adequacy and the Council's Decision on the conclusion of the agreement, on the grounds *inter alia* of breaching the fundamental principles of the Data Protection Directive and the right to privacy (*European Parliament* v. *Council and Commission (PNR))*.

The Court did not examine the European Parliament's plea that the transfer of such an amount of data to the US (some of which were even sensitive) without proper guarantees infringed the right to privacy of individuals. Instead it adopted a rather formalistic approach (de Witte, 2008, p.11) and annulled the Adequacy Decision on the sole ground that its subject matter was outside the material scope of the Data Protection Directive. It held that the transfer of PNR data constituted processing operations concerning 'public security and the activities of the State in areas of criminal law' as referred to in Article 3(2) of Directive 95/46, and thus the adequacy decision could not be adopted under this Directive. The Court distinguished between the initial collection of the PNR data by the airlines which constituted data processing necessary for a supply of services, and thus fell within the scope of Community law, from the data processing used for public security and law-enforcement purposes. Similarly, without engaging in an extensive analysis, the ECJ annulled the Council's Decision on the conclusion of the Agreement, on the basis that it could not be adopted on the legal basis of Article 95 EC, because it related to 'the same transfer of data as the decision on adequacy and therefore to data processing operations which, are excluded from the scope of the Directive' (*PNR*, para 68). The judgment has been criticized for a number of reasons. The ruling was characterized as a 'Pyrrhic victory' for the European Parliament (Gilmore & Rijpma, 2007, p. 1099). Cremona (2008) points out: 'The PNR case is a good example of the difficulty of allocating an international agreement to the correct legal base (and pillar), and of the consequences of getting it wrong' (p. 17). From the point of view of the fundamental right to privacy, it is certainly very disappointing. By transferring the PNR Agreement from the Community competence to the third pillar, with all the consequences regarding judicial review and democratic control arising therefrom, the Court created, as the EDPS noted, 'a loophole in the right of data protection' of the individual. More importantly, as a result of the ECJ's ruling, the EU had to negotiate and conclude new agreements with the USA, based this time on the correct legal basis, with even more serious implications on the right to data protection (Papakonstantinou & de Hert, 2009, p. 885).

4. CONCLUSION

As Simitis highlighted, the commitment of the Community to fundamental rights 'forces it to achieve not merely some level of protection, but protection of "a high degree," which in the Union's language means the maximum possible' (Simitis, 1995, p. 452). Is that statement true with respect to the right to information privacy in the EU?

The examination of the data protection legal framework has revealed an overall satisfactory picture. In the current state of affairs, the recent developments that mark the constitutional consecration of the right to data protection as an autonomous fundamental right within the EU are certainly to be considered as positive. As far as the legislative documents under the former first pillar are concerned, both the Data Protection Directive and the e-Privacy Directive provide for a high level of protection of fundamental rights, while ensuring at the same time the free movement of data. In particular, the Data Protection Directive represents a remarkable example of the promotion of a high level of protection of fundamental rights in the name of internal market concerns.

The dynamic of the existing data protection legislation can also be found in the outstanding zeal of bodies, such as the Article 29 Working Party and the European Data Protection Supervisor to put data protection concerns at the top of the agenda of the Union lawmaker. In particular, the opinions and recommendations of the Working Party, insofar as they are taken into account by the national Data Protection Authorities, contribute to the development of a common EU high standard of personal data protection. The role of the European courts should not be forgotten here. By reading broadly a common market measure, the European Court of Justice has enhanced the protection of the right to privacy in the Community.

However, there are a number of points that need to be taken into consideration. First of all, the exclusion from the scope of application of the Data Protection Directive and the e-Privacy Directive of activities concerning public security, defense, State security (including the economic well-being of the State when the processing operation relates to State security matters) and the activities of the State in areas of criminal law is rather problematic. Second, certain uncertainties still exist concerning the definitions of concepts that are central to the data protection regime such as the definition of 'personal data' itself, or of 'processing.' This certainly makes more difficult the full and effective compliance of national legislation with the EC data protection regime. Furthermore, there are some fields, such as for instance the employment relationship, that possible would require even further protective measures than those provided by the existing legal framework. A further crucial question concerns the effective implementation of the EC Data Protection framework at the national level. In particular, the independence problems and the limitation of competences of the national data protection authorities in certain Member States may constitute a violation of the EU Data Protection legislation. The role of the Commission at this point is crucial to employ its armory in order to safeguard the better application of EU legislation. Finally, recent technological developments in the field of surveillance cannot be disregarded and the fundamental question posed is whether the EU data protection regime can face effectively the new challenges.

Two recent Eurobarometer surveys reveal important information concerning the EU citizens' awareness with regard to their right to data protection. A first conclusion of these surveys is that the majority of EU citizens tend to see low levels of data protection in their own country. What's even worse, the national data protection authorities are relatively unknown to most EU citizens. The studies reveal that effective data protection in the EU is somehow affected by the low level of full awareness of EU citizens of their rights. Consequently, raising awareness is very important for the effective and comprehensive application of the existing EU legislation.

Following the terrorist attacks in New York, Madrid and London, the EU data protection regime has taken a new turn. Now the challenge is to safeguard privacy against security interests. In this respect, one might wonder whether the Data Retention Directive represents the beginning of the erosion of European privacy safeguards (Covington & Burling, 2003, p. 11). Although the present study concluded that this measure interferes disproportionately with the right to privacy, it will not adopt such a pessimistic analysis. Privacy watchdogs, civil liberties groups, national courts may still challenge before the ECJ the validity of the Directive on the basis of human rights. In such a case, it is submitted that the Court should uphold its role as guardian of fundamental rights within the EU legal order and annul this legislative measure.

The present contribution did not address the data protection regime in police and judicial cooperation (Hijmans & Scirocco, 2009, p. 1514), where – still, after the entry into force of the Lisbon Treaty- different levels of protection from the ones in the former first pillar continue to apply.

What should one expect from the future concerning data protection at the EU level? The answer is certainly not simple. The present study submits that there is a pressing need to put an end to the worrying increasing of provisions and measures limiting the protection of personal data on the most diverse grounds and to adopt common standards of protection of personal data –on the basis of the Data Protection Directive- in all areas, especially now that the abolition of the pillar structure of the EU is a reality.

REFERENCES

Andenas, M., & Zleptnig, S. (2003). Surveillance and data protection: Regulatory approaches in the EU and member Ssates. *European Business Law Review*, *14*(6), 765.

Article 29 Data Protection Working Party. (1998). Working Document on transfers of personal data to third countries: Applying Articles 25 and 26 of the EU data protection directive, 24 July 1998, WP 12. Retrieved May 5, 2009, from [REMOVED HYPERLINK FIELD]http://www.europa.eu.int/comm/internal_market/en/dataprot/wpdocs/wp12en.htm

Article 29 Data Protection Working Party. (2007, April). Opinion on the concept of personal data.

Article 29 Working Party. (2004). Opinion 9/2004 on a draft Framework Decision on the storage of data processed and retained for the purpose of providing electronic public communications services or data available in public communications networks with a view to the prevention, investigation, detection and prosecution of criminal acts, including terrorism. [Proposal presented by France, Ireland, Sweden and Great Britain (Council doc. 8958/04 – April 28, 2004)].

Article 29 Working Party. (2005a). Opinion 4/2005 on the Proposal for a Directive of the European Parliament and of the Council on the Retention of Data Processed in Connection with the Provision of Public Electronic Communication Services and Amending Directive 2002/58/EC (COM(2005)438 final of 21.09.2005).

Article 29 Working Party. (2005b). Opinion 113/2005 on the Proposal for a Directive of the European Parliament and of the Council on the Retention of Data Processed in Connection with the Provision of Public Electronic Communication Services and Amending Directive 2002/58/EC (COM (2005) 438 final of 21.09.2005).

Article 29 Working Party. (2006a). Opinion 3/2006 on the Directive 2006/XX/EC of the European Parliament and of the Council on the retention of data processed in connection with the provision of public electronic communication services and amending Directive 2002/58/EC, as adopted by the Council on 21 February 2006.

Article 29 Working Party. (2006b). Opinion 10/2006 on the processing of personal data by the Society for Worldwide Interbank Financial Telecommunication (SWIFT).

Balkin, J., & Levinson, S. (2006). The processes of constitutional change: From partisan entrenchment to the national surveillance state. *Fordham Law Review, 75*, 101-145. Retrieved May 5, 2009, from http://papers.ssrn.com/sol3/papers.cfm?abstract_id=930514

Banishar, D. (2000). *Privacy and human rights: An international survey of privacy laws and developments*. Washington, DC: Electronic Privacy Information Center.

Bennett, C. (1992). *Regulating privacy: Data protection and public policy in Europe and the United States*. Ithaca, NY: Cornell University Press.

Bergkamp, L. (2002). EU Data Protection Policy. *Computer Law & Security Report, 18*, 12.

Bignami, F. (2007). Privacy and law enforcement in the European Union: The Data Retention Directive. *Chicago Journal of International Law, 8*, 233.

Birnhack, M. (2008). The EU data protection directive: An engine of a global regime. *Computer Law & Security Report, 24*, 508. doi:10.1016/j.clsr.2008.09.001

Boehm, F. (2009). Confusing fundamental rights protection in Europe: Loopholes in Europe's fundamental rights protection exemplified on European data protection rules (Law Working Paper Series, no. 2009-01). Luxembourg: University of Luxembourg.

Bolman, E. (2002). Privacy in the age of information, *The Journal of Information, Law and Technology (JILT), 2002*(2). Retrieved from http://elj.warwick.ac.uk/jilt/02-2/bohlman.html

Breyer, P. (2005). Telecommunications data retention and human rights: the compatibility of blanket traffic data retention with ECHR. *European Law Journal, 11*(3), 365. doi:10.1111/j.1468-0386.2005.00264.x

Bygrave, L. A. (2004). Privacy protection in a global context: A comparative overview. *Scandinavian Studies in Law*, *47*, 319.

Covington & Burling. (2003). Memorandum of laws concerning the legality of data retention with regard to the rights guaranteed by the European Convention on Human Rights. London: Privacy International. Retrieved May 15, 2009, from http://www.statewatch.org/news/2003/oct/Data_Retention_Memo.pdf

Cremona, M. (2008). EU external action in the JHA domain: A legal perspective. EUI Working Papers, Law 2008/24.

Davies, S. (1996). *Big brother: Britain's web of surveillance and the new technological order.* London: Pan.

De Witte, B. (2008). Too much constitutional law in the European Union's foreign relations? In Cremona, M., & de Witte, B. (Eds.), *EU foreign relations law- constitutional fundamentals* (p. 3). Oxford: Hart.

Dougan, M. (2008). The Treaty of Lisbon 2007: Winning minds, not hearts. *Common Market Law Review*, *45*, 617.

Gallup Organization. (2009, February 21). Eurobarometer survey No. 225: Data protection. Retrieved May 5, 2009, from http://ec.europa.eu/public_opinion/flash/fl_225_en.pdf

Gallup Organization. (2009, February 21). Eurobarometer survey No. 226: Data perceptions among data controllers. Retrieved May 5, 2009, from http://ec.europa.eu/public_opinion/flash/fl_226_en.pdf

Gilmore, G., & Rijpma, J. (2007). Joined cases C-317/04 and C-318/04. *Common Market Law Review*, *44*, 1081.

Goemans, C., & Dumortier, J. (2003). Enforcement issues – mandatory retention of traffic data in the EU: possible impact on privacy and on-line anonymity. Retrieved May 5, 2009, from http://www.law.kuleuven.ac.be/icri/publications/440Retention_of_traffic_data_Dumortier_Goemans.pdf?where1/4

Gonzales-Fuster, G., & Gutwirth, S. (2006). Data protection in the EU: Towards 'reflexive governance'? Retrieved May 5, 2009, from http://refgov.cpdr.ucl.ac.be/?go=publications&dc=58b4b685f4bca1bece49dd9d296e3a2683ff7256

Gutwirth, S. (2002). *Privacy and the information age*. Oxford, UK: Rowman & Littlefield Publishers.

Heisenberg, D. (2005). *Negotiating privacy: The European Union, the United States and personal data protection*. London: Lynne Rienner Publishers. De Hert, P., & de Schutter, B. (2008). International transfers of data in the field of JHA: The lessons of Europol, PNR, and Swift. In Martenczuk, B., & van Thiel, S. (Eds.), *Justice, liberty, security: New challenges for EU external relations* (p. 303). Brussels: VUB Press.

Hijmans, H. (2006). The European data protection supervisor: The institutions of the EC controlled by an independent authority. *Common Market Law Review*, *43*, 1313.

Hijmans, H., & Scirocco, A. (2009). Shortcomings in EU Data protection in the third and the second pillars. Can the Lisbon Treaty be expected to help? *Common Market Law Review*, *46*, 1485.

House of Lords European Union Committee. (2005). After Madrid: The EU's response to terrorism. [Report with evidence, 5th Report of Session 2004-05].

Kosta, E., & Valcke, P. (2006). Retaining the data retention directive. *Computer Law & Security Report*, *22*, 370. doi:10.1016/j.clsr.2006.07.002

Michael, J. (1994). *Privacy and human rights*. Paris: UNESCO.

Newman, A. (2008). Building transnational civil liberties: Transgovernmental entrepreneurs and the European Data Privacy Directive. *International Organization, 62*, 103. doi:10.1017/S0020818308080041

Nugter, A. (1990). *Transborder flow of personal data within the EC*. Boston: Kluwer Law & Taxation Publishers.

Opinion of the European Data Protection Supervisor on the Proposal for a Directive of the European Parliament and of the Council on the Retention of Data Processed in Connection with the Provision of Public Electronic Communication Services and Amending Directive 2002/58/EC, 2005 OJ (C 298) 1.

Opinion of the European Data Protection Supervisor on the Proposal for a Directive of the European Parliament and of the Council on the retention of data processed in connection with the provision of public electronic communication services and amending Directive 2002/58/EC (COM (2005) 438 final).

Papakonstantinou, V., & de Hert, P. (2009). The PNR agreement and transatlantic anti-terrorism co-operation: No firm human rights framework on either side of the Atlantic. *Common Market Law Review, 46*, 885.

Poullet, Y. (2003). Pour une justification des articles 25 et 26 de la directive européenne 95/46/CE en matière de flux transfrontières et de protection des données. In Cools, M., & de Schutter, B. (Eds.), *Ceci n'est pas un juriste- Liber Amicorum* (p. 242). Brussels: VUB Press.

Poullet, Y. (2006). The Directive 95/46/EC: Ten Years After. *Computer Law & Security Report, 22*, 206. doi:10.1016/j.clsr.2006.03.004

Poullet, Y. (March 2007). *Transborder data flows and extraterritoriality: The European position*. Paper presented at the Public Seminar of the European Parliament: PNR/SWIFT/Safe Harbour: Are transatlantic data protected? Retrieved May 5, 2009, from http://www.europarl.europa.eu/hearings/20070326/libe/poullet_en.pdf

Rodota, S. (March 2007). *The European constitutional model for data protection*. Paper presented at the Public Seminar of the European Parliament: PNR/SWIFT/Safe Harbour: Are transatlantic data protected? (Transatlantic relations and data protection). Retrieved May 5, 2009, from http://www.europarl.europa.eu/hearings/20070326/libe/rodota_en.pdf

Simitis, S. (1995). From the market to the polis: The EU directive on the protection of personal data. *Iowa Law Review, 80*(3), 440.

Skandamis, N., Sigalas, F., & Stratakis, S. (2007). *Rival freedoms in terms of security: The case of data protection and the criterion of connexity* [CEPS Policy Briefs, Research Paper No.7]. Brussels: Centre for European Policy Studies. European Convention. (2003, June 9). Updated Explanations relating to the text of the Charter of Fundamental Rights, CONV 823/03.

Webb, P. (2003). A comparative analysis of data protection laws in Australia and Germany. *The Journal of Information, Law and Technology* (JILT). Retrieved May 5, 2009, from http://elj.warwick.ac.uk/jilt/03-2/webb.html

APPENDIX: TABLE OF CASES

European Court of Justice and Court of First Instance

Joined Cases C-465/00, C-138/01 & C-139/01, *Österreichischer Rundfunk*, Judgment of 20 May 2003, Full Court, [2003] ECR I-4989.

Case C-101/01 *Bodil Lindqvist* [2003] ECR I-12971.

Joined Cases C-317/04 and C-318/04, *European Parliament* v. *Council and Commission (PNR)*, Judgment of the Grand Chamber of 30 May 2006, [2006] ECR I-4721.

Case T- 194/04 *Bavarian Lager Co. Ltd v Commission*, judgment of 8 November 2007.

Case C-275/06 *Productores de Música de España (Promusicae) v Telefónica de España SAU*, judgment of 29 January 2008.

Case C-524/06 *Huber v Bundesrepublic Deutschland,* judgment of 16 December 2008.

Case C-73/07 *Satakunnan Markkinapörssi and Satamedia*, judgment of 16 December 2008.

Case C-301/06 *Ireland v. European Parliament and Council*, Judgment of the Grand Chamber of 10 February 2009.

Case C-557/07 *LSG-Gesellschaft*, judgment of 19 February 2009.

Case C-553/07 *Rijkeboer*, judgment of 7 May 2009.

Case C-518/07 *Commission v Germany*, judgment of 9 March 2010.

European Court of Human Rights

Klass and Others v Germany, (1978), Series A, No 28

Kruslin v France, (1990), Series A, No 176-A

Leander v. Sweden, judgment of 26 March 1987, Series A no. 116, p. 22

Rotaru v. Romania, judgment of 4 May 2000 (Application no. 28341/95)

Sunday Times v United Kingdom, (1979), Series A, No 30

Tyrer v UK (1978) Series A of the Publications of the European Court of Human Rights, No 26.

Z. v. Finland (Appl. No. 22009/93), judgment of 25 February 1997, *Rep.* 1997-I

German Constitutional Court

1 BvR 256/08, 1 BvR 263/08, 1 BvR 586/08, Urteil vom 2. März 2010

Chapter 17
Cross-Border Transfer of Personal Data:
The Example of Romanian Legislation

Grigore-Octav Stan
Salans, Romania and King's College London, UK

Georgiana Ghitu
DLA Piper, Romania

ABSTRACT

This chapter outlines the Romanian data protection legal regime governing the cross-border transfers of personal data, both to countries located in the European Union (EU) or in the European Economic Area (EEA), as well as to non-EU or non-EEA countries. In addressing the Romanian legal requirements related to international transfers of personal data, a high level insight into the background of Romanian data protection principles and main rules applicable in the broader context of privacy proves useful. Although this chapter analyzes mainly the Romanian legal regime of data protection, with a special emphasis on cross-border transfer of personal data, a similar interpretation and application of the data protection related requirements may also be encountered in other European jurisdictions. While expounding primarily on data transfer related matters, this chapter also looks at how the EU Data Protection Directive (Directive No. 95/46 EC), as well as the relevant secondary legislation in the field of data protection, has been implemented into Romanian law.

1. INTRODUCTION

In a world characterized by constant interaction between individuals' fundamental rights (including the right to privacy) and global corporate entities highly business oriented, data protection is a noteworthy area whose complexity and requirements may give rise to major practical concerns. In order to mitigate potential issues arising thereof (as their elimination may prove difficult, despite any intent to observe data protection requirements), both companies engaged in businesses covering a worldwide area, as well as locally based companies should be aware of the major importance that data protection requirements have over their businesses. As transfers of personal data frequently occur in the international business environment, and the processing of per-

DOI: 10.4018/978-1-60960-083-9.ch017

sonal data of the companies' clients, employees, partners etc. is usually inherent to the companies' day-to-day activity, consideration to the specific Romanian requirements for cross-border transfers of personal data should be given. Moreover, as such transfers of personal data represent a form of data processing (as such concept will be further explained herein), the present paper also reiterates the general principles applicable to the personal data processing, as set forth by Romanian legislation in force as of March 31, 2010.

In line with European legislation aimed at offering an adequate level of data protection, Romania has implemented the EU Data Protection Directive that sets out the legal framework for the processing of the individuals' personal data. The Romanian implementation law no. 677/2001 on the protection of individuals with regard to the processing of personal data and on the free movement of such data (the "Data Protection Law"), as well as the secondary domestic legislation, generally takes over the key concepts and principles of the EU Data Protection Directive, thus integrating itself into a system of supranational law focused on facilitating the free movement of personal data.

Although the main subject of this paper is represented by the requirements set forth by the Romanian legislation in the field of cross-border transfer of personal data, certain preliminary observations should be nevertheless made with respect to the general principles arising out of the Data Protection Law, as well as a brief outline of the main data protection related concepts.

2. BACKGROUND OF ROMANIAN DATA PROTECTION LAW

Giving effect to the EU Data Protection Directive that "seeks to establish an equivalent level of protection for personal data in all Member States, so as to facilitate the transfer of personal data across national boundaries within the European Union" (Carey, 2009, p. 6), the Romanian Data Protection Law has as its main purpose the protection of the individuals' fundamental rights and liberties, especially the right to intimacy, family and private life, with respect to the processing of personal data.

2.1. The Main Features of the Romanian Data Protection Law

The main features of the Romanian Data Protection Law are given by the following aspects:

2.1.1. Scope of Application

The Data Protection Law is intended to apply to personal data processed wholly or in part by automatic means, as well as to processing of personal data within an evidentiary system or data that are intended to be included in such system by other means than the automatic ones. The abovementioned law applies to the processing of personal data carried out by either natural or legal persons, Romanian or foreign, public or private entities, irrespective of whether the processing is performed in the public sector or in the private sector. Specifically, the Data Protection Law details the sphere of its application, setting out three categories of personal data processing that are subject to its requirements, namely:

(i) processing of personal data carried out in the context of the activities of a data controller established in Romania. Pursuant to the Romanian Data Protection Law, the data controller is defined as "any natural person or private or public legal person, including public authorities, institutions and their territorial structures, that determines the purposes and means of the processing of personal data; where the purposes and means of processing are determined by a legislative act or on the basis of a legislative act, the data controller is the natural person or the public or private legal person designated by the respective piece of legislation or on the basis of such act."

(ii) processing of personal data carried out in the context of the activities performed by Romanian diplomatic missions or by consular offices;

(iii) processing of personal data carried out in the context of the activities of data controllers that are not established in Romania, and that, for purposes of processing personal data, make use of means of whatever nature situated on the territory of Romania, unless such means are only used for purposes of transit through the territory of Romania. Under such circumstances, the data controller has the obligation to designate a representative that must be established in Romania that must also observe the provisions of the Data Protection Law.

In the latter case, the applicability of the legal requirements should be interpreted in a different light following the adherence of Romania to the European Union (EU) on 1 January 2007. Thus, the Romanian National Supervisory Authority for Personal Data Processing (the "Data Protection Authority") outlines that the obligation of the data controller to designate a representative established in Romania exists only in case the data controller is not located within the European Community (Data Protection Authority Activity report for 2008, 2008). Such interpretation is in line with both the requirements of the EU Data Protection Directive, as well as with the provisions of the Romanian Constitution and the principle of the priority of community law set forth by the Court of Justice of the European Communities. As a result, only the data controller that is not located within the Community shall assign a representative in Romania.

As regards the types of personal data exempted from the scope of application of the data protection requirements, the Romanian Data Protection Law expressly sets forth that its scope of application excludes the processing of personal data performed "by natural persons exclusively in the course of their purely personal activities, in case the respective data are not intended to be disclosed." Furthermore, the processing and the transfer of personal data carried out in the context of the activities relating to national defense and security are not subject to the Romanian Data Protection Law.

2.1.2. Principles for Personal Data Processing

The Romanian Data Protection Law sets forth the general rules that should be observed in case of personal data processing and that are significantly similar to the ones established by the EU Data Protection Directive. The processing of personal data under Romanian law is governed by the following principles:

(i) **Good-faith:** personal data must be processed in good-faith and in accordance with the relevant legal provisions. The lawful processing of personal data requires full compliance with the conditions provided by the Data Protection Law for any of the activities defining the concept of "processing of personal data," including collection, recording, organization, storage, adaptation or alteration, retrieval, consultation, use, disclosure by transmission, blocking, erasure or destruction of personal data.

(ii) **Legitimacy:** personal data must be collected for specified, explicit and legitimate purposes. The legitimacy of personal data processing mainly consists in both obtaining the consent of the data subject whose personal data are envisaged to be processed prior to the commencement of the data processing, as well in complying with the information requirements (including both the data controller's information obligation towards the data subject, as well as the notification given to the Data Protection Authority). Consequently, personal data cannot be processed for other purposes than those initially mentioned.

(iii) **Proportionality:** personal data processing must be adequate, relevant and not excessive in relation to the purposes for which they are collected and / or further processed.

(iv) **Accuracy:** personal data must be accurate and, where necessary, kept up to date; for such purpose, every necessary measures shall be undertaken to ensure that data which are inaccurate or incomplete, having regard to the purposes for which they are collected and for which they are further processed, are erased or rectified.

(v) **Limitation:** personal data subject to data processing must be kept in a form that permits identification of the data subjects for no longer than necessary in order to achieve the purposes for which the data were collected or for which they are further processed. The storage of personal data for a longer period than the one initially declared, for historical, statistical or scientific use, may occur provided that the safeguard measures for personal data processing are observed and for no longer periods than necessary for such purposes.

(vi) **Security:** the data controller is under the obligation to implement appropriate technical and organizational measures for the protection of personal data against accidental or unlawful destruction, loss, alteration, unauthorized disclosure or access, in particular where the data processing involves the transmission of data over a network, as well as against all other unlawful forms of data processing. Furthermore, when the data controller designates a data processor for processing personal data on its behalf, it must prove diligence in electing a person that offers sufficient guarantees with respect to the technical and organizational measures for the processing to be carried out and, moreover, it must supervise the data processor's compliance with such measures. The data processor's undertakings related to, *inter alia*, its obligation to act only on the basis of the instructions given by the data controller must be reflected in a written agreement concluded with the latter.

(vii) **Data transfer:** the Data Protection Law mandates that the transfer outside Romania of personal data that are subject to data processing or that are intended to be processed following the transfer may only take place provided that Romanian law requirements are observed, and that the country where the personal data are transferred ensures an adequate level of protection.

Under Romanian law, the concept of "transfer" falls within the wide meaning of "data processing" and, thus, all legal requirements have to be considered, including a legal basis for the transfer. However, the Data Protection Law does not provide for a definition of "data transfer," but sets forth the conditions under which personal data may be transferred outside Romania, either within the EU or outside the EU.

Such conditions provided by local law must be strictly complied with, notwithstanding the global standards regarding data protection. The Article 29 Working Party highlighted that

"global standards would also facilitate trans-border data flows which, due to globalisation, are becoming the rule rather than the exception. As long as global standards do not exist, diversity will remain. Trans-border data flows have to be facilitated whilst, at the same time, ensuring a high level of protection of personal data when they are transferred to and processed in third countries." (Joint contribution to the Consultation of the European Commission on the legal framework for the fundamental right to protection of personal data, 2009, p. 10).

After having briefly outlined the main key features of the Romanian Data Protection Law, the present paper will further detail the Romanian legal requirements that need to be observed when carrying out transfers of personal data outside Romania. As already mentioned, *data transfer* represents a form of *data processing* and, consequently, a lawful transfer of personal data will have to comply with all legal requirements. Before analyzing the concrete conditions for data transfer, it should be noted that there are certain special categories of personal data that benefit from a special legal protection, in the sense that the Data Protection Law allows their processing with the observance of specific rules.

Although they are not expressly named as such by the Data Protection Law, such special categories of personal data are referred to as "sensitive data" and they represent "a subset or category of personal data for which stronger protections apply" (Carey, 2009, p. 81).

2.2. Processing of Sensitive Data under Romanian Data Protection Law

Sensitive data are comprised of the following types of personal data: (i) personal data related to racial or ethnic origin, political opinions, religious or philosophical beliefs, trade union membership and data concerning health or sex life; (ii) personal data for identification purposes; (iii) personal data related to health; or (iv) personal data with respect to offences, criminal offences or security measures. Similar to the provisions of the EU Data Protection Directive stating basically that "such data may generally not be processed, except under certain clearly-defined circumstances" (Kuner, 2007, p. 10), the Romanian Data Protection Law generally prohibits the processing of sensitive personal data, except for certain expressly mentioned cases.

The Data Protection Law provides specific exceptional cases when each of the categories of sensitive data mentioned above may be processed. As a rule, the processing of sensitive data within the first category mentioned above is prohibited. By way of exception, such processing is allowed in certain cases expressly set forth by the Data Protection Law, including, *inter alia*, the cases when (i) the data subject "has given his/her express consent to the processing of those data"; (ii) processing "is necessary for the purposes of carrying out the obligations and specific rights of the controller in the field of employment law while observing the guarantees provided by law"; (iii) processing "is necessary to protect the vital interests of the data subject or for the purposes of preventive medicine and medical diagnosis."

The processing of the personal identification number or of any other identifier of general application may be performed provided that: (i) the data subject has given his/her express consent to the processing; or (ii) the processing of such data is expressly provided by law. The Data Protection Authority may establish other cases when the processing is allowed, provided that adequate guarantees for the protection of the data subject's rights are established.

The Romanian Data Protection Law expressly states that "the processing of data relating to criminal offences, criminal convictions, security measures, administrative fines applied to an individual may be carried out only by and under the control of public authorities, within the limits conferred to them by law and under the conditions provided by special regulations."

The abovementioned special categories of data are considered *data likely to trigger special risks for the rights and obligations of the data subject* and, thus, the provisions of the Decision No. 11/2009 issued by the Data Protection Authority must be observed. Pursuant to that Decision, the processing of the abovementioned categories of data is subject to a prior control carried out by the Data Protection Authority, under the conditions provided by the Data Protection Law. Moreover, the data controllers are under the obligation to notify to the Data Protection Authority the processing of such sensitive personal data at least 30 (thirty) days prior to the commencement of the processing. The Data Protection Authority is under the obligation to inform the data controller with respect to the result of the control and the decision taken following the control within maximum 30 (thirty) days from the moment it has been notified by the data controller.

2.3. Consent Requirements for the Collection and Cross-Border Transfer of the Personal Data

As mentioned above, the processing of personal data (including the cross-border transfer of such data) must be fair and lawful, and the legitimization of the processing is conferred by compliance with a set of conditions set out in the Data Protection Law.

Strengthening this idea and following the European principle of legitimacy, the Data Protection Law mandates that, as a rule, any processing of personal data may be carried out only provided that the data subject has given his/her express and unequivocal consent to such processing. As opposed to the EU Data Protection Directive that defines the concept of "consent" as "any freely given, specific and informed indication of his wishes by which the data subject signifies his agreement to personal data relating to him being processed," the Romanian Data Protection Law does not provide for a definition thereof. Moreover, while the EU Data Protection Directive provides as a condition for the fair processing of personal data an "unambiguous consent" and thus, it does not clearly indicate whether the consent should be "opt-in" (namely, it results from an action") or "opt-out" (as it does in Article 8 when dealing with the processing of sensitive personal data), the Romanian Data Protection Law provides for an "express" consent. However, the Data Protection Law does not require the consent to be in writing, except for one specific case of transfer of sensitive personal data abroad. Carey (2009) reiterates, with respect to the EU Data Protection Directive rules that "there is no requirement that consent must be in writing, although for the protection of the data controller it is suggested that some form of permanent record should be kept of those consents on which the data controller wishes to rely to legitimize its processing" (p. 67).

Nothwistanding the above, it should also be noted that the Data Protection Law sets out certain exceptional cases when the processing of personal data may be performed without the consent of the respective data subject, as follows:

(i) the processing is necessary in view of executing an agreement or a pre-agreement to which the data subject is a party or in view of taking some measures, at the data subject's request, before concluding an agreement or a pre-agreement;
(ii) the processing is necessary in view of protecting the life, physical integrity or health of the data subject or of another threatened person;
(iii) the processing is necessary for the fulfilment of the data controller's legal obligation;
(iv) the processing is necessary for the purposes of the legitimate interests pursued by the data controller or by the third party or parties to whom the data are disclosed, except where such interests are overridden by the interests or fundamental rights and freedoms of the data subject;
(v) the processing relates to data obtained from documents that are accessible to the public, pursuant to the law;
(vi) the processing is carried out exclusively for statistical purposes, for historic or scientific research, and the data processed remain anonymous throughout the processing;
(vii) the processing is necessary for the fulfilment of certain measures of public interest or that relate to the exercise of public authority prerogatives that the data controller or the

third party to whom the data is disclosed are vested with.

As in Romania the jurisprudence and common practices in the area of personal data protection are not yet sufficiently developed, the interpretation and identification of the sphere of application of each of the abovementioned exceptional cases lies with the Data Protection Authority. European doctrine and jurisprudence may prove useful tools in offering examples of what may fall within the exceptional cases when the consent of the data subject is not required by law for the processing of personal data.

By way of example, the contractual necessity referred to in the exception mentioned at point (i) above was exemplified in European doctrine (Carey, 2009, p. 68) with the case of a purchaser passing his details to the issuer of his credit card for payment purposes or with the case of sending a data subject's name and address to a courier for the delivery of items bought by the data subject. Moreover, Carey (2009) underlines that "significantly, the sending of direct marketing materials to a customer will not usually be a contractual necessity under the original purchase agreement" (p. 68).

Moreover, the exception grounded on the legal obligation placed on the data controller (mentioned at point (iii) above) could be successfully argued in case of a data controller providing "certain information to the police where such information is necessary for the investigation of a criminal offence," provided that the data controller ensures that it is "under a legal obligation to supply such information" (Carey, 2009, p. 69).

Serious health issues that may be faced by the data subject, as well as significant damages to the data subject's property could justify the exception provided by the Data Protection Law and mentioned at point (ii) above.

A controversial exception may be the one related to the data controller's "legitimate interests" due to the broad wording and lack of any further details regarding such concept. It is worth highlighting the guidance provided by the Article 29 Working Party on what is necessary in assessing whether the "legitimate interests" condition is satisfied in a particular case. The Opinion 10/2006 on the SWIFT processing of the Article 29 Working Party states that:

"Article 7 (f) of the Directive [implemented by the Romanian Data Protection Law in Article 5 paragraph (2) letter (e)] requires a balance to be struck between the legitimate interest pursued by the processing of personal data and the fundamental rights of data subjects. This balance interest test should take into account issues of proportionality, subsidiarity, the seriousness of the alleged offences that can be notified and the consequences for the data subjects. In the context of the balance of interest test, adequate safeguards will also have to be put in place."

It is recommendable that, whenever a data controller envisages raising the exception grounded on legitimate processing without the consent of the data subject, it bears in mind the individual's right to raise an objection at any time on compelling legitimate grounds to the processing of the data relating to them.

3. RESTRICTIONS AND REQUIREMENTS IN RELATION TO THE CROSS-BORDER TRANSFER OF PERSONAL DATA

3.1. General Comments Regarding Cross-Border Transfers of Personal Data

All the abovementioned general comments are entirely applicable to the cross-border transfer of personal data (including sensitive data) and, together with certain specific requirements provided by the Data Protection Law and secondary legislation (i.e., decisions issued by the president of the Data Protection Authority) set forth the framework for the trans-frontier flow of personal data.

The Romanian Data Protection Law does not provide a definition of the "data transfer" and neither does the EU Data Protection Directive. However, the conditions for legitimizing the cross-border data flow are expressly regulated so that the protection afforded by law is appropriately conferred to the data subjects.

Similar to the EU Data Protection Directive, the Romanian Data Protection Law sets out the general rule pursuant to which the cross-border transfer of personal data undergoing processing or intended for processing after transfer is permitted only if the receiving country in question ensures an adequate level of protection. This criterion also justifies the fact that the cross-border transfer of personal data to EU countries is subject to different requirements than the cross-border transfer of personal data to a non-EU country (hereinafter referred to as "third countries"). The abovementioned rule regarding cross-border transfers of personal data is referred to in the European doctrine and jurisprudence as the "Eighth Principle." This principle contains the personal data export ban that basically provides for the prohibition to transfer personal data to countries outside of the European Economic Area (i.e., third countries), "save for the cases where the exceptions or derogations can be claimed, unless the destination country [...] has an adequate level of personal data protection" (Jay, 2007, p. 298). A more detailed analysis of the Eighth Principle export ban and corresponding exemptions is presented below.

3.2. Legal Basis for the Processing of Personal Data

As already mentioned, the transfer of personal data abroad is deemed to be a form of "data processing" that must comply with all requirements for personal data processing provided by local law. This assertion is sustained by the Data Protection Law itself that states:

The transfer to another country of personal data which are undergoing processing or are intended for processing after transfer may take place only provided that the Romanian law is complied with, and the country where the personal data are transferred ensures an adequate level of protection. [Emphasis added by the authors]

The necessity of corroboration of the special provisions regulating the cross-border transfer of personal data with the general provisions regarding the principles and conditions for the processing of personal data in general is also stressed out by the Article 29 Working Party in its Opinion 10/2006 on the SWIFT processing. Thus, it is reiterated that:

"any transfer of data generated within EU territory that is to be used outside EU territory has to be subject to an adequacy assessment pursuant to the Directive [and, implicitly, pursuant to the national law implementing the Directive, i.e., the Romanian Data Protection Law]. Furthermore, the provisions of the Directive [and, implicitly, of the Romanian Data Protection Law] relating to transfers of personal data to third countries cannot be applied separately from other provisions of the Directive [and, implicitly, of the Romanian Data Protection Law]. As explicitly mentioned in Article 25(1), these provisions apply 'without prejudice to compliance with the national provisions adopted pursuant to the other provisions of this Directive.' This means that regardless of the provisions relied upon for the purpose of data transfer to a third country, other relevant provisions of the Directive [and, respectively, of the Romanian Data Protection Law] need to be respected."

Therefore, beyond the special requirements for the data transfer, all the other conditions for the lawful processing of personal data must be met by the exporting data controller. That is why

European doctrine (Kuner, 2007. p. 160) considers that the transfer of personal data abroad is a two-step procedure that consists in identifying: (i) a legal basis for carrying out a data transfer under the national law of the country of export, since a data transfer is a form of data processing which requires a legal basis; and (ii) a legal basis for the international transfer so as to ensure that the transferred data will enjoy "adequate protection" in the country of import.

As regards the first step that should be undertaken by any data controller before performing a data transfer, Data Protection Law generally requires the data subject's consent to the processing of its personal data and, thus, a legal basis for the transfer of personal data outside Romania will often consist in the consent of the data subject whose personal data are being transferred. However, as detailed above, Romanian law provides for several exemptions from the consent requirement.

3.3. Information Requirements

Nothwistanding the application of any of the exemptions provided by the Data Protection Law, it is worth mentioning that, in any case, the data subject must be informed of the data processing. This information requirements fall within the scope of the so-called "First Principle" that provides for a fair and lawful processing of personal data. Thus, "data are not to be treated as being processed fairly unless the data controller ensures [...] that the data subject is provided with certain information" (Jay, 2007, p. 221) (further referred to herein as the "required information"). The most common method used in practice for complying with this legal requirement is by providing the data subject with a notice that contains the required information.

The Romanian Data Protection Law does not require a certain form of the abovementioned notice, but expressly provides the nature of the elements that should be included in such document. Such elements, together with the timeline for complying with the information obligation, are stipulated depending on whether the personal data have been obtained directly from the data subject, or from a third party.

Although the Data Protection Law does not indicate a timeframe for providing the required information in case the personal data have been collected directly from the data subject, it may be construed that the data controller will have to comply with this obligation before or at the time when the data are collected from the data subject. When the personal data are not obtained directly from the data subject (e.g., the data have been obtained following a transfer from another data controller or from a relative of the data subject), the Data Protection Law mandates that the data controller is obliged to provide the required information (i) at the time the data are collected; or, (ii) in case a disclosure to a third party is envisaged, at the moment the data are first disclosed, at the latest.

While the abovementioned timeframe is being observed, the data subject whose personal data are processed by the data controller must be informed by the latter with respect to at least the following elements:

(a) the identity of the data controller;
(b) the identity of any nominated representative of the data controller (such requirement is relevant only if the data controller is located in a country outside of the EEA);
(c) the purpose for the processing of personal data;
(d) additional information, such as:
    - the category of personal data that is envisaged to be processed (e.g. images, voices, physical features);
    - the recipients or categories of recipients, namely the entities/persons to which the personal data is disclosed; and
    - the existence of the rights the respective data subject benefits from (more specifically the rights provided by the

Data Protection Law, mainly: (i) the right of access to the personal data, (ii) the right to interfere with the personal data, (iii) the opposition right, as well as (iv) the conditions under which such rights may be exercised by the respective data subject).

Moreover, the Data Protection Law allows certain exemptions from the obligation to provide the required information, but only in the case when the personal data are obtained from a person/entity other than the data subject. An interesting exemption may prove the one referring to the "disproportionate effort" that the provision of the required information would involve. However, difficulties for a data controller invoking this exemption are mainly generated by the fact that the term "disproportionate effort" is not defined by the Data Protection Law and, consequently, what amounts to disproportionate effort will be a question of fact analysed on a case-by-case basis.

3.4. Legal Basis for The Cross-Border Transfer of Personal Data

In short, a lawful cross- border transfer of personal data may occur in one of the following cases:

- an adequate level of data protection is ensured by the country where the personal data are transferred, including the adherence of the data importer to the US Safe Harbour arrangement;
- standard contractual clauses provided by the European Commission are included in the agreement between the data exporter and the data importer;
- "appropriate contractual clauses" are inserted in the agreement between the data exporter and the data importer;
- one of the exemptions provided by the Data Protection Law under which transfers of personal data are authorized by the Data Protection Authority is applicable.

3.5. Data Transfers to EEA Countries

The transfer of personal data is not subject to any restrictions, as far as the Eighth Principle export ban is concerned, in case the transfer is performed to countries within the EEA (namely, the 27 EU Member States, Iceland, Liechtenstein and Norway). Consequently, a transfer to such EEA countries would be governed by the same rules as those applicable to a disclosure of personal data made within Romania. Although there is no restriction on the transfer of personal data between EEA countries with respect to the legal grounds for the transfer, any exporting data controllers should bear in mind that a data transfer amounts to data processing and, consequently, the transfer will have to be made in compliance with all the other set of rules governing the handling of personal data.

As all EEA countries are deemed to offer an "adequate level of data protection," a transfer from Romania to another EEA country cannot be restricted on the basis of the lack of adequate level of data processing. If, by way of example, the transfer envisages sensitive personal data that, exceptionally, may be processed (and, implicitly, transferred) only if the data subject has expressly consented to such processing, the fulfilment of this condition constitutes a legal basis for the transfer. Such a transfer cannot be prohibited solely based on the level of data protection provided by the EEA country where the data is transferred. If, on the contrary, the consent requirement is not observed by the data exporter located in Romania, it may not lawfully transfer the sensitive data.

Under the Data Protection Law and corresponding secondary legislation, the transfer outside Romania of personal data that will be processed after the transfer in an EU or EEA member state must be notified to the Romanian Data Protection Authority prior to its occurrence. Such notification requirement is expressly provided by Decision No. 28/2007 of the Romanian Data Protection Authority and regarding personal data transfers in other countries. Moreover, this type of transfer is not subject to an authorization from the Data Protection Authority (as is the case when it comes to transfers of personal data to third countries not ensuring an adequate level of data protection).

As regards the notification requirement, the notification is made on the basis of a standard application form whose content and format have been approved by the Data Protection Authority. This single standard application has been established by the Data Protection Authority in view of simplifying the internal notification procedure and in order to ensure compliance with the recommendation of the Article 29 Working Party expressed in its Report on the obligation to notify the national supervisory authorities, the best use of exceptions and simplification and the role of the data protection officers in the European Union adopted on 18 January 2005.

The notification of a trans-border transfer of personal data to the Data Protection Authority can be made online by filling in the standard application on a free of charge basis. Assistance with filling in the standard notification application is provided by the Data Protection Authority, which produced a Notification Guide containing clarifications on each category of information that must be provided. Pursuant to this Notification Guide, the application must include information regarding the countries where the personal data are envisaged to be transferred (EEA countries or third countries), the purpose of the transfer and the categories of personal data being transferred, as well as other information such as the data controller's identification details, the data subjects whose personal data are being transferred, the persons to whom the personal data may be disclosed.

3.6. Data Transfers to Third Countries

As regards the transfer of data to non-EU/EEA countries, the data protection related requirements differ based on whether the third country where the personal data are transferred ensures or not an "adequate level of data protection". From this perspective, the analysis below will cover the following two situations:

(i) the third country (where the data is transferred) is recognized as ensuring an adequate level of data protection; and

(ii) the third country (where the data is transferred) is not recognized as ensuring an adequate level of data protection.

3.6.1. Third Countries Ensuring an Adequate Level of Data Protection

As regards the first hypothesis mentioned at point 3.6.(i) above, it should be pointed out that under Article 25 paragraph 6 of the EU Data Protection Directive, the European Commission is entitled to consider that certain countries "have data protection regimes that it considers provide a presumption of adequacy for personal data exports" (Carey, 2009, p. 108). Such power granted to the European Commission materialized in the issuance of a number of decisions at the EU level with respect to countries and territories that ensure an adequate level of data protection. These decisions were also transposed into Romanian legislation through the decisions of the Data Protection Authority. By way of example, the following countries have been recognized by the European Commission as complying with the adequate protection criteria: Argentina, Canada, the Bailiwick of Guernsey, the Isle of Man, Switzerland and the US Safe Harbor system.

There may be cases when, in the absence of a recognition by the European Commission of the adequacy of protection provided by a third country, the Data Protection Authority is able to determine such adequacy and assess that the transfer of personal data to the third country is lawful. In making such an assessment, the Data Protection Authority takes into account the following criteria provided by the Romanian Data Protection Law, while considering all the circumstances under which the personal data is transferred to the third country: (i) the nature of the personal data transferred; (ii) the purpose of the transfer; (iii) the duration envisaged for the personal data processing; (iv) the country of origin; (v) the country of the final destination; (vi) the legislation of the country requesting the transfer.

Helpful guidance with respect to the adequacy assessment was also provided by the Article 29 Working Party Working Document in a Working Document (Transfers of personal data to third countries: Applying Articles 25 and 26 of the EU data protection directive, 1998, p. 5) emphasising that:

"using Directive 95/46/EC as a starting point, [...], it should be possible to arrive at a 'core' of data protection 'content' principles and 'procedural/enforcement' requirements, compliance with which could be seen as a minimum requirement for protection to be considered adequate. Such a minimum list should not be set in stone. In some instances there will be a need to add to the list, while for others it may even be possible to reduce the list of requirements. The degree of risk that the transfer poses to the data subject will be an important factor in determining the precise requirements of a particular case. Despite this provision, the compilation of a basic list of minimum conditions is a useful starting point for any analysis."

The transfer of personal data to third countries that have been recognized as ensuring an adequate level of protection must be only notified to the Data Protection Authority, without authorization of the transfer by the Data Protection Authority being necessary. The rules provided at point 3.1 above are also applicable in case of cross-border transfers of data to third countries ensuring an adequate level of data protection. However, when the Data Protection Authority considers that the third country where the personal data are intended to be transferred does not meet such adequacy requirements, it may prohibit the respective transfer.

3.6.2. Third Countries not Ensuring an Adequate Level of Data Protection

Implementing Article 26 paragraph 2 of the EU Data Protection Directive, the Data Protection Law provides for the Data Protection Authority's option to authorize a transfer of personal data to a country whose legislation does not provide for an adequate level of protection at least equal to that offered by Romanian legislation "in case the data controller adduces sufficient guarantees with respect to the protection of the fundamental rights of individuals" (Data Protection Law, Article 29 paragraph 4). Moreover, it is expressly stated that such guarantees must result from agreements executed between the data controllers and the natural or legal persons from whose disposition the transfer takes place.

In light of the above legal provision, and also taking into account the Data Protection Authority's Decision No. 28/7.03.2007 regarding personal data transfers in other countries, it may be stated that the transfer of personal data to a third country that has not been recognized as ensuring an adequate data protection level must be both notified to and authorized by the Data Protection Authority. In that situation, the standard application form that must be submitted to the Data Protection Authority before performing the transfer must have attached a copy of the agreement between the data exporter and the data importer. However, there is no express timeline for submitting the notification application provided by the Data Protection Law.

3.6.2.1. Contractual Clauses

The use of contractual clauses is provided by both the EU Data Protection Directive and the Romanian Data Protection Law "as a method of providing safeguards necessary for circumnavigating the export ban" (Carey, 2009, p. 115) provided by Article 25 paragraph (1) and Article 29 paragraph (1) respectively. Although not expressly provided by the Data Protection Law, it may be construed, in line with European doctrine, that the export of personal data may be grounded on two types of contractual clauses, namely:

(i) *Standard contractual clauses* that represent contractual terms approved by the European Commission; and
(ii) *"Ad hoc" contracts,* containing the terms negotiated between the data exporter and the data importer.

The European Commission has adopted both controller to controller standard clauses, as well as controller to processor model standard clauses to be used for international transfers of personal data to countries not ensuring an adequate level of data protection, as follows:

- **Controller to controller standard clauses**

The European Commission has adopted two sets of model clauses to be used in controller to controller exports, referred to as: (i) Set I of Standard Contractual Clauses, to be used in case a data controller located in the EU transfers personal data to a data controller located outside the EEA in a country that does not ensure adequate protection; and (ii) Alternative Standard Contractual Clauses for the transfer of personal data from the EU to third countries (or Set II of Standard Contractual Clauses).

The first set of standard contractual clauses was criticised as being too restrictive and not commercially-friendly and, therefore, an alternative set of contractual clauses were proposed by the International Chamber of Commerce. Both sets of model clauses are currently applicable on an alternative basis and they provide for warranties and responsibilities for both the data exporter and the data importer.

Carrey (2009) underlines that "it should be noted that data controllers relying on model contractual clauses must do so on a "word for word" basis – no amendments to the clauses are permitted. [...] If the wording of the model clauses is changed then the automatic recognition of adequacy [*the advantage of using these standard contractual clauses consists in the fact that they are deemed to provide an adequate level of data protection throughout the EU and the EEA*] does not apply [...]" (p. 115).

Set I of Standard Contractual Clauses is reflected into Romanian legislation through Order No. 6/2003 on standard contractual clauses for the transfer of personal data to a data controller established in a country whose legislation does not ensure a level of protection at least equal to that offered by Romanian law. The Alternative Standard Contractual Clauses are not yet provided by Romanian legislation. However, as the European Commission's decisions are of direct applicability (i.e., there is no need for their transposition into local legislation), it may be argued that the Data Protection Authority may not exclude *de plano* the use of the Alternative Standard Contractual Clauses in case of a transfer of personal data from an operator located in Romania to an operator located in a non-EU or non-EEA state that has not been recognized as ensuring an adequate level of protection. This alternative set of standard contractual clauses may be used if they best suit the business interests of both the data exporter and the data importer. However, the Data Protection Authority will analyze the request for the authorization of such transfer taking into account various factors and also on the basis of the standard notification application that must be submitted for obtaining the authorization of the transfer. Consequently, it may be construed that the Data Protection Authority may not refuse the authorization of a transfer to a third country solely based on the fact that the data exporter and the data importer use Set II of Standard Contractual Clauses and not Set I of Standard Contractual Clauses (only the latter being reflected in the Romanian legislation).

- **Controller to processor standard clauses**

The European Commission also adopted standard contractual clauses to be used in case of a transfer to data processors located in a third country not ensuring an adequate level of data protection through Decision 2002/16/EC. Such model clauses have been reflected into Romanian data protection legislation through the Data Protection Authority's Decision No. 167 of 27 November 2006 on standard contractual clauses for the transfer of personal data to a data processor established in a third country whose legislation does not provide for a level of protection at least equal to that provided by Romanian law.

Nevertheless, in February 2010, the European Commission adopted Decision 2010/87/EC on standard contractual clauses for the transfer of personal data to processors established in third countries, which repealed Decision 2002/16/EC. However, this new decision has not been yet reflected into any corresponding Romanian legislation.

- **"Ad hoc" contracts**

Although not defined as such in the local law, "ad hoc" contracts may be used by data controllers in order to be submitted to the Data Protection Authority for the purposes of obtaining the authorization of the transfer of personal data to a third country not ensuring an adequate level of data protection. These contracts provide for the obligations of both the data exporter and the data importer with respect to the safeguards granted for the personal data processing.

It is however market practice that data controllers use the standard clauses instead of customized contracts, either those provided for the controller-to-controller relationship, or those established for a controller-to-processor relationship.

3.6.2.2. Exemptions from the Authorization Requirement

As mentioned above, the transfer of personal data to a third country not ensuring an adequate level of data protection should be authorized by the Data Protection Authority on the basis of a written agreement under which the data controller undertakes to guarantee an adequate level of data protection.

However, the Data Protection Law sets forth certain exceptional cases (derogations) that "operate independently of the rules concerning adequacy - it is not necessary to show adequacy where one of the derogations applies" (Carey, 2009, p. 123). In such exceptional cases, the transfer of personal data to other countries is always allowed, such as in situations when:

(i) the data subject has given his/her explicit consent to the proposed transfer; in case of transferring sensitive personal data, the consent must be expressed in writing;

As regards the consent requirement detailed above, it has been expressed in the European doctrine that "consent is most commonly used to justify one-off transfers as opposed to a set or series of transfers which may operate routinely or as part of a business system" (Carey, 2009, p. 125). The consent of the data subject to the cross-border transfer of his/her personal data must be informed and freely expressed.

(ii) the transfer is necessary for the performance of a contract between the data subject and the data controller, or for the implementation of pre-contractual measures taken in response to the data subject's request, or when the transfer is necessary for the execution or the performance of a contract concluded or that shall be concluded in the interest of the data subject between the data controller and a third party. Nevertheless, the European doctrine has been rather reserved as regards the applicability of this exception in case of the consent given by employees, as it is arguable whether employee consent can be considered freely expressed given the subordination relationship between the employer and the employees. Article 29 Working Party reiterated the same idea in its Opinion 8/2001 on the processing of personal data in the employment context adopted on 13 September 2001:

"The Article 29 Working Party has taken the view that where as a necessary and unavoidable consequence of the employment relationship an employer has to process personal data it is misleading if it seeks to legitimise this processing through consent. Reliance on consent should be confined to cases where the worker has a genuine free choice and is subsequently able to withdraw the consent without detriment."

(iii) the transfer is necessary for the protection of the data subject's life, physical integrity or health;
(iv) the transfer is necessary on grounds of major public interest, such as national defence, public order or national safety or for the establishment, exercise or defence of legal claims.

In such exceptional cases, the transfer of personal data to non-EU countries not ensuring an adequate level of protection must only be notified to the Data Protection Authority, and no authorization is required.

3.6.3. Special Rules Applicable to the Transfer of Personal Data to the United States

The restrictions imposed by the Data Protection Law on transfers to third countries (including the US) not ensuring an adequate level of data protection are overridden in the case of US-based data importers that have a "Safe Harbor" status. "The basis of the safe harbor system is provided by the safe harbor principles and a set of frequently asked questions (FAQ)" (Kuner, 2007, p. 180) that have been found adequate from a data protection standpoint by the European Commission. In order to comply with the Eighth Principle regarding adequate safeguards for the lawful transfer of personal data, an EU data controller must ensure that the data importer located in US has adhered to the Safe Harbor principles, and, thus, it is on the Safe Harbor List. Despite the reservations expressed towards the adequacy finding on the Safe Harbor arrangement, such as the ones expressed by the Article 29 Working Party in its Opinion 4/2000 on the level of protection provided by the Safe Harbor Principles, the Safe Harbor system "has established itself as a useful part of the data protection landscape" (Kuner, 2007, p. 191).

There are two scenarios that trigger different privacy requirements under Romanian Data Protection Law and secondary legislation in case of a cross-border transfer of personal data carried out towards a data importer located in the United States:

(i) if the US data controller to whom the personal data are exported has adhered to the Safe Harbor principles, and the FAQ, thus being recognized by the European Commission as ensuring an adequate level of personal data protection, the proposed transfer must be notified to the Data Protection Authority and authorization is not required;
(ii) if the US data controller to whom the personal data are exported has not adhered to the Safe

Harbor principles and the FAQ, it is deemed that it has not been recognized as ensuring an adequate level of personal data protection. In such case, the proposed transfer must be based on an agreement between the Romanian data controller and the relevant US data controller that contains sufficient guarantees with respect to the protection of the individuals' fundamental rights. Under such circumstances, the proposed transfer must be notified and authorized by the Data Protection Authority.

4. SOLUTIONS & RECOMMENDATIONS

Companies seem to understand that, although at a first glance data protection may not seem of crucial importance in the wide and complex picture of regulations to be observed for a lawful corporate behavior, data protection rules cannot be ignored. Although there is still a long way to go towards protecting privacy, especially due to the continuing developments in the field of technology that mostly interferes with the individuals' right to privacy, the involvement of the competent authorities and the improvement of legislation is a useful and primary step in developing a data protection oriented attitude. From this perspective, even though it may be subject to further improvement, the Romanian legislation in the field of data protection is a functional instrument regulating the data controllers' task to observe the individuals' privacy rights and to ensure compliance with the national and European requirements in the data protection field.

5. CONCLUSION

While this paper has endeavored to touch upon the main issues related to cross-border transfer of personal data which may be of interest for any entity aiming to export personal data outside Romania, the picture offered by this paper is a rather general one, without attempting to be anything else but a high level review of the relevant domestic and European legislation. However, when dealing with specific issues related to the processing and cross-border transfer of personal data, and in the absence of any publicly available guidelines, data controllers should also bear in mind that the official position of the national competent authorities may also be obtained, on a case-by-case basis, through specific clarification requests addressed to such authorities. The European doctrine and jurisprudence also offer very useful tools in understanding the main mechanisms and concepts of data protection that, in general lines, have been implemented into most European jurisdictions, including Romania.

Hopefully, should the data protection principles and instruments be observed and applied in the national and international context, a productive relationship between corporate entities and individuals may be ensured, while the privacy-related rights of individuals are also respected.

6. REFERENCES

Article 29 Data Protection Working Party & Working Party on Police and Justice, *The Future of Privacy: Joint contribution to the Consultation of the European Commission on the legal framework for the fundamental right to protection of personal data*, 02356/09/EN/WP 168 (December 1, 2009).

Article 29 Data Protection Working Party, *Article 29 Working Party report on the obligation to notify the national supervisory authorities, the best use of exceptions and simplification and the role of the data protection officers in the European Union*, 10211/05/EN/WP 106 (January 18, 2005).

Article 29 Data Protection Working Party, *Opinion 10/2006 on the processing of personal data by the Society for Worldwide Interbank Financial Telecommunication (SWIFT)*, 01935/06/EN/WP128 (November 22, 2006).

Article 29 Data Protection Working Party, *Opinion 2/2007 on information to passengers about transfer of PNR data to US authorities*, XXXX/07/EN/WP132 (February 15, 2007).

Article 29 Data Protection Working Party, *Opinion 4/2000 on the level of protection provided by the "Safe Harbor Principles"*, CA07/434/00/EN/WP 32 (May 16, 2000).

Article 29 Data Protection Working Party, *Opinion 8/2001 on the processing of personal data in the employment context*, 5062/01/EN/Final/WP 48, (September 13, 2001).

Carey, P. (2009). *Data protection: A practical guide to UK and EU Law* (3rd ed.). Oxford: Oxford University Press.

Commission Decision 2000/518 of 26 July 2000 on the adequate protection of personal data provided in Switzerland,2000 O.J. (L215/1).

Commission Decision 2000/520 of 26 July 2000 on the adequacy of the protection provided by the safe harbour privacy principles and related frequently asked questions issued by the US Department of Commerce, 2000 O.J. (L215/7).

Commission Decision 2001/497 of 15 June 2001 on standard contractual clauses for the transfer of personal data to third countries, under Directive 95/46/EC, 2001 O.J. (L 181/19).

Commission Decision 2002/16 of 27 December 2001 on standard contractual clauses for the transfer of personal data to processors established in third countries, under Directive 95/46/EC, 2002 O.J. (L 6).

Commission Decision 2002/2 of 20 December 2001 on the adequate protection of personal data provided by the Canadian Personal Information and Electronic Documents Act, 2002 O.J. (L2/13).

Commission Decision 2003/821 of 21 November 2003 on the adequate protection of personal data in Guernsey, 2003 O.J. (L308).

Commission Decision 2004/411 of 28 April 2004 on the adequate protection of personal data in the Isle of Man, 2004 O.J. (L151/1).

Commission Decision 2004/915 of 27 December 2004 amending Decision 2001/497/EC as regards the introduction of an alternative set of standard contractual clauses for the transfer of personal data to third countries, 2004 O.J. (L385/74).

Commission Decision 2010/87 of 5 February 2010 on standard contractual clauses for the transfer of personal data to processors established in third countries under Directive 95/46/EC, 2010 O.J. (L 39/5).

Commission Decision C(2003)1731 of 30 June 2003 on the adequate protection of personal data in Argentina, 2003 O.J. (L 168).

Commission, Directorate General XV, Working Party on the Protection of Individuals with regard to the Processing of Personal Data, *Working Document: Transfers of personal data to third countries: Applying Articles 25 and 26 of the EU data protection directive*, DG XV D/5025/98/WP 12 (July 24, 1998).

Constitution, R. published in the Official Gazette of Romania no. 767/31 October 2003. Rules of Procedure of the Article 29 Working Party. Retrieved March 31, 2010, from http://ec.europa.eu/justice_home/fsj/privacy/docs/wpdocs/rules-art-29_en.pdf

Council Directive 95/46 of 24 October 1995 on the protection of individuals with regard to the processing of personal data and on the free movement of such data, 1995 O.J. (L 281) 31 (EC). International Chamber of Commerce, Department of Policy and Business Practices, Commission on E-Business, IT and Telecoms: Task Force on Privacy and the Protection of Personal Data, *Final Approved Version of Alternative Standard Contractual Clauses for the Transfer of Personal Data from the EU to Third Countries (controller to controller transfers)*. Retrieved March 30, 2010, from http://www.internationalchamberofcommerce.org/uploadedFiles/ICC/policy/e-business/pages/ICC%20model%20clauses+FAQs%20final%20approved%20%20Jan%202005.pdf

Jay, R. (2007). *Data protection: Law and practice*. London: Sweet & Maxwell.

Kuner, C. (2007). *European data protection law: Corporate compliance and regulation* (2nd ed.). Oxford: Oxford University Press.

National Supervisory Authority for Personal Data Processing. (2008). Annual report 2008. Retrieved March 30, 2010, from http://www.dataprotection.ro/i ndex.jsp?page=Activity_Report_of_the_national_supervisory_authority_for_year_2008&lang=en.National Supervisory Authority for Personal Data Processing, Notification Guidance. Retrieved March 31, 2010, from http://www.dataprotection.ro/index.jsp?page=ghid_notificare&lang=en.National Supervisory Authority for Personal Data Processing, Order No. 6 of 28 January 2003 on standard contractual clauses for the transfer of personal data to a data controller established in a country whose legislation does not ensure a level of protection at least equal to that offered by Romanian law.

Law No. 677/2001 on the protection of individuals with regard to the processing of personal data and on the free movement of such data, published in the Official Gazette of Romania No. 720 of 12 December 2001.

Law No. 102/2005 regarding the establishment, organization and functioning of the Supervisory Authority for Personal Data Processing, published in the Official Gazette of Romania No. 391 of 9 May 2005.

Romanian Supervisory Authority for Personal Data Processing, Decision No. 173 /12 December 2006 regarding the adequate protection of personal data provided by the Canadian Personal Information and Electronic Documents Act of 13 April 2000.

Romanian Supervisory Authority for Personal Data Processing, Decision No. 95 /11 December 2008 regarding the establishing of the standard type notification form provided by the Law no. 677/2001 on the protection of individuals with regard to the processing of personal data and the free movement of such data.

Romanian Supervisory Authority for Personal Data Processing, Decision No. 10 /2 March 2009 for establishing a model of authorization for the transfer abroad of the personal data based on Article 29 paragraph (4) of Law No. 677/2001.

Romanian Supervisory Authority for Personal Data Processing, Decision No. 167 /27 November 2006 on standard contractual clauses for the transfer of personal data to a data processor established in a third country whose legislation does not provide for a level of protection at least equal to that provided by Romanian law.

Romanian Supervisory Authority for Personal Data Processing, Decision No. 172 /11 December 2006 regarding the adequate level of protection for the personal data in Argentina.

Romanian Supervisory Authority for Personal Data Processing, Decision No. 174 /13 December 2006 on the adequate protection of personal data provided in Switzerland.

Romanian Supervisory Authority for Personal Data Processing, Decision No. 175 /14 December 2006 on the adequate protection of personal data provided in Guernsey.

Romanian Supervisory Authority for Personal Data Processing, Decision No. 176 /15 December 2006 on the adequate protection of personal data provided in the Isle of Man.

Romanian Supervisory Authority for Personal Data Processing, Decision No. 28 /7 March 2007 regarding personal data transfers in other countries.

Romanian Supervisory Authority for Personal Data Processing, Decision No. 11 /5 March 2009 on the establishment of the categories of operations for the processing of personal data that are likely to trigger special risks for the individuals' rights and obligations.

U.S. Department of Commerce. (2007, July 21). Frequently asked questions (FAQs). Retrieved March 30, 2010, from http://www.export.gov/safeharbor/eg_main_018237.asp

U.S. Department of Commerce. (2007, July 21). Safe harbor privacy principles. Retrieved March 30, 2010, from http://www.export.gov/safeharbor/eu/eg_main_018475.asp

U.S. Department of Commerce. (n.d.). Safe harbor list. Retrieved March 31, 2010, from https://www.export.gov/safehrbr/list.aspx

Chapter 18
The Implementation of the Data Retention Directive: A Comparative analysis

Anna Pateraki
Humboldt University of Berlin, Germany

ABSTRACT

This paper aims to provide a comparative analysis regarding the implementation of the EC Data Retention Directive (2006/24/EC) in the most important Member States including Germany, Great Britain and France in order to provide the reader with the necessary information on the current controversial matters relating to it and display the differences in the speed, intensity and form of its implementation.

I. INTRODUCTION

Data retention has been the most controversial legal and political issue in the recent years in relation to data protection in Europe. As already analyzed in the previous papers the Data Retention Directive (2006/24/EC) refers to the obligation of providers of publicly available electronic communications services or of public communications networks to retain without occasion – which means without initial suspicion – traffic and location data of communications through fixed, mobile and internet telephony, internet access and e-mail for the purpose of investigation, detection and prosecution of serious crimes, as defined by the national law. The period of retention shall range between 6 months and 2 years; the content of the communication shall be exempted from the above obligation. The retained data shall be transferred to the competent authorities upon request and without undue delay, while certain data security principles are to be respected during the period of retention.

Ireland, supported by Slovakia, brought an action for the annulment of the Data Retention Directive before the European Court of Justice in 2006. Ireland's action related solely to the choice of legal basis and not to any possible infringement by the Directive of fundamental rights resulting from interference with the exercise of the right to privacy. In particular, the choice of Art. 95 EC former version (internal market) as the Directive's

DOI: 10.4018/978-1-60960-083-9.ch018

legal basis had been questioned. Nevertheless, the European Court of Justice dismissed this action on February 10, 2009 (C-301/06) and did not accept the argument made by Ireland that the "centre of gravity" of the Directive does not concern the functioning of the internal market, as its principal objective is the investigation, detection and prosecution of crime, and it should therefore be subjected to the third pillar and not to the Community competence under Article 95 EC former version. In fact, the Court held that the Directive was correctly adopted on the basis of the EC Treaty as it relates predominantly to the functioning of the internal market, with the argument that data retention has significant economic implications for service providers in so far as they may involve substantial investment and operating costs. Besides the Data Retention Directive amended the provisions of the Directive 2002/58/EC, which was itself based on Article 95 EC former version. In those circumstances, in so far as it amends an existing Directive which is part of the *acquis communautaire*, the Data Retention Directive could not be based on a provision of the EU Treaty.

This judgment was treated with criticism among commentators, since it contradicts an older decision (C-317/04) where the European Court of Justice annulled the Commission's Decision 2004/535/EC on the adequate protection of personal data contained in the Passenger Name Records (PNR) of air passengers transferred to US authorities on the grounds that it was not validly adopted on the basis of Art. 95 EC former version (Simitis, 2006). This decision made a crucial distinction between the purpose for which personal data are collected and processed and their further processing for public security purposes. The basic argument was that the processing of data collected for commercial purposes falls within the protective ambit of the data protection Directive, but when the same data are later transferred for public security reasons, they no longer enjoy the same protection (Kosta/ Dumortier, 2007). Nevertheless, the Court did not follow the same reasoning in the Ireland case. Moreover, it did not answer the compatibility question of the data retention obligation and the data protection principles such as the principles of necessity and proportionality, the finality principle or else purpose limitation and Art. 8 ECHR. At this point it is worthy of mention that if the European Court of Justice had accepted Ireland's action for annulment then many national constitutional courts of the Member States would have acquired the competence to question the compatibility of data retention with the above mentioned rights and principles.

Thus, since the primary aim of the Directive was to combat terrorism and serious crime, the unexceptional implementation of this measure on all citizens has been questioned. Further, as this legal framework contradicts in some cases the traditional national level of privacy protection, significant oppositions and contradictions have been raised in many Member States with respect to the proportionality of this measure. In Germany, for instance, several administrative courts have decided that data retention is incompatible with the principle of proportionality. On the other hand, strong legislative debates aiming at the application of retained data also to civil copyright cases in the future have also arisen.

Nevertheless, in this context it is worth noting that according to the legislation of the European Court of Justice Member States have to specify a time-limit for storage of personal data for as long as it is necessary for the purposes for which the data has been collected or for which it is further processed, in order to guarantee the right of access of the data subjects to their data as stated in Art. 12 lit. a) of the Directive 95/46/EC (ECJ C-553/07). In this respect, Article 12 lit. a) of the Directive 95/46/EC provides for a right of access to basic data and to information for the recipients or categories of recipients to whom the data has been disclosed. As stated in recital 41 in the preamble to the Directive 95/46/EC, the data subjects must have a right of access to the data relating to them which is being processed, in order to carry out the necessary checks. In particular, the data subjects may be certain that their personal data is processed in a correct and lawful manner, especially that the basic data regarding to them is accurate and that it is disclosed to authorized recipients only. This is considered to ensure a fair balance between the interest of the data subjects in protecting their privacy, in particular by way of their right to object and to bring legal proceedings and the burden which the obligation to store that information represents for the controller. It remains to be seen whether data retention will have implications for such a right of access in the telecommunications sector.

II. COMPARATIVE OVERVIEW OF THE IMPLEMENTATION OF THE DATA RETENTION DIRECTIVE IN THE MEMBER STATES

Member States were obliged to transfer the Directive into their national legal systems until the 16 of September, 2007. In addition, Member States had the right to declare that they will postpone the application of the Directive for a period of additionally 18 months, until March 2009, as provided in the body of the Directive. The Data Retention Directive has been implemented so far (Stand April 2010) by the Czech Republic, Denmark, Estonia, Finland, France, Germany, Great Britain, Hungary, Italy, Latvia, Lithuania, Luxemburg, Malta, the Netherlands, Portugal, Romania, Slovenia, Slovakia and Spain, whereas the Belgian transfer is expected within 2010. The average period of retention that has been chosen so far in the most Member States is 12 months, while there are examples that correspond to the minimum period of retention of 6 months such as the implementation in Luxemburg, the Czech Republic and Cyprus. Slovakia surprises to have selected the maximum period of retention of two years, with the exemption that for internet services only the minimum period of six months will apply. Nevertheless, the implementation of the Directive was declared as unconstitutional by the German Federal Constitutional Court on 2 March 2010 and the Romanian Constitutional Court on 8 October 2009.

Austria consciously refused until recently to transfer the Directive into national law because of legal and political concerns, especially due to serious doubts about its conformity with Art. 8 of the ECHR. After the EU Commission brought an action against Austria because of non-transfer of the Data Retention Directive, the Austrian Federal Ministry for Transport, Innovation and Technology assigned the Ludwig Boltzmann Institute of Human Rights (BIM) to elaborate a Draft Law on data retention (BIM Draft 2010). This draft is expected to amend the Austrian Telecommunications Act within 2010 in order to transfer the Directive in a way that would be in accordance to the fundamental rights acknowledged by the ECHR. Furthermore, it is considered that during the implementing legal procedure data retention considerations in regard of providing information for the identification of violations in civil copyright cases should be taken into account (Neubauer, 2008, p. 29).

Other Member States – such as Sweden, Greece and Ireland – were brought recently by the European Commission before the European Court of Justice for failing to implement the Data Retention Directive in a reasonable time frame (C-185/09 Commission v. Sweden of 4th February 2010; C-202/09 Commission v. Ireland and C-211/09 Commission v. Greece of 26th November 2009). Thus, Belgium and Ireland have not transferred the Directive yet. At this point it is worth-mentioning that before the Data Retention Directive was enacted only some Member States such as Belgium, France, Ireland, Italy and Great Britain had already applied retention measures in their domestic law. These internal data retention measures could reach in some cases a period of retention up to 36 months (Forgó/ Jlussi/ Klügel/ Krügel, 2008, p. 682).

a. Data Retention in Germany

Germany is in fact one of the member states that have already transferred the Directive into their national law. The implementing law has been the German Act for the Amendment of Telecommunications Surveillance ("Gesetz zur Neuregelung der Telekommunikations-überwachung und anderer verdeckter Ermittlungsmaßnahmen sowie zur Umsetzung der Richtlinie 2006/24/EG"), which came into force in January 2008 and transferred the Data Retention Directive into the body of the German Telecommunications Act (TKG). The German legislator distinguishes between traffic and customer data with respect to the processing of the retained data. Traffic data is legally defined in the TKG as any data collected, processed or used for the purpose of the conveyance of a communication. Traffic data may, *inter alia*, consist of data referring to the routing, duration, time or volume of a communication, to the protocol used, to the location of the terminal equipment of the sender or recipient, to the network on which the communication originates or terminates, to the beginning, end or duration of a connection.

The period of retention of such data has been stipulated to six months. This data shall be completely deleted one month after the expiration of the six month period of retention. On the contrary, customer data shall be kept until the expiration of the year after the termination of the contract; this means practically a period from one to two years beyond the termination of the contract. This information concerns the personal data of a user required for the justification, design of content or change of a contractual relationship regarding communications services such as name and address, bank account and description of the contractual service. The disclosure of information with respect to traffic data requires a previous court order and shall be provided for the prosecution of serious crime or telecommunication crime only. On the contrary, the disclosure of customer data is provided not only for the prosecution of crime but also in the context of specific administrative offences.

Over the past few years there were discussions as well as legislative debates concerning the potential use of retained data to combat product piracy on the internet, in particular illegal file sharing in peer-to-peer networks (Czychowski/ Nordemann 2008, p. 3095). The supporting arguments of this proposal were based on the legal construction that in the light of Art. 15 Sec. 1 Subsec. 2 of the Directive 2002/58/EC (known as the e-privacy Directive) data retention may also be used for purposes other than the investigation and prosecution of serious crime as provided by the Data Retention Directive, including civil copyright cases. In addition, recital 12 in the preamble to the Data Retention Directive in conjunction with Art. 15 Sec. 1a of the e-privacy Directive indicate that data retention measures for purposes beyond those of the investigation, detection and prosecution of serious crime as defined in the Data Retention Directive shall be admissible. Particularly, the explicit reference of Art. 15 of the e-privacy Directive to Art. 13 of the general data protection Directive (95/46/EC) concerning restriction measures for the protection of the *rights of others*, indicates a permissible use of retained data also in favor of right holders of intellectual property rights.

The reason for such a legal construction lays in the intention to practically reinforce the claims for information against access providers, designated in Art. 8 Sec. 1 lit. c) of the Directive 2004/48/EC concerning the enforcement of intellectual property rights (known as the enforcement Directive), as they provide on a commercial scale services used in infringing activities such as the internet access. The information provided concerns *inter alia* the origin of the services used for the infringement, including dynamic IP addresses and other traffic data that identifies the users on the internet.

Although this provision has been transferred into Art. 101 Sec. 2 Subsec. 2 of the German Copyright Act (Urhebergesetz), it is proved to be to a large extent void in practice as, according to German law, traffic data shall be deleted by the provider after the end of the communication and as long as it is no longer needed for accounting purposes. For instance, the retention of traffic data for accounting purposes in Germany is questionable in cases where flat rate internet is being used. In this context, the only data available for civil proceedings relating to infringements on Intellectual Property Rights (IPR) would be the data kept under the data retention provisions. Nevertheless, this is a theoretical understanding and thus it has not been yet adequately examined by any court decision on a national level.

Under similar circumstances, the European Court of Justice held in 2008 (C-275/06 – Promusicae Case) that the community law does not require that the Member States should lay down an obligation to communicate personal data in order to ensure effective protection of copyright in the context of civil proceedings. However, it did not prohibit it and emphasized that the Member States should provide a fair balance between the fundamental rights, such as the right to privacy and copyright – in particular hereunder the right to effective protection of intellectual property – when transferring community Directives relating to such matters. Furthermore, the authorities and courts of the Member States should respect the principle of proportionality, while implementing the measures of transferring such Directives.

Nevertheless, this discussion is expected to be placed on another basis after the recent developments in the German jurisprudence concerning data protection. On 2 March 2010 the Federal Constitutional Court ruled against German data retention legislation as unconstitutional and declared the implementing Articles of the German Telecommunication Act (Art. 113a Art. 113b TKG) as void. Furthermore, the Court ordered the destruction of the traffic and location data retained so far. The court decision was based on a massive constitutional complaint supported by 34.000 citizens. The arguments of the constitutional complaint were based on the fact that data retention infringes the secrecy of telecommunications as acknowledged in Art. 10 Sec. 1 of the German Basic Law (Grundgesetz), the right of the so-called "informational self-determination", in form of the capacity of the individual to determine basically the disclosure and the use of its personal data, and the principle of proportionality.

The Court held that a duty of storage for a period of six months, as provided by German law, is not in itself incompatible with Art. 10 of the Basic Law and therefore unconstitutional. However, this is not structured in its current form in a manner adapted to the principle of proportionality. Thus, the use and storage of data should have been subjected to stricter requirements than those acknowledged by the German legislator, so that a significant amendment of the respective legislation should be required. Furthermore, the Court proposed and formulated the criteria for a more restrictive access to and use of the retained data that substantiate in principal, the requirements of the Federal Data Protection Act. In particular, data should be collected and therefore retained only for specific, exclusive purposes, in order that the provisions made by the implementing legislation should be customized and concretized in a future version. Moreover, a minimum of transparency is required for the collection, processing and storage of data. Thus, the data subjects should be efficiently notified about data practices concerning their use, storage and process in order to have the possibility to assert – by occasion – their rights of information, amendment and deletion of such data or even to object to or to claim compensation for their unlawful use. Additionally, stricter requirements –though proportionate for the data controllers– should apply with respect to data security in case of data banks or of wide storing of data. For instance, encryption methods should be used, whereas access control and tamper-proof audit trail should be guaranteed on a high level in connection with the investigation and precaution of crime.

These criteria must be included in the national legislation in order to ensure that the data retention obligation is implemented without breaching the fundamental rights contained in the German Basic Law and specified in the Federal Data Protection Act. However, the court ruling did not annul the implementing legislation entirely and the Data Retention Directive was not therefore subjected to further legal doubts. In conclusion, it is predictable that after pertinent legislative improvements a reviewed data retention obligation will be re-enacted soon in order to correspond to the criteria set out by the German Federal Constitutional Court.

b. Data Retention in Great Britain

Data retention was first introduced in Great Britain in the context of the Anti-Terrorism, Crime and Security Act 2001 (ATCSA) that regulated the storage of telecommunications data on a voluntary basis. After the transfer of the data protection Directive in the national legal system in 2007 data retention became an obligation in the telecommunications area as regulated in the Statutory Instrument of 2007 (No. 2199). With respect to the scope of retention the content of the Statutory Instrument 2007 reflects in principal the content of the Part 11 of the previous ATCSA 2001. Furthermore, it complies entirely with the content of the Directive 2006/24/EC (BIM, 2008, p. 55). The period of retention shall be 12 months starting implementing Articles of the time of the collection of data.

The proportionality of the selected period of retention was discussed in the Consultation Paper for the transposition of the Directive. The Data Protection Act provides that personal data should be deleted if it is not anymore needed for the purpose that it had been collected initially. However, exceptions are made in view of public interest and for purposes related to national security. The proportionality of this period of time is therefore not questioned in the Regulatory Impact Assessment included in the Consultation Paper (Consultation Paper, Annex C). Furthermore, the Statutory Instrument 2007 (No. 2199) does not explicitly refer to the restriction of Art. 5 Sec. 2 of the Directive that exempts from the data retention provisions any data revealing the content of the communication. Nevertheless, this is indicated in the Consultation Paper (BIM, 2008, p. 56). Only telecommunications data used in usual business relations are to be retained and no other additional data. Only authorized persons should have access to data as provided by the law such as the Security Service, the Secret Intelligence Service and the Government Communications Headquarters as provided in the Regulation of Investigatory Powers Act. Telecommunications providers have to keep statistics of the access of data that is to be brought before the Minister of the Interior once a year (Statutory Instrument 2007 (No 2199), Regulation 9). Data should be deleted after the expiration of the period of retention. Nevertheless, in Great Britain no notification to the data subject is provided with regard to the data storage of its personal data.

However, it is worth mentioning that in Great Britain compensation is provided for the storage of telecommunications data. Within the framework of the ATCSA 2001 only appropriate contributions were provided towards costs incurred through the storage of data, whereas after the introduction of the data retention obligation in 2007 such contribution is provided for all costs incurred. In the event of violations against the provisions of the Statutory Instrument no legal sanctions shall apply on the providers. Instead, they have merely a financial incentive to comply with the provisions of the Statutory Instrument (BIM, 2008, p. 56). If an Act of Parliament had been chosen for the implementation of the Directive instead of a Statutory Instrument, this would also mean sanctions for the providers in case of infringement, especially criminal sanctions. However, this is not the case up to present.

In Great Britain there is no significant opposition in social life against the implementation of the Data Retention Directive in national law, especially in comparison with other close jurisdictions such as Ireland. Finally, the implications of the Data Retention Directive have been discussed in the media over the past few years in the context of criminal copyright cases that did not, however, find an adequate reaction in the legal literature (BIM, 2008, p. 60). Nevertheless, the House of Commons adopted recently the so-called "Three Strikes' Policy" to combat online infringement of copyright. This controversial Policy as provided by the Digital Economy Act 2010 will potentially suspend the internet connections of repeat file-swappers. The Act states that internet service providers have to send warning letters to subscribers suspected of illegal file-sharing at the behest of copyright holders. Should subscribers fail to heed several warnings, they could face slowed down or suspended Internet service. In addition, users who are caught downloading copyrighted material three times in the same year will have their names passed to rights holders, under the new proposals outlined by Ofcom (Office of Communications). To what extend means of data retention could be used for the identification of the users will predictably raise further concerns in the future.

c. Data Retention in France

Data retention in France is regulated in Art. 34 of the Telecommunications Act. The provision dates from the year 2000 and has been reviewed in 2006 to fully transfer the Data Retention Directive. As a general principle, the French legislation stipulates that providers should delete or anonymize traffic data. This applies also to services free of charge such as these of public libraries (BIM, 2008 p. 45). Data retention is considered to be an exception from this rule as provided in Art. 34 Section 2 Subs. 2 of the same Act. According to this regulation, providers have to retain certain technical data for a period of time that shall not exceed one year for the purposes of the investigation, detection and prosecution of specific crimes as provided by the national law. The Decree of the *Conseil d'Etat*, (No. 2006-358) that was enacted in 2006 after consulting with the *Commission nationale de l'informatique et des libertés* (CNIL) regulates further details with respect to data retention including the contribution towards costs incurred. Furthermore, according to Art. R 1013 of the Decree, within the scope of the data retention obligation fall data that enable the identification of the user of the communication, the communication device, the technical features of the user's telecommunications equipment, the date, time and duration of the communication, the required services and their providers as well as the receiving party of the communication (Lorrain/ Mathias 2006). The scope of data retention and the respective period of retention have been deemed to be in accordance with the principal of proportionality in France and compatible with Art. 8 ECHR (BIM, 2008, p. 47). Social opposition to data retention was not significant in France at the time of the transfer of the Directive, as this was implemented speedily in the French legal system.

In France no court order is provided for legitimating access to data. Furthermore, the form of the retention is not regulated. Although the content of communications shall be exempted from the data retention provisions, other legal provisions provide for the identification of the user that generated unlawful content on the internet (e.g. Loi n° 2004-575). Furthermore, providers should meet technical requirements regarding data security to ensure that the retained data will not be used for other purposes other than provided by law. Finally, infringements against retention obligations or with regard to the deletion of data could be punished with a fine of up to 75.000 Euros (Art. 39 Sec. 3 of the Telecommunications Act).

France also passed a "three strikes" law against internet piracy at the beginning of 2010 after a long struggle in parliament. The Higher Authority for the Distribution of Works and the Protection of Copyright on the Internet (Hadopi) will compile lists of alleged offenders, along with dates, number of infractions, penalties, etc. and will allow sanctions against internet users accused of copyright violations. If data retention is about to play a role with regard to the identification of the users, it remains to be seen in the future.

III. CONCLUSION

As stated in the Directive, its aim is to "harmonise" Member States' provisions on data retention (Art 1 Sec.1). Arguably, however, we cannot speak of a "harmonisation" in fact, as the Directive imposes data retention measures in the most of the Member States for the first time (Gitter/ Schnabel 2007, p. 411). Additionally, the Directive does not provide for reimbursement for additional costs incurred, but solely leaves this at the discretion of the Member States. Data retention includes high monetary costs that vary for service providers located in different Member States. Accordingly to a French report in 2006 the total annual costs for an internet service provider with one million customers were estimated up to 132 million Euros for a retention period of one year (Stampfel/ Gansterer/ Ilger 2008). Finally, we should not forget that serious concerns have been raised also on the part of the industry with respect to the financial impact of the data retention obligation. Members of the Data Retention Experts Group of the European Commission have stated jointly that a system of data retention would be much more effective if operators were obliged to retain the same data in the same format and the same rules were applied for access and handover of that data in all Member States. This lack of harmonization consequently has an impact on competition at the European level and, therefore, on the completion of the Internal Market (Statement of CableEurope, GSMA Europe, EuroISPA, ECTA and ETNO).

Viewed overall, Art. 29 Working Party notes that:

"the Directive lacks some adequate and specific safeguards as to the treatment of communication data and leaves room for diverging interpretation and implementation by the Member States in this respect. However, adequate and specific safeguards are necessary to protect the vital interests if the individual as mentioned by Directive 2002/58/EC. [...] The Working Party considers it also crucial that the provisions of the Directive are interpreted and implemented in a harmonised way to ensure that the European citizens can enjoy throughout the European Union the same level of protection" (Opinion 3/2006 WP on the Directive 2006/24/EC).

In conclusion, the implementation of the Data Retention Directive is controversial in many different aspects. The Data Retention Directive provides broad space for deviations in terms of data to be retained, periods of retention, such as cost compensation schemes. Thus, the non-binding recommendations of the Art. 29 Working Party regarding purpose specification, access limitation, data minimum scale, avoidance of data mining, authorized access to data, retention purpose, system separation and security measures with respect to data retention shall be taken into consideration by the Member States in the process of implementing or reviewing data retention legislative measures in order to ensure consistency throughout Europe.

REFERENCES

Article 29 Working Party. (2006). Opinion 3/2006 of Art. 29 Working Party on Directive 2006/24/ EC, adopted on 25 March 2006. Retrieved May 20, 2010, from http://ec.europa.eu/justice_home/ fsj/privacy/docswpdocs/2006/wp119 _en.pdf

Czychowski, C., & Nordemann, J. B. (2008). Vorratsdaten und Urheberrecht – Zulässige Nutzung gespeicherter Daten. *Neue Juristische Wochenschrift*, 3095–3099.

Department for Business. Innovation and Skills (BIS). (2010, April 21). Royal Assent for the Digital Economy Bill. London: BIS. Retrieved May 20, 2010, from http://interactive.bis.gov. uk/digitalbritain/digital-economy-bill

Digital Civil Rights in Europe. (2006, March 29). Telecom data to be retained for one year in France. Retrieved May 20, 2010, from http://www.edri.org/edrigram/number4.6/ franceretantion

Digital Civil Rights in Europe. (2010, February 10). Update on the Belgian transposition of the Data Retention Directive. Retrieved May 20, 2010, from http://www.edri.org/edrigram/number8.3/belgium-data-retention-draft-law

European Court of Justice. (2009). Press release no. 11/09 concerning the Judgment C-301/06 of February 10, 2009. Retrieved May 20, 2010, from http://www.statewatch.org/news/2009/feb/ eu-ecj-ireland-datret-judgment-prel.pdf

Federal Constitutional Court of Germany. (2010). Press release no. 11/2010 concerning the Judgment 1 BvR 256/08, 1 BvR 263/08, 1 BvR 586/08 of March 2, 2010. Retrieved May 20, 2010, from http://www.bundesverfassungsgericht.de/pressemitteilungen/bvg10-011

Forgó, N., Jlussi, D., Klügel, C., & Krügel, T. (2008). *Die Umsetzung der Richtlinie zur Vorratsdatenspeicherung* (pp. 680–682). Datenschutz und Datensicherheit.

Gitter, R., & Schnabel, C. (2007). *Die Richtlinie zur Vorratsspeicherung und ihre Umsetzung in das nationale Recht* (pp. 411–417). Multimedia und Recht.

Institute for Legal Informatics (IRI). (2008). Rechtsvergleichende Analyse im Hinblick auf die Umsetzung der Richtlinie 2006/24/EG über die Vorratsdatenspeicherung [Research on behalf of the Ludwig Boltzmann Institute of Human Rights (BIM)]. Hannover, Germany: Institute for Legal Informatics (IRI) of the Leibniz University of Hannover. Retrieved May 20, 2010, from http://bim.lbg.ac.at/files/sites/bim/Rechtsvergleich_Vorratsdatenspeicherung.pdf

Kosta, E., & Dumortier, J. (2007). *The Data Retention Directive and the principles of European data protection legislation* (pp. 130–135). Medien und Recht International.

Lorrain, A., & Mathias, P. (2006). Données de connexion: la publication du premier décret ou la premère pierre d'un édifice encore inachevé, Revue Lamy droit de l'immateriel, 35-38. Retrieved May 20, 2010, from http://www.aclorrain.fr/docs/donnees-de-connexion_06.pdf

Ludwig Boltzmann Institute of Human Rights (BIM). (2010). Draft Bill for the Amendment of the Austrian Telecommunications Act. Vienna: BIM. Retrieved May 20, 2010, from http://bim.lbg.ac.at/de/informationsgesellschaft/bimentwurf-zur-vorratsdatenspeicherung-begutachtung

Manolea, B., & Argesiu, A. (2009, October 8). Constitutional Court Decision no 1258. Retrieved May 20, 2010, from http://www.legi-internet.ro/english/jurisprudenta-it-romania/decizii-it/romanian-constitutional-court-decision-regarding-data-retention.html

Neubauer, M. (2008). *Aktuelles zu Unterlassungs- und Auskunftspflichten in Österreich mit einem Vergleich zur aktuellen Rechtslage in Deutschland im Zivil- und Strafrecht* (pp. 25–33). Medien und Recht International.

News, B. B. C. (2010, January 1). New internet piracy law comes into effect in France. Retrieved May 20, 2010, from http://news.bbc.co.uk/2/hi/europe/8436745.stm

Ofcom. (2010). Consultation on "Online Infringement of Copyright and the Digital Economy Act 2010". Retrieved May 20, 2010, from http://www.ofcom.org.uk/consult/condocs/copyrightinfringement/summary/

Ringland, K. (2009). The European Union's Data Retention Directive and the United States's data preservation laws: Finding the better model. *Shidler Journal of Law, Commerce & Technology, 5*(13). Retrieved May 20, 2010, from http://www.lctjournal.washington.edu/vol5/a13Ringland.html

Simitis, S. (2006). Übermittlung der Daten von Flugpassagieren in die USA: Dispens vom Datenschutz? *Neue Juristische Wochenschrift*, 2011–2014.

Stampfel, G., Gansterer, W. N., & Ilger, M. (2008). Implications of the EU Data Retention Directive 2006/24/EC. Vienna: Faculty of Computer Science, University of Vienna. Retrieved May 20, 2010, from http://www.informatik.univie.ac.at/upload//970/ImplicationsEUDR.pdf

Statement of CableEurope. GSMA Europe, EuroISPA, ECTA & ETNO. (n.d.). Data retention: Impact on economic operators. Retrieved May 20, 2010, from http://www.gsmeurope.org/documents/Joint_Industry_Statement_on_DRD.PDF

APPENDIX: LEGISLATION

European Legislation

Directive 2006/24/EC of the European Parliament and of the Council, 15 March 2006, on the retention of data generated or processed in connection with the provision of publicly available electronic communications services or of public communications networks and amending Directive 2002/58/EC, L 105/54, 13/04/2006.

Directive 2004/48/EC of the European Parliament and of the Council of 29 April 2004 on the

enforcement of intellectual property rights, L 195/ 16, 02/06/2004.

Directive 2002/58/EC of the European Council and of the Council of the 12 July 2002 concerning the processing of personal data and the protection of privacy in the electronic communications sector, L 201/37, 31/07/2002.

Directive 95/46/EC of the European Parliament and of the Council of 24 October 1995 on the protection of individuals with regard to the processing of personal data and on the free movement of such data, L 281/31, 23/11/1995.

Germany

German Act for the Amendment of Telecommunications Surveillance ("Gesetz zur Neuregelung der Telekommunikations-überwachung und anderer verdeckter Ermittlungsmaßnahmen sowie zur Umsetzung der Richtlinie 2006/24/EG"), from 21 December 2007.

German Telecommunications Act (Telekommunikationsgesetz – TKG), Art. 113a and Art. 113b (declared as void), as amended, from 23 Februar 2010.

Great Britain

Anti-Terrorism, Crime and Security Act 2001 (ATCSA), Part 11, Retention of Communications Data, 14 December 2001, Retrieved May 20, 2010, from http://www.opsi.gov.uk/acts/acts2001/ukpga_20010024_en_1#Legislation-Preamble .

Code of Practice on Voluntary Retention of Communications Data unter Part 11 ATCSA 2001, Retrieved May 20, 2010, from http://www.opsi.gov.uk/si/si2003/draft/5b.pdf .

Consultation Paper for the transposition of the Directive 2006/24/EC, August 2008, Retrieved May 20, 2010, from http://www.statewatch.org/news/2008/aug/uk-ho-consult-mand-ret-internet.pdf .

Digital Economy Act 2010, Retrieved May 20, 2010, from http://www.opsi.gov.uk/acts/acts2010/ukpga_20100024_en_1 .

Regulation of Investigatory Powers Act 2000, Retrieved May 20, 2010, from http://www.opsi.gov.uk/acts/acts2000/ukpga_20000023_en_1 .

Statutory Instrument of 2007 (No. 2199), 1 October 2007, Electronic Communications, The Data Retention (EC Directive) Regulations 2007, Retrieves May 20, 2010, from http://www.opsi.gov.uk/si/si2007/uksi_20072199_en_1 .

France

Decree no. 2006-358 of 24 March 2006 regarding electronic communications, from 26 March 2006, Retrieved May 20, 2010, from http://www.legifrance.gouv.fr/WAspad/UnTexteDe Jorf?numjo=JUSD0630025D (in French).

Loi n° 2004-575 du 21 juin 2004 pour la confiance dans l'économie numérique of 21 April 2004, version of 30 October 2009.

APPENDIX: CASES

Judgment, European Court of Justice, C-185/09 - Commission v. Sweden of 4 February, 2010.

Judgment, European Court of Justice, C-301/06 - Ireland v. Parliament and Council of 10 February, 2009.

Judgment, European Court of Justice, C-553/07 - College van burgemeester v. Rijkeboer of 7 May, 2009 .

Judgment, European Court of Justice, C-202/09 - Commission v. Ireland of 26 November, 2009.

Judgment, European Court of Justice, C-211/09 - Commission v. Greece of 26 November, 2009.

Judgment, European Court of Justice, C-275/06 - Promusicae v. Telefonica of 29 January, 2008.

Judgment, European Court of Justice, C-317/04 - European Parliament v. Council of 30 May, 2006.

Judgment, Federal Constitutional Court of Germany, 1 BvR 256/08, 1 BvR 263/08, 1 BvR 586/08 of 2 March, 2010.

Judgment, Romanian Constitutional Court, Decision no.1258 of 8 October, 2009.

Compilation of References

Aarts, E., & Encarnacao, J. (2006). *True visions: The emergence of ambient intelligence*. London: Springer Verlag.

Aarts, E., & Marzano, S. (2003). *The new everyday: Views on ambient intelligence*. Rotterdam, The Netherlands: 010 Publishers.

ABS-CBN News. (2010, January 13). LTO not ordered to reimburse RFID collection. Retrieved May 19, 2010, from http://www.abs-cbnnews.com/nation/01/13/10/lto-not-ordered-reimburse-rfid-collection

Act No. 3815, (otherwise known as the Revised Penal Code of the Philippines), December 8, 1930, as amended.

Agre, P., & Rotenberg, M. (1997). *Technology and privacy: The new landscape*. Cambridge, MA: MIT Press.

Akrivopoulou, C. M., & Stylianou, A. (2009). Navigating in internet: Privacy and the transparent individual. In Politis, D., Kozyris, P., & Igglezakis, I. (Eds.), *Socioeconomic and legal implications of electronic intrusion* (pp. 122–135). Hershey, PA: Information Science Reference. doi:10.4018/978-1-60566-204-6.ch007

Akrivopoulou, C. M. (2009). *Between autonomy and intimacy: Redefining the right to private life (Art. 9(1) of the Greek Constitution 1975/86/01/08)*. Thessaloniki: Aristotle University of Thessaloniki. Retrieved from http://invenio.lib.auth.gr/record/113367?In=el

Akrivopoulou, C. M. (2009, May 11-13). The jurisprudence of the ECHR as a common European constitution. Working paper presented at *The Many Constitutions of Europe* conference, Centre of Excellence in Foundations of European Law and Polity Research, Helsinki, Finland.

Albrecht, K., & McIntyre, L. (2005). *Spychips: How major corporations and government plan to track your every move with RFID*. Nashville, TN: Nelson Current Publishers.

Alderman, E., & Kennedy, C. (1997). *The right to privacy*. New York: Vintage Books.

Alivizatos, N. (2005). Privacy and disclosure [in Greek]. *Mass Media & Communication Law Review*, *1*, 14–23.

Alivizatos, N. (2007, December 16). Human rights in danger: The hidden side of the amendment on cameras. *Ta Nea* [in Greek]. Retrieved November 11, 2009, from http://www.tanea.gr/default.asp?pid=2&ct=1&artid=48419

Altman, I. (1975). *The environment and social behavior: Privacy, personal space, territory, crowding*. Monterey, CA: Brooks/Cole Pub. Co.

American Association of Advertising Agencies, Association of National Advertisers, Council of Better Business Bureaus, Direct Marketing Association, and Interactive Advertising Bureau. (2009). *Self-regulatory principles for online behavioral advertising*. Retrieved from http://www.iab.net/media/file/ven-principles-07-01-09.pdf

Anand, K. J. S. (2006, June). Fetal pain? *Pain: Clinical Updates*, *14*(2), 1–4.

Andenas, M., & Zleptnig, S. (2003). Surveillance and data protection: Regulatory approaches in the EU and member Ssates. *European Business Law Review*, *14*(6), 765.

Anderson, M., & den Boer, M. (Eds.). (1994). *Policing across national boundaries*. New York: Pinter Publishers.

Anderson, J., & Rainie, L. (2006). *The future of the Internet II*. New York: Pew Internet. Retrieved from http://www.elon.edu/e-web/predictions/2006survey.pdf

Anderson, J., & Rainie, L. (2008). *The future of the Internet III*. New York: Pew Internet. Retrieved from http://www.elon.edu/docs/e-web/predictions/2008_survey.pdf

Andrade, N. N. G. (2010). Technology and metaphors: From cyberspace to ambient intelligence. *Observatorio (OBS*). Journal*, *4*(1), 121–146.

Anthopoulos, H. (1992). *The constitutional right to freedom of conscience* [in Greek]. Thessaloniki: Sakkoulas Publications.

Anthopoulos, H. (2001). *New dimensions of fundamental rights* [in Greek]. Athens, Thessaloniki: Sakkoulas Publications.

Anthopoulos, H. (2004). Data protection and freedom of information [in Greek]. *Revue Hellénique des Droits de l'Homme*, *22*, 519–554.

Anthopoulos, H. (2006). Freedom & decency of work. The 'first-employ contract' before the French Constitutional Court. Comment on Case CC 2006-535DC (30.03.2006). [in Greek]. *Administrative Law Review*, *3*, 349–355.

Anthopoulos, H. (2005). State of prevention & the right to security. In H. Anthopoulos, X. Contiades & T. Papatheodorou (Eds.), *Security & human rights in the age of risk* [in Greek] (pp. 109-135). Athens-Komotini: Ant. N. Sakkoulas.

Araya, A. A. (1995). *Questioning ubiquitous computing*. Paper presented at the ACM 23rd Annual Conference on Computer Science, Nashville, TN.

Archard, D. (2006). The value of privacy. In Claes, E., Duff, A., & Gutwirth, S. (Eds.), *Privacy and the criminal law* (pp. 13–31). Antwerp, Belgium: Intersentia.

Article 29 data protection working party. (2007). Opinion 4/2007 on the concept of personal data. Retrieved March 15, 2010, from http://www.droit-technologie.org/upload/actuality/doc/1063-1.pdf

Article 29 Data Protection Working Party. (2001). Letter to Mr. Goran Persson, Acting President of the Council of the EU. Retrieved from http://www.statewatch.org/news/2001/jun/07Rodota.pdf

Article 29 Data Protection Working Party. (2006, March 25). Opinion 3/2006 on the Directive 2006/24/EC. Retrieved from http://europa.eu.int/comm/justice_home/fsj/privacy/docs/wpdocs/2006/wp119_en.pdf

Article 29 Data Protection Working Party. (1998). Working Document on transfers of personal data to third countries: Applying Articles 25 and 26 of the EU data protection directive, 24 July 1998, WP 12. Retrieved May 5, 2009, from [REMOVED HYPERLINK FIELD]http://www.europa.eu.int/comm/internal_market/en/dataprot/wpdocs/wp12en.htm

Article 29 Data Protection Working Party. (2007, April). Opinion on the concept of personal data.

Article 29 Working Party. (2004). Opinion 10/2004 on more harmonised information provisions. Retrieved May 1, 2010, from http://ec.europa.eu/justice_home/fsj/privacy/docs/wpdocs/2004/wp100_en.pdf

Article 29 Working Party. (2009). Opinion 2/2009 on the protection of children's personal data (General guidelines and the special case of schools). Retrieved May 1, 2010, from http://ec.europa.eu/justice_home/fsj/privacy/docs/wpdocs/2009/wp160_en.pdf

Article 29 Working Party. (2004). Opinion 9/2004 on a draft Framework Decision on the storage of data processed and retained for the purpose of providing electronic public communications services or data available in public communications networks with a view to the prevention, investigation, detection and prosecution of criminal acts, including terrorism. [Proposal presented by France, Ireland, Sweden and Great Britain (Council doc. 8958/04 – April 28, 2004)].

Article 29 Working Party. (2005a). Opinion 4/2005 on the Proposal for a Directive of the European Parliament and of the Council on the Retention of Data Processed in Connection with the Provision of Public Electronic Communication Services and Amending Directive 2002/58/EC (COM(2005)438 final of 21.09.2005).

Article 29 Working Party. (2005b). Opinion 113/2005 on the Proposal for a Directive of the European Parliament and of the Council on the Retention of Data Processed in Connection with the Provision of Public Electronic Communication Services and Amending Directive 2002/58/EC (COM (2005) 438 final of 21.09.2005).

Article 29 Working Party. (2006a). Opinion 3/2006 on the Directive 2006/XX/EC of the European Parliament and of the Council on the retention of data processed in connection with the provision of public electronic communication services and amending Directive 2002/58/EC, as adopted by the Council on 21 February 2006.

Article 29 Working Party. (2006b). Opinion 10/2006 on the processing of personal data by the Society for Worldwide Interbank Financial Telecommunication (SWIFT).

Article 29 Working Party. (2006). Opinion 3/2006 of Art. 29 Working Party on Directive 2006/24/EC, adopted on 25 March 2006. Retrieved May 20, 2010, from http://ec.europa.eu/justice_home/fsj/privacy/docswp-docs/2006/wp119 _en.pdf

Augusto, J. (2007). Ambient intelligence: The confluence of pervasive computing and artificial intelligence. In Schuster, A. (Ed.), *Intelligent computing everywhere*. London: Springer Verlag. doi:10.1007/978-1-84628-943-9_11

Aydın, S., & Keyman, E. F. (2004, August). *European integration and the transformation of Turkish democracy*. EU-Turkey Working Papers, No. 2. Brussels: Centre for European Policy Studies. Retrieved from http://www.ceps.be

Bainbridge, D. (1996). *EC Data Protection Directive*. London: Butterworths.

Baker, E. (2009). The European Union's "area of freedom, security and (criminal) justice" ten years on. *Criminal Law Review (London, England)*, *12*, 833–850.

Bakopoulos, G. (1995). *Freedom of assembly in Greek, French & British Public Law* [in Greek]. Athens-Komotini: Ant. N. Sakkoulas.

Baldassare, A. (1974). *Privacy e Constituzione*. Rome: Bulzoni.

Balkin, J. M. (2004). Digital speech and democratic culture. *New York University Law Review*, *79*(1), 1–58.

Balkin, J. M. (2008). Media access: A question of design. *The George Washington Law Review*, *76*(4), 933–951.

Balkin, J., & Levinson, S. (2006). The processes of constitutional change: From partisan entrenchment to the national surveillance state. *Fordham Law Review*, *75*, 101-145. Retrieved May 5, 2009, from http://papers.ssrn.com/sol3/papers.cfm?abstract_id=930514

Banishar, D. (2000). *Privacy and human rights: An international survey of privacy laws and developments*. Washington, DC: Electronic Privacy Information Center.

Banks, J., Pachano, M., Thompson, L., & Hanny, D. (2007). *RFID applied*. Hoboken, NJ: John Wiley & Sons. doi:10.1002/9780470168226

Barbaro, M., & Zeller, T., Jr. (2006, August 9). A face is exposed for AOL searcher no. 4417749. *The New York Times*, p. A1.

Barnard, C. (2004). *The substantive law of the EU*. Oxford: Oxford University Press.

Barron, J. A. (1967). Access to the press—A new first amendment right. *Harvard Law Review*, *80*, 1641–1678. doi:10.2307/1339417

Bartoli, E. (2009). Children's data protection vs. marketing companies. *International Review of Law Computers & Technology*, *23*(1-2), 35–45. doi:10.1080/13600860902742612

Bayan Muna et al. Petition in *Bayan Muna et al. v. Leandro R. Mendoza et al.*, G.R. No. 190431, (pending before the Supreme Court of the Republic of the Philippines)

BBC News. (2005, December 14). EU approves data retention rules.

BBC News. (2005, September 27) EU phone record proposal rejected.

BBC News. (2006, March 11). Madrid awaits end to bomb probe.

BBC News. (2010, March 2). German court orders stored telecoms data deletion.

BBC News. (November 17, 2009). T-Mobile staff sold personal data.

BBC. (March 20, 2009). *Google pulls some street images.* Retrieved from http://news.bbc.co.uk/2/hi/7954596.stm

Beattie, K. (2009). S and Marper v. United Kingdom: Privacy, DNA and crime rrevention. *EHRLR, 2009*(2), 229.

Beck, A. (1996). Foucault and law: The collapse of law's empire. *Oxford Journal of Legal Studies, 16*(3), 489–502. doi:10.1093/ojls/16.3.489

Beller, F. K., & Zlatnik, G. P. (1995). The beginning of human life. *Journal of Assisted Reproduction and Genetics, 12*(8), 477–483. doi:10.1007/BF02212909

Benetar, D., & Benetar, M. (2001). A pain in the fetus: Toward ending confusion about fetal pain. *Bioethics, 15*(1), 57–76. doi:10.1111/1467-8519.00212

Bennett, C. (1992). *Regulating privacy: Data protection and public policy in Europe and the United States.* Ithaca, NY: Cornell University Press.

Bennett, C. (1992). *Regulating privacy: Data protection and public policy in Europe and the United States.* Ithaca, NY: Cornell University Press.

Benyon, J. (1996). The politics of police co-operation in the European Union. *International Journal of the Sociology of Law, 24*, 353–379. doi:10.1006/ijsl.1996.0022

Ben-Ze'ev, A. (2003). Privacy, emotional closeness, and openness in cyberspace. *Computers in Human Behavior, 19*, 451–467. doi:10.1016/S0747-5632(02)00078-X

Bergkamp, L. (2002). EU Data Protection Policy. *Computer Law & Security Report, 18*, 12.

Berlin, I. (1958). Two concepts of liberty. In *Four Essays on Liberty* (1969 ed.). Oxford: Oxford University Press.

BeVier, L. R. (1995). Information about individuals in the hands of government: Some reflections on mechanisms for privacy protection. *The William and Mary Bill of Rights Journal, 4*(2), 455–506.

Bianca, C. M., & Busnelli, F. (2007). *La protezione dei dati personali.* Padova, Italy: Cedam.

Bibas, S. A. (1994). A contractual approach to data privacy. *Harvard Journal of Law & Public Policy, 17*(2), 591–611.

Bibas, S. (1994). A contractual approach to data privacy. *Harvard Journal of Law & Public Policy, 17*, 591–611.

Bignami, F. (2007). Privacy and law enforcement in the European Union: The Data Retention Directive. *Chicago Journal of International Law, 8*, 233.

Bilgin, P. (2008). The securityness of secularism? The case of Turkey. *Security Dialogue, 39*(6), 593–614.. doi:10.1177/0967010608098211

Bimber, B. (1994). The three faces of technological determinism. In Smith, M. R., & Marx, L. (Eds.), *Does technology drive history? The dilemma of technological determinism.* Cambridge, MA: MIT Press.

Birnhack, M. (2008). The EU data protection directive: An engine of a global regime. *Computer Law & Security Report, 24*, 508. doi:10.1016/j.clsr.2008.09.001

Black, E. (2001). *IBM and the Holocaust: The strategic alliance between Nazi Germany and America's most powerful corporation.* New York: Crown Publishers.

Blas, F. *Ople v. Ruben D. Torres, et al.*, G.R. No. 127685, July 23, 1998 (en banc), *citing* Burrows v. Superior Court of San Bernardino County, 13 Cal. 3d 238, 529 P 2d 590 (1974). See Katz v. United states (1967), 389 U.S. 347, 350-352, 88 S. Ct. 507, 19 L. Ed. 2d 576; People v. Krivda (1971) 5 Cal. 3d 357, 364, 96 Cal. Rptr. 62, 486 P. 2d 1262; 8 Cal. 3d 623-624,105 Cal. Rptr. 521, 504 P. 2d 457. Retrieved May 19, 2010, from http://www.lawphil.net/judjuris/juri1998/jul1998/gr_127685_1998.html

Boehm, F. (2009). Confusing fundamental rights protection in Europe: Loopholes in Europe's fundamental rights protection exemplified on European data protection rules (Law Working Paper Series, no. 2009-01). Luxembourg: University of Luxembourg.

Bohn, J., Coroama, V., Langheinrich, M., Mattern, F., & Rohs, M. (2005). Social, economic, and ethical implications of ambient intelligence and ubiquitous computing. In Weber, W., Rabaey, J. M., & Aarts, E. H. L. (Eds.), *Ambient intelligence* (pp. 5–29). Berlin: Springer. doi:10.1007/3-540-27139-2_2

Boisson de Chazournes, L. (2009). New technologies, the precautionary principle and public participation. In Murphy, T. (Ed.), *New technologies and human rights*. Oxford: Oxford University Press. doi:10.1093/acprof:oso/9780199562572.003.0005

Bolman, E. (2002). Privacy in the age of information, *The Journal of Information, Law and Technology (JILT), 2002*(2). Retrieved from http://elj.warwick.ac.uk/jilt/02-2/bohlman.html

Bonin, D. (2002). *Defense of abortion*. Cambridge, UK: Cambridge University Press. doi:10.1017/CBO9780511610172

Borenstein, J. (2008). Privacy: A non-existent entity. *IEEE Technology and Society Magazine, 27*(4), 20–26. doi:10.1109/MTS.2008.930565

Boussard, H. (2009). Individual human rights in genetic research: Blurring the line between collective and individual interests. In Murphy, T. (Ed.), *New technologies and human rights*. Oxford: Oxford University Press.

Boyle, J. (1997). *Foucault in cyberspace: Surveillance, sovereignty, and hard-wired censors*. Retrieved March 15, 2010, from http://www.law.duke.edu/boylesite/foucault.htm

Bozkurt, G. (2008, May 31). The corridor. *Hurriyet Daily News*. Retrieved from http://www.hurriyetdailynews.com/h.php?news=the-corridor-2008-05-31

Brewin, B. (2004, November 15). RFID gets FDA push. *Federal Computer Week*. Retrieved April 24, 2010, from http://fcw.com/articles/2004/11/14/rfid-gets-fda-push.aspx

Breyer, P. (2005). Telecommunications data retention and human rights: the compatibility of blanket traffic data retention with ECHR. *European Law Journal, 11*(3), 365. doi:10.1111/j.1468-0386.2005.00264.x

Brin, D. (1998). *The transparent society: Will technology force us to choose between privacy and freedom*. New York: Perseus Books.

Brobst, J. A. (2006, Spring). The prospect of enacting an unborn victims of violence act in North Carolina. *North Carolina Central Law Journal*, 127–171.

Brodeur, J. P. (1984). Policing: Beyond 1984. *Canadian Journal ofSociology, 9*(2), 195–207. doi:10.2307/3340216

Brody, B. (1975). *Abortion and the sanctity of human life*. Cambridge, MA: MIT Press.

Brody, B. (1988). *On the humanity of the fetus. What is a person?* (pp. 229–250). Clifton, NJ: Humana Press.

Bronitt, S., & Stellios, J. (2006). Regulating telecommunications interception and access in the twenty-first century: Technological evolution or legal revolution? *Prometheus, 24*(4), 413–428..doi:10.1080/08109020601030001

Brown, D. E. (2007). *RFID implementation*. New York: McGraw-Hill.

Bruening, P. J. (2004, July). *RFID technology: What the future holds for commerce, security, and the consumer*. Testimony before the Subcommittee on Commerce, Trade, and Consumer Protection of the House Committee on Energy and Commerce, Washington DC. Retrieved April 24, 2010, from http://cdt.info/testimony/20040714bruening.pdf

Burgess, J. A., & Tawai, S. A. (1996). When did you first begin to feel it? Locating the beginning of human consciousness. *Bioethics, 10*, 1–26. doi:10.1111/j.1467-8519.1996.tb00100.x

Burkell, J., Steeves, V., & Micheti, A. (2007). *Broken doors: Strategies for drafting privacy policies kids can understand*. Ottawa, Canada: On the Identity Trail. Retrieved from http://www.idtrail.org/files/broken_doors_final_report.pdf

Burkell, J., Steeves, V., & Micheti, A. (2007). Broken doors: Strategies for drafting privacy policies kids can understand. Retrieved May 1, 2010, from http://www.idtrail.org/files/broken_doors_final_report.pdf

Business Mirror Online. (2009, September 27). Transport leaders back RFID project. Retrieved May 19, 2010, from http://businessmirror.com.ph/index.php?option=com_content&view=article&id=16552:transport-leaders-back-rfid-project&catid=26:nation&Itemid=63

Buttarelli, G. (1997). *Banche dati e tutela della riservatezza*. Milano, Italy: Giuffrè.

Bygrave, L. A. (2004). Privacy protection in a global context: A comparative overview. *Scandinavian Studies in Law*, *47*, 319.

Bygrave, L. A. (2003). Digital rights management and privacy. In Becker, E., Buhse, W., Günnewig, D., & Rump, N. (Eds.), *Digital rights management: Technological, economic, legal and political aspects* (pp. 418–446). New York: Springer.

Bygrave, L. (2008). International agreements to protect personal data. In Rule, J. B., & Greenleaf, G. (Eds.), *Global privacy protection*. Cheltenham, UK: Edward Elgar Publishing.

Caballes v. Court of Appeals, G.R. No. 136292, January 15, 2002.

Cammilleri-Subrenat, A., & Levallois-Barth, C. (2007). *Sensitive data protection in the European Union*. Brussels: Bruylant.

Canotilho, J. G., & Moreira, V. (2007). *Constituição da República Portuguesa Anotada* (4th ed.). Coimbra, Portugal: Coimbra Editora.

Caplan, A., McCartney, J. J., & Sisti, D. (Eds.). (2006). *The case of Terri Schiavo: Ethics and the end of life*. New York: Prometheus Books.

Cappato, M. (2002, May). Session document on the Council common position for adopting a European Parliament and Council Directive (p. 3). Brussels: European Parliament. Retrieved from http://www.statewatch.org/news/2002/may/epamend.pdf

Carey, P. (2009). *Data protection: A practical guide to UK and EU law* (3rd ed.). New York: Oxford University Press.

Carolan, Mary. (2010, May 6). European court to rule on data storage law. *The Irish Times*.

Casarosa, F. (2009). Privacy in search engines: Negotiating Control. Retrieved May 1, 2010, from http://ssrn.com/abstract=1561571

Castro, C. S. (2005). O direito à autodeterminação informativa e os novos desafios gerados pelo direito à liberdade e à segurança no pós 11 de Setembro. In *Estudos em homenagem ao Conselheiro José Manuel Cardoso da Costa* (*Vol. II*). Coimbra, Portugal: Coimbra Editora.

Castro, C. S. (2006). *Protecção de dados pessoais na Internet. Sub Judice, 35*. Coimbra, Portugal: Almedina.

Chadwick, P. (2006). The value of privacy. *EHRLR, 2006*(5), 495-508.

Chandler, D. (2008). *Worldwide online backup services 2007-2011 forecast: A new market emerges*. Framingham, MA: IDC.

Chappell, D. (2008). *A short introduction to cloud platforms: An enterprise-oriented view*. Retrieved from http://www.davidchappell.com/CloudPlatforms--Chappell.pdf

Christofides, E., Muise, A., & Desmarais, S. (2009). Information disclosure and control on Facebook: Are they two sides of the same coin or two different processes? *Cyberpsychology & Behavior*, *12*, 341–345. doi:10.1089/cpb.2008.0226

Cisco, Inc. (2003). Wireless LAN benefits study. Retrieved April 24, 2010, from http://newsroom.cisco.com/dlls/2003_NOP_WLAN_Benefits_Study.pdf

Citron, D. K. (2009). Cyber civil rights. *Boston University Law Review. Boston University. School of Law*, *89*(1), 61–125.

Cizre, U. (2003). Demythologyzing the national security concept: The case of Turkey. *The Middle East Journal*, *57*(2), 213–229.

Cizre, Ü. (Ed.). (2006). *Almanac Turkey 2005: Security sector and democratic oversight*. İstanbul, Turkey: TESEV. Retrieved from http://www.tesev.org.tr/UD_OBJS/PDF/DEMP/Almanak-2005-Ingilizce-Tam%20Metin.pdf

CJEC. (2007). Opinion of Advocate General Kokott [Court of Justice of the European Communities Case C-275/06].

Clark, C. (1996). The answer to the machine is in the machine. In Bernt Hugenholtz, P. (Ed.), *The future of copyright in a digital environment*. The Hague: Kluwer Law International.

Clarke, R. (1994). The digital persona and its application to data surveillance. *The Information Society*, *10*(2), 77–92. doi:10.1080/01972243.1994.9960160

Clarke, R. (2010). The effectiveness of privacy policy statements: A pilot study against a normative template. In I. Kerr, J. Gammack & K. Bryant (Eds.), *Digital business security development: Management technologies*. Retrieved May 1, 2010, from http://www.rogerclarke.com/EC/PPSE0812.html

Clemens, B., Maghiros, I., Beslay, L., Centeno, C., Punie, Y., Rodriguez, C., & Maser, M. (2003). Security and privacy for the citizen in the post-September 11 digital age: A prospective overview. Report to the European Parliament Committee on Citizens' Freedom and Rights, Justice and Home Affairs (LIBE), Institute for Prospective Technological Studies, Seville, Spain. Retrieved from http://cybersecurity.jrc.es/docs/libe%20study/libestudy%20eur20823%20.pdf

CNIL. (2005, October 18). Délibération no. 2005-235. Retrieved March 27, 2010, from http://www.legifrance.gouv.fr/affichCnil.do?oldAction=rechExpCnil&id=CNILTEXT000017652059&fastReqId=137369379&fastPos=1

Coalition of Civil Liberties Organisations. (2002, May). Letter to the President of the European Parliament. Retrieved from http://www.gilc.org/cox_en.html

Cohen, J. (2000). Examined lives: Informational privacy and the subject as object. *Stanford Law Review*, *52*, 1373–1437. doi:10.2307/1229517

Cohen, J. (2002). *Regulating intimacy: A new legal paradigm*. Princeton, NJ: Princeton University Press.

Cohen, J. E. (2000). Examined lives: Informational privacy and the subject as object. *Stanford Law Review*, *52*, 1373–1438. doi:10.2307/1229517

Cohen, J. (1996). A right to read anonymously: A closer look at 'copyright management' in cyberspace. *Connecticut Law Review*, *28*, 981–1039.

Cohen, J. (1997). Some reflections on copyright management systems and laws designed to protect them. *Berkeley Technology Law Journal*, *12*, 161–190.

Cohen, J. (2003). DRM and privacy [Georgetown Public Law Research Paper No. 372741]. *Berkeley Technological Law Journal*, *18*, 575-617. Retrieved March 27, 2010, from http://ssrn.com/abstract=372741

Cohen, N. (2009, May 17). Law students teach Scalia about privacy and the web. *The New York Times*. Retrieved from http://www.nytimes.com/2009/05/18/technology/internet/18link.html

Cole, R. (2005). Authentic democracy: Endowing citizens with a human right in their genetic information. *Hofstra Law Review*, *33*, 1241–1303.

Collins, J. (2004). Hospitals get healthy dose of RFID. *RFID Journal*. Retrieved April 24, 2010, from http://www.rfidjournal.com/article/view/920http://www.rfidjournal.com/article/view/920http://www.rfidjournal.com/article/view/920http://www.rfidjournal.com/article/view/920http://www.rfidjournal.com/article/view/920

Colussi, I. A. (2011). Dati genetici e forze di polizia: intersezioni europee. In L. S. Rossi (Ed). *La protezione dei diritti fondamentali: Carta dei diritti UE e standards internazionali: xv Convegno, Bologna 10-11 June 2010 / SIDI*, Società italiana di diritto internazionale, Napoli: Editoriale scientifica (forthcoming).

Colvin, M. (Ed.). (2002). *Developing key privacy rights*. Oxford, UK: Hart.

Commission of the EC. (2005, September). Proposal for a directive of the European Parliament and of the Council on the retention of data. Retrieved from http://www.statewatch.org/news/2005/sep/com-438-data-retention.pdf

Commission, E. U. (2010). Recommendation of the council concerning guidelines governing the protection of privacy and transborder flow of personal data (23.09.1980). Retrieved May 1, 2010, from http://www.oecd.org/document/18/0,2340,en_2649_34255_1815186_1_1_1_1,00.html

Committee on Civil Liberties. Justice and Home Affairs. (2005, May). Report on the initiative for a Draft Framework Decision on the retention of data [European Parliament session document]. Retrieved from http://www.statewatch.org/news/2005/oct/ep-data-ret-june-05.pdf

Committee on Civil Liberties. Justice and Home Affairs. (2005, October). European Parliament Draft Report on Data Retention Directive. Retrieved from http://www.statewatch.org/news/2005/oct/alvaro-amendments.pdf

Committee on Civil Liberties. Justice and Home Affairs. (2005, November). *European Parliament report on data retention*. Retrieved from http://www.statewatch.org/news/2005/nov/EP_provdpreport.pdf

Contiades, X. (2002). *The new constitutionalism and fundamental rights after the 2001 revision* [in Greek]. Athens-Komotini: Ant. N. Sakkoulas.

Cook, D., Augusto, J. C., & Jakkula, V. R. (2009). Ambient intelligence: Technologies, applications and opportunities. *Pervasive and Mobile Computing*, *5*(4), 277–298. doi:10.1016/j.pmcj.2009.04.001

Cornell, S. E., & Karaveli, H. M. (2008, October). *Prospects for a 'Torn' Turkey: A secular and unitary future?* Washington, DC: Central Asia-Caucasus Institute & Silk Road Studies Program. Retrieved from http://www.silkroadstudies.org/new/docs/silkroadpapers/0810Turkey.pdf

Cortes, I. (1970). *The constitutional foundations of privacy*. Quezon City, Philippines: University of the Philippines Law Center.

Council of the EU. (2002, November). Answers to questionnaire on traffic data retention. Retrieved from http://www.effi.org/sananvapaus/eu-2002-11-20.html

Council of the EU. (2005, October). Outcome of proceedings on the subject of the Draft Framework Decision on the retention of data. Retrieved from http://www.statewatch.org/news/2005/oct/council-data-ret-draft-10-oct-05.pdf

Council of the European Union. (2004, April 28). Draft framework decision [Council Doc. 8958/04]. Brussels: EC. Retrieved from http://www.statewatch.orgg/soseurope.htm

Court: Tapping judges and prosecutors' phones prohibited. (2009, December 29). *Hurriyet Daily News*. Retrieved from http://www.hurriyetdailynews.com

Covington & Burling. (2003). Memorandum of laws concerning the legality of data retention with regard to the rights guaranteed by the European Convention on Human Rights. London: Privacy International. Retrieved May 15, 2009, from http://www.statewatch.org/news/2003/oct/Data_Retention_Memo.pdf

Cremona, M., & De Witte, B. (2008). *EU foreign relations law: Constitutional fundamentals*. Oxford: Hart.

Cremona, M. (2008). EU external action in the JHA domain: A legal perspective. EUI Working Papers, Law 2008/24.

Crum, G., & McCormack, T. (1992). *Abortion: Pro-choice or pro-life?* Washington, DC: American University Press.

Czychowski, C., & Nordemann, J. B. (2008). Vorratsdaten und Urheberrecht – Zulässige Nutzung gespeicherter Daten. *Neue Juristische Wochenschrift*, 3095–3099.

Dalangin-Fernandez, L. (2010, January 12). Supreme Court stops RFID. *Philippine Daily Inquirer.* Retrieved May 19, 2010 from http://newsinfo.inquirer.net/breakingnews/nation/view/20100112-246939/Supreme-Court-stops-RFID

Dalton, J., Ippolito, C., Poncet, I., & Rossini, S. (2005). *Using RFID technologies to reduce blood transfusion errors*. White Paper by Intel Corporation, Autentica, Cisco Systems, and San Raffaele Hospital. Retrieved April 24, 2010, from http://www.cisco.com/web/IT/local_offices/case_history/rfid_in_blood_transfusions_final.pdfhttp://www.cisco.com/web/IT/local_offices/case_history/rfid_in_blood_transfusions_final.pdfhttp://www.cisco.com/web/IT/local_offices/case_history/rfid_in_blood_transfusions_final.pdfhttp://www.cisco.com/web/IT/local_offices/case_history/rfid_in_blood_transfusions_final.pdfhttp://www.cisco.com/web/IT/local_offices/case_history/rfid_in_blood_transfusions_final.pdf

Dashwood, A. (2001). The Constitution of the European Union after Nice: Law-making procedures. *European Law Review*, *26*, 215–238.

Daskala, B., & Maghiros, I. (2007). *Digital territories: Towards the protection of public and private spaces in a digital and ambient intelligence environment* [IPTS report]. Luxemburg: OPOCE.

Davies, S. (1996). *Big brother: Britain's web of surveillance and the new technological order.* London: Pan.

De Burca, G. (1992). Giving effect to European Community directives. *The Modern Law Review*, *55*, 215–240.

De Hert, P. (2005). Balancing security & liberty within the European human rights framework: A critical reading of the court's case law in the light of surveillance & criminal law enforcement strategies after 9/11. *Utrecht Law Review*, *1*(1), 68–96.

De Hert, P., & Gutwirth, S. (2009). Data protection in the case law of Strasbourg and Luxembourg: Constitutionalisation in action. In Gutwirth, S., Poullet, Y., De Hert, P., Terwangne, C., & Nouwt, S. (Eds.), *Reinventing data protection?*Dordrecht, The Netherlands: Springer. doi:10.1007/978-1-4020-9498-9_1

De Hert, P. (2008). A right to identity to face the Internet of Things. [Also on the CD of Commission Nationale française pour l'Unesco, Ethique et droits de l'homme dans la societé d'information. Actes, synthèse et recommandations, 13-14 septembre 2007, Strasbourg.] Retrieved from http://portal.unesco.org/ci/fr/files/25857/12021328273de_Hert-Paul.pdf/de%2BHert-Paul.pdf

De Vries, K. (2010). Identity, profiling algorithms and a world of ambient intelligence. *Ethics and Information Technology*, *12*(1), 71–85. doi:10.1007/s10676-009-9215-9

De Witte, B. (2008). Too much constitutional law in the European Union's foreign relations? In Cremona, M., & de Witte, B. (Eds.), *EU foreign relations law- constitutional fundamentals* (p. 3). Oxford: Hart.

Deighton, J. (2003). Market solutions to privacy problems. In Nicoll, C., Prins, C., & Dellen, M. J. M. v. (Eds.), *Digital anonymity and the law: Tensions and dimensions*. The Hague: T.M.C. Asser Press.

Delany, H., & Murphy, C. (2007). Towards common principles relating to the protection of privacy rights? *EHRLR, 2007*(5), 568-582.

DeNoon, D. (2005, July 27). Chip implants: Better care or privacy scare? *WebMD Medical News*, Retrieved April 24, 2010, from http://www.webmd.com/healthy-aging/news/20050727/chip-implants-better-care-privacy-scarehttp://www.webmd.com/healthy-aging/news/20050727/chip-implants-better-care-privacy-scarehttp://www.webmd.com/healthy-aging/news/20050727/chip-implants-better-care-privacy-scarehttp://www.webmd.com/healthy-aging/news/20050727/chip-implants-better-care-privacy-scarehttp://www.webmd.com/healthy-aging/news/20050727/chip-implants-better-care-privacy-scare

Department for Business. Innovation and Skills (BIS). (2010, April 21). Royal Assent for the Digital Economy Bill. London: BIS. Retrieved May 20, 2010, from http://interactive.bis.gov. uk/digitalbritain/digital-economy-bill

Desierto, D. (2009). A universalist history of the 1987 Philippine constitution (I). *Historia Constitucional/Electronic Journal of Constitutional History, 10*, 383-444. Retrieved on May 19, 2010 from http://www.historiaconstitucional.com/index.php/historiaconstitucional/article/viewFile/236/209

Digital Civil Rights in Europe. (2006, March 29). Telecom data to be retained for one year in France. Retrieved May 20, 2010, from http://www.edri.org/edrigram/number4.6/franceretantion

Digital Civil Rights in Europe. (2010, February 10). Update on the Belgian transposition of the Data Retention Directive. Retrieved May 20, 2010, from http://www.edri.org/edrigram/number8.3/belgium-data-retention-draft-law

Directive 2009/136/EC of the European Parliament and of the Council. *Official Journal L337/11*.

Dix, A. (2005). Le tecniche Rfid. In G. Rasi (Ed.), *Innovazioni tecnologiche e privacy*. Rome: Ufficio grafico dell'Istituto Poligrafico e Zecca dello Stato.

Doe v. Cahill, 884 A.2d 451 (Del. 2005).

Donos, P. (2002). The data protection authority & its role in the advanced protection of human dignity. In Donos, P., Mitrou, L., Mittleton, P., & Papakonstantinou, E. (Eds.), *The data protection authority & the advanced protection of human rights* [in Greek]. Athens, Thessaloniki: Sakkoulas Publications.

Dorsen, N., Rosenfeld, M., Sajò, A., & Baer, S. (2003). *Comparative constitutionalism – Cases & materials*. Eagan, MN: West Group.

Dorsheidt, J. (1999). The unborn child and the UN Convention on Children's Rights: The Dutch perspective as a guideline. *The International Journal of Children's Rights, 7*, 303–347. doi:10.1163/15718189920494426

DOTC Circular No. 2009-06

Dougan, M. (2008). The Treaty of Lisbon 2007: Winning minds, not hearts. *Common Market Law Review, 45*, 617.

Downie, R., & Macnaughton, J. (2007). *Bioethics and humanities: Attitudes and perceptions*. London: Routledge-Cavendish.

Dreyer, E. (2005). Le respect de la vie privée objet d'un droit fondamental, *Lexis-Nexis Juris- Classeur, 5*(18).

Ducatel, K., Bogdanowicz, M., Scapolo, F., Leijten, J., & Burgelman, J. C. (2001). Scenarios for ambient intelligence in 2010. Final report EUR 19763, EC-JRC, IPTS, Seville, Spain. Retrieved from http://cordis.europa.eu/fp7/ict/istag/home_en.html

Durrant, P. (2006, July). *Data retention directive: Some ISP observations*. Paper presented at the Irish Centre for European Law, Privacy and Data Retention Directive Conference, Dublin, Ireland.

Dutch Data Protection Authority. (2007, January). Legislative proposal (Bill) for implementation of the European Directive on Data Retention. Retrieved from www.dutchdpa.nl/downloads_adv/z2006-01542.pdf

Eberle, E. J. (2002). *Dignity and liberty: Constitutional visions in Germany and the United States*. Westport, CT: Praeger Press.

Edwards, L., & Brown, I. (2009). Data control and social networking: Irreconcilable ideas? In Matwyshyn, A. M. (Ed.), *Harboring data: Information security, law and the corporation* (pp. 202–226). Stanford, CA: Stanford University Press.

Edwards, L. (2008). Data protection 2.0: This time is personal. Paper presented at the Gikii2 conference, Oxford, UK. Retrieved May 1, 2010, from http://www.law.ed.ac.uk/ahrc/gikii/docs3/edwards.pdf

Electronic Frontier Foundation. (2003). *Unsafe harbors: Abusive DMCA subpoenas and takedown demands*.

Elliston, S. (2007). *Best interests of the child in healthcare*. London: Routledge-Cavendish.

Elrick, M. L. (2001, July). Cops tap database to harass, intimidate. *Detroit Free Press*. Retrieved from http://www.sweetliberty.org/issues/privacy/lein1.htm

Ergenekon indictment may trouble Turkey. (2008, September 3). *Hurriyet Daily News.* Retrieved from http://www.hurriyetdailynews.com

Eschet, G. (2005). FIPs and PETs for RFID: Protecting privacy in the web of radio frequency identification. *Jurimetrics*, *45*, 301–331.

Estelle T. Griswold & C. Lee Buxton v. Connecticut (1965), 381 U.S. 479.

EU Commission. (1996a). Green paper on the protection of minors and human dignity in audiovisual and information services [COM (96) 483 fin].

EU Commission. (1996b). Communication on illegal and harmful content on the internet [COM (96) 487 fin].

EU Commission. (2003). First report on the implementation of the Data Protection Directive (95/46/EC) [COM(2003) 265 fin].

Eurobarometer. (2007). Safer internet for children: Qualitative study in 29 European countries. Retrieved May 1, 2010, from http://ec.europa.eu/public_opinion/quali/ql_safer_internet_summary.pdf

European Commission. (2007). Communication on the follow-up of the work program for better implementation of the Data Protection Directive [COM (2007) 87 final]. Retrieved from http://ec.europa.eu/justice_home/fsj/privacy/docs/lawreport/com_2007_87_f_en.pdf

European Council. (2008, November 27). Framework Decision 2008/977/JHA on the protection of personal data processed in the framework of police and judicial cooperation in criminal matters. Retrieved from http://eur-lex.europa.eu/LexUriServ/LexUriServ.do?uri=OJ:L:2008:350:0060:0071:EN:PDF

European Court of Justice. (2009). Press release no. 11/09 concerning the Judgment C-301/06 of February 10, 2009. Retrieved May 20, 2010, from http://www.statewatch.org/news/2009/feb/ eu-ecj-ireland-datret-judgment-prel.pdf

European Data Protection Supervisor. (2009). Opinion on the Communication from the Commission to the European Parliament, the Council and the European Economic and Social Committee towards a European e-Justice Strategy. *Official Journal of the European Union* (2009/C 128/02).

European Data Protection Supervisor. (2010). Opinion of the European Data Protection Supervisor on promoting trust in the information society by fostering data protection and privacy. Retrieved from http://www.edps.europa.eu/EDPSWEB/webdav/site/mySite/shared/Documents/Consultation/Opinions/2010/10-03-19_Trust_Information_Society_EN.pdf

Executive Order No. 269 (Creating the Commission on Information Communications and Technology), 12 January 2004. Retrieved on May 19, 2010 from http://www.ops.gov.ph/records/eo_no269.htm

Facebook. (2010). Press office statistics. Retrieved from http://www.facebook.com/press/info.php?statistics

Fanberg, H. (2004). The RFID revolution. *Marketing Health Services*, *24*(3), 43–44.

Fanuele, C. (2007). Un archivio centrale per i profili del DNA nella prospettiva di un "diritto comune" europeo. *Diritto penale e processo, 13*(3), 385.

FCC (1959), Allocation of frequencies in the bands above 890 Mcs, 27 FCC 359.

Federal Constitutional Court of Germany. (2010). Press release no. 11/2010 concerning the Judgment 1 BvR 256/08, 1 BvR 263/08, 1 BvR 586/08 of March 2, 2010. Retrieved May 20, 2010, from http://www.bundesverfassungsgericht.de/pressemitteilungen/bvg10-011

Federal Radio Frequency Device Regulations, 47 C.F.R. § 15.240.

Federal Trade Commission. (2005, March). *Radio frequency identification: Applications and implications for consumers*. Workshop report from the Staff of the Federal Trade Commission. Retrieved April 24, 2010, from http://www.ftc.gov/os/2005/03/050308rfidrpt.pdfhttp://www.ftc.gov/os/2005/03/050308rfidrpt.pdfhttp://www.ftc.gov/os/2005/03/050308rfidrpt.pdfhttp://www.ftc.gov/os/2005/03/050308rfidrpt.pdfhttp://www.ftc.gov/os/2005/03/050308rfidrpt.pdf

Federal Trade Commission. (1998). Privacy online: A report to congress. Retrieved May 1, 2010, from http://www.ftc.gov/reports/privacy3/priv-23a.pdf

Federal Trade Commission. (2000). Privacy online: Fair information practices in the electronic marketplace: A report to Congress. Retrieved May 1, 2010, from http://www.ftc.gov/reports/privacy2000/privacy2000.pdf

Federal Trade Commission. (2006). How to comply with the Children's Online Privacy Protection Rule. Retrieved May 1, 2010, from http://www.ftc.gov/bcp/edu/pubs/business/idtheft/bus45.shtm

Federal Trade Commission. (2010). Questions whether changes to technology warrant changes to agency rule. Retrieved May 1, 2010, from http://www.ftc.gov/opa/2010/03/coppa.shtm

Fendrick, S. (2008-2009). The role of privacy law in genetic research. *A Journal of Law & Policy for the Information, 4*, 803-820.

Fernandez-Barrera, M., Gomes De Andrade, N. N., De Filippi, P., Viola De Azevedo Cunha, M., Sartor, G., & Casanovas, P. (2009). *Law and technology: Looking into the future*. Florence: European Press Academic Publishing.

Ferola, L. (2002). The fight against organised crime in Europe: Building an area of freedom, security and justice in the European Union. *International Journal of Legal Information, 30*(1), 53–91.

Ferrajoli, L. (2001). Fundamental rights. *International Journal for the Semiotics of Law, 14*, 1–33. doi:10.1023/A:1011290509568

Fishkin, K., & Lundell, J. (2006). RFID in healthcare. In Garfinkel, S., & Rosenberg, B. (Eds.), *RFID: Applications, security, and privacy*. Reading, MA: Addison-Wesley.

Flaherty, D. H. (1989). *Protecting privacy in surveillance societies: The Federal Republic of Germany, France, Canada, and the United States*. Chapel Hill, NC: University of North Carolina Press.

Flichy, P. (2007). *Understanding technological innovation: A socio-technical approach*. Northampton, MA: Edward Elgar Publishing.

Floridi, L. (2007). A look into the future impact of ICT on our lives. *The Information Society, 23*(1), 59–64. doi:10.1080/01972240601059094

Forgó, N., Jlussi, D., Klügel, C., & Krügel, T. (2008). *Die Umsetzung der Richtlinie zur Vorratsdatenspeicherung* (pp. 680–682). Datenschutz und Datensicherheit.

Fotiadou, A. (2006). *Balancing freedom of speech* [in Greek]. Athens, Thessaloniki: Sakkoulas Publications.

Fotiadou, A. (2007). Protection of municipality property v. protection of citizens' privacy: Comment on data protection authority decision 51/2007 [in Greek]. *Administrative Law Review, 4*, 503–508.

Foucault, M. (1979). The history of sexuality: *Vol. I. An introduction*. London: Penguin Books.

Foucault, M. (2007). *Security, Territory, Population. Lectures at the Collège de France, 1977-78* (Burchell, G., Trans.). Basingstoke, UK: Palgrave Macmillan.

Foucault, M. (1980). *Power/knowledge selected interviews and other writings of Michael Foucault (1927-77)* (Gordon, C., Ed.). Brighton, UK: Harvester Press.

Foucault, M. (2003). *Society must be defended. Lectures at the Collège de France, 1975-1976* (Macey, D., Trans.). New York: Picador.

Foucault, M. (1991). *The Foucault reader* (Rabinow, P., Ed.). London: Penguin Books.

Freedom House. (2009). *Freedom on the Net 2009 – Turkey*. Geneva, Switzerland: The Office of the United Nations High Commissioner for Refugees. Retrieved from http://www.unhcr.org/refworld/docid/49d47595c.html

Fried, C. (1968). Privacy. *The Yale Law Journal, 77*(3), 475–493. doi:10.2307/794941

Friedewald, M., Vildjiounaite, E., Puniec, Y., & Wright, D. (2007). Privacy, identity and security in ambient intelligence: A scenario analysis. *Telematics and Informatics, 24*(1), 15–29. doi:10.1016/j.tele.2005.12.005

Friedman, M. (2003). *Autonomy, gender, politics*. New York: Oxford University Press. doi:10.1093/0195138503.001.0001

Frombolz, J. (2000). The European Union data privacy directive. *Berkeley Technology Law Journal, 15*, 461–484.

Froomkin, M. (2000). The death of privacy? *Stanford Law Review, 52*, 1461–1543. doi:10.2307/1229519

Gallup Organization. (2009, February 21). Eurobarometer survey No. 225: Data protection. Retrieved May 5, 2009, from http://ec.europa.eu/public_opinion/flash/fl_225_en.pdf

Gallup Organization. (2009, February 21). Eurobarometer survey No. 226: Data perceptions among data controllers. Retrieved May 5, 2009, from http://ec.europa.eu/public_opinion/flash/fl_226_en.pdf

Garber, D. (2001). COPPA: Protecting children's personal information on the Internet. *Journal of Law and Policy, 12*, 129–187.

Garcia, F. J. (2005). Bodil Lindqvist: A Swedish churchgoer's violation of the European Union's Data Protection Directive should be a warning to U.S. Legislators. *Fordham Intellectual Property. Media & Entertainment Law Journal, 15*, 1204–1243.

Garfinkel, S., DeAlmo, J., Leng, S., McAfee, P., & Puddington, J. P. (2006). RFID in the pharmacy: Q&A with CVS. In Garfinkel, S., & Rosenberg, B. (Eds.), *RFID: Applications, security, and privacy*. Reading, MA: Addison-Wesley.

Gatter, K. M. (2003). Genetic information and the importance of context: Implications for the social meaning of genetic information and individual identity. *Saint Louis University Law Journal, 47*(2), 423–462.

Gavaghan, C. (2007). *Defending the genetic supermarket: The law and the ethics of selecting the next generation*. London: Routledge-Cavendish.

Gavison, R. (1979-1980). Privacy and the limits of law. *The Yale Law Journal, 89*(3), 421–471. doi:10.2307/795891

Gavison, R. (1980). Privacy and the limits of law. *The Yale Law Journal, 89*, 421–471. doi:10.2307/795891

Geddes, R. (2000). Public utilities. In Bouckaert, B., & De Geest, G. (Eds.), *Encyclopedia of law and economics*. Northampton, MA: Edward Elgar Publishing.

Geiger, C. (2010). The future of copyright in Europe: Striking a fair balance between protection and access to information. *Intellectual Property Quarterly, 1*, 1–14.

Gerontas, A. (2002). *Citizen's protection from electronic processing of personal data* [in Greek]. Athens, Thessaloniki: Sakkoulas Publications.

Gever, S. (2006). Abortion legislation and the future of the 'counseling model'. *European Journal of Health Law, 13*, 27–40. doi:10.1163/157180906777036355

Gibson, D. G., Glass, J. I., Lartigue, C., Noskov, V. N., & Chuang, R. Y. Algire1, M. A.,...Venter, J. C. (2010, July 2). Creation of a bacterial cell controlled by a chemically synthesized genome. *AAS Science*. Retrieved from http://www.sciencemag.org/cgi/content/abstract/science.1190719

Gilbar, R. (2007). Communicating genetic information in the family: The familial relationship as the forgotten factor. *Journal of Medical Ethics, 33*, 390–393. doi:10.1136/jme.2006.017467

Gilbert, S., Tyler, A., & Zackin, E. (2005). *Bioethics and the new embryology: Springboards for debate*. Sunderland, MA: Sinauer Associates.

Gillespie, A. A. (2009). Regulation of internet surveillance. *EHRLR, 2009*(4), 552.

Gillon, R. (1994). Medical ethics: Four principles plus attention to scope. *British Medical Journal, 309*, 184–188.

Gilmore, G., & Rijpma, J. (2007). Joined cases C-317/04 and C-318/04. *Common Market Law Review, 44*, 1081.

Gitter, R., & Schnabel, C. (2007). *Die Richtlinie zur Vorratsspeicherung und ihre Umsetzung in das nationale Recht* (pp. 411–417). Multimedia und Recht.

Gleicher, N. (2008). John Doe subpoenas: Toward a consistent legal standard. *The Yale Law Journal, 118*(2), 320–368. doi:10.2307/20454712

Glendon, M. A. (1991). *Rights talk: The impoverishment of political discourse*. New York: Free Press.

Global Liberty Internet Campaign. (2001). Available from http://www.gilc.org/verhofstadt_letter.html

Goemans, C., & Dumortier, J. (2003). Enforcement issues – mandatory retention of traffic data in the EU: possible impact on privacy and on-line anonymity. Retrieved May 5, 2009, from http://www.law.kuleuven.ac.be/icri/publications/440Retention_of_traffic_data_Dumortier_Goemans.pdf?where1/4

Gonzales-Fuster, G., & Gutwirth, S. (2006). Data protection in the EU: Towards 'reflexive governance'? Retrieved May 5, 2009, from http://refgov.cpdr.ucl.ac.be/?go=publications&dc=58b4b685f4bca1bece49dd9d296e3a2683ff7256

Gostin, L. O. (1995). Genetic privacy. *The Journal of Law, Medicine & Ethics*, *23*, 320–330. doi:10.1111/j.1748-720X.1995.tb01374.x

Gostin, L. O., & Hodge, J. G. Jr. (1999). Genetic privacy and the law: An end to genetics exceptionalism. *Jurimetrics*, *40*, 21–58.

Goth, G. (2006). Tuning in to RFID. *Healthcare Informatics.* Retrieved April 24, 2010, from http://www.healthcare-informatics.com/ME2/dirmod.asp?sid=&nm=&type=Publishing&mod=Publications:Article&mid=8F3A7027421841978F18BE895F87F791&tier=4&id=B02C8A8740984CD7A7FDA241D324FAC1http://www.healthcare-informatics.com/ME2/dirmod.asp?sid=&nm=&type=Publishing&mod=Publications:Article&mid=8F3A7027421841978F18BE895F87F791&tier=4&id=B02C8A8740984CD7A7FDA241D324FAC1http://www.healthcare-informatics.com/ME2/dirmod.asp?sid=&nm=&type=Publishing&mod=Publications:Article&mid=8F3A7027421841978F18BE895F87F791&tier=4&id=B02C8A8740984CD7A7FDA241D324FAC1http://www.healthcare-informatics.com/ME2/dirmod.asp?sid=&nm=&type=Publishing&mod=Publications:Article&mid=8F3A7027421841978F18BE895F87F791&tier=4&id=B02C8A8740984CD7A7FDA241D324FAC1http://www.healthcare-informatics.com/ME2/dirmod.asp?sid=&nm=&type=Publishing&mod=Publications:Article&mid=8F3A7027421841978F18BE895F87F791&tier=4&id=B02C8A8740984CD7A7FDA241D324FAC1

Gov't to increase penalties against illegal wiretapping. (2009, November 17). *Hurriyet Daily News.* Retrieved from http://www.hurriyetdailynews.com

Graber, M., D'Alessandro, D., & Johnson-West, J. (2007). Reading level of privacy policies on Internet health web sites. *The Journal of Family Practice*, *51*(7), 642–646.

Gray, J. E., Suresh, G., Ursprung, R., Edwards, W. H., Nickerson, J., & Shiono, P. H. (2006). Patient misidentification in the neonatal intensive care unit: Quantification of risk. *Pediatrics*, *117*(1), 43–47. doi:10.1542/peds.2005-0291

Grayling, A. C. (2007). *Towards the light: The story of the struggles for liberty & rights that made the modern West*. London: Bloomsbury.

Greenfield, A. (2006). *Everyware: The dawning age of ubiquitous computing*. Berkeley, CA: New Riders.

Greenfield, K. (1991). Cameras in teddy bears: Electronic visual surveillance and the Fourth Amendment. *The University of Chicago Law Review. University of Chicago. Law School*, *58*(3), 1045–1077. doi:10.2307/1599996

Griswold v. Connecticut, 381 U.S. 479 (1965).

Guild, E. (2004). Editorial. *European Law Journal*, *10*, 147–149. doi:10.1111/j.1468-0386.2004.00208.x

Güngör, H. A. (2007). Yaşam Hakkı. Unpublished doctoral thesis. Istanbul Kultur University, Turkey.

Gutwirth, S. (2002). *Privacy and the information age*. Lanham, MD: Rowman & Littlefield Publishers.

Gutwirth, S. (2007). Biometrics between opacity and transparency. *Annali dell'Istituto Superiore di Sanita*, *43*(1), 61–65.

Gutwirth, S. (Ed.). (2009). *Reinventing data protection?* London: Springer. doi:10.1007/978-1-4020-9498-9

Gutwirth, S. (2002). *Privacy and the information age*. Oxford, UK: Rowman & Littlefield Publishers.

Häberle, P. (1993). *Le Libertá Fondamentali Nello Stato Constituzionale*. Rome: Carocci.

'Hands off,' judiciary tells government. (2008, May 22). *Hurriyet Daily News.* Retrieved from http://www.hurriyetdailynews.com

Hardt, M., & Negri, A. (2000). *Empire.* Cambridge, MA: Harvard University Press.

Haubenreicht, S. N. S. (2008). Parental rights in MySpace: Reconceptualising the state's parens patriae role in the digital age. Retrieved May 1, 2010, from http://ssrn.com/abstract=1217872

Hawkes, B. (2006, July). *The Data Retention Directive and data protection.* Paper presented at the Irish Centre for European Law, Privacy and Data Retention Directive Conference, Dublin, Ireland.

Hebenton, B., & Thomas, T. (1995). *Policing Europe: Co-operation, conflict and control.* Basingstoke, UK: Macmillan.

Hechinger, J. (2008, September 18). College applicants, beware: Your Facebook page is showing. *The Wall Street Journal.* Retrieved from http://online.wsj.com/article/SB122170459104151023.html

Heilbroner, R. (1967). Do machines make history? *Technology and Culture, 8*, 335–345. doi:10.2307/3101719

Heisenberg, D. (2005). *Negotiating privacy: The European Union, the United States and personal data protection.* London: Lynne Rienner Publishers. De Hert, P., & de Schutter, B. (2008). International transfers of data in the field of JHA: The lessons of Europol, PNR, and Swift. In Martenczuk, B., & van Thiel, S. (Eds.), *Justice, liberty, security: New challenges for EU external relations* (p. 303). Brussels: VUB Press.

Helberger, N., & Hugenholtz, P. B. (2007). No place like home for making a copy: Private copying in European copyright law and consumer law. *Berkeley Technology Law Journal, 22*, 1061–1098.

Henkin, L. (1974). Privacy and autonomy. *Columbia Law Review, 74*, 1410–1433. doi:10.2307/1121541

Hensen, W. F. (2005, Winter). The disabling impact of wrongful birth and wrongful life action. *Harvard Civil Rights-Liberties Law Review*, pp. 141-196.

Hijmans, H. (2006). The European data protection supervisor: The institutions of the EC controlled by an independent authority. *Common Market Law Review, 43*, 1313.

Hijmans, H., & Scirocco, A. (2009). Shortcomings in EU Data protection in the third and the second pillars. Can the Lisbon Treaty be expected to help? *Common Market Law Review, 46*, 1485.

Hildebrand, M., & Gurtwirth, S. (2007). *Profiling the European citizen.* London: Springer.

Hildebrandt, M., & Gutwirth, S. (2008). *Profiling the European citizen: Cross-disciplinary perspectives.* New York: Springer.

Hildebrandt, M. (2006). Privacy and identity. In Claes, E., Duff, A., & Gutwirth, S. (Eds.), *Privacy and the criminal law* (pp. 43–57). Antwerp, Belgium: Intersentia.

Hildebrandt, M. (2005). Privacy and identity. In Claes, E., Duff, A., & Gutwirth, S. (Eds.), *Privacy and the criminal Law*. Antwerp, Belgium: Intersentia.

Hildebrandt, M. (2009). Profiling and AmI. In Rannenberg, K., Royer, D., & Deuker, A. (Eds.), *The future of identity in the information society: Challenges and opportunities* (pp. 273–313). Berlin: Springer. doi:10.1007/978-3-642-01820-6_7

Hildebrandt, M. (2006). Privacy and Identity. In E. Claes, A. Duff & S. Gutwirth (Eds.), *Privacy and the criminal law* (pp. x, 199). Antwerp, Belgium: Intersentia.

Hildner, L. (2006). Defusing the threat of RFID: Protecting consumer privacy through technology-specific legislation at the state level. *Harvard Civil Rights-Civil Liberties Law Review, 41*, 133–176.

Hillard, D., & Kuzin, J. (2005, January). RFID experiences important growth and regulatory attention. *National Edition.*

HIPAA Privacy Rule, 45 C.F.R. § 164.512 (2009).

HIPAA Privacy Rule. 45 C.F.R § 160.103 (2009).

HIPAA Privacy Rule. 45 C.F.R. § 164.502(a) (2009).

HIPAA Privacy Rule. 45 C.F.R. § 164.502(a)-(b) (2009).

HIPAA Privacy Rule. 45 C.F.R. § 164.514(b) (2009).

Hirschl, R. (2004). Constitutional courts vs. religious fundamentalism: Three Middle Eastern tales. *Texas Law Review*, *82*, 1819–1860.

Hirschl, R. (2006). The new constitutionalism and the judicialization of pure politics worldwide. *Fordham Law Review*, *75*(2), 721–754. Retrieved from http://law2.fordham.edu/publications/articles/500flspub9554.pdf.

Hirschl, R. (2008). The judicialization of mega-politics and the rise of political courts. *Annual Review of Political Science*, *11*(1), 93–118. doi:10.1146/annurev.polisci.11.053006.183906

Hoikkaanen, A., Bacigalupo, M., Compano, R., Lusoli, W., & Maghiros, I. (2010). New challenges and possible policy options for the regulation of electronic identity. *Journal of International Commercial Law and Technology*, *5*(1).

Holtzapfel, M. (2002, Summer). The right to live, the right to choose, and the Unborn Victims of Violence Act. *The Journal of Contemporary Health Law and Policy*, 443–445.

Home Office task force on child protection on the internet. (2008). Good practice guidance for the providers of social networking and other user interactive services. Retrieved May 1, 2010, from http://police.homeoffice.gov.uk/publications/operational-policing/social-networking-guidance/

Horsey, K., & Biggs, H. (2006). *Human fertilization and embryology: Reproducing regulation*. London: Routledge-Cavendish.

House of Lords European Union Committee. (2005). After Madrid: The EU's response to terrorism. [Report with evidence, 5th Report of Session 2004-05].

Howanitz, P. J., Renner, S. W., & Walsh, M. K. (2002). Continuous wristband monitoring over 2 years decreases identification errors: A College of American Pathologists Q-tracks study. *Archives of Pathology & Laboratory Medicine*, *126*(7), 809–815.

Hrysogonos, K. (2003). *Civil & social rights* [in Greek]. Athens-Komotini: Ant.N.Sakkoulas.

http://www.hurriyetdailynews.com/h.php?news=the-empire-of-fear-2008-07-02

http://www.hurriyetdailynews.com/h.php?news=cost-of-uncertainty-2008-07-08

Human Right Commision. (2000). General Comment 28: Equality ofRights Between, Men and Women, 68th Session.

Hunt, A., & Wickham, G. (1994). *Foucault and law*. London: Pluto.

Ian, B. (2009). Regulation of converged communications surveillance. In Neyland, D., & Goold, B. (Eds.), *New directions in surveillance societies and privacy* (pp. 39–73). Exeter, UK: Willan.

Igglezakis, I. (2003). *Sensitive personal data* [in Greek]. Athens, Thessaloniki: Sakkoulas Publications.

Information Commissioner Office. (2007). Data protection: Topline report. Retrieved May 1, 2010 from http://www.ico.gov.uk/upload/documents/library/data_protection/detailed_specialist_guides/research_results_topline_report.pdf

Inness, J. C. (1996). *Privacy, intimacy and isolation*. Oxford: Oxford University Press. doi:10.1093/0195104609.001.0001

Institute for Legal Informatics (IRI). (2008). Rechtsvergleichende Analyse im Hinblick auf die Umsetzung der Richtlinie 2006/24/EG über die Vorratsdatenspeicherung [Research on behalf of the Ludwig Boltzmann Institute of Human Rights (BIM)]. Hannover, Germany: Institute for Legal Informatics (IRI) of the Leibniz University of Hannover. Retrieved May 20, 2010, from http://bim.lbg.ac.at/files/sites/bim/Rechtsvergleich_Vorratsdatenspeicherung.pdf

Inter-American Commission on Human Rights. (1981, October 6). Annual Report 1980-1981. OEA/Ser.L/V/II.54, Doc. 9 rev. 1.

International Affairs, *83*(2), 339–355. doi:10.1111/j.1468-2346.2007.00622.x

Irwing, D. (1999). When do human beings begin? Scientific myths and scientific facts. *International Sociology and Social Policy*, *19*(3/4), 22–46. doi:10.1108/01443339910788730

Ito, M., Horst, H., Bittanti, M., Boyd, D., Herr-Stephenson, B., Lange, P. G., & Pascoe, C. J. … Tripp, L. (2009). *Living and learning with new media: Summary of findings from the digital youth project (The MacArthur Foundation reports on digital media and learning)*. Cambridge, MA: MIT Press.

Jamal, A. (2009). Democratizing state-religion relations: A comparative study of Turkey, Egypt and Israel. *Democratization*, *16*(6), 1143–1171..doi:10.1080/13510340903271779

James, N. J. (2004). Handing over the keys: Contingency, power and resistance in the context of s 3LA of the Australian Crimes Act 1914. *The University of Queensland Law Journal*, *23*(1), 7–21.

Janis, M. W., Kay, R. S., & Bradley, A. W. (Eds.). (2007). *European human rights law: Text and materials* (3rd ed.). New York: Oxford University Press.

Janz, B. D., Pitts, M. G., & Otondo, R. F. (2005). Information systems and health care II: Back to the future with RFID: Lessons learned — Some old, some new. *Communications of the Association for Information Systems*, *15*(1), 132–148.

Jaques, R. (2004). Hospitals reluctant to deploy RFID. *Computing*. Retrieved April 24, 2010, from http://www.computing.co.uk/vnunet/news/2124641/hospitals-reluctant-deploy-rfidhttp://www.computing.co.uk/vnunet/news/2124641/hospitals-reluctant-deploy-rfidhttp://www.computing.co.uk/vnunet/news/2124641/hospitals-reluctant-deploy-rfidhttp://www.computing.co.uk/vnunet/news/2124641/hospitals-reluctant-deploy-rfidhttp://www.computing.co.uk/vnunet/news/2124641/hospitals-reluctant-deploy-rfid

Jaszi, P. (1998). Intellectual property legislative update: Copyright, paracopyright, and pseudo-copyright. Paper presented at the Association of Research Libraries conference: The Future Network: Transforming Learning and Scholarship, Eugene, OR. Retrieved March 27, 2010, from http://www.arl.org/resources/pubs/mmproceedings/132mmjaszi~print.shtml

Jenkins, G. (2007). Continuity and change: Prospects for civil–military relations in Turkey.

Jenkins, G. H. (2009, August). *Between fact and fantasy: Turkey's Ergenekon investigation*. Washington, DC: Central Asia-Caucasus Institute & Silk Road Studies Program. Retrieved from http://www.silkroadstudies.org/new/docs/silkroadpapers/0908Ergenekon.pdf

Jesus, P. *Morfe v. Amelito Mutuc as Executive Secretary et al.*, G.R. No. L-20387, January 31, 1968 (en banc). Retrieved on May 19, 2010 from http://www.lawphil.net/judjuris/juri1968/jan1968/gr_l-20387_1968.html

Joinson, A. N., Paine, C., Reips, U. D., & Buchanan, T. (2006). The role of situational and dispositional variables in online disclosures. Paper presented at the Workshop on Privacy, Trust and Identity Issues for Ambient Intelligence. Retrieved from http://www.cs.st-andrews.ac.uk/~pst/pti-ai-workshop/programme/joinson-privacy.pdf

Journal, R. F. I. D. (2010). *RFID Journal Live! Conference Brochure*, Retrieved April 24, 2010, from http://www.rfidjournalevents.com/live/live2010_brochure.pdfhttp://www.rfidjournalevents.com/live/live2010_brochure.pdfhttp://www.rfidjournalevents.com/live/live2010_brochure.pdfhttp://www.rfidjournalevents.com/live/live2010_brochure.pdfhttp://www.rfidjournalevents.com/live/live2010_brochure.pdf

Judicial board criticizes Justice Ministry over investigations. (2009, July 29) *Hurriyet Daily News*. Retrieved from http://www.hurriyetdailynews.com

Judicial decision on wiretapping shakes judiciary. (2009, November 12). *Hurriyet Daily News*. Retrieved from http://www.hurriyetdailynews.com

Kaltsonis, D. (2007). Political & social restrictions of freedom of assembly [in Greek]. *Utopia, 75*, 53–74.

Kamminga, M. T., & Sheinin, M. (2009). *The impact of human rights law on general international law*. Oxford: Oxford University Press. doi:10.1093/acprof:oso/9780199565221.001.0001

Kane, B., & Delange, B. D. (2009). A tale of two internets: Web 2.0 slices, dices, and is privacy resistant. *Idaho Law Review*, *45*(2), 317–347.

Kanlı, Y. (2008a, July 2). The empire of fear. *Hurriyet Daily News.* Retrieved from

Kanlı, Y. (2008b, July 8). Cost of Uncertainty. *Hurriyet Daily News.* Retrieved from

Kanlı, Y. (2009, November 12). Empire of fear or the AKP's Turkey. *Hurriyet Daily News.* Retrieved from http://www.hurriyetdailynews.com/n.php?n=empire-of-fear-or-akp8217s-turkey-2009-11-12

Karakas, C. (2007). *Turkey: Islam and laicism between the interests of state, politics, and society*. PRIF Reports, No. 78. Frankfurt, Germany: Peace Research Institute Frankfurt (PRIF). Retrieved from www.hsfk.de/downloads/prif78.pdf

Katrougalos, G. (2006). Freedom & security in the 'society of risk' [in Greek]. *Legal Review*, *54*, 360–374.

Katyal, S. (2004). The new surveillance. *Case Western Reserve Law Review*, *54*, 297–386.

Katz v. United States, 389 U.S. 347 (1967).

Keats Citron, D., & Henry, L. M. (2010). Visionary pragmatism and the value of privacy in the twenty-first century. *Michigan Law Review*, *108*, 1107–1126.

Kelleher, D. (2006). *Privacy and data protection law in Ireland*. London: Tottel.

Kerr, I., & Stevees, V. (2005, April). Virtual playgrounds and buddybots: A data-minefield for tinys & tweeneys. Paper presented at the meeting Panopticon, The 15th Annual Conference on Computers, Freedom & Privacy, Seattle, WA. Retrieved May 1, 2010, from http://idtrail.org/files/Kerr_Steeves_Virtual_Playgrounds.pdf

Khadija, R. P. (2009). Comparative architecture of genetic privacy. *Indiana International Journal & Comparative Law Review*, *19*, 89–170.

Killingsworth, S. (2000). Website privacy policies in principle and in practice. *PLI/Pat* 663-736.

Kosta, E., Zibushka, J., Scherner, T., & Dumortier, J. (2008). Legal considerations on privacy-enhancing location based services using PRIME technology. *Computer Law & Security Report*, *24*(2), 139–146. doi:10.1016/j.clsr.2008.01.006

Kosta, E., & Valcke, P. (2006). Retaining the data retention directive. *Computer Law & Security Report*, *22*, 370. doi:10.1016/j.clsr.2006.07.002

Kosta, E., & Dumortier, J. (2007). *The Data Retention Directive and the principles of European data protection legislation* (pp. 130–135). Medien und Recht International.

Kuner, C. (2003). *European data protection law and online business*. Oxford: Oxford University Press.

Kwok, A. (2010, March 2). Installation of more CCTV cameras on expressways pushed. *Philippine Daily Inquirer.* Retrieved on May 19, 2010, from http://newsinfo.inquirer.net/breakingnews/metro/view/20100302-256270/Installation-of-more-CCTV-cameras-on-expressways-pushed

Kyllo v. United States, 533 U.S. 27 (2001).

Lafollette, M., & Stine, J. (1991). Contemplating choice: Historical perspectives on innovation and application of technology. In Lafollette, M., & Kline, J. (Eds.), *Technology and choice: Reading from technology and culture*. Chicago: University of Chicago Press.

Lagerwall, A. (2008). *Privacy and secret surveillance from a European Convention perspective.* Unpublished master's thesis, Stockholm University, Sweden. Retrieved from http://www.adbj.se/2009/ht_2009_Anders_Lagerwall.pdf

Lancet. (2006, November 4). Executive summary of sexual and reproductive health series.

Laurie, G. (2002). *Genetic privacy: A challenge to medico-legal norms*. Cambridge: Cambridge University Press. doi:10.1017/CBO9780511495342

Law Reform Commission of Ireland. (1998). *Report on privacy: Surveillance and the interception of communications*. Dublin: Law Reform Commission of Ireland.

Le Metayer, D., & Monteleone, S. (2009). Automated consent through privacy agents: Legal requirements and technical architecture. *Computer Law & Security Report, 25*(2), 136–144. doi:10.1016/j.clsr.2009.02.010

Le Métayer, D. (2010). Privacy by design: A matter of choice. In Gutwirth, S., Poullet, Y., & De Hert, P. (Eds.), *Data protection in a profiled world*. London: Springer. doi:10.1007/978-90-481-8865-9_20

Leenes, R., Koops, B. J., & de Hert, P. (2008). *Constitutional rights and new technologies: A comparative study*. The Hague: T. M. C. Asser Press.

Leenes, R. (2008). Do you know me? Decomposing identifiability. *Tilburg University Legal Studies Working Paper* no. 01/2008.

Leinster, M. (1998). *First contacts: The essential Murray Leinster*. Framingham, MA: New England Science Fiction Association.

Lemelson-MIT Program. (1999). Lemelson-MIT survey finds high school students, their parents agree—and disagree—on the most important 20th century inventions [Press release]. Retrieved from http://web.mit.edu/invent/n-pressreleases/n-press-99index.html

Lenhart, A. (2009). *Adults and social network websites*. Washington, DC: Pew Internet & American Life Project.

Lessig, L. (2006). *Code 2.0*. New York: Basic Books.

Lessing, L. (1999). *The code and other laws of cyberspace*. New York: Basic Books.

Lillington, K. (2001, August 3). Government support for data plan at odds with own policies. *The Irish Times*.

Lillington, K. (2001, November 7). Retention of mobile call records queried [Article quotes M. Murphy, former co-chairperson of the Irish Council for Civil Liberties]. *The Irish Times*.

Lopucki, L. M. (2002-2003). Did privacy cause identity theft? *The Hastings Law Journal, 54*(4), 1277–1298.

Lorenc, M. (2007). Comment: The mark of the beast: U.S. Government use of RFID in government-issued documents. *Albany Law Journal of Science & Technology, 17*, 583–614.

Lorrain, A., & Mathias, P. (2006). Données de connexion: la publication du premier décret ou la premère pierre d'un édifice encore inachevé, Revue Lamy droit de l'immateriel, 35-38. Retrieved May 20, 2010, from http://www.aclorrain.fr/docs/donnees-de-connexion_06.pdf

LTO Memorandum Circular No. 87-038, otherwise known as Guidelines in the Verification of Motor Vehicles, 6 November 1987). June 16, 2009 Memorandum of Agreement (MOA) between DOTC and STRADCOM *EpieJr. et al. v. The Hon. Nelsonida T. Ulat-Marredo*, et al., G.R. No. 148117, March 22, 2007.

LTO Memorandum Circular No. ACL-2009-1199

Ludwig Boltzmann Institute of Human Rights (BIM). (2010). Draft Bill for the Amendment of the Austrian Telecommunications Act. Vienna: BIM. Retrieved May 20, 2010, from http://bim.lbg.ac.at/de/informationsgesellschaft/bimentwurf-zur-vorratsdatenspeicherung-begutachtung

Lugaresi, N. (2004). Protezione della privacy e protezione dei dati personali: i limiti dell'approccio comunitario. *Giustizia amministrativa* no. 03/2004. Rome: Istituto poligrafico e Zecca dello Stato.

Lugosi, C. I. (2007). Conforming to the rule of law: When person and human being finally mean the same thing in fourteenth amendment jurisprudence. *Issues in Law & Medicine, 22*, 119–303.

Lusoli, W., Maghiros, I., & Bacigalupo, M. (2009). eID policy in a turbulent environment: Is there a need for a new regulatory framework? *Identity in the Information Society, 1*(1), 173–187. doi:10.1007/s12394-009-0011-9

Lustgarten, L., & Leigh, I. (1994). *In from the cold: National security and parliamentary democracy*. Oxford: Clarendon Press.

Lyon, D. (2007). *Surveillance studies, an overview*. Cambridge: Polity.

Lyon, D., & Zureik, E. (1996). *Computer, surveillance and privacy*. Minneapolis, MN: University of Minnesota Press.

Magid, J. M., Tatikonda, M. V., & Cochran, P. L. (2009). Radio frequency identification and privacy law: An integrative approach. *American Business Law Journal*, *46*, 1–54. doi:10.1111/j.1744-1714.2009.01071.x

Manitakis, A. (2007). The necessity of constitutional revision in between majoritarian parliamentarism and revisional consensus [in Greek]. *Constitution (Foundation for the United States Constitution)*, *1*, 3–20.

Manolea, B., & Argesiu, A. (2009, October 8). Constitutional Court Decision no 1258. Retrieved May 20, 2010, from http://www.legi-internet.ro/english/jurisprudenta-it-romania/decizii-it/romanian-constitutional-court-decision-regarding-data-retention.html

Mantzoufas, P. (2006). *Constitutional protection of personal data in the age of risk* [in Greek]. Athens, Thessaloniki: Sakkoulas Publications.

Maragay, F. (2010, January 13). Birth pains of a high-tech project. *Manila Standard Today.* Retrieved May 19, 2010, from http://www.manilastandardtoday.com/insideOpinion.htm?f=2010/january/13/felmaragay.isx&d=2010/january/13

Marx, G. T. (1988). *Undercover: Police surveillance in America*. Berkeley, CA: University of California Press.

Marx, G. T. (2001). Technology and social control. In Smalser, N., & Baltes, P. (Eds.), *International encyclopedia of the social and behavioral sciences*. Oxford: Elsevier.

Mastyszczyk, C. (2009, February 26). Facebook entry gets office worker fired. *CNet News*. Retrieved from http://news.cnet.com/8301-17852_3-10172931-71.html

McIntyre v. Ohio Elections Comm'n, 514 U.S. 334 (1995).

McIntyre, T. J. (2007, November). *Data retention: Privacy, policy and proportionality*. Paper presented at the ICEL/ERA Conference on The Impact of the Fight Against Terrorism on EU Law, Dublin, Ireland.

McLean, S. A. M. (2010). *Autonomy, consent and the law*. London: Routledge-Cavendish.

Meiklejohn, A. (1960). *Political freedom: The constitutional powers of the people*. New York: Greenwood Press.

Meyer, R. J. (2006). Why we under-prepare for hazards. R. J. Daniels, D. F. Kettl, & H. Kunreuther (Eds.), *On risk and disaster: Lessons from Hurricane Katrina* (pp. 153-174). Philadelphia: University of Pennsylvania Press.

Mich. Comp. Laws § 28.304 (2009).

Michael, J. (1994). *Privacy and human rights*. Paris: UNESCO.

Microsoft. (2009). Cloud computing flash poll – Fact sheet. Seattle, WA: Microsoft. Retrieved from www.microsoft.com/presspass/presskits/cloudpolicy/docs/PollFS.doc

Mihm, S. (2003, December 21). Dumpster-diving for your identity. *The New York Times Magazine*. Retrieved from http://www.nytimes.com.

Mill, J. S. (1869). *On liberty*. Oxford: Oxford University Press.

Miller, A. R. (1971). *The assault on privacy: Computers, data banks, and dossiers*. Ann Arbor, MI: University of Michigan Press.

Miller, J. I. (2005). Don't be evil: Gmail's relevant text advertisements violate Google's own motto and your E-Mail privacy rights. *Hofstra Law Review*, *33*, 1607–1641.

Miller, J. (2003). *Police corruption in England and Wales: An assessment of current evidence*. London: Home Office.

Minister of justice: 'my phone has been tapped, too'. (2009, December 1). *Hurriyet Daily News.* Retrieved from http://www.hurriyetdailynews.com

Ministry announces number of people tapped. (2009, November 19). *Hurriyet Daily News.* Retrieved from http://www.hurriyetdailynews.com

Mitrou, L. (2001). Right to data protection: A new right? In D. Tsatsos, E. Venizelos & X. Contiades (Eds.), *The new constitution* [in Greek] (pp. 83–103). Athens-Komotini: Ant.N.Sakkoulas.

Mittleton, F. (2002). The right to informational self-determination and public safety. In Donos, P., Mitrou, L., Mittleton, P., & Papakonstantinou, E. (Eds.), *The data protection authority & the advanced protection of human rights* [in Greek]. Athens, Thessaloniki: Sakkoulas Publications.

MMDA., *et al. vs. Viron Transportation Co.,* G.R. No. 170656, 15 May 2007. Retrieved May 19, 2010, from http://www.lawphil.net/judjuris/juri2007/aug2007/gr_170656_2007.html

Mobile Aspects. (2005, February 9). *University of Chicago Comer Children's Hospital selects Mobile Aspects: RFID solutions deliver a higher quality of patient care, safety, and operational efficiency* [Press release]. Retrieved from http://www.mobileaspects.com/news_media/pressrelease/press_release_02.09.2005_University_of_Chicago.pdfhttp://www.mobileaspects.com/news_media/pressrelease/press_release_02.09.2005_University_of_Chicago.pdfhttp://www.mobileaspects.com/news_media/pressrelease/press_release_02.09.2005_University_of_Chicago.pdfhttp://www.mobileaspects.com/news_media/pressrelease/press_release_02.09.2005_University_of_Chicago.pdfhttp://www.mobileaspects.com/news_media/pressrelease/press_release_02.09.2005_University_of_Chicago.pdf

Monar, J., & Morgan, R. (Eds.). (1994). *The third pillar of the European Union.* Brussels: European University Press.

Monegain, B. (2005, September 12). Study: Passive RFID not ready for prime time in healthcare. *Healthcare IT News.* Retrieved April 24, 2010, from http://www.healthcareitnews.com/news/study-passive-rfid-not-ready-prime-time-healthcarehttp://www.healthcareitnews.com/news/study-passive-rfid-not-ready-prime-time-healthcarehttp://www.healthcareitnews.com/news/study-passive-rfid-not-ready-prime-time-healthcarehttp://www.healthcareitnews.com/news/study-passive-rfid-not-ready-prime-time-healthcarehttp://www.healthcareitnews.com/news/study-passive-rfid-not-ready-prime-time-healthcare

More than 50 judiciary members tabbed. (2009, November 13). *Hurriyet Daily News.* Retrieved from http://www.hurriyetdailynews.com

Moreham, N. (2006). Privacy in public spaces. *The Cambridge Law Journal, 65*(3), 606–635. doi:10.1017/S0008197306007240

Moreham, N. A. (2008). The right to respect for private life in the European Convention on Human Rights: A re-examination. *EHRLR, 2008*(1), 44.

Morowitz, H. J., & Trefil, J. (1992). *The facts of life: Science and the abortion controversy.* Oxford, UK: Oxford University Press.

Morris, A., & Saintier, S. (2003, Summer). To be or not to be: Is that the question? Wrongful life and misconception. *Medical Law Review*,167–191. doi:10.1093/medlaw/11.2.167

Mullane v. Hanover Bank & Trust Co., 339 U.S. 306 (1950).

Murphy, R. S. (1996). Property rights in personal information: An economic defense of privacy. *The Georgetown Law Journal, 84*(7), 2381–2417.

Narayanan, A., & Shmatikov, V. (2009). De-anonymizing social networks. In *IEEE Symposium on Security and Privacy*, Oakland, CA. New York: IEEE.

National Conference of State Legislatures. (2010, January). State statutes relating to radio frequency identification (RFID) and privacy. Retrieved April 24, 2010, from http://www.ncsl.org/default.aspx?tabid=13442http://www.ncsl.org/default.aspx?tabid=13442http://www.ncsl.org/default.aspx?tabid=13442http://www.ncsl.org/default.aspx?tabid=13442http://www.ncsl.org/default.aspx?tabid=13442

Neethling, J. (2005). Personality rights: A comparative overview. *The Comparative and International Law Journal of Southern Africa, 38*(2), 210–245.

Nelkin, D., & Andrews, L. (1999). DNA identification and surveillance creep. *Sociology of Health & Illness, 21*, 687–706. doi:10.1111/1467-9566.00179

Neubauer, M. (2008). *Aktuelles zu Unterlassungs- und Auskunftspflichten in Österreich mit einem Vergleich zur aktuellen Rechtslage in Deutschland im Zivil- und Strafrecht* (pp. 25–33). Medien und Recht International.

Neumann, F. (1953). The concept of political freedom. *Columbia Law Review*, *53*(7), 901–935. doi:10.2307/1119178

Nev. Rev. Stat. §§ 205.461-205.4675 (2009).

New Hampshire Commission on the Use of Radio Frequency Technology. (2008, November). *Final report.* Retrieved April 24, 2010, from http://www.gencourt.state.nh.us/statstudcomm/reports/1812.pdfhttp://www.gencourt.state.nh.us/statstudcomm/reports/1812.pdfhttp://www.gencourt.state.nh.us/statstudcomm/reports/1812.pdfhttp://www.gencourt.state.nh.us/statstudcomm/reports/1812.pdfhttp://www.gencourt.state.nh.us/statstudcomm/reports/1812.pdf

Newman, A. (2008). Building transnational civil liberties: Transgovernmental entrepreneurs and the European Data Privacy Directive. *International Organization*, *62*, 103. doi:10.1017/S0020818308080041

News, B. B. C. (2010, January 1). New internet piracy law comes into effect in France. Retrieved May 20, 2010, from http://news.bbc.co.uk/2/hi/europe/8436745.stm

Nissenbaum, H. (1998). Protecting privacy in an information age: The problem of privacy in public. *Law and Philosophy*, *17*, 559–596.

Nissenbaum, H. (2004). Privacy as contextual integrity. *Washington Law Review (Seattle, Wash.)*, *79*, 119–158.

No, W. G., Boritz, E., & Sundarraj, R. (2008). Do companies' online privacy policy disclosures match customer needs? Retrieved May 1, 2010, from http://ssrn.com/abstract_id=1082961

Noda, T. (2010, February). Service breakthroughs: Anytime, anywhere. *Computerworld Philippines.* Retrieved May 19, 2010, from http://computerworld.com.ph/service-breakthroughs-anytime-anywhere/

Noonan, J. T. (1970). *An almost absolute value in history. The morality of abortion: Legal and historical perspectives*. Cambridge, MA: Harvard University Press.

Nuechterlein, J., & Weiser, J. P. (2005). *Digital crossroads: American telecommunications policy in the Internet age*. Cambridge, MA: MIT Press.

Nugter, A. (1990). *Transborder flow of personal data within the EC*. Boston: Kluwer Law & Taxation Publishers.

O'Reilly, T. (2004). *The fuss about Gmail and privacy: Nine reasons why it's bogus*. Sebastopol, CA: O'Reilly. Retrieved from http://www.oreillynet.com/pub/wlg/4707

OECD. (2009, June 8-9). Using Sensor-based Networks to address Global Issues: Policy opportunities and Challenges. OECD Experts conference, Lisbon, Spain. Retrieved from http://www.oecd.org/document/41/0,3343,en_2649_34223_42616233_1_1_1_1,00.html

Ofcom. (2010). Consultation on "Online Infringement of Copyright and the Digital Economy Act 2010". Retrieved May 20, 2010, from http://www.ofcom.org.uk/consult/condocs/copyrightinfringement/summary/

Oğuzman, M. K., Seliçi, Ö., & Oktay, S. (2005). *Kişiler Hukuku*. Istanbul, Turkey: Filiz.

Olmstead v. United States, 277 U.S. 438 (1928).

Ong, E. (2009, November 1). Stradcom and LTO get close to people. *Manila Bulletin.* Retrieved May 19, 2010, from http://www.mb.com.ph/node/227466/

Opinion of the European Data Protection Supervisor on the Proposal for a Directive of the European Parliament and of the Council on the Retention of Data Processed in Connection with the Provision of Public Electronic Communication Services and Amending Directive 2002/58/EC, 2005 OJ (C 298) 1.

Opinion of the European Data Protection Supervisor on the Proposal for a Directive of the European Parliament and of the Council on the retention of data processed in connection with the provision of public electronic communication services and amending Directive 2002/58/EC (COM (2005) 438 final).

Palfrey, J. (2008). *Enhancing child safety and online technologies*. Cambridge, MA: The Berkman Center for Internet & Society, Harvard University. Retrieved from http://cyber.law.harvard.edu/pubrelease/isttf/

Papadopoulou, N. (2006). Electronic surveillance of sports fans: The contradiction of article 41E of Law 2725/1999 to higher legal rules (article 8 of the European Convention of Human Rights, articles 9, 9A & 5 of the Greek Constitution). In Thessaloniki Bar Association, *Scientific Review* [in Greek].

Papakonstantinou, V., & de Hert, P. (2009). The PNR agreement and transatlantic anti-terrorism co-operation: No firm human rights framework on either side of the Atlantic. *Common Market Law Review*, *46*, 885.

Pararas, P. (1996). *The Greek Constitution & the European Convention of Human Rights* [in Greek]. Athens-Komotini: Ant. N. Sakkoulas.

Paredes, D. (2010, January 25). On STRADCOM and the LTO. *Business Insight Malaya.* Retrieved May 19, 2010 from http://www.malaya.com.ph/01252010/edducky.html

Park, B. (2009, September). Ergenekon: Power and democracy in Turkey. *Open Democracy.* Retrieved from http://www.opendemocracy.net/article/ergenekon-power-and-democracy-in-turkey-0

Parker, R. B. (1974). A definition of privacy. *Rutgers Law Review*, *27*(2), 275–296.

Party, A. D. P. W. (2007). Opinion 4/2007 on the concept of personal data (pp. 1-26).

Pascual, F., Jr. (2009, October 20). Facts and figures on RFID car tags. *The Philippine Star.* Retrieved May 19, 2010, from http://www.philstar.com/Article.aspx?articleid=515822

Peoples Bank of Virgin Islands v. Figueroa, 559 F.2d 914 (3d Cir. 1977).

Philippine News Agency. (2008, February 22). Metro Manila crimes and traffic to be monitored by 56 CCTV cameras. Retrieved May 19, 2010 from http://www.encyclopedia.com/doc/1G1-180007363.html

Picker, R. (2009). *Online advertising, identity and privacy (University of Chicago Law & Economics, Olin Working Paper No. 475)*. Retrieved from http://ssrn.com/abstract=1428065

Pilia, R. (2002). *Tutela della privacy informatica e protezione dei dati personali: un'analisi comparata. Studi economico-giuridici della Facoltà di Giurisprudenza dell' Università degli Studi di Cagliari*. Torino, Italy: Giappichelli.

Pino, G. (2003). *Il diritto all'identità personale: Interpretazione costituzionale e creatività giurisprudenziale*. Bologna, Italy: Il mulino.

Polity, *39*(4), 479–501..doi:10.1057/palgrave.polity.2300086

Posner, R. (1978). The right of privacy. *Georgetown Law Review*, *12*, 393–422.

Posner, R. A. (1981). *The economics of justice and the criterion of wealth*. Cambridge, MA: Harvard University Press.

Poste, G. (1999). Privacy and confidentiality in the age of genetic engineering. *The Review of Law & Politics*, *4*, 25–32.

Poullet, Y. (1991). *Le fondement du droit à la protection des données nominatives: propriétés ou libertés. Nouvelles technologies et propriété*. Paris: Thémis.

Poullet, Y. (2001). *Conclude a contract through electronic agents? Electronic Commerce – DER Abschlub von Vertragen im Internet*. Baden Baden, Germany: Verlagsgesellschaft.

Poullet, Y. (2004). The fight against crime and/or the protection of privacy: A thorny debate? *International Review of Law Computers & Technology*, *18*(2), 251–273. doi:10.1080/1360086042000223535

Poullet, Y. (2005c). Comment réguler la protection des données? Réflexions sur l'internormativité. In *P. Delnoy, Liber amicorum*. Bruxelles: Larcier.

Poullet, Y. (2006). The Directive 95/46/EC: Ten Years After. *Computer Law & Security Report*, *22*, 206. doi:10.1016/j.clsr.2006.03.004

Poullet, Y. (2003). Pour une justification des articles 25 et 26 de la directive européenne 95/46/CE en matière de flux transfrontières et de protection des données. In Cools, M., & de Schutter, B. (Eds.), *Ceci n'est pas un juriste- Liber Amicorum* (p. 242). Brussels: VUB Press.

Poullet, Y. (2005a). The internet and private life. In Kenyon, A. T., & Richardson, M. (Eds.), *New dimensions in privacy law*. Cambridge: Cambridge University Press.

Poullet, Y. (2005b). Pour une troisième génération de réglementations de protection de données. *Jusletter, 3*(22).

Poullet, Y. (March 2007). *Transborder data flows and extraterritoriality: The European position.* Paper presented at the Public Seminar of the European Parliament: PNR/SWIFT/Safe Harbour: Are transatlantic data protected? Retrieved May 5, 2009, from http://www.europarl.europa.eu/hearings/20070326/libe/poullet_en.pdf

Presidency of the EU to the Council. (2005, May). On the subject of Draft Framework Decision on the retention of data. Retrieved from http://www.statewatch.org/news/2005/jul/8864-rev1-05.pdf

Presidency of the EU to the Council. (2005, October). Note on the subject of data retention (p. 2). Retrieved from http://www.statewatch.org/news/2005/oct/council-data-retention-oct-05.pdf

Privacy International. (2007a). *PHR 2006- Republic of Turkey*. London: Privacy International. Retrieved from http://www.privacyinternational.org/article.shtml?cmd[347]=x-347-559483

Privacy International. (2007b). *Leading surveillance societies in the EU and the world 2007.* London: Privacy International. Retrieved from http://www.privacyinternational.org/article.shtml?cmd[347]=x-347-559597

Privacy International. (2009). Privacy in Asia: Final report of scoping project. Retrieved May 19, 2010, from http://www.privacyinternational.org/issues/asia/privacy_in_asia_phase_1_report.pdf

Prosecutor in action to relieve court members' 'plight'. (2008, May 17). *Hurriyet Daily News.* Retrieved from http://www.hurriyetdailynews.com

Prudil, L. (2006). Privacy and confidentiality: Old concept, new challenges. *Medicine and Law*, *25*, 573–580.

Punay, E., & Ronda, R. (2010, January 12). Transport groups file support for RFID project before Supreme Court. *The Philippine Star.* Retrieved May 19, 2010 from http://www.philstar.com/Article.aspx?articleId=540015

Punie, Y. (2005). The future of ambient intelligent in Europe: The need for more everyday life. In Silverstone, R. (Ed.), *Media, technology and everyday life in Europe: From information to communication*. London: Ashgate Publishers Ltd.

Quirk, R. (2006, August 30). Commentary: Techlink: Barcodes on steroids. *The Daily Record* [Baltimore, MD].

Quittner, J. (1994, June). Anonymously yours—An interview with Johan Helsingius. *Wired*. Retrieved from http://www.wired.com/wired/archive/2.06/anonymous.1.html

Radin, M. J. (1982). Property and personhood. *Stanford Law Review*, *34*(5), 957–1015. doi:10.2307/1228541

Rannenberg, K., Royer, D., & Deuker, A. (2009). *The future of identity in the information society: Challenges and opportunities*. Berlin: Springer. doi:10.1007/978-3-642-01820-6

Reich, N. (2005). The constitutional relevance of citizenship and free movement in an enlarged Union. *European Law Journal*, *11*(6), 675–698. doi:10.1111/j.1468-0386.2005.00282.x

Reiman, J. (1996). Driving to the panopticon: A philosophical exploration of the risks to privacy posed by the highway technology of the future. *Santa Clara Computer and High-Technology Law Journal*, *11*, 27–44.

Remo, M. (2010, January 29). MMDA, WB sign 'bus reduction' for carbon credits project. *Philippine Daily Inquirer.* Retrieved May 19, 2010, from http://newsinfo.inquirer.net/breakingnews/metro/view/20100129-250154/MMDA-WB-sign-bus-reduction-for-carbon-credits-project

Republic Act No. 1405 (otherwise known as an Act Prohibiting Disclosure of or Inquiry into Deposits with any Banking Institution and providing penalties therefor), September 9, 1955, as amended.

Republic Act No. 386, (otherwise known as the Civil Code of the Philippines), June 18, 1949, as amended.

Republic Act No. 4136 (otherwise known as the Land Transportation and Traffic Code), June 20, 1964, as amended.

Republic Act No. 4200 (otherwise known as An Act to Prohibit and Penalize Wire Tapping and other Related Violations of Privacy of Communications, and for other purposes), June 19, 1965, as amended

Republic Act No. 6957, July 9, 1990, as amended by Republic Act No. 7718, (otherwise known as the Philippine BOT Law), May 8, 1994. Retrieved May 19, 2010, from http://www.neda.gov.ph/references/RAs/RAs%20 7718%20or%20the%20BOT%20Law.pdf

Republic Act No. 8293 (otherwise known as the Intellectual Property Code of the Philippines), June 6, 1997, as amended

Republic Act No. 8369, (otherwise known as the Family Courts Act of 1997), October 28, 1997

Republic Act No. 8505 (otherwise known as the Rape Victim Assistance and Protection Act of 1998), February 13, 1998

Republic Act No. 8792 (otherwise known as the Electronic Commerce Act), June 14, 2000

Response of Commission and other Member States. (2005, February). Report on the Draft Framework Decision on the retention of data (pp. 3-10). Retrieved from http://www.statewatch.org/news/2005/apr/draft-data-retention-proposal.pdf

Response of Council of the EU to proposals by EU Parliament, Council. (2005, October). Subject on data retention (p. 4). Retrieved from http://www.statewatch.org/news/2005/oct/coun-dat-ret-28-10.-5.pdf

Revised Rules of Evidence, Rules 128-134, Philippine Rules of Court [1997]

Ricœur, P. (1992). *Oneself as another*. Chicago: University of Chicago Press.

Ringland, K. (2009). The European Union's Data Retention Directive and the United States's data preservation laws: Finding the better model. *Shidler Journal of Law, Commerce & Technology, 5*(13). Retrieved May 20, 2010, from http://www.lctjournal.washington.edu/vol5/a13Ringland.html

Roberts, A., & Taylor, N. (2005). Privacy and the DNA database. *EHRLR, 2005*(4), 373.

Rodotà, S. (2006). *La Vita e Le Regole*. Milano, Italy: Feltrinelli.

Rodotà, S. (1997). *Repertorio di fine secolo*. Rome: Laterza.

Rodotà, S. (2009). *La vita e le regole, tra diritto e non diritto*. Milano, Italy: Feltrinelli.

Rodotá, S. (2009). Data protection as a fundamental right. In Gutwirth, S., Poullet, Y., De Hert, P., Terwangne, C., & Nouwt, S. (Eds.), *Reinventing data protection?* (pp. 77–82). Dordrecht, The Netherlands: Springer. doi:10.1007/978-1-4020-9498-9_3

Rodota, S. (March 2007). *The European constitutional model for data protection*. Paper presented at the Public Seminar of the European Parliament: PNR/SWIFT/Safe Harbour: Are transatlantic data protected? (Transatlantic relations and data protection). Retrieved May 5, 2009, from http://www.europarl.europa.eu/hearings/20070326/libe/rodota_en.pdf

Ronda, R. (2009, December 31). Transport groups back LTO's RFID project. *The Philippine Star.* Retrieved May 19, 2010, from http://www.philstar.com/Article.aspx?articleId=536960&publicationSubCategoryId=65

Ronda, R. (2010, April 12). LTO chief to respect Supreme Court ruling on RFID. *The Philippine Star.* Retrieved May 19, 2010, from http://www.philstar.com/Article.aspx?articleid=565639

Ronda, R. (2010, January 4). CHR says RFID tags wn't violate motorists' privacy. *The Philippine Star.* Retrieved May 19, 2010, from http://www.philstar.com/Article.aspx?articleId=537889

Rosen, J. (2000). *The unwanted gaze: The destruction of privacy in America.* New York: Random House.

Rotenberg, M. (1994, October). *Privacy and security for medical information systems.* Paper presented at American Health Information Management Association National Convention.

Rothstein, M. A., & Talbott, M. K. (2006). The expanding use of DNA in law enforcement: What role for privacy. *The Journal of Law, Medicine & Ethics, 34*, 153. doi:10.1111/j.1748-720X.2006.00024.x

Rouvroy, A. (2008). Privacy, data protection, and the unprecedented challenges of ambient intelligence. *Studies in Ethics, Law, and Technology, 2*(1), 51. doi:10.2202/1941-6008.1001

Rouvroy, A. (2009). Privacy, data protection, and the unprecedented challenges of ambient intelligence. *Studies in Ethics, Law, and Technology, 108*(2), 116–122.

Rouvroy, A., & Poullet, Y. (2008). The right to informational self-determination and the value of self-development: Reassessing the importance of privacy for democracy. In *Reinventing Data Protection: Proceedings of the International Conference*, Brussels, 12-13 October 2007. Berlin: Springer.

Rubenfeld, J. (1989). The right of privacy. *Harvard Law Review, 102*(4), 737–807. doi:10.2307/1341305

Rubenfeld, J. (2008). The end of privacy. *Stanford Law Review, 61*(1), 101–161.

Rubin, P. H. (2001). Privacy in commercial world. Statement before the 106th Congress.

Ruiz, J. C. (2010, January 6). Motorists assured on RFID plan. *Manila Bulletin.* Retrieved May 19, 2010, from http://www.mb.com.ph/articles/237228/motorists-assured-rfid-plan

Ruiz, J. C., & Panesa, E. F. (2010, January 11). RFID stirs protests. *Manila Bulletin.* Retrieved May 19, 2010, from http://www.mb.com.ph/node/238026/rfid-stirs-protests

Salamat, M. (2009, December 20). Solons, Drivers Ask SC to Void Anomalous RFID Project. *Bulatlat.* Retrieved May 19, 2010, from http://www.bulatlat.com/main/2009/12/20/solons-drivers-ask-sc-to-void-anomalous-rfid-project/ and http://www.satur4senator.com/news/2009/12/15/solons-drivers-ask-high-court-void-rfid-project

Samatras, M. (2004). *Surveillance in Greece: From anticommunist to consumer surveillance.* New York: Pella Publishing.

Samuelson, P. (2000). Privacy as intellectual property? *Stanford Law Review, 52*(5), 1125–1173. doi:10.2307/1229511

Sarafianos, D. (2004). Freedom of assembly. In Tsapogas, M., & Hristopoulos, D. (Eds.), *Human rights in Greece: 1953-2003* [in Greek]. Athens: Kastaniotis.

Sartor, G. (2006). Privacy, reputation and trust: Some implications for data protection. *EUI Working Papers*, Law no. 2006/04. Florence, Italy: European University Institute.

Sartor, G., & Viola de Azevedo Cunha, M. (2010). The Italian Google-case: Privacy, freedom of speech and responsibility for user-generated contents [Working paper]. *Social Science Research Network.* Retrieved from http://papers.ssrn.com/sol3/papers.cfm?abstract_id=1604411

Scaffardi, L. (2009). Le banche dati genetiche per fini giudiziari e i diritti della persona. In Casonato, C., Piciocchi, C., & Veronesi, P. (Eds.), *Forum biodiritto 2008 La circolazione dei modelli nel biodiritto.* CEDAM.

Scheinin, M. (2010). Report of the special rapporteur to the Human Rights Council of United Nations on human rights and counter-terrorism [A/HRC/13/37]. Retrieved from http://www2.ohchr.org/english/issues/terrorism/rapporteur/srchr.htm

Schwartz, P. M. (2003). German and U.S. telecommunications privacy law: Legal regulation of domestic law enforcement surveillance. *The Hastings Law Journal, 54*(4), 751–804.

Schwartz, P. M. (2004). Evaluating telecommunications surveillance in Germany: The lessons of the Max Planck Institute's study. *The George Washington Law Review, 72*(6), 1244–1263.

Schwartz, P. M. (2008). Reviving telecommunications surveillance law. *The University of Chicago Law Review. University of Chicago. Law School, 75*(1), 287–315.

Schwartz, P. M. (2009). Warrantless wiretapping, FISA reform, and the lessons of public liberty: A comment on Holmes's Jorde lecture. *California Law Review, 97*(2), 407–432.

Schwartz, P. M. (2004). Property, privacy, and personal data. *Harvard Law Review, 117*, 2055. doi:10.2307/4093335

Schwartz, P. M. (2009). Preemption and privacy. *The Yale Law Journal, 118*, 902.

Schwartz, P. M. (2006). Privacy inalienability and personal data chips. In Strandburg, K., & Raicu, D. S. (Eds.), *Privacy and technologies of identity: A cross-disciplinary conversation* (pp. 93–114). New York: Springer. doi:10.1007/0-387-28222-X_6

Şen, E. (2010). *Türk Hukunda Telefon Dinleme, Gizli Soruşturmacı, X Muhabir*. Ankara, Turkey: Seçkin.

Sewell, G., & Barker, J. R. (2001). Neither good, nor bad, but dangerous: Surveillance as an ethical paradox. *Ethics and Information Technology, 3*, 181–194. doi:10.1023/A:1012231730405

Shah, M. K. (2001). Inconsistencies in the legal status of unborn child: Recognition of a fetus as a potential life. *Hofstra Law Review, 29*(3), 931–969.

Shambayati, H., & Kirdis, E. (2009). In pursuit of "contemporary civilization": Judicial empowerment in Turkey. *Political Research Quarterly, 62*(4), 767–780.. doi:10.1177/1065912909346741

Shambayati, H. (2004). A tale of two mayors: Courts and politics in Iran and Turkey. *International Journal of Middle East Studies, 36*(2), 253–275. doi: 10.1017.S0020743804362057

Shanon, T. A., & Wolter, A. B. (1990). Reflection on the moral status of the pre-embryo. *Theological Studies, 5*, 603–626.

Sheinin, M. (2009). *Law and security: Facing the dilemmas. EUI working papers, Law 2009/11*. Florence, Italy: European University Institute.

Siegal, G., Siegal, N., & Weisman, Y. (2001). Physicians' attitudes toward patients' rights legislation. *Medicine and Law, 20*(1), 63–78.

Simeonidou-Kastanidou, E. (2007, December 11). Cameras in public assemblies. *Ta Nea* [in Greek]. Retrieved November 11, 2009, from http://digital.tanea.gr/Default.aspx?d=20071211&nid=6844132

Simitis, S. (1995). From the market to the polis: The EU directive on the protection of personal data. *Iowa Law Review, 80*(3), 440.

Simitis, S. (2006). Übermittlung der Daten von Flugpassagieren in die USA: Dispens vom Datenschutz? *Neue Juristische Wochenschrift*, 2011–2014.

Simon, H. (1971). Designing organizations for an information-rich world. In Greenberger, M. (Ed.), *Computers, communications, and the public interest*. Baltimore, MD: Johns Hopkins Press.

Simpson, H. S., Lynch, R., Grant, J., & Alroomi, L. (2004). Reducing medication errors within the neonatal intensive care unit. [Special fetal neonatal issue]. *Archives of Disease in Childhood, 89*(6), F480–F482.

Simpson, B. (2005). Identity manipulation in cyberspace as a leisure option: Play and the exploration of self. *Information & Communications Technology Law, 14*(2), 115–131. doi:10.1080/13600830500042632

Simpson, R., Schreckenghost, D., LoPresti, E. F., & Kirsch, N. (2006). Plans and planning in smart homes. In Augusto, J. C., & Nugent, C. D. (Eds.), *Designing smart homes: The role of artificial intelligence*. London: Springer- Verlag. doi:10.1007/11788485_5

Sincan judge investigated as part of Ergenekon probe. (2009, August 6). *Today's Zaman*. Retrieved from http://www.todayszaman.com

Sinclair, D. (1997). Self-regulation versus command and control? Beyond false dichotomies. *Law & Policy*, *19*, 529–559. doi:10.1111/1467-9930.00037

Skandamis, N., Sigalas, F., & Stratakis, S. (2007). *Rival freedoms in terms of security: The case of data protection and the criterion of connexity* [CEPS Policy Briefs, Research Paper No.7]. Brussels: Centre for European Policy Studies. European Convention. (2003, June 9). Updated Explanations relating to the text of the Charter of Fundamental Rights, CONV 823/03.

Skouris, V. (1996). *Orientations in public law I* [in Greek]. Thessaloniki: Sakkoulas.

Slaughter-Defoe, T. D., & Wang, Z. (2009). From "ego" to "social comparison": Cultural transmission and child protection policies and laws in a digital age. In Matwyshyn, A. M. (Ed.), *Harboring data: Information security, law and the corporation* (pp. 145–157). Stanford, CA: Stanford University Press.

Slobogin, C. (2002). Public privacy: Camera surveillance of public places & the right to anonymity. *Mississippi Law Journal*, *72*, 213–299.

Slutsman, J., Kass, N., McGready, J., & Wynia, M. (2005). Health information, the HIPAA privacy rule, and health care: What do physicians think? *Health Affairs*, *24*(3), 832–841. doi:10.1377/hlthaff.24.3.832

Smith, M., & Marx, L. (Eds.). (1994). *Does technology drive history? The dilemma of technological determinism*. Mass: MIT Press.

Smith, B. (2010, January 20). Cloud computing for business and society. *The Huffington Post*. Retrieved from http://www.huffingtonpost.com/brad-smith/cloud-computing-for-busin_b_429466.html

Social Justice Society et al. v. Dangerous Drugs Board et al., G.R. No. 157870, November 3, 2008 (en banc).

Solove, D. J. (2001). Privacy and power: Computer databases and metaphors for information privacy. *Stanford Law Review*, *53*(6), 1393–1462. doi:10.2307/1229546

Solove, D. J. (2008). *Understanding privacy*. Cambridge, MA: Harvard University Press.

Solove, D. J. (2002). Conceptualizing privacy. *California Law Review*, *90*, 1087–1155. doi:10.2307/3481326

Solove, D. J. (2004). *The digital person*. New York: New York University Press.

Solove, D. (2008). *Understanding privacy*. Cambridge, MA: Harvard University Press.

Solove, D. (2007). "I've got nothing to hide" and other misunderstandings of privacy. *The San Diego Law Review*, *44*, 745.

Sommer, K. (2009). Riding the wave: The uncertain future of RFID legislation. *Journal of Legislation*, *35*, 48.

Sotiropoulos, V. (2006). *Constitutional protection of personal data* [in Greek]. Athens, Thessaloniki: Sakkoulas Publications.

Sotiropoulos, V., & Armamentos, P. (2005). *Personal data: An interpretation of law 2472/1997* [in Greek]. Athens, Thessaloniki: Sakkoulas Publications.

Sotto, L. J. (2005). An RFID code of conduct. *RFID Journal*. Retrieved April 24, 2010, from http://www.rfidjournal.com/article/view/1624/http://www.rfidjournal.com/article/view/1624/http://www.rfidjournal.com/article/view/1624/http://www.rfidjournal.com/article/view/1624/http://www.rfidjournal.com/article/view/1624/

Sprenger, P. (1999, January 16). Sun on privacy: 'Get over it'. *Wired.* Retrieved from http://www.wired.com/news/politics/0,1283,17538,00.html

Staksrud, E., & Livingstone, S. (2009). Children and online risk: Powerless victims or resourceful participants? *Information Communication and Society*, *12*(3), 364–387. doi:10.1080/13691180802635455

Staksrud, E., & Lobe, B. (2010). *Evaluation of the implementation of the Safer Social Networking Principles for the EU.* European Commission Safer Internet Programme, Luxembourg. Retrieved May 1, 2010, from http://ec.europa.eu/information_society/activities/social_networking/eu_action/implementation_princip/index_en.htm#final_report

Stampfel, G., Gansterer, W. N., & Ilger, M. (2008). Implications of the EU Data Retention Directive 2006/24/EC. Vienna: Faculty of Computer Science, University of Vienna. Retrieved May 20, 2010, from http://www.informatik.univie.ac.at/upload//970/ImplicationsEUDR.pdf

Stanton, J. M. (2008). ICAO and the biometric RFID passport. In Bennett, C. J., & Lyon, D. (Eds.), *Playing the identity card: Surveillance, security and identification in global perspective* (pp. 253–267). New York: Routledge.

Statement of CableEurope. GSMA Europe, EuroISPA, ECTA & ETNO. (n.d.). Data retention: Impact on economic operators. Retrieved May 20, 2010, from http://www.gsmeurope.org/documents/Joint_Industry_Statement_on_DRD.PDF

Steeves, V. (2008). If the Supreme Court were on Facebook: Evaluating the reasonable expectation of privacy test from a social perspective. *Canadian Journal of Criminology and Criminal Justice*, *50*, 331–347. doi:10.3138/cjccj.50.3.331

Stein, R. (2006, March 15). Use of implanted patient-data chips stirs debate on medicine vs. privacy. *Washington Post*. Retrieved April 24, 2010, from http://www.washingtonpost.com/wp-dyn/content/article/2006/03/14/AR2006031402039.htmlhttp://www.washingtonpost.com/wp-dyn/content/article/2006/03/14/AR2006031402039.htmlhttp://www.washingtonpost.com/wp-dyn/content/article/2006/03/14/AR2006031402039.htmlhttp://www.washingtonpost.com/wp-dyn/content/article/2006/03/14/AR2006031402039.htmlhttp://www.washingtonpost.com/wp-dyn/content/article/2006/03/14/AR2006031402039.html

Stephen, J. F. (1991). *Liberty, equality and fraternity*. Chicago, IL: University of Chicago Press.

Stevees, V. (2006). It's not child's play: The online invasion of children's privacy. *University of Ottawa Law & Technology Journal*, *3*(1), 169–188.

Streisand v. Adelman, No. SC 077 257 (Super. Ct. Cal. decided Dec. 31, 2003).

Strickland, L. S., & Hunt, L. E. (2005). Technology, security, and individual privacy: New tools, new threats, and new public perceptions. *Journal of the American Society for Information Science and Technology*, *56*(3), 221–234. doi:10.1002/asi.20122

Strowel, A. (2009). Internet piracy as a wake-up call for copyright law makers – Is the "graduated response" a good reply? *World Intellectual Property Organization Journal*, *1*, 75–86.

Stubb, A. (1996). A categorisation of differentiated integration. *Journal of Common Market Studies*, *34*(2), 283–295. doi:10.1111/j.1468-5965.1996.tb00573.x

Stylianou, K. (2009). ELSA copyright survey: What does the young generation believe about copyright? *Intellectual Property Quarterly*, *2009*(3), 391-395.

Sudre, F. (2005). La "construction" par le Juge européen du droit au respect de la vie privée. In Sudre, F. (Ed.), *Le droit au respect de la vie privée au sens de la Convention européenne des droits de l'homme*. Brussels: Bruylant.

Sullivan, C. (2008). Privacy or identity? *International Journal of Intellectual Property Management*, *2*(3), 289–324.

Sun Star. (2010, May 19). LTO unveils modernized services. Retrieved May 19, 2010, from http://www.sunstar.com.ph/manila/lto-unveils-modernized-services

Sunstein, G. R. (2007). *Republic.com 2.0*. Princeton, NJ: Princeton University Press.

Suresh, G., Horbar, J. D., Plsek, P., Gray, J., Edwards, W. H., & Shiono, P. H. (2004). Voluntary anonymous reporting of medical errors for neonatal intensive care. *Pediatrics*, *113*(6), 1609–1618. doi:10.1542/peds.113.6.1609

Sweeney, L. (1998). *Re-identification of de-identified medical data. Testimony before the National Center for Vital Health Statistics on the subject of medical data and privacy*. Baltimore, MD: HIPAA.

Swire, P. (1997). Markets, self-regulation, and government enforcement in the protection of personal information. In Daley, W. M., & Irving, L. (Eds.), *Privacy and self-regulation in the information age*. Washington, DC: U.S. Department of Commerce.

Tadros, V. (1998). Between governance and discipline: The law and Michel Foucault. *Oxford Journal of Legal Studies*, *18*(1), 75–103. doi:10.1093/ojls/18.1.75

Taipale, K. A. (2004). Technology, security and privacy: The fear of Frankenstein, the mythology of privacy and the lessons of King Ludd. *Yale Journal of Law and Technology*, *7*(123), 125–201.

Talley v. California, 362 U.S. 60 (1960).

Tan, O. (2008, June). Articulating the complete Philippine right to privacy in constitutional and civil law: A tribute to Chief Justice Fernando and Justice Carpio. *Philippine Law Journal*, *82*(4), 78–238.

Taylor, H. (2003). *Most people are "privacy pragmatists" who, while concerned about privacy, will sometimes trade it off for other benefits*. New York: Harris Interactive.

Taylor, M. J. (2007). Regulating personal data in a shared world: Limitations of the EU's approach to data protection. *Personalized Medicine*, *4*, 471–477. doi:10.2217/17410541.4.4.471

Tension rises in the judiciary. (2009, December 1). *Hurriyet Daily News.* Retrieved from http://www.hurriyetdailynews.com

Tensions rise between Turkish judicial board, Justice Ministry. (2009, July 30). *Hurriyet Daily News.* Retrieved from http://www.hurriyetdailynews.com

Tessling, R. v. (2004). 3 S. *CR (East Lansing, Mich.)*, 432.

Tezcur, G. M. (2009). Judicial activism in perilous times: The Turkish case. *Law & Society Review*, *43*(2), 305–336. doi:10.1111/j.1540-5893.2009.00374.x

Tezcur, G. M. (2007). Constitutionalism, judiciary, and democracy in Islamic societies.

The Constitution of the Republic of the Philippines [1987], Constitutional Commission, Quezon City, Philippines

The Philippine Star. (2009, November 2). Technology brings LTO into the 21st century. Retrieved May 19, 2010, from http://www.philstar.com/ArticlePrinterFriendly.aspx?articleId=519585

Thomas, K. (1992). Beyond the privacy principle. *Columbia Law Review*, *92*, 1431–1516. doi:10.2307/1122999

Top court's decision on Paksüt to challenge Ergenekon prosecutors. (2009, July 19). *Hurriyet Daily News.* Retrieved from http://www.hurriyetdailynews.com

Torres, T. (2010, January 11). Transport groups to SC: Car ID system OK. *Philippine Daily Inquirer*". Retrieved May 19, 2010, from http://newsinfo.inquirer.net/breakingnews/nation/view/20100111-246744/Transport-groups-to-SC-Car-ID-system-OK

Tracy, P. E., & Morgan, V. (2000). Big Brothers and his science kit: DNA databases for 21st century crime control? *The Journal of Criminal Law & Criminology*, *90*(2), 635. doi:10.2307/1144232

Tsatsos, D. (1994). *Constitutional law* (*Vol. A*). Athens: Ant. N. Sakkoulas. [in Greek]

Tsiris, P. (1988). *The constitutional guarantee of freedom of assembly* [in Greek]. Athens: Ant. N. Sakkoulas.

Turkey's dark side: Party closures, conspiracies and the future of democracy. (2008, April 2). *European Stability Initiative (ESI).* ESI Briefing Berlin – Istanbul. Retrieved from http://www.esiweb.org/pdf/esi_document_id_104.pdf

Turow, J. (2003). *Americans and privacy: The system is broken*. Philadelphia, PA: Annenberg Public Policy Center of the University of Pennsylvania. Retrieved May 1, 2010 from http://www.annenbergpublicpolicycenter.org/Downloads/Information_And_Society/20030701_America_and_Online_Privacy/20030701_online_privacy_report.pdf

Turow, J., King, J., Hoofnagle, C. J., Bleakley, A., & Hennessy, M. (2009). *Americans reject tailored advertising and three activities that enable it*. Retrieved from http://ssrn.com/abstract=1478214

U.S. Department of Health and Human Services. (2003, May). *OCR privacy brief: Summary of the HIPAA privacy rule*. Retrieved April 24, 2010, from http://www.hhs.gov/ocr/privacy/hipaa/understanding/summary/privacysummary.pdfhttp://www.hhs.gov/ocr/privacy/hipaa/understanding/summary/privacysummary.pdfhttp://www.hhs.gov/ocr/privacy/hipaa/understanding/summary/privacysummary.pdfhttp://www.hhs.gov/ocr/privacy/hipaa/understanding/summary/privacysummary.pdfhttp://www.hhs.gov/ocr/privacy/hipaa/understanding/summary/privacysummary.pdf

UK Home Office. (2005, October). Letter to the European Parliament. Retrieved from http://www.statewatch.org/news/2005/oct/data-ret-clarke-to-cavada-17-10-05.pdf

Ulatowski, L. M. (2008). Recent development in RFID technology: Weighing technology against potential privacy concerns. *Journal of Law and Policy For The Information Society*, *3*, 623.

UN Human Right Commission. (2000). General Comment 28: Equality of Rights Between, Men and Women, CCPR/C/21/Rev.1/Add.10, 68th Session.

UN Human Rights Committee. (1998, August 18). CCPR/C/79/Add.92, Ecuador.

United States Mission to the European Union. (2001, October). Retrieved from http://www.statewatch.org/news/2001/nov/06Ausalet.htm

Uno, K. M., et al. *v. The Director General et al.*, G.R. No. 167798, April 19, 2006 (en banc). Retrieved May 19, 2010, from http://www.lawphil.net/judjuris/juri2006/apr2006/gr_167798_2006.html

Ünver, H. A. (2009). *Turkey's "deep-state" and the Ergenekon conundrum*. The Middle East Institute, Policy Brief, No. 23. Retrieved from http://www.mei.edu/Portals/0/Publications/turkey-deep-state-ergenekon-conundrum.pdf

Vedral, V. (2010). *Decoding reality: The universe as quantum information*. Oxford: Oxford University Press.

Venizelos, E. (2005). The relationship between the Greek Constitution & EU Law after the Signing of the Treaty Establishing a European Constitution & the Greek Constitutional Revision of 2001 [in Greek]. *Hellenic European Law Review*, *1*, 1–36.

Venizelos, E. (2001). Overview of the constitutional revision. In D. Tsatsos, E. Venizelos, & X. Contiades (Eds.), *The new constitution* [in Greek] (pp. 473 - 484). Athens-Komotini: Ant. N. Sakkoulas.

Venizelos, E. (2007). Les Formes Modernes de Crises de l'État de droit démocratique. Le binôme 'liberté/securité' comme garantie et sapement des droits fondamentaux. *Annuaire International des Droits de l'homme, II*, pp. 227-234.

VeriChip. (2006). *VeriMed patient identification*. Retreived April 24, 2010, from http://www.verimedinfo.com/files/Patient_VM-003R2(web).pdfhttp://www.verimedinfo.com/files/Patient_VM-003R2(web).pdfhttp://www.verimedinfo.com/files/Patient_VM-003R2(web).pdfhttp://www.verimedinfo.com/files/Patient_VM-003R2(web).pdfhttp://www.verimedinfo.com/files/Patient_VM-003R2(web).pdf

VeriChip. (2006, March 20). *VeriChip Corporation expands infrastructure rollout of VeriMed patient identification system — 172 new physicians elect to offer VeriMed ID system to patients* [Press release]. Retrieved from http://www.redorbit.com/news/health/435457/verichip_corporation_expands_infrastructure_rollout_of_verimed_patient_identification_system/http://www.redorbit.com/news/health/435457/verichip_corporation_expands_infrastructure_rollout_of_verimed_patient_identification_system/http://www.redorbit.com/news/health/435457/verichip_corporation_expands_infrastructure_rollout_of_verimed_patient_identification_system/http://www.redorbit.com/news/health/435457/verichip_corporation_expands_infrastructure_rollout_of_verimed_patient_identification_system/http://www.redorbit.com/news/health/435457/verichip_corporation_expands_infrastructure_rollout_of_verimed_patient_identification_system/

Verloop, P. (2005, June). *Wie wat bewaart die heeft wat.* Eramus University Rotterdam Report: Investigation into the use of and need for a retention duty for historical traffic data from telecommunication traffic. Government of the Netherlands.

Vilasu, M. (2007). Traffic data retention v data protection: The new European framework. *Computer and Telecommunications Law Review, 13*(2), 52–59.

Vildjiounaite, E., Mäkelä, S. M., Lindholm, M., Riihimäki, R., Kyllönen, V., Mäntyjärvi, J., & Ailisto, H. (2006). Unobtrusive multimodal biometrics for ensuring privacy and information security with personal devices. In *Pervasive Computing* [Proceedings of the 4th International Conference, PERVASIVE 2006, Dublin, Ireland, May 7-10, 2006]. Berlin-Heidelberg: Springer.

Vincents, O. B. (2007). Interception of internet communications and the right to privacy. *European Human Rights Law Review, 6*, 637–648.

Volokh, E. (2000). Freedom of speech and information privacy: The troubling implications of a right to stop people from speaking about you. *Stanford Law Review, 52*(5), 1049–1124. doi:10.2307/1229510

Volti, R. (2006). *Society and technological change*. New York: Worth Publishers.

Wacks, R. (1980). The poverty of privacy. *The Law Quarterly Review, 96*, 73.

Wagner DeCew, J. (1997). *In pursuit of privacy, law, ethics and the rise of technology*. Ithaca, NY: Cornell University Press.

Wagner DeCew, J. (2004). Privacy and policy for genetic research. *Ethics and Information Technology, 6*, 5–14. doi:10.1023/B:ETIN.0000036155.29288.f9

Walker, N. (1998). Sovereignty and differential integration in the European Union. *European Law Journal, 4*(4), 355–388. doi:10.1111/1468-0386.00058

Wang, S., Chen, W., Ong, C., Liu, L., & Chuang, Y. (2006). RFID applications in hospitals: A case study on a demonstration RFID project in a Taiwan hospital. In *Proceedings of the 39th Hawaii International Conference on System Sciences*.

Warbrick, C. J. (1998). The structure of Article 8. *EHRLR, 1998*(1), 32.

Warren, S. D., & Brandeis, L. D. (1890). The right to privacy. *Harvard Law Review, 4*(5), 193–220.

Weatherill, S., & Beaumont, P. (1999). *EU Law*. London: Penguin Books.

Webb, P. (2003). A comparative analysis of data protection laws in Australia and Germany. *The Journal of Information, Law and Technology* (JILT). Retrieved May 5, 2009, from http://elj.warwick.ac.uk/jilt/03-2/webb.html

Weinberg, J. (2008). RFID and Privacy. In Chander, A., Gelman, L., & Radin, M. J. (Eds.), *Securing privacy in the internet age* (pp. 245–269). Stanford, CA: Stanford Law Books.

Weinberg, J. (2007-2008). Tracking RFID. *I/S: A Journal of Law & Policy for the Information Society, 3*, 777-836.

Werbach, K. (2007). Sensors and sensibilities. *Cardozo Law Review, 28*, 2321–2371.

Werra, J. (2001). Le regime juridique des mesures techniques de protection des oeuvres selon les Traités de l'OMPI, le Digital Millennium Copyright Act, les Directives Européennes et d'autres legislations (Japon, Australie). *Revue Internationale du Droit d'Auteur, 189*, 66–213.

Westin, A. F. (1967). *Privacy and freedom*. New York: Atheneum Press.

Westin, A. F. (1967). *Privacy and freedom* (1st ed.). New York: Atheneum.

Westin, A. (1966). Science, privacy, and freedom: Issues and proposals for the 1970's: The current impact of surveillance on privacy. *Columbia Law Review, 66*, 1003–1050. doi:10.2307/1120997

White, L. (1949). *The science of culture*. New York: Farrar, Straus & Giroux.

Williams, R., & Johnson, P. (Eds.). (2008). *Genetic policing: The use of DNA in criminal investigations*. Cullompton, UK: Willan.

Winn, P. (2009). Katz and the origins of the 'Reasonable Expectations of Privacy' test. *McGeorge Law Review*, *40*, 1–13.

Winner, L. (1978). *Autonomous technology: Technics-out-of-control as a theme in political thought*. Cambridge, MA: MIT Press.

Wiretapping scandal still echoes in Turkish capital. (2009, November 16). *Hurriyet Daily News*. Retrieved from http://www.hurriyetdailynews.com

Wolgemuth, L. (2009, June 19). In Bozeman, giving up privacy for a chance at a paycheck. *U.S. News & World Report*. Retrieved from http://www.usnews.com/blogs/the-inside-job/2009/06/19/in-bozeman-giving-up-privacy-for-a-paycheck.html

Wood, D. M. (2009). The 'surveillance society': Questions of history, place and culture. *European Journal of Criminology*, *6*(2), 179–194..doi:10.1177/1477370808100545

Wood, D. M. (Ed.). (2006). *A report on the surveillance society for the Information Commissioner*. London: Surveillance Studies Network.

Wright, D., Gutwirth, S., Friedewald, M., De Hert, P., Langheinrich, M., & Moscibroda, A. (2009). Privacy, trust and policy-making: Challenges and responses. *Computer Law & Security Report*, *25*(1), 69–83. doi:10.1016/j.clsr.2008.11.004

Wright, D., Gutwirth, S., Friedewald, M., Vildjiounaite, E., & Punie, Y. (2008). *Safeguards in a world in ambient intelligence*. London: Springer.

Wright, D. (2005). The dark side of AmI. *The Journal of policy, regulation and strategies for Telecommunications, 7*(6), 33-51.

Yardımcı, M. M. (2009). *İletişimin Denetlenmesi*. Ankara, Turkey: Seçkin.

Yücel, G. (2002, February). *New dilemmas of Turkish national security politics: Old and new security concerns and national development in the post-1980 era*. Paper presented at the Fourth Kokkalis Graduate Student Workshop at JFK School of Government, Harvard University. Retrieved from http://www.hks.harvard.edu/kokkalis/GSW4/YucelPAPER.PDF

Zittrain, J. (2003). Internet points of control. *Boston College Law Review. Boston College. Law School*, *44*(2), 653–688.

Zittrain, J. (2006). The generative internet. *Harvard Law Review*, *119*(7), 1974–2040.

Zittrain, J. (2008). Privacy 2.0. *The University of Chicago Legal Forum*, 65–119.

Zucca, L. (2008). *Constitutional dilemmas*. Oxford: Oxford University Press. doi:10.1093/acprof:oso/9780199552184.001.0001

About the Contributors

Christina Akrivopoulou holds a PhD in Constitutional Law. Her main research interests concern human and constitutional rights, the protection of the right to privacy, data protection, the private-public distinction, and citizenship. She teaches law as a Special Scientist in the faculty of Political Sciences of the Democritus University of Thrace, in Greece, where she currently lives. She also works as an attorney at law at the Thessaloniki Law Bar Association. She is collaborating with several Greek law reviews, and she is a member of many non-governmental human rights organizations in Greece and abroad.

Athanasios-Efstratios Psygkas is a JSD candidate at Yale Law School. He holds an LLB from the Aristotle University of Thessaloniki, Greece, an LLM in Public Law and Political Science from the same law school and an LLM from Yale where he was a Fulbright scholar. He served as editor of the Yale Journal of Law and Technology and the Yale Journal of International Law. From January to July 2009, Psygkas was the Oscar M. Ruebhausen visiting research fellow at Yale Law School and a visiting fellow at the Institut d'Etudes Politiques (Sciences Po) in Paris in 2010-2011. He has published in the area of comparative public law.

***

Norberto Nuno Gomes de Andrade is a legal researcher and a PhD candidate at the Law Department of the European University Institute (EUI, Italy). He graduated in Law at the Faculty of Law of the University of Lisbon, and he holds a Master of Arts in International Relations and European Studies from the Central European University (CEU, Hungary), as well as a Master of Research from the European University Institute. He has previously worked as a legal expert at the External Relations Department of the Portuguese Regulatory Authority for Communications (ANACOM, Portugal). In 2009 he co-edited and published "Law and Technology: Looking into the Future – Selected Essays."

Haralambos Anthopoulos is currently an assistant professor of Law and Public Administration in the Hellenic Open University and he lives in Athens, Greece. He has published several books in Greek concerning the protection of fundamental rights, the freedom of conscience, the freedom of information, political anonymity, racism, and social seclusion as well as articles in relation to democracy, freedom of assembly, and the role of political parties in the modern democracies. He is editor of the Greek Review of Administrative Law.

Federica Casarosa (MA, European University Institute, 2004; PhD, European University Institute, 2007) is a Jean Monnet Fellow at the Robert Schuman Centre, Italy. Her main research interests are consumer protection in electronic contracts, privacy policy in European and comparative perspectives, protection of children in information and communication technologies. In addition to several book chapters, her publications include articles in the journals European Review of Private Law, Danno e responsabilità, Revue Internationale de droit economique, Diritto dell'informazione e dell'informatica.

Cristina Contartese (MA, University of Birmingham, 2004; PhD, University of Bologna, 2010) is a Post-PhD researcher at the University of Bologna. Her main research interests are the European Union as an international actor, the European Convention of Human Rights, and the protection of foreigners' human rights.

Diane A. Desierto is a Law Reform Specialist at the University of the Philippines (UP) Institute of International Legal Studies; Professorial Lecturer at the law faculties of UP and Lyceum of the Philippines; and litigation partner at Desierto Ammuyutan Purisima & Desierto Law. Desierto earned degrees from UP (BS Economics, summa cum laude; Law, cum laude) and Yale Law School (LLM/Master of Laws). Presently, she is a JSD candidate (under Professor W. Michael Reisman's supervision), Howard M. Holtzmann Fellow in International Arbitration and Dispute Resolution, Lillian Goldman Perpetual Scholar, and the 2010-2011 University Trainee (clerk) at the International Court of Justice.

Nikolaos Garipidis is Attorney at Law in the Thessaloniki Bar Association in Greece. He has an LLM in Legal Theory from EALT Brussels and an LLM in History, Philosophy and Methodology of Law from the Aristotle University of the Thessaloniki, where he is currently concluding his doctoral thesis. His main research interests concern democratic theory, the counter majoritarian difficulty, constitutional power, redistributive justice, and the right to disobedience.

Georgiana Ghitu is an attorney at law and member of the Bucharest Bar Association in Romania. She has been a member of the finance & projects and employment practices of DLA Piper Bucharest since November 2008. She previously worked for the Bucharest office of Linklaters LLP, where she gained valuable experience in various banking, employment and restructuring matters. She holds an LLB from the University of Bucharest, Faculty of Law, and has completed an LLM in business law at the same faculty. In addition to the above, Ghitu attended numerous professional development programmes, including the Jean Monnet module on European integration at the University of Bucharest.

Hasan Atilla Güngör has an LLB from the Istanbul University Law Faculty. He has an MA degree in history from the Istanbul University Institute of Ataturk's Principles and Reforms and a PhD degree in Public Law from the Istanbul Kultur University Social Science Institute. He has worked as a research assistant at the Istanbul Kultur University Law Faculty between 2000 and 2009. He is currently working as an assistant professor at the same university. His research areas include constitutional law, human rights law, and environmental law.

Melike Akkaraca Köse has a BA in International Relations and Political Sciences from Marmara University. She holds an LLM and a PhD in European Union Law from Marmara University. She also has an LLM in legal theory from the European Academy of Legal Theory (Brussels). She has worked as a lecturer at the Department of International Relations, Istanbul Kultur University between 2000 and 2008, as a senior lecturer at Girne American University, and at Near East University between 2008 and 2010. Her research areas include legal theory, political philosophy and European Union law.

Shara Monteleone is a graduate of the Law Faculty of Florence (Italy) and received a PhD in IT Law from the Media Integration and Communication Centre (MICC) of Florence in 2007. As a post-doc researcher at INRIA (France) she has worked on the PRIAM project (Privacy Issues in Ambient Intelligence) and has previously conducted research in Media Law, with special attention to Privacy issues. Her research interests also include copyright law and computer forensics. Currently she is an LLM researcher at the European Institute of Florence (EUI).

Nóra Ní Loideain (BA, LLB, LLM, National University of Ireland, Galway) is a Legal Research Officer in the Office of the Director of Public Prosecutions of Ireland. She was previously a Judicial Researcher for the Courts' Service of Ireland, including the Supreme Court and was Senior Researcher in the Rape and Justice in Ireland Report, an independent research study into the process of prosecuting rape cases in Ireland. Her main research interests are in the areas of privacy, State surveillance, criminal justice, and law reform.

Szilvia Papp obtained her MA in English and American Studies from the University of Szeged, Hungary. She speaks fluently English, Italian, Greek, Russian, German and Hungarian. After several years of working as an interpreter and translator in various countries, including Italy and Hungary, she is currently living in Thessaloniki, Greece where she is professionally teaching English legal terminology.

Anna Pateraki is attorney-at-law, admitted to the Thessaloniki Bar Association, Greece. She studied law in Thessaloniki, at the University of Marburg, and the Humboldt University of Berlin (LLM). Her thesis concerned data retention and copyright. At present she is a doctoral candidate in the field of data protection at the Humboldt University and researches on the so-called list privilege in German data protection legislation. She specializes in Intellectual Property and Information Technology Law. During her legal clerkship she worked as a legal intern at the law firms Oppenhoff & Partner in Cologne and Olswang LLP in Berlin. After that she worked as a research associate in the IP/IT practice groups of the law firms Beiten Burkhardt Rechtsanwaltsgesellschaft mbH and Bird & Bird LLP in Frankfurt. Pateraki worked as a trainee at the European Data Protection Supervisor, and she lives and works in Frankfurt.

Pedro Pina is an attorney at law and teaches law in the Oliveira do Hospital School of Technology and Management at the Polytechnic Institute of Coimbra. He holds a law degree from the University of Coimbra Law School and a post-graduation degree in Territorial Development, Urbanism and Environmental Law from the Territorial Development, Urbanism and Environmental Law Studies Center (CEDOUA) at the University of Coimbra Law School. He holds a master's degree in Procedural Law Studies from the University of Coimbra Law School and is currently a PhD student in the Doctoral Program "Law, Justice, and Citizenship in the Twenty First Century" at the University of Coimbra Law School and Economics School.

Grigore-Octav Stan is a Romanian qualified attorney at law and member of the Bucharest Bar Association in Romania. He is currently an associate in the Corporate department of Salans Bucharest, specialising in corporate law and mergers and acquisitions. Earlier in his career, Octav worked for Gugerbauer & Partners in Vienna and for the Bucharest offices of DLA Piper and Linklaters LLP.

Octav is also a PhD candidate at King's College London, School of Law, with a thesis focusing on the topic of compensation in international investment arbitration. He holds an LLM from the University of Vienna, School of Law (Austria), an LLB degree from the University of Iasi (Romania), and was a visiting scholar at the University of Porto (Portugal).

Konstantinos Stylianou is an S.J.D. candidate at the University of Pennsylvania Law School under the supervision of Professor Christopher Yoo. Before joining Penn Law he completed the LL.M. Degree at Harvard Law School as a Fulbright scholar specializing in Intellectual Property, Telecommunications and Cyberlaw. He holds an LL.B. from Aristotle University of Thessaloniki, and a Master's Degree in International and European Law from the same university. He has worked for the Council of Europe and for YouthMedia, and he has published in the fields of copyright, media and internet freedoms.

Christopher Suarez is a student fellow of the Information Society Project at the Yale Law School. His research areas include information privacy law, education law, and antitrust. In 2006, Suarez graduated from the Massachusetts Institute of Technology with dual degrees in Electrical Engineering/Computer Science and Political Science. He has served as a law clerk at the Electronic Privacy Information Center, and his most recent research has focused on the antitrust implications of the Google Book Search Settlement.

Bradley T. Tennis is a third year student at Yale Law School. He is Managing Online Editor of the Yale Law Journal and a co-chair of the Morris Tyler Moot Court of Appeals. Bradley received an MS in Computer Science, focusing on graphics and human-computer interaction, from Stanford University in 2008 and a BS in Computer Science and Mathematics with highest honors from Harvey Mudd College in 2006.

Anna Tsiftsoglou is a PhD Candidate in Public Law at the University of Athens, Greece. Her research interests include security & human rights from a comparative perspective. She studied Law at the University of Thessaloniki, Greece (LLB) and under a University of California scholarship at Berkeley Law School (LLM), where she served as an Associate Editor of Berkeley Technology Law Journal (BTLJ). She has worked for the European Commission in Brussels and as a lawyer in private practice in Greece. Currently, she is a contributor to the Greek legal periodical Administrative Law Review.

Maria Tzanou is a PhD Candidate at the European University Institute, Florence, Italy. Her doctoral thesis focuses on EU counter-terrorism measures in the area of Freedom, Security and Justice and their implications on privacy and data protection. She holds a Master degree in Comparative, European and International Law from the EUI, a Master II in 'Specialized Public Law' from the Universities of Athens and Bordeaux IV, and an LLM in European Law from the University of Cambridge. She has published articles in the German Law Journal and the Yearbook of European Law, and has written (as a co-author) several reports for the EU Fundamental Rights Agency (FRA).

Index

E

F

G

V

W

X